D1556768

Type Directory

A B C D E F G H I
J K L M N O P Q R
R S T U V W X Y Z
1 2 3 4 5 6 7 8 9 0
& , . “ ” ‘ ’ ; : ! ?

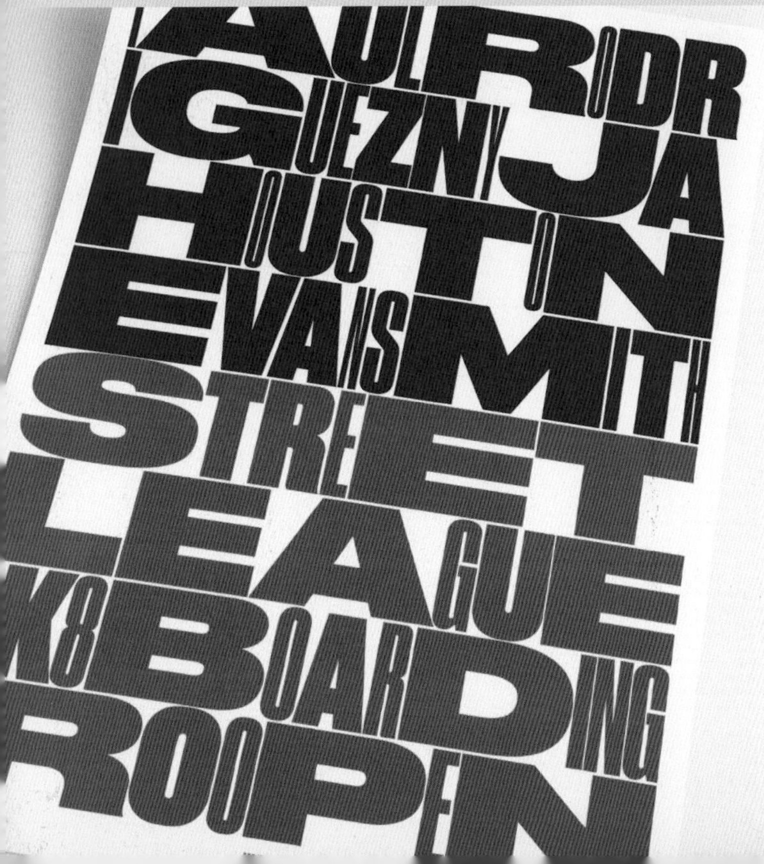
STRE
LEA
GUE
K8
BOAR
ING
ROO

1.INTRO

Natürlich: Mann und Frau gehören beide zur Spezies „Mensch“, sie sind aber auch unterschiedlich und weisen viele Gegensätze auf. In meiner Kollektion sollen diese Unterschiede nicht miteinander kollidieren, sondern ästhetisch miteinander harmonieren. Ich möchte sie zu etwas Gemeinsamem verschmelzen lassen, so dass es praktisch kein destruktives Gegeneinander mehr gibt. Unterschiede an sich sind es, die mich interessieren, wie Tag und Nacht, wie Schwarz und Weiß, wie Mann und Frau. Ich will keineswegs behaupten, dass ich alle Antworten zum Thema Mann und Frau kenne; man kann wohl ewig darüber diskutieren, und vermutlich wird die Diskussion auch ebenso lange weitergehen.
Was ich hiermit vorhabe, ist der Versuch, mir meine und nur meine Meinung zu bilden vor dem Hintergrund mir bekannter wissenschaftlicher Artikel, gelesener Bücher, und auch unter Einbeziehung meines Umfeldes und meiner eigenen Erfahrungen.
Jeder Mann ist einzigartig. Jede Frau ist einzigartig. Jeder Mensch ist einmalig, unwiederholbar. Dennoch haben wir etwas Universelles: unsere geschlechtsspezifische Persönlichkeit. Wir sind in unterschiedlichem Maß männlich oder weiblich geprägt. Die Details und die Unterschiede sind es ja gerade, die uns so interessant machen. Und diese Unterschiede zwischen Mann und Frau werden von mir in einer Unisex-Kollektion verbunden. Innere und äußere Eigenschaften und Verhaltensweisen von Geschlechtern werden in Charakeristika von Textilien und modische Gestaltungsmittel übersetzt. So entstehen aus diversen Analysen viele interessante, experimentielle Prozesse zur Farb-, Material-, Print- und Formfindung.

2.INSPIRATION

Die Inspiration für meine Unisex-Kollektion beziehe ich aus dem Thema „Mann und Frau/ Was uns verbindet - was uns unterscheidet“. Das Thema „Mann und Frau“ war und bleibt wahrscheinlich auch weiterhin ein großes Thema. Es gibt kaum etwas Interessanteres, als unser Dasein zu betrachten. Der Mensch an sich und die Unterschiede zwischen beiden Geschlechtern faszinieren nach zig Jahrtausenden der Evolution heute noch immer. Aber auch gleiche Eigenschaften an uns sind nicht weniger interessant. Jeder und jede hat sowohl männliche als auch weibliche Eigenschaften, der eine mehr, die andere weniger. Sie spiegeln sich sowohl im Äußeren einer Person als auch im Inneren wieder. Das Aussehen kann Vieles über einen Menschen sagen, aber das Innere, das uns bewegt und treibt, bleibt meistens unentdeckt.
Meine Kollektion möchte sich fachlich-thematisch also dem Maskulinen und Femininen gleichermaßen nähern und möglichst viele Aspekte berücksichtigen, die einerseits das jeweils geschlechtstypische und andererseits die gemeinsamen Schnittmengen der beiden Geschlechter im Fokus hat.
Die Dynamik, die sich aus Unterschieden und Gemeinsamkeiten ergibt, soll sich in nige recht interessante Fakten und Aspekte zum Beispiel zu folgenden Themen: Hormone, Aussehen und Empfinden, Fähigkeiten, Verhaltensweisen, Wertvorstellungen...
Hormone: Im Großen und Ganzen begründen Gene und Hormone bzw. andere biologisch bedingte Komponenten den Kern eines Menschen. Die Entwicklung des Menschen und damit auch der Geschlechter hängt aber auch in nicht unwesentlichem Maße vom sozialen Umfeld und seinen Einflüssen ab. Kaum öffnet ein Baby das erste Mal die Augen, prägen Geschlechterstereotype seine Welt. Von Söckchen bis Lätzchen teilt sich sein Kosmos in Rosarot und Himmelblau, jedenfalls in bestimmten Regionen der Erde. Selbst wenn die Eltern diese Klischees umschiffen: Großeltern, Gleichaltrige und später die Medien impfen den Kleinen oft genug stereotype Vorlieben ein.[1]
1.Die Gehirne von Ungeborenen entwickeln sich im Mutterleib unter dem Einfluss verschiedener Hormoncocktails. Die Botenstoffe prägen die geistigen Talente und psychologischen Eigenarten von Mann und Frau ein Leben lang in erheblichem Maße.[2]
2.Es häufen sich die Hinweise darauf, dass die Geschlechtshormone das Verhalten in weit größerem Umfang beeinflussen als bislang angenommen. Je mehr männlichem Geschlechtshormon (Testosteron) ein Fötus ausgesetzt ist, um so männlicher wird der Erwachsene in seinem Verhalten. Je geringer die Menge an männlichem Geschlechtshormon, um so weiblicher wird das Verhalten als Erwachsener.[3]
3.Untersuchungen zeigen, dass Mädchen, die vor der Geburt größeren Mengen Testosteron als den normalen ausgesetzt waren, "jungenhafter" sind als andere kleine Mädte sagen, und dem, was sie meinen, und hören viel besser die Nuancen heraus, die die wahren Gefühle eines anderen offenbaren“, sagte Joyce Brothers.
Mehrere Forscher haben bestätigt gefunden, dass eine Gruppe von Neuronen im Hypothalamus bei Männern mehr als doppelt so groß ist wie bei Frauen. Eben dieser Bereich steuert die vier Urtriebe, nämlich: Essen, Flüchten, Kämpfen und - na, was wohl- Sex. Das Zusammenspiel von strukturellen Unterschieden und Hormonen hat bei Männern ein mehr lineares Denken - d.h. in einer geraden Linie von A zu B zu C - zur Folge, wohingegen die Denkweise von Frauen eher breitgefächert und "multidimensional" ist. Aufgrund dieses Unterschieds können sich Männer leichter auf eine Aufgabe konzentrieren, ohne sich ablenken zu lassen (aber sie können sich in Details verzetteln und den großen Zusammenhang vergessen), während Frauen, die viele unterschiedliche Reize gleichzeitig wahrnehmen, leichter abgelenkt werden, jedoch besser den Gesamtzusammenhang im Auge behalten können.
Körpersprache: Die Körpersprache ist der Große Kommunikator. Sie ist oft ehrlicher als die gesprochene Sprache. Wenn Sie die Haltung der Leute beobachten, werden Sie sehen, wie Frauen sich oft zu ihrem Gegenüber hinbeugen, während Männer sich eher wegbeugen. Diese Beobachtung ist einer der besten Beweise dafür, dass Frauen mehr auf andere bezogen sind als Männer. Sich zu jemand hinbeugen ist eine unbewusste Geste der Verbundenheit, während es eine psychische Distanzierung widerspiegelt, wenn man auf Einhaltung einer körperlichen Distanz achtet. Das ist aber nicht der einzige Unterschied in der Körpersprache der Geschlechter.
Die Körperhaltung bei Mann und Frau: Die Psychologin Shirley Weit z.B. nennt in ihrem Buch über nonverbale Kommunikation einige Studien zum Thema Körpersprache und stellt fest: 'Männer sind in Körperhaltung und Bewegung raumgreifender; Frauen nehmen sich weniger Raum, was für Menschen mit niedrigerem Status und weniger Macht charakteristisch ist. 'Frauen orientieren sich mehr zum Gesprächspartner hin. 'Frauen bewegen sich freier, wenn sie mit anderen Frauen zusammen sind. Bei Männern nehmen sie eine engere Körperhaltung ein. Männer verhalten sich Männern und Frauen gegenüber gleich. 'Bei Männern kommen Phasen völliger Reglosigkeit häufiger vor.'

3. ZIEL
DER ARBEIT

Entwickelt wird eine handgefertigte Unisex-Kollektion mit experimentellen Details. Eine Unisex-Kollektion zeichnet sich durch Handarbeit und selbstgezeichneten Prints aus. Hohe Qualität und die Fertigung der Einzelteile zeichnen sich aus durch besondere Schnitte, aufwendige Nähte und gute Passform. Die Outfits sind handgefertigt, aber auch für die Massenproduktion gedacht. Preislich hat diese Kollektion einen etwas höheren Wert, da sie handgefertigt ist; die Prints sind per Hand gezeichnet. Da die Kollektion handeeherer Wert. Die Outfits sind auch für eine Massenproduktion gedacht: durch einfache Schnitte lassen sie sich schnell produzieren.
Zielsetzung in der Entwicklung der Kollektion ist es, dass sich der Träger/-in den Outfits wohlfühlt und sich alltagsentsprechend bewegen kann. Es soll ein Gefühl von Freiheit und Leichtigkeit übermittelt werden, wobei die entsprechenden Details und Form der Outfits den Trägern Besonderheit und Individualität signalisieren. Generell sollen sie das Gefühl haben, sowohl im Berufsleben wie auch in der Freizeit jeweils entsprechend gekleidet zu sein. Die Kleiderstücke dieser Kollektion sind praktisch, miteinander kombinierbar und eignen sich für jegliche Anlässe. Die Kollektion orientiert sich einerseits an der Zielgruppe, andererseits an entsprechenden Trends.

4. ZIELGRUPPE

Die Menschen, die ich mit der Kollektion ansprechen möchte, will ich nicht in Kategorien unterteilen. Der Ausdruck Unisex impliziert hier ja nicht, dass ich Frauen Männerkleidung anziehen möchte oder umgekehrt. Unisex ist auch keine Gleichmacherei, vielmehr spiegelt sich darin eine ganz bestimmte Philosophie wider. Die von mir entworfenen Outfits können von Frauen und Männern getragen werden. Unisex bedeutet, dass diese Kleidung neutral ist und nicht einem bestimmten Geschlecht zugeordnet werden kann. Dabei ist „neutral“ keinesfalls gleichzusetzen mit Adjektiven wie zum Beispiel langweilig, charakterlos, beliebig o.ä. - ganz im Gegenteil.

für Bewegung zwischen den beiden Farben sorgt. Die unterschiedlichsten Materialien und deren Strukturen sorgen für die Vielfältigkeit der Farben.

6. KOLLEKTIONSPLAN

Meine Kollektion basiert auf einer Umfrage. Es wurden ca. 100 Personen, männlich/ weiblich, im Alter von 25 und aufwärts befragt. Es entspricht dem Alter meiner Zielgruppe. Es wurden keine Angaben zu Jahreszeiten gemacht, da die Outfits fast für jede Jahreszeit gedacht sind. Die Befragten sollten ohne viel zu überlegen/ spontan die Antwort geben.
Die Umfrage bestand aus 3 folgenden Fragen: 1. Nennen Sie die 5 notwendigsten Kleidungsstücke aus Ihrer Garderobe. 2. Nennen Sie Ihre 2 Lieblingskleidungsstücke. 3. Welches Teil würde Sie glücklich machen? Mit diesen Fragen bzw. den Antworten wollte ich herausfinden, was den Befragten das Wichtigste ist , was ihre Persönichkeit ausmacht und inwiefern sie sich durch Mode beeinflußen lassen. Es entstand eine Aufzählung der unterschiedlichsten Kleidungsstücke: Jeans, Hemd, Pullover, Sakko, Mantel/ Trenchcoat, Cardigan, Jacke, Kleid, Anzug, Shorts, Rock, Leggins, Sporthose, T-Shirt kurz/ lang, Longshirt, Hose, Rucksack.
Basierend auf dieser Liste entstand die endgültige Auswahl. Das heißt, dass mehrere Teile zu einem Teil fusionierten, mit dem Ziel, mehr UNISEX- Look zu erreichen. Es wurden aber spezifische Merkmale für beide Geschlechter beibehalten. Jedes entstandene Teil bekam ein entsprechendes, auf das Minimale reduzierte Symbol, das markante Linien/ Silhouetten/ Formen wiedergibt.

7. VORGEHENSWEISE
(Parallele zwischen Eigenschaften und modischen Mitteln)

EIGENSCHAFTEN VON BEIDEN GESCHLECHTERN	*EIGENSCHAFTEN VON DEN OUTFITS*
HORMONE	
Muskelwachtum	Volumen
Stimmbruch	Übertriebene Länge
Körperbehaarung	Wärme/ Schutz
Logisches Denken	Transformation
Lineares Denken	Grade/ Klare Linien
Fingerspitzengefühl	Deko
Multidimensional	2 in 1
WAHRNEHMUNG	
Details schärfer erkennen	Kleine Details
Bewegung besser wahrnehmen	Farbkontraste
Feinere Farbunterschiede wahrnehmen	Farbverlauf S/W
KÖRPERSPRACHE	
Selbstbewusst	Klare Konturen
Herausfordernd	Steifer Griff
Ausdrucklos	Durchsichtig
Teilnahmslos	Lockerer Schnitt
Dominanz	Ausgeprägte Farben/ Print
Freundlich	Fließender/ weicher Fall
Verbindlich	Strapazierfähig/ Haltbar
Verführerisch	Enganliegend/ Figurbetont

8. MATERIAL

Parallelen, die zwischen menschlichen
genschaften und den Eigenschaften der K
dungsstücke gezogen wurden, führen zu un
schiedlicher Materialauswahl. Jedes De
hat einen eigenen Charakter, ist auf ei
Art und Weise individuell und trotzdem
sehr frei kombinierbar. Die Textilstrukt
ermöglichen es, die Kleidungsstücke in
rer besonderen Form zu verstärken. Es wu
folgende Merkmale der Teilnehmor berücks
tigt:
1. Jeans - Volumen (bequem im Alltag) V
men erreicht durch erweiterten Schnitt
100% BW mit Beschichtung; 2. Hemd - ge
Linien (helle Farben) gerade Linien d
Form und Schnitt aus 95% BW, 5% Elast
3. Pullover - durchsichtig (Grau/ grob
strickt) Locker handgestrickt aus Misch
(30% Schurwolle, 40% Polyester und 30%
lyacryl); 4. Sakko - 2 in 1 (lässig) wend
von beiden Seiten tragbar aus leichter
Viskose; 5. Mantel/ Trenchcoat - Kontr
in Stoffen (aussergewöhlich) aus besch
tetem Polyester, schwarzem, durchsicht
Petticoat Tuell (100% Polyamid), aus we
100% Polyamid; 6. Cardigan - klare Kont
(Oversize/ ohne Verschluß) Schwarzem Chi
(100% Polyester) und einer Maschenware
Wolle, 20% Polyester); 7. Jacke - ste
Griff (Übergangsjacke) steifer Griff d
3-Lagen-Laminat (100% Polyester mit Nano
schichtung), stretch Futter (96% Acetat
Elasthan); 8. Overall - warm/ Schutz
Kälte (schlicht/ casual) Schutz durch T
(100% Polyethylen), der bei Schutzklei
angewendet wird mit eingesetzten Bünd
aus Strickschlauch (96% BW, 4% Elasthan
Shorts/ Rock - Vielfältigkeit + übertrie
Länge Zusammengesetzt aus Zwei untersch
lichen Teilen: Shorts und Rock aus Misc
webe (60% Wolle, 38% Polyester, 2% Elast
10. Leggins - enganliegend (Schwarz) en
liegend durch elastischen Jerseystoff
lyester); 11. Sporthose - weiter und lo
rer Schnitt (bequem) Bequemlichkeit d
Lockeren Schnitt und angenehmen Stoff
BW, 20% Polyester); 12. T-Shirt kurz -
geprägte Farben (Print) ausgeprägte Fa
durch selbstgezeichneten Print (Textil
be für Seide), aus Jersey (95% Viskose
Elasthan), 100% Polyester; 13. T-Shirt
- (Weiß) ausgeprägte Farben durch sel
gezeichneten Print (Textilfarbe für Se
aus Jersey (95% Viskose, 5% Elasthan),
Polyester; 14. Longshirt - zart (einfar
zarter Jersey Stoff (Polyester); 15. Ho
Transformation (Schwarz/ breit/ bequem)
Lässt sich zu einer Jacke transformie
aus Mischgewebe (43% Wolle, 53% Polye
4% Elasthan); 16. Rucksack - strapazie
hig (groß) strapazierfähig durch besond
Stoff, der bei Tragbahren angewendet wi

9. QUELLEN

Es gibt keinen Un
terschied

STOUT | PALE ALE | EXPORT STOUT | STOUT

BREWERY · REDCHURCH · PARADISE PALE ALE

BREWERY · REDCHURCH · BRICK LANE LAGER

BREWERY · REDCHURCH · BETHNAL PALE ALE

BREWERY · REDCHURCH · SHOREDITCH BLONDE

BREWERY · REDCHURCH · BETHNAL PALE ALE

BREWERY · REDCHURCH · HOXTON STOUT

BREWERY · REDCHURCH · GREAT EASTERN IPA

BREWERY · REDCHURCH · PARADISE PALE ALE

BREWERY · REDCHURCH · BRICK LANE LAGER

BREWERY · REDCHURCH · GREAT EASTERN IPA

BREWERY · REDCHURCH · SHOREDITCH BLONDE

BREWERY · REDCHURCH · OLD FORD EXPORT STOUT

16

Museu del Disseny
de Barcelona

Gabriel Lluelles

Leopoldo Milá

23

Museu del Disseny
de Barcelona

79

Museu del Disseny
de Barcelona

Amaya Arzuaga

ASTRONAUT OF INNER SPACES: SUNDRIDGE PARK, SOHO, LONDON … MARS

MARLBOROUGH
CENTURY
CATTLE & SON
PORTLAND
St JAMES
BERWICK
CHARITY

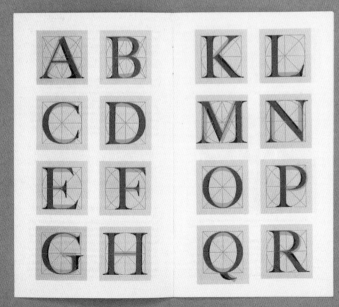

Quintessentializes
Photosynthesised
College of Justice
E Pluribus Unum
Bank of England
Gamesomeness

Exposició

**Extraordinàries!
Col·leccions d'arts
decoratives i arts
d'autor (segles III-XX)**

2

-1B01   Exposició **Extraordinàries!
Col·leccions d'arts
decoratives i arts
d'autor (segles III-XX)**   234

Diese Woche:
21.8.23.8.25.8.27.8.

19.30 h
Bayerische Staatsoper
Cuvilliéstheater
Titus (Originalsprache)
von Wolfgang Amadeus Mozart
20 h
Bayerisches Staatsschauspiel
Neues Residenztheater
Professor Bernhardi
von Arthur Schnitzler
20 h
Bayerische Staatsoper
Nationaltheater
Salome
von Richard Strauss
20 h
Bayerisches Staatstheater
am Gärtnerplatz
Ballettabend
20 h
Münchner Kammerspiele
im Schauspielhaus
Die Hose
von Carl Sternheim
20 h
Staatliche Hochschule für Musik
Kammermusikalische Volksmusik
Volksmusikalische Kammermusik
20 h
Cirkus Krone Bau
Internationales Folklorefestival 1972
Marokko, Senegal
20 h
Haus der Kunst, Klangzentrum
Chinesisches Schattenspiel

22.8.
19.30 h
Bayerische Staatsoper
Nationaltheater
Carmina Burana
Geschlossene Vorstellung
19.30 h
Bayerisches Staatsschauspiel
Neues Residenztheater
Troilus und Cressida
von William Shakespeare
20 h
Bayerisches Staatstheater
am Gärtnerplatz
Der Barbier von Sevilla
von Gioacchino Rossini
20 h
Bayerisches Staatsschauspiel
Der Zerrissene
von Johann Nestroy
20 h
Münchner Kammerspiele
im Schauspielhaus
Dantons Tod
von Georg Büchner
20 h
Allerheiligen-Hofkirche in der Residenz
Sondergastspiel
Theaterlaboratorium
Jerzy Grotowski, Wroclaw/Breslau
20 h
Cirkus Krone Bau
Internationales Folklorefestival 1972
Rumänien

24.8.
16.30–2.30 h
Haus der Kunst, Klangzentrum
Musik mit und ohne Lautsprecher
Konzerte Non Stop der Groupe de
Recherches Musicales und Solisten
der Chöre der O.R.T.F.
19.30 h
Bayerisches Staatsschauspiel
Neues Residenztheater
Professor Bernhardi
von Arthur Schnitzler
20 h
Bayerische Staatsoper
Nationaltheater
Symphonie Nr. IX d-moll op. 125
von Ludwig van Beethoven
Geschlossene Veranstaltung
20 h
Bayerisches Staatstheater
am Gärtnerplatz
Der Arzt wider Willen
von Charles Gounod
20 h
Bayerisches Staatsschauspiel
Der Zerrissene
von Johann Nestroy
20 h

26.8.
10 h
Eröffnung der Spielstraße
im Olympia Park
16.30–2.30 h
Haus der Kunst, Klangzentrum
Musik mit und ohne Lautsprecher
Konzerte Non Stop der Groupe
de Recherches Musicales und Solisten
der Chöre der O.R.T.F.
19 h
Klosterkirche Schäftlarn
Schäftlarner Konzerte
20 h
Bayerisches Staatsschauspiel
Neues Residenztheater
Professor Bernhardi
von Arthur Schnitzler
20 h
Schloß Schleißheim, Großer Barocksaal
Schleißheimer Schloßmusik

19 h
Bayerische Staatsoper
Nationaltheater
Der Hochzeit des Figaro (Originalsprache)
von Wolfgang Amadeus Mozart
19.30 h
Bayerisches Staatsschauspiel
Nationaltheater
Ballettabend
Eugen Onegin
von Peter Tschaikowsky
19 h
Bayerische Staatsoper
Cuvilliéstheater
Capriccio
von Richard Strauss
19.30 h
Bayerisches Staatsschauspiel
Neues Residenztheater
Troilus und Cressida
von William Shakespeare
20 h
Bayerische Staatstheater
am Gärtnerplatz
Fra Diavolo
von François Auber
20 h
Bayerisches Staatsschauspiel
Der Zerrissene
von Johann Nestroy
20 h
Münchner Kammerspiele
im Schauspielhaus
Dantons Tod
von Georg Büchner
20 h
Münchner Marionettentheater
Der Mond
von Carl Orff
21 h
Historischer Münzhof, Hofgarten 4
Münchner Kammeroper
Gianni Schicchi
von Giacomo Puccini
20 h
Allerheiligen-Hofkirche in der Residenz
Sondergastspiel
Theaterlaboratorium
Jerzy Grotowski, Wroclaw/Breslau
20 h
Cirkus Krone Bau
Internationales Folklorefestival 1972
Rumänien

16.30–2.30 h
Haus der Kunst, Klangzentrum
Musik mit und ohne Lautsprecher
Konzerte Non Stop der Groupe
de Recherches Musicales und Solisten
der Chöre der O.R.T.F.
20 h
Bayerisches Staatstheater
am Gärtnerplatz
Gaeta May
Chanson
Nationalpreisträgerin DDR
20 h
Münchner Kammerspiele
im Schauspielhaus
Dantons Tod
von Georg Büchner
20 h
Allerheiligen-Hofkirche in der Residenz
Sondergastspiel
Theaterlaboratorium
Jerzy Grotowski, Wroclaw/Breslau
20 h
Herkulessaal der Residenz
Orchester der Welt
Symphonieorchester und
Chor des Bayerischen Rundfunks
Dirigent Rafael Kubelík
20 h
Cirkus Krone Bau
Internationales Folklorefestival 1972
Rumänien

19.30 h
Prunkhof des Rathauses
Bläserserenade der Münchner
Petersturm-Musik
15 h
Wallfahrtskirche am Wies
Festlicher Sommer in der Wieskirche 1972
20 h
Basilika Ottobeuren
Symphonie Nr. IX d-moll op. 125
von Ludwig van Beethoven
Dirigent Ladislav Slovák
19 h
Bayerische Staatsoper
Nationaltheater
Der Hochzeit des Figaro (Originalsprache)
von Wolfgang Amadeus Mozart
14 h
Urfaust
von Johann Wolfgang von Goethe
19 h
Bayerisches Staatsschauspiel
Neues Residenztheater
Troilus und Cressida
von William Shakespeare
19.30 h
Schloß Schleißheim, Großer Barocksaal
Schleißheimer Schloßmusik
16 h
Der Mann von La Mancha
von Dale Wassermann
23 h
Bayerisches Staatstheater
am Gärtnerplatz
Gaeta May
Chanson
20 h
Kongreßsaal des Deutschen Museums
Bayerische Folklore
Vita Bavarica – ein bayerischer Bilderbogen
20 h
Theater in der Leopoldstraße
Gastspiel
Moskauer Puppentheater
Serge Obrastow

Haus der Kunst, Klangzentrum
20 h
Zeitgenössische Musik, Lateinamerikas
27 h
Cage-Nacht
24 h
Musik mit und ohne Lautsprecher
Konzerte Non Stop der Groupe
de Recherches Musicales
und Solisten der Chöre der O.R.T.F.
20 h
Bayerisches Staatstheater
am Gärtnerplatz
Wiederaufführung
Liebeserregin
Katechismus mit Muse
von Gerhard Wimberger
20 h
Bayerisches Staatsschauspiel
Cuvilliéstheater
Der Zerrissene
von Johann Nestroy
20 h
Münchner Kammerspiele
im Schauspielhaus
Dantons Tod
von Georg Büchner
20 h
Allerheiligen-Hofkirche in der Residenz
Sondergastspiel
Theaterlaboratorium
Jerzy Grotowski, Wroclaw/Breslau
20 h
Cirkus Krone Bau
Internationales Folklorefestival 1972
Mexiko

**Manuel Aires Mateus
Manuel Graça Dias
Maria Helena Barreiros
Pedro Campos Costa
Ricardo Agarez
Ricardo Carvalho**

/ UAL
00-185 Lisboa
na.pt

Habitar
pensar
nvestigar
fazer

Peter Dawson

Foreword by
Tobias Frere-Jones

Type Directory

 **Thames & Hudson**

Contents

Script 560

Foundry Profiles

Designer Profiles

Foreword
by Tobias Frere-Jones

Looking back on the recent history of type design, it's tempting to see a story of technology, liberating makers and users alike. In the last few decades, the tools for making digital type became available to anyone with a computer and enough patience. Designing a typeface – let alone preparing it for the marketplace – was a lengthy and daunting task. Throughout most of the 20th century, this had been an industrial-scale undertaking (literally). It was thrilling to watch the old ways being usurped and swept away. As it turned out, that was really the smaller part of the story.

The quieter and more profound change has been in education. Those slow, onerous ways of making type were also the venue for training young designers. No school taught these very particular skills, so the young and eager would learn on the job, as they had for centuries. Techniques were closely guarded from competitors, with most designers ('punch-cutters' for many years) declining to publish any detailed guide to their craft. It was a black art, and deliberately so.

But in the digital age, access to tools begat the demand for skills. And now typeface design is a regular feature of design programs around the world, with a few schools in Europe and the United States even offering degrees or certificates in this very specialized discipline. The spread of type education has brought digital type to its more mature state. And now there are more trained type designers than at any point in history. This discipline has never been so thoroughly populated.

But the question is often posed: why do we need more typefaces? Depending on how you hear it, the question may imply not only a redundancy but an ongoing dilution: the more we make the less it means. But the opposite is true. That diversity – even in fine shades – is a source of strength. If we all used the same type, that choice would become meaningless and we'd lose a chance for expression.

We can (and should) discuss the associations the type will accrue through use: the typeface that was used for this ad campaign, this political candidate, that movie poster. But it glosses over an important point: these choices, any choices, have the chance to mean more because other designers used something else. That constant refresh of inventory is the foundation of power. As long as the flavour is distinct and the execution is sound, typefaces will support one another regardless of style. Not in spite of their differences but because of them.

Gathering typefaces from the last centuries as well as the present day, this book hopes to consider that expanding world.

Opposite. Specimen examples of sans serif design Mallory. It was the first typeface released under Frere-Jones Type (see p. 80), the independent type design studio of Tobias Frere-Jones. A humanist design combining British and US typographic traditions to provide a distinctive and unique sans serif font family.

FREQUENTS HERZEGOVINA

World Leagues Grand Prix

Every December Sunday

€207 ₺214 ₦981 ₹835 ₽160

MEN'S NATIONAL TEAM

5408 SAN FRANCISCO BLVD

QUILTING WORKSHOPS!

Unjustifiable Alternatives

Gjøvik to Logroño quickest

RYE WHISKEY TASTINGS

Introduction

I had my first forays into working with type in my youth, when I spent my later school studies honing my skills to become a commercial illustrator. My ambition was to illustrate graphic novels. Designing posters and graphic ephemera, I used type mainly in the form of hand drawings with a liberal dash of Letraset dry-transfer lettering. At such a tender age, I was not fully aware of the existence of typeface designers or typefaces as a commercial craft and industry.

I was formally introduced to typography and typefaces during my first year of studying for a degree in Graphic Design at Kingston University, Surrey, when my lecturer, the designer Eugenie Dodd, asked me to complete a typographic project. It was a momentous moment as I realized that a whole world of typefaces and their infinite possibilities lay before me. I changed tack in my studies and never looked back. Gone was my ambition of becoming a comic-book illustrator as my attentions turned to becoming a typographic graphic designer.

More than twenty-five years later, I am writing the introduction to *Type Directory*, having enjoyed a career that has been more like a vocation. I love my role and, more importantly, I am still learning. Over the years, I have used numerous typefaces on a wide variety of projects and have always admired the creative ingenuity, dedication, craftsmanship and attention to detail of the unsung heroes of the world of type design. These highly skilled members of the creative community past and present number in their thousands. Many are revered as icons in the typographic world thanks to their creative genius and unassuming daily passion. What are invariably their labours of love enable those who work with type to have their creations read in print or online across the world.

Type Directory aims to pay tribute to these heroes of type by presenting a selection of the many typefaces that are available for a designer. The book is a visual celebration of the craft, innovation and beauty of these letterforms. It is a comparative guide across a range of type styles and their subcategories, providing the historical background to their creation as well as insight into the evolution of the international industry and community that revolves around typefaces. There are now more than 250,000 individual fonts that make up typeface families, and they comprise the good, the bad and the excellent. This collection presents a portfolio of diverse creations with the aim of being an essential and informative sourcebook for the graphic designer and design studio. Given there are so many types available, not all can be included here and inevitably there are typefaces that have been omitted but which are popular with practitioners. (Other factors are the extent, permissions and contributions offered.) This collection comprises more than 1,800 typefaces with all manners of style, geographical location and historical periods, as well as aesthetic appeal and practicality. *Type Directory* also profiles some of the world's most innovative type design studios and their work, as well as significant type designers who have created landmark typefaces and contributed to the development of type design and graphic design.

The *Type Directory* is a typographic time capsule. It is by no means complete but it provides a snapshot of what has come before, shows where typeface design is now and signals the directions it is heading. Type design evolves, not simply according to fashion, designers' interests and aesthetic urges, but most importantly in keeping with the technological advances in how people read information in print and on screen. In recent years, there has been a wealth of highly crafted typefaces with extensive families that bridge the gap between print and online legibility, working across all media at all sizes. A number of these typefaces are commissions specifically created for brands and organizations, large and small, to communicate their position and messages, but as is often the case, the typefaces created become the visual essence of the brands.

Designing new and ever-more refined and advanced types is a perpetual benefit to all, from the largest studios to the independent designer.

Above. A typesetter in the late 1940s assembles letters of lead type into a block at the Wick printing works of Partridge & Love, Bristol. This traditional method of printing with blocks of individual type remained in use by some printers for small jobs until the 1970s. It was labour-intensive but provided high-quality impressions.

Above right. Editors and typesetters working in the composing room of the *Washington Times-Herald* newspaper in 1954.

Right. Phototypesetting systems became prevalent by the 1970s (shown here in Germany *c.* 1980s). As a result of their introduction, the use of metal type for commercial mass-market printing declined and eventually ceased. Phototypesetting systems projected letterforms onto photographic material for use in offset lithographic printing.

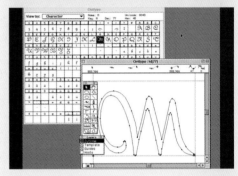

Top. When the Apple Macintosh computer was released in 1984, it triggered a seismic change in the ways that users could work with type and how type could be designed. Early type-design software such as Font Studio and Fontographer led the way.

Above. Today, the same design principles, attention to detail and lengthy processes still apply to the creation of any new typefaces. Shown above are on-screen refinements being undertaken at Fontsmith and, right, the numerous workings for Fedra Serif by Typotheque.

The encouragement of businesses, cultural organizations and media empires to engage with type, and the desires of type foundries to create beautifully crafted, aesthetically pleasing and technically competent typefaces will ensure that the craft of these individuals across the world continues. Just as their predecessors have influenced today's designers, so contemporary creations become cultural, creative and historical reference points in their turn.

Peter Dawson

About the Book

To compile the final edit of the 1,800-plus typefaces included in this book took six months of research, examination, addition, deletion and refinement, with a further eight months for building the book and evolving the content. Many foundries from around the globe were invited to participate; sadly, several could not contribute due to commercial, logistical or timing reasons.

Once all the classic and key historical types and subsequent variations and revivals were included, the foundries who kindly contributed their libraries were added. This has resulted in a diverse range of contemporary and highly crafted submissions.

The final collection is of typefaces that work as a resource and reference point to help graphic designers in selecting typefaces for their projects, as well as acting as an encyclopaedia of type development and history.

Each typeface is presented with uppercase and lowercase alphabetical letterforms along with numerals, key punctuation marks and symbols. All typeface examples are presented at 20-point size on 22-point leading, thereby creating a direct comparison across the entire book for letter spacing, x-height and cap height. In addition, readers can see the line length occupied by each typeface. However, because of the structure of the book and page size it is not possible on some occasions to present the whole of the uppercase alphabet. Those typefaces that appear only in uppercase will have no lowercase option and some of the typefaces possess alternate characters, so discrete differences in their letter designs or certain of the characters are shown.

A short descriptive text accompanies each entry, explaining its origin and / or significant design features. Each entry also contains a section that provides information on the foundry, the name of the designer/s, the designer's nationality and the type's date of origination. Earlier dates invariably refer to metal production, whether punches or hot metal. Later dates refer to phototypesetting and digital production. The team of writers who assisted in this extensive challenge were confronted by many cases of conflicting information regarding origination credits and dates of typefaces that in some instances are centuries old and come from all over the world. The hope is that their diligence has achieved clarity and historical accuracy. Typefaces of particular value, visual interest or innovative contemporary designs are presented as half-, single- or double-page spread features. This allows for additional information and images showcasing how they were created or their usage. At the end of the book there are several indexes to help readers locate typeface entries: an A to Z index of typefaces, an index of typefaces by designer and an index by foundry.

Glossary

Anti-aliasing
The addition of intermediate pixels (especially on curves) on screen, where bitmapped type possesses stepped pixels to create smooth transitions by blurring the edges.

Antiqua
A classification or grouping of serif types with calligraphic Old Style letterforms. Used as a German and Scandinavian common name for serif types.

Aperture
The opening of a part-closed counter, such as 'C' and 'S', or the upper half of a lowercase double-storey 'a'.

Apex
The point where two strokes meet at the top of a letter, such as on an uppercase 'A' or 'M'.

Arc
Any part of a curve of a letter, leading into a stem.

Arm
The horizontal stroke in a character that does not connect to a stem at one side such as on an 'E', or on both sides such as a 'T'.

Ascender
The vertical stroke or feature of a lowercase letter that rises above the font's x-height, as in 'b', 'd', 'f' and 'k'.

Axis (stress)
A key feature of most typefaces, an invisible line that runs through the character, from top to bottom, through its thinnest points, creating direction in its form. This assists in classification, with Old Style typefaces having a slanted axis and transitional types having invariably a vertical stress.

Back slant
A reverse italic /oblique with a left tilt or lean.

Ball terminal
A circular rounded shape found at the end of a stroke instead of a serif or a sharp cut-off. To be found on lowercase double-storey serif letters such as 'a', 'c' and 'f'.

Baseline
Invisible line on which all lower- and uppercase letters sit.

Beak
A decorative pronounced stroke, similar to a serif, found at the end of the arm of a letter, such as capital 'S'.

Bitmap
Character or form defined by pixels set within a grid. What was a part of PostScript fonts containing information for the typeface to display correctly on-screen on older computer systems that had no rasterizing capability. Also referred to as 'screen fonts'.

Blackletter
A classification or grouping of heavy calligraphic script types, also known as Gothic Script and Old English script, employing broad-nibbed uniform vertical strokes connected by angular lines. Created from the Middle Ages onwards and used commonly for manuscript books and documents throughout Europe at the time.

Body
The full height of a typeface including ascenders, descenders and clearance space. The height of the body is equal to the point size.

Bold
A heavier drawn variation of a regular weight of a typeface.

Bowl
The enclosed rounded /oval form found on letterforms such as 'b', 'o' and 'p'.

Bracket
The curved or wedge-shaped element found between the serif and the stem that joins them together.

Calligraphy
The craft of writing elegant letterforms by hand using a writing tool.

Cap height
The height of a capital or uppercase letter from its baseline to the letterform's highest point.

Capital
A large set of initial letters. Also referred to as 'uppercase' and 'caps'.

Character
Any individual letter, number, punctuation mark, symbol or sign within a typeface.

Colour (typographic)
The tonal value of a block of text when it is set on a page. Referred to in shades of grey to black.

Condensed
Typeface appearance designed with a narrower character width over Roman types.

Constructivist
Russian 20th-century art and architectural movement, influenced by Cubism and Futurism, and which was an influence at the Bauhaus schools in Germany.

Contrast
The difference between thick and thin strokes of a character design. Can also be referred to in terms of size, colour and weight of differing types.

Counter
The enclosed or partially enclosed negative space within a letter, such as in 'b' and the lower part of 'e'.

Cross stroke
The horizontal strokes across the stem found in lowercase letterforms, such as 't' and 'f'.

Crossbar
The horizontal strokes found in letterforms, such as 'A' and 'H'. Also known as a 'bar'.

Crotch
Inside angle where two strokes join, such as in a 'V'.

Cursive
Type reminiscent of handwritten letterforms. Also known as 'script' or 'longhand' with characters joined up.

Descender
The part of a lowercase letter that sits below the baseline, such as on a 'g' or 'p'.

Didone
A serif family that possesses very high stroke contrast with unbracketed hairline serifs. Also referred to as 'modern'.

Dingbat
A non-alphabetical character consisting of a symbol, shape or other pictorial element.

Display
Typefaces designed for title or headline applications rather than for reading texts. Commonly used in advertising or banner applications, often decorative and used for larger settings rather than the setting of extended lengths of text.

Double-storey
Lowercase 'a' and 'g' that possess two counters over each other. Single-storey types have just the one.

Drop shadow
Creation of an offset replication of a letterform positioned behind a character to provide a 3D effect or shadow design.

Ear
Decorative flourish found on a lowercase double-storey 'g' on the upper right of the top bowl.

Egyptian
Serif type with low stroke contrast and large, heavy, squared serifs.

English roundhand
Calligraphic connecting handwritten script originating from England in the mid 17th century. Features include a low stroke contrast as drawn with metal pointed nibs.

Expanded (extended)
A type design whereby the letterforms are created as if stretched across the horizontal axis to make wider character widths than in a regular design.

Expert
A reference for a font that possesses an extended character set such as non-aligning numerals and other alternative characters.

Eye
Specifically the counter within a lowercase 'e'.

Family
A collection of fonts of varying weights and styles sharing a common design approach and construction.

Fat Face
Heavily emboldened serif display typefaces. The earliest recorded designs were in England during the early 19th century, where they were used for posters and lottery bills.

Figures
Alternative name for numbers and numerals.

Finial
A tapered or curved end to a stroke.

Fleuron
Decorative typographic ornament such as a flower or botanical symbol that is placed at the beginning or ends of paragraphs.

Font / fount
A collection of all the letterforms, punctuation marks, numerals and font metrics attributed to a single typeface design and weight such as Roman. A typeface family is made up of several fonts, each of its own style and weight.

Foot
The element of a stem that sits on the baseline.

Foundry
The historical name of a place used for casting hot-metal type. It is employed today to describe type studios.

Fraktur
A form of decorative blackletter type, commonly found in Germany from the 16th century and widely used there until the mid 20th century.

Glyph
A single character (number or letter), punctuation mark or symbol within a typeface.

Grotesque
From the German 'grotesk'; a type classification of sans serif typefaces.

Hot metal
A process that involved the injection of molten metal into a cast formed of differing glyphs to create type blocks (slugs) to be used for printing, when inked up and pressed into the paper. Developed in the late 19th century, it fell out of fashion for mass-market printing with the appearance of phototypesetting in the late 1950s. It became obsolete with the advent of digital processes in the 1980s. Also known as 'mechanical typesetting'.

Humanist
A classification of serif and sans serif typefaces based on calligraphic minuscule letterforms dating to the 7th and 9th centuries and the proportions of the Roman capital.

Ink trap
A feature within a typeface's design where counters and corners of letterforms are removed to counter the build-up of ink when printed, negating dark spots, especially if material is of a low quality such as newsprint.

Italic
A slanted, script version of a Roman typeface; a bespoke design incorporating distinctive and individual letterforms that appear handwritten. More often found in serif designs. See 'oblique'.

Italienne
Decorative display type inspired by the large wood type of the American Wild West identified by large, heavy banded serifs and extreme contrast in stroke weight.

Junction
Intersection at which the end of one stroke meets a point in another stroke in a letter.

Kerning
The spacing and plus / minus adjustment between individual pairs of letters to improve readability and appearance.

Leading
The term dates to the use of metal type when compositors inserted thin strips of lead between lines to increase line spacing. Traditionally, it refers to the adjustment and addition of vertical distance between lines of horizontal type, expressed in points, fractions of points or millimetres. Today, the term is widely used to describe line spacing.

Leg
The downward sloping stroke on a 'k' and 'R'.

Legibility
The ability of one letter to be easily distinguished and recognizable from another.

Letter spacing
The adjustment of space between letters in typesetting, either uniformly or optically, to achieve optimum positioning.

Ligature
Two characters joined to form one letterform such as 'fi', 'ff' or 'fl'.

Light
A thinner drawn variation of a regular weight of a typeface.

Line spacing
The vertical distance between lines of horizontal type, expressed in points, fractions of points or millimetres. Measured from the baseline of one line to the baseline of the next.

Lining figures
Numeral characters of common size and cap height resting on the baseline.

Lithographic (litho) printing
Printing onto paper from inked etched metal plates. The most common form of printing worldwide today. It is used for the printing of books, catalogues and posters due to its high quality.

Loop
The lower portion of a double-storey lowercase 'g' that sits below the baseline.

Lowercase
Small letters of the Latin alphabet derived from handwritten minuscules. The name derives from the use of metal type, when the letterforms were kept in tray. The lower part of the tray contained the lowercase letter whereas the capitals were in the upper trays and were hence named 'uppercase'.

Metrics
Numerical values and units of measure contained within a digital font file to ensure accurate spacing and positioning of type.

Minuscule
The small or lowercase letters of the alphabet based on cursive letterforms from the 7th to 9th century.

Modern
A serif family that possesses very high stroke contrast often with unbracketed hairline serifs. Also referred to as 'didone'.

Monoline
A typeface where the letterform's stroke weight possesses a constant width.

Monospaced
A typeface where each of its character occupies the same amount of space, irrespective of its width. Commonly seen in typefaces based on manual typewriters.

Neo-grotesque
A type classification of sans serif typefaces. These types are simpler in appearance than earlier grotesque counterparts with more consistent stroke contrast and increased legibility.

Non-aligning figures
Numeral characters of varying height and position on the baseline. Also referred to as 'Old Style' numerals.

Oblique
Slanted (mechanically sheared) Roman letter forms; not to be confused with 'Italic', which has a more cursive construction. More often seen with sans serif than serif types. See 'Italic'.

OCR
Abbreviation of 'optical character recognition'. A typeface that can be scanned and read by a machine as well as read by people. Invariably used when large amounts of data require processing.

Old Style
A classification for serif types that appear with low stroke contrast, an angled stress to the left, bracketed serifs and angled head serifs. Originally created between the late 15th and mid 18th centuries.

OpenType
Cross-platform font format by Microsoft and Adobe, which was developed in the late 1990s and became widespread in the industry after 2000. Not only does the typeface allow for cross-platform compatibility working on both PCs and Macs but it also allows for very large character sets to be created and contained within a single file. As OpenType fonts support Unicode, one font can contain more than 65,000 glyphs, making it possible to work with multiple languages within one file.

Phototypesetting (photocomposition)
Typesetting process whereby typefaces were created on glass negatives and were exposed to photo-sensitive paper by shining light through them to create hard-copy versions. Became obsolete with the introduction of the personal computer and desktop-publishing software.

Pica
An Anglo-American standard typographic unit of measure possessing a width of 12 points.

Pixel
Smallest unit of a digital image and a display screen.

Point
A standard typographic unit of measure equal roughly to $1/72$nd of an inch (0.351 mm) with 72.27 points to the inch.

Point size
A unit of measure of type based on roughly $1/72$ in. In the Anglo-American point system, one point typically equals 0.01383 in. (0.351 mm). In desktop publishing the figure is usually rounded off to exactly $1/72$ in., which matches with screen display resolutions of 72 pixels to the inch.

PostScript
Adobe's page-description programming language that allows for vector-based elements to be accurately rendered. Now replaced by OpenType.

Proportional spacing
A typeface whose characters possess spacing based on their individual character widths rather than a uniform, identical spacing, thus creating better readability within running text.

Punch (punch-cutter)
A steel die faced with an individual letter hand-carved in relief. This die was then punched into a softer metal with other letter punches to create text blocks / page layouts and the resultant printing blocks to reproduce them.

Readability
The ability of being able to read and absorb lengthy typeset text when composed with ease.

Regular
A classification term for a standard weight of typeface.

Roman
Regular, upright style of letter. Also used as a term for a typeface of book / normal weight as opposed to a bolder weight.

Running text
Continuous typeset reading text, as commonly seen in textbooks.

Sans serif
A typeface classification of a group of typefaces with no serif features in its construction. First became popular in the early 19th century.

Semibold
An intermediary weight between Roman /Medium and Bold.

Serif
The small stroke that appears at the beginning or end of a serif letter stroke. There are a number of differing shapes that include bracketed, slab, hairline, banded and wedge.

Slab serif
A typestyle where the serifs are squared in construction and equal, or close to, the optical weight of the strokes.

Slope
Oblique simulated Roman letterforms, more often used with sans serif.

Small caps (capitals)
Capital letterforms but with a height roughly that of lowercase letters.

Spacing
See 'Letter spacing'.

Spine
The central curved stroke in both lower- and uppercase 's'.

Stem
The main vertical stroke in a letter.

Stress
See 'Axis'.

Stroke
The line that creates the letterform /character.

Style
Typographic term that describes the varieties of a single typeface, such as Roman, Bold and Italic.

Swash
An elegant addition, usually to uppercase italics or script types, which is a decorative extension to the letterform.

Tabular figures
Numerals that share a fixed width so that when they are employed in columns for accounting purposes they can be aligned to be easily read.

Tail
Decorative stroke on uppercase letter 'Q' that sits below the baseline.

Thicks and thins
Terminology to describe the widths of the stroke.

Titling
A display style of typeface designed for large settings, capitals and numerals only.

Tittle
The dot of a lowercase 'i' and 'j'.

Tracking
Spacing applied to characters in a line of text as a whole, adjusting the inter-letter spacing as a consistent unit rather than kerning that focuses on just a pair of letters.

Transitional
A group of typefaces emerging in the 18th century which are the bridge between their predecessors' Old Style types with elements of the soon to emerge modern-style serifs. Possessing a higher contrast stroke weight and a more vertical stress to their construction. Many contemporary serif designs can be categorized as transitional.

Typeface
The harmonious design of a font as a collection of all the character elements (letters, numerals and punctuation marks) that share the same design principles and / or construction elements.

Unicase
Typeface where both uppercase and lowercase share the same height so that they can be mixed together.

Unicode
The international computer industry standard for the handling and presentation of text.

Uppercase
The capital letters in a typeface.

Vector
Mathematical formula that creates and defines a curved or straight line that is at the heart of every digital font. The vector outlines allow for the typeface to be scaled at any size without loss of quality and the information is translated into a bitmap representation for screen use as pixels.

Weight
Definition for the lightness or heaviness of a typeface's design.

x-height
The height of lowercase letters from the baseline exemplified by the letter 'x', ignoring both ascenders and descenders. Typefaces with a large x-height appear much bigger than typefaces with a smaller x-height even if they share the same point size when set.

Type Directory

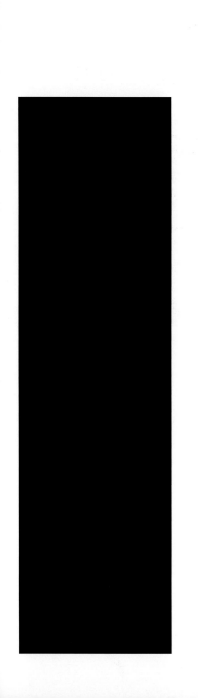
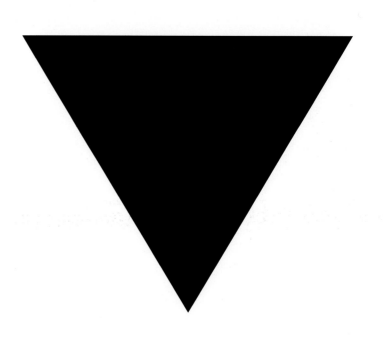

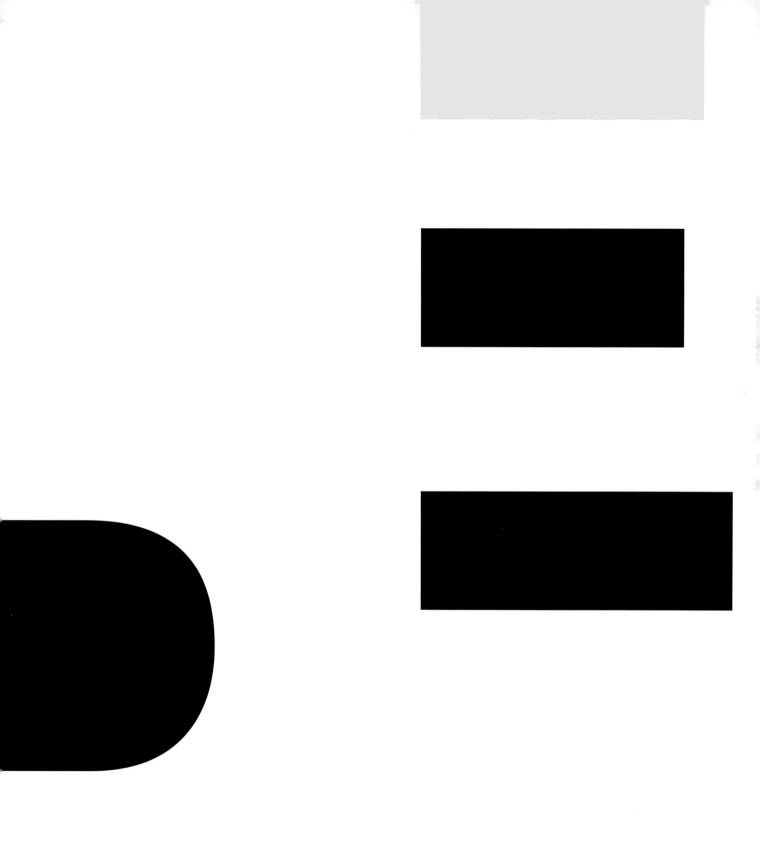

ES TALENTS *of* RIDICUL

ut pleaded excuse for

much the rather

N NEW YORK C

y that nasty wee

ndeterminately

AID THE SPANI

nd smiled at her apprehension

Serif

Opposite. Detail of specimen of Emigre foundry's MrsEavesXL. Designed by Zuzana Licko in 2009; this variant is built upon the success of the original Mrs Eaves design but with more consideration to designs where space is at a premium.

The earliest serif forms date to Roman times, when Latin letterforms were carved into stone. Research indicates that these inscriptions were first painted or marked on to the stone for stone carvers to follow as a guide, hence the introduction of a serif flare at the end of a line to close the stroke. This provided a tidy and clean closure, as well as neatening the end of the lines once carved.

In the 1400s, all type had to be carved before it was set and printed, and type cutters adopted existing Roman forms in their designs. Soon the Blackletter (see p. 562) forms of the day were replaced by the handwriting-influenced designs of these early Roman forms. The earliest serif forms, described as Venetian or humanist (see p. 71), had a more calligraphic feel. The stress of the drawn letter reflected a handwritten approach with the stroke contrast being less markedly different.

In the 1500s, these types gave way to what is referred to as Old Style (see p. 110). This was a period of great invention and innovation as designers and printers created their own designs. These Old Style letterforms built further on the handwritten aspect of their construction. The axis of their curved strokes inclined to the left, the serifs were almost always bracketed and the head serifs were angled. These types had a more upright composure and, as letter-cutting and printing techniques improved, more refinement was introduced into the stroke weights. Printers worked closely with type designers experimenting with letterforms, ink mixtures and paper manufacture.

By the mid to late 1700s, the fashion for an increased contrast between the thick and thin strokes and a vertical stress, or close to vertical, in the construction of the letters with flat bracketed serifs resulted in the evolution of transitional typefaces (see p. 150). This was the period where type forms evolved from Old Style to the Modern / Didone (see p. 93) typeface designs. One of the lead innovators of the time was English type designer and printer John Baskerville. His tireless efforts researching and developing all aspects of producing the printed word had a huge impact on type design and his principles still apply. As such, many contemporary serif typefaces fall into this category.

By the 1800s, technological developments in type design and printing resulted in the creation of Modern / Didone or neoclassical typefaces. Notable exponents of these styles include Italy's Giambattista Bodoni and France's Firmin Didot.

Because printing was at a relatively sophisticated point by then, these types possessed very high contrast in their stroke weights with hairline thins and heavyweight thicks. Their serifs were often unbracketed, allowing for sharp junctures between horizontal and vertical strokes and the serifs.

At the start of the 20th century, type design and manufacture began to expand industrially as a global *tour de force*. Slab-serif designs (also referred to as square serif or Egyptian) had emerged. These types were primarily born out of increased newspaper usage and the need to create bold headlines with impact. The rise in consumerism resulted in their use for product advertising too, notably including Clarendon (see p. 38), Rockwell (see p. 58) and later ITC Lubalin Graph (see p. 55). Their forms have minimal stroke contrast, so as to be more impactful on the page, and invariably come with unbracketed serifs. Slab serifs can be further broken down from the accepted subcategories of serif to Clarendon-style slab serifs (see p. 35), geometric-style slab serifs (see p. 419) and humanist slab serifs (see p. 521).

Amalia

ABCDEFGHIJKLMNOPQRSTUVWXYZ
abcdefghijklmnopqrstuvwxyz
1234567890 !@#?:;"*&

Foundry: Typotheque
Designer: Nikola Djurek
Designer Nationality: Croatian
Date: 2006

While taking inspiration from Dutch classical typography in general, Amalia has a moderate contrast that is similar to modern faces such as Didot and Bodoni. *Typographica* review chose Amalia as one of its 'Favorite Typefaces of 2006'. The font was remastered in 2018.

Barbedor

ABCDEFGHIJKLMNOPQRSTUVWXYZ
abcdefghijklmnopqrstuvwxyz
1234567890 !@#?:;"*&

Foundry: Hell
Designer: Hans Eduard Meier
Designer Nationality: Swiss
Date: 1987

Created for the Hell Digiset machine (but sketched out on paper), Barbedor is influenced by 15th-century humanist book scripts. Its characters appear as if they have been formed by broad-tipped pens, and its handwritten nature is further emphasized by its subtle serif elements.

Bernhard Modern

ABCDEFGHIJKLMNOPQRSTUVWXYZ
abcdefghijklmnopqrstuvwxyz
1234567890 !@#?:;"*&

Foundry: American Type Founders
Designer: Lucian Bernhard
Designer Nationality: German
Date: 1937

Originally named 'Booklet', Bernhard Modern has a low x-height, reminiscent of the engravers' Old Style faces that were popular in the 1930s. The difference in line weight gives it a handwritten flavour, which is emphasized by its rounded line terminals and gently tapered serifs.

Brioni

ABCDEFGHIJKLMNOPQRSTUVWXYZ
abcdefghijklmnopqrstuvwxyz
1234567890 !@#?:;"*&

Foundry: Typotheque
Designer: Nikola Djurek
Designer Nationality: Croatian
Date: 2008

Nikola Djurek received the Icograda Excellence Award for Brioni (along with Plan Grotesque and Marlene) in 2010. Three years later, a Greek version by Peter Biľak and a Cyrillic version Alexander Tarbeev was added. It is a sophisticated serif designed for use in books and magazines.

Byngve

ABCDEFGHIJKLMNOPQRSTUVWXYZ
abcdefghijklmnopqrstuvwxyz
1234567890 !@#?:;"*&

Foundry: Linotype
Designer: Bo Berndal
Designer Nationality: Swedish
Date: 2004

This unpronounceable font is an amalgamation of the designer's two Christian names, 'Bo' and 'Yngve'. Byngve takes its inspiration from elegant 15th-century Italian calligraphic letterforms. Swedish typographer Bo Berndal drew the laid-back serif entirely by hand before digitizing it.

Calligraphic 810

ABCDEFGHIJKLMNOPQRSTUVWXYZ
abcdefghijklmnopqrstuvwxyz
1234567890 !@#?:;"*&

Foundry: Stempel / Bitstream
Designer: Gudrun Zapf von Hesse
Designer Nationality: German
Date: 1952 / c. 1980s

Calligraphic 810 is Bitstream's cut of Gudrun Zapf von Hesse's serif Diotima originally made for Stempel in 1952 and available in roman and italic. Linotype released a new four-weight cut in 2008 as Diotima Classic, which includes additional light and heavy weight.

Cataneo

ABCDEFGHIJKLMNOPQRSTUVWXYZ
abcdefghijklmnopqrstuvwxyz
1234567890 !@#?:;"*&

Foundry: Bitstream
Designer: Richard Lipton / Jacqueline Sakwa
Designer Nationality: American
Date: 1993

This elegant cursive serif was inspired by the 16th-century Italian master calligrapher Bernardino Cataneo, who is best known for his single manuscript copy book of twenty pages. It has three weights – Light, Regular and Bold – as well as complementary swash characters and extensions.

Corvallis

ABCDEFGHIJKLMNOPQRSTUVWXYZ
abcdefghijklmnopqrstuvwxyz
1234567890 !@#?:;"*&

Foundry: ITC
Designer: Philip Bouwsma
Designer Nationality: American
Date: 1994

This beautifully crafted serif came as a result of Philip Bouwsma's lifetime appreciation of the classics and the craft of calligraphy. Like many of his typefaces, Corvallis is clearly influenced by the broad-pen calligraphy of historic scripts. It is available in regular and oblique.

De Worde

ABCDEFGHIJKLMNOPQRSTUVWXYZ
abcdefghijklmnopqrstuvwxyz
1234567890 !@#?:;"&*

This expertly crafted seven-weight font was inspired by the early italic used extensively by the 16th-century printer and publisher Wynkyn de Worde, who is known as the Father of Fleet Street. It was released to coincide with the 60th anniversary of the Wynkyn de Worde Society.

Foundry: Jeremy Tankard Typography
Designer: Jeremy Tankard
Designer Nationality: British
Date: 2016

Diotima

ABCDEFGHIJKLMNOPQRSTUVWXYZ
abcdefghijklmnopqrstuvwxyz
1234567890 !@#?:;"*&

A delicate, rounded serif, Diotima is named after a slim and beautiful Greek priestess in one of Plato's texts. This typeface, originally released as a hot-metal typeface with a single weight, is complemented perfectly by Gudrun Zapf von Hesse's headline type Smaragd, and Ariadne Initials.

Foundry: Stempel
Designer: Gudrun Zapf von Hesse
Designer Nationality: German
Date: 1951

Ellington

ABCDEFGHIJKLMNOPQRSTUVWXYZ
abcdefghijklmnopqrstuvwxyz
1234567890 !@#?:;"*&

This calligraphy-influenced font was named for the jazz musician Duke Ellington and was designed by lettering artist and stone carver Michael Harvey. Its condensed letterforms were developed with utility in mind, to be both legible and distinctive in body text and display contexts.

Foundry: Monotype
Designer: Michael Harvey
Designer Nationality: British
Date: 1990

Empirica

ABCDEFGHIJKLMNOPQRSTUVWXYZ
abcdefghijklmnopqrstuvwxyz
1234567890 !@#?:;"*&

Empirica is a combination of the grand style of Ancient Rome and the French tradition, and its close spacing and delicate serifs make it a perfect headline font. It comprises six weights plus italics, and there are alternate short descenders for tighter line spacing at the largest headline settings.

Foundry: Frere-Jones Type
Designer: Tobias Frere-Jones / Nina Stössinger
Designer Nationality: American / Swiss
Date: 2018

Exlibris

ABCDEFGHIJKLMNOPQRSTUVWXYZ
abcdefghijklmnopqrstuvwxyz
1234567890 !@#?:;"*&

Foundry: ITC
Designer: Bo Berndal
Designer Nationality: Swedish
Date: 1993

Bo Berndal's remarkable seventy-year-long career spanned book design, illustration, calligraphy, advertising and teaching, and he created more than 200 typefaces over the course of his life. This graceful yet robust serif, available in three weights, was his first design for ITC.

Footlight

ABCDEFGHIJKLMNOPQRSTUVWXYZ
abcdefghijklmnopqrstuvwxyz
1234567890 !@#?:;"*&

Foundry: Monotype
Designer: Ong Chong Wah
Designer Nationality: Malaysian
Date: 1986

Malaysian designer Ong Chong Wah first created Footlight as an italic, before expanding his design to include the roman. This approach is reflected in the distinctive, calligraphic appearance of the font, which was made widely available by Microsoft within many of its products.

FS Olivia

ABCDEFGHIJKLMNOPQRSTUVWXYZ
abcdefghijklmnopqrstuvwxyz
1234567890 !@#?:;"*&

Foundry: Fontsmith
Designer: Eleni Beveratou
Designer Nationality: Greek
Date: 2012

Eleni Beveratou's design for FS Olivia was inspired in part by the work of Dutch type designer Sjoerd Hendrik de Roos, and was created to capture a sense of the movement of pen on paper. It is an expressive, textural serif, and the Pro edition also includes Cyrillic and Greek character sets.

Gilgamesh

ABCDEFGHIJKLMNOPQRSTUVWXYZ
abcdefghijklmnopqrstuvwxyz
1234567890 !@#?:;"*&

Foundry: Letraset
Designer: Michael Gills
Designer Nationality: British
Date: 1994

Michael Gills's exploration of calligraphic type styles during his time at Letraset resulted in a range of new designs, among them Gilgamesh. This Old Style typeface features narrower letterforms and counterbalanced serifs, making it a useful and legible choice for body text.

GT Sectra

ABCDEFGHIJKLMNOPQRSTUVWXYZ
abcdefghijklmnopqrstuvwxyz
1234567890 !@#?:;"*&

Foundry: Grilli Type
Designer: Marc Kappeler /
Dominik Huber / Noël Leu
Designer Nationality: Swiss
Date: 2011 / 2014

GT Sectra was originally created for use in the reportage magazine *Reportagen*. The typeface combines 'the calligraphic influence of the broad nib pen with the sharpness of the scalpel knife'. *Reportagen* was designed by Zurich-based studio Moiré and the journal required a typeface that was flexible and extensive in weights following expenditure on its start-up.

At first, *Reportagen* used Times Bold for headlines and a typewriter typeface for texts, but once more funding was achieved a typeface was commissioned to work with the many hierarchies and sizes being employed in the magazine, whose impact was nearly all typographic. This sole use of text throughout was also at the core of the magazine's visual identity, from the cover through to the articles it contained.

Swiss foundry Grilli Type (see p. 238) published the design by Marc Kappeler and Dominik Huber of Moiré. The typeface's edgy appearance and distinctive, cut calligraphic forms, led to its name Sectra, derived from the Latin for 'to cut', *secare*.

Sectra has undergone many iterations since its inception in 2011. Moiré joined forces with Noël Leu from Grilli Type to refine the concept behind it, and every issue of *Reportagen* saw improvements to the typeface. Initially, the letterforms possessed a softer and more traditional feel, but gradually curves were replaced by cuts, resulting in simpler shapes. The result is a design with a high legibility factor and strong, angular lines. The family contains fifteen weights divided into three subfamilies.

Below. GT Sectra was created for use in the current affairs magazine *Reportagen*, designed in conjunction with Zurich-based studio Moiré.

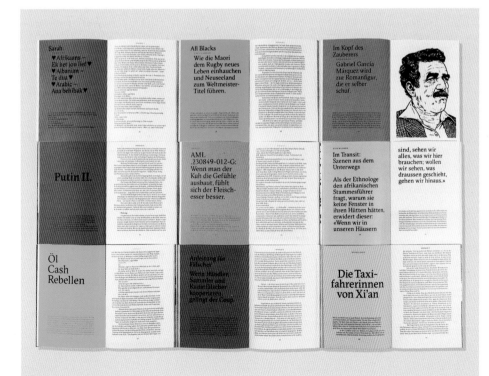

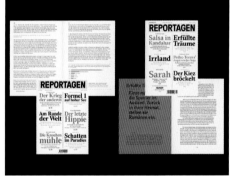

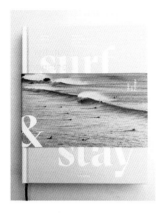

Above. Travel guide *Surf & Stay* highlights the best spots on the coastlines of Spain and Portugal to camp and surf. Written by Veerle Helsen and designed by Elke Treunen of Antwerp-based design studio MAFF.

Left. Designed by London studio Land of Plenty, GT Sectra is employed on the cover of *The Association of Photographers Annual* and used at both headline and text sizes.

Hiroshige

ABCDEFGHIJKLMNOPQRSTUVWXYZ
abcdefghijklmnopqrstuvwxyz
1234567890 !@#?:;”*&

Foundry: AlphaOmega Typography
Designer: Cynthia Hollandsworth Batty
Designer Nationality: American
Date: 1986

Hiroshige was originally commissioned to appear in a book of woodcuts by renowned 19th-century Japanese artist Andō Hiroshige. The calligraphic details within the font's letterforms are very reminiscent of brushstrokes and could be seen as a nod to its namesake.

ITC Anima

ABCDEFGHIJKLMNOPQRSTUVWXYZ
abcdefghijklmnopqrstuvwxyz
1234567890 !@#?:;”*&

Foundry: ITC
Designer: Olivera Stojadinovic
Designer Nationality: Serbian
Date: 2006

For ITC Anima, Serbian designer Olivera Stojadinovic set out to create a font that captured a sense of movement and vivacity within its forms. She hand-drew Anima before making digital amendments, and its angled serifs and calligraphic feel reflect the spontaneity of the sketching process.

ITC Cerigo

ABCDEFGHIJKLMNOPQRSTUVWXYZ
abcdefghijklmnopqrstuvwxyz
1234567890 !@#?:;”*&

Foundry: ITC
Designer: Jean-Renaud Cuaz
Designer Nationality: French
Date: 1993

This distinctive serif was created by French type designer Jean-Renaud Cuaz, who wanted to develop a new interpretation of Renaissance calligraphic lettering styles that stood apart from existing revivals, such as Chancery by Hermann Zapf (see p. 574). It is available in three weights.

ITC Kallos

ABCDEFGHIJKLMNOPQRSTUVWXYZ
abcdefghijklmnopqrstuvwxyz
1234567890 !@#?:;”*&

Foundry: ITC
Designer: Phill Grimshaw
Designer Nationality: British
Date: 1996

Phill Grimshaw was taught by typographer Tony Forster at Bolton College of Art, Greater Manchester, England before studying at London's Royal College of Art. ITC Kallos is an elegant, calligraphic text typeface and one of more than forty fonts he designed in his career.

ITC New Veljovic

ABCDEFGHIJKLMNOPQRSTUVWXYZ
abcdefghijklmnopqrstuvwxyz
1234567890 !@#?:;"'*&

Foundry: ITC
Designer: Jovica Veljović
Designer Nationality: Serbian
Date: 2014

This revised version of Serbian designer Jovica Veljović's eponymous first typeface was published by ITC thirty years after the original, with the addition of several weights, styles and character sets. Veljović's amendments enhance the typeface's suitability for a broad range of applications.

ITC Syndor

ABCDEFGHIJKLMNOPQRSTUVWXYZ
abcdefghijklmnopqrstuvwxyz
1234567890 !@#?:;"*&

Foundry: ITC
Designer: Hans Eduard Meier
Designer Nationality: Swiss
Date: 1992

Swiss type designer Hans Eduard Meier held a fascination with the evolution of written letterforms; his book on the subject, *Die Schriftenwicklung* (*The Development of Script and Type*, 1959), remains in print to this day. This elegant humanist serif design of his was published by ITC in 1992.

Mariposa

ABCDEFGHIJKLMNOPQRSTUVWXYZ
abcdefghijklmnopqrstuvwxyz
1234567890 !@#?:;"'*&

Foundry: Agfa Compugraphic
Designer: Philip Bouwsma
Designer Nationality: American
Date: 1994

US graphic designer Philip Bouwsma has a background in calligraphy and an interest in historical scripts. This is evident in this distinctive serif that features subtle curves and small, square serifs. Mariposa comes in Book and Bold, with italics, and can be paired with Mariposa Sans.

Nocturno

ABCDEFGHIJKLMNOPQRSTUVWXYZ
abcdefghijklmnopqrstuvwxyz
1234567890 !@#?:;"'*&

Foundry: Typotheque
Designer: Nikola Djurek
Designer Nationality: Croatian
Date: 2013

Nocturno comes in four weights, with italics, from the Dutch foundry Typotheque (see p. 90), which describes it as an 'unapologetically calligraphic typeface with slightly oblique stress and sculpted, concave, almost flare serifs'. It is easy on the eyes as a text face due to its large x-height.

Oxalis

ABCDEFGHIJKLMNOPQRSTUVWXYZ
abcdefghijklmnopqrstuvwxyz
1234567890 !@#?:;"*&

Foundry: Creative Alliance
Designer: Franck Jalleau
Designer Nationality: French
Date: 1996

Oxalis is a quirky, calligraphic font with minimal serifs. It was created by French type designer Franck Jalleau, a teacher at the École Estienne, Paris and designer of typefaces for French passports. Oxalis was made for the Creative Alliance and is also available from Monotype in four weights.

Runa Serif

ABCDEFGHIJKLMNOPQRSTUVWXYZ
abcdefghijklmnopqrstuvwxyz
1234567890 !@#?:;"*&

Foundry: Monotype
Designer: Lennart Hansson
Designer Nationality: Swedish
Date: 1996

For Runa Serif, Swedish calligrapher Lennart Hansson was influenced by the forms of ancient Viking runes, which were used to write various Germanic languages. His design won the Nordic Typeface Competition in Copenhagen in 1993 and the Runa Serif family was published three years later.

Semper

ABCDEFGHIJKLMNOPQRSTUVWXYZ
abcdefghijklmnopqrstuvwxyz
1234567890 !@#?:;"*&

Foundry: Omnibus
Designer: Franko Luin
Designer Nationality: Swedish
Date: 1993

Semper is named after the Latin for 'always'. It is a transitional serif inspired by the expressive forms of calligraphic lettering. Franko Luin's design balances the angular strokes and stresses of calligraphic forms with the moderate contrast and symmetrical serifs of the transitional style.

Thema

ABCDEFGHIJKLMNOPQRSTUVWXYZ
abcdefghijklmnopqrstuvwxyz
1234567890 !@#?:;"*&

Foundry: Typotheque
Designer: Nikola Djurek
Designer Nationality: Croatian
Date: 2012

Thema is a versatile, calligraphic serif face designed for both continuous text and striking headlines. The distinct contrast between strokes, alongside the sharp serifs and open counters, make it highly legible at small sizes, as well as being very effective in larger formats.

Algebra

ABCDEFGHIJKLMNOPQRSTUVWXYZ
abcdefghijklmnopqrstuvwxyz
1234567890 !@#?:;"*&

Algebra was informed by Granger, the headline face designed by Susana Carvalho and Kai Bernau for the US edition of *Esquire* magazine in 2011.

Algebra was conceived for flexible editorial use, and has loose spacing and little contrast, so it sits comfortably in long runs of text.

Foundry: Commercial Type
Designer: Susana Carvalho / Kai Bernau
Designer Nationality: Portuguese / German
Date: 2016

Algebra Display

ABCDEFGHIJKLMNOPQRSTUVWXYZ
abcdefghijklmnopqrstuvwxyz
1234567890 !@#?:;"*&

Algebra Display is the beefier sibling of Algebra, which is designed to inject authority into headlines and initials. While the broad strokes and serifs

feature a considerable addition of muscle, the thin strokes are made even slimmer, to help maintain the font's dynamic balance.

Foundry: Commercial Type
Designer: Susana Carvalho / Kai Bernau
Designer Nationality: Portuguese / German
Date: 2017

Amariya

ABCDEFGHIJKLMNOPQRSTUVWXYZ
abcdefghijklmnopqrstuvwxyz
1234567890 !@#?:;"*&

Created primarily for on-screen use, this refined nine-weight font family supports the Arabic, Persian and Urdu languages. It shares many qualities with

traditional Middle Eastern text faces, but has been optimized for on-screen reading by its lower level of stroke contrast.

Foundry: Monotype
Designer: Nadine Chahine
Designer Nationality: Lebanese
Date: 2017

Ascender Serif

ABCDEFGHIJKLMNOPQRSTUVWXYZ
abcdefghijklmnopqrstuvwxyz
1234567890 !@#?:;"*&

Created for on-screen legibility, this serif is metrically compatible with Times New Roman, offering a width-compatible font for developers

to use across different platforms. The Ascender foundry worked closely with type developers for the Xbox 360, Android phone and Windows core fonts.

Foundry: Ascender
Designer: Steve Matteson
Designer Nationality: American
Date: 2005

Bonobo

ABCDEFGHIJKLMNOPQRSTUVWXYZ
abcdefghijklmnopqrstuvwxyz
1234567890 !@#?:;"*&

Foundry: Typodermic
Designer: Ray Larabie
Designer Nationality: Canadian
Date: 2006

Bonobo is a relaxed slab serif with distinctive curls on letters 'a', 'c' and 's'. This playful typeface was created by Canadian Ray Larabie, a video games art director turned typeface designer. Larabie is based in Nagoya, Japan where he has set up his own foundry, Typodermic.

Bookman Old Style

ABCDEFGHIJKLMNOPQRSTUVWXYZ
abcdefghijklmnopqrstuvwxyz
1234567890 !@#?:;"*&

Foundry: Monotype
Designer: Alexander Phemister / Ong Chong Wah
Designer Nationality: British / Malaysian
Date: 1858 / 1990

This typeface has its origins in Alexander Phemister's Old Style Antique created *c.* 1858 for the Scottish foundry Miller & Richard. Many versions were made of the typeface, which became known as Bookman. This version is based on models for Lanston Monotype and American Type Founders.

Century Expanded

ABCDEFGHIJKLMNOPQRSTUVWXYZ
abcdefghijklmnopqrstuvwxyz
1234567890 !@#?:;"*&

Foundry: American Type Founders
Designer: Linn Boyd Benton / Morris Fuller Benton
Designer Nationality: American
Date: 1900

Century Expanded is a very legible text font. It is a version of Century Broadface, which is a version of Linn Boyd Benton's font Century, commissioned by *Century Magazine* in 1894. This expanded version was designed with his son, Morris Fuller, and references the Bruce Type foundry's #16 Roman.

CG Clarendon

ABCDEFGHIJKLMNOPQRSTUVWXYZ
abcdefghijklmnopqrstuvwxyz
1234567890 !@#?:;"*&

Foundry: Fann Street
Designer: Robert Besley
Designer Nationality: British
Date: 1845

Clarendon is a sturdy serif with a large x-height, short ascenders and descenders and strong bracketed serifs. It has inspired numerous copies and revivals. The slab serif became immediately popular, although many designers consider the later 20th-century versions to be superior.

Claridge

ABCDEFGHIJKLMNOPQRSTUVWXYZ
abcdefghijklmnopqrstuvwxyz
1234567890 !@#?:;"*&

Foundry: Cofino
Designer: Adrian Williams
Designer Nationality: British
Date: 1979

The lowercase 'g' of this distinguished slab serif has a distinctive central join to its loop. Its designer Adrian Williams collaborated with Dr Rosemary Sassoon in 1985 to create typefaces for children; the partnership has produced some of the most notable educational typefaces for British schools.

Clarion

ABCDEFGHIJKLMNOPQRSTUVWXYZ
abcdefghijklmnopqrstuvwxyz
1234567890 !@#?:;"*&

Foundry: Monotype
Designer: Robin Nicholas
Designer Nationality: British
Date: 1985

Clarion is derived from Robin Nicholas's font Nimrod (1980) and made use of much of the research he completed for it, but with very distinctive detailing. He designed this sturdy serif with a large x-height specifically to be compatible with the emerging newspaper technology of the 1980s.

Congress

ABCDEFGHIJKLMNOPQRSTUVWXYZ
abcdefghijklmnopqrstuvwxyz
1234567890 !@#?:;"*&

Foundry: Elsner+Flake
Designer: Adrian Williams
Designer Nationality: British
Date: 1980

Congress is designed to look good when used in different European languages and was shown for the first time to an appreciative audience at the ATypI Congress held by the Association Typographique Internationale in Kiel, Germany in 1980. Adrian Williams added a sans version in 1985.

Cosmiqua

ABCDEFGHIJKLMNOPQRSTUVWXYZ
abcdefghijklmnopqrstuvwxyz
1234567890 !@#?:;"*&

Foundry: Linotype
Designer: Akira Kobayashi
Designer Nationality: Japanese
Date: 2007

This 1950s inspired serif sits somewhere between formal italic types and casual handwriting scripts. Its name is an amalgamation of the French word *cosmique* (cosmic) and the German word *Antiqua* (the term for 'serif'). Cosmiqua's distinctive serifs and terminals give it an informal, almost kitsch feel.

Clarendon LT

ABCDEFGHIJKLMNOPQRSTUVWXYZ
abcdefghijklmnopqrstuvwxyz
1234567890 !@#?:;"*&

Clarendon LT is a revival of the English slab-serif typeface Clarendon created in 1953 by Hermann Eidenbenz of the Haas Type Foundry (Haas'sche Schriftgiesserei), a Swiss manufacturer of types that went on to produce Helvetica. Its distinctive bracketed square serifs, known as slab serifs, make for a more refined, Egyptian-style design. When employed with lighter serif typefaces, its heavier appearance helps to bring definition, and significantly aids access and navigation in expansive texts such as dictionaries.

This particular version of the typeface was refined from early slab-serif designs that emerged from England in the early decades of the 19th century. The first Clarendon was created by Robert Besley of the Fann Street Foundry in London in 1845 and it was named after the Clarendon Press in Oxford. The origins of the design were from wooden display types, and Clarendon is often used for titles and display work. However, the Clarendon LT Light variant is perfectly adaptable for text applications.

Clarendon has influenced many slab-serif designs and its popularity has resulted in the name being employed as a generic term for fonts of this style. Its characterful appearance and timeless design still make it a strong candidate for use in contemporary designs.

Foundry: Fann Street Foundry / Linotype
Designer: Robert Besley / Hermann Eidenbenz
Designer Nationality: British / Swiss
Date: 1845 / 1953

Below. A selection of prints from the calendar series 'Cats Let Nothing Darken Their Roar', created by multi-discipline Spanish designer, Noa Bembibre Clarendon is employed to convey a selection of abstract and emotive phrases.

I FELT BRIEFLY THAT YOU LIKED ARGUING SYNTAX

SENDING A POETIC, TENDER MOMENT BACK TO EARTH

LITTLE INFINITY

Right. *Inimigo Público* (Public Enemy) is a series of political protest posters, designed by the Brazilian husband and wife team of graphic designer and illustrator Johnny Brito and visual artist and photographer Maria Clara Feitosa, who collaborate as Vertentes Coletivo. The posters focus on four political figures from the 2018 elections and feature controversial comments they had made. The background is typeset in Fit by David Jonathan Ross, an ultra squared-off display type with keyline counters and apertures.

"Não falta água em São Paulo"

"Não te estupro porque você não merece"

"Pobre não tem hábito alimentar"

"Tem que manter isso aí"

Delima

ABCDEFGHIJKLMNOPQRSTUVWXYZ
abcdefghijklmnopqrstuvwxyz
1234567890 !@#?:;"*&

Foundry: Monotype
Designer: Ong Chong Wah
Designer Nationality: Malaysian
Date: 1993

Delima has similarities to the slab-serif Clarendon, and combines open counters and generous lowercase x-heights. Its serifs are short but sturdy, thus allowing closer letter spacing, which makes it extremely space efficient and therefore perfect for use as a text font.

Devin

ABCDEFGHIJKLMNOPQRSTUVWXYZ
abcdefghijklmnopqrstuvwxyz
1234567890 !@#?:;"*&

Foundry: Omnibus
Designer: Franko Luin
Designer Nationality: Swedish
Date: 1994

Despite being created primarily as a display typeface, Devin still remains surprisingly legible at smaller point sizes. The typeface is loosely influenced by Egyptian fonts. It is named after a ruined castle in Bratislava, Slovakia by its ex-Ericsson designer Franko Luin.

Digi Antiqua

ABCDEFGHIJKLMNOPQRSTUVWXYZ
abcdefghijklmnopqrstuvwxyz
1234567890 !@#?:;"*&

Foundry: Hell
Designer: Hell Design Studio
Designer Nationality: German
Date: 1968

The Hell Design Studio created Digi Antiqua primarily for use with its Digiset typesetting machines. Its letterforms were influenced by the slab-serif fonts produced in England in the early 19th century. Its clear and elegant forms make it extremely legible at small point sizes.

Egizio

ABCDEFGHIJKLMNOPQRSTUVWXYZ
abcdefghijklmnopqrstuvwxyz
1234567890 !@#?:;"*&

Foundry: Nebiolo
Designer: Aldo Novarese
Designer Nationality: Italian
Date: 1955–58

Influential typeface designer Aldo Novarese created the heavily Clarendon-influenced Egizio. It comes with an italic, and was initially designed for the Italian foundry Nebiolo. Subsequent cuts have appeared courtesy of the German type foundries URW and Elsner+Flake.

Egyptian 505

ABCDEFGHIJKLMNOPQRSTUVWXYZ
abcdefghijklmnopqrstuvwxyz
1234567890 !@#?:;"*&

Foundry: Bitstream
Designer: André Gürtler
Designer Nationality: Swiss
Date: 1966 / c. 1980s

This is Bitstream's version of a typeface by Swiss designer André Gürtler. He worked on the font with his lettering class at the Allgemeine Gewerbeschule in Basle, which was held in classroom number 505. It won first prize in Visual Graphics Corporation's typeface design competition in 1966.

Egyptian 710

ABCDEFGHIJKLMNOPQRSTUVWXYZ
abcdefghijklmnopqrstuvwxyz
1234567890 !@#?:;"*&

Foundry: Figgins Foundry / Bitstream
Designer: Figgins Foundry
Designer Nationality: British
Date: 1860 / 1987

This is Bitstream's version of Antique No. 3. 'Antique' was an early name for Egyptian types. The London-based Figgins Foundry cast a number of these types in the mid 19th century, which helped to define the contemporary styles of British printing. Bitstream digitized its font based on the original design.

Egyptienne F

ABCDEFGHIJKLMNOPQRSTUVWXYZ
abcdefghijklmnopqrstuvwxyz
1234567890 !@#?:;"*&

Foundry: Deberny & Peignot
Designer: Adrian Frutiger
Designer Nationality: Swiss
Date: 1956

Egyptienne F is the first attempt at a slab serif font by Adrian Frutiger (see p. 290). Later, he produced the Serifa typeface in 1966 and the recut Glypha in 1980. Egyptienne F is a sturdy Clarendon-style Egyptian with a medium x-height and excellent legibility at small sizes.

Else NPL

ABCDEFGHIJKLMNOPQRSTUVWXYZ
abcdefghijklmnopqrstuvwxyz
1234567890 !@#?:;"*&

Foundry: Norton Photosetting
Designer: Robert Norton
Designer Nationality: British
Date: 1982

This lively interpretation of the Century tradition was designed by Robert Norton, a shrewd businessman keen to engage with developing type technologies. He went on to join Microsoft in the 1990s, and was instrumental in the development of the company's TrueType font library.

Excelsior

ABCDEFGHIJKLMNOPQRSTUVWXYZ
abcdefghijklmnopqrstuvwxyz
1234567890 !@#?:;"*&

Foundry: Linotype
Designer: Chauncey H. Griffith
Designer Nationality: American
Date: 1931

Designer Chauncey H. Griffith consulted an optometrists' legibility survey before beginning work on Excelsior, which is an Ionic slab serif created with newspapers in mind. It is one of five designs by Griffith for Linotype's Legibility Group of typefaces and remains highly regarded within editorial design.

FS Clerkenwell

ABCDEFGHIJKLMNOPQRSTUVWXYZ
abcdefghijklmnopqrstuvwxyz
1234567890 !@#?:;"*&

Foundry: Fontsmith
Designer: Phil Garnham / Jason Smith
Designer Nationality: British
Date: 2003

The asymmetric details and upwardly angled leading serifs of this characterful font were the result of extensive experimentation by Phil Garnham and Jason Smith. Their resulting design is a distinctive, contemporary interpretation of the slab-serif style, available in four weights.

ITC Bookman

ABCDEFGHIJKLMNOPQRSTUVWXYZ
abcdefghijklmnopqrstuvwxyz
1234567890 !@#?:;"*&

Foundry: ITC
Designer: Ed Benguiat
Designer Nationality: American
Date: 1975

Ed Benguiat (see p. 514) designed ITC Bookman based on several 19th-century antique or slab-serif typefaces that themselves referenced Old Style serifs such as Caslon. Its bold texture and set of decorative swashes made the typeface popular within advertising after its release.

ITC Century

ABCDEFGHIJKLMNOPQRSTUVWXYZ
abcdefghijklmnopqrstuvwxyz
1234567890 !@#?:;"*&

Foundry: ITC
Designer: Linn Boyd Benton / Morris Fuller Benton / Tony Stan
Designer Nationality: American
Date: 1894 / 1980

This ITC typeface is based on a late 19th-century design for *Century Magazine* by Linn Boyd Benton, whose son Morris Fuller Benton further extended the font family for American Type Founders over the following decades. Tony Stan's revival of the original Century features narrower letter spacing.

ITC Charter

ABCDEFGHIJKLMNOPQRSTUVWXYZ
abcdefghijklmnopqrstuvwxyz
1234567890 !@#?:;"*&

Foundry: ITC
Designer: Matthew Carter
Designer Nationality: British
Date: 1987

Matthew Carter (see p. 616) designed Charter for ITC in 1987, with the intention of creating a typeface that would perform well in both high-resolution digital contexts and in lower-quality print conditions. ITC Charter's square skeleton ensures it reproduces well even at small point sizes.

ITC Cheltenham

ABCDEFGHIJKLMNOPQRSTUVWXYZ
abcdefghijklmnopqrstuvwxyz
1234567890 !@#?:;"*&

Foundry: ITC
Designer: Bertram Goodhue / Tony Stan
Designer Nationality: American
Date: 1896 / 1975

ITC stalwart Tony Stan was enlisted in the mid 1970s to fine-tune the proportions of the original Cheltenham, designed in 1896 by architect Bertram Goodhue. A subsequent condensed version for headlines, designed by Matthew Carter (see p. 616), was commissioned in 2003 by *The New York Times*.

ITC Cushing

ABCDEFGHIJKLMNOPQRSTUVWXYZ
abcdefghijklmnopqrstuvwxyz
1234567890 !@#?:;"*&

Foundry: ITC
Designer: J. Stearns Cushing / Vincent Pacella
Designer Nationality: American
Date: 1897 / 1992

Cushing was based on a design by New England printer and typographer J. Stearns Cushing from 1897, which was licensed and released by several other foundries more than a century after its appearance. Vincent Pacella's update adjusts the design of the uppercase letterforms.

ITC Pacella

ABCDEFGHIJKLMNOPQRSTUVWXYZ
abcdefghijklmnopqrstuvwxyz
1234567890 !@#?:;"*&

Foundry: ITC
Designer: Vincent Pacella
Designer Nationality: American
Date: 1987

This sturdy typeface by US designer Vincent Pacella was influenced by the highly legible forms of Century Schoolbook and Corona, among others. Characterful details such as the open bowls of the uppercase P and R ensure that it displays a distinct personality all of its own.

Designer Profile

Margaret Calvert

Typographer and graphic designer Margaret Calvert is renowned for her work, alongside design partner Jock Kinneir, creating the typographical and pictorial architecture and typefaces for British airports, road and rail networks in the 1960s.

She was born in South Africa and moved to the UK, where she studied at the Chelsea College of Art. There Kinneir, a graphic designer, was her tutor and mentor. In 1957, he asked for her assistance with the design of the wayfinding signage at the UK's second largest airport, Gatwick. Their first-ever foray into a project of this magnitude resulted in a solution of employing a black on yellow scheme as a highly effective way to aid passenger navigation. Calvert went on to work further with Kinneir and in 1966, they formed Kinneir Calvert Associates. Soon, the firm was appointed by the government's Anderson Committee to design the system for the UK's road and motorway network.

A key factor of this daunting challenge was designing a new typeface, one to be employed across the nation that could be easily read at high speeds, provide concise information and in varying light conditions. After much testing, Calvert created and drew a mixed-case sans serif design using Akzidenz-Grotesk as a starting point, which gave rise to a new typeface, Transport. In addition to this hugely successful typeface and graphical structure for the signage, Calvert developed an easy-to-understand pictogram system for warnings and instructions, taking their cue from pre-existing European road signs. The structures for these signs were formed of triangular frames for warnings, circles for instructions and squares for information.

Calvert and Kinneir then designed the Rail Alphabet typeface used on the British railway system in the early 1960s. Its first outing was in National Health Service hospitals. It was then adopted by the British Rail network and later by all British Airports Authority airports as well as the Danish railway corporation, DSB. It was employed until the early 1990s, when the privatization of the networks meant an amalgam of identities and differing typefaces were introduced. In 2009, a digital version of Rail Alphabet was created from Calvert's original drawings and letterforms. Called New Rail Alphabet, it was created by A2-Type's Henrik Kubel and Scott Williams, who worked closely with Calvert on the project.

Calvert has also designed a number of commercial fonts for Monotype, including the slab-serif design Calvert (see p. 51) in 1980. She served as a lecturer and head of graphic design at London's Royal College of Art between 1961 and 2001. In 2004, she was granted an honorary degree by the University of the Arts London and in 2016 was awarded the Order of the British Empire for services to typography and road safety.

Date: 1936–
Nationality: British
Notable typefaces:
Calvert (see p. 51)

Below left. The plethora of differing styles, sizes and formats of the UK's road signs prior to Calvert and Kinneir's redesign. Here newly made road signs are being stored at the RAC sign factory in London, 1936.

Below middle / right. Margaret Calvert, Jock Kinneir.

Opposite. Examples of the redesigned warning and road signs employing the Transport sans serif and the new graphical structure. Motorway signs are always in blue with all white lettering with non-primary routes in black lettering on white backgrounds as shown in the London Design Museum show *This is Design*. A green background on signs signifies the routes are primary with destinations in white and road numbers in yellow.

ITC Stone Informal

ABCDEFGHIJKLMNOPQRSTUVWXYZ
abcdefghijklmnopqrstuvwxyz
1234567890 !@#?:;"*&

Foundry: ITC
Designer: Sumner Stone / Bob Ishi
Designer Nationality: American
Date: 1988

US type designer Sumner Stone studied sociology and mathematics before moving into typeface design, a field in which he has since had a distinguished career. This rounded serif style, part of the extensive Stone superfamily, was designed with a colleague of his at Adobe, Bob Ishi.

ITC Stone Serif

ABCDEFGHIJKLMNOPQRSTUVWXYZ
abcdefghijklmnopqrstuvwxyz
1234567890!@#?:;"*&

Foundry: ITC
Designer: Sumner Stone
Designer Nationality: American
Date: 1987

This stately predecessor to ITC Stone Informal was designed to complement the other members of the Stone family, offering a versatile toolkit to serve a range of typesetting needs. Type designer John Renner added more than 300 phonetic characters to the typeface in 1992.

Kleukens-Egyptienne FSL

ABCDEFGHIJKLMNOPQRSTUVWXYZ
abcdefghijklmnopqrstuvwxyz
1234567890 !@#?:;"+&

Foundry: Forgotten Shapes
Designer: Friedrich Wilhelm Kleukens / Reymund Schröder
Designer Nationality: German
Date: 1929 / 2018

Kleukens-Egyptienne FSL is Reymund Schröder's digitization of German designer Friedrich Wilhelm Kleukens's design of 1929. Schröder worked from a low-resolution scan of the trial proof, alongside three initial sketches, to reproduce the strength and details of Kleukens's original concept.

Marlene

ABCDEFGHIJKLMNOPQRSTUVWXYZ
abcdefghijklmnopqrstuvwxyz
1234567890 !@#?:;"*&

Foundry: Typotheque
Designer: Nikola Djurek
Designer Nationality: Croatian
Date: 2008

Marlene is a high-contrast Egyptian face designed by Nikola Djurek. It has long vertical serifs with square edges, a sharp italic and a large x-height. It comes in four weights, ranging from Light to Bold. The family also contains three display faces: Marlene Grand, Stencil and Display.

Melior

ABCDEFGHIJKLMNOPQRSTUVWXYZ
abcdefghijklmnopqrstuvwxyz
1234567890 !@#?:;"'*&

Foundry: Stempel
Designer: Hermann Zapf
Designer Nationality: German
Date: 1952

Melior is a fairly heavy and square roman serif by Hermann Zapf (see p. 574). It has short ascenders and descenders, and an italic that is the roman at an angle, although the 'a' switches from two-storey to single in the italic. Zapf was inspired by the squared-off circle shape of a superellipse.

Monotype Century Schoolbook

ABCDEFGHIJKLMNOPQRSTUVWXYZ
abcdefghijklmnopqrstuvwxyz
1234567890 !@#?:;"*&

Foundry: Monotype
Designer: Morris Fuller Benton / Monotype Studio
Designer Nationality: American
Date: 1894 / 1915

Linn Boyd Benton designed Century for *Century Magazine* in 1894. Schoolbook, which has prominent slab serifs and open spacing, was an adaption by his son, Morris Fuller, intended for school textbooks and young readers in 1915. Legibility, clarity and easy reading were the key aims.

Monotype Clarendon

ABCDEFGHIJKLMNOPQRSTUVWXYZ
abcdefghijklmnopqrstuvwxyz
1234567890 !@#?:;"*&

Foundry: Monotype
Designer: Robert Besley / Monotype Studio
Designer Nationality: British
Date: 1845 / c. 1960s

Clarendon was initially released by London's Fann Street Foundry as an evolution of the Egyptian style. It introduced varied stroke widths but kept the large, square serifs. Clarendon is a robust, friendly face best used for headlines and display, rather than body text.

Monotype Ionic

ABCDEFGHIJKLMNOPQRSTUVWXYZ
abcdefghijklmnopqrstuvwxyz
1234567890 !@#?:;"*&

Foundry: Monotype
Designer: Vincent Figgins
Designer Nationality: British
Date: 1821

Ionic was designed by London based typefounder Vincent Figgins in the early 19th century. Its large x-height, short ascenders and descenders, and prominent serifs, makes it highly readable at small sizes. Its legibility has made it a popular choice for newspapers for well over a century.

Monotype New Clarendon

ABCDEFGHIJKLMNOPQRSTUVWXYZ
abcdefghijklmnopqrstuvwxyz
1234567890 !@#?:;"*&

Foundry: Monotype
Designer: Robert Besley / Monotype Studio
Designer Nationality: British
Date: 1845 / 1960

New Clarendon has slightly more contrast and thinner serifs than the standard Clarendon, and also has a much shorter 't' and no top serif on the 'q'. Monotype released this update in 1960 following Clarendon's popularity during the 1950s. It is available in regular and bold versions.

New Century Schoolbook

ABCDEFGHIJKLMNOPQRSTUVWXYZ
abcdefghijklmnopqrstuvwxyz
1234567890 !@#?:;"*&

Foundry: Linotype
Designer: Morris Fuller Benton / Matthew Carter
Designer Nationality: American / British
Date: 1915 / 1980

New Century Schoolbook is an update of Morris Fuller Benton's typeface Century Schoolbook, made in 1980 by Matthew Carter (see p. 616) for Linotype. It is an extremely legible text face, with a large x-height, a vertical axis and strong, bracketed serifs. It is available in roman and bold with italics.

News 701

ABCDEFGHIJKLMNOPQRSTUVWXYZ
abcdefghijklmnopqrstuvwxyz
1234567890 !@#?:;"*&

Foundry: Bitstream
Designer: Chauncey H. Griffith
Designer Nationality: American
Date: 1925

News 701 is Bitstream's version of Chauncey H. Griffith's Ionic No. 5 of 1925, which was the first release from Linotype's Legibility Group, a series of easily read faces designed to be used by newspapers with Linotype's hot-metal typesetting system. News 701 comes in regular, italic and bold.

News 702

ABCDEFGHIJKLMNOPQRSTUVWXYZ
abcdefghijklmnopqrstuvwxyz
1234567890 !@#?:;"*&

Foundry: Bitstream
Designer: Chauncey H. Griffith
Designer Nationality: American
Date: 1931

News 702 is Bitstream's version of Chauncey H. Griffith's Excelsior, the second release from Linotype's Legibility Group in 1931, created for newspapers printing with rubber-roller presses. News 702 is a newspaper text face with horizontal serifs and a fairly even colour.

Nimrod

ABCDEFGHIJKLMNOPQRSTUVWXYZ
abcdefghijklmnopqrstuvwxyz
1234567890 !@#?:;"*&

Foundry: Monotype
Designer: Robin Nicholas
Designer Nationality: British
Date: 1980

Monotype produced the Nimrod superfamily of eighteen fonts in response to the needs of the modern newspaper industry. It is an evolution of traditional Ionic newspaper faces with less fine detail, making it easier to read when small and less prone to degradation when cast in metal.

Scherzo

ABCDEFGHIJKLMNOPQRSTUVWXYZ
abcdefghijklmnopqrstuvwxyz
1234567890 !@#?:;"*&

Foundry: Monotype
Designer: Albert Boton
Designer Nationality: French
Date: 1996

Scherzo is a Clarendon serif designed for both body text and headlines. The minimal stroke contrast, elongated serifs and abrupt brackets provide muscle in the demi and bold weights, while also ensuring the face has character and clarity in the regular weight.

Superclarendon

ABCDEFGHIJKLMNOPQRSTUVWXY
abcdefghijklmnopqrstuvwxyz
1234567890 !@#?:;"*&

Foundry: Typodermic
Designer: Ray Larabie
Designer Nationality: Canadian
Date: 2007

Superclarendon is a salute to Robert Besley's Clarendon font family from the mid 1800s, and is both a revival and expansion of Besley's design. Alongside the original features, details from other popular 19th-century faces were added to enhance its character and complexion.

Ysobel

ABCDEFGHIJKLMNOPQRSTUVWXYZ
abcdefghijklmnopqrstuvwxyz
1234567890 !@#?:;"*&

Foundry: Monotype
Designer: Robin Nicholas / Delve Withrington / Alice Savoie
Designer Nationality: British / American / French
Date: 2009

Ysobel is a clarendon serif designed for the diverse needs of editorial design. In all four weights, including a redrawn Display version, Ysobel fuses the approachability of open, gentle forms with the precision of incised serifs and robust strokes for optimal legibility.

Belwe Mono

ABCDEFGHIJKLMNOPQRSTUVWXYZ
abcdefghijklmnopqrstuvwxyz
1234567890 !?:;”*&

With unusual detailing and proportions, Belwe is an Art Nouveau-inspired slab serif with blackletter influences. Its many quirky characters, angled serifs and calligraphic flourishes made it a popular choice when released by Schelter & Giesecke. After its first revival by Letraset, it was reissued many times.

Foundry: Letraset
Designer: Georg Belwe / Alan Meeks
Designer Nationality: German / British
Date: 1926 / 1976

Beton

ABCDEFGHIJKLMNOPQRSTUVWXYZ
abcdefghijklmnopqrstuvwxyz
1234567890 !@#?:;”*&

Beton's name references the French term *Béton* (raw concrete). A geometric slab serif, it shares many similarities with Memphis, its competitor when it was released in the 1930s. What distinguishes this monoline typeface is its double-storey 'a'. It was updated later by URW and Linotype.

Foundry: Bauersche Giesserei
Designer: Heinrich Jost
Designer Nationality: German
Date: 1931–36

Courier 10 Pitch

ABCDEFGHIJKLMNOPQRSTUVWXYZ
abcdefghijklmnopqrstuvwxyz
1234567890 !@#?:;”*&

Bitstream's version of the instantly recognizable monospaced slab serif displays all the characteristics of the original typewriter font designed by Howard Kettler for IBM. The typeface was made freely available and soon became the industry standard typeface for all machines.

Foundry: Bitstream
Designer: Howard Kettler
Designer Nationality: American
Date: 1955

Courier LT Round

ABCDEFGHIJKLMNOPQRSTUVWXYZ
abcdefghijklmnopqrstuvwxyz
1234567890 !@#?:;”*&

Linotype's version of this well-known IBM typewriter font has Regular and Bold weights, with obliques and rounded terminals. Its sister version, Courier, has flat terminals, an optional oblique, a Medium weight, and Central European and Cyrillic companions.

Foundry: Linotype
Designer: Howard Kettler
Designer Nationality: American
Date: 1955

Calvert

ABCDEFGHIJKLMNOPQRSTUVWXYZ
abcdefghijklmnopqrstuvwxyz
1234567890 !@#?:;"*&

Foundry: Monotype
Designer: Margaret Calvert
Designer Nationality: British
Date: 1980

Calvert takes its name from Margaret Calvert (see p. 44), who is renowned for having worked with Jock Kinneir to design most of the British road and traffic-warning signs of the 1950s and 1960s. This typeface is based on a commission for the Tyne and Wear Metro system in north-east England during the 1980s.

Calvert is a timeless slab serif, and its contemporary appearance and unique design come from the fact many of the characters have only half serifs, such as the 'A', 'M' and 'X'. This design choice results in a typeface with a constructed aesthetic that still retains a humanist quality to the characters. The typeface possesses a beautiful consistency in its letterforms, making for a very clear presentation in display applications.

Margaret Calvert is known for her typeface designs on British transportation signage. Her notable creations include Transport, which was created between 1957 and 1963 and is used on road signs throughout Britain, and Rail Alphabet, which was devised in 1964 and is employed on the nation's railway system.

Below. Cartlidge Levene's wayfinding system employing Margaret Calvert's eponymously titled slab serif typeface in the Royal College of Arts Dyson Building. The signage features a specially created reduced stencil version of Calvert, titled Calvert Brody, which was created by three generations of RCA type design luminaries: Margaret Calvert, Neville Brody and Henrik Kubel of A2-Type.

Courier New

ABCDEFGHIJKLMNOPQRSTUVWXYZ
abcdefghijklmnopqrstuvwxyz
1234567890 !@#?:;"*&

Foundry: Monotype
Designer: Howard Kettler /
Adrian Frutiger
Designer Nationality: American /
Swiss
Date: 1955 / 2008

Howard Kettler and the Monotype Studio designed Courier in 1955 as a commission for IBM. The highly recognizable monospaced slab serif is the original typewriter typeface, spawning many variants from other foundries big and small. This was possible because IBM decided not to seek any form of copyright or trademark over the design.

Courier's monospacing reflects the charm of old typewritten letters where all the characters were evenly spaced out when struck, therefore creating unsightly gaps when set. By incorporating this mechanical restraint within its design, Courier has a certain rawness when used as text. However, in lists or tables it can be used as an advantage in aligning content. Despite the awkwardness of the typeface's setting and the distinctive appearance of emulating typewriter's letterforms, it has remained incredibly

popular. Its functional and basic appearance have meant it has been widely used in everything from official-looking documents, through to designs emulating telegrams and letters, and on advertising.

Renowned Swiss type designer Adrian Frutiger (see p. 290) redrew this later version, Courier New, for Monotype. The font family includes Courier New, Courier New Bold, Courier New Italic and Courier New Bold Italic. Primarily used on IBM's popular model range of Selectric electric typewriters in the early 1960s, the family was later used as a system font appearing on Windows 3.1 and has remained the default font for monospaced typesetting and plain text usage on PCs.

Below left. Graphic identity, infographics and UI design for an exhibition about language in the Estonian National Museum by Margus Tamm.

Below right. Acoustic by Noize MC. Contributed by Mikhail Rul on 26 February 2016. Artwork published in 2015.

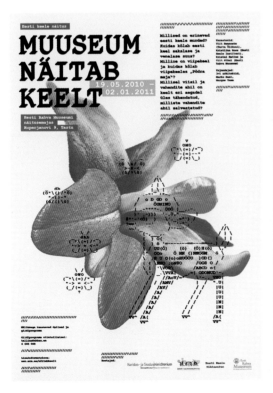

Cumberland

ABCDEFGHIJKLMNOPQRSTUVWXYZ
abcdefghijklmnopqrstuvwxyz
1234567890 !@#?:;"*&

Foundry: Monotype
Designer: Monotype Studio
Designer Nationality: British
Date: 1999

This monospaced typewriter-style typeface is very much in the same genre as the ubiquitous Courier. Cumberland was designed and digitized in-house at the Monotype Studio in Redhill, Surrey, England to offer as an alternative to. It supports up to fifty languages.

Egyptian Slate

ABCDEFGHIJKLMNOPQRSTUVWXYZ
abcdefghijklmnopqrstuvwxyz
1234567890 !@#?:;"*&

Foundry: Monotype
Designer: Rod McDonald
Designer Nationality: Canadian
Date: 2008

Rod McDonald developed Egyptian Slate from the Slate sans serif typeface he created in 2006. It is a poised slab serif available in six weights from Light to Black with complementary italics. Following on from Slate, the typeface was later reissued as Gibson in 2011.

Gelo

ABCDEFGHIJKLMNOPQRSTUVWXYZ
abcdefghijklmnopqrstuvwxyz
1234567890 !@#?:;"*&

Foundry: Dalton Maag
Designer: Tom Foley / Sebastian Losch
Designer Nationality: Irish / German
Date: 2017

Gelo is an expressive font family that merges the structural authority of a slab serif with the approachable strokes of brush lettering. While the font's shape is principally geometric, the serifs and joints hint towards a more organic construction. It was designed for both print and digital use.

Geometric Slabserif 703

ABCDEFGHIJKLMNOPQRSTUVWXYZ
abcdefghijklmnopqrstuvwxyz
1234567890 !@#?:;"*&

Foundry: Bitstream
Designer: Rudolf Wolf
Designer Nationality: German
Date: 1929 / 1990

This Bitstream typeface is a digitization of Rudolf Wolf's Memphis of 1929, which added slab serifs to the geometric forms popularized within Modernist type designs such as Futura. Bitstream's revival of this popular font adds a range of condensed weights to the original family.

Geometric Slabserif 712

ABCDEFGHIJKLMNOPQRSTUVWXYZ
abcdefghijklmnopqrstuvwxyz
1234567890 !@#?:;"*&

This is a Bitstream digitization of an earlier slab serif. Its monolinear design is based on Monotype's popular Rockwell typeface of 1934, which was itself based on a US slab-serif design from 1910, Litho Antique. Rockwell is more suited for display type than lengthy body text.

Foundry: Bitstream
Designer: William Schraubstadter / Frank Hinman Pierpont / Manvel Shmavonyan / Isay Slutsker
Designer Nationality: American / American / Armenian / Russian
Date: 1910 / 1934 / 1999

HoTom

ABCDEFGHIJKLMNOPQRSTUVWXYZ
abcdefghijklmnopqrstuvwxyz
1234567890 !@#?:;"*&

The uncluttered design of this orderly slab serif is particularly well-suited to long passages of body text. HoTom was submitted to Linotype for its International Digital Type Design Contest in 1994 and later released as part of the foundry's TakeType Library that features competition winners.

Foundry: Linotype
Designer: Thomas Hofmann
Designer Nationality: German
Date: 1994

ITC American Typewriter

ABCDEFGHIJKLMNOPQRSTUVWXYZ
abcdefghijklmnopqrstuvwxyz
1234567890 !@#?:;"*&

Foundry: ITC
Designer: Joel Kaden / Tony Stan
Designer Nationality: American
Date: 1974

International Typeface Corporation (ITC) launched the ITC American Typewriter typeface as part of the celebrations in 1974 to commemorate the 100th anniversary of the invention of the office typewriter. ITC adopted the charm of this genre of letterforms as an homage to the forerunners of today's digital machines, yet reworked them to be a far more usable and aesthetically pleasing experience. The foundry chose to break away from the monospaced setting of existing designs and create a proportionally spaced font. This change allows the design to be used for a wider range of applications, just as a conventional text typeface would. The accompanying improvement in readability means it also works far better in roles such as text setting.

ITC Lubalin Graph

ABCDEFGHIJKLMNOPQRSTUVWXYZ
abcdefghijklmnopqrstuvwxyz
1234567890 !@#?:;"*&

Foundry: ITC
Designer: Herb Lubalin /
Ed Benguiat / Tony DiSpigna /
Joe Sundwall
Designer Nationality: American
Date: 1974

ITC Lubalin Graph is a giant among the extensive range of geometric slab-serif, or Egyptian types. Lubalin Graph's striking rectangular slab serifs and powerful circular forms create a practical yet friendly design. It is ideal for display and titling work or short extents of text, and the larger the typeface when used, the more striking any design becomes.

Designer Herb Lubalin (see p. 62) based the design of Lubalin Graph around that of his ITC Avant Garde Gothic san serif. The two faces share the basic geometric character shapes, tight letter spacing and generous x-height. When paired together, they make for an ideal marriage between sans and serif.

To create the design, Lubalin collaborated with Ed Benguiat (see p. 514). It was then drawn up to fit the requirements of typographic reproduction by Tony DiSpigna and Joe Sundwall in 1974. Condensed weights, including small caps and Old Style figures, were added to the family by Helga Jörgenson and Sigrid Engelmann in 1992.

Below. Vinyl single cover design employing ITC Lubalin Graph Extra Light for Aretha Franklin and George Benson released in 1981.

Lexia Mono

ABCDEFGHIJKLMNOPQRSTUVWXYZ
abcdefghijklmnopqrstuvwxyz
1234567890 !@#?:;"*&

Lexia Mono is a monospaced slab serif designed intentionally for complex, text-heavy compositions. Its clean rhythm helps make it easy to read. Unlike most monospaced fonts, Lexia Mono is available in several weights, each with a true italic, and has an elevated x-height for readability in small sizes.

Foundry: Dalton Maag
Designer: Ron Carpenter / Elí Castellanos / Spike Spondike
Designer Nationality: British / Mexican / American
Date: 2018

Memphis

ABCDEFGHIJKLMNOPQRSTUVWXYZ
abcdefghijklmnopqrstuvwxyz
1234567890 !@#?:;"*&

Rudolf Wolf designed the Memphis slab serif for Stempel at the end of the 1920s. Its timeless look helped it remain popular throughout the 20th century and it is considered one of the first Egyptian revivals. Initially, Memphis was available in four weights: Light, Medium, Bold and Extra Bold.

Foundry: Stempel
Designer: Rudolf Wolf
Designer Nationality: German
Date: 1929

Memphis Soft Rounded

ABCDEFGHIJKLMNOPQRSTUVWXYZ
abcdefghijklmnopqrstuvwxyz
1234567890 !@#?:;"*&

Memphis Soft Rounded is an adaption of Rudolf Wolf's Memphis slab serif of 1929 done in-house by Linotype. It takes the original and replaces all of the right angles with soft curves. The result is a far friendlier typeface that comes in three weights: Medium, Bold and Extra Bold.

Foundry: Linotype
Designer: Rudolf Wolf / Linotype Design Studio
Designer Nationality: German
Date: 1929 / Unknown

Monotype Courier 12

ABCDEFGHIJKLMNOPQRSTUVWXYZ
abcdefghijklmnopqrstuvwxyz
1234567890 !@#?:;"*&

Courier 12 is a version of the monospaced typewriter font Courier, which was created by US designer Howard Kettler for IBM in 1955. Courier 12 comes in one weight, which is lighter, finer and more widely spaced than the regular weight of the standard Courier.

Foundry: Monotype
Designer: Howard Kettler
Designer Nationality: American
Date: 1955

November Slab

ABCDEFGHIJKLMNOPQRSTUVWXYZ
abcdefghijklmnopqrstuvwxyz
1234567890 !@#?:;"*&

Foundry: Typotheque
Designer: Peter Biľak
Designer Nationality: Slovakian
Date: 2018

A functional, robust slab-serif, Biľak's November Slab is a large type family available in three widths – regular, condensed and compressed – and nine weights – hairline to black, all with italics for Latin, Cyrillic and Greek. The original sans serif November was released in 2016.

Peggs

ABCDEFGHIJKLMNOPQRSTUVWXYZ
abcdefghijklmnopqrstuvwxyz
1234567890 !@#?:;"*&

Foundry: Colophon
Designer: The Entente
Designer Nationality: British
Date: 2009

Based on monospaced typewriter fonts and the quirks that appear from using unsophisticated printing techniques and materials, Peggs was first created in a singular bold weight for the identity of Brighton fashion shop Peggs & Son. It was later redrawn, re-spaced and extended.

Prestige 12 Pitch

ABCDEFGHIJKLMNOPQRSTUVWXYZ
abcdefghijklmnopqrstuvwxyz
1234567890 !@#?:;"*&

Foundry: Bitstream
Designer: Clayton Smith
Designer Nationality: American
Date: 1953 / c. 1980s

Prestige 12 Pitch is Bitstream's digitization of Clayton Smith's Prestige Elite Typewriter design of 1953. Smith designed typewriter fonts at IBM, Lexington and developed this monospaced slab serif to improve both the character and legibility of typewriter text.

Rockwell Nova

ABCDEFGHIJKLMNOPQRSTUVWXYZ
abcdefghijklmnopqrstuvwxyz
1234567890 !@#?:;"*&

Foundry: Monotype
Designer: Monotype Studio
Date: Unknown

Rockwell Nova builds upon the original Rockwell font family. It retains all the quintessential qualities of the design while adding depth and diversity. The expanded font family includes thirteen variations, ranging from Condensed to Extra Bold, and suits both display and text uses.

Rockwell

ABCDEFGHIJKLMNOPQRSTUVWXYZ
abcdefghijklmnopqrstuvwxyz
1234567890 !@#?:;"*&

Foundry: Monotype
Designer: Frank Hinman Pierpont
Designer Nationality: American
Date: 1934

Slab serifs, or Egyptian, types were derived from early wood-carved typefaces and were used for large display types. Because of the difficulty in carving wood and the inability to create intricate and subtle shapes, these types adopted slab serifs for ease of creation. Rockwell's ancestry is no different; it is based on the Litho Antique font cast in 1910 by William A. Schraubstadter for the Inland Type Foundry. It, and similar typefaces, became popular over the next twenty years in the United States and Europe. Consequently, in 1931, the American Type Founders foundry asked Morris Fuller Benton to create a reissue with added characters and refinements, called Rockwell Antique.

However, Rockwell's evolution was still not over. In 1934, the esteemed type designer Frank Hinman Pierpont, in partnership with Monotype, created the Rockwell typeface family that exists today. This final design incorporated many refinements in spacing, letter weights and glyphs.

Rockwell is highly versatile, can be used in both display and text applications and is available in nine variations, including italics, differing weights and condensed versions. As with most slab serifs, its consistency and boldness allow it to be used in signage, wayfinding applications and branding.

Below. Rockwell employed on the walls of the Achievement First Endeavor Middle School in Brooklyn, New York. Created by renowned Pentagram partner Paula Scher with Andrew Freeman and Drea Zlanabitnig.

Rockwell WGL

ABCDEFGHIJKLMNOPQRSTUVWXYZ
abcdefghijklmnopqrstuvwxyz
1234567890 !@#?:;"*&

Foundry: Monotype
Designer: Monotype Studio
Date: 1934 / c. 1980s

Rockwell WGL is an update of the original Rockwell font family, designed for enhanced compatibility with Microsoft's Windows operating system. Unlike other Rockwell font families, Rockwell WGL includes the Windows Glyph List character set. It supports more than seventy-nine languages.

Serifa

ABCDEFGHIJKLMNOPQRSTUVWXYZ
abcdefghijklmnopqrstuvwxyz
1234567890 !@#?:;"*&

Foundry: Bauer
Designer: Adrian Frutiger
Designer Nationality: Swiss
Date: 1968

Serif is a traditional slab serif designed by Adrian Frutiger (see p. 290) and adapted from Univers, the sans serif face that he created in the 1950s. By lowering the x-height, Frutiger was able to balance the addition of block serifs with the original frame and geometry of Univers.

Square Slabserif 711

ABCDEFGHIJKLMNOPQRSTUVWXYZ
abcdefghijklmnopqrstuvwxyz
1234567890 !@#?:;"*&

Foundry: Bitstream
Designer: Georg Trump
Designer Nationality: German
Date: c. 1900–10 / 1990

Square Slabserif 711 is a revival of the slab-serif types of the early 20th century. It was republished by Bitstream for the digital devices that emerged in the 1990s, because its geometric frame balances right angles and opposing curves, ensuring readability on screen and in print.

Stymie

ABCDEFGHIJKLMNOPQRSTUVWXYZ
abcdefghijklmnopqrstuvwxyz
1234567890 !@#?:;"*&

Foundry: ATF / Bitstream
Designer: Morris Fuller Benton / Sol Hess / Gerry Powell
Designer Nationality: American
Date: 1931 / c. 1980s

Stymie is Bitstream's digitization of an early 20th-century slab serif of the same name by Morris Fuller Benton. American Type Founders (ATF) commissioned it as a reworking of popular slab serifs of the time. Weights were added later by Sol Hess at Lanston Monotype and Gerry Powell at ATF.

Tesla Slab

ABCDEFGHIJKLMNOPQRSTUVWXYZ
abcdefghijklmnopqrstuvwxyz
1234567890 !@#?:;"*&

Tesla Slab is an expressive slab serif with smooth curves, which boasts true italics and six different weights, from Hairline to Bold. Unlike many slabs, the strong strokes of Nikola Djurek's design features a slight variation in their width in order to convey both eloquence and industry.

Foundry: Typotheque
Designer: Nikola Djurek
Designer Nationality: Croatian
Date: 2015

Tribunal

ABCDEFGHIJKLMNOPQRSTUVWXYZ
abcdefghijklmnopqrstuvwxyz
1234567890 !@#?:;"*&

Tribunal was conceived as a custom typeface for a cross-platform Slovenian student magazine, *Tribuna*, and was always intended for both printed and digital environments. The type family won the Brumen Award for typeface design at the 5th Slovene Biennale of Visual Communication in 2011.

Foundry: Typotheque
Designer: Aljaž Vindiš
Designer Nationality: Slovenian
Date: 2011

Trilogy Egyptian

ABCDEFGHIJKLMNOPQRSTUVWXYZ
abcdefghijklmnopqrstuvwxyz
1234567890 !@#?:;"*&

Trilogy Egyptian is a bold, headline slab serif inspired by the visual richness of 19th-century printed ephemera. Unlike the geometric forms of most early 20th-century slabs, the typeface combines a modern shape with the decorative details of late Victorian type design.

Foundry: Jeremy Tankard Typography
Designer: Jeremy Tankard
Designer Nationality: British
Date: 2009

Typewriter

ABCDEFGHIJKLMNOPQRSTUVWXYZ
abcdefghijklmnopqrstuvwxyz
1234567890 !@#?:;"*&

The Typewriter font family is a fixed-pitch, slab-serif typeface, designed to imitate the letterforms produced on a typewriter. The characters are monospaced and mix symmetrical, flat serifs with bulbous terminals, alongside artificial ink traps and dark spots.

Foundry: Monotype
Designer: Monotype Studio
Date: Unknown

Albertus

ABCDEFGHIJKLMNOPQRSTUVWXYZ
abcdefghijklmnopqrstuvwxyz
1234567890 !@#?:;"✻&

Foundry: Monotype
Designer: Berthold Wolpe
Designer Nationality: German
Date: 1932

Albertus was designed by German type designer and typographer Berthold Wolpe to satisfy a commission by renowned British typographer Stanley Morrison for Monotype in 1932. The typeface was inspired by raised letterform inscriptions carved out of bronze, and the first release was in an all-capital, titling weight in 1935. A Roman upper- and lowercase design followed in 1938 and a Light weight in 1940. Albertus's bold simple strokes with subtle, minimal glyphic serifs make it an elegant and highly legible typeface used for display and titling applications. In 1941, Wolpe joined book publisher Faber & Faber in London, where he remained until his retirement in 1975. He became one of the great book-cover designers of the time, publishing more than 1,500 covers and dust jackets.

Right: Page designs from the exhibition catalogue to accompany the exhibition *David Bowie Is* at the V&A Museum, London. Albertus was used as the headline face in the book and the exhibition. Design by Barnbrook studio.

Albertus Nova

ABCDEFGHIJKLMNOPQRSTUVWXYZ
abcdefghijklmnopqrstuvwxyz
1234567890 !@#?:;"✻&

Foundry: Monotype
Designer: Berthold Wolpe / Toshi Omagari
Designer Nationality: German / Japanese
Date: 1932 / 2017

Berthold Wolpe's distinctive Albertus design is famous for its use on signage in the City of London. Toshi Omagari's Albertus Nova revives and extends it, revisiting some of the compromises made for metal typesetting. It comprises five weights, Greek and Cyrillic characters and alternative caps.

Americana

ABCDEFGHIJKLMNOPQRSTUVWXYZ
abcdefghijklmnopqrstuvwxyz
1234567890 !@#?:;"*&

Foundry: American Type Founders
Designer: Richard Isbell
Designer Nationality: American
Date: 1965

Americana was named in honour of the United States Bicentennial in 1976 and is the last face cut by American Type Founders. The stylized design features generous letterforms, large counters, short ascenders and descenders, flared serifs and a large x-height. It is best suited for short text.

Herb Lubalin

Herb Lubalin was a giant in the field of US graphic and type designers of the 1960s and 1970s. His groundbreaking and cutting-edge designs as designer/art director for the design and creative journal *Avant Garde* and the International Typeface Corporation's (ITC) magazine *U&lc*, along with his typeface ITC Avant Garde Gothic influenced design in the United States and internationally.

Born in New York in 1918, it wasn't until art school at the Cooper Union that his drawing pastime was directed into a passion for typography. From 1939, he was a freelance designer and typographer and then art director at a number of New York advertising agencies for more than two decades. It was during this period that his reputation was established as a master of 'expressive typography' – conceptual ideas embedded within typographical arrangements as imagery. In 1964, he set up his own studio, Herb Lubalin, and quickly established a reputation for excellence. Three years later, he joined with Ernie Smith and Tom Carnase to found Lubalin, Smith, Carnase.

At this time, Lubalin had a working relationship with Ralph Ginzburg. An author, editor, publisher and photojournalist, Ginzburg had gained notoriety for publishing books and journals on erotica and in 1963 was convicted for violating obscenity laws. He worked with Lubalin on a number of revolutionary magazines: *Eros* (1962), *Fact* (1964–67) and *Avant Garde* (1968–71). The latter had the greatest impact on Lubalin's output and legacy.

In 1970, Lubalin formed ITC with partners Aaron Burns and Edward Rondthaler. A new foundry, and one of the first created, which had no history or materials emanating from the period of type design from the hot-metal era. One of its first official releases was ITC Avant Garde Gothic, based around the masthead Lubalin had created for *Avant Garde* magazine, an entire typeface was developed from its geometric sans serif design that made full use of the advantages of phototypesetting. In addition to a set of standard characters, it possessed special characters and ligatures that were constructed around 45° angles allowing the designer to experiment with the letters when setting. Although coming under some criticism at the time for its grid-based approach and consistency, it has proved to be a highly legible and one of the most successful and popular sans serif display typeface designs of all time.

In 1973, ITC launched its quarterly journal, *U&lc* with Lubalin as editor and art director. His experimentation and ideas were given free rein and he worked on the journal until his death in 1981. *U&lc* was not only an international success it was a must-have journal with a circulation of more than 170,000 readers. These are impressive numbers for a journal on creative typography and reflect the immeasurable impact had Lubalin had on the field of design and typography.

Date: 1918–1981
Nationality: American
Notable typefaces:
ITC Avant Garde Gothic (see p. 202)
ITC Lubalin Graph (see p. 55)

Below. Lubalin's famous Mother & Child logotype and the *Avant Garde* journal masthead designed by Lubalin and drawn by colleague Tom Carnase under Lubalin's direction.

Opposite top. Specimen booklet for ITC Serif Gothic typeface, designed by Lubalin and fellow partner at Lubalin Associates Tony di Spigna.

Opposite middle. Herb Lubalin Inc. logo (left); Herb Lubalin; and a selection of the numerous logos created and collaborated with by Lubalin over his career.

Opposite bottom. Striking logotypes (from left) for Families (1980), proposed New York City logo NY, NY (1966), masthead for *Fact* magazine (1967).

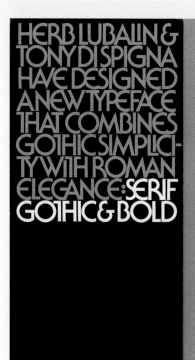

HERB LUBALIN &
TONY DI SPIGNA
HAVE DESIGNED
A NEW TYPEFACE
THAT COMBINES
GOTHIC SIMPLICI-
TY WITH ROMAN
ELEGANCE: SERIF
GOTHIC & BOLD

ITC SERIF GOTHIC & BOLD
ALTERNATE CHARACTERS

JOHN ALCORN VIA DEI SERRAGLI 132 · 50124 FIRENZE ITALIA TEL: (055) 220033

TRUMAN CAPOTE'S OTHER VOICES, OTHER ROOMS

PEACE ON EARTH GOOD WILL TO ALL MEN & JOY TO THE WORLD

ITC Serif Gothic with bold is also avail-able for headline use on our photo display typesetting machines.
Several alternate characters have been designed but unless specifically requested normal font characters will always be used.

FLAT FILE
Nº 1 — FEB 16, 2016

Herb Lubalin Study Center
of Design & Typography

Amerigo BT

ABCDEFGHIJKLMNOPQRSTUVWXYZ
abcdefghijklmnopqrstuvwxyz
1234567890 !@#?:;"*&

Foundry: Bitstream
Designer: Gerard Unger
Designer Nationality: Dutch
Date: 1987

Amerigo BT is the result of a commission to create a font similar to Optima. Gerard Unger's design is narrower and sharper than Optima, with wider ending terminals, and a greater contrast between thick and thin. The font is available in three weights with matching true italics.

Baker Signet

ABCDEFGHIJKLMNOPQRSTUVWXYZ
abcdefghijklmnopqrstuvwxyz
1234567890 !@#?:;"*&

Foundry: VGC
Designer: Arthur Baker
Designer Nationality: American
Date: 1965

Calligrapher Arthur Baker created this serif with its delicate strokes and triangular serifs. The lowercase 'y' and capital 'Q' have spirited descenders that demonstrate the typeface's close connection to handwriting. Coca-Cola adopted Baker Signet Bold for the word 'Coke' in its product branding.

Canela Deck

ABCDEFGHIJKLMNOPQRSTUVWXYZ
abcdefghijklmnopqrstuvwxyz
1234567890 !@#?:;"*&

Foundry: Commercial Type
Designer: Miguel Reyes
Designer Nationality: Mexican
Date: 2018

Canela Deck is a glyphic serif, with sturdy strokes and wedged feet, crafted for use in the middle sizes of editorial layouts. Its graceful and imposing characters are suited to texts of between 20 and 40 points in size, such as headlines on web pages or a printed pull-quote.

Canela Text

ABCDEFGHIJKLMNOPQRSTUVWXYZ
abcdefghijklmnopqrstuvwxyz
1234567890 !@#?:;"*&

Foundry: Commercial Type
Designer: Miguel Reyes
Designer Nationality: Mexican
Date: 2018

Canela Text is optimized for small sizes and designed to preserve the character and precision of Canela Deck, while adding the many features required for text use. This includes the addition of a full range of weights, alongside small caps, fractions and tabular figures.

Cantoria

ABCDEFGHIJKLMNOPQRSTUVWXYZ
abcdefghijklmnopqrstuvwxyz
1234567890 !@#?:;"'*&

Foundry: Monotype
Designer: Ron Carpenter
Designer Nationality: British
Date: 1986

With its open counters and large capitals, Cantoria is a low-key but charming serif based on marks typical of stone-cut letters. It was inspired by Thomas Maitland Cleland's typeface Della Robbia of 1902, which was in turn inspired by 15th-century Florentine inscriptional capitals.

Charlotte Serif

ABCDEFGHIJKLMNOPQRSTUVWXYZ
abcdefghijklmnopqrstuvwxyz
1234567890 !@#?:;"'*&

Foundry: ITC
Designer: Michael Gills
Designer Nationality: British
Date: 1992

Charlotte Serif is a modern roman typeface influenced by the 18th-century French type designer Pierre-Simon Fournier. It is a formal serif with strong vertical stress and unbracketed serifs. Described as having an authoritative tone, it is suitable for use in most text applications.

Flareserif 821

ABCDEFGHIJKLMNOPQRSTUVWXYZ
abcdefghijklmnopqrstuvwxyz
1234567890 !@#?:;"'*&

Foundry: Bitstream
Designer: Berthold Wolpe / Matthew Carter
Designer Nationality: German / British
Date: 1938 / 1998

This version of Berthold Wolpe's perennially popular Albertus was one of several similar digitizations released in the late 20th century. Wolpe's work was a key source of inspiration for Bitstream founder Matthew Carter (see p. 616), who revived several of his fonts over the course of his career.

Foundry Wilson

ABCDEFGHIJKLMNOPQRSTUVWXYZ
abcdefghijklmnopqrstuvwxyz
1234567890 !@#?:;"'*&

Foundry: The Foundry
Designer: David Quay / Freda Sack
Designer Nationality: British
Date: 1993

Scotsman Alexander Wilson was a fascinating figure – an astronomer, surgeon and meteorologist, he also established a successful foundry in St Andrews in 1742. This respectful revival of one of his designs includes a set of ornamental printers' flowers reproduced from the original source.

FS Benjamin

ABCDEFGHIJKLMNOPQRSTUVWXYZ
abcdefghijklmnopqrstuvwxyz
1234567890 !@#?:;"*&

Foundry: Fontsmith
Designer: Stuart de Rozario / Jason Smith
Designer Nationality: British
Date: 2018

FS Benjamin is designed by Stuart de Rozario, senior type designer at leading London foundry Fontsmith (see p. 272), with creative direction from company founder and creative director Jason Smith. The typeface is de Rozario's tribute to the capital city he calls home, and it was inspired by London's sounds and contrasts.

The font's name references Big Ben, the nickname given to the Great Bell in the clock at the Houses of Parliament. This may refer to Sir Benjamin Hall, who oversaw the bell's installation, or a contemporary English heavyweight boxer called Benjamin 'Big Ben' Caunt.

FS Benjamin is a highly versatile design with an elegant flared serif. Despite Benjamin's elegant and delicate nature, the design features brutal chiselled angles on closer inspection, reflecting the traditional roots of the craft. However, this is no retrospective design and it aims to work in a contemporary setting. The classic proportions of the design's x-height to cap height and ascender to descender ratio help make it accessible and highly legible across a wide variety of media. It comes in six weights with matching italics.

Below. For the launch of FS Benjamin, Fontsmith worked with London design studio DixonBaxi and released *Sounds of London*. In collaboration with Zelig Sound, they produced a unique track that remixed field recordings taken from across the capital by the studio staff, into a soundtrack of London, which was then pressed into a limited-edition vinyl release.

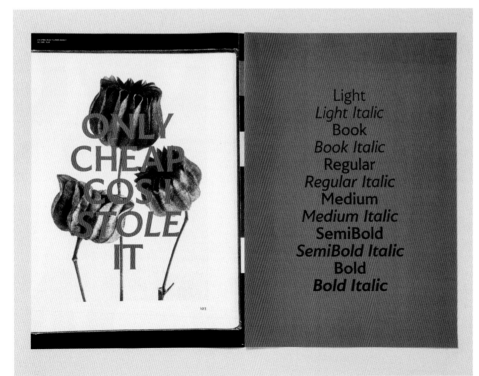

Light
Light Italic
Book
Book Italic
Regular
Regular Italic
Medium
Medium Italic
SemiBold
SemiBold Italic
Bold
Bold Italic

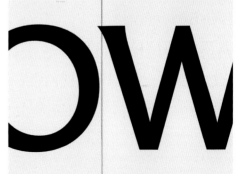

Friz Quadrata

ABCDEFGHIJKLMNOPQRSTUVWXYZ
abcdefghijklmnopqrstuvwxyz
1234567890 !@#?:;"*&

Foundry: VGC
Designer: Ernst Friz
Designer Nationality: Swiss
Date: 1965

Ernst Friz designed this distinctive, display-friendly serif for a competition held by phototypesetting foundry Visual Graphics Corporation (VGC). ITC reissued it in 1974 with the addition of a bold cut by Victor Caruso; Thierry Puyfoulhoux contributed italics two decades later.

FS Maja

ABCDEFGHIJKLMNOPQRSTUVWXYZ
abcdefghijklmnopqrstuvwxyz
1234567890 !@#?:;"*&

Foundry: Fontsmith
Designer: Jason Smith
Designer Nationality: British
Date: 2013

FS Maja was developed by Fontsmith (see p. 272) for a commission from Channel 4, which briefed the foundry to create a new typeface for its Freeview channel, E4. FS Maja is rounded and approachable, and designed to work well in physical and screen-based contexts, as well as at a variety of scales.

Icone

ABCDEFGHIJKLMNOPQRSTUVWXYZ
abcdefghijklmnopqrstuvwxyz
1234567890 !@#?:;"*&

Foundry: Linotype
Designer: Adrian Frutiger
Designer Nationality: Swiss
Date: 1980

The inscriptional style of this expansive font family features swollen, flared serifs, inspired by carved stone type found in northern France and Ireland. It was designed by Adrian Frutiger (see p. 290) to explore the intersection of classical type styles with developing digital type technology.

ITC Barcelona

ABCDEFGHIJKLMNOPQRSTUVWXYZ
abcdefghijklmnopqrstuvwxyz
1234567890 !@#?:;"*&

Foundry: ITC
Designer: Ed Benguiat
Designer Nationality: American
Date: 1981

Type designer and jazz musician Ed Benguiat (see p. 514) has designed more than 600 typefaces over the course of his career; he is widely renowned for his work both at Photo-Lettering and ITC. His design for ITC Barcelona features wedged brackets and distinctive curled curve terminals.

ITC Novarese

ABCDEFGHIJKLMNOPQRSTUVWXYZ
abcdefghijklmnopqrstuvwxyz
1234567890 !@#?:;"*&

Foundry: ITC
Designer: Aldo Novarese
Designer Nationality: Italian
Date: 1978

Aldo Novarese developed this typeface after his departure from the Nebiolo foundry in Turin and it can be seen as a consolidation of ideas expressed within many of his published typefaces. He took elements from what he considered to be his most successful typefaces to create this new design.

Masqualero

ABCDEFGHIJKLMNOPQRSTUVWXYZ
abcdefghijklmnopqrstuvwxyz
1234567890 !@#?:;"*&

Foundry: Monotype
Designer: Jim Ford
Designer Nationality: American
Date: 2017

Masqualero was designed by Jim Ford at Monotype and named after a song by jazz legend Miles Davis. It is a sophisticated, high-contrast contemporary serif that comes in six weights with italics. There are also two attractive, decorative display versions in uppercase: Stencil and Groove.

Memento

ABCDEFGHIJKLMNOPQRSTUVWXYZ
abcdefghijklmnopqrstuvwxyz
1234567890 !@#?:;"*&

Foundry: Omnibus
Designer: Franko Luin
Designer Nationality: Swedish
Date: 1993

Memento has little, triangular serifs reminiscent of Dutch typefaces of the 17th century. This is a versatile serif with a large x-height, which makes it legible at small sizes, and a distinctive 'g' with an open lower loop. It is available in four different weights with italics.

Memo

ABCDEFGHIJKLMNOPQRSTUVWXYZ
abcdefghijklmnopqrstuvwxyz
1234567890 !@#?:;"*&

Foundry: Monotype
Designer: Albert Boton
Designer Nationality: French
Date: 1998

Memo was designed by French typographer Albert Boton, who trained under, and later worked with, leading Swiss designer Adrian Frutiger (see p. 290). The typeface has very minimal, triangular serifs and is a very slight variation on Agora, which Boton created for Berthold in 1990.

Meridien

ABCDEFGHIJKLMNOPQRSTUVWXYZ
abcdefghijklmnopqrstuvwxyz
1234567890 !@#?:;"*&

Foundry: Deberny & Peignot
Designer: Adrian Frutiger
Designer Nationality: Swiss
Date: 1957

A classical roman text face, Meridien was the fourth font created by Adrian Frutiger (see p. 290) and it established his name. Meridien was hard to obtain outside of France, leading to Monotype commissioning Frutiger to create the very similar Apollo, released in 1964.

Odense

ABCDEFGHIJKLMNOPQRSTUVWXYZ
abcdefghijklmnopqrstuvwxyz
1234567890 !@#?:;"*&

Foundry: Omnibus
Designer: Franko Luin
Designer Nationality: Swedish
Date: 1994

Named after a Danish town, Odense is like Optima but with tiny flared serifs. The family contains seventeen fonts: Roman to Extra Bold with italics; two weights of small caps; compressed, condensed and condensed bold with italics; and a display version, Odense Neon.

Pompei

ABCDEFGHIJKLMNOPQRSTUVWXYZ
abcdefghijklmnopqrstuvwxyz
1234567890 !@#?:;"*&

Foundry: Monotype
Designer: Albert Boton
Designer Nationality: French
Date: 1996

Albert Boton's Pompei is a glyphic serif with a muscular body that has been designed for great readability at small sizes. The font family features four weights, which range from Regular to Bold, with accompanying italics for both the Light and Regular weights.

Pompei New

ABCDEFGHIJKLMNOPQRSTUVWXYZ
abcdefghijklmnopqrstuvwxyz
1234567890 !@#?:;"*&

Foundry: Monotype
Designer: Albert Boton
Designer Nationality: French
Date: 2004

Pompei New is an update and expansion of Albert Boton's original font family of 1996. Alongside the initial styles, Pompei New includes the addition of a small caps design and an Old version, which includes extended ascenders and shrunken lowercase characters.

Versailles

ABCDEFGHIJKLMNOPQRSTUVWXYZ
abcdefghijklmnopqrstuvwxyz
1234567890 !@#?:;"*&

Foundry: Linotype
Designer: Adrian Frutiger
Designer Nationality: Swiss
Date: 1984

Versailles is inspired by the liberated letterforms of 19th-century French lithography, as well as the characters found on the memorial to French architect Charles Garnier in Paris. The shapes are modern in style, but the triangular serifs are reminiscent of earlier forms carved by hand.

Weiss

ABCDEFGHIJKLMNOPQRSTUVWXYZ
abcdefghijklmnopqrstuvwxyz
1234567890 !@#?:;"*&

Foundry: Bauer
Designer: Emil Rudolf Weiss
Designer Nationality: German
Date: 1928

Weiss was inspired by typefaces from the Italian Renaissance. It is one of the earliest contemporary serif types with italics based on the chancery style of writing. Originally known as Weiss Antiqua, it has sharp apex points and tall ascenders and its uppercase characters have a low-slung midsection.

Wolpe Pegasus

ABCDEFGHIJKLMNOPQRSTUVWXYZ
abcdefghijklmnopqrstuvwxyz
1234567890 !@#?:;"*&

Foundry: Monotype
Designer: Berthold Wolpe / Toshi Omagari
Designer Nationality: German / Japanese
Date: 1937 / 2017

Wolpe Pegasus is an update and digitization of Berthold Wolpe's serif Pegasus created in 1937. True to Wolpe's original design, Monotype's font maintains the initial quirks, which include varying stroke thicknesses, the occasional oversized serif and atypical loops and links.

Xenois Serif

ABCDEFGHIJKLMNOPQRSTUVWXYZ
abcdefghijklmnopqrstuvwxyz
1234567890 !@#?:;"*&

Foundry: Linotype
Designer: Erik Faulhaber
Designer Nationality: German
Date: 2013

Xenois Serif is a glyphic serif designed as part of a larger font family whose typefaces all interrelate well. It is notable for its expansive counters and apertures, reminiscent of those found in a sans serif, and its omission of serifs on several of the lowercase characters.

Alda

ABCDEFGHIJKLMNOPQRSTUVWXYZ
abcdefghijklmnopqrstuvwxyz
1234567890 !@#?:;"*&

Foundry: Emigre
Designer: Berton Hasebe
Designer Nationality: American
Date: 2008

Berton Hasebe conceived Alda during his master's at the Royal Academy of Art in The Hague. His idea was to generate different weights according to characteristics of physical objects, with the boldest weight echoing the tension of bent steel, and the lightest being as slight as a rubber band.

Breughel

ABCDEFGHIJKLMNOPQRSTUVWXYZ
abcdefghijklmnopqrstuvwxyz
1234567890 !@#?:;"*&

Foundry: Linotype
Designer: Adrian Frutiger
Designer Nationality: Swiss
Date: 1981

Breughel is inspired by 16th-century fonts and is one of the more experimental designs by Adrian Frutiger (see p. 290). It appears to slant to the right, due to the right sides of the stems being vertical and at 90° to the baseline, and the left sides curving into the serifs.

Cardea

ABCDEFGHIJKLMNOPQRSTUVWXYZ
abcdefghijklmnopqrstuvwxyz
1234567890 !@#?:;"*&

Foundry: Emigre
Designer: David Cabianca
Designer Nationality: Canadian
Date: 2004

David Cabianca created Cardea as part of his master's in Type Design at the University of Reading, Berkshire, England. With its high contrast and crisp edges, it has a strong, sculptural feel. Designed as a text face, it has three weights with accompanying italics and small caps.

Demos

ABCDEFGHIJKLMNOPQRSTUVWXYZ
abcdefghijklmnopqrstuvwxyz
1234567890 !@#?:;"*&

Foundry: Linotype
Designer: Gerard Unger
Designer Nationality: Dutch
Date: 1975

Gerard Unger's Demos was one of the first commercially available digital typefaces created for Hell's Digiset composing machines. It has a smooth appearance with an unusually tall x-height and relatively little difference between its thick vertical and thin horizontals.

Demos Next

ABCDEFGHIJKLMNOPQRSTUVWXYZ
abcdefghijklmnopqrstuvwxyz
1234567890 !@#?:;"*&

Demos Next is the latest incarnation of Gerard Unger's original Demos font from 1975. It follows on from 2001's Demos Neue, which was the typeface of the German federal government for more than ten years. Demos Next has been extended to several weights and adjusted for multiple languages.

Foundry: Linotype
Designer: Gerard Unger / Linda Hintz / Dan Reynolds
Designer Nationality: Dutch / German / American
Date: 1975 / 2015

Enigma

ABCDEFGHIJKLMNOPQRSTUVWXYZ
abcdefghijklmnopqrstuvwxyz
1234567890 !@#?:;"*&

For Enigma, Jeremy Tankard drew upon his research into innovations in 16th-century Dutch type design, the blending of Roman and Gothic styles, and the work of William A. Dwiggins. Since its initial release, Enigma now includes more weights and optical versions – Enigma Text, Enigma Display and Enigma Fine.

Foundry: Jeremy Tankard Typography
Designer: Jeremy Tankard
Designer Nationality: British
Date: 1999

Fairplex Wide

ABCDEFGHIJKLMNOPQRSTUVWXYZ
abcdefghijklmnopqrstuvwxyz
1234567890 !@#?:;"*&

Fairplex Wide is a low-contrast serif that is reminiscent of a sans serif. Its intermediate weights were created by interpolating the Book and Black, with the exception of several characters, such as 'n', which needed specially designed features to yield a pleasing weight balance and avoid serifs colliding.

Foundry: Emigre
Designer: Zuzana Licko
Designer Nationality: Slovakian
Date: 2002

FF Meta Serif

ABCDEFGHIJKLMNOPQRSTUVWXYZ
abcdefghijklmnopqrstuvwxyz
1234567890 !@#?:;"*&

This serif counterpart to FF Meta was designed by Erik Spiekermann (see p. 304) along with Christian Schwartz and Kris Sowersby, who developed its form over three years. It is versatile and warm, with subtle idiosyncrasies that sit comfortably alongside the sans serif original.

Foundry: FontFont
Designer: Erik Spiekermann / Christian Schwartz / Kris Sowersby / Ralph du Carrois / Botio Nikoltchev
Designer Nationality: German / American / New Zealander / German / Bulgarian
Date: 2007

Fedra Serif

ABCDEFGHIJKLMNOPQRSTUVWXYZ
abcdefghijklmnopqrstuvwxyz
1234567890 !@#?:;"'*&

Foundry: Typotheque
Designer: Peter Biľak
Designer Nationality: Slovakian
Date: 2003

Fedra Serif is a contemporary serif typeface designed in 2003 by Peter Biľak, the founder and type designer of Typotheque (see p. 90). It is a truly global and comprehensive typeface with each style supporting more than ninety languages. Biľak based his design on humanistic roots and the 'rhythm' of handwriting married with the 'rational drawing' of 'a coarse computer-screen grid'.

The typeface comes in two versions with varying stem heights. Version A has short ascenders and descenders, and low contrast; it can be used at very small sizes and for low-quality print applications, such as newspapers. Version A also matches the proportions of the sister sans serif typeface Fedra Sans for partnering serif and sans serif. Version B has longer stems and more contrast. Both versions have the same character widths and kerning pairs, so are interchangeable without texts reflowing. In 2005, the OpenType Pro version was released with a wealth of features. The Fedra Serif Pro OpenType font supports all European languages, with Latin-based (Western, Central and Eastern European, Baltic and Turkish), Cyrillic-based and Greek-based versions. Arabic and Hebrew versions are available separately.

The detailing on some of the characters include a diamond-shaped point above the letter 'i'; open counters for 'P', 'b', 'g' and '6'; and curved terminating and sharp, angled connections for joining the strokes. Each weight has a collection of symbols, arrows, pictograms and alternative characters, and a set of characters for science and mathematics.

Below. The elegant Fedra Serif, here shown in its Display cut at various sizes and mixed cases, includes details such as diamond-shaped points above the letter 'i' and alternate characters such as the extended leg to the capital R, and custom ligatures for the T and U.

HEADLINE
maximum impact
LIGATURES

FF Scala

ABCDEFGHIJKLMNOPQRSTUVWXYZ
abcdefghijklmnopqrstuvwxyz
1234567890 !@#?:;"*&

This humanist serif takes its name from La Scala opera house in Milan and was commissioned by the Bredenburg Music Center of Utrecht. FF Scala Sans is its companion sans serif, along with FF Scala Jewels, which has a Dutch Baroque influence and decorative capitals.

Foundry: FontFont
Designer: Martin Majoor
Designer Nationality: Dutch
Date: 1990

Freight Text Pro

ABCDEFGHIJKLMNOPQRSTUVWXYZ
abcdefghijklmnopqrstuvwxyz
1234567890 !@#?:;"*&

Freight was first published by David Carson's GarageFonts foundry in 2005; an extensive set of variant styles and weights have since been added. Freight Text Pro offers clarity and legibility thanks to its generous x-height, and it includes an expressive italic counterpart.

Foundry: GarageFonts
Designer: Joshua Darden
Designer Nationality: American
Date: 2009

Frutiger Serif

ABCDEFGHIJKLMNOPQRSTUVWXYZ
abcdefghijklmnopqrstuvwxyz
1234567890 !@#?:;"*&

This serif counterpart to the eponymous sans from Adrian Frutiger (see p. 290) was developed from another of his designs, Meridien, first published by Deberny & Peignot in 1957. Frutiger Serif features a slightly narrower width than Meridien and contains an expanded range of sizes and weights.

Foundry: Linotype
Designer: Adrian Frutiger / Akira Kobayashi
Designer Nationality: Swiss / Japanese
Date: 1957 / 2008

Givens Antiqua

ABCDEFGHIJKLMNOPQRSTUVWXYZ
abcdefghijklmnopqrstuvwxyz
1234567890 !@#?:;"*&

George Ryan began his career at Mergenthaler Linotype, and spent more than a decade at Bitstream before joining Monotype in 2003. He developed Givens Antiqua from sketches inspired by hand-drawn magazine typography; the font was named for Monotype co-founder Robert M. Givens.

Foundry: Monotype
Designer: George Ryan
Designer Nationality: American
Date: 2007

Greta Text

ABCDEFGHIJKLMNOPQRSTUVWXYZ
abcdefghijklmnopqrstuvwxyz
1234567890 !@#?:;"*&

Foundry: Typotheque
Designer: Peter Biľak
Designer Nationality: Slovakian
Date: 2007

Greta Text was designed with the practicalities and limitations of newspaper use and web offset printing in mind. It is available in several grades of each weight for fine control of its visual texture, and its character set is tailored to the demands of a range of journalistic contexts.

ITC Resavska

ABCDEFGHIJKLMNOPQRSTUVWXYZ
abcdefghijklmnopqrstuvwxyz
1234567890 !@#?:;"*&

Foundry: ITC
Designer: Olivera Stojadinovic
Designer Nationality: Serbian
Date: 2004

This is Olivera Stojadinovic's serif counterpart to ITC Resavska Sans, which she designed for editorial use. She added geometric serifs to the original design to create four weights in serif and sans serif subfamilies. She went on to co-found the Serbia-based foundry Typolis in 2017.

Kingfisher

ABCDEFGHIJKLMNOPQRSTUVWXYZ
abcdefghijklmnopqrstuvwxyz
1234567890 !@#?:;"*&

Foundry: Jeremy Tankard Typography
Designer: Jeremy Tankard
Designer Nationality: British
Date: 2005

Jeremy Tankard intended Kingfisher to be ideal for continuous reading, especially for books. He found inspiration in the subtleties of letterpress typefaces such as Bembo and Ehrhardt, paying attention to their printed image. He added a slight irregularity to the letters to make the type appear less rigid.

Marathon

ABCDEFGHIJKLMNOPQRSTUVWXYZ
abcdefghijklmnopqrstuvwxyz
1234567890 !@#?:;"*&

Foundry: Monotype
Designer: Rudolf Koch / Ute Harder
Designer Nationality: German
Date: 1930 / 2003

Marathon is a digitization of one of the last fonts by Rudolf Koch, who is best known for his Kabel sans serif. Marathon was his serif text face, for which he cut the punches himself. Ute Harder based her digitization on a 48-point metal alphabet of Marathon, improving the spacing and adding characters.

Amasis

ABCDEFGHIJKLMNOPQRSTUVWXYZ
abcdefghijklmnopqrstuvwxyz
1234567890 !@#?:;"*&

Foundry: Monotype
Designer: Ron Carpenter
Designer Nationality: British
Date: 1992

Ron Carpenter created Amasis during his twenty-five-year-long stint at Monotype. The slab serif is unusual in that it takes a humanist rather than geometric approach. It was designed to work well at small sizes, and had the advantage of being suited for use with low-resolution printers and faxes.

Aptifer Slab

ABCDEFGHIJKLMNOPQRSTUVWXYZ
abcdefghijklmnopqrstuvwxyz
1234567890 !@#?:;"*&

Foundry: Linotype
Designer: Mårten Thavenius
Designer Nationality: Swedish
Date: 2006

This wedge slab serif channels two very different influences: the robust American Gothic and the more open humanist traditions. It shares many similarities, including stroke contrast and vertical stress, with its sister typeface, Aptifer Sans, which Swedish designer Mårten Thavenius also created.

Bariol Serif

ABCDEFGHIJKLMNOPQRSTUVWXYZ
abcdefghijklmnopqrstuvwxyz
1234567890 !@#?:;"*&

Foundry: Atipo
Designer: Raúl García del Pomar / Ismael González
Designer Nationality: Spanish
Date: 2015

Bariol Serif is a modern, functional serif designed as a sister typeface to the popular rounded sans serif Bariol. This accessible typeface is free for Regular and italic versions, or whatever a potential user can afford for the full set, and has proved popular as a low-budget option.

Brighton

ABCDEFGHIJKLMNOPQRSTUVWXYZ
abcdefghijklmnopqrstuvwxyz
1234567890 !@#?:;"*&

Foundry: ITC
Designer: Alan Bright
Designer Nationality: British
Date: 1979

Brighton was conceived as a text face but became more popular as a display face. Its rounded shapes and curved corners are often likened to Art Nouveau letters. It is perhaps most recognizable as the font used since 1984 in the logo of US supermarket chain Whole Foods Market.

Archer

ABCDEFGHIJKLMNOPQRSTUVWXYZ
abcdefghijklmnopqrstuvwxyz
1234567890 !@#?:;"'*&

Foundry: Hoefler & Co.
Designer: Tobias Frere-Jones / Jonathan Hoefler
Designer Nationality: American
Date: 2001

US foundry Hoefler & Co. (then called Hoefler & Frere-Jones) designed this elegant slab serif in 2001 for *Martha Stewart Living* magazine. It possesses a humanist and gentle character yet retains the geometry of a slab serif that meets the challenges of editorial demands. From information graphics to reading text through to headlines and tables, Archer is a typeface family that is incredibly flexible and legible but also personable and inviting to read.

The rationale behind the design was that slab serifs generally fall into two camps. One is the Antique style, which comes from the 19th-century tradition that produced the Modern and Scotch styles with a more old-fashioned feel. The other is the geometric style, which is a Bauhaus type with a more rationalized discipline to the design. Archer combines the two approaches to get the best of both.

The typeface has fifty-five styles, including italics. Such a large range means not only that it is perfect for print applications but also that it can be employed on screen, ideally for headline sizes and larger. Details such as ball terminals on a number of the lowercase characters add to its unique character and friendliness. Such details are also seen on the typeface's uppercase, thus reinforcing its accessibility and legibility.

Below. The redesign of the identity and the packaging for Weingut Zähringer by Schmidt / Thurner / von Keisenberg features Archer with a vertical umlaut over the a in Zähringer.

PMN Caecilia

ABCDEFGHIJKLMNOPQRSTUVWXYZ
abcdefghijklmnopqrstuvwxyz
1234567890 !@#?:;"*&

Foundry: Linotype
Designer: Peter Matthias Noordzij
Designer Nationality: Dutch
Date: 1990

The first-ever Neo-humanist slab serif, PMN Caecilia is Peter Matthias Noordzij's debut typeface. Replicating the writing style of a broad nib pen, it has subtle variations in stroke thickness and a large x-height, providing excellent legibility. It is used as the default font on Kindle e-readers.

Candida

ABCDEFGHIJKLMNOPQRSTUVWXYZ
abcdefghijklmnopqrstuvwxyz
1234567890 !@#?:;" *&

Foundry: Ludwig & Mayer / Bitstream
Designer: Jakob Erbar
Designer Nationality: German
Date: 1935–45 / c. 1980s

Candida was released after the designer's death in 1935, with subsequent weights drawn by other people. It was reworked in 1945, with a digitized version subsequently released by Bitstream. Described as a modest serif, it retains its legibility when used in text at small sizes.

Charlie

ABCDEFGHIJKLMNOPQRSTUVWXYZ
abcdefghijklmnopqrstuvwxyz
1234567890 !@#?:;"*&

Foundry: Typotheque
Designer: Ross Milne
Designer Nationality: Canadian
Date: 2010

This affable serif was originally Ross Milne's thesis project when he was studying for his master's on the Type and Media course at the Royal Academy of Art, The Hague. A versatile slab serif, Charlie has narrow proportions, high x-height and some unique finishing details.

Compatil Letter

ABCDEFGHIJKLMNOPQRSTUVWXYZ
abcdefghijklmnopqrstuvwxyz
1234567890 !@#?:;"*&

Foundry: Linotype
Designer: Olaf Leu
Designer Nationality: German
Date: 2001

Compatil Letter is a robust serif that is described as being 'informative yet poetic'. It forms part of German font designer Olaf Leu's Compatil system. Compatil Letter is comprised of four weights and can easily be combined with the other typefaces in the Compatil family.

DIN Next Slab

ABCDEFGHIJKLMNOPQRSTUVWXYZ
abcdefghijklmnopqrstuvwxyz
1234567890 !@#?:;"*&

Foundry: Linotype
Designer: Akira Kobayashi / Tom Grace / Sandra Winter
Designer Nationality: Japanese / American / German
Date: 1931 / 2014

This is a new slab serif version of the typeface introduced by the Deutsches Institut für Normung (German Institute for Standardization) in the 1930s.

DIN Next Slab is available in seven weights from Ultra Light to Black. Its sister typefaces are DIN Next and DIN Next Rounded.

Diverda Serif

ABCDEFGHIJKLMNOPQRSTUVWXYZ
abcdefghijklmnopqrstuvwxyz
1234567890 !@#?:;"*&

Foundry: Linotype
Designer: Daniel Lanz
Designer Nationality: Swiss
Date: 2004

Diverda is a contemporary and very legible ornament-free serif with small x-heights and proportions that stay true to those of the Roman alphabet. Swiss designer Daniel Lanz was inspired by pen on paper, and Diverda's downstrokes are heavier than its upstrokes.

Elante

ABCDEFGHIJKLMNOPQRSTUVWXYZ
abcdefghijklmnopqrstuvwxyz
1234567890 !@#?:;"*&

Foundry: Compugraphic
Designer: William A. Dwiggins
Designer Nationality: American
Date: 1935

Elante is Compugraphic's cold-type revival of Electra, a modern roman typeface designed by William A. Dwiggins in 1935 with long-form reading in mind. This version, which has since been digitized, incorporates the set of shorter descenders included in Dwiggins's metal type original.

Exchange

ABCDEFGHIJKLMNOPQRSTUVWXYZ
abcdefghijklmnopqrstuvwxyz
1234567890 !@#?:;"*&

Foundry: Frere-Jones Type
Designer: Tobias Frere-Jones
Designer Nationality: American
Date: 2017

Exchange was originally designed as a newspaper text font, as is evident in its condensed proportions and wide range of historical references, from the Depression-era United States to 19th-century Britain. Its additional MicroPlus styles make it ideal for use across all forms of digital media.

Frere-Jones Type

Tobias Frere-Jones is a superstar in the typographic world. He is one of the United States' leading and most prolific typeface designers and has designed more than 500 typefaces for retail, personal work and private commissions. He also has numerous awards to his name for his contributions to design, typography and type education.

After graduating with a Bachelor of Fine Arts degree from the Rhode Island School of Design he started his career at Font Bureau in Boston, where he went on to be senior designer. There he designed some of the foundry's best-known types, including Interstate and Garage Gothic. He went on to become a partner at New York foundry Hoefler & Frere-Jones, where he collaborated on many projects, creating some of his most recognizable designs such as Gotham (see p. 198), Surveyor and Whitney.

In 2015, he founded his own type studio, Frere-Jones Type. In a short time, the new foundry's offerings received recognition. The first release was Mallory, a humanist sans serif, which includes twenty-six fonts – sixteen standard styles and ten MicroPlus styles that address the challenges of small print text and screen text simultaneously.

Working closely with Frere-Jones in the creation of typefaces are senior type designer Nina Stössinger and type designer Fred Shallcrass. Nina, originally from Switzerland, studied multi-media design in Germany, where she discovered her passion for type, and went on to an MA in Type and Media at Royal Academy of Art in The Hague. She also teaches type design at Yale School of Art, and currently serves on the Board of Directors of the Type Directors Club.

Fred, who gained editorial, brand and lettering experience in New Zealand, moved to New York in 2015 and joined Frere-Jones soon after. He is also a teaching assistant at Type@Cooper Extended program.

Founded: 2015
Country: America
Website: frerejones.com
Notable typefaces:
Conductor (see p. 458)

Below, clockwise from left. With British and American traits, sans serif Mallory is available in twenty-six fonts; inspired by Ancient Rome, headline face Empirica offers a full palette and is ideal for editorial and branding projects; display typeface Conductor is inspired by the letterforms on Bulgarian lottery tickets.

Opposite. Slab serif Exchange was originally designed as a newspaper text face.

DER GROßE DUDEN (1957)
FREQUENTS HERZEGOVINA
World Leagues Grand Prix
Every December Sunday
€207 ₺214 ₦981 ₹835 ₽160
MEN'S NATIONAL TEAM
5408 SAN FRANCISCO BLVD
QUILTING WORKSHOPS!
Unjustifiable Alternatives
Gjøvik to Logroño quickest
RYE WHISKEY TASTINGS
New Small Lizard Research

Quintessentializes
Photosynthesised
College of Justice
E Pluribus Unum
Bank of England
Gamesomeness

Overcompensating
Acts of Parliament
Goodbye to Berlin
Radiotherapeutic
Metamorphosed
Antimonarchist

Queensboro Plaza
Concept Album
Understated
Lineament

Track Connections
Revolving Mass
Photosphere
Quicksilver

PROBLEM SOLVING

CONSERVATION OF MATTER

BINARY NOTATION

PICKLED MUSTARD GREENS

ELECTRIC HEATER

APPROACH WHILE DRIVING

HOMEMADE WINE

CORRUGATED CARDBOARD

KEYNOTE SPEECH

FF Unit Slab

ABCDEFGHIJKLMNOPQRSTUVWXYZ
abcdefghijklmnopqrstuvwxyz
1234567890 !@#?:;"*&

This counterpart to the existing sans serif typeface FF Unit was developed from the early sketches for Meta Serif by New Zealand typeface designer Kris Sowersby. The precise, humanist slab-serif design is suitable for both body text and headline use, and it also pairs well with typefaces from the Meta family.

Foundry: FontFont
Designer: Erik Spiekermann / Christian Schwartz / Kris Sowersby
Designer Nationality: German / American / New Zealander
Date: 2009

FS Rufus

ABCDEFGHIJKLMNOPQRSTUVWXYZ
abcdefghijklmnopqrstuvwxyz
1234567890 !@#?:;"*&

The extended letterforms of FS Rufus feature exaggerated ink traps – a detail traditionally incorporated into metal type that was designed for use at small point sizes. With more than eighty discretionary ligatures included, Rufus offers plenty of scope for creative typesetting.

Foundry: Fontsmith
Designer: Emanuela Conidi / Mitja Miklavčič / Jason Smith
Designer Nationality: Italian / Slovenian / British
Date: 2009

FS Silas Slab

ABCDEFGHIJKLMNOPQRSTUVWXYZ
abcdefghijklmnopqrstuvwxyz
1234567890 !@#?:;"*&

Fontsmith (see p. 272) created this angular serif as a counterpart to FS Silas Sans, and its design is more blunt and square than in the foundry's other explorations of the slab style. Its forms display an effective balance of expressiveness and clarity, and it is equally suitable for both print and digital use.

Foundry: Fontsmith
Designer: Phil Garnham / Jason Smith
Designer Nationality: British
Date: 2015

Generis Slab

ABCDEFGHIJKLMNOPQRSTUVWXYZ
abcdefghijklmnopqrstuvwxyz
1234567890 !@#?:;"*&

German font designer Erik Faulhaber designed the comprehensive Generis type system to offer a versatile, complementary palette of typefaces that could be easily and harmoniously combined. The economical proportions of Generis Slab work well alongside its Serif, Sans and Simple siblings.

Foundry: Linotype
Designer: Erik Faulhaber
Designer Nationality: German
Date: 2006

Glypha

ABCDEFGHIJKLMNOPQRSTUVWXYZ
abcdefghijklmnopqrstuvwxyz
1234567890 !@#?:;"*&

Foundry: Stempel
Designer: Adrian Frutiger
Designer Nationality: Swiss
Date: 1977

Adrian Frutiger (see p. 290) designed this balanced serif. It is one of two such slab styles that he developed from the skeleton of Univers; its predecessor, Serifa, displays slightly more extended letterforms. True to its heritage, Glypha works well alongside Univers and other Neo-grotesques.

HFJ Sentinel

ABCDEFGHIJKLMNOPQRSTUVWXYZ
abcdefghijklmnopqrstuvwxyz
1234567890 !@#?:;"*&

Foundry: Hoefler & Frere-Jones
Designer: Tobias Frere-Jones / Jonathan Hoefler
Designer Nationality: American
Date: 2009

Sentinel was designed to address some of the shortcomings of earlier slab-serif fonts, which frequently featured inconsistent character sets, missing italics and a limited range of weights. Sentinel Screensmart, a version design specially for screen use, is also available.

Humanist Slabserif 712

ABCDEFGHIJKLMNOPQRSTUVWXYZ
abcdefghijklmnopqrstuvwxyz
1234567890 !@#?:;"*&

Foundry: Bitstream
Designer: Adrian Frutiger
Designer Nationality: Swiss
Date: 1956

This Bitstream digitization is based on Egyptienne F, which was designed by Adrian Frutiger (see p. 290) for Deberny & Peignot in 1956; it was the first font to be created specifically for phototypesetting. Its bracketed serifs set it apart from Frutiger's later explorations of the slab style.

ITC Napoleone Slab

ABCDEFGHIJKLMNOPQRSTUVWXYZ
abcdefghijklmnopqrstuvwxyz
1234567890 !@#?:;"*&

Foundry: ITC
Designer: Silvio Napoleone
Designer Nationality: American
Date: 2002

This contemporary slab serif is the work of award-winning type and graphic designer Silvio Napoleone, co-founder of the Canadian consultancy Nubrand. Its chiselled, calligraphy-inspired forms make it a distinctive and legible choice for print and screen-based applications.

ITC Officina Serif

ABCDEFGHIJKLMNOPQRSTUVWXYZ
abcdefghijklmnopqrstuvwxyz
1234567890 !@#?:;"*&

Foundry: ITC
Designer: Erik Spiekermann
Designer Nationality: German
Date: 1990–98

This highly functional and very legible typeface was conceived for use in office correspondence and business documentation, and has proved suitable for many different applications. It is also available in sans serif and display versions (plus dingbats), each with five weights and matching italics.

ITC Tactile

ABCDEFGHIJKLMNOPQRSTUVWXYZ
abcdefghijklmnopqrstuvwxyz
1234567890 !@#?:;"*&

Foundry: ITC
Designer: Joseph Stitzlein
Designer Nationality: American
Date: 2002

This typeface, which won the Type Directors Club Award, features an intriguing blend of contradictory details, including both straight slab and bracketed serifs, and calligraphic diagonal line endings. It is available in a range of weights, each with its own distinctive tone of voice.

ITC Tyke

ABCDEFGHIJKLMNOPQRSTUVWXYZ
abcdefghijklmnopqrstuvwxyz
1234567890 !@#?:;"*&

Foundry: ITC
Designer: Tomi Haaparanta
Designer Nationality: Finnish
Date: 2005

The soft and friendly letterforms of ITC Tyke were developed by Finnish type designer Tomi Haaparanta to communicate in a similar tone to Cooper Black, but this contemporary typeface is available in a much broader range of weights, plus italics. It was published by ITC in 2005.

Jeunesse Slab

ABCDEFGHIJKLMNOPQRSTUVWXYZ
abcdefghijklmnopqrstuvwxyz
1234567890 !@#?:;"*&

Foundry: Monotype
Designer: Johannes Birkenbach
Designer Nationality: German
Date: 1993

Jeunesse Slab was created by German typographer Johannes Birkenbach, who had worked at Stempel, Linotype and then Monotype. He designed it to complement Jeunesse and Jeunesse Sans; all were conceived as a full family in 1993. It is a slab-serif available in one weight with italics.

Joanna

ABCDEFGHIJKLMNOPQRSTUVWXYZ
abcdefghijklmnopqrstuvwxyz
1234567890 !@#?:;"*&

Foundry: Monotype
Designer: Eric Gill
Designer Nationality: British
Date: 1930–31

Eric Gill designed Joanna following the release of Gill Sans, and named it after his daughter. He first used the typeface for the text in his book *An Essay on Typography* (1931). Joanna pairs very well with Gill Sans and is economical due to its narrow width and almost vertical italics.

Joanna Nova

ABCDEFGHIJKLMNOPQRSTUVWXYZ
abcdefghijklmnopqrstuvwxyz
1234567890 !@#?:;"*&

Foundry: Monotype
Designer: Eric Gill / Ben Jones
Designer Nationality: British
Date: 1930–31 / 2015

Monotype released this extensive update of Joanna, along with Gill Sans Nova and Joanna Sans, as part of the Eric Gill Series collection of seventy-seven fonts across the families. Ben Jones revisited Eric Gill's original drawings to reinstate some lost features while also improving usability.

Karloff Neutral

ABCDEFGHIJKLMNOPQRSTUVWXYZ
abcdefghijklmnopqrstuvwxyz
1234567890 !@#?:;"*&

Foundry: Typotheque
Designer: Peter Biľak / Pieter van Rosmalen / Nikola Djurek
Designer Nationality: Slovakian / Dutch / Croatian
Date: 2012

Designed by a team lead by Peter Biľak, the Karloff family explores extremes. Neutral was an attempt to find a middle ground between high-contrast didone serifs and reverse-contrast Italian typefaces; the result is a slab-serif that shares some of the humanistic features of a grotesque.

LinoLetter

ABCDEFGHIJKLMNOPQRSTUVWXYZ
abcdefghijklmnopqrstuvwxyz
1234567890 !@#?:;"*&

Foundry: Linotype
Designer: André Gürtler / Reinhard Haus
Designer Nationality: Swiss / German
Date: 1992

LinoLetter is a slab serif that is ideal for newspaper work and mass-produced printing thanks to its heavy forms, low contrast and legibility at small sizes. It was the result of a collaboration, began during the 1980s, between the Linotype foundry and the Basel School of Design, Switzerland.

Lumin

ABCDEFGHIJKLMNOPQRSTUVWXYZ
abcdefghijklmnopqrstuvwxyz
1234567890 !@#?:;"*&

Foundry: Typotheque
Designer: Nikola Djurek
Designer Nationality: Croatian
Date: 2013

Lumin is a dark slab serif by Croatian Nikola Djurek and forms part of a family that contains sans serif, condensed and display faces. It has a big x-height, large counters and horizontal terminals on unbracketed serifs. Lumin was designed with editorial usage in mind and comes in four weights.

Madawaska

ABCDEFGHIJKLMNOPQRSTUVWXYZ
abcdefghijklmnopqrstuvwxyz
1234567890 !@#?:;"*&

Foundry: Typodermic
Designer: Ray Larabie
Designer Nationality: Canadian
Date: 2008

Madawaska is a clean slab serif named after a county in New Brunswick, Canada. It is available in eight weights – Ultra Light to Heavy – each with italics and small caps. Canadian Ray Larabie, the proprietor of Typodermic, also designed two digitally distressed versions, Madawaska Jeans and River.

Malaga

ABCDEFGHIJKLMNOPQRSTUVWXYZ
abcdefghijklmnopqrstuvwxyz
1234567890 !@#?:;"*&

Foundry: Emigre
Designer: Xavier Dupré
Designer Nationality: French
Date: 2007

Malaga is a characterful sans serif inspired by everything from blackletter script to Latin fonts, and from the first Venetian Antiquas of the 15th century to brushstroke types. It has a number of unorthodox details but is still legible when used for extended text as well as display.

Mantika News

ABCDEFGHIJKLMNOPQRSTUVWXYZ
abcdefghijklmnopqrstuvwxyz
1234567890 !@#?:;"*&

Foundry: Linotype
Designer: Jürgen Weltin
Designer Nationality: German
Date: 2016

The newest of the Mantika family, News is a robust, contemporary serif in four weights, with Light and ExtraBold display versions that have shorter ascenders and a lower x-height. The Mantika family has shared character widths, making them ideal to use in tandem.

Marconi

ABCDEFGHIJKLMNOPQRSTUVWXYZ
abcdefghijklmnopqrstuvwxyz
1234567890 !@#?:;"'*&

Foundry: Hell
Designer: Hermann Zapf
Designer Nationality: German
Date: 1976

Hermann Zapf (see p. 574) designed Marconi for the Digiset early digital typesetting system produced by Hell. It has a large x-height, very open lowercase letters and less height difference between upper and lowercases, all of which were suggested by the results of readability tests.

Museo Slab

ABCDEFGHIJKLMNOPQRSTUVWXYZ
abcdefghijklmnopqrstuvwxyz
1234567890 !@#?:;"'*&

Foundry: exljbris
Designer: Jos Buivenga
Designer Nationality: Dutch
Date: 2009

Dutch designer Jos Buivenga of foundry exljbris added a slab serif to the family in 2009, a year after the successful release of Museo, his first commercial typeface. The standard Museo has square serifs, which are more prominent in the slab version that comes in six weights.

Neue Aachen

ABCDEFGHIJKLMNOPQRSTUVWXYZ
abcdefghijklmnopqrstuvwxyz
1234567890 !@#?:;"'*&

Foundry: Monotype
Designer: Alan Meeks / Colin Brignall / Jim Wasco
Designer Nationality: British / British / American
Date: 1969 / 2012

Colin Brignall and Alan Meeks designed Aachen or Letraset in 1969. Jim Wasco gave the heavy, tightly spaced headline font an extensive update in 2012. Wasco designed nine weights with italics, a vast increase on the original Aachen, which came in just regular and bold.

Pica 10 Pitch

ABCDEFGHIJKLMNOPQRSTUVWXYZ
abcdefghijklmnopqrstuvwxyz
1234567890 !@#?:;"'*&

Foundry: Bitstream
Designer: Bitstream
Designer Nationality: American
Date: 1953 / 1990

Pica 10 Pitch is named after the measuring system used for typewriter faces. Bitstream's revival is a digitization of the Pica typeface designed for the IBM Standard and Selectric typewriters. Pica 10 Pitch is fixed width, monospaced and features capitals but no bold or italics.

Prima Serif

ABCDEFGHIJKLMNOPQRSTUVWXYZ
abcdefghijklmnopqrstuvwxyz
1234567890 !@#?:;"*&

Foundry: Bitstream
Designer: Jim Lyles
Designer Nationality: American
Date: 1998

Prima Serif was released in the middle of the dot-com boom when there was a period of rapid growth in internet usage. It was designed to provide outstanding quality at low screen resolutions, making it an ideal font for prolonged periods of web browsing or on-screen reading.

Proteus

ABCDEFGHIJKLMNOPQRSTUVWXYZ
abcdefghijklmnopqrstuvwxyz
1234567890 !@#?:;"*&

Foundry: ITC
Designer: Freda Sack
Designer Nationality: British
Date: 1983

British designer Freda Sack created the Proteus squared slab serif in the style of 16th-century poster and handbill typography. Similar to letterforms of this period, its design is expressive and robust, a formula that resonates in each of its four weights: Light, Book, Medium and Bold.

Quitador

ABCDEFGHIJKLMNOPQRSTUVWXYZ
abcdefghijklmnopqrstuvwxyz
1234567890 !@#?:;"*&

Foundry: Linotype
Designer: Arne Freytag
Designer Nationality: German
Date: 2014

German designer Arne Freytag created the Quitador slab serif for multiple platforms, from mobile devices to magazine headlines. The font's shape is based on the superellipse, providing the letterforms with an open character that works at both small and large sizes.

Schadow

ABCDEFGHIJKLMNOPQRSTUVWXYZ
abcdefghijklmnopqrstuvwxyz
1234567890 !@#?:;"*&

Foundry: Bitstream
Designer: Georg Trump
Designer Nationality: German
Date: 1938–52

German font designer Georg Trump's Schadow was originally released by the Weber type foundry to rival Ludwig & Mayer's Candida typeface. Bitstream chose to digitize Schadow because its geometric letterforms suit the small sizes typically required for screen displays.

Siseriff

ABCDEFGHIJKLMNOPQRSTUVWXYZ
abcdefghijklmnopqrstuvwxyz
1234567890 !@#?:;"'*&

Foundry: Linotype
Designer: Bo Berndal
Designer Nationality: Swedish
Date: 2002

Swedish designer Bo Berndal created the Siseriff slab serif to accommodate the various hierarchies of editorial design. Comprised of nine styles, the font family includes weights from Light to Black, and unlike the majority of slab-serif families, features true italics instead of standard obliques.

Soho

ABCDEFGHIJKLMNOPQRSTUVWXYZ
abcdefghijklmnopqrstuvwxyz
1234567890 !@#?:;"'*&

Foundry: Monotype
Designer: Seb Lester
Designer Nationality: British
Date: 2007

The product of three years of work, Soho is a slab-serif family comprised of forty fonts and 32,668 characters. With a catalogue of weights that range from Condensed Extra Light to Ultra Extended, Soho is a typeface designed for the multiple platforms of 21st-century typography.

Vectipede

ABCDEFGHIJKLMNOPQRSTUVWXYZ
abcdefghijklmnopqrstuvwxyz
1234567890 !@#?:;"'*&

Foundry: Typodermic
Designer: Ray Larabie / Chikako Larabie
Designer Nationality: Canadian / Japanese
Date: 2010

Vectipede is a technical slab serif with seven weights, ranging from Ultralight to Black, for maximum versatility. The letterforms have a squared character, smooth curves and short serifs. Unlike most slab serifs, Vectipede combines curled terminals with keen edges.

Venus Egyptienne

ABCDEFGHIJKLMNOPQRSTUVWXYZ
abcdefghijklmnopqrstuvwxyz
1234567890 !@#?:;"'*&

Foundry: Linotype
Designer: Bauersche Giesserei / Linotype Design Studio
Designer Nationality: German
Date: Unknown

Venus Egyptienne is Linotype's revival of the Bauersche Giesserei's font family, initially designed as a highly legible slab serif for German map production. Contrary to many slab-serif designs, Venus Egyptienne has a narrow width, curved brackets and no bold weight.

Typotheque

Based in a former school building in The Hague, Netherlands, Typotheque is a foundry that offers an expansive range of high-quality retail typefaces while also providing custom solutions for a range of applications and languages. It was established by founder Peter Biľak, who is committed to continuing the traditions of independent type foundries by creating typefaces that will stand the test of time but also reflect and serve today's needs. This is a concept they describe as 'contemporaneity'.

Typotheque focuses on extended language support for its typefaces, with its range of fonts covering most Latin-based languages as well as those based on Greek, Cyrillic, Arabic, Armenian and Devanagari scripts. This comprehensive consideration for languages is visible in most of their releases, such as Fedra Sans (see p. 261), which is also available in Bengali, Tamil and Inuktitut. In 2009, Typotheque was the first

commercial type foundry to license its entire type library for use on the web.

Typotheque is also a publisher and a design studio managed by Peter along with his Slovak partner, Johanna, and Croatian designer Nikola Djurek. As a design studio, Typotheque has created an impressive body of cultural and commercial work over the years, using its own typefaces. This ranges from postage stamps to posters, and ceramic tiles to exhibition architecture and design.

Founded: 1999
Country: Netherlands
Website: typotheque.com
Notable typefaces:
Fedra Sans (see p. 261)
Fedra Serif (see p. 73)
Julien (see p. 429)

Below left. 'Threesome' for the Karloff typeface family showing its three personalities: Positive, Neutral and Negative.

Below middle. Specimen for Greta Sans and its extensive type system and language variants.

Below right. Experimental display typeface Calcula.

Right. The History typeface system conceived and designed by Peter Biľak (with assistance from Eike Dingler, Ján Filípek, Ondrej Jób, Ashfaq Niazi and Ilya Ruderman) is a typeface that is based on the skeleton of Roman inscriptional capitals. The end design for History consists of twenty-one independent typefaces that share widths and other metric information so that they can be combined to reflect the evolution of typography. With the potential to create thousands of different designs with the twenty-one layers, the designer is provided with a huge opportunity for experimentation and play.

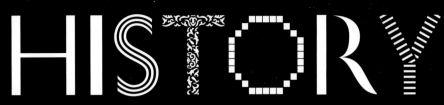

HISTORY

HISTORY is the longest project that Typotheque has undertaken. Its beginnings trace to mid 1990s when Peter Biľak experimented with decorative layering systems inspired by 19th century Tuscan types. HISTORY goes a step forward and based on a skeleton of Roman inscriptional capitals creates 21 layers, 21 independent typefaces which share widths and other metric information, so they can be recombined. Potentially thousands of different unique styles can be created by superimposition of layers, ranging from conventional rennaissance, transitional, baroque, script like, commercial accidental, to digital fantasy. Since they can share different all elements, the most interesting is when various seamingly incompatible elements are combines. Just try putting on pixel letters the Didot-like serifs, or put 19th century slab serifs on top of a rennaisance construction. Happy accidents are not only amusing but suprisingly fresh and usable.

Realizing that controling 21 different layers can be a daunting task, Typotheque delivers history not only as a set of OpenType fonts, but provides an application entitled History Remixer. This web based application uses single text input, and familiar Photoshop-like interface, where users select which layers should be on, layer order, colour and luminosity, and application generates an open PDF files.

Designed by Peter Biľak
Published by Typotheque, 2008

Vista Slab

ABCDEFGHIJKLMNOPQRSTUVWXYZ
abcdefghijklmnopqrstuvwxyz
1234567890 !@#?:;"*&

Foundry: Emigre
Designer: Xavier Dupré
Designer Nationality: French
Date: 2008

Vista Slab, by French typographer and type designer Xavier Dupré, was published in 2008 along with Vista Sans Narrow as an extension to the Vista Sans typeface he created three years earlier. The addition of the new versions extended the family to 108 fonts.

Dupré's intention for the design of the Vista family was to combine the simpler forms of a sans serif typeface with the 'humanist appeal of calligraphic forms'. When enlarged, the typeface provides insight into the many refined details it possesses, such as bulging edges on a selection of the stroke endings, ink traps in some of the characters and squared-up notches on inside cusps. Overall, it is a slab serif that provides a warmth and character to any texts set using it.

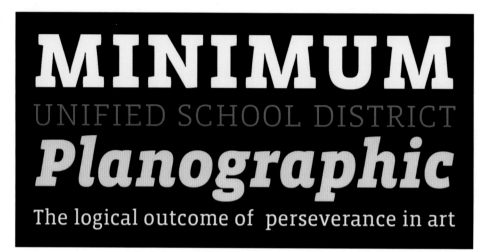

Xenois Slab

ABCDEFGHIJKLMNOPQRSTUVWXYZ
abcdefghijklmnopqrstuvwxyz
1234567890 !@#?:;"*&

Foundry: Linotype
Designer: Erik Faulhaber
Designer Nationality: German
Date: 2013

Xenois Slab is a further component of the extensive Xenois font family. The characters provide the font with a unique disposition while retaining the proportions and stroke weights of other Xenois fonts, allowing each style to harmonize across platforms and projects.

Zico

ABCDEFGHIJKLMNOPQRSTUVWXYZ
abcdefghijklmnopqrstuvwxyz
1234567890 !@#?:;"*&

Foundry: Typotheque
Designer: Marko Hrastovec
Designer Nationality: Croatian
Date: 2016

Marko Hrastovec's Zico is a humanist slab serif, influenced by the muscular letterforms found on sports jerseys. Throughout its seven weights, from Thin to Black, the characters propose a sporting aesthetic, seen primarily in their dynamic joints and robust strokes.

Archive

ABCDEFGHIJKLMNOPQRSTUVWXYZ
abcdefghijklmnopqrstuvwxyz
1234567890 !@#?:;"*&

Archive was initially created for a publication by Brighton-based photographic publisher Photoworks, and has small indents on the top and bottom of each serif that align parallel to the baseline and cap height. It is available in four weights plus italics, and a monospaced version.

Foundry: Colophon
Designer: The Entente
Designer Nationality: British
Date: 2013

Basilia

ABCDEFGHIJKLMNOPQRSTUVWXYZ
abcdefghijklmnopqrstuvwxyz
1234567890 !@#?:;"*&

Basilia has a classical look, expressed by the strong contrast between its robust verticals and fine horizontal strokes and serifs. Its round forms and softer strokes differentiate it from traditional Modern faces, with straight horizontal serifs set at right angles to the strokes.

Foundry: Haas
Designer: André Gürtler
Designer Nationality: Swiss
Date: 1978

Boberia

ABCDEFGHIJKLMNOPQRSTUVWXYZ
abcdefghijklmnopqrstuvwxyz
1234567890 !@#?:;"*&

Bo Berndal's expressive serif won the Linotype International Digital Type Design Contest in 1994. It is inspired by early 20th-century neoclassicism, and its narrow letterforms, large x-height and high stroke contrast give it a sophisticated feel, reminiscent of Art Deco designs.

Foundry: Linotype
Designer: Bo Berndal
Designer Nationality: Swedish
Date: 1994

Bodoni Classico

ABCDEFGHIJKLMNOPQRSTUVWXYZ
abcdefghijklmnopqrstuvwxyz
1234567890 !@#?:;"*&

This is one of the numerous variations on Giambattista Bodoni's hugely influential design of 1767, which was dominant until the end of the 19th century. Franko Luin's take is notable for displaying less stroke contrast than Bodoni's original design, making it ideal for use at smaller point sizes.

Foundry: Omnibus
Designer: Giambattista Bodoni / Franko Luin
Designer Nationality: Italian / Swedish
Date: 1767 / 1995

Bauer Bodoni

ABCDEFGHIJKLMNOPQRSTUVWXYZ
abcdefghijklmnopqrstuvwxyz
1234567890 !@#?:;"*&

Foundry: Bauer
Designer: Giambattista Bodoni / Heinrich Jost
Designer Nationality: Italian / German
Date: 1798 / 1926

Bauer Bodoni was designed for the Bauer Type Foundry in 1926 by Heinrich Jost, the German typographer and type designer, and is a revival of the famous Didone cut in 1798 by Italian typographer and printer Giambattista Bodoni. Bodoni's design was heavily influenced by the first of the modern faces cut by the Frenchman Firmin Didot, his contemporary and rival, in the early 1780s in Paris.

Bodoni and Didot were the key instigators in the development of serif typefaces from the transitional to the modern, along with Frenchman Pierre-Simon Fournier. However, it is the former pair who are most recognized, and the term 'didone' is a combination of both of their surnames.

Bodoni pushed at the boundaries of what was achievable to be cut and printed. His typeface design was revolutionary; discarding brackets, with serifs just defined by a thin stroke and creating a huge contrast between the thick and thin strokes that defined each character. The technical precision and elegance of the typeface made for a classic.

The Bauer version of Bodoni is most often seen employed in graphic design for fashion, and in display and headline applications. This version retains the high contrast of Bodoni's original design and more of its features than many other published versions from different foundries, which have sometimes aimed to improve legibility by reducing the extreme tolerances of the overall design.

Below. f32 is an American trend-watching company. Blok Design, based in Canada, worked with the organization to create both its name (f32 comes from photography terminology, a setting that provides the most depth of field), and its visual identity across print, including stationery, trend reports and a new website. The san-serif employed is Montserrat, a geometric sans serif by Argentinian designer Julieta Ulanovsky.

Bodoni LT

ABCDEFGHIJKLMNOPQRSTUVWXYZ
abcdefghijklmnopqrstuvwxyz
1234567890 !@#?:;"*&

Foundry: ATC
Designer: Giambattista Bodoni / Morris Fuller Benton
Designer Nationality: Italian / American
Date: 1767 / 1911

Giambattista Bodoni was a prolific type designer, and many interpretations of his 18th-century typeface have been created. Although some of the finer details of the original are missing from this cut, the high contrast and vertical stress typical of this style of serif are very much present.

Brenner

ABCDEFGHIJKLMNOPQRSTUVWXYZ
abcdefghijklmnopqrstuvwxyz
1234567890 !@#?:;"*&

Foundry: Typotheque
Designer: Nikola Djurek
Designer Nationality: Croatian
Date: 2018

Although inspired by the high-contrast fonts of Giambattista Bodoni and Firmin Didot, Brenner has the feel of handwritten pointed-pen writing. The typeface forms part of a superfamily with a Serif, Sans, Display, Mono, Script, Condensed and Slab. It is best used at 14 point and above.

Bressay

ABCDEFGHIJKLMNOPQRSTUVWXYZ
abcdefghijklmnopqrstuvwxyz
1234567890 !@#?:;"*&

Foundry: Dalton Maag
Designer: Stuart Brown
Designer Nationality: British
Date: 2015

A revision of 19th-century Scotch Roman letterforms, Bressay is a versatile serif designed for use at all sizes. Slight modifications to classical features, such as the ball terminals, ensure character and readability across both print and digital platforms.

Chiswick Deck

ABCDEFGHIJKLMNOPQRSTUVWXYZ
abcdefghijklmnopqrstuvwxyz
1234567890 !@#?:;"*&

Foundry: Commercial Type
Designer: Paul Barnes
Designer Nationality: British
Date: 2017

Informed by a collection of 18th- and 19th-century types, Chiswick Deck is a lively modern serif. While the strokes are high in contrast and largely formal, the serifs and tails, especially those in the wonderfully rich italics, are treated with the more expressive forms of hand-lettering.

Didot

ABCDEFGHIJKLMNOPQRSTUVWXYZ
abcdefghijklmnopqrstuvwxyz
1234567890 !@#?:;”*&

Swiss type designer Adrian Frutiger (see p. 290) drew on the type designs and letterforms of Parisian designer Firmin Didot when he created Didot for Linotype in 1991. Frutiger's sensitive revival typeface captures the spirit and innovation of the Enlightenment, yet is also representative of Firmin Didot's later designs drawn up in the first decade of the 19th century.

Firmin Didot was working at a time when advances in type design, printing techniques and paper technology led to huge improvements in letter-cutting. This contributed to increased innovation and the creation of ever-more sophisticated types. Didot's Modern approach (so-called because of its position after Old Style and Transitional) type design reflected the progression of these types, as did those of French designer Pierre-Simon Fournier and Italian designer Giambattista Bodoni in developing increasingly refined type designs.

A key design feature in the construction of Didot is the greater contrast between the thick and thin strokes making up the characters. In the 18th and 19th centuries, this feature pushed the boundaries of printing reproduction, but its style captured the pioneering zeitgeist of the time. The lack of curved serifs and the use of horizontal strokes is also part of the aesthetic for this typeface. Its elegance and refinement have made it a go-to typeface for fashion and classical-art applications.

Foundry: Linotype
Designer: Firmin Didot / Adrian Frutiger
Designer Nationality: French / Swiss
Date: c. 1810 / 1991

Below left. Identity and branding for American Friends Musée d'Orsay using Linotype Didot with the sans serif Cantarell. Design: Trüf Creative, USA.

Below. Detail from an advert for The JFK Presidential Library and Museum. Design: The Martin Agency, USA.

Chiswick Text

ABCDEFGHIJKLMNOPQRSTUVWXYZ
abcdefghijklmnopqrstuvwxyz
1234567890 !@#?:;”*&

Foundry: Commercial Type
Designer: Paul Barnes
Designer Nationality: British
Date: 2017

Chiswick Text is a serif designed in the modern style and intended for texts that require smaller sizes. Like Chiswick Deck, its characters are informed by British lettering at the dawn of the Industrial Revolution and combine formal precision with lively, calligraphic flourishes.

Electra

ABCDEFGHIJKLMNOPQRSTUVWXYZ
abcdefghijklmnopqrstuvwxyz
1234567890 !@#?:;”*&

Foundry: Linotype
Designer: William A. Dwiggins
Designer Nationality: American
Date: 1935

William A. Dwiggins, the polymath and graphic-design pioneer, created Electra as a celebration of the new machine age within typography. Its crisp forms proved popular among US book designers following its release, and it has since been the subject of several digital revivals.

Estrella

ABCDEFGHIJKLMNOPQRSTUVWXYZ
abcdefghijklmnopqrstuvwxyz
1234567890 !@#?:;”*&

Foundry: Neutura
Designer: Alexander McCracken
Designer Nationality: American
Date: 2009

Created by San Francisco-based type designer Alexander McCracken for his foundry Neutura (see p. 472), this dignified, high-contrast Didone font supports more than thirty Latin-based languages. Alongside Regular and Hairline Regular weights, a decorative cut, Estrella Neuvo, is also available.

Fournier

ABCDEFGHIJKLMNOPQRSTUVWXYZ
abcdefghijklmnopqrstuvwxyz
1234567890 !@#?:;”*&

Foundry: Monotype
Designer: Pierre-Simon Fournier / Stanley Morison
Designer Nationality: French / British
Date: c. 1700s / 1924

Fournier MT was created under the direction of British typographer Stanley Morison. It is based on the designs of 18th-century French typefounder Pierre-Simon Fournier, whose work has been the subject of several revivals and influenced the development of modern-style serifs such as Bodoni.

Filosofia

ABCDEFGHIJKLMNOPQRSTUVWXYZ
abcdefghijklmnopqrstuvwxyz
1234567890 !@#?:;"*&

Foundry: Emigre
Designer: Zuzana Licko
Designer Nationality: Slovakian
Date: 1996

The Filosofia typeface family was designed by type designer Zuzana Licko, the founder of the type foundry Emigre (see p. 106). It is her interpretation of a Bodoni font design. Licko's creation incorporates slightly bulging round serif endings, which reflect the appearance of original Bodoni fonts printed in letterpress. She has also reduced the contrast between the thick and thin strokes of the characters to allow her design to be used in small text sizes for text either in print or on a computer.

Filosofia is a family of seven fonts, featuring a regular, bold, italic and small caps, for use in a variety of text applications. The Grand character set has been further refined and is more delicate, with increased contrast in the stroke weights, and is intended for use at larger sizes. An additional style included in the Grand family package is a Unicase version that sets the characters at a single height irrespective of upper or lowercase.

Below. Specimen examples created by the Emigre foundry presenting Filosofia in both titling and text applications.

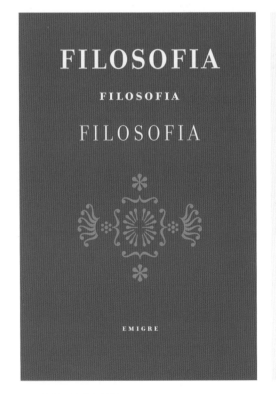

THE YOSEMITE
John Muir

THE APPROACH TO THE VALLEY

When I set out on the long excursion that finally led to California I wandered afoot and alone, from Indiana to the Gulf of Mexico, with a plant-press on my back, holding a generally southward course, like the birds when they are going from summer to winter. From the west coast of Florida I crossed the gulf to Cuba, enjoyed the rich tropical flora there for a few months, intending to go thence to the north end of South America, make my way through the woods to the headwaters of the Amazon, and float down that grand river to the ocean.

Excerpt from the book *The Yosemite* by John Muir. Copyright © 1912 by The Century Company, New York.

Text set in Filosofia Regular, designed by Zuzana Licko in 1996.

55 | *The Yosemite*

WWW.EMIGRE.COM

NINE LITERARY TYPES | FILOSOFIA

Right. Specimen example showing the unicase version (manifest destiny) where both lower and uppercase characters are set at the same height.

Below. Designed by Vignelli Associates in 1996, this poster was created to promote the Filosofia typeface. It describes Licko's underlying approach to the process of the design of their Bodoni tribute.

moccasin
UNIFIED SCHOOL DISTRICT
manifest destiny
The logical outcome of perseverance in art

My Favorite Typeface

Before the age of personal computers, when I used to spec typefaces out of photo typesetters' style books, my favorite typeface was Bodoni. I was attracted to its clean lines and geometric shapes, and the variety of headline style choices. However, for practical reasons, I often decided against using Bodoni for long texts, as the extreme contrast made it difficult to read at small sizes.

Since then, there have been many digital font revivals and reworkings of Bodoni's typefaces, some of which

have brought to light the numerous variations in Bodoni's type designs not evident in the earlier photo types. For example, the recent ITC Bodoni was released in three variants, each optimized for a range of sizes, and each with very distinct features, reflecting the variety of Bodoni's work.

In fact, Bodoni spent his entire life building a large collection of over 400 fonts. He started with Fournier's types as a model, and over time developed a personal style that tended toward simplicity, austerity and a greater contrast between the vertical stems and hairlines than previously seen, resulting in what we know today as the modern face.

In the preface of his "Manuale Tipografico" Bodoni stated: "It is proper here to offer the four different heads under which it seems to me are derived the beauties of type, and the first to these is regularity: conformity without ambiguity, variety without dissonance, and equality and symmetry without confusion".

This apparent development toward the geometry of Modern Face may explain the prevalence of excessively geometric Bodoni revivals which may have gone a step further in this progression than Bodoni intended.

Bodoni's many fonts also included small increments in sizes, sometimes down to half point sizes. As was common practice at the time, each size varied in design to accommodate the effects of the printing process. The characters comprising small text sizes were slightly widened to accommodate ample counters which resisted the tendency to clog up, as well as reduced contrast to ensure that the hairlines would not break up. The display sizes, in turn, were slightly narrower with more contrast, yielding graceful and delicate features which the letterpress process could only maintain at the larger sizes.

This practice disappeared with the introduction of photo type since it became most efficient to simply settle a single design to the various sizes as needed. Since then, technical advancements, including improvements in the printing process itself, have made it less necessary to have size specific design variations. However, it does remain a necessity for the optimum legibility of certain designs, such as Bodoni, which were designed for different manufacturing and printing processes

than those used today. In fact, the extreme contrast problem of many Bodoni revivals may be the result of choosing a display size for the model, which subsequently cause the hairlines to erode when reduced to small text sizes.

Although the computer is capable of addressing multiple size masters more readily than photo type did, Adobe's Multiple Master format can accommodate this), optical scaling remains to be added as a standard feature to the popular font formats, and probably never will, since most contemporary typefaces which are designed for today's technology do not so critically demand such technical wizardry.

Because Bodoni created so many variations, many different Bodoni revivals and interpretations are possible. However, determining which most truly reflect Bodoni's work can be eternally debated. Filosofia is my interpretation of a Bodoni. It shows my personal preference for a geometric Bodoni, while incorporating such features as the slightly bulging round serif endings which often appeared in printed samples of Bodoni's work and reflect Bodoni's origins in letterpress technology. The Filosofia Regular family is designed for text applications. It is somewhat rugged with reduced contrast to withstand the reduction to text sizes. The Filosofia Grand family is intended for display applications and is therefore more delicate and refined.

An additional variant, included in the Grand package, is a Unicase version which uses a single height for characters that are otherwise separated into upper and lower case. This is similar to Bradbury Thompson's Alphabet Twenty Six, except that Thompson's goal was to create a text alphabet free of such redundancies as the two different forms which represent the character "a" or "A," whereas Filosofia Unicase does have stylistic variants to provide flexibility for headline use.

Zuzana Licko

'It's their Bodoni'

Industrial 736

ABCDEFGHIJKLMNOPQRSTUVWXYZ
abcdefghijklmnopqrstuvwxyz
1234567890 !@#?:;"*&

Foundry: Bitstream
Designer: Alessandro Butti
Designer Nationality: Italian
Date: 1908

Industrial 736 is a Bitstream digitization of the Torino font family, a neoclassical design for the Nebiolo foundry in Turin in 1908. Some attribute the design to the Italian type designer Alessandro Butti, who was director of the Nebiolo foundry from 1936 to 1952, when he was succeeded by Aldo Novarese.

Iridium

ABCDEFGHIJKLMNOPQRSTUVWXYZ
abcdefghijklmnopqrstuvwxyz
1234567890 !@#?:;"*&

Foundry: Stempel
Designer: Adrian Frutiger
Designer Nationality: Swiss
Date: 1972

This warm and delicate interpretation of the neoclassical style was commissioned by Stempel as one of the foundry's first fonts for phototypesetting. Adrian Frutiger (see p. 290) paid especially close attention to the harmony between its letterforms, and cut the final films himself, by hand.

ITC Bodoni Seventytwo

ABCDEFGHIJKLMNOPQRSTUVWXYZ
abcdefghijklmnopqrstuvwxyz
1234567890 !@#?:;"*&

Foundry: ITC
Designer: Giambattista Bodoni / Janice Fishman / Holly Goldsmith / Jim Parkinson / Sumner Stone
Designer Nationality: Italian / American / American / American / American
Date: 1790 / 1994

Bodoni Seventytwo is the display cut of ITC's Bodoni revival, and was developed by a four-strong team of type designers who travelled to Parma, Italy to research Giambattista Bodoni's original steel punches first-hand. Its design is carefully tailored for headline use.

ITC Bodoni Six

ABCDEFGHIJKLMNOPQRSTUVWXYZ
abcdefghijklmnopqrstuvwxyz
1234567890 !@#?:;"*&

Foundry: ITC
Designer: Giambattista Bodoni / Janice Fishman / Holly Goldsmith / Jim Parkinson / Sumner Stone
Designer Nationality: Italian / American / American / American / American
Date: 1790 / 1994

ITC's interpretation of Bodoni was cut in three different optical styles, of which this version was specifically developed for small type. With lower contrast than its display counterpart, ITC Bodoni Seventytwo, it remains legible within contexts such as captions and footnotes.

ITC Bodoni Twelve

ABCDEFGHIJKLMNOPQRSTUVWXYZ
abcdefghijklmnopqrstuvwxyz
1234567890 !@#?:;”*&

Designed for text use, ITC Bodoni Twelve is an archetypal modern design reflecting the fine details of Giambattista Bodoni's original. This meticulous ITC revival includes a set of delicate typographic ornaments derived from examples found in Bodoni's *Manuale tipografico* (*Manual of Typography*, 1818).

Foundry: ITC
Designer: Giambattista Bodoni / Janice Fishman / Holly Goldsmith / Jim Parkinson / Sumner Stone
Designer Nationality: Italian / American / American / American / American
Date: 1790 / 1994

ITC Fenice

ABCDEFGHIJKLMNOPQRSTUVWXYZ
abcdefghijklmnopqrstuvwxyz
1234567890 !@#?:;”*&

Aldo Novarese is well known for his work at the Italian foundry Nebiolo, but he also designed typefaces for several other companies over the course of his career. This neoclassical serif builds on the high-contrast forms of Bodoni, but with contemporary details added throughout.

Foundry: ITC
Designer: Aldo Novarese
Designer Nationality: Italian
Date: 1980

ITC Jamille

ABCDEFGHIJKLMNOPQRSTUVWXYZ
abcdefghijklmnopqrstuvwxyz
1234567890 !@#?:;”*&

Jamille was US designer Mark Jamra's first typeface, begun during his postgraduate studies, and ITC acquired it for publication in 1988. The Pro version, sold through Jamra's own TypeCulture foundry, includes an expanded character set, and an attractive alphabet of swash caps.

Foundry: ITC
Designer: Mark Jamra
Designer Nationality: American
Date: 1988

ITC Modern No 216

ABCDEFGHIJKLMNOPQRSTUVWXYZ
abcdefghijklmnopqrstuvwxyz
1234567890 !@#?:;”*&

This Didone typeface displays a warmth that is characteristic of many of the designs by Ed Benguiat (see p. 514), with balanced, shapely curves evident within many of its letterforms. Offering eight different styles, the ITC Modern No 216 family performs at its best in display contexts.

Foundry: ITC
Designer: Ed Benguiat
Designer Nationality: American
Date: 1982

ITC Týfa

ABCDEFGHIJKLMNOPQRSTUVWXYZ
abcdefghijklmnopqrstuvwxyz
1234567890 !@#?:;"*&

Foundry: Grafotechna / ITC
Designer: Josef Týfa /
František Štorm
Designer Nationality: Czech
Date: 1959 / 1998

A fine example of mid 20th-century Czech type design, this distinctive serif was designed by Josef Týfa in 1959 and released by Grafotechna. It was digitized for ITC by František Štorm, working in collaboration with Týfa, nearly forty years later. Its delicate set of true italics has a distinctive character.

ITC Zapf Book

ABCDEFGHIJKLMNOPQRSTUVWXYZ
abcdefghijklmnopqrstuvwxyz
1234567890 !@#?:;"*&

Foundry: ITC
Designer: Hermann Zapf
Designer Nationality: German
Date: 1976

Zapf Book was created by Hermann Zapf, the illustrious German type designer and calligrapher (see p. 290), and was his first typeface for ITC. It is a blend of elements and characteristics from the existing typefaces Walbaum and Melior, and with the contrasting strokes of a modern typeface such as Bodoni.

Though it was designed as a text face, Zapf suggested the addition of swashes for display purposes, but these were never designed and realized. Highly distinctive in appearance, Zapf Book has been crafted in keeping with Zapf's ethos that an alphabet should not just work as a collection of single letters but also have a sense of unity in itself. Zapf designed his fonts using pen and paper, and was a master of calligraphy.

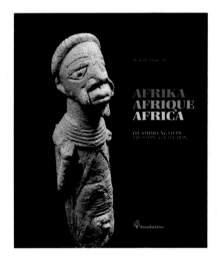

Karloff Positive

ABCDEFGHIJKLMNOPQRSTUVWXYZ
abcdefghijklmnopqrstuvwxyz
1234567890 !@#?:;"*&

Foundry: Typotheque
Designer: Peter Biľak / Pieter van Rosmalen / Nikola Djurek
Designer Nationality: Slovakian / Dutch / Croatian
Date: 2012

Inspired by the high-contrast of Didot and Bodoni, Karloff Positive is the beauty in this experimental family, while the reverse-contrast Karloff Negative is the beast, and Karloff Neutral is a mixture of both. The name is a nod to Boris Karloff, the actor famed for playing the monster in *Frankenstein* (1931).

Linotype Didot eText

ABCDEFGHIJKLMNOPQRSTUVWXYZ
abcdefghijklmnopqrstuvwxyz
1234567890 !@#?:;"*&

Foundry: Linotype
Designer: Adrian Frutiger
Designer Nationality: Swiss
Date: 2013

This modification of Didot by Adrian Frutiger (see p. 290) was specifically created for use in text-heavy digital contexts, such as e-readers, tablets, mobile devices and websites. eText fonts are made with higher x-heights, wider spacing and modulated stroke weights to improve on-screen legibility.

Linotype Gianotten

ABCDEFGHIJKLMNOPQRSTUVWXYZ
abcdefghijklmnopqrstuvwxyz
1234567890 !@#?:;"*&

Foundry: Linotype
Designer: Giambattista Bodoni / Antonio Pace
Designer Nationality: Italian
Date: 1790 / 1999

Linotype Gianotten took Italian designer Antonio Pace more than five years to develop and it is his attempt to adapt Bodoni's modern text faces for the digital age. Hairlines are thicker and serifs shorter to aid readability. It was named after the Dutch typographer Henk W. J. Gianotten.

Madison Antiqua

ABCDEFGHIJKLMNOPQRSTUVWXYZ
abcdefghijklmnopqrstuvwxyz
1234567890 !@#?:;"*&

Foundry: Stempel
Designer: Heinrich Wilhelm Hoffmeister
Designer Nationality: German
Date: 1965

Madison Antiqua is based on Amts-Antiqua, designed by Heinrich Wilhelm Hoffmeister between 1909 and 1919. Stempel rereleased six of the original eight weights of Hoffmeister's design in 1965 as Madison Antiqua. It shares its name with the Manhattan Avenue famed for advertising agencies.

Menhart

ABCDEFGHIJKLMNOPQRSTUVWXYZ
abcdefghijklmnopqrstuvwxyz
1234567890 !@#?:;"*&

Foundry: Monotype
Designer: Oldrich Menhart
Designer Nationality: Czech
Date: 1934

Named after its creator Oldrich Menhart, the Czech type designer, calligrapher and book designer, this is a roman with small serifs and an almost cursive feel to the lowercase alphabet. The Czech alphabet has fifteen accented letters and Menhart included these diacritics as an integral part of his design.

Modern 880

ABCDEFGHIJKLMNOPQRSTUVWXYZ
abcdefghijklmnopqrstuvwxyz
1234567890 !@#?:;”*&

Foundry: Bitstream
Designer: Walter Tracy
Designer Nationality: British
Date: 1969

Modern 880 is Bitstream's version of Linotype Modern, a typeface designed by Walter Tracy, who worked at Linotype for more than thirty years from 1948. Modern 880, which comes in roman, italic and bold, is a highly legible book type. Roman has square dots on the 'i' and 'j'.

Modern No. 20

ABCDEFGHIJKLMNOPQRSTUVWXYZ
abcdefghijklmnopqrstuvwxyz
1234567890 !@#?:;”*&

Foundry: Stephenson, Blake & Co. / Bitstream
Date: 1905 / c. 1980s

Modern No. 20 is an attractive didone serif face released by British foundry Stephenson, Blake & Co. at the start of the 20th century, but like all of the many numbered modern faces it was inspired by the earlier forms of Bodoni and Didot. Modern No. 20 comes in roman and italic.

Monotype Bodoni

ABCDEFGHIJKLMNOPQRSTUVWXYZ
abcdefghijklmnopqrstuvwxyz
1234567890 !@#?:;”*&

Foundry: Monotype
Designer: Giambattista Bodoni
Designer Nationality: Italian
Date: 1790

Monotype Bodoni comes in five weights with italics and has a condensed bold too. Designed by Giambattista Bodoni and one of the first modern faces, it is high-contrast with vertical stress and has flat, unbracketed serifs. Monotype's cut is heavier than that of other foundries.

Monotype Modern

ABCDEFGHIJKLMNOPQRSTUVWXYZ
abcdefghijklmnopqrstuvwxyz
1234567890 !@#?:;”*&

Foundry: Monotype
Designer: Monotype Studio
Date: 1896

The first typeface produced by Monotype – then known as the Lanston Monotype Machine Company – was the condensed cut of Modern, an upright, high-contrast serif face with thin hairlines. It is available in four versions: bold, condensed, extended and wide, all with italics.

Nara

ABCDEFGHIJKLMNOPQRSTUVWXYZ
abcdefghijklmnopqrstuvwxyz
1234567890 !@#?:;"*&

Foundry: Typotheque
Designer: Andrej Krátky /
Nikola Djurek / Peter Biľak
Designer Nationality: Czech /
Croatian / Slovakian
Date: 2009

Nara is a distinctive hybrid serif designed by Andrej Krátky between 1989 and 2009, and finished with help from Nikola Djurek and Peter Biľak. It comes in five weights, with two types of italic – both regular and an upright cursive. Originally called Adriq, it was renamed Nara after the Japanese city in Honshu.

New Caledonia

ABCDEFGHIJKLMNOPQRSTUVWXYZ
abcdefghijklmnopqrstuvwxyz
1234567890 !@#?:;"*&

Foundry: Linotype
Designer: William A. Dwiggins /
Alex Kaczun
Designer Nationality: American
Date: 1939 / 2007

Caledonia is a serif face designed for Mergenthaler Linotype in 1939 by William A. Dwiggins – the US designer credited with coining the term 'graphic design'. It is a popular choice for book text. New Caledonia is a digital update made by Alex Kaczun at Linotype in the late 1980s.

Otama

ABCDEFGHIJKLMNOPQRSTUVWXYZ
abcdefghijklmnopqrstuvwxyz
1234567890 !@#?:;"*&

Foundry: Tim Donaldson Design
Designer: Tim Donaldson
Designer Nationality: New
Zealander
Date: 2012

It took New Zealander Tim Donaldson more than two years to design this high-contrast didone serif. Otama features more than 8,000 different characters in the twenty-eight fonts that make up the superfamily, which contains regular, display and text versions, in six weights, all with italics.

Parma

ABCDEFGHIJKLMNOPQRSTUVWXYZ
abcdefghijklmnopqrstuvwxyz
1234567890 !@#?:;"*&

Foundry: Monotype
Designer: Monotype Studio
Date: 2008

Named after the Italian city where Giambattista Bodoni worked, Parma is a high-contrast didone available in regular, italic, display and bold, with support for the Latin, Greek and Cyrillic alphabets. It was designed by the Monotype Studio using research conducted at the Museo Bodoniano, Parma.

Emigre

Founded in 1984, Emigre can rightly be described as a pioneer and an innovator in the world of type, its launch coinciding with the arrival of the Macintosh computer in the design industry. The impact of these two events on design can never be underestimated. Founded in Berkeley, California by the Dutch designer Rudy VanderLans and his wife, Slovak designer Zuzana Licko, the foundry gained worldwide acclaim through its quarterly magazine, *Emigre*. An often-controversial journal, it challenged the conventions of legibility and explored readability through adventurous and experimental layouts that used its own digital typefaces, which were some of the very first to be created. *Emigre* magazine drew both acclaim and criticism worldwide because it altered the understanding of what could be achieved using a PC to design typefaces and create layouts.

As one of the first foundries distributing digital fonts, Emigre created systems that have been adopted by many smaller foundries across the world and still used today. Having won numerous awards for its own work and huge contribution to type design, Emigre has also collaborated with many esteemed type designers around the world using the Emigre platform to distribute their designs. Key contributors include Barry Deck, Miles Newlyn, Jonathan Barnbrook, P. Scott Makela, Jeffery Keedy and Xavier Dupré.

In 2011, five digital typefaces from the *Emigre* Type Library were honoured when they were acquired by the Museum of Modern Art in New York for its permanent design and architecture collection. The final issue of *Emigre* magazine, No. 69, was published in 2005 and sold out, as has most of the back catalogue. This was a fitting tribute to the creativity and invention of the Emigre foundry and its influential library of design, which continues to have an impact today.

Founded: 1984
Country: America
Website: emigre.com
Notable typefaces:
Mrs Eaves (see p. 171)
Base 900 (see p. 190)
Filosofia (see p. 98)

Below and opposite. As a ground-breaking showcase of not only their design abilities but also their innovative typeface creations, the *Emigre* magazines are still highly coveted publications today and reflect the digital revolution in graphic design through the years. From left, front covers of Issue Nos. 11, 14, 68 and 70.

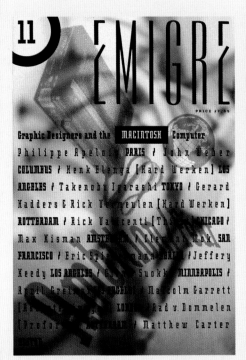

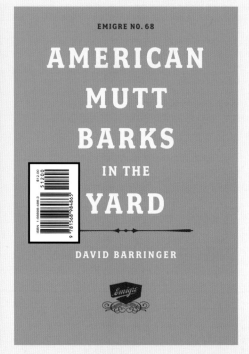

EMIGRE

No.70

The Look Back Issue

SELECTIONS FROM EMIGRE MAGAZINE #1 ~ #69

1984 ~ 2009

CELEBRATING 25 YEARS

In Graphic Design

Parmigiano Text

ABCDEFGHIJKLMNOPQRSTUVWXYZ
abcdefghijklmnopqrstuvwxyz
1234567890 !@#?:;”*&

Parmigiano Text is part of the Parmigiano superfamily by Italians Riccardo Olocco and Jonathan Pierini. It is the family's Bodoni-inspired text face in six weights with italics. The Cyrillic was designed by Ilya Ruderman and Irina Smirnova, a Greek version by Irene Vlachou followed in 2015.

Foundry: Typotheque
Designer: Riccardo Olocco / Jonathan Pierini
Designer Nationality: Italian
Date: 2014

Pax

ABCDEFGHIJKLMNOPQRSTUVWXYZ
abcdefghijklmnopqrstuvwxyz
1234567890 !@#?:;”*&

Pax, which takes its name from the Latin for 'peace', is a narrow didone designed by Franko Luin. A versatile family, Pax comes in roman, semibold and bold, with italics; a condensed version comes in regular and bold, with italics. There are small-cap versions for roman and condensed.

Foundry: Omnibus
Designer: Franko Luin
Designer Nationality: Swedish
Date: 1995

Pax 2

ABCDEFGHIJKLMNOPQRSTUVWXYZ
abcdefghijklmnopqrstuvwxyz
1234567890 !@#?:;”*&

Released by Franko Luin the same year as the first Pax (1995), Pax 2 is almost identical, but since the original was somewhat narrow, Luin decided to create a second version that was a little broader and darker. Less versatile than its forebear, Pax 2 has no condensed versions.

Foundry: Omnibus
Designer: Franko Luin
Designer Nationality: Swedish
Date: 1995

Scotch Roman

ABCDEFGHIJKLMNOPQRSTUVWXYZ
abcdefghijklmnopqrstuvwxyz
1234567890 !@#?:;”*&

Scotch Roman is modelled on Pica No. 2, a typeface designed in Edinburgh by William Miller in the 19th century and believed to be the first example of the style with a marked contrast in stroke weight. The font's name was applied to a recasting of Miller's type by the A. D. Farmer Foundry of New York.

Foundry: A. D. Farmer
Designer: William Miller / A. D. Farmer Foundry
Designer Nationality: Scottish / American
Date: 1813 / 1904

Tiemann

ABCDEFGHIJKLMNOPQRSTUVWXYZ
abcdefghijklmnopqrstuvwxyz
1234567890 !@#?:;"*&

Foundry: Kingspor
Designer: Walter Tiemann
Designer Nationality: German
Date: 1923

The Tiemann font family, designed early in the 20th century, is a serif that both respects and challenges the modern style. While the significant stroke contrasts and flat serifs remain conventional, the shapes and proportions take their cue from neoclassical letterforms.

VentiQuattro

ABCDEFGHIJKLMNOPQRSTUVWXYZ
abcdefghijklmnopqrstuvwxyz
1234567890 !@#?:;"*&

Foundry: Playtype
Designer: Jonas Hecksher
Designer Nationality: Danish
Date: 2009

This elegant didone-style serif was designed by Jonas Hecksher, award-winning partner and creative director at the Danish design agency e-Types. VentiQuattro means 'twenty-four' in Italian. It comprises four weights from Regular to Bold, plus an italic.

Walbaum

ABCDEFGHIJKLMNOPQRSTUVWXYZ
abcdefghijklmnopqrstuvwxyz
1234567890 !@#?:;"*&

Foundry: Monotype
Designer: Justic Erich Walbaum / Charles Nix / Carl Crossgrove / Juan Villanueva
Designer Nationality: German / American / American / Peruvian
Date: c. 1800s / 2018

A restoration of a typeface designed by Justus Erich Walbaum in the 19th century, Monotype's Walbaum is a 21st-century take on the modern serif. Designed for multiplatform use, Walbaum consists of thirty-two weights, and unlike earlier modern serifs, includes a wealth of ornaments.

WTC Our Bodoni

ABCDEFGHIJKLMNOPQRSTUVWXYZ
abcdefghijklmnopqrstuvwxyz
1234567890 !@#?:;"*&

Foundry: Monotype
Designer: Giambattista Bodoni / Tom Carnase / Massimo Vignelli
Designer Nationality: Italian / American / American
Date: 1767 /1989

WTC Our Bodoni was commissioned by the World Typeface Center, New York and is a redesign of the 18th-century modern serif cut by Giambattista Bodoni. Designed by Tom Carnase and Massimo Vignelli, this face takes the original forms of Bodoni and applies the ratios of the Helvetica font.

Adobe Caslon

ABCDEFGHIJKLMNOPQRSTUVWXYZ
abcdefghijklmnopqrstuvwxyz
1234567890 !@#?:;”*&

Foundry: Adobe
Designer: William Caslon / Carol Twombly
Designer Nationality: British / American
Date: *c.* 1720s / 1990

This revival by esteemed US type designer Carol Twombly for Adobe as part of its Adobe Originals programme was developed from her studies of specimen pages printed by English typefounder William Caslon in the mid-1700s. It is considered by many to be the best text typeface ever to come out of the Adobe design studio and it retains an elegance no matter what the application.

A gunsmith and engraver by trade, William Caslon created his first typefaces in 1722, basing them on Old Style designs from the Netherlands. His typefaces proved to be a success at home and internationally, and were employed widely because of their simplicity, practicality and legibility. His work contributed greatly to the development of English type design and towards creating an English national typographic style.

After Caslon's death in 1766, the usage of his typefaces declined until the mid to late 1800s, when they gained favour thanks to the Arts and Crafts movement in Britain. They remain a popular choice for printers and typesetters even to this day. The success of Caslon's types means there have been many revivals and the number of types referred to as 'Caslon' is extensive. In addition, there is much variation between foundries and technological developments have also impacted on the way type is produced.

As a standard over three centuries, Caslon can rightly be said to be one of the most significant typefaces of all time. It has been used as text on the American Declaration of Independence, in classic works of literature by writers including George Bernard Shaw, and in *The New Yorker* magazine.

Right. Detail from *The First Six Books of the Elements of Euclid* annotated with Caslon Roman and Italic.

THE FIRST SIX BOOKS OF

THE ELEMENTS OF EUCLID

IN WHICH COLOURED DIAGRAMS AND SYMBOLS

ARE USED INSTEAD OF LETTERS FOR THE

GREATER EASE OF LEARNERS

BY OLIVER BYRNE

SURVEYOR OF HER MAJESTY'S SETTLEMENTS IN THE FALKLAND ISLANDS
AND AUTHOR OF NUMEROUS MATHEMATICAL WORKS

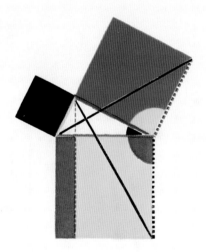

LONDON
WILLIAM PICKERING
1847

Administer

ABCDEFGHIJKLMNOPQRSTUVWXYZ
abcdefghijklmnopqrstuvwxyz
1234567890 ! @ #?:;" * &

Foundry: Typsettra
Designer: Les Usherwood / Steve Jackaman
Designer Nationality: British
Date: *c.* 1980s / 2000

British-born designer Les Usherwood moved to Canada in 1957, where he co-founded the Typsettra foundry. His Administer now forms part of the Red Rooster Collection. Steve Jackaman digitized the new version of this elegant Old Style serif, which remains true to Usherwood's original drawings.

Adobe Garamond Pro

ABCDEFGHIJKLMNOPQRSTUVWXYZ
abcdefghijklmnopqrstuvwxyz
1234567890 !@#?:;"*&

Foundry: Adobe
Designer: Claude Garamond / Robert Slimbach
Designer Nationality: French / American
Date: 1480–1561 / 1989

This is considered an Old Style face due to the oblique nature of the slimmest parts of the letterforms. It is based on Claude Garamond's 16th-century design cut by Garamond's assistant Robert Granjon and is regarded as a more faithful interpretation than earlier versions.

Agmena

ABCDEFGHIJKLMNOPQRSTUVWXYZ
abcdefghijklmnopqrstuvwxyz
1234567890 !@#?:;"*&

Foundry: Linotype
Designer: Jovica Veljović
Designer Nationality: Serbian
Date: 2012

Created by Serbian designer Jovica Veljović, Agmena shares many traits with the group of Renaissance Antiqua fonts. Its generous x-height, large counters and open forms all help its legibility at small sizes, making it an ideal book font. It was a Type Directors Club Typeface Design Winner in 2013.

Alcuin

ABCDEFGHIJKLMNOPQRSTUVWXYZ
abcdefghijklmnopqrstuvwxyz
1234567890 !@#?:;" * &

Foundry: Linotype
Designer: Gudrun Zapf von Hesse
Designer Nationality: German
Date: 1991

Gudrun Zapf von Hesse's expressive design retains the flow of handwritten letters, and Alcuin is based on the Carolingian minuscule calligraphic script that was introduced so the Latin alphabet could be recognized from region to region. It is named after an advisor to Emperor Charlemagne.

Aldine 401

ABCDEFGHIJKLMNOPQRSTUVWXYZ
abcdefghijklmnopqrstuvwxyz
1234567890 !@#?:;"★&

Foundry: Bitstream
Designer: Francesco Griffo
Designer Nationality: Italian
Date: c. 1495

This digitized Old Style serif was released by Bitstream and later updated by Paratype. It is based on Bembo, which itself was based on a design from c. 1495 cut by the Italian punch-cutter Francesco Griffo for Aldus Manutius, the Venetian scholar, printer and founder of the Aldine Press.

Aldine 721

ABCDEFGHIJKLMNOPQRSTUVWXYZ
abcdefghijklmnopqrstuvwxyz
1234567890 !@#?:;"★&

Foundry: Bitstream
Designer: Frank Hinman Pierpont
Designer Nationality: American
Date: 2000

One of many digitized versions of typefaces originally designed by Frank Hinman Pierpont (the engineer-turned-type-designer who became President of Monotype in 1899), this classic Old Style font is based on Plantin, itself based on a 16th-century design by Robert Granjon.

Aldus

ABCDEFGHIJKLMNOPQRSTUVWXYZ
abcdefghijklmnopqrstuvwxyz
1234567890 !@#?:;"*&

Foundry: Stempel
Designer: Hermann Zapf
Designer Nationality: German
Date: 1954

Initially called Palatino Light but later named Aldus, this was originally created as a text weight by Hermann Zapf (see p. 574) for his Palatino family. It was released in its own right with italic, small caps and Old Style figures, and its narrow forms and light weight made it a popular choice for book typography.

Aldus Nova

ABCDEFGHIJKLMNOPQRSTUVWXYZ
abcdefghijklmnopqrstuvwxyz
1234567890 !@#?:;"*&

Foundry: Linotype
Designer: Hermann Zapf / Akira Kobayashi
Designer Nationality: German / Japanese
Date: 1954 / 2005

Hermann Zapf (see p. 574) collaborated with Akira Kobayashi to rework his designs for Palatino to form a new typeface family, Palatino Nova. It includes this updated version of his Aldus typeface from 1954, plus two titling weights based on Zapf's metal typeface Michelangelo and all caps Sistina.

Alisal

ABCDEFGHIJKLMNOPQRSTUVWXYZ
abcdefghijklmnopqrstuvwxyz
1234567890 !@#?:;"*&

Foundry: Monotype
Designer: Matthew Carter
Designer Nationality: British
Date: 1995

This handsome calligraphic font was a labour of love for Matthew Carter (see p. 616), who worked on the design for many years. Influenced by 15th- and 16th-century Italian Old Style fonts, Alisal is heavier and has distinctive serifs with no bracketing, which appear to cross the main vertical.

Arrus BT

ABCDEFGHIJKLMNOPQRSTUVWXYZ
abcdefghijklmnopqrstuvwxyz
1234567890 !@#?:;"*&

Foundry: Bitstream
Designer: Richard Lipton
Designer Nationality: American
Date: 1991

Arrus BT is influenced by classic Roman inscriptions and displays vertical strokes that gently expand. It is based on calligraphic alphabets that US designer Richard Lipton drew by hand using a brush rather than a pen. Lipton also created its distinctive sister typeface, Arrus Black.

Aurelia

ABCDEFGHIJKLMNOPQRSTUVWXYZ
abcdefghijklmnopqrstuvwxyz
1234567890 !@#?:;"*&

Foundry: Hell
Designer: Hermann Zapf
Designer Nationality: German
Date: 1963

Named after the Roman emperor Aurelianus, this typeface is based on Nicolas Jenson's classic Old Style typeface Jenson, created in 1470. Hermann Zapf (see p. 574) added his own personal flourishes, and updated it for use with the typesetting machines introduced in the 1960s by Rudolf Hell.

Bara

ABCDEFGHIJKLMNOPQRSTUVWXYZ
abcdefghijklmnopqrstuvwxyz
1234567890 !@#?:;"*&

Foundry: Typotheque
Designer: Nikola Djurek
Designer Nationality: Croatian
Date: 2016

Bara is a loose interpretation of a 16th-century typeface Schefferletter (or Enschedé English-bodied Roman No. 6). It is a slim, refined family, which has many of the idiosyncrasies found in the original metal type, such as the abruptly ended strokes of the letters 'c' and 'e'.

Bembo

ABCDEFGHIJKLMNOPQRSTUVWXYZ
abcdefghijklmnopqrstuvwxyz
1234567890 !@#?:;"★&

Foundry: Monotype
Designer: Francesco Griffo /
Stanley Morison
Designer Nationality: Italian /
British
Date: 1496 / 1929

Bembo's origins date to the 15th century, when legendary Italian Renaissance printer Aldus Manutius of the Aldine Press in Venice, published a short book *De Aetna* (1496) on the travels of scholar and poet Pietro Bembo and his ascent of Mount Etna. Manutius employed a new roman typeface for the dialogue, which was created by punch-cutter Francesco Griffo. The type's design adopted less of a heavy calligraphic, hand-drawn approach in favour of the more elegant appearance seen in serif types today. This resulted in many type designers of the time moving away from the established approach towards the evolution of serif roman designs.

In 1929, Monotype consultant Stanley Morison oversaw the recreation of the typeface as part of Monotype's restoration of historic typeface designs and titled it 'Bembo'. The 15th-century design had a number of characters refined and redrawn to meet the technical requirements of contemporary machine typesetting. Bembo comes in thirty-one weights, with small caps, Old Style figures and expert characters. It is ideal for book typography but also functions as an all-rounder. Bembo has also had great influence on well-known typefaces such as Garamond, Times Roman and, in recent times, Robert Slimbach's Minion.

Section 25–Always now friend
ly fires dirty disco c.p. loose tal
k costs lives inside out melt clos
e hit babies in the bardo be bra
ve new horizon produced by
martin hannett engineer joh
n caffrey recorded at brittania
row disegnatori : grafica indu
stria e typografica berthold a
factory records product fact 45

16.5 mm (60p)   10   20

Above. Vinyl album cover *Always Now* from English post-punk and electronic band Section 25. Released in 1981, the cover was designed by renowned British graphic designer Peter Saville and Grafica Industria, his studio at the time.

Bembo Book

ABCDEFGHIJKLMNOPQRSTUVWXYZ
abcdefghijklmnopqrstuvwxyz
1234567890 !@#?:;"★&

Foundry: Monotype
Designer: Francesco Griffo /
Stanley Morison / Robin Nicholas
Designer Nationality: Italian /
British
Date: 1496 / 1929 / 2005

Stanley Morison's version (1929) of the typeface inspired by Francesco Griffo's 15th-century design was followed by a number of revisions by Monotype.

Robin Nicholas's Bembo Book is widely considered to be the most faithful interpretation of this classic and much-copied Old Style serif.

Bembo Infant

ABCDEFGHIJKLMNOPQRSTUVWXYZ
abcdefghijklmnopqrstuvwxyz
1234567890 !@#?:;"★&

Foundry: Monotype
Designer: Francesco Griffo /
Monotype Studio
Designer Nationality: Italian /
British
Date: 1495–1501 / 1929

One of many versions of Francesco Griffo's Bembo, this friendly serif has different forms for the letters 'a', 'g' and 'y', the first two of which are both single

storey. The traditional 'Infant' or 'Schoolbook' versions of typefaces were designed to help children with their reading.

Berling

ABCDEFGHIJKLMNOPQRSTUVWXYZ
abcdefghijklmnopqrstuvwxyz
1234567890 !@#?:;"*&

Foundry: Berlingska Stilgjuteriet
Designer: Karl-Erik Forsberg
Designer Nationality: Swedish
Date: 1951

This elegant serif with its sharp, beak-like serifs was designed for the Berlingska Stilgjuteriet foundry in Lund in 1951. It was followed by several

more weights in 1958. A full-scale redesign was commissioned in 2004 by the Swedish publisher Verbum, under the title 'Berling Nova'.

Bertham

ABCDEFGHIJKLMNOPQRSTUVWXYZ
abcdefghijklmnopqrstuvwxyz
1234567890 !@#?:;"*&

Foundry: Continental
Designer: Frederic W. Goudy /
Steve Matheson
Designer Nationality: American
Date: 1936 / 2009

Frederic W. Goudy named this refined serif in memory of his wife Bertha, who had died the year before. It was commissioned by *American Printer*

magazine and inspired by a design used by Lienhart Holle for Ptolemy's *Geographica* (*Geography*) in 1482. It was revived by Ascender as Bertham Pro.

Binny Old Style

ABCDEFGHIJKLMNOPQRSTUVWX
abcdefghijklmnopqrstuvwxyz
1234567890 !@#?:;"*&

Foundry: MacKellar, Smiths & Jordan
Designer: Alexander Kay
Designer Nationality: Scottish
Date: c. 1863 / 1908

Adapted by Alexander Kay, this sophisticated serif was itself an adaptation from Old Style No. 77, a typeface from the Philadelphia-based foundry MacKellar, Smiths & Jordan, dating from c. 1863. While influenced by Caslon, Binny Old Style is a more modern take on the classic typeface.

Buccardi

ABCDEFGHIJKLMNOPQRSTUVWXYZ
abcdefghijklmnopqrstuvwxyz
1234567890 !@#?:;"*&

Foundry: Agfa Compugraphic
Designer: Bo Berndal
Designer Nationality: Swedish
Date: 2003

This jaunty serif is designed by the calligrapher, author and lecturer Bo Berndal, one of Sweden's most prolific type designers. Buccardi features a distinctive, almost top-heavy lowercase 'a'. It is available in both Pro and Standard versions in regular and bold, and with matching italics.

Calisto

ABCDEFGHIJKLMNOPQRSTUVWXYZ
abcdefghijklmnopqrstuvwxyz
1234567890 !@#?:;"*&

Foundry: Monotype
Designer: Ron Carpenter
Designer Nationality: British
Date: 1986

A graceful Old Style serif, with classical proportions and minimal stroke contrast, Calisto is reminiscent of typefaces such as Palatino and Belwe. Highly legible, its terminals are cut on an angle to the baseline and concavely indented. It was created by British typographer Ron Carpenter.

Cardamon

ABCDEFGHIJKLMNOPQRSTUVWXYZ
abcdefghijklmnopqrstuvwxyz
1234567890 !@#?:;"*&

Foundry: Linotype
Designer: Brigitte Schuster
Designer Nationality: Swiss
Date: 2015

Swiss designer Brigitte Schuster's first typeface was conceived while she was still a student at the Royal Academy of Art in The Hague. This legible, well-crafted serif was inspired by 16th-century punch-cutters. It has angular forms, slightly inclined characters and tapering stems.

Carmina BT

ABCDEFGHIJKLMNOPQRSTUVWXYZ
abcdefghijklmnopqrstuvwxyz
1234567890 !@#?:;"*&

Foundry: Bitstream
Designer: Gudrun Zapf von Hesse
Designer Nationality: German
Date: 1987

Also known as Calligraphic 811, Carmina forms part of a calligraphic series commissioned by Bitstream from German designer Gudrun Zapf von Hesse.

The adaptable serif font displays the designer's love of calligraphy and is suitable for use in everything from books to signage.

Carré Noir

ABCDEFGHIJKLMNOPQRSTUVWXYZ
abcdefghijklmnopqrstuvwxyz
1234567890 !@#?:;"*&

Foundry: Monotype
Designer: Albert Boton
Designer Nationality: French
Date: 1996

French font designer Albert Boton became head of the type department at the Paris-based agency Carré Noir in 1981; fifteen years later he created this

sophisticated serif typeface with the same name, which is available in four weights, from Light to Bold, plus an italic and small caps.

Cartier Book

ABCDEFGHIJKLMNOPQRSTUVWXYZ
abcdefghijklmnopqrstuvwxyz
1234567890 !@#?:;"*&

Foundry: Linotype
Designer: Carl Dair / Rod McDonald
Designer Nationality: Canadian
Date: 1967 / 1997

Carl Dair's CG Cartier was not suitable as a text font. Rod McDonald redrew the original typeface thirty years later, when it became Cartier Book.

He referenced the original drawings and removed inconsistencies, creating a functional but elegant face with three weights, an italic and small caps.

Caslon 540

ABCDEFGHIJKLMNOPQRSTUVWXYZ
abcdefghijklmnopqrstuvwxyz
1234567890 !@#?:;"*&

Foundry: American Type Founders
Designer: William Caslon / American Type Founders
Designer Nationality: British / American
Date: 1725 / 1902

This is the second version of Caslon to be released by American Type Founders. Caslon 540 has shortened descenders, which allow for tighter line

spacing. It features Old Style figures, small caps and an italic, which was distributed by Letraset with a matching set of swashes.

Caslon Classico

ABCDEFGHIJKLMNOPQRSTUVWXYZ
abcdefghijklmnopqrstuvwxyz
1234567890 !@#?:;"*&

This five-weight version of Caslon, which is one of many cuts, was based closely on the 18th-century original by William Caslon. He was known as the first great English punch-cutter, and typeface as 'the script of kings'. It was the type chosen for the United States Declaration of Independence in 1776.

Foundry: Omnibus
Designer: William Caslon / Franko Luin
Designer Nationality: British / Swedish
Date: 1725 / 1993

Caslon Old Face

ABCDEFGHIJKLMNOPQRSTUVWXYZ
abcdefghijklmnopqrstuvwxyz
1234567890 !@#?:;"*&

The Bitstream version of Caslon Old Face is based largely on the hot-metal revival of the original Caslon fonts by English type founder William Caslon, and was created in digital form by George Ostrochulski at Mergenthaler Linotype. As with other revivals, it is a faithful recreation of the original.

Foundry: Bitstream
Designer: William Caslon / George Ostrochulski
Designer Nationality: British / German
Date: 1725 / c. 1950s

Caxton

ABCDEFGHIJKLMNOPQRSTUVWXYZ
abcdefghijklmnopqrstuvwxyz
1234567890 !@#?:;"*&

Fully justified (meaning that all the lines fit to the same margin), with concave-shaped serifs and diamond-shaped dots on the letters 'i' and 'j', Caxton is named after the font created in 1478 by printer William Caxton, which has been revised a number of times over the years.

Foundry: ITC
Designer: Leslie Usherwood
Designer Nationality: American
Date: 1981

Centaur

ABCDEFGHIJKLMNOPQRSTUVWXYZ
abcdefghijklmnopqrstuvwxyz
1234567890 !@#?:;"*&

An elegant and very slender humanist Old Style serif loosely based on Nicolas Jenson's 15th-century designs, this revival by Bruce Rogers first appeared as titling capitals in 1914 for the Metropolitan Museum of Art. The completed family, including lowercase and italics, was released in 1929.

Foundry: Monotype
Designer: Bruce Rogers
Designer Nationality: American
Date: 1914 / 1929

Cochin

ABCDEFGHIJKLMNOPQRSTUVWXYZ
abcdefghijklmnopqrstuvwxyz
1234567890 !@#?:;"*&

Foundry: G. Peignot et Fils
Designer: Charles Malin
Designer Nationality: French
Date: 1914

This serif is named after the 18th-century French engraver Charles-Nicolas Cochin and is based on his copperplate engravings. The typeface was made for the Paris foundry G. Peignot et Fils (later Deberny & Peignot). It has particularly wide letterforms and was popular at the start of the 20th century.

Columbus

ABCDEFGHIJKLMNOPQRSTUVWXYZ
abcdefghijklmnopqrstuvwxyz
1234567890 !@#?:;"*&

Foundry: Monotype
Designer: David Saunders / Patricia Saunders
Designer Nationality: British
Date: 1992

Columbus was created to celebrate the 400th anniversary of Christopher Columbus crossing the Atlantic Ocean and the 1992 Summer Olympic Games in Barcelona. It is an interpretation of a typeface used by printer Jorge Coci in Spain c. 1513, which still retains traces of the Antique letterforms.

Della Robbia

ABCDEFGHIJKLMNOPQRSTUVWXYZ
abcdefghijklmnopqrstuvwxyz
1234567890 !@#?:;"*&

Foundry: American Type Founders
Designer: Thomas Maitland Cleland
Designer Nationality: American
Date: 1902

Inspired by a trip to Rome, US type designer Thomas Maitland Cleland created this serif in 1902 and named it after the Florentine sculptor Luca della Robbia. Its lowercase has long ascenders and short descenders. It was cast as Westminster Oldstyle by British foundry Stephenson, Blake & Co. in 1907.

Dutch 766

ABCDEFGHIJKLMNOPQRSTUVWXYZ
abcdefghijklmnopqrstuvwxyz
1234567890 !@#?:;"*&

Foundry: Bitstream
Designer: Gerard Meynell / John Henry Mason / F. Ernest Jackson / Edward Johnston
Designer Nationality: British
Date: 1913 / c. 1980s

This is Bitstream's digital version of Imprint Antiqua, a restrained large x-height serif that was heavily inspired by Caslon. Imprint Antiqua was created as the text face for *The Imprint*, a short-lived periodical published in London in 1913 about typography, lettering and fine printing.

Elysium

ABCDEFGHIJKLMNOPQRSTUVWXYZ
abcdefghijklmnopqrstuvwxyz
1234567890 !@#?:;"*&

Foundry: Letraset
Designer: Michael Gills
Designer Nationality: British
Date: 1992

Designed during Michael Gills's time at Letraset, Elysium has distinctive, crisp letterforms and calligraphic details that were influenced by the work of Czech type designer Oldrich Menhart. It was designed for body text, to accompany Gills's earlier headline typeface, Prague (1991).

Engravers Oldstyle 205

ABCDEFGHIJKLMNOPQRSTUVWXYZ
abcdefghijklmnopqrstuvwxyz
1234567890 !@#?:;"*&

Foundry: Bitstream
Designer: Georges Peignot / Sol Hess / Matthew Carter
Designer Nationality: French / American / British
Date: 1912 / 1921 / 1977

This generously proportioned font is a revival of Cochin, designed by Georges Peignot in 1912. Building upon Sol Hess's work on Cochin Bold (1921), it adds further weights and corresponding italics to the original roman, whose design was based on 18th-century copper engravings.

Fairfield

ABCDEFGHIJKLMNOPQRSTUVWXYZ
abcdefghijklmnopqrstuvwxyz
1234567890 !@#?:;"*&

Foundry: Linotype
Designer: Rudolph Ruzicka
Designer Nationality: Czech
Date: 1939

Linotype recruited Rudolph Ruzicka on the recommendation of William A. Dwiggins. Ruzicka's economical approach to type design prioritized the reader's experience. His original designs for Fairfield Light and Medium were later developed by Alex Kaczun into an extensive digital font family.

Figural

ABCDEFGHIJKLMNOPQRSTUVWXYZ
abcdefghijklmnopqrstuvwxyz
1234567890 !@#?:;"*&

Foundry: ITC
Designer: Oldrich Menhart / Michael Gills
Designer Nationality: Czech / British
Date: 1940 / 1992

Figural was first published by Czech foundry Grafotechna in 1940; like much of Oldrich Menhart's work, it was designed to convey a sense of the spirit of Czech culture. This revival by Michael Gills preserves the character of the original, while smoothing some of its sharper edges.

Fleischman BT

ABCDEFGHIJKLMNOPQRSTUVWXYZ
abcdefghijklmnopqrstuvwxyz
1234567890 !@#?:;"'*&

Charles Gibbons based this design on the work of German punch-cutter Johann Fleischmann, whose 8-point roman (1739) inspired several revivals. This Old Style serif was well-received upon its release, offers an extensive character set, and supports a range of Latin-based languages.

Foundry: Bitstream
Designer: Johann Fleischmann / Charles Gibbons
Designer Nationality: German / American
Date: 1739 / 2002

FS Brabo

ABCDEFGHIJKLMNOPQRSTUVWXYZ
abcdefghijklmnopqrstuvwxyz
1234567890 !@#?:;"'*&

Fernando Mello's design for FS Brabo draws inspiration from classic book serifs such as Garamond and Bembo, reinterpreting their key characteristics to create a rounded and highly readable font. Its selection of OpenType swashes and ligatures offer versatility and flair.

Foundry: Fontsmith
Designer: Fernando Mello
Designer Nationality: Brazilian
Date: 2015

Garamond Classico

ABCDEFGHIJKLMNOPQRSTUVWXYZ
abcdefghijklmnopqrstuvwxyz
1234567890 !@#?:;"'*&

This Garamond revival builds upon the work of Jean Jannon, whose designs were for many years mistaken for Claude Garamond's originals. Of his choice to create yet another interpretation of this popular font, Franko Luin remarked 'if so many others have done it, why not me too?'

Foundry: Omnibus
Designer: Franko Luin
Designer Nationality: Swedish
Date: 1993

Gloucester

ABCDEFGHIJKLMNOPQRSTUVWXYZ
abcdefghijklmnopqrstuvwxyz
1234567890 !@#?:;"'*&

Originally known as Gloucester Old Style, this typeface was developed by Monotype from a font drawn by renowned US architect Bertram G. Goodhue for the Cheltenham Press. Goodhue's design proved popular, and numerous digitizations of his design have since been released.

Foundry: Monotype
Designer: Bertram G. Goodhue / Monotype Studio
Designer Nationality: American
Date: 1896 / 1911

Goudy

ABCDEFGHIJKLMNOPQRSTUVWXYZ
abcdefghijklmnopqrstuvwxyz
1234567890 !@#?:;"*&

Foundry: Monotype
Designer: Frederic W. Goudy /
Morris Fuller Benton
Designer Nationality: American
Date: 1915 / 1916 / 1927

Monotype's digitization of this enduringly popular font, created by the prolific US type designer Frederic W. Goudy, incorporates five styles and an elegant set of fleurons. Its bold and extrabold cuts were first created by Morris Fuller Benton in 1916 and 1927 respectively.

Goudy Catalogue

ABCDEFGHIJKLMNOPQRSTUVWXYZ
abcdefghijklmnopqrstuvwxyz
1234567890 !@#?:;"*&

Foundry: American Type
Founders
Designer: Morris Fuller Benton
Designer Nationality: American
Date: 1919

Sporting a slightly heavier weight than the original Goudy Old Style, this Catalogue cut was designed in 1919 by Morris Fuller Benton, who led the design department at American Type Founders for nearly forty years. An italic counterpart to Goudy Catalogue, also by Benton, was published in 1921.

Goudy Old Style

ABCDEFGHIJKLMNOPQRSTUVWXYZ
abcdefghijklmnopqrstuvwxyz
1234567890 !@#?:;"*&

Foundry: American Type
Founders
Designer: Frederic W. Goudy
Designer Nationality: American
Date: 1915

While this Old Style serif might appear visually similar to many Renaissance-era Italian typefaces, it was an original design by Frederic W. Goudy rather than a revival. Extensively expanded since its first release, the font is accompanied by a range of alternate cuts and weights.

Griffo Classico

ABCDEFGHIJKLMNOPQRSTUVWXYZ
abcdefghijklmnopqrstuvwxyz
1234567890 !@#?:;"*&

Foundry: Omnibus
Designer: Francesco Griffo /
Franko Luin
Designer Nationality: Italian /
Swedish
Date: 1496 / 1993

Franko Luin designed several accomplished revivals over the course of his career; this example builds upon the work of Francesco Griffo, a punch-cutter for the influential printer and scholar Aldus Manutius. Its design was developed from Griffo's 1496 roman cut for Piero Bembo's book *De Aetna*.

Guardi

ABCDEFGHIJKLMNOPQRSTUVWXYZ
abcdefghijklmnopqrstuvwxyz
1234567890 !@#?:;"*&

Foundry: Linotype
Designer: Reinhard Haus
Designer Nationality: German
Date: 1986

Reinhard Haus's elegant design for Guardi was influenced by Venetian typefaces from the 15th century. It incorporates subtle calligraphic characteristics throughout, with a dynamic diagonal emphasis evident in both its letterforms and in the angle of its serifs.

Haarlemmer

ABCDEFGHIJKLMNOPQRSTUVWXYZ
abcdefghijklmnopqrstuvwxyz
1234567890 !@#?:;"*&

Foundry: Monotype
Designer: Jan van Krimpen / Frank E. Blokland
Designer Nationality: Dutch
Date: c. 1930s / 1998

Jan van Krimpen created the first drawings for Haarlemmer in the 1930s, but its production was thwarted by the outbreak of World War II. Freed from the limitations of metal typecasting, this revival presents a comprehensive realization of Van Krimpen's ambitions for the original.

Hadriano

ABCDEFGHIJKLMNOPQRSTUVWXYZ
abcdefghijklmnopqrstuvwxyz
1234567890 !@#?:;"*&

Foundry: Monotype
Designer: Frederic W. Goudy
Designer Nationality: American
Date: 1918

First released in uppercase only, Hadriano was developed from rubbings taken by Frederic W. Goudy of carved type on display in the Louvre. His later lowercase letterforms were not included in its earliest Monotype release; they would finally be incorporated within a much later digitization.

Hollander

ABCDEFGHIJKLMNOPQRSTUVWXYZ
abcdefghijklmnopqrstuvwxyz
1234567890 !@#?:;"*&

Foundry: Hell
Designer: Gerhard Unger
Designer Nationality: German
Date: 1983

Gerhard Unger designed Hollander during his time at Rudolf Hell's eponymous foundry, which pioneered digital-typesetting technology and went on to merge with Linotype in 1990. The generous curves and large x-height of its letterforms retain legibility within a wide range of contexts.

Commercial Type

Collaborating designers Paul Barnes and Christian Schwartz have worked together across the Atlantic since 2004 and formalized their arrangement as Commercial Type three years later. A joint venture, the foundry is based in New York and London and publishes retail fonts developed by Barnes and Schwartz as well as creations from their design team and third-party collaborators. Contributors from an international Who's Who in type design include Erik van Blokland, Susana Carvalho, Kai Bernau, Sandrine Nugue and Ilya Ruderman.

As well as designing their own typefaces Commercial Type takes on numerous commissions, and one of Barnes and Schwartz's first and most ambitious projects – and one of the most ambitious undertaken by any foundry in recent years – was the creation of a new typeface family for the British newspaper the *Guardian* in 2005. As part of the redesign of the newspaper, headed up by its creative director Mark Porter, the title underwent a change in size from a broadsheet to the smaller Berliner format. Porter needed a new typeface suite to get the most out of the new format. The result was the award-winning Guardian Egyptian, a contemporary slab serif with accompanying sans serif consisting of more than 130 styles. As a result of their work, the redesign team was awarded the coveted Black Pencil by D&AD and in 2006, *Wallpaper** magazine named Barnes and Schwartz two of the forty most influential designers under the age of forty. Other notable commissions include typefaces for the Empire State Building and *The Wall Street Journal*.

Founded: 2007
Countries: Britain / America
Website: commercialtype.com
Notable typefaces:
Portrait (see p. 143)
Druk (see p. 463)

Below. Britain's largest heritage organization, the National Trust, with over 3 million members, asked Commercial Type to produce their new corporate typeface. The new design was to replace its existing mixed usage of Helvetica, Bembo and Albertus. Paul Barnes' final design takes its cues from 19th-century British vernacular types yet incorporates the necessities that a contemporary corporate typeface is required to possess.

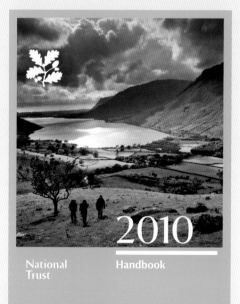

National Trust

2010

Handbook

Antony

Torpoint, Cornwall PL11 2QA

Map ① E8

'**Because Antony is still a family experience of visiting is unique. coming back again and again**.'
Helen Munzer, York

Faced in silver-grey Pentewan stone by colonnaded wings of mellow bric classically beautiful house is a beguil of the formal and informal. Still the I Carew Pole family, it contains fine cc of paintings, furniture and textiles. T bordering the Lynher estuary, lands

GG
Guardian
Egyptian Text
Regular

GG
Guardian
Egyptian Text
Medium

GG
Guardian
Egyptian Text
Bold

GG
Guardian
Egyptian Text
Black

GG
Guardian
Egyptian Headline
Hairline

GG
Guardian
Egyptian Headline
Thin

GG
Guardian
Egyptian Headline
Light

GG
Guardian
Egyptian Headline
Regular

GG
Guardian
Egyptian Headline
Medium

GG
Guardian
Egyptian Headline
Semibold

GG
Guardian
Egyptian Headline
Bold

GG
Guardian
Egyptian Headline
Black

GG
Guardian
Agate
Regular

GG
Guardian
Agate
Medium

GG
Guardian
Agate
Bold

GG
Guardian
Agate
Black

GG
Guardian
Sans Text
Regular

GG
Guardian
Sans Text
Medium

GG
Guardian
Sans Text
Bold

GG
Guardian
Sans Text
Black

GG
Guardian
Sans Headline
Hairline

GG
Guardian
Sans Headline
Thin

GG
Guardian
Sans Headline
Light

GG
Guardian
Sans Headline
Regular

GG
Guardian
Sans Headline
Medium

GG
Guardian
Sans Headline
Semibold

GG
Guardian
Sans Headline
Bold

GG
Guardian
Sans Headline
Black

GG
Guardian
Sans Headline
Ultra

GG
Guardian
Sans Headline
Narrow
Hairline

GG
Guardian
Sans Headline
Narrow
Thin

GG
Guardian
Sans Headline
Narrow
Light

GG
Guardian
Sans Headline
Narrow
Regular

GG
Guardian
Sans Headline
Narrow
Medium

GG
Guardian
Sans Headline
Narrow
Semibold

GG
Guardian
Sans Headline
Narrow
Bold

GG
Guardian
Sans Headline
Narrow
Black

GG
Guardian
Sans Headline
Narrow
Ultra

GG
Guardian
Sans Headline
Condensed
Hairline

GG
Guardian
Sans Headline
Condensed
Thin

GG
Guardian
Sans Headline
Condensed
Light

GG
Guardian
Sans Headline
Condensed
Regular

GG
Guardian
Sans Headline
Condensed
Medium

GG
Guardian
Sans Headline
Condensed
Semibold

GG
Guardian
Sans Headline
Condensed
Bold

GG
Guardian
Sans Headline
Condensed
Black

GG
Guardian
Sans Headline
Condensed
Ultra

GG
Guardian
Sans Headline
XCondensed
Hairline

GG
Guardian
Sans Headline
XCondensed
Thin

GG
Guardian
Sans Headline
XCondensed
Light

GG
Guardian
Sans Headline
XCondensed
Regular

GG
Guardian
Sans Headline
XCondensed
Medium

GG
Guardian
Sans Headline
XCondensed
Semibold

GG
Guardian
Sans Headline
XCondensed
Bold

GG
Guardian
Sans Headline
XCondensed
Black

GG
Guardian
Sans Headline
XCondensed
Ultra

Above. The multi-award-winning typeface for the UK's *Guardian* newspaper was commissioned by Mark Porter for the *Guardian* and designed by Paul Barnes and Christian Schwartz with Berton Hasebe and Vincent Chan. The complete family took from 2009 through to 2012 to design and comprises a slab-serif Egyptian (Guardian Egyptian), with accompanying italics used for headlines, and an accompanying version for text usage as well. There is also a sans serif variant for headline text and an agate version.

The full family is employed across all print and online media and apps, from titling and texts through to infographics and tables.

Horley Old Style

ABCDEFGHIJKLMNOPQRSTUVWXYZ
abcdefghijklmnopqrstuvwxyz
1234567890 !@#?:;''"*&

Foundry: Monotype
Designer: Frank Hinman Pierpont
Designer Nationality: American
Date: 1925

This cheerful, well-crafted serif was developed by Monotype in response to the popularity of similar typefaces designed by Frederic W. Goudy – in particular, Kennerley and Goudy Old Style. A version suitable for phototypesetting systems was designed by Robert Norton in 1977.

Imprint

ABCDEFGHIJKLMNOPQRSTUVWXYZ
abcdefghijklmnopqrstuvwxyz
1234567890 !@#?:;"*&

Foundry: Monotype
Designer: Frank Hinman Pierpont / Fritz Stelzer
Designer Nationality: American
Date: 1912

This Caslon-influenced design was commissioned by publisher Gerard Meynell for his short-lived print trade journal *The Imprint*, which counted type designers Edward Johnston and Stanley Morison among its contributors. It has since proved a popular choice for book typesetting.

Iowan Old Style BT

ABCDEFGHIJKLMNOPQRSTUVWXYZ
abcdefghijklmnopqrstuvwxyz
1234567890 !@#?:;"*&

Foundry: Bitstream
Designer: John Downer
Designer Nationality: American
Date: 1991

Designer and sign-painter John Downer first created this hard-working font for ITC, but after plans to publish it were shelved, Bitstream stepped in. Its tall x-height, comprehensive character set and compact form make Iowan Old Style BT a versatile choice for book designers.

ITC Berkeley Old Style

ABCDEFGHIJKLMNOPQRSTUVWXYZ
abcdefghijklmnopqrstuvwxyz
1234567890 !@#?:;"*&

Foundry: ITC
Designer: Frederic W. Goudy / Tony Stan
Designer Nationality: American
Date: 1938 / 1983

This legible design is based on Frederic W. Goudy's University of California Old Style typeface (1938), which was created for exclusive use by the University of California Press. Tony Stan's revival of the font for ITC made it available to designers worldwide for the first time.

ITC Caslon No 224

ABCDEFGHIJKLMNOPQRSTUVWXYZ
abcdefghijklmnopqrstuvwxyz
1234567890 !@#?:;"*&

Foundry: ITC
Designer: Ed Benguiat
Designer Nationality: American
Date: 1982

Another design by Ed Benguiat (see p. 514), this revival of William Caslon's eponymous 18th-century font was developed with the methodologies and demands of contemporary graphic design in mind. Designed for body text, it was preceded by a version optimized for display use, ITC Caslon 223.

ITC Galliard

ABCDEFGHIJKLMNOPQRSTUVWXYZ
abcdefghijklmnopqrstuvwxyz
1234567890 !@#?:;"*&

Foundry: Linotype / ITC
Designer: Matthew Carter
Designer Nationality: British
Date: 1978 /1982

This interpretation of Robert Granjon's 16th-century design by Matthew Carter (see p. 616) was not intended as a direct revival; instead he wanted to capture the spirit of Granjon's designs in a contemporary typeface. ITC's reissue of the Linotype original is in the Museum of Modern Art collection.

ITC Galliard eText

ABCDEFGHIJKLMNOPQRSTUVWXYZ
abcdefghijklmnopqrstuvwxyz
1234567890 !@#?:;"*&

Foundry: ITC
Designer: Matthew Carter / Carl Crossgrove
Designer Nationality: British / American
Date: 2013

Type designer Carl Crossgrove developed this version of Galliard in 2013 for screen-based use. It is part of Monotype's eText offering, optimized to appear legible and true to its original forms on a range of screens, and at many different pixel resolutions.

ITC Garamond

ABCDEFGHIJKLMNOPQRSTUVWXYZ
abcdefghijklmnopqrstuvwxyz
1234567890 !@#?:;"*&

Foundry: ITC
Designer: Tony Stan
Designer Nationality: American
Date: 1975

This revival of Jean Jannon's 16th-century Garalde was originally developed by Tony Stan for ITC as a display typeface in two weights; its popularity and regular misuse as a text face prompted the development of a more extensive family, which now includes sixteen different styles.

ITC Giovanni

ABCDEFGHIJKLMNOPQRSTUVWXYZ
abcdefghijklmnopqrstuvwxyz
1234567890 !@#?:;"*&

Designed by Robert Slimbach shortly before he joined Adobe in 1987, ITC Giovanni is a contemporary reinterpretation of classic Old Style serifs such as Garamond and Bembo. The result is a clean and legible typeface, with a generous x-height and an open visual texture.

Foundry: ITC
Designer: Robert Slimbach
Designer Nationality: American
Date: 1986

ITC Golden Cockerel

ABCDEFGHIJKLMNOPQRSTUVWXYZ
abcdefghijklmnopqrstuvwxyz
1234567890 !@#?:;"*&

This ITC typeface is a revival of a design by British type designer and sculptor Eric Gill in 1929 for the Golden Cockerel Press, a publisher renowned for finely crafted editions of classic works featuring wood-engraved illustrations. Gill's original design displays the influence of his work as a stone-carver.

Foundry: ITC
Designer: Eric Gill / Richard Dawson / David Farey
Designer Nationality: British
Date: 1929 / 1996

ITC Legacy Serif

ABCDEFGHIJKLMNOPQRSTUVWXYZ
abcdefghijklmnopqrstuvwxyz
1234567890 !@#?:;"*&

Nicolas Jenson's type was designed for a 1470 edition of Eusebius's *De praeparatione evangelica* (*Preparation for the Gospel*), and Ronald Arnholm began this revival for his master's thesis at Yale; he refined its design over several decades, improving its fidelity to Jenson's original.

Foundry: ITC
Designer: Ronald Arnholm
Designer Nationality: American
Date: 1993

ITC Legacy Square Serif

ABCDEFGHIJKLMNOPQRSTUVWXYZ
abcdefghijklmnopqrstuvwxyz
1234567890 !@#?:;"*&

Ron Arnholm built on the success of his Legacy typeface following its release, designing numerous variant styles to develop an extensive superfamily. This square cut, traced from specimens of the serif and sans letterforms, was a Type Directors Club Typeface Design Winner in 2010.

Foundry: ITC
Designer: Ronald Arnholm
Designer Nationality: American
Date: 2009

ITC Mendoza Roman

ABCDEFGHIJKLMNOPQRSTUVWXYZ
abcdefghijklmnopqrstuvwxyz
1234567890 !@#?:;"*&

Foundry: ITC
Designer: José Mendoza y Almeida
Designer Nationality: French
Date: 1991

This Old Style serif, created by renowned French illustrator and type designer José Mendoza y Almeida, features low-contrast letterforms with subtly cupped serifs. The regularity of its forms makes it a useful choice for body text at small point sizes, and in suboptimal printing conditions.

ITC New Esprit

ABCDEFGHIJKLMNOPQRSTUVWXYZ
abcdefghijklmnopqrstuvwxyz
1234567890 !@#?:;"*&

Foundry: ITC
Designer: Jovica Veljović
Designer Nationality: Serbian
Date: 2010

Jovica Veljović won the coveted ATypI Prix Charles Peignot award in 1985, the same year he designed the first letterforms of this typeface for ITC. Revisiting his work several years later, he expanded the original design to encompass separate cuts for display and body text use.

ITC New Winchester

ABCDEFGHIJKLMNOPQRSTUVWXYZ
abcdefghijklmnopqrstuvwxyz
1234567890 !@#?:;"*&

Foundry: ITC
Designer: Jim Speice
Designer Nationality: American
Date: 1999

William A. Dwiggins' design for Winchester, through which he tested several ideas that he hoped would improve the legibility of serif faces, was never properly published. Jim Speice's revival of the font, more than five decades later, finally made its distinctive forms available digitally.

ITC Souvenir

ABCDEFGHIJKLMNOPQRSTUVWXYZ
abcdefghijklmnopqrstuvwxyz
1234567890 !@#?:;"*&

Foundry: ITC
Designer: Morris Fuller Benton / Ed Benguiat
Designer Nationality: American
Date: 1914 / 1972

This revival of Morris Fuller Benton's 1914 design went on to wildly outstrip its predecessor in popularity. One of ITC's first releases, the typeface is indelibly associated with 1970s graphic design, though its ubiquity prompted something of a backlash in subsequent decades.

ITC Souvenir Monospaced

ABCDEFGHIJKLMNOPQRSTUVWXYZ
abcdefghijk1mnopqrstuvwxyz
1234567890 !@#?:;"*&

Foundry: ITC
Designer: Ed Benguiat /
Ned Bunnel
Designer Nationality: American
Date: 1972 / 1983

This monospaced cut of Souvenir was designed by Ned Bunnel, who was also responsible for the monospaced cut of ITC AvantGarde. First developed to accommodate the limitations of typewriters and early digital displays, such styles now offer a distinctive character of their own.

ITC Usherwood

ABCDEFGHIJKLMNOPQRSTUVWXYZ
abcdefghijklmnopqrstuvwxyz
1234567890 !@#?:;"*&

Foundry: ITC
Designer: Leslie Usherwood
Designer Nationality: Canadian
Date: 1983

Designed for ITC by Leslie Usherwood and the team at his Canadian foundry Typsettra, this approachable serif features asymmetrical styles throughout, and is well-suited for the setting of body text. ITC Usherwood is available in four weights, with corresponding italics.

ITC Veljovic

ABCDEFGHIJKLMNOPQRSTUVWXYZ
abcdefghijklmnopqrstuvwxyz
1234567890 !@#?:;"*&

Foundry: ITC
Designer: Jovica Veljović
Designer Nationality: Serbian
Date: 1984

Before ITC commissioned Jovica Veljović to design this, his eponymous first typeface, his calligraphic work appeared on the pages of the foundry's type journal, *U&lc*. His design for ITC Veljovic was influenced by the work of Hermann Zapf (see p. 574) and Henri Friedlaender.

ITC Weidemann

ABCDEFGHIJKLMNOPQRSTUVWXYZ
abcdefghijklmnopqrstuvwxyz
1234567890 !@#?:;"*&

Foundry: ITC
Designer: Kurt Weidemann
Designer Nationality: German
Date: 1983

Originally called Biblica, this typeface was commissioned for a new German edition of the Bible; its condensed letterforms reflect the need to set large volumes of text economically and legibly. Kurt Weidemann took inspiration from early Venetian faces for the design of the font.

Jenson Classico

ABCDEFGHIJKLMNOPQRSTUVWXYZ
abcdefghijklmnopqrstuvwxyz
1234567890 ! @#?:;"*&

In 1458, the French King Charles VII sent Nicolas Jenson to Mainz to learn about movable type. The type Jenson later used as a printer working in Venice from 1470 to 1480 has been called the original roman; it survived in books, providing a source for this digitization by Franko Luin.

Foundry: Linotype
Designer: Nicolas Jenson / Franko Luin
Designer Nationality: French / Swedish
Date: 1470 / 1993

King's Caslon

ABCDEFGHIJKLMNOPQRSTUVWXYZ
abcdefghijklmnopqrstuvwxyz
1234567890 !@#?:;"*&

King's Caslon is a reinterpretation of William Caslon's 16th-century letterforms, designed with two optical sizes. The Text style is more transitional in character, with symmetrical serifs and moderate contrast, while the Display version combines strong contrast with softer details.

Foundry: Dalton Maag
Designer: Marc Weymann / Ron Carpenter
Designer Nationality: British
Date: 2007

Kuenstler 480

ABCDEFGHIJKLMNOPQRSTUVWXYZ
abcdefghijklmnopqrstuvwxyz
1234567890 !@#?:;"*&

Kuenstler 480 is a Bitstream version of Trump Mediaeval (1954). It has features of both an Old Style serif and a Venetian, as well as a sloping roman italic and angular serifs. In 2010, ParaType released a Cyrillic version of Kuenstler 480 by Vladimir Yefimov and Isabella Chaeva.

Foundry: Bitstream
Designer: Georg Trump
Designer Nationality: American
Date: 1954

Latin 725

ABCDEFGHIJKLMNOPQRSTUVWXYZ
abcdefghijklmnopqrstuvwxyz
1234567890 !@#?:;"*&

Latin 725 is Bitstream's version of the sharp-serifed Latin typeface Méridien by Adrian Frutiger (see p. 290), which was released by Deberny & Peignot in 1957. It was later re-envisioned as Frutiger Serif by Frutiger and Akira Kobayashi for Linotype. Latin 725 is ideal for setting large amounts of text.

Foundry: Bitstream
Designer: Adrian Frutiger
Designer Nationality: Swiss
Date: 1955

Lava

ABCDEFGHIJKLMNOPQRSTUVWXYZ
abcdefghijklmnopqrstuvwxyz
1234567890 !@#?:;"*&

Foundry: Typotheque
Designer: Peter Biľak
Designer Nationality: Slovakian
Date: 2013

Peter Biľak created Lava for his magazine *Works That Work* (2013–18). The first issue was designed by Carvalho Bernau and used Lava alone. A highly legible face designed for both digital and print, Lava is available in four weights and has a Cyrillic alphabet designed by Ilya Ruderman.

Linotype Syntax Serif

ABCDEFGHIJKLMNOPQRSTUVWXYZ
abcdefghijklmnopqrstuvwxyz
1234567890 !@#?:;"*&

Foundry: Linotype
Designer: Hans Eduard Meier
Designer Nationality: Swiss
Date: 2000

Syntax Serif was released as part of the Syntax Next family forty-five years after Swiss designer Hans Eduard Meier originally began drawing Syntax, its sans serif partner. A highly legible face, described by Linotype as a 'workhorse', Syntax Serif has a double-storey 'g' and is ideal for long text.

Mantika Book

ABCDEFGHIJKLMNOPQRSTUVWXYZ
abcdefghijklmnopqrstuvwxyz
1234567890 !@#?:;"*&

Foundry: Linotype
Designer: Jürgen Weltin
Designer Nationality: German
Date: 2014

Mantika Book is the Antiqua serif of the Mantika superfamily, which also has a sans and an informal sans, by German designer Jürgen Weltin of Type Matters. Mantika Book comes in two weights – regular and bold – each of which has an italic that is relatively upright.

Matt Antique

ABCDEFGHIJKLMNOPQRSTUVWXYZ
abcdefghijklmnopqrstuvwxyz
1234567890 !@#?:;"*&

Foundry: Bitstream
Designer: John Matt
Designer Nationality: American
Date: 1979

Although drawn in the 1960s by US designer and Pratt Institute graduate John Matt, this elegant calligraphic serif was not released by Compugraphic until 1979. It was first known as Garth Graphic, after the company's founder William W. Garth Jr, and Bitsteam's version comes in roman, italic and bold.

Right. An example specimen page for Monotype Garamond, published by the Monotype Corporation, *c.* 1960s.

"MONOTYPE" SERIES No. 156
GARAMOND
Unit Arrangement 37 (6 point to 12D)

156—6 (6D) 6 Set   Line ·1186
THE invention of Printing from movable types was one of the chief events affecting the history of European civilization. The task of duplicating texts without variance was impossible before Gutenberg equipped the scholar with the accuracy of type. Prejudiced connoisseurs in the fifteenth century deplored the new mass-production *The invention of Printing from movable types was one of the chief events* THE INVENTION OF PRINTING FROM MOVABLE TYPES

156—8 (8D) 8 Set   Line ·125
DIE Erfindung des Buchdrucks mit beweglichen Lettern war eines der wichtigsten Ereignisse in der Geschichte der Zivilisation, denn die originalgetreue *Die Erfindung des Buchdrucks mit beweglichen Lettern war* DIE ERFINDUNG DES BUCHDRUCKS MIT

156—9 (8D) 8¼ Set   Line ·1268
L'INVENTION de l'Imprimerie au moyen de caractères mobiles fut l'un des principaux événements de l'histoire de la civilisation européenne, car *L'invention de l'Imprimerie au moyen de caractères* L'INVENTION DE L'IMPRIMERIE AU M

156—10 (9D) 9½ Set   Line ·1276
THE invention of Printing from movable types was one of the chief events affecting *The invention of Printing from movable types was* THE INVENTION OF PRINTING FRO

156—11 (10D) 10¼ Set   Line ·13
DIE Erfindung des Buchdrucks mit beweglichen Lettern war eines der wich- *Die Erfindung des Buchdrucks mit beweglichen* DIE ERFINDUNG DES BUCHDRU

156—12 (12D) 11¼ Set   Line ·1338
L'INVENTION de l'Imprimerie au moyen de caractères mobiles fut l'un *L'invention de l'Imprimerie au moyen de* L'INVENTION DE L'IMPRIME

156—12D 12¼ Set (cast on 13 point E.) Line ·1368
THE invention of Printing from movable types was one of the *The invention of Printing from movable* THE INVENTION OF PRINT

156—14 (14D) 12¼ Set ·2″ × ·2″   Line ·1486
Unit Arrangement 99
The invention of Printing from movable types was one of the *The invention of Printing from mova* THE INVENTION OF PRIN

156—14 12¾ Set   Unit Arrangement 114   Line ·1395
His family has farmed the land for two hundred years, and although the estate, since the bad time, HAS PASSED FROM HIS POSSESSION HE

156—14   Display Matrices   Line ·1395
Fashions change, and each succeeding generation has its own tastes. That is to say, of the most infinite OF NATURE'S ASPECTS SOME MAY GIVE

156—16   14 Set   Unit Arrangement 114   Line ·1599
There are few more striking indications of the changes in manners and customs that time has BROUGHT ABOUT THAN THESE OLD

156—18   16 Set   Unit Arrangement 114   Line ·181
By that time the great green slope that rises away from the farmhouse garden IS TOUCHED WITH AN AUTUMN

156—18   Display Matrices   Line ·181
His family has farmed the land for two HUNDRED YEARS AND SINCE A

156—24   21½ Set   Unit Arrangement 114   Line ·2364
There are so many changes in ALL OUR MANNERS OR

156—24   Display Matrices   Line ·2364
Having arrived, we can now EXPLAIN IN A MANNER

156—30   Display Matrices   Line ·2918
This family has farmed the LANDS FOR OVER A

ABCDEFGHIJKLMNOPQRSTUVWXYZÆŒ&   *ABCDEFGHIJKLMNOPQRSTUVWXYZÆŒ&*
abcdefghijklmnopqrstuvwxyzæœ   ABCDEFGHIJKLMNOPQRSTUVWXYZÆŒ   *abcdefghijklmnopqrstuvwxyzæœ*
ÀÁÂÄÈÉÊËÌÍÏÒÓÔÖÙÚÛÜÑÇ   Q U   Qu *Qu*   *AÁÂÄÈÉÊËÌÍÏÒÓÔÖÙÚÛÜÑÇ*
àáâäèéêëìíïòóôöùúûüñç   ÀÁÂÄÈÉÊËÌÍÏÒÓÔÖÙÚÛÜÑÇ   *àáâäèéêëìíïòóôöùúûüñç*
1234567890   .,:;-!?"-.().·[]*†‡§¶...£–$ fiflffffiffl   ij ß *ij ß*   *,.:;'!?*   *fiflffffiffl*   *1234567890*
Alternative Figures: F214 1234567890 and F341 *1234567890*   Alternative *h* (75H) *s* (669S)   Qu Qu qu QU *QU*
A B C D E F G H J K M P T V Ex Na Ne Ni No Nu Qu Qu Ra Re Ri Ro Ru
as ct e et fr q gg gj gy is k ky ll m nt sa sb se sh si sk so sa st su ssa sse sti st ssu sp st ta tt us v zy

LONDON: THE MONOTYPE CORPORATION LTD   PARIS: SOCIÉTÉ ANONYME MONOTYPE   BERLIN: SETZMASCHINEN-FABRIK MONOTYPE G.M.B.H.
(Printed in Great Britain)   (Imprimé en Grande-Bretagne)   (Gedruckt in Großbritannien)

Monotype Goudy

ABCDEFGHIJKLMNOPQRSTUVWXYZ
abcdefghijklmnopqrstuvwxyz
1234567890 !@#?:;''"*&

Foundry: Monotype
Designer: Frederic W. Goudy
Designer Nationality: American
Date: 1915

The acclaimed Goudy typeface was made by the master of US type design, Frederic W. Goudy, who designed more than one hundred typefaces over fifty years. The typeface is valued for its legibility and readability in print, its flexibility and its range of weights, which means it is equally at home on a billboard as on the printed page.

When the American Type Foundry released the typeface in roman form only as Goudy Old Style in 1915, it was an immediate success. Its use became widespread because of its legibility as a text face compared to its contemporaries, thanks to its rounder curves and a softer design. Such features were partly due to the Renaissance types from which it drew its inspiration. However, it was also because of Goudy's clever hand in adding many personal and distinct touches to the character designs. He created an italic and a revision, Goudy Modern, in 1918, and a Heavyface in 1925. Other variants have also been drawn up by other designers, including Morris Fuller Benton who created Goudy Bold (1916–19), Goudy Extra Bold (1927) and the shaded version, Goudy Handtooled (1922). Today, the Goudy family is wide and extensive with a number of foundries offering versions.

Early in the 21st Century, THE TYRELL CORPORATION advanced Robot evolution into the NEXUS phase — a being virtually identical to a human — known as a *Replicant.* The NEXUS 6 *Replicants* were superior in strength and agility, and at least equal in intelligence, to the genetic engineers

Left. Goudy employed in the opening titles for director Ridley Scott's 1982 science-fiction classic *Bladerunner*.

Monotype Century Old Style

ABCDEFGHIJKLMNOPQRSTUVWXYZ
abcdefghijklmnopqrstuvwxyz
1234567890 !@#?:;"*&

Foundry: Monotype
Designer: Morris Fuller Benton
Designer Nationality: American
Date: 1906

Century Old Style is an evolution of Century Expanded (1900), which Morris Fuller Benton cut as an extension of his father Linn Boyd Benton's Century (1894). He kept similar weights and proportions to Expanded but replaced the modern characteristics with more restrained Old Style features.

Monotype Goudy Catalogue

ABCDEFGHIJKLMNOPQRSTUVWXYZ
abcdefghijklmnopqrstuvwxyz
1234567890 !@#?:;"*&

Foundry: Monotype
Designer: Frederic W. Goudy / Morris Fuller Benton
Designer Nationality: American
Date: 1915 / 1919

Goudy Catalogue is Morris Fuller Benton's adaption of Goudy Old Style (1915); it comes in one weight with an italic and is heavier than the original Goudy. As the name implies, it is a good choice for book text. The typeface has short descenders and once had a display version called Goudy Handtooled.

Monotype Goudy Modern

ABCDEFGHIJKLMNOPQRSTUVWXYZ
abcdefghijklmnopqrstuvwxyz
1234567890 !@#?:;"*&

Foundry: Monotype
Designer: Frederic W. Goudy
Designer Nationality: American
Date: 1918

The result of prolific designer Frederic W. Goudy filling in the white spaces he had left in Goudy Open (1918), an earlier decorative face, Goudy Modern has sturdy, flat serifs. Monotype has held a version since 1928 which is available digitally in regular and bold with italics.

Monotype Italian Old Style

ABCDEFGHIJKLMNOPQRSTUVWXYZ
abcdefghijklmnopqrstuvwxyz
1234567890 !@#?:;"*&

Foundry: Monotype
Designer: Frederic W. Goudy
Designer Nationality: American
Date: 1924

Frederic W. Goudy designed this for Lanston Monotype, which wanted a competitor to Morris Fuller Benton's Cloister Old Style (1913). Italian Old Style was inspired by the forms of 15th-century Italian typefaces. It is available in regular and bold with italics, and is ideal as a book face.

Monotype Old Style

ABCDEFGHIJKLMNOPQRSTUVWXYZ
abcdefghijklmnopqrstuvwxyz
1234567890 !@#?:;"*&

Foundry: Monotype
Designer: Alexander Phemister
Designer Nationality: Scottish
Date: 1860 / 1901

Monotype Old Style is a Lanston Monotype recut of a typeface first produced by the Scottish foundry Miller & Richard in 1860 as an update of Caslon Old Style. It is a mixture of Old Style and modern serifs, with vertical stress and sharp, straight serifs, and is ideal for text use.

Nevia BT

ABCDEFGHIJKLMNOPQRSTUVWXYZ
abcdefghijklmnopqrstuvwxyz
1234567890 !@#?:;"*&

Foundry: Bitstream
Designer: Hal Taylor
Designer Nationality: American
Date: 2002

Nevia is a characterful serif with many nuances and distinctive letters. The terminal of the 'a' joins with the lower loop, the 'M' has two different top serifs, and the crossbars of the 'B', 'P' and 'R' do not meet their stems. The typeface is available in regular and bold with italics.

Orion

ABCDEFGHIJKLMNOPQRSTUVWXYZ
abcdefghijklmnopqrstuvwxyz
1234567890 !@#?:;"*&

Foundry: Monotype
Designer: Hermann Zapf
Designer Nationality: German
Date: 1974

Legendary typographer Hermann Zapf (see p. 574) started Orion in 1963. It was finally released in 1974 for the Linofilm photocomposing machine and was intended to be a neutral, legible text face for newspapers and books. Orion is available in roman and italic, which has a distinctive 'et' ampersand.

Palatino

ABCDEFGHIJKLMNOPQRSTUVWXYZ
abcdefghijklmnopqrstuvwxyz
1234567890 !@#?:;"*&

Foundry: Stempel
Designer: Hermann Zapf
Designer Nationality: German
Date: 1950

Palatino is an Old Style serif by Hermann Zapf (see p. 574). It is named after the 16th-century Italian calligrapher Giovanni Battista Palatino, and inspired by the Renaissance typefaces of other Italian typographers such as Aldus Manutius. The German foundry Stempel released Palatino in 1950.

Palatino Linotype

ABCDEFGHIJKLMNOPQRSTUVWXYZ
abcdefghijklmnopqrstuvwxyz
1234567890 !@#?:;"'*&

Foundry: Linotype
Designer: Hermann Zapf
Designer Nationality: German
Date: 1950 / 1999

Palatino was an instant hit when it was released, garnering much acclaim for Hermann Zapf (see p. 290). This led to many new versions – and copies – such as Linotype's, which became even more prominent when it was included in Windows 2000 and bundled with all Microsoft software.

Palatino Nova

ABCDEFGHIJKLMNOPQRSTUVWXYZ
abcdefghijklmnopqrstuvwxyz
1234567890 !@#?:;"'*&

Foundry: Linotype
Designer: Hermann Zapf / Akira Kobayashi
Designer Nationality: German / Japanese
Date: 2005

Many foundries released sanctioned digitizations of Palatino, including Bitstream and URW, while Monotype put out the almost identical Book Antiqua. In 2005, Hermann Zapf (see p. 574) worked with Akira Kobayashi on a redesign called Palatino Nova to provide a definitive digitized version.

Pastonchi

ABCDEFGHIJKLMNOPQRSTUVWXYZ
abcdefghijklmnopqrstuvwxyz
1234567890 !@#?:;"'*&

Foundry: Monotype
Designer: Francesco Pastonchi / Eduardo Cotti / Robin Nicholas
Designer Nationality: Italian / Italian / British
Date: 1927 / 1998

When poet Francesco Pastonchi was commissioned to produce a new edition of classic Italian books he failed to find a type he felt suitable, so he set about designing his own, with help from Eduardo Cotti at the Royal School of Typography in Turin. Pastonchi was digitized by Robin Nicholas in 1998.

Pescadero

ABCDEFGHIJKLMNOPQRSTUVWXYZ
abcdefghijklmnopqrstuvwxyz
1234567890 !@#?:;"'*&

Foundry: Ascender
Designer: Steve Matteson
Designer Nationality: American
Date: 2006

Taking its name from the historic farming and ranching valley on California's coastline, Pescadero is an Old Style serif that references the calligraphic style of inscriptional letterforms. The characters strike a balance between swelling curves and stringent strokes.

Plantin

ABCDEFGHIJKLMNOPQRSTUVWXYZ
abcdefghijklmnopqrstuvwxyz
1234567890 !@#?:;"*&

Foundry: Monotype
Designer Frank Hinman
Pierpont / Fritz Stelzer
Designer Nationality: American /
German
Date: 1913

Though it possesses his name, the hugely influential 16th-century French printer and publisher Christophe Plantin did not design the Plantin typeface. Rather, it is an homage to the types he collected and employed as founder of the Plantin Press in Antwerp, Belgium.

Plantin was first cut in 1913 by German draughtsman Fritz Stelzer under the guidance of Frank Hinman Pierpont, a US engineer and works manager at Monotype in Surrey, England. Pierpoint instigated the creation of Plantin after a visit to the Plantin-Moretus Museum in Antwerp. He took away copies of a vast wealth of material, including unused types by 16th-century French type designer and printer Robert Granjon. Many believe that these, together with samples of Granjon's work printed by the Plantin Press, were the foundations of Plantin.

In the 21st century, Plantin has seen a resurgence in its use, especially in editorial and publishing arenas; it is highly legible and has a distinctive design, while its thicker characters allow it to hold more ink on press, aiding the printing process. Plantin has also influenced a number of designs, including another Monotype creation, Times New Roman. The Plantin family includes Light, Regular, Semi Bold and Bold weights with a suite of small caps, ligatures and Old Style figures for the text weights.

Below and opposite. The joint overall winner in the 2014 International Society of Typographic Designers International Typographic Awards was *Eros und Thanatos*. Written by Mark Gisbourne and published by Lubok Verlag in Germany, this stunning book is wholly set in Plantin, and was art directed and designed by Maria Magdalena Meyer with Maria Ondrej of studio MMKoehn in Leipzig. Its classic, understated style belies a highly crafted and elegant design solution with Plantin at the core of its success. Plantin's flexibility and suitability as a titling and text face is used to maximum effect from cover to cover.

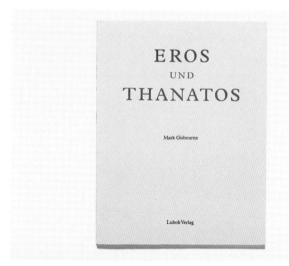

ns in Geis Bild mit Justine Ottos *Lonestar I,* könn
r ein Mädchen ähnlichen Alters dar, zeigt aber zu
. kultureller Differenzen.[87] Weniger skizzenhaft un
n von unten, wie sie stolz ihre perspektivisch ver
hten falschen Fingernägeln präsentiert. Während
hsene imaginiert, konzentriert sie sich ganz dar
nte sagen, dass zwischen Sargents kleinem Mädch
Jahrhundert der Kinderpsychologie steht. Ihr Se
ken Eindruck proto-adoleszenter sexueller Selb
ch ist das Mädchen noch ein Mädchen, nicht älte

:MPORARY PAINTING

hardly surprising given that Thomas Rusche, who
ch Baroque paintings, is deeply concerned with ide
ion that link both his Baroque and contemporary
aroque Age and the contemporary practice of painti
ne.[4] The idea of a monad-like parallelism, or "linea
modernist ideas of linear cause and effect (argu
used recently as a powerful analogous argument
extension the plurality of different approaches from
lso a fundamental corollary that profoundly links
amely Eros (desire, the 'life drive') and Thanatos
which we must all succumb in our different ways
d through 'deistic' principles, and in the Moder
l' or libidinal structures of explanation.[6] However,
ning emotive power or experiences that these impul
que and contemporary parallels are no less signific
understanding of the motives and meaning behind
orks.

ual aesthetic medium, has always been deeply conn
the isolation of the studio, long hours of solitude a
form of personal expression, and the dissatisfactio
s of a painter's life. Similarly, to a passionate collec
esire to possess the un-possessable, to grasp the tan
ors no less a sense of personal and unresolved fru
uously seeking out, a yearning for the complete im
the creative aesthetics of 'Eros' and 'Thanatos', is
ut inescapable. But desire and the death of desire a
merely different aspects of human identity forged i
e civilising processes of life, as binary necessities to
reciprocity is the shadow that exists because the
n simultaneously at a sense of discovery, and at an i
que personal and ever deepening relationship to pa
through his extensive acquisitions over recent years
ut a very small part of Thomas Rusche's contempor
reflect upon the aforementioned affinities. A featu
hirty years is the return to genre categories that in
ries of landscape and still life, and many sub-gen
first born of seventeenth century painting, and cur
nting practitioners.[8] It not only reflects a Nietzsche
ng as a practice has the continuous ability to recre
painting, it has returned and facilitates the contin
nporary world.[10] With the abandonment of so-call
rminism, the end game often argued by minimalis
s to the historical past, and the great traditions of pa

BAROCKE UND ZEITGENÖSSISCHE MALEREI

VOR dem bisher Gesagten erstaunt es nicht, dass Thomas Rusche, der auch über eine umfangreiche Sammlung niederländischer Barockmalerei verfügt, sich intensiv mit den Konzepten und unterschiedlichen Verfahren der Überlieferung beschäftigt, die seine barocken und zeitgenössischen Kunstwerke miteinander verbinden.[3] Bemerkenswerterweise war das Verhältnis zwischen den barocken und zeitgenössischen Praktiken nie relevanter als zum gegenwärtigen Zeitpunkt.[4] Die Vorstellung von parallelen Monaden oder von „variablen Inflexionslinien" (Deleuze) wurde – im Gegensatz zu den vormals üblichen Ideen der Moderne von Ursache und Wirkung (die verschiedene Modi des stilistischen Determinismus begründeten) – in letzter Zeit oft als überzeugendes Argument verwendet, um mittels der Analogie die häufig so titulierte Postmoderne und, im weiteren Sinn, auch die Vielfalt der unterschiedlichen Zugänge zeitgenössischer Malpraktiken zu erklären.[5] Es gibt zudem eine grundlegende logische Konsequenz, die das 17., 20. und 21. Jahrhundert tiefgreifend miteinander verbindet: die Prinzipien von Eros (Begehren, Lebenstrieb) und Thanatos (Todestrieb). Sie sind die menschlichen variablen „Inflexionslinien", nach denen wir uns alle auf unsere jeweils eigene Art und Weise ausrichten müssen. Im Zeitalter des Barock waren diese beiden Impulse üblicherweise Teil von „deistischen" Prinzipien, an deren Stelle in der Moderne weitgehend vielfältige „psychologische" oder libidinöse Erklärungsmuster getreten sind.[6] Aber nichts vermag jene emotive Macht und die Erfahrungen abzumildern, mit denen diese Impulse noch immer unsere zeitgenössischen menschlichen Leben konfrontieren. Diese Parallelen zwischen dem Barock und der Gegenwart sind aber auch hilfreich, um die Beweggründe und Bedeutungen, die der SØR Rusche Sammlung mit ihren weit über zweitausend Arbeiten zugrunde liegen, zu verstehen.

Die Praxis der Malerei war schon immer mehr als jede andere visuelle ästhetische Sprache tief mit Eros und Thanatos, dem Lebens- und Todestrieb verbunden: Die Isolation im Atelier, lange Stunden der Einsamkeit und Innenschau, das ehrgeizige Verlangen, eine vollkommene Form des persönlichen Ausdrucks zu finden und die Unzufriedenheit, wenn dies nicht gelingt, bestimmen die gespannte Unruhe im Leben eines Malers. Ähnlich spürt ein leidenschaftlicher Sammler wie Thomas Rusche das unstillbare Drängen und Begehren, Unbesitzbares besitzen und das Greifbare im nicht greifbaren Inhalt eines Gemäldes erfassen zu wollen, und er erlebt nicht weniger das Gefühl persönlicher, nicht zu besänftigender Enttäuschung. Das Sammeln ist naturgemäß ein Akt kontinuierlichen Aufspürens, ein Verlangen nach einem erfüllten Innenleben persönlicher ästhetischer Vertiefung. In diesem Zusammenhang sind die schöpferischen Ästhetiken von Eros und Thanatos, als Ausdruck sowohl des Lebens im Tod als auch des Todes im Leben, unausweichlich. Begehren und Tod des Begehrens sind jedoch nicht als schlichtweg entgegengesetzte Kräfte zu verstehen, sondern lediglich als verschiedene Aspekte der menschlichen Identität – parallel ausgebildet wohnen sie uns ein. Als duale Grundbedingungen der Malerei und der conditio humana sind sie Teil und ermöglichen sie die zivilisierenden Prozesse des Lebens. Sie bedingen einander wie der Schatten und das Licht.[7] Die in dieser Edition reproduzierten Werke zielen gleichzeitig auf den Sinn für Entdeckung sowie auf Vermittlung und Assimilation ab. Sie reflektieren Thomas Rusches einzigartige persönliche und sich stets vertiefende Beziehung zur Malerei, die er mit seinen umfassenden Erwerbungen der letzten Jahre bewiesen hat.

Die fünfzig ausgewählten Arbeiten sind nur ein kleiner Teil von Thomas Rusches Sammlung zeitgenössischer Kunst. Sie wurden ausgesucht, weil sich an ihnen die genannten Affinitäten gut verdeutlichen lassen. Ein Merkmal postmoderner oder zeitgenössischer Malerei der letzten dreißig Jahre ist die Rückkehr zu Genrekategorien, die auch im Barock verwendet wurden. Die Genres der Landschafts- und Stillebenmalerei, aber auch Subgenres wie Vanitas-Darstellungen oder das Memento-mori-Motiv wurden zuerst von der Malerei des 17. Jahrhunderts hervorgebracht und kehrten nun zurück, und viele zeitgenössische Maler beschäftigen sich mit ihnen.[8] Darin zeigt sich nicht nur eine nietzscheanische Geisteshaltung, sondern auch, dass die Praxis der Malerei sich beständig selbst wieder zu beleben vermag.[9] Weit entfernt vom „Betrauern" oder dem Tod der Malerei, ist sie lebendig und zeitigt heute eine enorme Vielfalt an Ausdrucksformen und Anwendungsweisen.[10] Mit dem Ungültigwerden der sogenannten „großen Erzählungen", der starren Ideen des historischen Determinismus und der oft von den Minimalisten behaupteten Endphase hat sich die Malerei ein neues Leben geschaffen, das sie nicht nur mit der Vergangenheit und den großen Traditionen der Malerei verbindet, sondern zudem ihre Praxis bereichert und weiterführt.

3
Zeitgenössische Kunst der SØR Rusche Sammlung wurde gemeinsam mit Rusches Werken barocker Meister gezeigt: Gera *Landscapes: Landschaft entdecken;* Anhaltische Gemäldegalerie Dessau *Still Lifes: Stilleben – Niederländische Kunst des 17. Jahrhunderts im Dialog mit zeitgenössischen Positionen der Sammlung SØR Rusche;* Schloss Corvey *Genre: Von Liebeslust und Lebenslast – der inszenierte Alltag;* Museum Abtei Liesborn *Portraits: Menschenbilder 1629–2009;* Anhaltische Gemäldegalerie Dessau *Portraits: Blickkontakte – Niederländische Portraits des 17. Jahrhunderts im Dialog mit Kunst der Gegenwart, Sammlung SØR Rusche.* In den letzten drei Jahren wurden mehr als 1200 Gemälde der SØR Rusche Sammlung an über zwanzig Museen verliehen.

4
„Was ist barock?", 3. Kapitel in Deleuze, Gilles: Die Falte. Leibniz und der Barock. Frankfurt am Main: Suhrkamp 2000. S. 49–67. Der Text widmet sich den verwandten Ästhetiken barocker und zeitgenössischer Malerei und Architektur. (Originalausgabe: Deleuze, Gilles: Le Pli. Leibniz et le Baroque. Paris: Les Editions de Minuit 1988).

5
Lyotard, Jean-François: Beantwortung der Frage: Was ist postmodern? In: Wege aus der Postmoderne. Schlüsseltexte der Postmoderne-Diskussion. Hrsg. von Wolfgang Welsch. Weinheim: VCH Acta Humanoria 1988. S. 193–203. „Ein Werk ist nur modern, wenn es zuvor postmodern war. So gesehen, bedeutet der Postmodernismus nicht das Ende des Modernismus, sondern dessen Geburt, dessen permanente Geburt." S. 201. (Originalausgabe: Lyotard, Jean-François: La Condition postmoderne: Rapport sur le savoir. Paris: Les Editions de Minuit 1979).

6
Es gibt viele moderne psychologische Theorien von Eros und Thanatos, aber sie alle leiten sich ab von den Definitionen, die Freud in seinen berühmten Aufsätzen „Die Widerstände gegen die Psychoanalyse" (1925) und „Jenseits des Lustprinzips" (1920) formulierte. Ursprünglich nutzte Freud nicht den Begriff „Eros" (er bevorzugte „Lebenstrieb"), stellte ihn jedoch mit „Libido" (libidinöse oder sexuelle Energie) gleich, jedoch nicht, um ihn als Geschlechtlichkeit im genitalen Sinn verstanden zu wissen, sondern als lebensschaffende Kraft im schöpferischen Sinn. Thanatos (der Todesinstinkt oder Todestrieb), ein Begriff, der in der Psychoanalyse zuerst von Freuds Anhänger Wilhelm Stekel geprägt wurde, taucht bei Freud als ungelöste, in sich gegensätzliche Neigung, die den Menschen denaturiert und ihn oft zu Wiederholungen und Nachstellungen traumatischer Ereignisse zwingt, deren Funktion es sei vorauszusetzen, dass der Organismus seinem eigenen Weg des Todes folgen solle. In einen nicht-freudschen Sprachrahmen gebracht und die theistisch-philosophische Beschreibung nutzend, ist dies der menschliche Hang, über die Sterblichkeit und über den letztendlichen Ausgang des menschlichen Lebens, den Tod, zu meditieren. In gewissem Grade entwickelte Freud diese Idee (wie auch die Idee des Es) aus Werk des deutschen Philosophen des Pessimismus, Arthur Schopenhauer (1788–1860), und dessen Vorstellung vom „Willen zum Leben" und anderen menschlichen Neigungen als „Verneinung d[ies]es Willens". Siehe dazu: Schopenhauer, Arthur: Die Welt als Wille und Vorstellung (1918).

7
„Das Gemälde ändert seinen Status, die Dinge tauchen vor dem Hintergrund auf, die Farben definieren den gemeinsamen Grund [‚fond'], der ihre dunkle Natur bezeugt, die Figuren definieren sich eher durch ihre Deckung als durch ihren Umriß. Das aber geschieht nicht im Gegensatz zum Licht, sondern im Bereich aufgrund der neuen Herrschaft des Lichts. Leibniz sagt in der *Confessio philosophi:* ‚Es gleitet durch einen Spalt in die Mitte der Finsternis.'" Deleuze, G.: Die Falte. S. 57.

8
Allgemeine Publikationen jüngeren Datums dazu sind: Buttner, Nils: Landscape Painting. A History. New York: Abbeville Press 2006; Meijer, Fred G.: Dutch and Flemish Still-life Paintings. Zwolle: Waanders 2005; Sander, Jochen: Die Magie der Dinge. Stillebenmalerei 1500–1800. Ostfildern: Hatje Cantz 2008.

9
Friedrich Nietzsches Theorie der ewigen Wiederkunft erschien zuerst in seinem Buch Die fröhliche Wissenschaft (1882) und wurde ausgiebig von Martin Heidegger analysiert. **Siehe** „Die ewige Wiederkunft des Gleichen" in: Heidegger, **Martin:** Nietzsche II. 7. Auflage. Stuttgart: Klett-Cotta 2008. S. 254–261.

10
Bois, Yve-Alain: Painting. The Task of Mourning. In: Ders.: Painting as Model. Cambridge, Mass.: The MIT Press (1990) 1993. S. 229–244. Der Bois' Aufsatz beigefügte Aphorismus stammt von Sherry Levine: „[Meine Gemälde] behandeln auf gewisse Art den Tod, den unbehaglichen Tod des Modernismus."

Pilgrim

ABCDEFGHIJKLMNOPQRSTUVWXYZ
abcdefghijklmnopqrstuvwxyz
1234567890 !@#?:;"*&

Foundry: Linotype
Designer: Eric Gill / Walter Tracy / Linotype Design Studio
Designer Nationality: British
Date: 1934 / 1953 / 2005

Pilgrim is an Old Style serif informed by Eric Gill's design for a book published for the Limited Editions Club in New York in 1934. Much like Gill's original face, Pilgrim combines the traditional shapes and contrasts of an Old Style serif with the incised strokes typical of monumental Roman lettering.

Plantin Headline

ABCDEFGHIJKLMNOPQRSTUVWXYZ
abcdefghijklmnopqrstuvwxyz
1234567890 !@#?:;"*&

Foundry: Monotype
Designer: Monotype Studio
Date: 1913

Plantin Headline is one of several designs based on the 16th-century specimens held in the Plantin-Moretus Museum in Antwerp. Intended for use at larger sizes, Plantin Headline maintains the shape of Old Style letterforms while adding contrast to the strokes and serifs.

Plantin Infant

ABCDEFGHIJKLMNOPQRSTUVWXYZ
abcdefghijklmnopqrstuvwxyz
1234567890 !@#?:;"*&

Foundry: Monotype
Designer: Monotype Studio
Date: 1913

Plantin Infant is an Old Style text face based on the 16th-century specimens held in the Plantin-Moretus Museum in Antwerp. Like other traditional serifs designed in the French tradition, it combines pronounced strokes with a lowered x-height, for legibility at small sizes.

Poliphilus

ABCDEFGHIJKLMNOPQRSTUVWXYZ
abcdefghijklmnopqrstuvwxyz
1234567890 !@#?:;"*&

Foundry: Monotype
Designer: Francesco Griffo / Monotype Studio
Designer Nationality: Italian
Date: 2001

Poliphilus is an exact replica of a text face cut by Francesco Griffo and used in *Hypnerotomachia Poliphili* (*The Dream of Poliphilus*), a romantic tale published by Aldus Manutius in 1499. Monotype's design even replicates the ink spreads caused by its original printing on handmade paper.

Portrait

ABCDEFGHIJKLMNOPQRSTUVWXYZ
abcdefghijklmnopqrstuvwxyz
1234567890 !@#?:;"'*&

Foundry: Commercial Type
Designer: Berton Hasebe
Designer Nationality: American
Date: 2013

The distinctive Portrait typeface by New York-based type designer Berton Hasebe was inspired by the forms of French Renaissance types produced by designers such as Claude Garamond and Robert Granjon. It encompasses his love of types from the period and is a marriage of classical proportions but with an edge.

Portrait has a striking clean and aggressively sharp tone, employing pointed Latin serifs across the design. It started out as a display typeface and possesses nuanced details that are clearly visible when scaled up. However, it comes in four families – Portrait, Portrait Text, Portrait Condensed and Portrait Inline – and thirty-five styles, so it can be employed in every scenario. Its hard, chiselled serifs and minimal yet confident appearance make it ideal for contemporary publications; it has been used in influential art, design and fashion magazines such as *Document Journal* and *Wallpaper**.

Hasebe was born in Hawaii and studied design and typography in Los Angeles and the Netherlands. When he was completing his master's on the Type and Media course at the Royal Academy of Art in The Hague, he designed the Alda typeface, which was released by Emigre in 2008. Hasebe went on to become an in-house type designer at Commercial Type (see p. 124) from 2008 to 2013, after which he left to form his own studio. Through Commercial Type he has also released Platform (2010) and Druk (2014).

Below. Example setting for Portrait – from left, regular, medium and bold. Possessing many traits of type with classical proportions, Hasebe's design contemporizes these serif types of old with minimal, triangular sharp chiselled serifs for lighter and roman weights and with heavier woodcut type forms with the bold weights. Portrait's main inspiration comes from a design attributed to French punch-cutter Maitre Constantin (*c.* 1530) for the printer Robert I Estienne in Paris.

Cabin boys
BOUNCE
Macédoine

PORTRAIT REGULAR 100 PT

Dandelion
YAWNER
Porquerías

PORTRAIT MEDIUM 100 PT

Ultimates
X-RATED
Tabulator

PORTRAIT BOLD 100 PT

Łódź & Kęty
OBESITIES
Fired Games

PORTRAIT REGULAR ITALIC 100 PT

Tuscan Sun
EQUINOX
N'est-ce pas

PORTRAIT MEDIUM ITALIC 100 PT [SWASH, Q]

Affiliations
MÖGÖTT
Littérateur

PORTRAIT BOLD ITALIC 100 PT [LIGATURE, ffi]

Portrait Condensed

ABCDEFGHIJKLMNOPQRSTUVWXYZ
abcdefghijklmnopqrstuvwxyz
1234567890 !@#?:;”*&

Foundry: Commercial Type
Designer: Berton Hasabe
Designer Nationality: American
Date: 2013

Portrait Condensed is a narrow, Old Style serif, inspired by the Vendôme Condensed font family, designed by François Ganeau in 1952. Like Ganeau's design, Portrait Condensed takes its cues, such as the sharp, triangular serifs, from the type designs of the French Renaissance.

Portrait Text

ABCDEFGHIJKLMNOPQRSTUVWXYZ
abcdefghijklmnopqrstuvwxyz
1234567890 !@#?:;”*&

Foundry: Commercial Type
Designer: Berton Hasabe
Designer Nationality: American
Date: 2013

Portrait Text is a streamlined Old Style serif that first appeared in style-led magazines such as the *Document Journal* and *Wallpaper**. The characters are trim and articulate, and are reminiscent of the faces used by 16th-century French printer and scholar Robert I Estienne.

Raleigh

ABCDEFGHIJKLMNOPQRSTUVWXYZ
abcdefghijklmnopqrstuvwxyz
1234567890 !@#?:;”*&

Foundry: Linotype
Designer: Carl Dair / David Anderson / Adrian Williams / Robert Norton
Designer Nationality: Canadian / Canadian / British / British
Date: 1967 / 1978

An Old Style serif, Raleigh is based on the Cartier typeface designed by Carl Dair in 1967 for the Canadian Centennial and the Expo held in Montreal. It was renamed after Dair's death that year. The Raleigh font family includes Robert Norton's text version and Adrian Williams's three display weights.

Renner Antiqua

ABCDEFGHIJKLMNOPQRSTUVWXYZ
abcdefghijklmnopqrstuvwxyz
1234567890 !@#?:;”*&

Foundry: Linotype
Designer: Paul Renner / Patrick Strietzel
Designer Nationality: German
Date: 1939 / 2008

Renner Antiqua was initially designed by Paul Renner in 1939 and later updated by Patrick Strietzel in 2008. Strietzel's design was produced in both text and display sizes and maintains the distinctive features of the original, such as bowed serifs and heightened stroke contrasts.

Revival 555

ABCDEFGHIJKLMNOPQRSTUVWXYZ
abcdefghijklmnopqrstuvwxyz
1234567890 !@#?:;"*&

Foundry: Bitstream
Designer: Frank Hinman Pierpont
Designer Nationality: American
Date: 1951

A romantic revival of Old Style letterforms, supervised by Frank Hinman Pierpont and later published by Bitstream, Revival 555 is a font family in the style of 15th- and 18th-century faces. The design features low x-heights, long ascenders and minimal stroke contrasts.

Rotation

ABCDEFGHIJKLMNOPQRSTUVWXYZ
abcdefghijklmnopqrstuvwxyz
1234567890 !@#?:;"*&

Foundry: Linotype
Designer: Arthur Ritzel
Designer Nationality: German
Date: 1971

Rotation is a serif font family designed for use on the rotation printing press; it was intended for newspapers and for setting at small point sizes. Unlike Ionic style font families, which dominated newsprint after the end of World War II, Rotation utilizes the more traditional qualities of Old Style letterforms.

Rustika

ABCDEFGHIJKLMNOPQRSTUVWXYZ
abcdefghijklmnopqrstuvwxyz
1234567890 !@#?:;"*&

Foundry: Linotype
Designer: Franko Luin
Designer Nationality: Swedish
Date: 1995

The Rustika font family is a traditional Old Style serif with a rough edge. It takes its name from the Esperanto spelling of 'rustic' and was designed to emulate the process of shaping characters by chisel. The resulting jagged letterforms give Rustika a historical feel.

Simoncini Garamond

ABCDEFGHIJKLMNOPQRSTUVWXYZ
abcdefghijklmnopqrstuvwxyz
1234567890 !@#?:;"*&

Foundry: Ludwig & Mayer
Designer: Francesco Simoncini / Wilhelm Bilz
Designer Nationality: Italian / German
Date: 1961

This was created by Italian font designer Francesco Simoncini and the art director of German type foundry Ludwig & Mayer, Wilhelm Bilz. It is based on the Jean Jannon model, and is lighter and more delicate than other Garamonds. Variations are Garamond Simoncini and Italian Garamond.

Stempel Garamond

ABCDEFGHIJKLMNOPQRSTUVWXYZ
abcdefghijklmnopqrstuvwxyz
1234567890 !@#?:;"*&

Foundry: Stempel
Designer: Claude Garamond /
David Stempel
Designer Nationality: French /
German
Date: 1592 / 1925

Based on the Egenolff-Berner specimen, produced in 1592, Stempel Garamond is a restoration of the original Garamond types. One of the most popular renditions of the style, Stempel Garamond distinguishes itself through its keen curves and sharp terminals.

Stempel Schneidler

ABCDEFGHIJKLMNOPQRSTUVWXYZ
abcdefghijklmnopqrstuvwxyz
1234567890 !@#¿:;"*&

Foundry: Linotype
Designer: F. H. Ernst
Schneidler / Linotype
Design Studio
Designer Nationality: German
Date: 1936 / 1982

First designed by Friedrich Hermann Ernst Schneidler in 1936, and titled Schneidler Old Style, this font family is a humanist serif inspired by the Renaissance typefaces of Venice. The Stempel foundry in Frankfurt later reworked the design, before being acquired by Linotype.

Thesaurus

ABCDEFGHIJKLMNOPQRSTUVWXYZ
abcdefghijklmnopqrstuvwxyz
1234567890 !@#?:;"*&

Foundry: Typotheque
Designer: Fermín Guerrero
Designer Nationality:
Uruguayan
Date: 2017

Thesaurus is an Old Style serif but with a modern feel. It was inspired by the metal types that Robert Estienne took from Paris to Geneva in the 16th century. Unlike the original letterforms, Thesaurus features an extended x-height, a narrower width and multiple weights.

Thorndale

ABCDEFGHIJKLMNOPQRSTUVWXYZ
abcdefghijklmnopqrstuvwxyz
1234567890 !@#?:;"*&

Foundry: Monotype
Designer: Monotype Studio
Date: 1999

Thorndale is a traditional Old Style serif, manufactured for the digital age. Thorndale was designed primarily for web browsers, but its asymmetrical serifs, low-contrast strokes and classical characters ensure optimal legibility across multiple digital platforms.

Tribute

ABCDEFGHIJKLMNOPQRSTUVWXYZ
abcdefghijklmnopqrstuvwxyz
1234567890 !@#?:;"*&

Foundry: Emigre
Designer: Frank Heine
Designer Nationality: American
Date: 2003

Inspired by a photocopied type specimen from 1565 featuring letters cut by the French punch-cutter François Guyot, and echoing his idiosyncratic approach, Tribute is a contemporary interpretation that features a roman and an italic and an accompanying set of ornaments.

Truesdell

ABCDEFGHIJKLMNOPQRSTUVWXYZ
abcdefghijklmnopqrstuvwxyz
1234567890 !@#?:;"*&

Foundry: Monotype
Designer: Frederic Goudy / Steve Matteson
Designer Nationality: American
Date: 1930 / 1994

Originally drawn by Frederic W. Goudy in 1930, Truesdell was subsequently lost in the fire that destroyed Goudy's studio in 1939. Almost sixty years later, using the only surviving examples of the initial design, Steve Matteson revived the Old Style serif for digital use.

Trump Mediaeval

ABCDEFGHIJKLMNOPQRSTUVWXYZ
abcdefghijklmnopqrstuvwxyz
1234567890 !@#?:;"*&

Foundry: Weber
Designer: Georg Trump
Designer Nationality: German
Date: 1954

Trump Mediaeval is a reworking of the traditional Old Style font family. It was designed for use with mid 20th-century technology, such as fax machines, so the letterforms utilize angled strokes and joints alongside sliced serifs and brackets to remain legible in low-resolution outputs.

Trump Mediaeval Office

ABCDEFGHIJKLMNOPQRSTUVWXYZ
abcdefghijklmnopqrstuvwxyz
1234567890 !@#?:;"*&

Foundry: Linotype
Designer: Georg Trump / Akira Kobayashi
Designer Nationality: German / Japanese
Date: 1954 / 2006

Trump Mediaeval Office is Linotype's revival of Trump Mediaeval for use in the 21st-century office. Reworking Georg Trump's original, Akira Kobayashi adds a variety of features to adapt the face to updated technology, such as the synchronization of character shapes across weights.

Van Dijck

ABCDEFGHIJKLMNOPQRSTUVWXYZ
abcdefghijklmnopqrstuvwxyz
1234567890 !@#?:;"★&

Foundry: Monotype
Designer: Christoffel van Dijck /
Jan van Krimpen
Designer Nationality: Dutch
Date: c. 1600s / 1935

Van Dijck is Jan van Krimpen's revision of an Old Style serif attributed to 17th-century typefounder Christoffel van Dijck. Despite persisting doubts over the initial specimen's true author, the font family exhibits all the characteristics of Dutch type design in the 1600s.

Vendetta

ABCDEFGHIJKLMNOPQRSTUVWXYZ
abcdefghijklmnopqrstuvwxyz
1234567890 !@#?:;"*&

Foundry: Emigre
Designer: John Downer
Designer Nationality: American
Date: 1999

Vendetta is a homage to the roman types of 15th-century punch-cutters, who were themselves influenced by the work of Nicholas Jenson, and displays a very distinctive blend of old and new. The typeface comes in four weights from Light to Volume, and two matching italics.

Vendome

ABCDEFGHIJKLMNOPQRSTUVWXYZ
abcdefghijklmnopqrstuvwxyz
1234567890 !@#?:;"*&

Foundry: Olive
Designer: François Ganeau
Designer Nationality: French
Date: 1952

Vendome is an Old Style serif and the single result of French artist and sculptor François Ganeau's foray into the field of type design. The characters are calligraphic in their strokes and irregular in shape, with decorative features found in both the upper- and lowercase families.

Venetian 301

ABCDEFGHIJKLMNOPQRSTUVWXYZ
abcdefghijklmnopqrstuvwxyz
1234567890 !@#?:;"*&

Foundry: Bitstream
Designer: Bruce Rogers / Dmitry Kirsanov
Designer Nationality: American / Russian
Date: 1914 / 2006

Venetian 301 is Bitstream's digital version of Bruce Rogers's font family, Centaur (1914). Dmitry Kirsanov's design maintains the distinguishing features of the initial design, such as the arching strokes and gradual brackets, but favours smooth curves over the original angular shapes.

Whitenights

ABCDEFGHIJKLMNOPQRSTUVWXYZ
abcdefghijklmnopqrstuvwxyz
1234567890 !@#?:;"'*&

Foundry: Linotype
Designer: Lars Bergquist
Designer Nationality: Swedish
Date: 2002

Whitenights is a versatile serif with variants that include Titling for headlines, Math for mathematical glyphs and a series of supplementary ligatures in all weights. Its characters are moderate in contrast and maintain a standard x-height for legibility in continuous text.

Wile

ABCDEFGHIJKLMNOPQRSTUVWXYZ
abcdefghijklmnopqrstuvwxyz
1234567890 !@#?:;"*&

Foundry: Monotype
Designer: Cynthia Hollandsworth Batty
Designer Nationality: American
Date: 1998

Wile is an Old Style serif, designed as a gift to the Agfa Compugraphic executive Don Wile upon his retirement. Its characters exhibit the influence of inscriptional letterforms, as seen in the wedged serifs, and are designed to work in both text and display sizes.

Wilke

ABCDEFGHIJKLMNOPQRSTUVWXYZ
abcdefghijklmnopqrstuvwxyz
1234567890 !@#?:;"*&

Foundry: Linotype
Designer: Martin Wilke
Designer Nationality: German
Date: 1988

Wilke is an energetic serif font family influenced by the styles of Irish handwriting found in the *Book of Kells*, a 9th-century illuminated manuscript. The strokes are somewhat typical of an Old Style face, but the serifs and terminals, especially in the numerals, express the idiosyncrasy of penmanship.

William Text

ABCDEFGHIJKLMNOPQRSTUVWXYZ
abcdefghijklmnopqrstuvwxyz
1234567890 !@#?:;"'*&

Foundry: Typotheque
Designer: Maria Doreuli
Designer Nationality: Russian
Date: 2016

William Text is an elegant serif inspired by the legacy of English typefounder William Caslon. As with Caslon's 16th-century designs, William Text has a large x-height and is intended primarily for book text. The standard characters are accompanied by 200 refined ornaments.

Apollo

ABCDEFGHIJKLMNOPQRSTUVWXYZ
abcdefghijklmnopqrstuvwxyz
1234567890 !@#?:;''"*&

Apollo is one of the lesser known fonts by Adrian Frutiger (see p. 290). He designed it to print accurately on smooth paper stocks. One of the first fonts created for Monotype's new phototypesetting machine, the robust design has a small x-height, open counters, bracketed serifs and a primarily oblique axis.

(see p. 290)

Foundry: Monotype
Designer: Adrian Frutiger
Designer Nationality: Swiss
Date: 1964

Austin News Deck

ABCDEFGHIJKLMNOPQRSTUVWXYZ
abcdefghijklmnopqrstuvwxyz
1234567890 !@#?:;"*&

Austin News Deck is a flexible transitional serif. It was conceived to work as an intermediate between the delicacy of the original Austin, designed by British graphic designer and typographer Paul Barnes for *Harper's Bazaar* fashion magazine in 2014, and the full body of Austin Text.

Foundry: Commercial Type
Designer: Paul Barnes
Designer Nationality: British
Date: 2016

Austin News Headline

ABCDEFGHIJKLMNOPQRSTUVWXYZ
abcdefghijklmnopqrstuvwxyz
1234567890 !@#?:;"*&

Making its debut in Jon Hill's redesign of the *Daily Telegraph* in 2015, Austin News Headline is a transitional serif suited to the demands of news media. It is an update of Austin, its increased x-height and shorter ascenders and descenders improving both readability and spatial economy.

Foundry: Commercial Type
Designer: Paul Barnes
Designer Nationality: British
Date: 2016

Austin News Headline Condensed

ABCDEFGHIJKLMNOPQRSTUVWXYZ
abcdefghijklmnopqrstuvwxyz
1234567890 !@#?:;"*&

Like its Austin News siblings, Austin News Headline Condensed was designed to meet the spatial requirements of 21st-century news media. Building on the economic forms of Austin News Headline, this font is a true condensed serif and includes a family of eight distinct weights.

Foundry: Commercial Type
Designer: Paul Barnes
Designer Nationality: British
Date: 2016

Austin Text

ABCDEFGHIJKLMNOPQRSTUVWXYZ
abcdefghijklmnopqrstuvwxyz
1234567890 !@#?:;"*&

Foundry: Commercial Type
Designer: Paul Barnes
Designer Nationality: British
Date: 2014

Designed specifically for use at smaller sizes, Austin Text is a robust transitional serif informed by the original types of 18th-century English punch-cutter Richard Austin. The letterforms are each proportionally balanced to suit easy reading in long runs of dense text.

Baskerville Classico

ABCDEFGHIJKLMNOPQRSTUVWXYZ
abcdefghijklmnopqrstuvwxyz
1234567890 !@#?:;"*&

Foundry: Omnibus
Designer: John Baskerville / Franko Luin
Designer Nationality: British / Swedish
Date: 1724 / 1995

John Baskerville was a highly influential 18th-century writer, stonecutter and printer, known internationally for his innovative ideas and fastidious approach to his craft. One of numerous versions of Baskerville's classic serif, this cut was created by the Swedish type designer Franko Luin.

Baskerville LT

ABCDEFGHIJKLMNOPQRSTUVWXYZ
abcdefghijklmnopqrstuvwxyz
1234567890 !@#?:;"*&

Foundry: Mergenthaler Linotype
Designer: John Baskerville / George W. Jones
Designer Nationality: British
Date: 1724 / 1923

George W. Jones, the master printer and typeface designer, was hired by the British branch of Mergenthaler to develop a series of typefaces for its hot-metal typesetting machines. He created this faithful revival of Baskerville's dignified serif in partnership with Linotype draughtsman Harry Smith.

Baskerville No 2

ABCDEFGHIJKLMNOPQRSTUVWXYZ
abcdefghijklmnopqrstuvwxyz
1234567890 !@#?:;"*&

Foundry: Monotype / Bitstream
Designer: John Baskerville
Designer Nationality: British
Date: 1724 / 1924 / 1980

Bitstream's version of Baskerville was digitized following Monotype's version of 1924, which was created from proofs of John Baskerville's Great Primer (16 point) rather than the metal. There are many versions of Baskerville, which was the first transitional (between old-face and modern) type.

Jeremy Tankard Typography

British type designer Jeremy Tankard started his career after his studies at London's Central St Martins and then the Royal College of Art. He worked in corporate graphic design, advising and creating typography for many well-known international brands. Tankard established his own studio in 1998 to concentrate on his designs and since then has gone on to create an enviable portfolio of award-winning typefaces and a worldwide reputation for the outstanding quality and innovative designs of his types. They include the highly lauded Bliss (see p. 255), Enigma, Shire Types (see p. 483) and Hawkland (see p. 162).

Tankard has produced typographic solutions for commercial clients and design / advertising studios for several decades (such as Corbel for Microsoft and Blue Island for Adobe), and the typefaces he has created are highly flexible and adaptable to changes in technology and usage. The studio offers a diverse range of styles for nearly every application, providing both excellence and functionality, whether for a pre-established font or a bespoke commission typeface or logotype.

Founded: 1998
Country: Britain
Website: typography.net
Notable typefaces:
Bliss (see p. 255)
Hawkland (see p. 162)
Shire Types (see p. 483)

Below left. De Worde typeface specimen designed by Alistair Hall at We Made This.

Below. Fenland specimen page.

Opposite. Promotional fold-out poster highlighting a selection of varying typefaces on offer.

Fenland a 14 font typeface

JEREMY TANKARD
- REDISTURBED REGULAR -

HAS
- TRILOGY EGYPTIAN HEAVY WIDE -

A FRESH NEW
- BLISS HEAVY -

SITE
- TRILOGY FATFACE REGULAR -

THAT'S QUITE WONDERFULLY EASY TO USE
- KINGFISHER ITALIC -

AND REPLETE WITH MANY
- ALCHEMY -

MARVELLOUS
- DE WORDE EXTRA BOLD -

TYPEFACES
- CAPLINE REGULAR -

Bell

ABCDEFGHIJKLMNOPQRSTUVWXYZ
abcdefghijklmnopqrstuvwxyz
1234567890 !@#?:;"*&

Richard Austin cut Bell in 1788 for John Bell, who used it in his newspaper *The Oracle*, and Monotype typographer Stanley Morison considered it to be the first English modern face. In 1931, Monotype cut a new version for hot metal based on original designs, with updates added over the years.

Foundry: British Letter / Monotype
Designer: Richard Austin / Monotype Studio
Designer Nationality: British
Date: 1788 / 1931

Berling Nova

ABCDEFGHIJKLMNOPQRSTUVWXYZ
abcdefghijklmnopqrstuvwxyz
1234567890 !@#?:;"*&

This redesign of Swedish designer Karl-Erik Forsberg's classic was created using much of his original source material from Linotype and is available in two weights. It has an increased x-height and bigger, more curved serifs, as well as the addition of small caps and Old Style figures.

Foundry: Verbum
Designer: Karl-Erik Forsberg / Örjan Nordling
Designer Nationality: Swedish
Date: 1951 / 2004

Berndal

ABCDEFGHIJKLMNOPQRSTUVWXYZ
abcdefghijklmnopqrstuvwxyz
1234567890 !@#?:;"*&

A refined serif from Sweden's master typographer, Berndal has large x-heights, open counters and short ascenders. Legible at small sizes, its letterforms are relatively wide, but consistent in width. There is a contrast in the thickness of the strokes, and a subtle calligraphic influence.

Foundry: Linotype
Designer: Bo Berndal
Designer Nationality: Swedish
Date: 2003

Birka

ABCDEFGHIJKLMNOPQRSTUVWXYZ
abcdefghijklmnopqrstuvwxyz
1234567890 !@#?:;"*&

Birka is named after the ancient Viking town near Stockholm. It is the first typeface that Franko Luin designed from scratch and he said it taught him everything he knows about type design. Inspired by the classic forms of Garamond, this polished serif has been described as 'unmistakably Swedish'.

Foundry: Omnibus
Designer: Franko Luin
Designer Nationality: Swedish
Date: 1992

Bohemia

ABCDEFGHIJKLMNOPQRSTUVWXYZ
abcdefghijklmnopqrstuvwxyz
1234567890 !@#?:;”*&

Foundry: Linotype
Designer: Eduardo Manso
Designer Nationality: Spanish
Date: 2004

Bohemia was influenced by the refined design of transitional typefaces, such as Baskerville, but its more curvy letterforms give it a distinctive appearance. In 2003, it won first prize in the text category of Linotype's International Digital Type Design Contest.

Bruce Old Style

ABCDEFGHIJKLMNOPQRSTUVWXYZ
abcdefghijklmnopqrstuvwxyz
1234567890 !@#?:;”*&

Foundry: Monotype / Bitstream
Designer: Sol Hess
Designer Nationality: American
Date: 1909 / c. 1980s

This was originally Bruce Foundry's Old Style No. 20 (1869), which was based on Miller & Richard's Old Style (1858). Sol Hess recut the typeface at Lanston Monotype in 1909, and this was digitized by Bitstream. It is used as the complementary typeface in the Sears mail-order catalogue.

Bulmer

ABCDEFGHIJKLMNOPQRSTUVWXYZ
abcdefghijklmnopqrstuvwxyz
1234567890 !@#?:;”*&

Foundry: ATF / Monotype
Designer: Morris Fuller Benton / Robin Nicholas
Designer Nationality: American / British
Date: 1792 / 1995

A late transitional face heavily influenced by Baskerville, Bulmer has a greater contrast, along with sharper serifs and a distinctive curved-tailed uppercase 'R'. It was revived in the early 20th century by Morris Fuller Benton at American Type Founders, and then by Robin Nicholas at Monotype.

Burgess

ABCDEFGHIJKLMNOPQRSTUVWXYZ
abcdefghijklmnopqrstuvwxyz
1234567890 !@#?:;“*&

Foundry: Colophon
Designer: The Entente
Designer Nationality: British
Date: 2014

This subjective reinterpretation of mid-century cuts by Photostat (an early projection photocopier) of Times New Roman Bold and Bold Italic is named after William Starling Burgess. Some historians credit him, rather than Lardent and Morison, with the original design of Times New Roman in 1904.

Byington

ABCDEFGHIJKLMNOPQRSTUVWXYZ
abcdefghijklmnopqrstuvwxyz
1234567890 !@#?:;"*&

Foundry: Typodermic
Designer: Ray Larabie
Designer Nationality: Canadian
Date: 2005

Byington was inspired by the carvings on Trajan's Column in Rome and shares their classical lines, but its serifs are bolder and its curves more defined, making it ideal for low-resolution applications. Its lowercase letterforms are influenced by Sabon and Garamond, but retain the uppercase's elegant lines.

Carniola

ABCDEFGHIJKLMNOPQRSTUVWXYZ
abcdefghijklmnopqrstuvwxyz
1234567890 !@#?:;" *&

Foundry: Omnibus
Designer: Franko Luin
Designer Nationality: Swedish
Date: 1993

Swedish designer Franko Luin has described Carniola as 'a pastiche of different type designs from the beginning of the 20th century, mostly American'. In a reference to Luin's Slovene origins, the typeface takes its name from a historical region that comprised parts of present-day Slovenia.

CG Adroit

ABCDEFGHIJKLMNOPQRSTUVWXYZ
abcdefghijklmnopqrstuvwxyz
1234567890 !@#?:;"*&

Foundry: TypeSpectra
Designer: Phil Martin
Designer Nationality: American
Date: 1981

With its a distinctive lowercase 'g', diagonal stress and strong contrast between thick and thin strokes, Adroit is available in six weights, from Light to Extra Bold. Its designer Phil Martin spent many years designing cartoons, before setting up the foundry TypeSpectra in Dallas, Texas in 1974.

Charter BT

ABCDEFGHIJKLMNOPQRSTUVWXYZ
abcdefghijklmnopqrstuvwxyz
1234567890 !@#?:;"*&

Foundry: Bitstream
Designer: Matthew Carter
Designer Nationality: British
Date: 1987

Charter is an economical serif with squared-off serifs and moderate curves and diagonals. It was created to deal with the limitations of low-resolution printers in the late 1980s. A new version, Charter Pro, was released in 2004 and was later added to Apple's OSX operating system.

Compatil Exquisit

ABCDEFGHIJKLMNOPQRSTUVWXYZ
abcdefghijklmnopqrstuvwxyz
1234567890 !@#?:;"*&

Foundry: Linotype
Designer: Olaf Leu
Designer Nationality: German
Date: 2001

Compatil Exquisit is a refined serif forming part of the Compatil type system, created specifically for use in annual reports. This system comprises four compatible typefaces each with four weights, making it possible to set any combination of different styles effortlessly.

Compatil Text

ABCDEFGHIJKLMNOPQRSTUVWXYZ
abcdefghijklmnopqrstuvwxyz
1234567890 !@#?:;"*&

Foundry: Linotype
Designer: Olaf Leu
Designer Nationality: German
Date: 2001

An authoritative serif, Compatil Text is designed for setting large blocks of text. It comes in four styles and supports ninety-three different languages. As it has identical letter spacing within individual heights, it can easily be combined with any of the other typefaces in the Compatil type superfamily.

Corona

ABCDEFGHIJKLMNOPQRSTUVWXYZ
abcdefghijklmnopqrstuvwxyz
1234567890 !@#?:;"*&

Foundry: Mergenthaler Linotype
Designer: Chauncey H. Griffith
Designer Nationality: American
Date: 1941

With its narrow widths and large x-height giving a strong, modern feel, Corona forms part of Chauncey H. Griffith's Legibility Group, which contained typefaces especially suited to printing on newsprint. He commenced work on the series of typefaces in 1922, with Ionic No. 5 being the first face.

Dante

ABCDEFGHIJKLMNOPQRSTUVWXYZ
abcdefghijklmnopqrstuvwxyz
1234567890 !@#?:;"*&

Foundry: Monotype
Designer: Giovanni Mardersteig / Charles Malin
Designer Nationality: German / French
Date: c. 1950s / 1991

Dante is one of Giovanni Mardersteig's most frequently used typefaces. It is a classic book face designed with an italic to work harmoniously with the roman. The face is named after the first book in which it was used, a biography of Dante, published by Mardersteig's private press Officina Bodoni in 1955.

Dante eText

ABCDEFGHIJKLMNOPQRSTUVWXYZ
abcdefghijklmnopqrstuvwxyz
1234567890 !@#?:;"★&

Foundry: Monotype
Designer: Giovanni Mardersteig / Ron Carpenter
Designer Nationality: German / British
Date: c. 1950s / 1993

One of a number of digitized versions of the original serif by German publisher and typographer Giovanni Mardersteig, this version was revised by Ron Carpenter for Monotype. It comprises three weights with titling capitals and was designed to be especially effective for screen use.

Diotima Classic

ABCDEFGHIJKLMNOPQRSTUVWXYZ
abcdefghijklmnopqrstuvwxyz
1234567890 !@#?:;"★&

Foundry: Linotype
Designer: Gudrun Zapf von Hesse / Akira Kobayashi
Designer Nationality: German / Japanese
Date: 1948 / 2008

Diotima Classic is a four-weight cut of the original single-weight design created in 1948. It includes a heavy weight added by Gudrun Zapf von Hesse, as well as a light, regular and italic. With more robust serifs and thicker hairlines, the regular weight is ideal for text sizes.

Dutch 801

ABCDEFGHIJKLMNOPQRSTUVWXYZ
abcdefghijklmnopqrstuvwxyz
1234567890 !@#?:;"*&

Foundry: Bitstream
Designer: Stanley Morison / Victor Lardent
Designer Nationality: British
Date: 1931 / c. 1980s

Bitstream's Dutch 801 is one of many variants of Times New Roman, the typeface created by Stanley Morison for *The Times* newspaper. It was in use for forty years from 1931, though the newspaper had exclusive rights for just one year before it was released for general use.

Dutch 809

ABCDEFGHIJKLMNOPQRSTUVWXYZ
abcdefghijklmnopqrstuvwxyz
1234567890 !@#?:;"*&

Foundry: Bitstream
Designer: Günter Gerhard Lange
Designer Nationality: German
Date: 1969 / 1990

Dutch 809 is Bitstream's version of Concorde, the face created by Berthold art director Günter Gerhard Lange in 1969 as opposed to the typeface of the same name created by Adrian Frutiger (see p. 290). It is a highly legible typeface that is particularly well-suited for use in large areas of text.

Dutch 811

ABCDEFGHIJKLMNOPQRSTUVWXYZ
abcdefghijklmnopqrstuvwxyz
1234567890 !@#?:;"*&

Foundry: Bitstream
Designer: Matthew Carter
Designer Nationality: British
Date: 1970 / *c.* 1980s

This confident serif is Bitstream's version of the Olympian typeface created in 1970 by Matthew Carter (see p. 616). It was one of the next generation of newspaper fonts, combining old-face, transitional and modern forms, and was later customized by Carter & Cone Type for *The Philadelphia Inquirer*.

Dutch 823

ABCDEFGHIJKLMNOPQRSTUVWXYZ
abcdefghijklmnopqrstuvwxyz
1234567890 !@#?:;"*&

Foundry: Bitstream
Designer: Francesco Simoncini
Designer Nationality: Italian
Date: 1958 / *c.* 1980s

Bitstream's version of Francesco Simoncini's Aster typeface, which he designed in 1958 for his Bologna-based Simoncini foundry and line-caster manufacturer. This typeface has delicate detailed serifs and was originally intended to be employed in books and newspapers.

Emona

ABCDEFGHIJKLMNOPQRSTUVWXYZ
abcdefghijklmnopqrstuvwxyz
1234567890 !@#?:;"*&

Foundry: Omnibus
Designer: Franko Luin
Designer Nationality: Swedish
Date: 1992

Franko Luin was born to Slovenian parents in Trieste in 1941 and immigrated to Sweden in 1961. He created more than fifty fonts during his career, working on original designs and digital revivals. Emona is a Luin original built on a superelliptical skeleton. Its letterforms share some similarities with Bodoni.

Esperanto

ABCDEFGHIJKLMNOPQRSTUVWXYZ
abcdefghijklmnopqrstuvwxyz
1234567890 !@#?:;"*&

Foundry: Omnibus
Designer: Franko Luin
Designer Nationality: Swedish
Date: 1992

Esperanto's design was inspired by the letterforms found in Renaissance manuscripts. It was named after an auxiliary language developed in the late 1800s to foster global peace and understanding; ironically, the Esperanto character set is not compatible with its namesake language.

Foundry Form Serif

ABCDEFGHIJKLMNOPQRSTUVWXYZ
abcdefghijklmnopqrstuvwxyz
1234567890 !@#?:,"*&

Foundry: The Foundry
Designer: Freda Sack /
David Quay
Designer Nationality: British
Date: 1999

Designed concurrently with Foundry Form Sans, this open, legible typeface with a pronounced horizontal emphasis upholds the reputation of The Foundry (see p. 284) for well-formed fonts. Offering a comprehensive character set, it also includes a genuine italic, small caps and Old Style figures.

FS Sally

ABCDEFGHIJKLMNOPQRSTUVWXYZ
abcdefghijklmnopqrstuvwxyz
1234567890 !@#?:,"*&

Foundry: Fontsmith
Designer: Phil Garnham /
Jason Smith
Designer Nationality: British
Date: 2009

Fontsmith (see p. 272) expanded the versatile and elegant FS Sally family in 2016 to include support for Cyrillic and Greek alphabets, reflecting an increasing global demand for multilingual fonts. Available in five weights with corresponding italics, it boasts an exhaustive character set.

Garth Graphic

ABCDEFGHIJKLMNOPQRSTUVWXYZ
abcdefghijklmnopqrstuvwxyz
1234567890 !@#?:,"*&

Foundry: Compugraphic
Designer: John Matt /
Constance Blanchard /
Renee LeWinter
Designer Nationality: American
Date: c. 1960s / 1979

Garth Graphic was developed from a single surviving proof of Matt Antique, a serif created during the 1960s by John Matt for use with the American Type Founders phototypesetter. This revival of Matt's design was named for Compugraphic founder William W. Garth Jr.

Gazette

ABCDEFGHIJKLMNOPQRSTUVWXYZ
abcdefghijklmnopqrstuvwxyz
1234567890 !@#?:,"*&

Foundry: Intertype / Linotype
Designer: Edwin W. Shaar
Designer Nationality: American
Date: 1954 / 1977

As its name implies, Gazette was created for newspaper text, with compact proportions designed to retain legibility. The font was originally published by Intertype in 1954 as Imperial; details of its reissue as Gazette are the subject of debate within the typographic community.

Granjon

ABCDEFGHIJKLMNOPQRSTUVWXYZ
abcdefghijklmnopqrstuvwxyz
1234567890 !@#?:;"*&

Foundry: Linotype
Designer: George W. Jones
Designer Nationality: British
Date: 1928

Based on a cut of Garamond from 1592, this interpretation of the French Renaissance style was well-received following its release. To avoid confusion with other Garamond revivals it was named for Robert Granjon, whose italic designs were often paired with Garamond's original romans.

GT Alpina

ABCDEFGHIJKLMNOPQRSTUVWXYZ
abcdefghijklmnopqrstuvwxyz
1234567890 !@#?:;"*&

Foundry: Grilli Type
Designer: Reto Moser
Designer Nationality: Swiss
Date: 2019

GT Alpina is a large workhorse serif family designed by Swiss designer Reto Moser of Grilli Type (see p. 238) and Studio RM. It is a typeface that pushes the boundaries but never sacrifices function for form: its letters are robust and finely crafted, yet show a healthy disregard for convention.

Hawkhurst

ABCDEFGHIJKLMNOPQRSTUVWXYZ
abcdefghijklmnopqrstuvwxyz
1234567890 !@#?:;"*&

Foundry: Linotype
Designer: Richard Yeend
Designer Nationality: British
Date: 2002

Alongside his successful career in the editorial field as a designer, art director and cartoonist, Richard Yeend was also an accomplished type designer, creating numerous fonts for both Monotype and Linotype. Hawkhurst, released in 2002, is expressive and transitional in style.

Imperial

ABCDEFGHIJKLMNOPQRSTUVWXYZ
abcdefghijklmnopqrstuvwxyz
1234567890 !@#?:;"*&

Foundry: Intertype
Designer: Edwin W. Shaar
Designer Nationality: American
Date: 1954

US type designer Edwin W. Shaar designed this compact, newspaper-friendly font for Intertype; it was created to compete with Linotype's legibility group of typefaces, which were also designed for editorial use. Imperial has been used within *The New York Times* since 1967.

Hawkland

ABCDEFGHIJKLMNOPQRSTUVWXYZ
abcdefghijklmnopqrstuvwxyz
1234567890 !@#?:;"*&

Foundry: Jeremy Tankard
Typography
Designer: Jeremy Tankard
Designer Nationality: British
Date: 2018

Hawkland is the result of British type designer Jeremy Tankard's aim to create a transitional typeface with an unbracketed serif. Tankard was inspired by type styles from the late 18th century, and Hawkland owes more to type models drawn along mechanical lines using a ruler and compass than the calligraphic structure that lies at the heart of Old Style typefaces. At the end of the 17th century, French type engraver Philippe Grandjean cut a new type for the Imprimerie Royale printing works. Compared to Old Style, it had a vertical axis in the rounded letters and the serifs were sharper and flatter. Termed *roman du roi*, it is the forerunner of modern letters. This approach underlined Hawkland's development, and its serifs are much sharper and unbracketed compared to existing transitional types and owe more to those of a modern design.

The development work for Hawkland began in 2012 after Tankard completed his Fenland sans serif typeface and initially explored ideas for a serif based on Fenland. However, because of other commitments, the design of Hawkland was a stop-start process until 2017, when Tankard recommenced work on it towards completion.

The Hawkland family comes in six weights in roman and italic styles. It is suitable within a variety of contexts from editorial design to packaging and brand styling. Tankard also developed Hawkland Fine for larger display use. Hawkland Fine comes in a greater range of weights, and its thinner weights in particular evoke an engraved appearance.

Below. Jeremy Tankard's sketchbook below provides insight into the thought processes and experimentation – even at the initial stages – in establishing the design principles behind a new typeface.

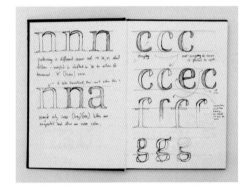

Isolde

ABCDEFGHIJKLMNOPQRSTUVWXYZ
abcdefghijklmnopqrstuvwxyz
1234567890 !@#?:;"*&

Foundry: Omnibus
Designer: Franko Luin
Designer Nationality: Swedish
Date: 1993

The wide letterforms, exaggerated serifs and heavily slanted italics of this Caslon-influenced typeface are well-suited for headline and display use. Designer Franko Luin named the font after the story of Tristan and Isolde, and created its specimen in the form of a fairy tale.

ITC Leawood

ABCDEFGHIJKLMNOPQRSTUVWXYZ
abcdefghijklmnopqrstuvwxyz
1234567890 !@#?:;"*&

Foundry: ITC
Designer: Leslie Usherwood
Designer Nationality: Canadian
Date: 1985

Leslie Usherwood's designs for this characterful serif were completed by the team at Typsettra, his Toronto-based phototypesetting company, following his death in 1983. Its confident strokes, distinct serifs and generous x-height aid legibility when close character spacing is required.

ITC Slimbach

ABCDEFGHIJKLMNOPQRSTUVWXYZ
abcdefghijklmnopqrstuvwxyz
1234567890 !@#?:;"*&

Foundry: ITC
Designer: Robert Slimbach
Designer Nationality: American
Date: 1987

Robert Slimbach designed this serif typeface for ITC on a freelance basis during the mid 1980s. It displays the influence of his training in calligraphy. Slimbach joined Adobe during the year of its release, and went on to be instrumental in the development of the company's digital typefaces.

ITC Zapf International

ABCDEFGHIJKLMNOPQRSTUVWXYZ
abcdefghijklmnopqrstuvwxyz
1234567890 !@#?:;"*&

Foundry: ITC
Designer: Hermann Zapf
Designer Nationality: German
Date: 1976

Zapf International is named after its designer, the leading German typographer Hermann Zapf (see p. 574). He designed the typeface for ITC in 1976 after a ten-year type design hiatus. Various flourishes indicate his calligraphic background, such as the long tail of the 'Q' and the open bowl of the 'g'.

ITC New Baskerville

ABCDEFGHIJKLMNOPQRSTUVWXYZ
abcdefghijklmnopqrstuvwxyz
1234567890 !@#?:;"*&

Foundry: ITC
Designer: John Baskerville /
John Quaranda
Designer Nationality: British /
American
Date: 1762 / 1982

This revival of one of the world's most widely used typefaces was created in 1978 by US type designer John Quaranda and arguably remains one of the most popular of all the Baskerville designs. The original Baskerville was created in the 18th century by English printer, stonecutter, writer and type designer John Baskerville. This classic was then punch-cut by his assistant, John Handy.

When John Baskerville designed this typeface, his ambition was to improve on the letterforms created by his contemporary, the English typefounder William Caslon. Baskerville brought in a more refined, elegant cut to the serifs, increased contrast and introduced thinner stroke weights. He also employed a more consistent design across the characters, which helped to increase legibility and recognition.

John Baskerville was also known as a perfectionist and his experimentation as a printer in all aspects of the printing process caused long delays to his own work. He invested his energies in all aspects of the printing process; from how the paper was made, the ink mixtures, the construction of the printing presses and the type itself. Consequently, although he set up his printing company in 1750, he did not produce his first book until 1757. However, his contribution to the creation of type foundries and printing in England is immeasurable. Although his endeavours were not so well-received at home, his work was greatly admired by his contemporaries in Europe and North America.

In its earliest incarnation, Baskerville was released in roman and italic. ITC New Baskerville comes in four weights with matching italics.

Right/opposite. Thirty-six-page promotional booklet for specifying ITC foundry's ITC New Baskerville, printed 1982.

abcdefghijklmnopqrstuv
ABCDEFGHIJKLMNOP

30

abcdefghijklmnopqr
ABCDEFGHIJKLNP

36

abcdefghijklmn
ABCDEFGHIK

48

abcdefghijkn
ABCDEFGH

60

abcdehikn
ABCDEHI

72

abcdeh
ABCDI

1" on Caps

Above display sizes, 30 pt to 1" are based on cap heights and are not necessarily in direct relation to text heights.

abcdefghijklmnopqrstuvwxyz
ABCDEFGHIJKLMNOPQRSTUVWXYZ
1234567890&1234567890$$¢ƒ£%@
ÇŁØÆŒßçłøæœfi ˘ ˜ ˚
(·:;,.!?·-—""''/#*)[†‡§»«1234567890]aeilmorst

COMPLETE ITC DISPLAY ALPHABET

26
good
reasons
to use
ITC New
Baskerville™
Roman

6

7

Jante Antiqua

ABCDEFGHIJKLMNOPQRSTUVWXYZ
abcdefghijklmnopqrstuvwxyz
1234567890 !@#?:;"*&

Foundry: ITC
Designer: Poul Søgren
Designer Nationality: Danish
Date: 1992

Danish type and graphic designer Poul Søgren studied in Copenhagen before going to Paris to study under French type designer José Mendoza y Almeida at the Imprimerie Nationale. Søgren designed Jante Antiqua with newspaper usage in mind, and its ample x-height makes it ideal for body text.

Kalix

ABCDEFGHIJKLMNOPQRSTUVWXYZ
abcdefghijklmnopqrstuvwxyz
1234567890 !@#?:;"*&

Foundry: Linotype
Designer: Franko Luin
Designer Nationality: Swedish
Date: 1994

Designer Franko Luin named Kalix after a town in northern Sweden. He suggested that it be used 'mainly for books and magazines'. The typeface is a transitional serif, with many reference points. It comes in three weights – Roman, Semi Bold and Bold – with italics and small caps.

Kis

ABCDEFGHIJKLMNOPQRSTUVWXYZ
abcdefghijklmnopqrstuvwxyz
1234567890 !@#?:;"*&

Foundry: Bitstream
Designer: Miklós Tótfalusi Kis
Designer Nationality: Hungarian
Date: 1685 / 1985

Kis is Bitstream's digital revival of Miklós Tótfalusi Kis's Old Style serif Janson. Kis was a Hungarian printer working in Amsterdam during the late 17th century and was revealed as the originator of the font, rather than the Dutch punch-cutter Anton Janson, thanks to the work of type scholars in 1954.

Kis Classico

ABCDEFGHIJKLMNOPQRSTUVWXYZ
abcdefghijklmnopqrstuvwxyz
1234567890 !@#?:;"*&

Foundry: Omnibus
Designer: Franko Luin
Designer Nationality: Swedish
Date: 1993

Kis Classico is the work of Swedish type designer Franko Luin at his own studio, Omnibus, and comes in five weights. The typeface is named after a Hungarian monk called Miklós Kis, who travelled to Amsterdam towards the end of the 17th century to discover the art of printing.

Lapidary 333

ABCDEFGHIJKLMNOPQRSTUVWXYZ
abcdefghijklmnopqrstuvwxyz
1234567890 !@#?:;"*&

Foundry: Bitstream
Designer: Eric Gill
Designer Nationality: British
Date: 1929–32 / c. 1980s

Lapidary 333 is Bitstream's release of Eric Gill's Perpetua and comes in five styles. In 1925, Monotype's Stanley Morison commissioned Gill to make a roman for use in books; it was released commercially in 1932. Its small, angled serifs were inspired by Gill's background in stone carving.

Laurentian

ABCDEFGHIJKLMNOPQRSTUVWXYZ
abcdefghijklmnopqrstuvwxyz
1234567890 !@#?:;"*&

Foundry: Monotype
Designer: Rod McDonald
Designer Nationality: Canadian
Date: 2001

Canadian designer Rod McDonald created Laurentian as a commission for *Maclean's* magazine, which wanted a new masthead and a neutral, custom type family. Usage in tight columns meant the face needed to be slightly narrow, while economical printing meant contrast had to be modest.

Lector FSL

ABCDEFGHIJKLMNOPQRSTUVWXYZ
abcdefghijklmnopqrstuvwxyz
1234567890 !@#?:;"*&

Foundry: Forgotten Shapes
Designer: Gert Wunderlich / Reymund Schröder
Designer Nationality: German
Date: 1963 / 2018

Lector FSL is a revision and extension of Lector, a font initially designed by Gert Wunderlich for the Typoart foundry in the 1960s. The typeface is a collaboration between Wunderlich and his former student Reymund Schröder, and retains the character of a sharp, transitional serif.

Levato

ABCDEFGHIJKLMNOPQRSTUVWXYZ
abcdefghijklmnopqrstuvwxyz
1234567890 !@#?:;"*&

Foundry: Monotype
Designer: Felix Bonge
Designer Nationality: German
Date: 2011

Levato is German designer Felix Bonge's debut font and grew out of his studies at Hamburg University of Applied Sciences, taking inspiration from Renaissance Antiqua typefaces. It comes in five weights with a cursive italic, many ligatures and swatch options for some letters.

Life

ABCDEFGHIJKLMNOPQRSTUVWXYZ
abcdefghijklmnopqrstuvwxyz
1234567890 !@#?:;"*&

Foundry: Ludwig & Mayer
Designer: Wilhelm Bilz /
Francesco Simoncini
Designer Nationality: German /
Italian
Date: 1965

Life's co-designer Francesco Simoncini grew up with type as his father Vincenzo ran a repair shop for typesetting machines. After World War II, they worked on matrices for Linotype and Intertype systems. Life is a newsprint font mainly inspired by Times, which mixes elements of many serif forms.

Linotype Centennial

ABCDEFGHIJKLMNOPQRSTUVWXYZ
abcdefghijklmnopqrstuvwxyz
1234567890 !@#?:;"*&

Foundry: Linotype
Designer: Adrian Frutiger
Designer Nationality: Swiss
Date: 1986

Adrian Frutiger (see p. 290) created Centennial to honour Linotype's 100th anniversary. It was inspired by Linn Boyd Benton and Morris Fuller Benton's Century, released by American Type Founders in the late 19th century. Frutiger deviated considerably from Century, enhancing it for a modern audience.

Linotype Really

ABCDEFGHIJKLMNOPQRSTUVWXYZ
abcdefghijklmnopqrstuvwxyz
1234567890 !@#?:;"*&

Foundry: Linotype
Designer: Gary Munch
Designer Nationality: American
Date: 1999

Really, by American designer Gary Munch, is available in six weights with italics and small caps. It functions well as a clean, legible text face, blending details from Caslon, Baskerville and Bodoni. Munch later updated it as Really No. 2 with more weights and language support.

Marion

ABCDEFGHIJKLMNOPQRSTUVWXYZ
abcdefghijklmnopqrstuvwxyz
1234567890 !@#?:;"*&

Foundry: Typodermic
Designer: Ray Larabie
Designer Nationality: Canadian
Date: 2006

Ray Larabie is a Canadian font designer who lives in Nagoya, Japan. He describes his Marion typeface family as an 'unambiguous transitional serif typeface with an 18th-century flair'. It comes in regular and bold with italics, ligatures and the occasional flamboyant swash option.

Maxime

ABCDEFGHIJKLMNOPQRSTUVWXYZ
abcdefghijklmnopqrstuvwxyz
1234567890 !@#?:;"*&

Foundry: Monotype
Designer: Éric de Berranger
Designer Nationality: French
Date: 1999

French designer Éric de Berranger has created fonts for Monotype, ITC, Agfa, Linotype, T-26 and 2Rebels. His Maxime design is a highly legible serif available in regular and bold with italics. The family also contains Maxime Ornaments, which consists of twenty-six custom typographic ornaments.

Mentor

ABCDEFGHIJKLMNOPQRSTUVWXYZ
abcdefghijklmnopqrstuvwxyz
1234567890 !@#?:;"*&

Foundry: Monotype
Designer: Michael Harvey / Andy Benedek
Designer Nationality: British
Date: 2004

According to Michael Harvey, three designers influenced the development of his Mentor serif: Eric Gill, Hermann Zapf (see p. 574) and Harvey's former boss, Reynolds Stone. Harvey and Andy Benedek designed type for Monotype before starting their own foundry, Fine Fonts, in 2000.

Monotype Baskerville

ABCDEFGHIJKLMNOPQRSTUVWXYZ
abcdefghijklmnopqrstuvwxyz
1234567890 !@#?:;"*&

Foundry: Monotype
Designer: John Baskerville / Monotype Studio
Designer Nationality: British
Date: 1754 / 1923

The Monotype Baskerville font family is a transitional serif created by the Monotype Studio in 1923, based on the original by John Baskerville in the mid 18th century. It is a popular choice for text in books and magazines, having a higher contrast and sharper serifs than Caslon.

Monotype Janson

ABCDEFGHIJKLMNOPQRSTUVWXYZ
abcdefghijklmnopqrstuvwxyz
1234567890 !@#?:;"*&

Foundry: Monotype
Designer: Miklós Tótfalusi Kis / Robin Nicholas / Patricia Saunders
Designer Nationality: Hungarian / British / British
Date: 1685 / c. 1930s

Monotype's cut of Miklós Tótfalusi Kis's Old Style serif Janson comes in regular and bold, with italics. Its legibility and even colour make it perfect for text use in publications. An earlier Monotype version created in the 1930s was slightly less condensed and named Ehrhardt, after the foundry in Leipzig.

Monotype Sabon

ABCDEFGHIJKLMNOPQRSTUVWXYZ
abcdefghijklmnopqrstuvwxyz
1234567890 !@#?:;"'*&

Foundry: Monotype
Designer: Jan Tschichold
Designer Nationality: German
Date: 1967

German graphic designer, type designer and typographer Jan Tschichold was an advocate of modernist design and inspired by the principles of the Bauhaus. Sabon came about from a joint commission in the early 1960s by three German foundries – Monotype, Linotype and Stempel – to create a unifying design that would provide consistency in printing across the metal type technology of the day, either through mechanical composition or set by hand.

Released in 1967, the design of Sabon is loosely based on a 14-point Garamond Roman sample sheet printed in 1592 by Konrad Berner, a German printer based in Frankfurt. Berner married the widow of Jaques Sabon, a French typefounder, who brought some Garamond matrices to Frankfurt. The story is the inspiration behind Sabon's name as well as its appearance.

Although inspired by Old Style principles to letterforms, there is a reduced level of calligraphic construction and the characters are more balanced with rounded forms, resulting in a design with a moderate contrast in its stroke weights. This aids printing and reading in poor conditions. Another innovative feature, one of many in the design, was that the differing weights of roman, italic and bold would occupy the same width, thus reducing the time required to do calculations for working out text extents. In addition, the typeface was fractionally narrower, meaning more characters could be set on line, reducing paper and ink costs.

Sabon is a truly classic typeface that is flexible, legible and resilient with an elegant presentation, and it works as well for editorial tasks as for display settings.

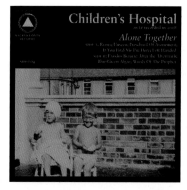

Left. To achieve differentiation for their record releases, which are set entirely with Sabon (bold, italic and regular), Sacred Bones Records use a template system, employing varying colour and illustration styles. The independent record label is based in Brooklyn, New York.

Mrs Eaves

ABCDEFGHIJKLMNOPQRSTUVWXYZ
abcdefghijklmnopqrstuvwxyz
1234567890 !@#?:;"*&

Foundry: Emigre
Designer: Zuzana Licko
Designer Nationality: Slovakian
Date: 1996

Mrs Eaves is a revival of Baskerville by Zuzana Licko, the co-founder of the type foundry Emigre (see p. 106). In the best traditions of transitional serif typeface design, it appears traditional and elegant but offers a contemporary take on the past.

The softer appearance and yet heavier weight of Mrs Eaves when compared to other transitional designs is intentional. It reflects Licko's desire to give the impression it has been formed using lead type so that texts set on paper appear as if printed with letterpress. This distinguishes it from types with the crispness typical of modern reproduction.

Mrs Eaves is named after Sarah Eaves, who was housekeeper and then mistress to the 18th-century English printer and type designer John Baskerville. The pair married after her estranged husband died. Mrs Eaves's character and charm are further enhanced by its notable ligatures. There are 213 ligatures in all, which range from the standard to the ornate, with a number of elegant swash designs featured. As well as the standard ligatures, Mrs Eaves also contains the 18th-century variations of 'ct' and 'st'.

In 2009, several variations were launched. Mrs Eaves XL features a larger x-height that makes it more suitable for body text. Mr Eaves and Mr Eaves XL are sans serif humanist variants that echo the designs of Gill Sans and Johnston.

Below. This ever-popular design is not only one of Emigre's most popular typefaces but is also one of the best-selling serif types from the last two decades, thanks to its elegant aesthetic and its flexibility, being ideal for both titling and text usages.

FABLE LIII. **The Trumpeter.**
— [SET IN MRS EAVES XL NARROW] —

A Trumpeter in a certain army happened to be taken prisoner.
HE WAS ORDERED *immediately* TO EXECUTION
but pleaded **excuse** for
HIMSELF,
that it was *unjust*
a person should suffer *death*, who, far from an intention
of mischief, *did not even wear* an offensive weapon.
So much the rather,
replied one of the enemy
SHALT THOU DIE;
since without any design of *fighting thyself*,
THOU EXCITEST OTHERS TO THE
bloody business:
for he that is the *abettor* of a
BAD ACTION
IS AT LEAST EQUALLY WITH HIM THAT
commit it.

FABLE LII. **The Mock-bird.**
— [SET IN MRS EAVES XL] —

There is a certain bird
in the West-Indies,
WHICH HAS THE *faculty* OF
MIMICKING THE NOTES
of *every* other songster,
without being able himself to add *any* original strains to the concert.
As one of these Mock-birds was displaying
HIS TALENTS *of* RIDICULE
among the branches of a venerable wood:
'Tis very well,
SAID A LITTLE WARBLER,
speaking in the name of all the rest.
we grant you that our music
is *not* without its faults:
but why will you not favour us
with a strain of
YOUR OWN?

ed **excuse**
[SEI
was unj
leath, who, far from an
en wear an offensive we
the rath

Monticello

ABCDEFGHIJKLMNOPQRSTUVWXYZ
abcdefghijklmnopqrstuvwxyz
1234567890 !@#?:;"*&

Foundry: Linotype
Designer: Chauncey H. Griffith / Matthew Carter
Designer Nationality: American / British
Date: 1946 / 2002

Chauncey H. Griffith based Monticello on James Ronaldsons' Roman No. 1 (c. 1796) and American Type Founders' Oxford (1892). He created it as a historically apt face for Princeton University Press' publication of *The Papers of Thomas Jefferson*. Matthew Carter (see p. 616) refined the family for Linotype in 2002.

New Aster

ABCDEFGHIJKLMNOPQRSTUVWXYZ
abcdefghijklmnopqrstuvwxyz
1234567890 !@#?:;"*&

Foundry: Linotype
Designer: Francesco Simoncini / Linotype Design Studio
Designer Nationality: Italian
Date: 1958

Aster was first designed in 1958 by Italian designer Francesco Simoncini for newspaper and book text; thus it has a large x-height, fine serifs and short ascenders and descenders. New Aster, available in four weights with italics, was the result of improvements made by Linotype.

News Plantin

ABCDEFGHIJKLMNOPQRSTUVWXYZ
abcdefghijklmnopqrstuvwxyz
1234567890 !@#?:;"*&

Foundry: Monotype
Designer: Frank Hinman Pierpont
Designer Nationality: American
Date: 1979

Designed by Monotype for use by the British newspaper *The Observer*, News Plantin is slightly more condensed, and therefore efficient, than the standard Plantin typeface. Plantin was named after an Antwerp printer, and created by Frank Hinman Pierpont based on fonts from the 16th century.

Nicolas Cochin

ABCDEFGHIJKLMNOPQRSTUVWXYZ
abcdefghijklmnopqrstuvwxyz
1234567890 !@#?:;"*&

Foundry: Deberny & Peignot
Designer: Charles Malin / Georges Peignot
Designer Nationality: French
Date: 1912

Named after the 18th-century French artist, writer and critic Charles-Nicolas Cochin, whose engraved lettering provided inspiration to Georges Peignot, this typeface cut by Charles Malin for Deberny & Peignot in 1912 is a distinct serif with wide capitals and very tall, slender ascenders.

Octavian

ABCDEFGHIJKLMNOPQRSTUVWXYZ
abcdefghijklmnopqrstuvwxyz
1234567890 !@#?:;"*&

Foundry: Monotype
Designer: Will Carter /
David Kindersley
Designer Nationality: British
Date: 1961

Will Carter and David Kindersley designed Octavian for Monotype in 1961. They were inspired by the letterforms of classical inscriptions cut in stone; however, they reduced the width of letters and added weight to make it more economical in print. The typeface is available in one weight with an italic.

Old Style 7

ABCDEFGHIJKLMNOPQRSTUVWXYZ
abcdefghijklmnopqrstuvwxyz
1234567890 !@#?:;"*&

Foundry: Miller & Richard
Designer: Alexander Phemister
Designer Nationality: Scottish
Date: 1860

Alexander Phemister cut Old Style 7 at the Scottish foundry Miller & Richard. It was one of the first of the much-imitated 'modernized old face' types, which updated the forms of Caslon for the needs of the mid-19th-century printing industry, removing details considered to be old-fashioned.

Olympian

ABCDEFGHIJKLMNOPQRSTUVWXYZ
abcdefghijklmnopqrstuvwxyz
1234567890 !@#?:;"*&

Foundry: Linotype
Designer: Matthew Carter
Designer Nationality: British
Date: 1970

British typographer Matthew Carter (see p. 616) designed Olympian for economical newspaper text use in 1970. It has a large x-height and is suited to being set in narrow columns. Available in roman and bold with italics, Olympian is believed to be the first copyrighted typeface in the United States.

Omnibus

ABCDEFGHIJKLMNOPQRSTUVWXYZ
abcdefghijklmnopqrstuvwxyz
1234567890 !@#?:;"*&

Foundry: Omnibus
Designer: Franko Luin
Designer Nationality: Swedish
Date: 1993

Franko Luin was inspired by Baskerville when designing Omnibus, which shares its name with his type foundry, but decided to aim for a darker colour. A legible serif text face, it is available in roman, semibold and bold, all with italics, plus a single weight of small capitals.

Oranda

ABCDEFGHIJKLMNOPQRSTUVWXYZ
abcdefghijklmnopqrstuvwxyz
1234567890 !@#?:;"*&

Foundry: Bitstream
Designer: Gerard Unger
Designer Nationality: Dutch
Date: 1992

Dutch printer manufacturer Océ commissioned Dutch typographer Gerard Unger to design Oranda as a custom project in 1986. The typeface is named after the Japanese word for 'Holland'. Unger said he 'had a look at typewriter fonts and came up with a subtler and more modern variant'.

Paperback

ABCDEFGHIJKLMNOPQRSTUVWXYZ
abcdefghijklmnopqrstuvwxyz
1234567890 !@#?:;"*&

Foundry: House Industries
Designer: John Downer
Designer Nationality: American
Date: 2005

Paperback is a transitional font family intended for both headline and text purposes. Unlike most serif designs, which develop characters for use at a single scale, Paperback has features that are designed to shift with its size, enabling the letterforms to adapt to their context.

Parkinson Electra

ABCDEFGHIJKLMNOPQRSTUVWXYZ
abcdefghijklmnopqrstuvwxyz
1234567890 !@#?:;"*&

Foundry: Linotype
Designer: William A. Dwiggins / Jim Parkinson
Designer Nationality: American
Date: c. 1930s / 2010

In 2010, Jim Parkinson undertook a remodelling and digitization of the 1930s serif text face Electra to bring it into the modern age. Parkinson, who reworked Electra before for the *San Francisco Chronicle* in the 1990s, looked to William A. Dwiggins's original drafts for inspiration.

Perrywood

ABCDEFGHIJKLMNOPQRSTUVWXYZ
abcdefghijklmnopqrstuvwxyz
1234567890 !@#?:;"*&

Foundry: Monotype
Designer: Johannes Birkenbach
Designer Nationality: German
Date: 1993

German designer Johannes Birkenbach, who worked at Monotype in the UK from 1988 to 1993, took inspiration from Bembo and Plantin when designing Perrywood, a legible text face with an even colour. A family of thirty fonts, Perrywood includes three versions in five weights with italics.

Perpetua

ABCDEFGHIJKLMNOPQRSTUVWXYZ
abcdefghijklmnopqrstuvwxyz
1234567890 !@#?:;"*&

Foundry: Monotype
Designer: Eric Gill
Designer Nationality: British
Date: 1929–32

This serif classic by English sculptor and type designer Eric Gill is as popular today as it was upon release. Monotype's Stanley Morison commissioned Gill in 1925, but the design process was a struggle and not without setbacks. Not only did Morison have to contend with his management's dislike for his new ideas and proposals, he also had to deal with Gill's dislike for the mechanical arts. Yet Gill had recently become involved in making books, and fonts were an essential part of that process, so he agreed to take on the project. He based Perpetua on old engravings, and using his sculpting skills patterned it after epigraphic, rather than calligraphic, letters.

However, despite progressing with the serif design, Gill was reassigned to a more pressing matter, the design of Gill Sans, which put Perpetua on hold. Perpetua was first set in a limited edition of a new edition of *The Passion of Perpetua and Felicity* (*c*. 203) in 1929. When finally ready for release in 1930, further issues gathered apace. Perpetua was to be released with an accompanying italic called Felicity, a sloped roman, rather than a cursive italic. Despite Morison favouring the sloped approach, the Monotype management disliked the italic intensely, and with no italic, there was no release. So Gill returned to the drawing board and the completed family was finally launched in 1932. Perpetua is the culmination of a lengthy, drawn-out process, but it is a timeless design that has become Gill's most popular and enduring typeface.

Below. Designed by John Overton, then production manager at Penguin Books, these original Penguin Classic covers employ Eric Gill's Perpetua for titling. The series was redesigned after seven titles by Jan Tschichold in 1947.

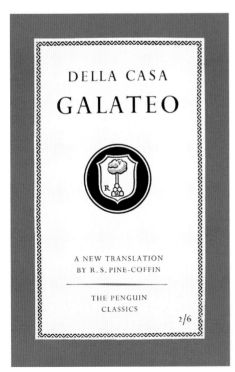

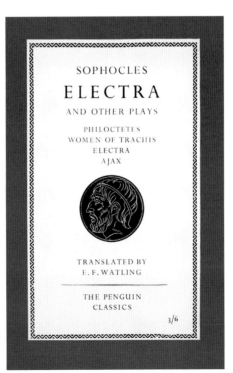

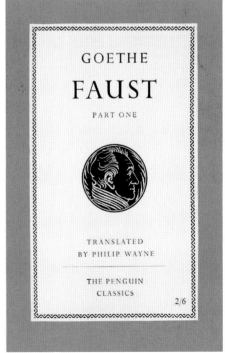

Photina

ABCDEFGHIJKLMNOPQRSTUVWXYZ
abcdefghijklmnopqrstuvwxyz
1234567890 !@#?:;"*&

Foundry: Monotype
Designer: José Mendoza y Almeida
Designer Nationality: French
Date: 1971

Photina was only the third serif produced by Monotype specifically for phototypesetting systems. Its sharp serifs and robust frame indicate the new forms made possible by phototypesetting technology. The face's high typographic quality made it popular for magazine and book text.

Rabenau

ABCDEFGHIJKLMNOPQRSTUVWXYZ
abcdefghijklmnopqrstuvwxyz
1234567890 !@#?:;"*&

Foundry: Linotype
Designer: Alex Bertram / Andreas Frohloff
Designer Nationality: German
Date: 2011

Rabenau is the result of more than a decade of research and experimentation by its co-creators, the German type designers Alex Bertram and Andreas Frohloff. The typeface mixes high-contrast strokes with smoothly curved serifs in each of its sixteen weights.

Really No. 2

ABCDEFGHIJKLMNOPQRSTUVWXYZ
abcdefghijklmnopqrstuvwxyz
1234567890 !@#?:;"*&

Foundry: Linotype
Designer: Gary Munch
Designer Nationality: American
Date: 1999 / 2008

Really No. 2 is an update of the Really serif Gary Munch designed for Linotype in 1999. It offers an expanded seven weights alongside extended language capabilities. Much like the initial design, Really No. 2 balances impact in the bold weights with clarity in the lighter versions.

Res Publica

ABCDEFGHIJKLMNOPQRSTUVWXYZ
abcdefghijklmnopqrstuvwxyz
1234567890 !@#?:;"*&

Foundry: Linotype
Designer: Franko Luin
Designer Nationality: Swedish
Date: 1992

Res Publica is a serif designed in the transitional style. Its name means 'public matters' in Latin, from which is also derived the word 'republic'. The font's title is an indication of its purpose: to provide clarity in text-heavy documents, such as official reports, magazines and school books.

Romana

ABCDEFGHIJKLMNOPQRSTUVWXYZ
abcdefghijklmnopqrstuvwxyz
1234567890 !@#?:;”*&

Foundry: Bitstream
Designer: Theophile Beaudoire /
Gustav F. Schroeder
Designer Nationality: French /
German
Date: 1892 / c. 1990s

Romana is Bitstream's digitization of a popular 19th-century transitional serif face of the same name. The narrow and nimble frame of the lighter weights makes Romana legible at smaller sizes, while its compact design in the heavier styles increases its impact at display sizes.

Sabon eText

ABCDEFGHIJKLMNOPQRSTUVWXYZ
abcdefghijklmnopqrstuvwxyz
1234567890 !@#?:;”*&

Foundry: Linotype
Designer: Jan Tschichold /
Linotype Design Studio
Designer Nationality: German
Date: 1967 / 2013

Designed specifically for the screens of e-readers, mobile phones and computers, Sabon eText is a conversion of Jan Tschichold's original design of 1967. Sabon eText contains several adjustments, to counters, line thickness and x-height, to optimize the face for smaller sizes.

Sabon Next

ABCDEFGHIJKLMNOPQRSTUVWXYZ
abcdefghijklmnopqrstuvwxyz
1234567890 !@#?:;”*&

Foundry: Linotype
Designer: Jan Tschichold /
Jean François Porchez
Designer Nationality: German /
French
Date: 1967 / 2002

Sabon Next is Jean François Porchez's revival of Jan Tschichold's Sabon, itself based on a Claude Garamond typeface. Working from both Tschichold's design and Garamond's original specimens, Porchez designed four extra weights and a series of alternate characters and ornaments.

Selune

ABCDEFGHIJKLMNOPQRSTUVWXYZ
abcdefghijklmnopqrstuvwxyz
1234567890 !@#?:;”*&

Foundry: Monotype
Designer: Jean Lochu
Designer Nationality: French
Date: 1999

Selune is a transitional serif by French designer Jean Lochu of Studio Hollenstein in Paris. Lochu, whose early passion for calligraphy reveals itself in the refined strokes and bowls, designed the font in four weights, from Pale to Sombre, alongside a set of typographic accessories.

Spectrum MT

ABCDEFGHIJKLMNOPQRSTUVWXYZ
abcdefghijklmnopqrstuvwxyz
1234567890 !@#?:;"*&

Foundry: Enschedé Foundry / Monotype
Designer: Jan Van Krimpen / Monotype Studio
Designer Nationality: Dutch / British
Date: 1952–1955

Dutch typographer, book designer and type designer Jan van Krimpen created his Spectrum typeface in the early 1950s for a Bible project for the Spectrum publishing house in Utrech while he was employed by the Koninklijke Joh. Enschedé type foundry and printer in Haarlem. However, the book project was cancelled.

Fortunately, Van Krimpen had a relationship with Monotype in England, which released many of his designs outside the Netherlands. The company was so enamoured by the design's refinement, elegance and balance, it acquired the typeface, completing it for release in 1955. The process of getting it published was a fractious one, with many letters passing between Van Krimpen and Monotype's Stanley Morison over disagreements in the design process. Spectrum's enlarged x-height and calligraphic nature make for a precise and incisive tone. It possesses some similar forms to Eric Gill's Perpetua: both share distinctive Old Style figures and numerals, and each is very legible across all ranges of size.

Van Krimpen was also a leading book designer with an international reputation, designing titles in the Netherlands and for the Limited Editions Club of New York. Spectrum's crisp and precise nature made it ideal as a book typeface although it was rarely used in contemporary publishing.

Swift

ABCDEFGHIJKLMNOPQRSTUVWXYZ
abcdefghijklmnopqrstuvwxyz
1234567890 !@#?:;"*&

Foundry: Linotype
Designer: Gerard Unger
Designer Nationality: Dutch
Date: 1984–89

Dutch typeface designer and professor of typography Gerard Unger developed Swift between 1984 and 1989. His design brief was to create a modern digital type for newspapers that could maintain legibility and consistency on ever higher speed printing presses yet on low-quality paper.

Swift's appearance with its sturdy stems, low-contrast strokes, enlarged serifs, tall x-height and open counters, all contribute towards increasing legibility for what has become a contemporary classic. Ever popular among graphic designers, its versatility has meant its usage has stretched far beyond that of the newspaper industry: it is often seen employed in corporate identities, editorial and publishing applications.

Right. *Typografische Monatsblätter* (*Swiss Typographic Monthly Magazine*) No. 4 created in 1987 by Swiss type designer and lecturer Max Caflisch.

Tempera Biblio

ABCDEFGHIJKLMNOPQRSTUVWXYZ
abcdefghijklmnopqrstuvwxyz
1234567890 !@#?:;"*ɞ

Tempera Biblio is a transitional book face designed for continuous text. The font family features calligraphic features and low contrast, and comprises three weights, each maintaining a standard width, which allows the text to facilitate a variety of styles without altering its length.

Foundry: Typotheque
Designer: Nikola Djurek
Designer Nationality: Croatian
Date: 2006

Times Eighteen

ABCDEFGHIJKLMNOPQRSTUVWXYZ
abcdefghijklmnopqrstuvwxyz
1234567890 !@#?:;"*&

Times Eighteen is a transitional serif, designed specifically for headline type. Unlike the Times New Roman variation, this design is ideally suited to sizes of 18 point and above and features slightly condensed letterforms and finer hairline strokes for a bolder character.

Foundry: Linotype
Designer: Stanley Morison / Victor Lardent / Walter Tracy
Designer Nationality: British
Date: 1931 / 1972

Times Europa

ABCDEFGHIJKLMNOPQRSTUVWXYZ
abcdefghijklmnopqrstuvwxyz
1234567890 !@#?:;"*&

Walter Tracy's Times Europa is a sweeping update of Stanley Morison's Times New Roman (1931). The muscular forms and wide counters of Tracy's design preserve legibility while adapting to the faster printing presses and lower-quality paper of the 1970s newspaper industry.

Foundry: Linotype
Designer: Stanley Morison / Victor Lardent / Walter Tracy
Designer Nationality: British
Date: 1931 / 1972

Times Europa Office

ABCDEFGHIJKLMNOPQRSTUVWXYZ
abcdefghijklmnopqrstuvwxyz
1234567890 !@#?:;"*&

Times Europa Office is a revision of Times Europa to optimize Walter Tracy's design for office use. Akira Kobayashi, Linotype's type director, removed several irregularities, which were initially included to smooth the text in print, and redrew them to suit the clarity of digital displays.

Foundry: Linotype
Designer: Stanley Morison / Victor Lardent / Walter Tracy / Akira Kobayashi
Designer Nationality: British / Japanese
Date: 1931 / 1972 / 2006

Times New Roman

ABCDEFGHIJKLMNOPQRSTUVWXYZ
abcdefghijklmnopqrstuvwxyz
1234567890 !@#?:;'"*&

Foundry: Monotype
Designer: Stanley Morison / Victor Lardent
Designer Nationality: British
Date: 1931

Times New Roman was created in 1931 by Monotype typographic consultant Stanley Morison and *The Times* newspaper lettering artist Victor Lardent. Their historic font was first used by the British newspaper on 3 October 1932, and was made available to purchase in 1933.

By 1929, Morison was typographic advisor not only to Monotype but also to *The Times*. In 1931, he criticized the newspaper for the poor quality of its printing, and so the publication commissioned him to create a typeface to replace the existing outdated 19th-century face. The new typeface needed to be clearer, larger and heavier on the page without taking up more space.

Morison and Lardent's design starting point was another of Monotype's existing serifs, Plantin, but Perpetua and Baskerville were also considered. For more than two years, Morison as art director and Lardent as designer laboured to achieve their goal. The new typeface was incredibly successful and was used for forty years.

Although the newspaper no longer uses this particular version of Times New Roman, with many updates and revisions having been created over the years due to changes in production techniques, digital technologies and format changes, the typeface's popularity has endured. It is still widely used in book and general printing while also being Monotype's biggest selling metal type of all time.

Today, Times New Roman is available on all computer operating systems as standard. However, it is still available to purchase with a wider range of styles and optical sizes offered for differing and more precise print applications.

Right. Monotype's Stanley Morison and Victor Lardent present their brand new Times New Roman typeface in the 3rd October, 1932 edition of *The Times*.

Right. Herb Lubalin's designs as art director for Ralph Ginzburg's *Fact* journal in the 1960s employed Times New Roman as the main text face throughout, creating dramatic typographic statements for each front cover. The *Fact* logo was drawn-up by Tom Carnase and was created from modifications to Caslon 540.

fact:
JANUARY/FEBRUARY 1964   VOLUME ONE, ISSUE ONE · $1.25

Bertrand Russell considers *Time* magazine to be "scurrilous and utterly shameless in its willingness to distort." **Ralph Ingersoll:** "In ethics, integrity, and responsibility, *Time* is a monumental failure." **Irwin Shaw:** *Time* is "nastier than any other magazine of the day." **Sloan Wilson:** "Any enemy of *Time* is a friend of mine." **Igor Stravinsky:** "Every music column I have read in *Time* has been distorted and inaccurate." **Tallulah Bankhead:** "Dirt is too clean a word for *Time*." **Mary McCarthy:** "*Time*'s falsifications are numerous." **Dwight Macdonald:** "The degree of credence one gives to *Time* is inverse to one's degree of knowledge of the situation being reported on." **David Merrick:** "There is not a single word of truth in *Time*." **P.G. Wodehouse:** "*Time* is about the most inaccurate magazine in existence." **Rockwell Kent:** *Time* "is inclined to value smartness above truth." **Eugene Burdick:** *Time* employs "dishonest tactics." **Conrad Aiken:** "*Time* slants its news." **Howard Fast:** *Time* provides "distortions and inaccuracies by the bushel." **James Gould Cozzens:** "My knowledge of inaccuracies in *Time* is first-hand." **Walter Winchell:** "*Time*'s inaccuracies are a staple of my column." **John Osborne:** "*Time* is a vicious, dehumanizing institution." **Eric Bentley:** "More pervasive than *Time*'s outright errors is its misuse of truth." **Vincent Price:** "Fortunately, most people read *Time* for laughs and not for facts." **H. Allen Smith:** "*Time*'s inaccuracies are as numerous as the sands of the Sahara." **Taylor Caldwell:** "I could write a whole book about *Time* inaccuracies." **Sen. John McClellan:** "*Time* is prejudiced and unfair."

fact:
VOLUME ONE, ISSUE FIVE $1.25

1,189 Psychiatrists Say Goldwater Is Psychologically Unfit To Be President!

fact:
VOLUME ONE, ISSUE FOUR $1.25

"Bobby Kennedy is the most vicious, evil _ _ _ _ in American politics today," says lawyer Melvin Belli.

fact:
VOLUME ONE, ISSUE THREE $1.25

American Cars Are Death Traps
This issue reveals which car makes are the most dangerous of all

Times Ten

ABCDEFGHIJKLMNOPQRSTUVWXYZ
abcdefghijklmnopqrstuvwxyz
1234567890 !@#?:;"*&

Foundry: Linotype
Designer: Stanley Morison
Designer Nationality: British
Date: 1931

Times Ten is a transitional serif and a member of the Times font family, which Stanley Morison designed explicitly for typography of twelve point and below. To retain character and legibility at such sizes, Times Ten features a wider build and additional muscle in the strokes.

Transitional 511

ABCDEFGHIJKLMNOPQRSTUVWXYZ
abcdefghijklmnopqrstuvwxyz
1234567890 !@#?:;"*&

Foundry: Bitstream
Designer: William A. Dwiggins
Designer Nationality: American
Date: 1938 / c. 1980s

Transitional 511 is Bitstream's digitization of William A. Dwiggins's transitional serif Caledonia from the 1930s. While most of the details were faithfully translated, such as the contrast of the joints and the calligraphic cross strokes, Transitional 511 has distinctly shorter descenders.

Transitional 521

ABCDEFGHIJKLMNOPQRSTUVWXYZ
abcdefghijklmnopqrstuvwxyz
1234567890 !@#?:;"*&

Foundry: Bitstream
Designer: William A. Dwiggins
Designer Nationality: American
Date: 1935 / c. 1980s

Transitional 521 is Bitstream's digitized version of William A. Dwiggins's 1930s serif, Electra, which became a standard book face. Taking its cue from Dwiggins's original metal design, Transitional 521 has distinctly sharp characters, as seen in the right-angled brackets and keen terminals.

Transitional 551

ABCDEFGHIJKLMNOPQRSTUVWXYZ
abcdefghijklmnopqrstuvwxyz
1234567890 !@#?:;"*&

Foundry: Bitstream
Designer: Rudolf Ruzicka
Designer Nationality: Czech
Date: 1939 / c. 1980s

Transitional 551 is Bitstream's digital translation of the Fairfield serif by Czech-born US illustrator and designer Rudolf Ruzicka. The significance of this font, designed for book text, lies in its unique design, with each letterform, from stem to serif, designed separately to provide the utmost legibility.

Vega

ABCDEFGHIJKLMNOPQRSTUVWXYZ
abcdefghijklmnopqrstuvwxyz
1234567890 !@#?:;"*&

Foundry: Omnibus
Designer: Franko Luin
Designer Nationality: Swedish
Date: 1994

Vega takes its name from several sources, which vary from a constellation, to a mathematician, to a research ship. Vega finds its shape in typefaces from the 16th and 17th centuries but includes its own unique details, seen in the blunt serifs of the 's'. It is ideal not only for print but also for web usage.

Winthorpe

ABCDEFGHIJKLMNOPQRSTUVWXYZ
abcdefghijklmnopqrstuvwxyz
1234567890 !@#?:;"*&

Foundry: Typodermic
Designer: Ray Larabie
Designer Nationality: Canadian
Date: 2007

Ray Larabie's Winthorpe is a transitional serif designed to cover the breadth of styles required in 21st-century typesetting. The Winthorpe font family includes small caps, Old Style and lining numerals, ordinals, fractions, inferiors and superiors, in each of its three weights.

Zapf Calligraphic 801

ABCDEFGHIJKLMNOPQRSTUVWXYZ
abcdefghijklmnopqrstuvwxyz
1234567890 !@#?:;"*&

Foundry: Bitstream
Designer: Hermann Zapf
Designer Nationality: German
Date: 1950 / c. 1980s

Zapf Calligraphic 801 is Bistream's digitization of the Palatino family from the 1950s by Hermann Zapf (see p. 574). As with the original design, produced for the Stempel foundry in Germany, Bitstream's version preserves the calligraphic styling of the letterforms which defines the lowercase of the font.

Zapf Elliptical 711

ABCDEFGHIJKLMNOPQRSTUVWXYZ
abcdefghijklmnopqrstuvwxyz
1234567890 !@#?:;"*&

Foundry: Bitstream
Designer: Hermann Zapf
Designer Nationality: German
Date: 1952 / c. 1980s

This font is Bitstream's version of Melior, a modern font family initially designed in 1952 for newsprint by Hermann Zapf (see p. 574). Zapf Elliptical 711 takes both its name and character from the superellipse, a squared circle that was central to Zapf's original design.

EFGHIJK
LMNOP
QRSTUV
WXYZ

Now see the movie:

Helvetica

Sans Serif

Opposite. Detail from the film poster for *Helvetica*, directed by US filmmaker Gary Hustwit, to celebrate the global popularity of Max Meidinger and Eduard Hoffmann's typeface on its 50th anniversary.

Sans serif forms have been found in Greek inscriptions as early as the 5th century BC, but more readily available sans serif types emerged towards the end of the 18th century, which is far later than for their serif equivalents. Sans serif forms are not constructed with serifs and, compared to serif forms, the stroke thickness has far less variation. Initially, printers adopted sans serifs for use in newspaper advertisements, theatre programmes, posters and tickets because of their simplicity, legibility, utilitarian appearance and immediacy.

William Caslon IV printed one of the first sans serif specimens in England in *c.* 1816, 'Two Lines English Egyptian'. It was subsequently digitized as Caslon Egyptian, although that design has monoline stroke widths and circular forms for its rounded letters. This became a reference point for many ensuing designs.

The development of sans serif types took off in the early 20th century. Many classic sans serif types were created after World War I (1914–18) through to the 1960s. After the horrors of the war, people anticipated a modern technological age of peace and innovation. Art and cultural movements such as the Bauhaus led to the creation of early geometric types such as Jakob Erbar's Erbar (*c.* 1920s) and Paul Renner's Futura (1928). These types reflected a purist and mechanical consideration to their construction with a simplicity formed around geometric shapes, producing circular, squared-up and triangular forms, in contrast to earlier types influenced by handwritten rhythms. Such types were popular throughout the 1920s and 1930s. In the 1970s, designs such as ITC Avant Garde Gothic by Tom Carnase and Herb Lubalin (see p. 62) re-energized interest in these purist types. More recent designs for geometric typefaces, such as Avenir (1988) by Adrian Frutiger (see p. 290) and Gotham (2000) by Tobias Frere-Jones (see p. 80) maintained their international design appeal.

The term 'grotesque' (also 'grotesk' and 'Gothic') is used to describe sans serifs with subtle variations of construction. It is a general term, although nuances do exist between grotesk and Gothic, the latter being a US approach to the design of grotesque fonts which is less geometric and more based on oval shapes. Invariably, Gothic has an increased contrast in stroke weight, regular proportions, uniform widths and a lowercase of double-storey construction with relatively closed apertures. More modern grotesque designs are referred to as Neo-grotesque and for the purpose of comparison on the page they have been grouped together here. They usually have a greater range in weights within their families and possess slightly more geometric qualities to their designs. They also provide better legibility than their earlier counterparts. These designs aim to offer readability as well as legibility and can be used for far greater lengths of texts than their predecessors in print and online and digital media. This classification came to the fore in the 1950s thanks to a movement known as the International Typographic Style (aka Swiss Style). However, the starting point was the Akzidenz Grotesk design dating to the end of the 19th century, which inspired the titan sans serifs Helvetica and Univers, both of which are employed across the globe in a vast array of applications.

Humanist sans serifs take their inspiration from more classical Roman letterforms. They adopt stroke contrast and construction forms from traditional serif types. Their italic variants are true italic designs based on a calligraphic approach rather than slanted variants. Humanist types are regarded as being the most legible and readable among the sans serif for lengthy texts, given their association with serif influences. They are ideal for headline and text purposes. Such flexibility gives them an edge when used by designers and means they are increasingly popular and are being created for screen applications.

Square sans serifs adopt many of the traits of grotesque and geometric designs but with the rounded ovals forming letter shapes being squared off to create a far more rectangular appearance. Sans serif designs over the last twenty years have drawn on a melting pot of influences and historical references. The result of this wealth of resources is that the distinctions between newer sans serifs are blurring. Sans serif types are ever increasing as many new and established foundries strive for perfection and innovation in creating designs that evoke modernity and simplicity.

Aperçu

ABCDEFGHIJKLMNOPQRSTUVWXYZ
abcdefghijklmnopqrstuvwxyz
1234567890 !@#?:;"*&

Foundry: Colophon
Designer: Anthony Sheret /
Edd Harrington
Designer Nationality: British
Date: 2010

From the award-winning independent type foundry Colophon (see p. 210), which is based in London and Los Angeles, comes Aperçu, a contemporary geometric sans serif whose forms are drawn from classic typefaces such as Johnston (see p. 278), Gill Sans (see p. 276) and Franklin Gothic (see p. 235). Its elegant, rounded forms possess much charm and upon closer examination reveal quirks and details that make it stand out from similar designs. Its cleanliness and readability make it ideal for print and online use.

Developing Aperçu was one of Colophon's earliest projects, and it was trialled and tested on a number of live commissions during the creative process, the final design being published in August 2010. An extensive and highly flexible family, it has been expanded over the years to accommodate differing languages (with an Arabic version released in 2018) and enhanced OpenType features. Its four core weights consist of Light, Regular, Medium and Bold with matching italics.

Since its release, Aperçu has been employed by cultural institutions such as New York's Museum of Modern Art, the Jewish Museum in London and the Walker Art Center, Minneapolis. It has also been used in journals such as *Zeit Magazin* and by a host of commercial organizations.

Right. Aperçu specimen book (second edition), which includes overviews of both language support extensions and new cuts in Black, Black Italic and Mono Bold. Design by Colophon.

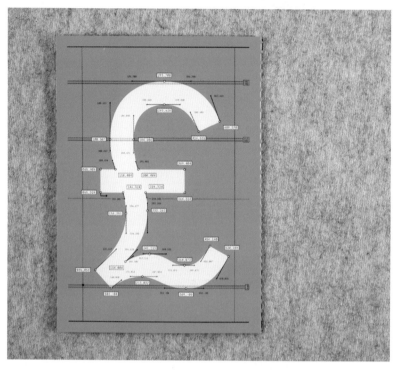

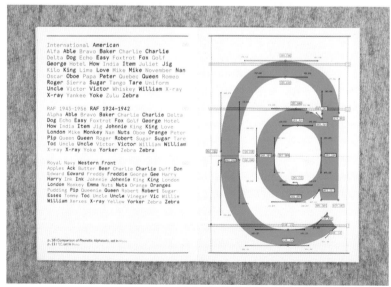

Black
ÀÁÂÃÄÅÆÇÐÈÉÊËÌÍÎÏŁÑ
ÒÓÔÕÖØŒÞŠÙÚÛÜÝŸŽ
№ ¼½¾⅓⅔⅛⅜⅝⅞
@& +©® £€¶# − [({!?})]

Black Italic
ÀÁÂÃÄÅÆÇÐÈÉÊËÌÍÎÏŁÑ
ÒÓÔÕÖØŒÞŠÙÚÛÜÝŸŽ
№ ¼½¾⅓⅔⅛⅜⅝⅞
@& +©® £€¶# − [({!?})]

Black & *Black Italic*
←→↑↓↖↗↙↘ *←→↑↓↖↗↙↘*

p. 28 : 'E!' Waterfall, set in Black
p. 29 : Additional Characters, set in Black and *Black Italic*

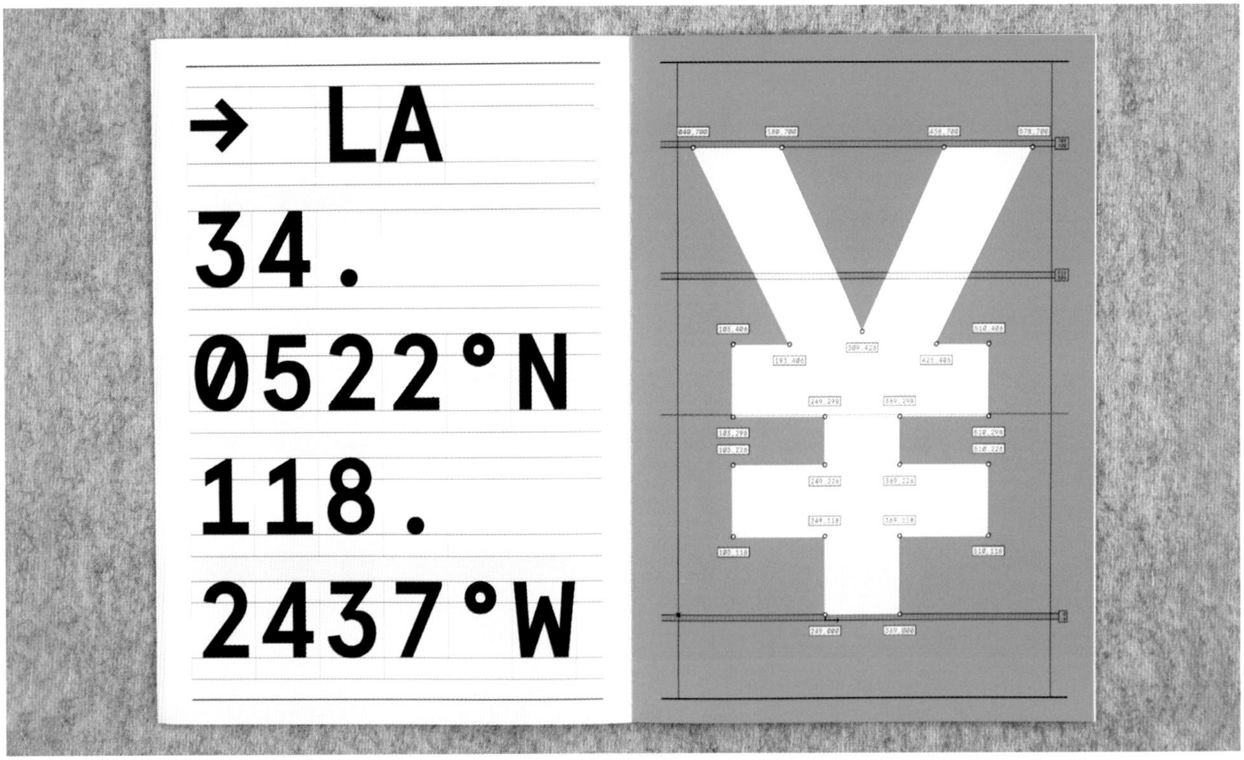

→ LA
34.
Ø522°N
118.
2437°W

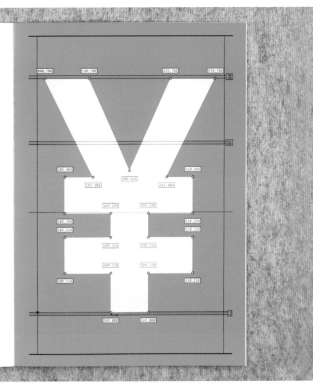

Aperture

ABCDEFGHIJKLMNOPQRSTUVWXYZ
abcdefghijklmnopqrstuvwxyz
1234567890 !@#?:;"*&

Foundry: Neutura
Designer: Alexander McCracken
Designer Nationality: American
Date: 2009

Aperture was created by graphic designer and type designer Alexander McCracken, founder of Neutura (see p. 472) in San Francisco. Its geometric forms are based around an increased x-height, a strong use of vertical construction in its letterforms, low contrast in its stroke weights and particular details such as unbracketed serifs on certain characters (see lowercase 'i' and 'r'). Its vertical extended appearance is offset by the use of shallow sloping diagonals for the continuation of the stroke in many of the characters, creating a consistency and modernity yet retaining legibility. Aperture is available as Extra Light, Regular and Heavy.

 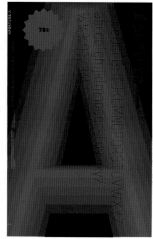 

Avenir Next

ABCDEFGHIJKLMNOPQRSTUVWXYZ
abcdefghijklmnopqrstuvwxyz
1234567890 !@#?:;"*&

Foundry: Linotype
Designer: Adrian Frutiger /
Akira Kobayashi / Akaki Razmadze
Designer Nationality: Swiss /
Japanese / Georgian
Date: 2004

Adrian Frutiger (see p. 290) and the in-house team at Linotype designed Avenir Next as an expanded version of the original from 1988. It features six weights with a roman and italic and two widths, Normal and Condensed. Small caps, text figures and ligatures were also added.

Avenir Next Rounded

ABCDEFGHIJKLMNOPQRSTUVWXYZ
abcdefghijklmnopqrstuvwxyz
1234567890 !@#?:;"*&

Foundry: Linotype
Designer: Adrian Frutiger /
Akira Kobayashi / Sandra Winter
Designer Nationality: Swiss /
Japanese / German
Date: 2012

This version of Avenir Next featuring rounded terminals was created by the in-house team at Linotype in consultation with Adrian Frutiger (see p. 290). Comprising of four weights along with complementary italics, it is a playful and welcoming version of the popular sans serif.

Avenir

ABCDEFGHIJKLMNOPQRSTUVWXYZ
abcdefghijklmnopqrstuvwxyz
1234567890 !@#?:;"*&

Foundry: Linotype
Designer: Adrian Frutiger
Designer Nationality: Swiss
Date: 1988

The elegant geometric sans serif created by Swiss type designer Adrian Frutiger (see p. 290) takes its inspiration from the structured geometric typefaces of the early 20th century yet is endowed with a humanist touch, creating a warmer, more approachable typeface that is more akin in tone to his typeface Frutiger. Avenir reflects the aesthetic approaches of the later 20th century rather than the hardened perfection of its ancestors and inspiration, the typefaces Futura and Erbar.

'Avenir' means 'future' in French and it has become a most appropriate title. Linotype released this refined and pure typeface in 1988, and it has become a timeless classic. The family includes three weights with matching italics. As with Univers, Frutiger employed a double-digit naming system to convey weight and width for each of the styles.

Avenir has many subtle details such as thicker vertical strokes and shortened ascenders, which all contribute towards its heightened legibility.

In 2004, Frutiger created a revised version with Linotype type director Akira Kobayashi, titled Avenir Next (see p. 188). It contains true italics, condensed styles and small caps.

Below. The famous letters standing on Amsterdam's Museumplein, *I am amsterdam*, were hugely popular wth residents and tourists alike. Introduced in 2014 as part of a marketing campaign for the city, the logotype is set in Avenir. Sadly their popularity was so great, and crowds so large, that they were removed by the council at the end of 2018 but are now on tour, being sited in other areas across the Dutch city.

Base 900

ABCDEFGHIJKLMNOPQRSTUVWXYZ
abcdefghijklmnopqrstuvwxyz
1234567890 !@#?:;"*&

Foundry: Emigre
Designer: Zuzana Licko
Designer Nationality: Slovakian
Date: 2010

Developed from a bitmap typeface, Base 900 from Emigre (see p. 106) is a typeface born from technological restraint. Refined from a simple bitmap form to a full, high-resolution typeface, Base 900 reflects its origins in early computer type in appearance and modular geometry, both enhanced to create an elegant and distinguished design.

Base 900 takes its origins from an earlier design by Zuzana Licko, Base 9, created in 1994, which was formed from a simple grid construction. Licko's aim with the Base 9 design was to create a comprehensive family of screen and printer fonts, similar to Verdana by British type designer Matthew Carter (see p. 616). These forms were primarily worked in a reverse manner to how modern fonts are designed, in that the screen-based appearance took dominance over the printer version. The design and adjustment of a grid-based letterform is far harder to adjust than the vector line-based forms of the printer fonts, so it was tackled first. In addition, a bitmap form is quite crude in its makeup and can be very limiting when designing letters, so it is necessary to get the screen version correct first.

It was from this simple Base 9 design that Base 900 was developed. It takes on a number of the quirks of Base 9, such as the triangular spur element that appears on many of the letterforms and the narrowed 'm' that follows the grid construction over regular forms, which all originated in the Lo-Res 9 Bold bitmap. These features were incorporated and adapted as stylistic elements, giving the family its own highly distinctive geometric appearance.

IJANTING
SOJOURN
1,395,456,780
1,395,456,780
AWARD
AWARD AWARD
5037
5037

13

Base 900 : TYPE SPECIMEN

Boutique

ABCDEFGHIJKLMNOPQRSTUVWXYZ
abcdefghijklmnopqrstuvwxyz
1234567890 !@#?:;"*&

Foundry: Milieu Grotesque
Designer: Timo Gaessner
Designer Nationality: German
Date: 2012

Boutique is a sans serif with several geometric gestures. It was initiated as an experiment in 2008, and developed for the rebranding of German fashion label A. D. Deertz in 2009. The font family, finally released in 2012, features distinctly linear characters and a high stroke contrast.

Castledown

ABCDEFGHIJKLMNOPQRSTUVWXYZ
abcdefghijklmnopqrstuvwxyz
1234567890 !@#?:;"*&

Foundry: Colophon
Designer: The Entente
Designer Nationality: British
Date: 2014

Colophon (see p. 210) initiated Castledown in 2012 as a bespoke typeface for Castledown Primary School in Hastings, UK. It is a geometric sans serif with both Regular and Fun versions. Both styles include proportional weights, alongside variants such as Dotted and Cursive.

Century Gothic

ABCDEFGHIJKLMNOPQRSTUVWXYZ
abcdefghijklmnopqrstuvwxyz
1234567890 !@#?:;"*&

Foundry: Monotype
Designer: Monotype Studio
Date: 1991

Heavily influenced by geometric fonts Futura and Avant Garde, Century Gothic is a version of Futura created to match the proportions of Avant Garde. It also has its roots in Sol Hess's typeface Twentieth Century, but lacks the slanted characters and visual flair of the classic by Herb Lubalin (see p. 62).

Chalet

ABCDEFGHIJKLMNOPQRSTUVWXYZ
abcdefghijklmnopqrstuvwxyz
1234567890 !@#?:;"*&

Foundry: House Industries
Designer: Ken Barber /
Paul van der Laan
Designer Nationality: American /
Dutch
Date: 1993

Credited to the fictional 1940s designer René Albert Chalet, this functional sans serif has three variations: Chalet 1960, Chalet 1970 and Chalet 1980. Each has three weights: Paris (Light), London (Regular) and New York (Bold). Chalet also comes with more than one hundred useful silhouette images.

Chapeau

ABCDEFGHIJKLMNOPQRSTUVWXYZ
abcdefghijklmnopqrstuvwxyz
1234567890 !@#?:;"*&

Foundry: Milieu Grotesque
Designer: Timo Gaessner
Designer Nationality: German
Date: 2016

Chapeau's geometric design is inspired by IBM's proportionally aligned typeface Doric, which Timo Gaessner encountered in a letter written by Johnny Cash on an IBM typewriter. Since its first release in 2010, Chapeau has been updated to include six weights and two monospaced styles.

DIN Neuzeit Grotesk

ABCDEFGHIJKLMNOPQRSTUVWXYZ
abcdefghijklmnopqrstuvwxyz
1234567890 !@#?:;"*&

Foundry: Stempel
Designer: Wilhelm Pischner
Designer Nationality: German
Date: 1928

Neuzeit Grotesk was once the standard typeface used by the print industry. In 1970 the *Deutsches Institut für Normung* (German Institute for Industrial Standards) chose a version for use in signage and traffic directional systems across Germany, and the abbreviation 'DIN' was then added to its name.

Drescher Grotesk BT

ABCDEFGHIJKLMNOPQRSTUVWXYZ
abcdefghijklmnopqrstuvwxyz
1234567890 !@#?:;"*&

Foundry: Bitstream
Designer: Arno Drescher / Nicolai Gogoll
Designer Nationality: German
Date: 1930 / 2001

This geometric design is Nicolai Gogoll's award-winning revival of Arno Drescher's Super Grotesk created in 1930, which became known as the 'East German Futura' because Futura was unavailable. It is available in six weights, plus a special weight for use at small point sizes.

Erbar

ABCDEFGHIJKLMNOPQRSTUVWXYZ
abcdefghijklmnopqrstuvwxyz
1234567890 !@#?:;"*&

Foundry: Ludwig & Mayer
Designer: Jakob Erbar
Designer Nationality: German
Date: c. 1920s / 1995

Erbar is a revival of Erbar Grotesk, one of the first geometric sans serifs that predates Futura. Erbar has eleven extra styles, including two weights with a smaller x-height, longer ascenders and two condensed weights. There are a number of different digitized versions, including CJ Type's Dunbar.

Erbar AT

ABCDEFGHIJKLMNOPQRSTUVWXYZ
abcdefghijklmnopqrstuvwxyz
1234567890 !@#?:;"*&

Foundry: Ludwig & Mayer
Designer: Jakob Erbar
Designer Nationality: German
Date: c. 1920s / 1995

Jakob Erbar's groundbreaking typeface was one of the first geometric sans serifs and predates both Rudolf Koch's Kabel and Paul Renner's Futura by five years. The original Erbar has Light Condensed and Bold Condensed weights, whereas this version has Light Condensed and Medium Condensed.

FS Alvar

ABCDEFGHIJKLMNOPQRSTUVWXYZ
abcdefghijklmnopqrstuvwxyz
1234567890 !@#?:;"*&

Foundry: Fontsmith
Designer: Phil Garnham / Jason Smith
Designer Nationality: British
Date: 2009

A departure from the type styles for which Fontsmith (see p. 272) has traditionally been known, this Modernist-inspired sans serif was developed from sketches made by Phil Garnham during his undergraduate studies. Available in three weights, its stencilled letterforms are built on a modular grid.

FS Emeric

ABCDEFGHIJKLMNOPQRSTUVWXYZ
abcdefghijklmnopqrstuvwxyz
1234567890 !@#?:;"*&

Foundry: Fontsmith
Designer: Phil Garnham
Designer Nationality: British
Date: 2013

FS Emeric presents a departure from the neutral, impersonal feel of many 20th-century sans serif typefaces. Created to demonstrate that demonstrate that utility within a sans serif design need not prevail over personality, its extensive family of weights and styles is both versatile and legible.

FS Lucas

ABCDEFGHIJKLMNOPQRSTUVWXYZ
abcdefghijklmnopqrstuvwxyz
1234567890 !@#?:;"*&

Foundry: Fontsmith
Designer: Stuart de Rozario
Designer Nationality: British
Date: 2016

In response to the trend for geometric, circular forms within typography and branding in the mid 2010s, Fontsmith (see p. 272) set out to develop its own optically balanced font family to offer brands a comprehensive typographic toolkit. FS Lucas, released in 2016, is the result.

Futura

ABCDEFGHIJKLMNOPQRSTUVWXYZ
abcdefghijklmnopqrstuvwxyz
1234567890 !@#?:;"*&

Foundry: Linotype
Designer: Paul Renner
Designer Nationality: German
Date: 1928

German designer Paul Renner was a hugely influential graphic artist, type designer, writer and teacher. He created the Futura typeface according to his Constructivist beliefs and to reflect Bauhaus principles, although he was never actually associated or affiliated to the famous German arts and crafts school.

Renner was commissioned to create the typeface by the Bauer Type Foundry based in Frankfurt am Main, Germany. His belief that a modern typeface should be based around the purest of geometric forms of the circle, square and triangle was tempered by the foundry's need for a practical and usable product. Renner's earliest sketches were deemed to be extreme and unworkable, with characters losing their ability to be recognized clearly.

The foundry and Renner redrew and refined the designs, resulting in what is a timeless classic that was marketed by Bauer as capturing the spirit of modernity, using the slogan *die Schrift unserer Zeit* ('the typeface of our time'). In fact, Futura is as relevant and as popular today as it was when it first appeared in the early 20th century.

Futura's near constant stroke weight and crisp geometric forms have made it the most successful of these forms of type. It has had a great influence on sans serif types designed with a similar rationale because of the purity of its design. Efficient, elegant, and versatile, Futura is employed from print to branding on a global scale. A wide variety of weights are available: its lighter weights suit text setting, while the typeface is ideal for display applications thanks to its Bold and Condensed styles.

Below left. Futura promotion and specimen from The Bauer Type Foundry's New York office.

Below right. Tourist map of Berlin for visitors to the 1936 Berlin Olympic Games.

Opposite. Barbican Arts Centre Identity and Interior. Identity guidelines by North with interior wayfinding by Cartlidge Levene with Studio Myerscough working with architects Allford Hall Monaghan Morris. The particular variant of Futura used for the wayfinding is Futura SH by Scangraphic, designed specifically for use at larger sizes.

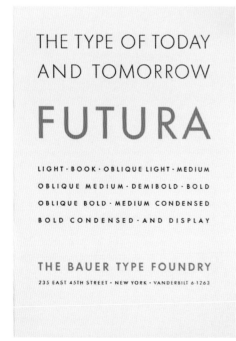

Typeface

41

Futura is our voice

We only use one font.

Futura is at the core of our visual identity and synonymous with our brand.

futura

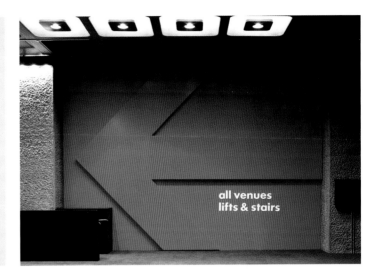

all venues
lifts & stairs

Typeface

Three weights

The Barbican likes to be bold and strong in its communications, however with Futura we can also be quieter, more restrained and classical. Use a weight that best suits the message.

The version of Futura that we use belongs to the Scangraphic font library. Details about purchasing the font are at the back of this guide.

extra-light
book
bold

Typeface

Three type sizes

Keeping things consistent and simple makes communication quicker and easier. When the audience is familiar with the hierarchy of information, it takes them just an instant to find what they're interested in.

Our system only utilises up to three sizes:

Size one for headlines or titles
Size two for descriptor/subheading
Size three for additional information

Our wordmark is not a typesize.

one
two
three

46

FS Sinclair

ABCDEFGHIJKLMNOPQRSTUVWXYZ
abcdefghijklmnopqrstuvwxyz
1234567890 !@#?:;"*&

Foundry: Fontsmith
Designer: Phil Garnham / Jason Smith
Designer Nationality: British
Date: 2009

Phil Garnham and Jason Smith designed this modular, grid-based typeface in 2009, inspired by the blocky letterforms gracing the display of the ZX Spectrum home computer. Their careful refinements of each letterform have resulted in a technologically inspired typeface with a humanist touch.

Generica Condensed

ABCDEFGHIJKLMNOPQRSTUVWXYZ
abcdefghijklmnopqrstuvwxyz
1234567890 !@#?:;"*&

Foundry: Monotype
Designer: Jim Parkinson
Designer Nationality: American
Date: 1994

Jim Parkinson worked as a lettering artist for Hallmark Cards before beginning his freelance type design career, and is well known for his design of editorial mastheads and logos for titles such as *Newsweek*, *Esquire* and *Rolling Stone*. He designed this condensed sans for Monotype in 1994.

Generika

ABCDEFGHIJKLMNOPQRSTUVWXYZ
abcdefghijklmnopqrstuvwxyz
1234567890 !@#?:;"*&

Foundry: Milieu Grotesque
Designer: Alexander Colby
Designer Nationality: Swiss
Date: 2008

Generika is a geometric sans serif, inspired by the letterforms produced on an old Alder typewriter with an unreliable carbon ribbon and low-quality paper. The characters mimic the blurred aesthetics of the typewritten letters, seen primarily in Generika's rounded corners.

Geometric 212

ABCDEFGHIJKLMNOPQRSTUVWX
abcdefghijklmnopqrstuvwxyz
1234567890 !@#?:;"*&

Foundry: Bauer Type Foundry / American Type Founders / Linotype / Bitstream
Designer: Paul Renner / ATF Staff
Designer Nationality: German / American
Date: 1927 / 1936

This enigmatic Bitstream typeface is based on Linotype and American Type Founders' metal matrices for Spartan released in 1936, which was itself a version of Paul Renner's perennially popular Futura, first published by Bauer Type. It is available in four weights, including two condensed cuts.

Geometric 231

ABCDEFGHIJKLMNOPQRSTUVWXYZ
abcdefghijklmnopqrstuvwxyz
1234567890 !@#?:;"*&

Foundry: Klingspor / Bitstream
Designer: Rudolf Koch
Designer Nationality: German
Date: 1927

German designer Rudolf Koch created Kabel, on which this Bitstream digitization is based, for the Klingspor foundry in 1927. Stempel republished it later. The typeface features tall ascenders, a low x-height and geometric letters based on the interplay between circular forms and straight lines.

Geometric 415

ABCDEFGHIJKLMNOPQRSTUVWXYZ
abcdefghijklmnopqrstuvwxyz
1234567890 !@#?:;"*&

Foundry: Linotype / Bitstream
Designer: William A. Dwiggins
Designer Nationality: American
Date: 1937 / 1990

Geometric 415 is Bitstream's copy of Metro No. 2 by US designer William A. Dwiggins, originally published by Linotype in 1932. It was commissioned to compete with popular European sans serifs such as Futura. Dwiggins developed its lowercase letters to add further visual interest.

Geometric 706

ABCDEFGHIJKLMNOPQRSTUVWXYZ
abcdefghijklmnopqrstuvwxyz
1234567890 !@#?:;"*&

Foundry: Stempel / Bitstream
Designer: Wilhelm Pischner
Designer Nationality: German
Date: 1928 / 1990

Wilhelm Pischner's geometric Neuzeit Grotesk font has been the subject of several revivals, adaptations and digitizations since its release in 1928; it was selected by the German Standards Committee in 1970 for use on official and traffic signage. Bitstream's version was published in 1990.

Gotham Rounded

ABCDEFGHIJKLMNOPQRSTUVWXYZ
abcdefghijklmnopqrstuvwxyz
1234567890 !@#?:;"*&

Foundry: Hoefler & Frere-Jones
Designer: Tobias Frere-Jones
Designer Nationality: American
Date: 2005

Tobias Frere-Jones developed this cut of Gotham for the redesign of the US graphic-arts magazine *Print* in 2005; it was subsequently released as a retail typeface following the expiry of that exclusive licence. Its rounded forms build upon the approachability and warmth of the original.

Gotham

ABCDEFGHIJKLMNOPQRSTUVWXYZ
abcdefghijklmnopqrstuvwxyz
1234567890 !@#?:;"*&

Foundry: Hoefler & Co.
Designer: Tobias Frere-Jones
Designer Nationality: American
Date: 2000

Gotham started life as a commission for US men's magazine *GQ* to design a bespoke sans serif to be employed in its publication. Tobias Frere-Jones (see p. 80), the principal and type director of New York foundry Hoefler, Frere & Jones (now Hoefler & Co.), used the project as a stepping stone to develop and design a typeface based on his interest and fascination with the architectural display lettering and signage seen around New York from the mid 20th century.

A key reference point in Frere-Jones's research was the letterforms found on 'one of the city's most mundane buildings', the Port Authority Bus Terminal on Eighth Avenue in Manhattan. These vernacular letterforms, created and formed by engineers and draughtsmen from steel and bronze, were the inspiration for this highly popular geometric sans.

When *GQ*'s exclusive licence ended in 2002, the foundry marketed Gotham as a commercial typeface. It gained in popularity and was nominated as 'the font of the decade' by *USA Today*. Such was its success that it was used by Coca-Cola and on former President Barack Obama's presidential campaign in 2008; it has even been employed for the cornerstone of the One World Trade Center building.

Gotham is uniquely American in tone, and its clean lines, generous width and elegant forms mark a typeface that offers an honesty with clear readability no matter the application. Gotham offers an extremely large family of sixty-six styles with four widths, eight weights, separate fonts for screen use and a Rounded variant containing eight styles.

Below left. The iconic Barack Obama HOPE poster from 2008 by artist Shepard Fairey, which came to symbolize the future president's political campaign.

Below right. CD cover design for *Live 2002,* a recording of a concert near Newcastle, UK, by sound artist Carsten Nicolai (aka Alva Noto), and fellow musicians Ryoji Ikeda and the late Mika Vainio.

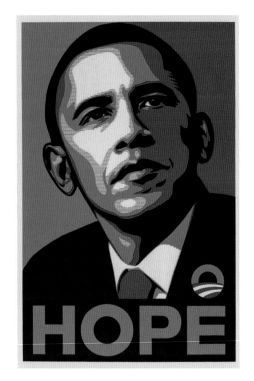

Left. Book cover for *Twice Upon A Time: Listening to New York* by Hari Kunzru, designed by award-winning New York graphic designer and writer Chip Kidd.

Below left. Wayfinding design using extruded Gotham Book by Cómo Design Studio, Barcelona for Biblioteca Camp de l'Arpa Caterina Albert.

Below. One of a series of posters for New York's Tribeca Film Festival by J. Walter Thompson.

GT Cinetype

ABCDEFGHIJKLMNOPQRSTUVWXYZ
abcdefghijklmnopqrstuvwxyz
1234567890 !@#?:;"*&

Foundry: Grilli Type
Designer: Mauro Paolozzi / Rafael Koch
Designer Nationality: Swiss
Date: 2015

Based on a design created for a now defunct cinema subtitling machine, GT Cinetype is a typeface that does not contain any curves. A laser that can only move in straight lines is used to erase the coloured layer of the film, and small, brilliant white letters appear.

GT Eesti

ABCDEFGHIJKLMNOPQRSTUVWXYZ
abcdefghijklmnopqrstuvwxyz
1234567890 !@#?:;"*&

Foundry: Grilli Type
Designer: Reto Moser
Designer Nationality: Swiss
Date: 2016

Based on Anatoly Schukin's typeface Zhurnalnaya Roublennaya of 1947, and sourced from Estonian children's books, GT Eesti is described as 'a free-spirited interpretation' of the geometric Soviet sans serif. It has two subfamilies, text and display, and Latin and Cyrillic versions.

GT Flexa

ABCDEFGHIJKLMNOPQRSTUVWXYZ
abcdefghijklmnopqrstuvwxyz
1234567890 !@#?:;"*&

Foundry: Grilli Type
Designer: Dominik Huber
Designer Nationality: Swiss
Date: 2019

This energetic sans serif started life as part of a branding project for a fashion label by Swiss agency Moiré. As its name implies, its curves flex from very narrow to very wide shapes. Its ink traps provide the glue that makes this family of extremes work so well together.

GT Walsheim

ABCDEFGHIJKLMNOPQRSTUVWXYZ
abcdefghijklmnopqrstuvwxyz
1234567890 !@#?:;"*&

Foundry: Grilli Type
Designer: Noël Leu
Designer Nationality: Swiss
Date: 2010

GT Walsheim is a geometric sans serif, informed by the lettering of Swiss designer Otto Baumberger. Drawing on poster designs from the 1930s, it revives a variety of Baumberger's hand-drawn idiosyncrasies, most notably the jovial uppercase 'g' or the oversized counter of the uppercase 'r'.

Gubia

ABCDEFGHIJKLMNOPQRSTUVWXYZ
abcdefghijklmnopqrstuvwxyz
1234567890 !@#?;;"*&

Foundry: Graviton
Designer: Pablo Balcells
Designer Nationality: Argentinian
Date: 2013

The rounded, rectangular forms of Pablo Balcells's Gubia typeface are well suited for display use, and its alternate characters offer the capacity to add further visual interest. Vertically extended tittles within the font's lowercase letterforms emphasize its condensed feel.

Harmonia Sans

ABCDEFGHIJKLMNOPQRSTUVWXYZ
abcdefghijklmnopqrstuvwxyz
1234567890 !@#?:;"*&

Foundry: Monotype
Designer: Jim Wasco
Designer Nationality: American
Date: 2010

Jim Wasco studied classic geometric designs such as Futura and Avant Garde when developing Harmonia Sans; the result is an evenly proportioned sans serif with its own distinct character. Details such as the single-storey 'a' and 'g' give the typeface a friendly, informal feel.

ITC Bauhaus

ABCDEFGHIJKLMNOPQRSTUVWXYZ
abcdefghijklmnopqrstuvwxyz
1234567890 !@#?:;"*&

Foundry: ITC
Designer: Herbert Bayer / Ed Benguiat / Victor Caruso
Designer Nationality: German / American / American
Date: 1925 / 1975

In 1975, Ed Benguiat (see p. 514) and Victor Caruso developed this ITC release from Herbert Bayer's typeface prototypes created at the Bauhaus in Dessau, Germany. Its unmistakably geometric, semi-stencilled design is available in five different weights, though it does not include italics.

ITC Conduit

ABCDEFGHIJKLMNOPQRSTUVWXYZ
abcdefghijklmnopqrstuvwxyz
1234567890 !@#?:;"*&

Foundry: ITC
Designer: Mark van Bronkhorst
Designer Nationality: American
Date: 1997

Conduit has long been regarded as something of an ugly duckling within the ITC roster – Erik Spiekermann (see p. 304) called it 'wonderfully stupid', and designer Mark van Bronkhorst seems to agree. Nonetheless, its geometric, oversimplified forms have a certain inscrutable appeal.

ITC Avant Garde Gothic

ABCDEFGHIJKLMNOPQRSTUVWXYZ
abcdefghijklmnopqrstuvwxyz
1234567890 !@#?:;"*&

Foundry: ITC
Designer: Herb Lubalin /
Tom Carnase
Designer Nationality: American
Date: 1970

Graphic designer and lettering artist Herb Lubalin (see p. 62) drew up a logotype for the masthead of *Avant Garde* magazine, which was published in the United States in the late 1960s. Tom Carnase, fellow type designer and lettering artist, as well as partner at their agency Lubalin, Smith, Carnase, was charged with the task of creating the typeface from his sketches and workings. The result was an innovative and ever popular design that draws its appearance from past versions of geometric sans serifs, from the Bauhaus in Germany but also the first sans serif, all capitals design, produced in 1816 by the Caslon Foundry in London.

Its elegant construction from circular forms and straight lines masks the complexity of this elegant typeface. The typeface itself consists of monoline characters, overlapping characters, tightly set letters and the distinctive leaning uppercase 'A's. More often used for display work, it is also highly popular with branding and logotype applications, as seen with sports-equipment company Adidas.

The ITC Avant Garde Gothic family is made up of five weights and four condensed designs, all with matching italics. The later condensed designs were created in 1974 by a friend and peer of Lubalin's, Ed Benguiat (see p. 514), with obliques being designed by André Gürtler, Erich Gschwind and Christian Mengelt in 1977.

The most recent OpenType version, ITC Avant Garde Gothic Pro, includes a range of alternate upper- and lowercase characters and a collection of bitform characters (lowercase letters with capital proportions). A serif version exists where Lubalin and Benguiat added large rectangular slab serifs, which is called Lubalin Graph (see p. 55) and was released in 1974.

Below. ITC *Avant Garde* magazine covers for Issues No. 8, 1969 (the Picasso edition) and 13, 1971 (a photo essay of America by Alwyn Scott Turner).

Opposite. Adverts for the Audi Fox designed by renowned American art director Helmut Krone in 1975, employing Avant Garde Gothic in both headline and text applications.

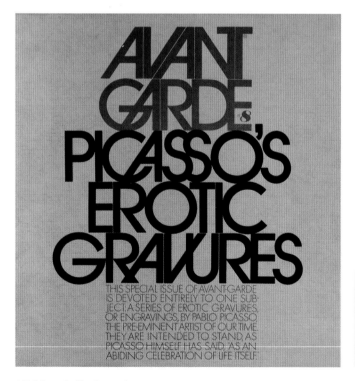

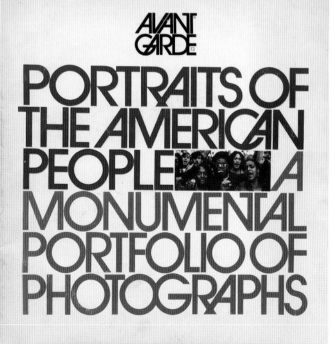

SURE
FOOTED
THE
FOX
BY AUDI

TALE OF THE FOX
BY AUDI

Once upon a time, all cars were more or less the same. Then along came sports cars, economy cars, compact cars, you name it cars.

The latest of which is the "sports sedan." Which is supposed to be a sedan that has sports car features. But how many of them really are, though?

Enter the Fox by Audi: a real, true sports sedan.

Its front-wheel drive makes it incredibly surefooted. (It also gives you that traction you need to help get you through the snow.)

It has the same type of rack-and-pinion steering and independent front suspension that are found on some of the finest sports cars. This allows it to take turns with an agility remarkable for a sedan.

We also put something in the Fox so advanced, sports cars don't even have it yet. A special front axle design that helps prevent swerving when you stop under certain adverse conditions. (Speaking of stopping, the Fox's front disc brakes and radial-ply tires enable it to stop practically on a dime.)

Most extraordinary of all, despite the fact that this peppy little creature's overhead-cam engine can do 0 to 50 in 8.4 seconds and has a top speed of 97 mph, it has an amazingly small appetite: 25 miles per gallon. Its price is relatively small also: $3975.*

The interior, we might mention, is relatively large: seats five, comfortably. And it has an amount of trunk space almost unbelievable for a car this size. Its interior, by the way, is fairly smart, too, with things like fully-reclining contoured seats and door-to-door pile carpeting.

If you're in the market for a "sports sedan," try a true sports sedan: the Fox by Audi. You'll drive happily ever after.

TAKES TURNS NIMBLY.

STOPS STRAIGHT IN ITS TRACKS.

TROTS AT 97 MPH.

DOESN'T EAT MUCH.

QUICK TO THE CHASE, CLEVER IN TIGHT CORNERS, LEAN PERFORMANCE

A Fox knows how to take care of himself. He can run when he has to. Get out of tight places. Stop in his tracks. Just like an Audi Fox.

Ours takes off fast. 0 to 50 in 8.5 seconds. (In 10 seconds with automatic transmission.) It runs all day without tiring. And stops surely with the help of power-front disc brakes.

Corner our Fox and what happens? Rack-and-pinion steering, along with independent front suspension and a torsion crank axle in the rear, lets you maneuver nimbly and easily. Follow the trail wherever it leads. And take the sharpest turns in stride.

Though Foxes like to run in uncrowded places, ours performs well in town too. It calmly sits through traffic jams. Starts and stops again without complaints. Gets in and out of tight parking spaces with agility. Then it's back to the open road, where once again the chase is on.

FOX BY AUDI

A Fox is smart. Sleek. And ours is no different. The Audi Fox is a smart little sports sedan that's precisely engineered, inside and out. How does it run? Like a sports car. How spacious is it? Like a sedan.

The Audi Fox is nobody's hand-me-down. It's a special combination of sports car precision and sedan comfort. It has a brand new engine, chassis and body. It has excellent performance and above average acceleration in its class, along with interior roominess and luggage space. Features you won't find combined in other cars. Not even other Audis. Our Fox is easy to take care of. Doesn't eat much either. About 23 mpg.

So don't fall for another fable. Take a look at the Fox. It's a true sports sedan. And that's no story.

NOT JUST ANOTHER FABLE, A TRUE SPORTS SEDAN. FOX BY AUDI.

*DIN 70030

ITC Handel Gothic

ABCDEFGHIJKLMNOPQRSTUVWXYZ
abcdefghijklmnopqrstuvwxyz
1234567890 !@#?:;"*&

Foundry: Fotostar / ITC
Designer: Donald J. Handel /
Rod McDonald
Designer Nationality: American
Date: 2008

Designed by Donald J. Handel in the 1960s for phototypesetting, Handel Gothic will be familiar to science-fiction fans thanks to its use on the *Star Trek* TV series. This ITC update adjusts the proportions of the original and expands its character set; Nadine Chahine designed its Arabic counterpart.

ITC Kabel

ABCDEFGHIJKLMNOPQRSTUVWXYZ
abcdefghijklmnopqrstuvwxyz
1234567890 !@#?:;"*&

Foundry: Klingspor / ITC
Designer: Rudolf Koch /
Victor Caruso
Designer Nationality: German /
American
Date: 1927 / 1975

Victor Caruso's revival of Kabel for ITC turned the design on its head, switching the diminutive x-height of the original for much shorter ascenders and descenders. Though extreme in this case, this approach, which can aid legibility, is characteristic of many ITC revivals.

ITC Octone

ABCDEFGHIJKLMNOPQRSTUVWXYZ
abcdefghijklmnopqrstuvwxyz
1234567890 !@#?:;"*&

Foundry: ITC
Designer: Éric de Berranger
Designer Nationality: French
Date: 1999

Alongside his typeface design work, Éric de Berranger has worked on brand identity and logotype design for corporations including Renault. This upright sans serif, designed by De Berranger for ITC in 1999, features flared letterforms reminiscent of stone-carved lettering.

Leroy

ABCDEFGHIJKLMNOPQRSTUVWXYZ
abcdefghijklmnopqrstuvwxyz
1234567890 !@#?:;"*&

Foundry: Colophon
Designer: Oscar & Ewan
Designer Nationality: British
Date: 2012

Leroy is a geometric sans serif inspired by a technical drawing found in a 1960s model car magazine. Despite being drawn with a lettering set from the same period, Leroy features several quirks, such as the angular cross stroke of the lowercase 'e' and the uneven bowls of the uppercase 'b'.

Litera

ABCDEFGHIJKLMNOPQRSTUVWXYZ
abcdefghijklmnopqrstuvwxyz
1234567890 !@#?:;"*&

Foundry: Letraset
Designer: Michael Neugebauer
Designer Nationality: Austrian
Date: 1983

Originally designed for Letraset by Austrian Michael Neugebauer, Litera is a geometric sans serif, inspired by the Bauhaus and the purity of the circle, square and triangle. Distinctive features include the wide crossbar of the 'G' and the stencil construction of the 'e', 'B', 'P' and 'R'.

Mabry

ABCDEFGHIJKLMNOPQRSTUVWXYZ
abcdefghijklmnopqrstuvwxyz
1234567890 !@#?:;"*&

Foundry: Colophon
Designer: Benjamin Critton / Colophon Foundry
Designer Nationality: American
Date: 2018

First commissioned by fashion brand Nasty Gal in 2014, and initially titled NB Grotesque, Mabry is a simultaneously grotesque and geometric sans serif. Referencing and integrating features from each style, the letterforms draw inspiration from both 19th- and 20th-century faces.

Madera

ABCDEFGHIJKLMNOPQRSTUVWXYZ
abcdefghijklmnopqrstuvwxyz
1234567890 !@#?:;"*&

Foundry: Monotype
Designer: Malou Verlomme
Designer Nationality: French
Date: 2018

Designed in 2018 by Malou Verlomme, a French designer working for Monotype in London, Madera comes in eight weights with italics. A versatile, geometric sans serif, Madera was designed with graphic designers and corporate identities in mind. It has diamond-shaped tittles and full stops.

Mont

ABCDEFGHIJKLMNOPQRSTUVWXYZ
abcdefghijklmnopqrstuvwxyz
1234567890 !@#?:;"*&

Foundry: Fontfabric
Designer: Mirela Belova / Svet Simov
Designer Nationality: Bulgarian
Date: 2018

Designed by two of the six Bulgarian designers working for Sofia-based Fontfabric, Mont is a versatile, geometric sans with a large x-height and support for more than 130 languages thanks to Latin, Greek and Cyrillic characters. Mont comes in ten weights; hairline to black, with italics.

Neo Sans

ABCDEFGHIJKLMNOPQRSTUVWXYZ
abcdefghijklmnopqrstuvwxyz
1234567890 !@#?:;"*&

Foundry: Monotype
Designer: Seb Lester
Designer Nationality: British
Date: 2004

Designed by British typographer Sebastian 'Seb' Lester, now better known for his calligraphy, Neo Sans is a rounded, square sans with a technical, futuristic feel. It comes in six weights, light to ultra, with italics, and has been used by Intel, the British Labour Party and car company Kia Motors.

Neo Tech

ABCDEFGHIJKLMNOPQRSTUVWXYZ
abcdefghijklmnopqrstuvwxyz
1234567890 !@#?:;"*&

Foundry: Monotype
Designer: Seb Lester
Designer Nationality: British
Date: 2004

A sister typeface to Neo Sans, Neo Tech is more minimal with some letters stripped of detail, a single-storey 'g', and softer shapes in some places. Seb Lester, who worked at Monotype for nine years, has more than one million followers on Instagram where he shares calligraphy videos.

Neue Kabel

ABCDEFGHIJKLMNOPQRSTUVWXYZ
abcdefghijklmnopqrstuvwxyz
1234567890 !@#?:;"*&

Foundry: Monotype
Designer: Rudolf Koch / Marc Schütz
Designer Nationality: German
Date: 2016

An update of Kabel, the early geometric sans originally drawn by Rudolf Koch in 1927 for the Klingspor foundry, Neue Kabel was designed by German typographer Marc Schütz, and came out of extensive archival research. Schütz reinstated italics and added new weights and missing characters.

Neue Plak

ABCDEFGHIJKLMNOPQRSTUVWXYZ
abcdefghijklmnopqrstuvwxyz
1234567890 !@#?:;"*&

Foundry: Monotype
Designer: Paul Renner / Linda Hintz / Toshi Omagari
Designer Nationality: German / German / Japanese
Date: 2018

Released by Stempel in 1928, Plak was overshadowed by Paul Renner's first font, also a geometric sans, Futura. Neue Plak, Linda Hintz and Toshi Omagari's update, is a versatile family of sixty styles. The oversized tittle and circle and rectangle construction of the 'r' can be seen in the heavier cuts.

Noir Text

ABCDEFGHIJKLMNOPQRSTUVWXYZ
abcdefghijklmnopqrstuvwxyz
1234567890 !@#?:;"*&

Foundry: Playtype
Designer: Jonas Hecksher
Designer Nationality: Danish
Date: 2005

Noir Text is a geometric sans serif font family, designed in Light, Book, Regular and Bold weights. The stroke contrast varies for individual joints, heavy on shoulders but minimal on bowls, and the hooks of letters such as 'f' and 't' are flattened in order to balance the character widths.

November

ABCDEFGHIJKLMNOPQRSTUVWXYZ
abcdefghijklmnopqrstuvwxyz
1234567890 !@#?:;"*&

Foundry: Typotheque
Designer: Peter Biľak
Designer Nationality: Slovakian
Date: 2016

Peter Biľak described November as 'a rational, utilitarian typeface inspired by street signage'. It comes in nine weights with italics, and many travel-related signs, symbols and directional arrows are included as glyphs. Slab, Stencil, Condensed and Compressed versions also exist.

Objektiv

ABCDEFGHIJKLMNOPQRSTUVWXYZ
abcdefghijklmnopqrstuvwxyz
1234567890 !@#?:;"*&

Foundry: Dalton Maag
Designer: Bruno Mello
Designer Nationality: Brazilian
Date: 2015–19

Designed in three styles, Mk1 for display, Mk2 and Mk3 for text, the Objektiv family combines geometry with humanism. While the display style utilizes the severity of geometric forms for impact, the text styles are softer in their principles, enabling a greater legibility. Objektiv is also available as a variable font.

October

ABCDEFGHIJKLMNOPQRSTUVWXYZ
abcdefghijklmnopqrstuvwxyz
1234567890 !@#?:;"*&

Foundry: Typotheque
Designer: Peter Biľak
Designer Nationality: Slovakian
Date: 2016

A rounded sans serif, October was first carved in wood by the rotary cutters of a computer numerical control router, then optically corrected digitally. A large family, October comes in Latin, Hebrew, Cyrillic and Greek in nine weights with italics. Condensed and compressed versions are also available.

Orange

ABCDEFGHIJKLMNOPQRSTUVWXYZ
abcdefghijklmnopqrstuvwxyz
1234567890 !@#?:,"*&

Foundry: Neutura
Designer: Alexander McCracken
Designer Nationality: American
Date: 2006

Orange is a monoline geometric sans serif designed by Alexander McCracken and released in 2006 by his foundry Neutura (see p. 472). It is available in four weights; Light to Extra Bold, without italics. Neutura is the name of McCracken's foundry and design studio, whose clients include Nike and Sony.

Orange Round

ABCDEFGHIJKLMNOPQRSTUVWXYZ
abcdefghijklmnopqrstuvwxyz
1234567890 !@#?:,"*&

Foundry: Neutura
Designer: Alexander McCracken
Designer Nationality: American
Date: 2011

Released five years after Orange, Orange Round follows the exact same structure and comes in the same weights, but features rounded rather than flat terminals. Alexander McCracken's typefaces show interest in geometry, and he often uses them in work for his clients in the music industry.

Pembroke

ABCDEFGHIJKLMNOPQRSTUVWXYZ
abcdefghijklmnopqrstuvwxyz
1234567890 !@#?:,"*&

Foundry: Jeremy Tankard Typography
Designer: Jeremy Tankard
Designer Nationality: British
Date: 2014

Jeremy Tankard's Pembroke was inspired by the square proportions and geometry of Caslon Old Face and other early English types, as well as sans serif inscriptions from late 18th-century British buildings. It is a crisp, clean geometric sans serif available in regular and italic in eight weights.

Raisonné

ABCDEFGHIJKLMNOPQRSTUVWXYZ
abcdefghijklmnopqrstuvwxyz
1234567890 !@#?:,"*&

Foundry: Colophon
Designer: Benjamin Critton / Colophon Foundry
Designer Nationality: American
Date: 2018

First designed in a single Demibold weight in 2010, Raisonné was expanded in 2018 to add both Light and Regular weights. The geometric letterforms reference the aesthetic eccentricities of various 20th-century designs, including Avant Garde by Herb Lubalin (see p. 62) and Rudolf Koch's Kabel.

Refuel

ABCDEFGHIJKLMNOPQRSTUVWXYZ
abcdefghijklmnopqrstuvwxyz
1234567890 !@#?:;"*&

Foundry: Typodermic
Designer: Ray Larabie
Designer Nationality: Canadian
Date: 2016

An octagonal sans serif inspired by the type used on military aircraft, Refuel is a versatile family of six widths and six weights with italics, and support for Latin, Cyrillic, Greek and Vietnamese. A clever feature is the capital 'L', which gains serifs when set next to a lowercase 'l'.

Scene

ABCDEFGHIJKLMNOPQRSTUVWXYZ
abcdefghijklmnopqrstuvwxyz
1234567890 !@#?:;"*&

Foundry: Monotype
Designer: Seb Lester
Designer Nationality: British
Date: 2002

Seb Lester, who studied at Central Saint Martins College of Arts and Design and joined Monotype in 2000, was the designer of Scene, a versatile sans serif available in six weights with italics. Lester aimed to create a 'clean, calm and highly legible' sans and developed Scene for over two years.

Styrene A

ABCDEFGHIJKLMNOPQRSTUVWXYZ
abcdefghijklmnopqrstuvwxyz
1234567890 !@#?:;"*&

Foundry: Commercial Type
Designer: Berton Hasebe
Designer Nationality: American
Date: 2016

Styrene A is geometric sans serif initially inspired by Breede Schreeflooze, a sans serif from a type specimen published by the Enschedé Typefoundry in 1932. Alongside its strict geometry, Styrene A is distinctive for its treatment of narrow forms, such as 'f', 'j' and 'r', which are stretched and flattened.

Styrene B

ABCDEFGHIJKLMNOPQRSTUVWXYZ
abcdefghijklmnopqrstuvwxyz
1234567890 !@#?:;"*&

Foundry: Commercial Type
Designer: Berton Hasebe
Designer Nationality: American
Date: 2016

Styrene B is a narrower version of its sibling font Styrene A, designed for less spacious texts and environments. It is not truly condensed and the letterforms retain the guiding geometric principles, but with slightly more flexibility, and preserve the characteristic features of the design.

Colophon

Founded in 2009 by Edd Hàrrington and Anthony Sheret, Colophon is an international, award-winning independent type foundry based in London and Los Angeles, creating, publishing and distributing high-quality retail and custom typefaces for analogue and digital media. It was initially formed as a design studio, The Entente, and Colophon Foundry was launched three months later.

Colophon's prominence within typeface design came to the fore when it released its grotesque sans serif Aperçu (see p. 186) in 2010. Adopted by organizations such as New York's Museum of Modern Art and a favoured choice for contemporary editorial work, Aperçu soared in popularity, as did the foundry behind it.

Colophon's approach has been to task itself with producing fonts that are composed with aesthetic and technological care. Consequently, its reputable library of typefaces are considered modern classics that couple typographic history with contemporary sensibilities. In addition to its own designs, the foundry hosts and distributes original typefaces drawn by influential type designers and practitioners from varied design disciplines. The extensive catalogue offers graphic designers and typographers a wealth of opportunity with highly crafted considered fonts. In addition to offering a diverse retail portfolio of more than thirty typefaces, Colophon takes on commissions for custom fonts, font families and logotypes, as well as tailoring bespoke versions of its existing typefaces, which include language extensions.

Colophon also provides an innovative and fun buying guide online, which enables the user to navigate the issues regarding licensing for different media and allowances for foreign-language versions incorporating Greek or Cyrillic fonts.

Founded: 2009
Countries: Britain / America
Website: colophon-foundry.org
Notable typefaces:
Aperçu (see p. 186)
Lisbon (see p. 554)

Below. A 24-page catalogue showcasing the concept and technical aspects of the Relative typeface family.

Opposite top and middle rows. Central Avenue typeface family specimen booklet. The unbound booklet also works as a series of four posters.

Opposite bottom row. Future II poster designed by Colophon Foundry.

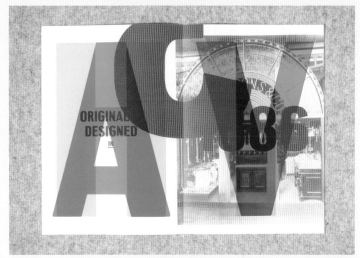

Twentieth Century

ABCDEFGHIJKLMNOPQRSTUVWXYZ
abcdefghijklmnopqrstuvwxyz
1234567890 !@#?:;"*&

Foundry: Monotype
Designer: Sol Hess
Designer Nationality: American
Date: 1936–47

Twentieth Century is a geometric sans serif, drawn between 1936 and 1947, and informed by the Bauhausian typefaces produced in Germany in the 1920s. Designed for function over form, the geometric shapes are disrupted only by the sharp, cutting junctures, which add distinction.

Ulissa

ABCDEFGHIJKLMNOPQRSTUVWXYZ
abcdefghijklmnopqrstuvwxyz
1234567890 !@#?:;"*&

Foundry: Monotype
Designer: Johannes Birkenbach
Designer Nationality: German
Date: 1993

Ulissa is a geometric sans serif, designed in Johannes Birkenbach's final year at Monotype before he returned to Germany to establish his own design studio, ABC Design. Ulissa's narrow, geometric frame is combined with acute joints and stroke endings to ensure legibility in all sizes.

Uni Grotesk

ABCDEFGHIJKLMNOPQRSTUVWXYZ
abcdefghijklmnopqrstuvwxyz
1234567890 !@#?:;"*&

Foundry: Typotheque
Designer: Peter Biľak / Nikola Djurek / Hrvoje Živčić
Designer Nationality: Slovakian / Croatian / Croatian
Date: 2016

Uni Grotesk is a modern adaptation of Universal Grotesk, a popular font from Communist Czechoslovakia, and is a geometric sans serif with the details of a 20th-century European grotesque. Unlike the original, Uni Grotesk also includes an italic version based upon the upright styles.

VAG Rounded

ABCDEFGHIJKLMNOPQRSTUVWXYZ
abcdefghijklmnopqrstuvwxyz
1234567890 !@#?:;"*&

Foundry: Linotype
Designer: Gerry Barney / David Bristow / Terence Griffin / Ian Hay / Kit Cooper
Designer Nationality: British
Date: 1979

Initially released as a corporate typeface for Volkswagen in 1979, VAG Rounded is a circular, geometric sans serif. The font family was released publicly in 1989 and alongside general release, it has been used by corporations such as Apple, Skype and Myspace.

VAG Rounded Next

ABCDEFGHIJKLMNOPQRSTUVWXYZ
abcdefghijklmnopqrstuvwxyz
1234567890 !@#?:;"*&

Foundry: Linotype
Designer: Steve Matteson / Tom Grace
Designer Nationality: American
Date: 2018

VAG Rounded Next is an update and extension of the VAG Rounded font family. Maintaining its characteristically curved stroke endings and light informality, VAG Rounded Next includes the addition of two extra styles, Shine and Rough, and much expanded European language support.

Value Sans

ABCDEFGHIJKLMNOPQRSTUVWXYZ
abcdefghijklmnopqrstuvwxyz
1234567890 !@#?:;"*&

Foundry: Colophon
Designer: The Entente
Designer Nationality: British
Date: 2012 / 2018

Value Sans is a geometric sans serif, designed in 2012 to contemplate the benefits of cultural and economic exchange. The design, which was expanded in 2018 to comprise four weights, finds inspiration in the style of typefaces such as the German Elegant Grotesk and the British Granby.

Visuelt

ABCDEFGHIJKLMNOPQRSTUVWXYZ
abcdefghijklmnopqrstuvwxyz
1234567890 !@#?:;"*&

Foundry: Colophon
Designer: The Entente
Designer Nationality: British
Date: 2013 / 2015 / 2016

Visuelt is a geometric sans serif, initially designed in 2013 for the National Norwegian Design Awards, commonly known as the 'Visuelt'. In 2015, the designers added light and black weights to the existing regular, while Medium and Bold weights were introduced in 2016.

Vita

ABCDEFGHIJKLMNOPQRSTUVWXYZ
abcdefghijklmnopqrstuvwxyz
1234567890 !@#?:;"*&

Foundry: Typotheque
Designer: Nikola Djurek
Designer Nationality: Croatian
Date: 2016

Vita is a 21st-century geometric sans serif, designed to perform effectively on both high- and low-resolution screens. Its modest yet distinctive characters, which feature minimalist serifs to distinguish between similar shapes, maintain its legibility at smaller sizes.

Akkurat Pro

ABCDEFGHIJKLMNOPQRSTUVWXYZ
abcdefghijklmnopqrstuvwxyz
1234567890 !@#?:;"*&

Foundry: Lineto
Designer: Laurenz Brunner
Designer Nationality: Swiss
Date: 2004

A contemporary take on the 'pragmatic' traditions of Swiss typography, Akkurat, created by German type designer Laurenz Brunner, is an acclaimed modern-day classic of grotesque sans serif design. Sometimes referred to as a 'Helvetica killer', it is available in three weights, with accompanying italics, and an alternate monospaced variation was made available in 2005. Ideal for a range of applications, the design allows for optimum readability for text set at nearly all sizes. Widely used in print because of its excellent legibility in editorial and publishing applications, Akkurat has become increasingly popular for web use in recent years. Its slightly widened letter spacing, more vertical forms and clean, simple character shapes improve on-screen readability greatly, even at reduced text sizes or on the poorest of displays.

Below. Part of a series of striking typographic poster designs by Portuguese studio Atelier Pedro Falcão employing Lineto's Akkurat Pro for the *Departamento de Arquitectura Universidade Autónoma de Lisboa.*

Aktiv Grotesk

ABCDEFGHIJKLMNOPQRSTUVWXYZ
abcdefghijklmnopqrstuvwxyz
1234567890 !@#?:;"*&

A typeface that goes all out to be a 'Helvetica killer', Dalton Maag (see p. 594) first released Aktiv Grotesk in 2010 as a passion project for the studio founder and type designer Bruno Maag. Describing Helvetica as the 'vanilla ice cream' of a designer's type library, Maag was determined to create an alternative grotesque to the most ubiquitous of Swiss grotesques, one that stayed true to the grotesque tradition – no humanist aspects, but remaining neutral and authoritative while retaining an element of 'warmth' in its design with characters being simple, clear and consistent.

Aktiv Grotesk is a hugely comprehensive and diverse design with twenty-four weights and matching italics, from Hairline to Black, with support for more than 130 languages. It can truly be described as a global grotesque and one that can be employed in every conceivable application across all media.

Foundry: Dalton Maag
Designer: Bruno Maag / Alex Blattmann / Pilar Cano / Fernando Caro / Kalapi Gajjar / Fabio Haag
Designer Nationality: Swiss / Swiss / Spanish / Brazilian / Indian / Brazilian
Date: 2010–18

Below. Example of weight scaling for Condensed, Standard and Extended styles and Dalton Maag promotional print to launch Aktiv Grotesk.

" So success for Aktiv would be to see Helvetica driven from the face of the earth?
BM Yes! When I do lectures I always have a little rant about Helvetica and at the end I say if everyone in the world used Univers instead from now on I'd happily retire, but it ain't going to happen.
PB When this is out can you let Helvetica go? Have you exorcised the demon?
BM **Yes, it's catharsis. It's done now.**

PB **So let's talk about Aktiv, Dalt Maag's new Helvetica killer. Ca design a typeface in oppositic something? Is that what you s to do or were you just trying to as good a grotesk as you coul general use?** BM Clearly, because we are competing against Uni Helvetica there are a lot of close similarities. The : higher than Helvetica but the rounds have a little l them that Helvetica's don't have. The differences are really subtle but give it just that bit of p pronged really. One was the fact that we were looking at our font library and felt that we were in a Univers style, purely as a commercial entity. It has been at the back of our minds to do th years now. We wanted to have a grotesk font positioned somewhere between Helvetica and as Univers but devoid of all the quirks of Helvetica. To have a font that is beautifully crafted, s chink in a curve or anything – perfectly drawn but hopefully with a bit of personality. We wan

Albany

ABCDEFGHIJKLMNOPQRSTUVWXYZ
abcdefghijklmnopqrstuvwxyz
1234567890 !@#?:;"*&

Foundry: Monotype
Designer: Monotype Studio
Date: 2016

Possessing identical metrics to Robin Nicholas's ubiquitous Arial, this patriotic sans serif differs from both Arial and its arch rival Helvetica by having square dots over the letters 'i' and 'j'. In contrast to its predecessors, it also has more open letterforms with larger apertures and counters.

Angro

ABCDEFGHIJKLMNOPQRSTUVWXYZ
abcdefghijklmnopqrstuvwxyz
1234567890 !@#?:;"*&

Foundry: Linotype
Designer: Erwin Koch
Designer Nationality: German
Date: 1989

Designed to be used with Hell typesetting machines, Angro has two weights, Light and Bold, and a distinctive lowercase 'g'. Based on a rectangular form, it has short 'W's and descenders and a high x-height, meaning that it can be set with very close line spacing.

Applied Sans

ABCDEFGHIJKLMNOPQRSTUVWXYZ
abcdefghijklmnopqrstuvwxyz
1234567890 !@#?:;"*&

Foundry: Monotype
Designer: Akira Kobayashi / Sandra Winter
Designer Nationality: Japanese / German
Date: 2016

Applied Sans was designed as a refined and more human version of early 'jobbing' or 'trade' grotesques from the late 19th and early 20th centuries. The typeface has open counters, large apertures, a generous x-height and terminals that are at 90° to the character strokes.

Arial

ABCDEFGHIJKLMNOPQRSTUVWXYZ
abcdefghijklmnopqrstuvwxyz
1234567890 !@#?:;"*&

Foundry: Monotype
Designer: Robin Nicholas / Patricia Saunders
Designer Nationality: British
Date: 1982

Allegedly commissioned by IBM because Microsoft did not want to license Helvetica – with which it shares the same metrics – Arial has appeared in Windows 3.1 onwards and also on the Mac operating systems. This generic sans serif comes in numerous weights and styles, including a rounded version.

Arial Nova

ABCDEFGHIJKLMNOPQRSTUVWXYZ
abcdefghijklmnopqrstuvwxyz
1234567890 !@#?:;”*&

Foundry: Monotype
Designer: Robin Nicholas /
Patricia Saunders / Monotype
Studio
Designer Nationality: British
Date: 1982 / 2014

Forever associated with the Windows operating system, Arial Nova is a reboot of Robin Nicholas's and Patricia Saunders's original version of Arial created for IBM laser printers in 1982. It features three weights of roman and three weights of condensed, all with matching italics.

Basic Commercial

ABCDEFGHIJKLMNOPQRSTUVWXYZ
abcdefghijklmnopqrstuvwxyz
1234567890 !@#?:;”*&

Foundry: Linotype
Designer: Linotype Design Studio
Date: 1900 / 1999

Basic Commercial is a type family based on sans serifs launched by the Berthold foundry in Germany in 1898, as the Akzidenz Grotesk series. These typefaces were marketed as the Standard family elsewhere. Linotype made its version of Standard in 1957, and Basic Commercial follows those designs.

Basis

ABCDEFGHIJKLMNOPQRSTUVWXYZ
abcdefghijklmnopqrstuvwxyz
1234567890 !@#?:;“*&

Foundry: Colophon
Designer: The Entente
Designer Nationality: British
Date: 2015

Initially produced for the redesign of photography magazine *Hotshoe* in 2012, Basis is a sans serif font family with sixteen styles. Informed by early Monotype grotesques, but intentionally given more shape, Basis is defined by its tight apertures, curvy terminals and refined counters.

Bell Centennial

ABCDEFGHIJKLMNOPQRSTUVWXYZ
abcdefghijklmnopqrstuvwxyz
1234567890 !@#?:;”*&

Foundry: Mergenthaler Linotype
Designer: Matthew Carter
Designer Nationality: British
Date: 1978

Commissioned by AT&T, this economical sans serif saved the telecoms company millions of dollars. Compared to the previously used Bell Gothic, it saved space and it also provided increased legibility under difficult printing conditions, which in turn reduced calls to the help desk.

Berthold Akzidenz Grotesk

ABCDEFGHIJKLMNOPQRSTUVWXYZ
abcdefghijklmnopqrstuvwxyz
1234567890 !@#?:;"*&

Foundry: Berthold
Designer: Günter Gerhard Lange
Designer Nationality: German
Date: 1958

Often referred to as the 'original' sans serif, Akzidenz Grotesk has clean lines and forms that mean it is often mistaken for Helvetica (see p. 229) or Univers (see p. 248). However, its subtle varying stroke weights, more circular counters and bowls gives it a warmer and slightly softer appearance than its rivals.

Akzidenz Grotesk dates to a period of design much further back than the aforementioned 1950s' typefaces. The original design is believed to date to the 1880s, and understood to have been developed from Didone serif fonts such as the Walbaum and Didot typefaces. With their serifs removed, the proportions of the types are similar to a sans serif font resembling Akzidenz Grotesk.

As the years passed, Akzidenz Grotesk became a collection of differing grotesque types carrying the same name until the 1950s, when Günter Gerhard Lange, the art director for the renowned German type foundry Berthold, revised and improved upon the existing arrangement of designs to create the version of Akzidenz Grotesk of today. His efforts in increasing legibility and flexibility with a variety of weights led Akzidenz Grotesk to become one of the most widely used and successful typefaces in the world today, as well as an instant classic.

Below left. *Fikkefuchs* movie poster by Johannes Stoll employing Akzidenz Grotesk and its condensed variant.

Below right. One of a series of posters, entitled *Swissted*, an ongoing project by US graphic designer Mike Joyce. Each poster is designed around lowercase Berthold Akzidenz Grotesk Medium and the designer's love of punk rock and Swiss Modernism.

Opposite. The School of Life special events poster designed by Tako Chabukiani.

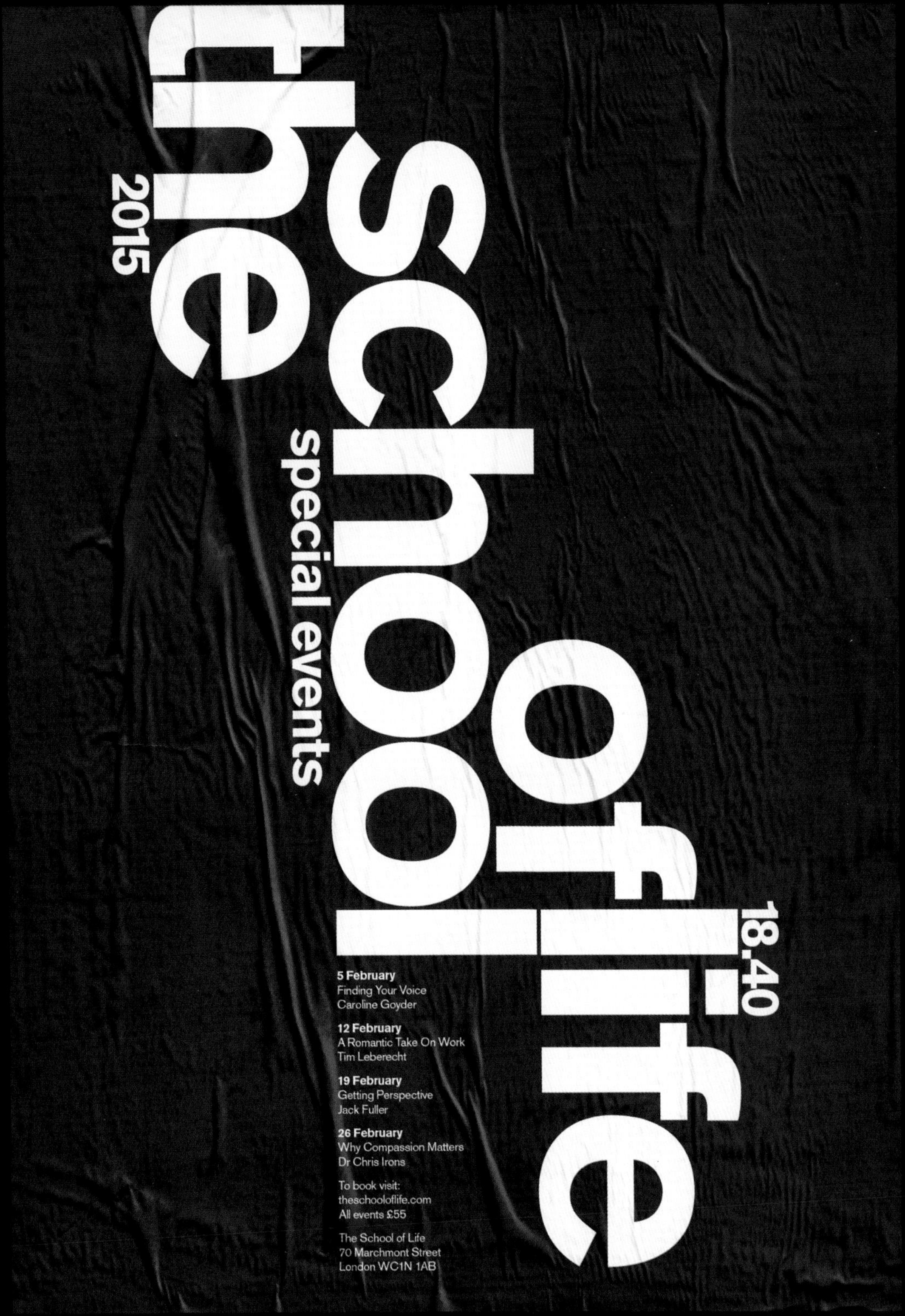

the school of life

2015

special events

18.40

5 February
Finding Your Voice
Caroline Goyder

12 February
A Romantic Take On Work
Tim Leberecht

19 February
Getting Perspective
Jack Fuller

26 February
Why Compassion Matters
Dr Chris Irons

To book visit:
theschooloflife.com
All events £55

The School of Life
70 Marchmont Street
London WC1N 1AB

Bell Gothic

ABCDEFGHIJKLMNOPQRSTUVWXYZ
abcdefghijklmnopqrstuvwxyz
1234567890 !@#?:;"*&

AT&T used Bell Gothic as its principal typeface for telephone books and other printed materials until 1978, when it became available for use by the public. Chauncey H. Griffith designed the typeface in 1938, when he was head of type development at Linotype. His experience with Excelsior, the highly successful newspaper typeface he created, earmarked him for the AT&T commission. The new typeface was required to be read at very small sizes and yet printed at very high speed, so the design had to overcome these challenging factors and ensure that legibility and readability were not compromised in any way. Griffith also had to optimize the restricted space it would be set within. The result, Bell Gothic, stood the test of time, and is still a popular choice within the design and publishing industries.

Foundry: Linotype
Designer: Chauncey H. Griffith
Designer Nationality: American
Date: 1938

Right. Promotional poster for director Alejandro G. Iñárritu's Oscar-winning film *Birdman*. Bell Gothic was the primary typeface for the marketing materials and also employed on the film's opening credits in an all capitals treatment.

Beret

ABCDEFGHIJKLMNOPQRSTUVWXYZ
abcdefghijklmnopqrstuvwxyz
1234567890 !@#?:;"*&

Foundry: Linotype
Designer: Eduardo Omine
Designer Nationality: Brazilian
Date: 2003

A jaunty sans serif, Beret has distinctive terminals at the ends of its vertical strokes which are slightly bent, suggesting a subtle flare and giving the impression that the letters are leaning. It comes with a set of obliques rather than traditional italics and is suitable for many applications, in both text and display sizes.

Between

ABCDEFGHIJKLMNOPQRSTUVWXYZ
abcdefghijklmnopqrstuvwxyz
1234567890 !@#?:;"*&

Foundry: Monotype
Designer: Akira Kobayashi
Designer Nationality: Japanese
Date: 2016

Between comprises one typeface with three different styles. Between 1, 2 and 3 have subtly different characteristics but share some of the same key characters, as well as caps and x-heights, which means that they have a harmonious feel when used together.

Brezel Grotesk

ABCDEFGHIJKLMNOPQRSTUVWXYZ
abcdefghijklmnopqrstuvwxyz
1234567890 !@#?:;"*&

Brezel Grotesk, as its name implies, is informed by the character of traditional 19th-century sans serif grotesques and the looping shape of a Bavarian pretzel. Initially designed in 2011 by Stefanie Preis, Brezel Grotesk was revised and extended by Milieu Grotesque in 2015.

Foundry: Milieu Grotesque
Designer: Stefanie Preis / Milieu Grotesque
Designer Nationality: German / Swiss
Date: 2011 / 2015

Bureau Grotesque

ABCDEFGHIJKLMNOPQRSTUVWXYZ
abcdefghijklmnopqrstuvwxyz
1234567890 !@#?:;"*&

Developed from original specimens of the grotesques made by the Stephenson, Blake & Co. foundry in Sheffield, Yorkshire, David Berlow added further weights to Bureau Grotesque. Jill Pichotta, Christian Schwartz and Richard Lipton expanded it further. It also goes under the name of 'Bureau Grot'.

Foundry: Font Bureau
Designer: David Berlow / Jill Pichotta / Christian Schwartz / Richard Lipton
Designer Nationality: American
Date: 1989–2006

CG Symphony

ABCDEFGHIJKLMNOPQRSTUVWXYZ
abcdefghijklmnopqrstuvwxyz
1234567890 !@#?:;"*&

Comprising Regular, Regular Italic, Bold and Black, CG Symphony is a restrained serif that started life as Hans Eduard Meier's Syntax (sometimes known as Syntax-Antiqua), and was one of the first one hundred PostScript faces released by Compugraphic in 1988.

Foundries: Stempel / Compugraphic
Designer: Hans Eduard Meier / Compugraphic Design Studio
Designer Nationality: German
Date: 1968 / 1988

Chiswick Grotesque

ABCDEFGHIJKLMNOPQRSTUVWXYZ
abcdefghijklmnopqrstuvwxyz
1234567890 !@#?:;"*&

Chiswick Grotesque is a grotesque sans serif, the kind of style commonly seen in the early 19th century. The burly, industrial characters merge geometric frames with eccentric strokes, as seen in the loop of the lowercase 'g' or the leg of the 'k'. It comes in eight weights plus italics.

Foundry: Commercial Type
Designer: Paul Barnes
Designer Nationality: British
Date: 2016

Cisalpin

ABCDEFGHIJKLMNOPQRSTUVWXYZ
abcdefghijklmnopqrstuvwxyz
1234567890 !@#?:;"*&

Foundry: Linotype
Designer: Felix Arnold
Designer Nationality: Swiss
Date: 2004

A linear typeface designed specifically to be used for cartography Cisalpin is naturally very compact and legible at small sizes. Its letterforms have flattened curves, open interior forms and tall x-heights, with a capital height that almost reaches the tops of the ascenders.

Classic Grotesque

ABCDEFGHIJKLMNOPQRSTUVWXYZ
abcdefghijklmnopqrstuvwxyz
1234567890 !@#?:;"*&

Foundry: Monotype
Designer: Frank Hinman Pierpont / Rod McDonald
Designer Nationality: American / Canadian
Date: 1926 / 2008

This is a new take on the original Monotype Grotesque, with seven weights from Light to Extra Bold. A restrained sans serif, it bears the hallmark of a traditional grotesque but has some subtle variations in its uppercase letters, including bevelled terminals and curved descenders.

Compatil Fact

ABCDEFGHIJKLMNOPQRSTUVWXYZ
abcdefghijklmnopqrstuvwxyz
1234567890 !@#?:;"*&

Foundry: Linotype
Designer: Olaf Leu / Linotype Design Studio
Designer Nationality: German
Date: 2001

Compatil Fact is a refined sans serif forming part of the Compatil type system, created specifically for use in annual reports. This system comprises four compatible typefaces, each with four weights, making it possible to set any combination of different styles effortlessly.

Corinthian

ABCDEFGHIJKLMNOPQRSTUVWXYZ
abcdefghijklmnopqrstuvwxyz
1234567890 !@#?:;"*&

Foundry: ITC
Designer: Colin Brignall
Designer Nationality: British
Date: 1981

Colin Brignall designed Corinthian when he was type director of Letraset. It is an unassuming monolineal sans serif for text and display use, which takes inspiration from the typefaces of Edward Johnston and Eric Gill. Corinthian is available in four weights: Light, Medium, Bold and Condensed.

Dialog

ABCDEFGHIJKLMNOPQRSTUVWXYZ
abcdefghijklmnopqrstuvwxyz
1234567890 !@#?:;"'*&

Foundry: Omnibus
Designer: Franko Luin
Designer Nationality: Swedish
Date: 1993

Available in weights from Light to Extra Bold, all with a condensed and italic version, this is the first sans serif typeface designed by Franko Luin. After several false starts, and despite preferring serifs, he created Dialog – a confident sans serif suitable for multiple applications.

Divulge

ABCDEFGHIJKLMNOPQRSTUVWXYZ
abcdefghijklmnopqrstuvwxyz
1234567890 !@#?:;"'*&

Foundry: Typodermic
Designer: Ray Larabie
Designer Nationality: Canadian
Date: 2008

Divulge is a modern grotesque inspired by metal type of the 19th and early 20th centuries. It is a handsome but restrained sans serif with some idiosyncratic features, which is available in three weights – Light, Medium and Bold – with two widths and matching italics.

Elastik

ABCDEFGHIJKLMNOPQRSTUVWXYZ
abcdefghijklmnopqrstuvwxyz
1234567890 !@#?:;"'*&

Foundry: BB-Bureau
Designer: Benoit Bedhuin
Designer Nationality: French
Date: 2017

Elastik is a grotesque sans serif with elasticated punctuation and diacritical marks, designed in four styles. The A style is small, B is regular, C is oversized, and D is extra-oversize. As the sizes increase, the mark's proportions stretch like elasticated materials.

Endurance

ABCDEFGHIJKLMNOPQRSTUVWXYZ
abcdefghijklmnopqrstuvwxyz
1234567890 !@#?:;"'*&

Foundry: Ascender
Designer: Steve Matteson
Designer Nationality: American
Date: 2004

Created as a more refined, less industrial-looking Neo-grotesque sans serif, Endurance is designed to function well under challenging conditions, from mobile to billboard-sized applications. Optimized for on-screen legibility, it has careful detailing in order to give a refined appearance in large sizes.

Esseltube

ABCDEFGHIJKLMNOPQRSTUVWXYZ
abcdefghijklmnopqrstuvwxyz
1234567890 !@#?:;"*&

Foundry: Linotype
Designer: Stig Åke Möller /
Bo Berndal
Designer Nationality: Swedish
Date: 1955

Also known as 'SL-Grotesk' and 'Esseltub', the Esseltube sans serif typeface was originally created for the Stockholm underground system. It was designed by Stig Åke Möller and digitized by Bo Berndal. In the 1980s, it was replaced with black and white signs using Helvetica.

Folio

ABCDEFGHIJKLMNOPQRSTUVWXYZ
abcdefghijklmnopqrstuvwxyz
1234567890 !@#?:;"*&

Foundry: Bauer Type
Designer: Konrad F. Bauer /
Walter Baum
Designer Nationality: German
Date: 1957

Released at the same time as Helvetica and Univers, Folio is a realist sans serif that is also modelled on Akzidenz Grotesk but follows its proportions more closely than Helvetica and Univers, which have larger x-heights. Extra Bold and Condensed versions were added in 1963.

FF Sizmo

ABCDEFGHIJKLMNOPQRSTUVWXYZ
abcdefghijklmnopqrstuvwxyz
1234567890 !@#?:;"*&

Foundry: FontFont
Designer: Verena Gerlach
Designer Nationality: German
Date: 2017

FF Sizmo is available in five weights from Light to Bold. It is unusual in that all its weights come in a separate 'Line' version, in which a line runs along the bottom of the letterforms – with the exception of letters that drop below or are open to the baseline – and joins them up.

Foundry Context

ABCDEFGHIJKLMNOPQRSTUVWXYZ
abcdefghijklmnopqrstuvwxyz
1234567890 !@#?:;"*&

Foundry: The Foundry
Designer: David Quay
Designer Nationality: British
Date: 2005

Foundry Context is a grotesque sans serif designed for universal use and inspired by the utilitarian sans serifs of the 19th century. The letterforms are modest in stroke contrast and neutral in character, resisting the superfluous details usually found in terminals or joints.

FS Industrie

ABCDEFGHIJKLMNOPQRSTUVWXYZ
abcdefghijklmnopqrstuvwxyz
1234567890 !@?:;"*&

Foundry: Fontsmith
Designer: Phil Garnham /
Fernando Mello
Designer Nationality: British /
Brazilian
Date: 2018

FS Industrie is an incredibly versatile type system, with seventy variants within its family, consisting of five differing widths (Condensed, Narrow, Standard, Wide and Extended) and seven different weights (ranging from Thin to Black). It was created by the type design director Phil Garnham and senior type designer Fernando Mello of London foundry Fontsmith (see p. 272). The key approach behind the design was to create a typeface that embraces 'variable design', an inbuilt flexibility within the system that adapts to the changing needs of brands. As more communications go online, digital platforms evolve and in turn create new opportunities in how they present the written word.

The core design is based on fonts from Germany in the 1930s, whose origins emanate from manufacturing and signage applications. FS Industrie harnesses the clean and considered approach of these functional and highly legible fonts. The design adapts through the styles and the weights. Each character is hand drawn, and careful consideration has been given to the letterforms, with subtle changes in the terminals and angles according to the weight and style required. This creates a consistent visual design that evolves, as seen in the closed terminals of the Condensed version, which gradually open up across the styles and form open terminals in the Extended version. Given its flexibility and functionality, FS Industrie is likely to be future-proof.

Below. Fontsmith launched FS Industrie with a limited-edition promotion of 1,000 printed specimen books, each design being unique. After a survey of hundreds of design professionals, each design had the recipient's name die-cut in the cover using a punched-card system. The content from the survey was then used inside to promote the typeface's abilities.

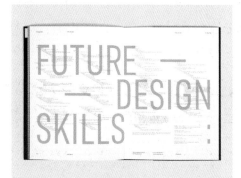

FS Jack

ABCDEFGHIJKLMNOPQRSTUVWXYZ
abcdefghijklmnopqrstuvwxyz
1234567890 !@#?:;"*&

Jason Smith and Fernando Mello designed FS Jack to include certain distinctive quirks within key letterforms, and it is particularly expressive in its heavier weights. In 2010, the typeface family won the Families category at the Tipos Latinos type design biennial in Mello's home country, Brazil.

Foundry: Fontsmith
Designer: Fernando Mello / Jason Smith
Designer Nationality: Brazilian / British
Date: 2010

FS Koopman

ABCDEFGHIJKLMNOPQRSTUVWXYZ
abcdefghijklmnopqrstuvwxyz
1234567890 !@#?:;"*&

The lighter cuts of FS Koopman display the influence of classic Swiss sans serif typography; its bold weights, however, feature details reminiscent of 20th-century British grotesques. Designers Andy Lethbridge and Stuart de Rozario also added an American Gothic flavour to the mix.

Foundry: Fontsmith
Designer: Andy Lethbridge / Stuart de Rozario
Designer Nationality: British
Date: 2018

Gerstner-Programm FSL

ABCDEFGHIJKLMNOPQRSTUVWXYZ
abcdefghijklmnopqrstuvwxyz
1234567890 !@#?:;"*&

Gerstner-Programm FSL is the digital reissue of an original type design by Karl Gerstner drawn between 1964 and 1967. Berthold first marketed the design with its Diatype phototypesetting system in 1967. Forgotten Shapes' published the reissue with Gerstner's permission

Foundry: Forgotten Shapes
Designer: Karl Gerstner / Stephan Müller
Designer Nationality: Swiss
Date: 1964–67 / 2007–17

GGX88

ABCDEFGHIJKLMNOPQRSTUVWXYZ
abcdefghijklmnopqrstuvwxyz
1234567890 !@#?:;"*&

Ray Larabie developed his Swiss-influenced design for GGX88 with screen use in mind. Its letterforms are optimized to be clear and legible in a range of digital contexts, such as TV screens, phones and watches. It includes seven weights with corresponding italics for each.

Foundry: Typodermic
Designer: Ray Larabie
Designer Nationality: Canadian
Date: 2010

Gothic 720

ABCDEFGHIJKLMNOPQRSTUVWXYZ
abcdefghijklmnopqrstuvwxyz
1234567890 !@#?:;"*&

This Bitstream font was modelled on the letterforms of Frank Hinman Pierpont's series of grotesque typefaces published by Monotype in the 1920s. The Monotype grotesques were themselves based on Berthold's Ideal Grotesk, and also referenced the Bauer type foundry's popular Venus typeface.

Foundries: Monotype / Bitstream
Designer: Frank Hinman Pierpont
Designer Nationality: American
Date: 1926

Graphik

ABCDEFGHIJKLMNOPQRSTUVWXYZ
abcdefghijklmnopqrstuvwxyz
1234567890 !@#?:;"*&

Graphik is a muted grotesque sans serif designed for efficacy across a variety of contexts and platforms. Instead of looking to the mainstays of utilitarian sans serifs, such as Helvetica or Univers, designer Christian Schwartz took inspiration from lesser known types such as Plak and Folio.

Foundry: Commercial Type
Designer: Christian Schwartz
Designer Nationality: American
Date: 2009

Graphik Compact

ABCDEFGHIJKLMNOPQRSTUVWXYZ
abcdefghijklmnopqrstuvwxyz
1234567890 !@#?:;"*&

Graphik Compact is a narrow alternative to the full-bodied Graphik and is intended for designs that require a strict economy of space, such as signage and user interfaces. While reduced in width, its letterforms retain a strong frame and open counters for maximum legibility.

Foundry: Commercial Type
Designer: Christian Schwartz
Designer Nationality: American
Date: 2017

Graphik Condensed

ABCDEFGHIJKLMNOPQRSTUVWXYZ
abcdefghijklmnopqrstuvwxyz
1234567890 !@#?:;"*&

Unlike Graphik Compact, which aims to maintain the physique of the original design, Graphik Condensed is closer to traditional condensed styles. While the vertical strokes are lengthened, the type's character is preserved in the curved upper and lower parts of the letterforms.

Foundry: Commercial Type
Designer: Christian Schwartz
Designer Nationality: American
Date: 2017

Graphik Wide

ABCDEFGHIJKLMNOPQRSTUVWXY
abcdefghijklmnopqrstuvwxyz
1234567890 !@#?:;"*&

Foundry: Commercial Type
Designer: Christian Schwartz
Designer Nationality: American
Date: 2018

Graphik Wide is a wide-set grotesque font family, inspired by the extended sans serifs that emerged in the 19th century, as well as those designed in the systematic tradition of the 20th century. The characters maintain a distinctly rounded shape, as per the original Graphik design.

GT America

ABCDEFGHIJKLMNOPQRSTUVWXYZ
abcdefghijklmnopqrstuvwxyz
1234567890 !@#?:;"*&

Foundry: Grilli Type
Designer: Noël Leu / Seb McLauchlan
Designer Nationality: Swiss
Date: 2016

GT America is named after channelling the design origins of 20th-century European Neo-grotesques and 19th-century American Gothics, with a pragmatic, Swiss approach. The letterforms have tapered stems and angled spurs, with eighty-four styles available across six widths and seven weights.

GT Pressura

ABCDEFGHIJKLMNOPQRSTUVWXYZ
abcdefghijklmnopqrstuvwxyz
1234567890 !@#?:;"*&

Foundry: Grilli Type
Designer: Marc Kappeler / Dominik Huber
Designer Nationality: Swiss
Date: 2012

Independent Swiss foundry Grilli Type (see p. 238) released GT Pressura in 2012. Inspired by the visual effect of ink spreading under pressure, Pressura is a robust sans available in regular and monospace, in three weights with italics. It was revised and extended with Cyrillic support in 2017.

GT Zirkon

ABCDEFGHIJKLMNOPQRSTUVWXYZ
abcdefghijklmnopqrstuvwxyz
1234567890 !@#?:;"*&

Foundry: Grilli Type
Designer: Tobias Rechsteiner
Designer Nationality: Swiss
Date: 2018

GT Zirkon is a grotesque sans serif that foregrounds the details typically found in small-scale body copy. Features such as ink traps, tapered curves and a high contrast between strokes are utilized as stylistic devices to enhance its character and utility.

Helvetica

ABCDEFGHIJKLMNOPQRSTUVWXYZ
abcdefghijklmnopqrstuvwxyz
1234567890 !@#?:,"*&

Foundry: Haas Type Foundry
Designer: Max Miedinger /
Eduard Hoffmann
Designer Nationality: Swiss
Date: 1957

Swiss typeface designer Max Miedinger, under the direction of Eduard Hoffmann, Haas director and fellow type designer, was responsible for designing perhaps the most widely used sans serif typeface, and possibly any typeface, of all time. Created in 1957 and originally titled Neue Haas Grotesk, it was renamed Helvetica in 1959 when released by Haas's new owners Stempel for the Linotype, which led to global success and domination in many quarters. At the Haas Type Foundry in Münchenstein, Switzerland, the two collaborated in creating a grotesque sans serif that would compete with the existing and popular Akzidenz Grotesk (see p. 218) released in 1898 by the Berthold Foundry of Berlin. Neither would envisage the phenomenal success that Helvetica would become once their work was done.

Miedinger trained as a typesetter from 1926, entering the School of Arts and Crafts, Abendkurse in Zurich. From 1947 to 1956, he worked at Haas before going freelance and picking up a commission from his now previous employer for the Neue Haas Grotesk project. The renaming of the typeface was undertaken by Haas's parent company Stempel and is a variation on the Latin word for Switzerland, Helvetia. Despite the designers expressing concern over the new name, it benefited from the positive attention the Swiss design movement had at the time of its release, and its universal appeal led to widespread usage. When Miedinger died in 1980 his legacy was the creation of one of the most specified and used typefaces of the 20th century. In 2007, US filmmaker Gary Hustwit directed the film *Helvetica* to celebrate its 50th anniversary.

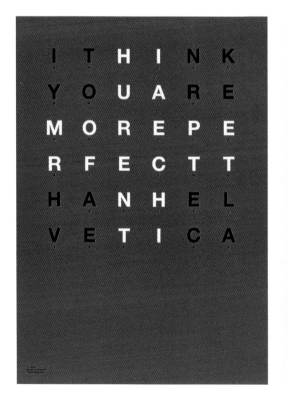

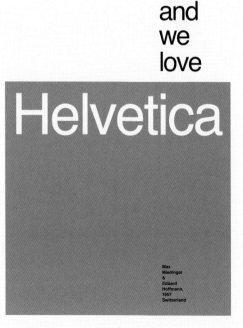

Far left. Poster design by Spanish studio Bisgràfic and their 2015 tribute to Helvetica.

Left. Taiwanese graphic designers Leslie Chan Wing Kei and Pei Lin share their feelings and the love for Miedinger and Hoffmann's sans serif, although Helvetica is not without its critics – in part due to its success. This is a typeface with a global reach.

Helvetica Neue

ABCDEFGHIJKLMNOPQRSTUVWXYZ
abcdefghijklmnopqrstuvwxyz
1234567890 !@#?:;"*&

Foundry: Stempel / Linotype
Designer: Max Meidinger /
Linotype Design Studio
Designer Nationality: Swiss
Date: 1957 / 1983

Helvetica soon found global success after its release in 1957. Since then, a range of variations have been created, as well as derivative clones released, in an attempt to gain a share of the original's market. The variations that exist are wide and diverse. Among them there are a number that are highly considered and which follow the principles of neutrality and aesthetic simplicity seen in the original designs.

Variations were not just created for commercial gain. As there were technological improvements in typesetting, from hot-metal composition through to digital fonts, so stresses were placed on the original designs that had in some ways been compromised by the technologies of the day. This meant the design warranted a revisit to embrace the opportunities and benefits that digital could bring to it.

The first digital version was Helvetica Neue, released by Linotype subsidiary Stempel. It is a complete reworking of the original Helvetica,

which, like Univers, follows a strict numerical classification system with a wider range of Condensed, Regular and Extended families to convey width, weight or Roman / Italic for each of the fonts. Its design has also been enriched with improved legibility, refined spacing, enhanced characters and a wider range of weights. The cap height is the same throughout the family and its improved legibility resulted in an incredibly popular typeface being more flexible than ever.

Truly global typefaces, both Helvetica and Helvetica Neue have been employed on every conceivable piece of graphic design: from corporate logos and identity programmes through to signage and wayfinding, packaging and publishing, film and TV, and even on the side of the now defunct Space Shuttle orbiters. Such overuse and domination means that there are many designers who are averse to using the typeface today. Nevertheless, it remains hugely popular and is one of the most successful typefaces ever created.

Below right. Postcard designs by Dutch studio Experimental Jetset for the De Theatercompagnie, now part of the MoMa New York collection.

Below left. Gold Award winner at the Graphis poster awards by Husmee Studio for their 60th anniversary poster design as part of the 60helvetica project.

Right. Poster design for FHNW HGK Visual Communication Institute, The Basel School of Design by Konstantin Eremenko, Russia. The final version was printed by silkscreen with white colour on a black paper.

Helvetica Now

ABCDEFGHIJKLMNOPQRSTUVWXYZ
abcdefghijklmnopqrstuvwxyz
1234567890 !@#?:;"*&

The first major revision of Helvetica in thirty-five years was released in 2019 by Monotype. The process spanned four years and was led by Jan Hendrik Weber and Charles Nix, and involved dozens of designers and engineers from the Monotype Studio. An exhaustive update of the most famous typeface of all time, the project has reinvigorated this classic sans serif for an evolving digital age. The redrawing resolves issues of legibility and readability at very small sizes (a perennial problem with Neue Helvetica) – and issues of spacing and style at large sizes.

Helvetica Now consists of forty-eight fonts in three optical sizes: Micro, Text and Display. The twenty Helvetica Now Display fonts, in a weight range from Hairline to ExtraBlack, are ideal for setting short amounts of text in sizes fourteen point and above. The sixteen Helvetica Now Text fonts, in a weight range from Thin to Black, are optimized for setting type in a range from eight to twelve point. The Helvetica Now Micro fonts, in ExtraLight to ExtraBold weights, are ideal for type in the micro-range of three to seven point and type in low-resolution environments. Within twenty-four hours of its release, Helvetica Now shot to number one in the sales charts – offering a new lease of life for a classic family.

Foundry: Monotype
Designer: Max Miedinger / Eduard Hoffmann / Jan Hendrik Weber / Charles Nix / Monotype Studio
Nationality: Swiss / Swiss / German / American / British
Date: 1957 / 2019

Below left. Promotional design conveying the three distinctive optical sizes, Display, Text and Micro and ideal applications.

Opposite. The full range of characters (glyphs) in a single weight of Helvetica Now number 812, resulting in a total of 38,976 characters across the entire family. In addition, the new release also contains alternate characters (shown in red) and additional glyphs such as arrows and sets of circled and squared figures.

A Á Ă Â Ä À Ā Ą Å Ǻ Ã Æ Ǽ B C Ć Č Ç Ĉ Ċ D Đ Ď Ð E É Ĕ Ě Ê Ë Ė È Ē
Ę F G Ǵ Ğ Ĝ Ģ Ġ H Ħ Ĥ I IJ Í Ĭ Î Ï İ Ì Ī Į Ĩ J Ĵ K Ķ L Ĺ Ľ Ļ Ŀ Ł M N Ń Ň Ņ Ŋ Ñ
O Ó Ŏ Ô Ö Ò Ő Ō Ø Ǿ Õ Œ P Þ Q R Ŕ Ř Ŗ S Ś Š Ş Ŝ Ș ß Ə T Ŧ Ť Ţ Ț U
Ú Ŭ Û Ü Ù Ű Ū Ų Ů Ũ V W Ẃ Ŵ Ẅ Ẁ X Y Ý Ŷ Ÿ Ỳ Z Ź Ž Ż Ä Ċ Ë Ġ Ï İ
Ķ Ļ Ŀ Ņ Ö Ŗ Ş Ţ Ü Ẅ Ÿ Ż G Ǵ Ğ Ĝ Ģ Ġ G Ġ R Ŕ Ř Ŗ Ŗ a á ă â ä à ā ą å ǻ
ã æ ǽ b c ć č ç ĉ ċ d ð ď đ e é ĕ ě ê ë ė è ē ę ə f g ǵ ğ ĝ ġ ġ h ħ ĥ i ı í ĭ î ï
i ì ij ī į ĩ j ĵ k ķ ĸ l ĺ ľ ļ ŀ ł m n ń ' n ň ņ ŋ ñ o ó ŏ ô ö ò ő ō ø ǿ õ œ p þ q r ŕ ř
ŗ s ś š ş ŝ ș ß t ŧ ť ţ ț u ú ŭ û ü ù ű ū ų ů ũ v w ẃ ŵ ẅ ẁ x y ý ŷ ÿ ỳ z ź ž ż
ä ċ ë ė ġ ï i ij j ķ ļ ŀ ' n ņ ö ŗ ş ţ ẅ ÿ ż a á ă â ä à ā ą å ǻ ã ä ţ ü ŧ ŧ ť ţ ţ
ü ů ú ŭ û ü ù ű ū ų ů ũ ÿ y ý ŷ ÿ ỳ l ĺ ľ ļ ŀ ł ļ ŀ fi fl fi fl ᵃ ᵒ ᵃ ʰ ⁿ ʳ ˢ ᵗ Δ Ω µ π
ᵈ ₙ ᵗ 0 1 2 3 4 5 6 7 8 9 ❶ ❷ ❸ ❹ ❺ ❻ ❼ ❽ ❾ 0 1 2 3 4 5
6 7 8 9 ⓪ ① ② ③ ④ ⑤ ⑥ ⑦ ⑧ ⑨ 0 1 2 3 4 5 6 7 8 9 0
0 1 2 3 4 5 6 7 8 9 0 1 2 3 4 5 6 7 8 9 0 1 2 3 4 5 6 7 8 9 0 1 2 3 4 5 6 7 8 9 / ½ ⅓ ⅔
¼ ¾ ⅕ ⅖ ⅗ ⅘ ⅙ ⅚ ⅛ ⅜ ⅝ ⅞ 0 1 2 3 4 5 6 7 8 9 0 . , : ; … ! ¡ ? ¿
· • * ? ¿ # / \ . , : ; … ! ¡ ? ¿ · • ? ¿ ₍ ₎ ( ) { } [ ] ⁽ ⁾ ( ) { } [ ] - - — - _ - - —
, „ " " ' ' « » ‹ › " ' « » ‹ › , „ " " ' ' - ( ) { } [ ] . , ⁻ ⁽ ⁾ ⁽ ⁾ · . , . , ' - { } [ ]
. , - { } [ ] . , ₿ ¢ ¤ $ € ƒ ₭ ₥ ₮ £ ₸ ¥ € ₺ ₮ ₴ ¥ • / + − × ÷ = ≠ > < ≥ ≤ ±
≈ ~ ¬ ∧ ∞ ∫ Ω Δ Π Σ √ µ ∂ % ‰ ₌ ⁼ ₋ ⁻ ₊ ⁺ • ÷ ↑ ↗ → ↘ ↓ ↙ ← ↖ ↔ ↕
● ○ ◇ ■ □ ʰᵉˡ ᵛᵉ ᵗⁱᶜᵃ @ & ¶ § © ® ℗ ™ ‰ ° | ¦ ℓ † ‡ Ө № ¢ $ € + − = ¢ $ € + −
= ¢ $ € ¢ $ € ⁻ ‾ ̆ ˊ ˋ ˝ ˘ ˇ ˚ ˜ ⁻ ‾ ˆ ˙ ˙ "
‾ ˚ ˜ , ¨ ¨ ˝ ˆ ^ ˘ ˇ ˚ ̃ ̈ · · ₒ ‚ ˛ ⌣ ‐ · ̃
̦ · ‿ · ̦ · ˛ · ̦

Incised 901

ABCDEFGHIJKLMNOPQRSTUVWXYZ
abcdefghijklmnopqrstuvwxyz
1234567890 !@#?:;"*&

Foundry: Bitstream
Designer: Roger Excoffon
Designer Nationality: French
Date: 1962

This Bitstream typeface is based on Antique Olive, designed in 1962 by Roger Excoffon for Fonderie Olive in France. Although originally created to compete with other European grotesques such as Helvetica, this expressive design took the finished typeface in a much less neutral direction.

Interstate

ABCDEFGHIJKLMNOPQRSTUVWXYZ
abcdefghijklmnopqrstuvwxyz
1234567890 !@#?:;"*&

Foundry: Font Bureau
Designer: Tobias Frere-Jones
Designer Nationality: American
Date: 1993

Frere-Jones based the design of Interstate on the typeface created in 1949 by Ted Forbes and his team of J. E. Penton and E. E. Radek for the US Federal Highway Administration, Highway Gothic. Interstate's wide letter spacing and generous x-height make it particularly suitable for signage and display use.

Italian Plate No. 2 Expanded

ABCDEFGHIJKLMNOPQRSTUVWXYZ
abcdefghijklmnopqrstuvwxyz
1234567890 !@#?:;"*&

Foundry: Playtype
Designer: Jonas Hecksher
Designer Nationality: Danish
Date: 2014

Similar to Italian Plate No. 1, the characters of this font are informed by the Italian vehicle number plates of the 1960s. However, the design of Italian Plate No. 2 Expanded includes the addition of width and space in the letterforms, alongside sharper terminals, for greater readability.

ITC Franklin

ABCDEFGHIJKLMNOPQRSTUVWXYZ
abcdefghijklmnopqrstuvwxyz
1234567890 !@#?:;"*&

Foundry: American Type Founders / ITC
Designer: Morris Fuller Benton / David Berlow
Designer Nationality: American
Date: 1902–05 / 2008

Font Bureau founder David Berlow comprehensively reworked Franklin Gothic to marshal existing cuts of the font into a superfamily of forty-eight grotesque styles. This suite of typefaces built upon his work in the early 1990s to create condensed cuts of Franklin for ITC.

ITC Franklin Gothic

ABCDEFGHIJKLMNOPQRSTUVWXYZ
abcdefghijklmnopqrstuvwxyz
1234567890 !@#?:;"*&

Franklin Gothic's expansion into a full font family from the first weight published by the American Type Founders in 1902 took several decades. This ITC version, created by Victor Caruso, adds lighter weights to the family while preserving the robust spirit of Morris Fuller Benton's original design.

Foundry: American Type Founders / ITC
Designer: Morris Fuller Benton / Victor Caruso
Designer Nationality: American
Date: 1902–05 / 1980

La Fabrique

ABCDEFGHIJKLMNOPQRSTUVWXYZ
abcdefghijklmnopqrstuvwxyz
1234567890 !@#?:;"*&

This font was originally designed in 2012 as part of an installation for La Fabrique, an exhibition staged at the 23rd International Poster and Graphic Design Festival in Chaumont, France. The La Fabrique family was expanded in 2017 to include five weights, Italics and extended language support.

Foundry: Colophon
Designer: The Entente
Designer Nationality: British
Date: 2017

Linotype Gothic

ABCDEFGHIJKLMNOPQRSTUVWXYZ
abcdefghijklmnopqrstuvwxyz
1234567890 !@#?:;"*&

Linotype Gothic is based on Morris Fuller Benton's News Gothic, which was first published in 1908 by American Type Founders, and on Stempel's digitization of the face in 1984, News Gothic 2. The Linotype in-house team designed a new Italic counterpart for this updated version.

Foundry: Linotype
Designer: Linotype Design Studio
Date: 2005

Maison

ABCDEFGHIJKLMNOPQRSTUVWXYZ
abcdefghijklmnopqrstuvwxyz
1234567890 !@#?:;"*&

Maison is a grotesque sans serif, designed to evoke an industrial aesthetic without an over-reliance on optical adjustments or symbolic elements. It was initially produced in 2010 as a monospaced font family and then expanded in 2018 to include a partnering standard alignment.

Foundry: Milieu Grotesque
Designer: Timo Gaessner
Designer Nationality: German
Date: 2018

Maison Neue

ABCDEFGHIJKLMNOPQRSTUVWXYZ
abcdefghijklmnopqrstuvwxyz
1234567890 !@#?:;"*&

Foundry: Milieu Grotesque
Designer: Timo Gaessner
Designer Nationality: German
Date: 2017

Maison Neue is a revision of the initial Maison design. Unlike the original, Maison Neue's expanded font family, which includes forty styles, lessens its focus on geometry. Instead, Maison Neue favours an optical construction, producing a style closer to a traditional grotesque.

Monotype Grotesque

ABCDEFGHIJKLMNOPQRSTUVWXYZ
abcdefghijklmnopqrstuvwxyz
1234567890 !@#?:;"*&

Foundry: Monotype
Designer: Frank Hinman Pierpont
Designer Nationality: American
Date: 1926

Frank Hinman Pierpont supervised the designs of this family of numbered grotesques at Monotype in 1926, which were inspired by Berthold's Ideal Grotesk. Monotype Grotesque was digitized in 1992 and the numbering system was dropped in favour of descriptive names for the twelve styles in the family.

Monotype Lightline Gothic

ABCDEFGHIJKLMNOPQRSTUVWXYZ
abcdefghijklmnopqrstuvwxyz
1234567890 !@#?:;"*&

Foundry: Monotype
Designer: Morris Fuller Benton
Designer Nationality: American
Date: 1908

Morris Fuller Benton designed Lightline Gothic for the American Type Founders (ATF) in 1908. A thin sans serif with fairly narrow characters, it was conceived as a lighter alternative to his popular Franklin Gothic, which was released by ATF in 1904 but came in only one Bold weight.

Monotype News Gothic

ABCDEFGHIJKLMNOPQRSTUVWXYZ
abcdefghijklmnopqrstuvwxyz
1234567890 !@#?:;"*&

Foundry: Monotype
Designer: Morris Fuller Benton
Designer Nationality: American
Date: 1908

Morris Fuller Benton created News Gothic for the American Type Founders in 1908 to accompany his other sans serifs, the bolder Franklin Gothic and thinner Lightline Gothic. News Gothic became a popular choice for newspapers and magazines during the 20th century.

Mote

ABCDEFGHIJKLMNOPQRSTUVWXYZ
abcdefghijklmnopqrstuvwxyz
1234567890 !@#?:;”*&

Foundry: Typotheque
Designer: Hrvoje Živčić
Designer Nationality: Croatian
Date: 2013

Designed by Hrvoje Živčić, a Croatian designer educated on the Type and Media course at the Royal Academy of Arts in The Hague and now based in Zagreb, Mote is a utilitarian grotesque sans serif with low contrast. Mote comes in six weights with italics and many alternative characters.

Nationale

ABCDEFGHIJKLMNOPQRSTUVWXYZ
abcdefghijklmnopqrstuvwxyz
1234567890 !@#?:;”*&

Foundry: Playtype
Designer: Jonas Hecksher
Designer Nationality: Danish
Date: 2013

Jonas Hecksher designed Nationale as part of a new visual identity for the National Museum of Denmark. Informed by the timeless aesthetics of Futura, Avenir and Gill Sans, the design of his streamlined grotesque sans serif resists stylistic details to transcend the periodization of history.

Neue Haas Grotesk Display

ABCDEFGHIJKLMNOPQRSTUVWXYZ
abcdefghijklmnopqrstuvwxyz
1234567890 !@#?:;”*&

Foundry: Linotype
Designer: Max Miedinger / Christian Schwartz / Berton Hasebe
Designer Nationality: Swiss / American / American
Date: 1957 / 2010

Christian Schwartz drew Neue Haas Grotesk Display for Richard Turley's redesign of *Bloomberg Businessweek* in 2010. It takes its name from Helvetica's first incarnation. Schwartz aimed to capture the spirit of Helvetica's original design, which he felt had been lost in digitizations.

Neue Haas Unica

ABCDEFGHIJKLMNOPQRSTUVWXYZ
abcdefghijklmnopqrstuvwxyz
1234567890 !@#?:;”*&

Foundry: Monotype
Designer: André Gürtler / Christian Mengelt / Erich Gschwind / Toshi Omagari
Designer Nationality: Swiss / Swiss / Swiss / Japanese
Date: 2014–15

Designed at Haas, Unica began as a Helvetica update for phototypesetting, but the rise of computers made this neutral Swiss sans redundant. Toshi Omagari based his Unica on files found in Linotype's archive. The Lineto foundry released its Unica digitization by Christian Mengelt in 2015.

Grilli Type

Grilli Type is an independent Swiss type foundry offering original retail and custom typefaces. Beautifully crafted, these are created in the Swiss tradition, marrying a classic design approach to a contemporary aesthetic. Based in Lucerne, the foundry was set up by Noël Leu and Thierry Blancpain in 2009. Today team Grilli also includes Reto Moser, Tobias Rechsteiner and Anna Lind Haugaard. The foundry often collaborates with other designers, artists and developers, including Josh Schaub, Pieter Pelgrims, Refurnished+, XXIX and David Elsener.

Notable releases include GT Sectra (see p. 30), a contemporary serif typeface combining the 'calligraphy of the broad nib pen with the sharpness of the scalpel knife'. The GT America sans serif bridges the American Gothic and European Grotesque typeface genres, combining design features from both traditions to unite them in a contemporary family. The versatile system consists of eighty-four styles across six widths and seven weights.

Founded: 2009
Country: Switzerland
Website: grillitype.com
Notable typefaces:
GT Sectra (see p. 30)

Below. NeoCon is the USA's largest contract design trade show. For its 50th edition, Maiarelli Studio created a new visual identity, using GT America as the main typeface across print and online materials.

Opposite top. Stereo Associates' catalogue for the Danish Architecture Center's opening exhibition for Politikens Forlag. The catalogue is the first publication using their new visual identity, which prominently features GT Pressura.

Opposite, middle and bottom. Designed by Morphoria Design Collective in cooperation with Jazek Porallathe, GT Walsheim was employed within the new corporate design for the Museum Kunsthaus NRW.

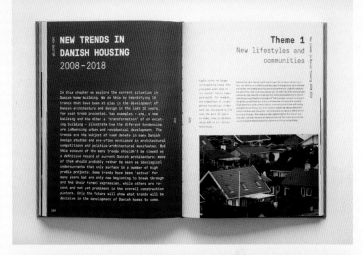

Neutral

ABCDEFGHIJKLMNOPQRSTUVWXYZ
abcdefghijklmnopqrstuvwxyz
1234567890 !@#?:;"*&

Foundry: Typotheque
Designer: Kai Bernau
Designer Nationality: German
Date: 2014

Neutral was designed by German Kai Bernau of Dutch design studio Atelier Carvalho Bernau. The typeface began as a graduate project on the Design & Typography course at the Royal Academy of Arts in The Hague. As its name implies, Neutral aims to be objective, free of connotations and character.

Neuzeit Office

ABCDEFGHIJKLMNOPQRSTUVWXYZ
abcdefghijklmnopqrstuvwxyz
1234567890 !@#?:;"*&

Foundry: Linotype
Designer: Wilhelm Pischner / Akira Kobayashi
Designer Nationality: German / Japanese
Date: 1928 / 2006

Wilhelm Pischner designed the Neuzeit Grotesk geometric sans serif for the German foundry Stempel in 1928. It was then updated in 1959 and 1966. Akira Kobayashi created Neuzeit Office for Linotype in 2006, adding obliques and optimizing it for on-screen text usage.

Neuzeit Office Soft Rounded

ABCDEFGHIJKLMNOPQRSTUVWXYZ
abcdefghijklmnopqrstuvwxyz
1234567890 !@#?:;"*&

Foundry: Linotype
Designer: Wilhelm Pischner / Akira Kobayashi
Designer Nationality: German / Japanese
Date: 1928 / 2006

Like many prominent sans serif typefaces, such as Arial and Helvetica, Neuzeit received a rounded version that softened it and made it appear friendlier. The Soft Rounded approach was applied to only two cuts of Neuzeit Office, Regular and Bold, without obliques.

Neuzeit S

ABCDEFGHIJKLMNOPQRSTUVWXYZ
abcdefghijklmnopqrstuvwxyz
1234567890 !@#?:;"*&

Foundry: Linotype
Designer: Wilhelm Pischner / Arthur Ritzel
Designer Nationality: German
Date: 1928 / 1966

Neuzeit S is an update of Wilhelm Pischner's Neuzeit Grotesk of 1928 made by Arthur Ritzel at Linotype in 1966. 'Neuzeit' is German for 'new time' and the 'S' in the name stands for 'Siemens', which adopted a version as its corporate font. It comes in two weights, Book and Heavy.

News Gothic BT

ABCDEFGHIJKLMNOPQRSTUVWXYZ
abcdefghijklmnopqrstuvwxyz
1234567890 !@#?:;"*&

Foundry: Bitstream
Designer: Morris Fuller Benton
Designer Nationality: American
Date: 1908

Morris Fuller Benton designed News Gothic for the American Type Founders (ATF) in 1908. The ATF ceased to exist in 1993 and since then numerous foundries have created variants, among them Adobe, Monotype and Linotype. Bitstream's version, News Gothic BT, is one of many variants of the original revived in digital font form. It comes in four weights and three widths – Regular, Condensed and Extra Condensed.

As with Benton's other notable sans serif design Franklin Gothic, News Gothic shares the same proportions but is a lighter design with a slightly condensed appearance. It was originally developed as two lighter weight designs, with another, Lightline Gothic, being dropped. Dmitry Kirsanov of the Russian foundry Paratype created a Cyrillic version in 2005 and then a Greek glyphs variant in 2009.

News Gothic was a popular grotesque sans serif throughout the 20th century. The original design was widely used in newspaper and magazine publishing because of its availability on Monotype and similar machines employed for hot-metal typesetting. However, perhaps News Gothic's most notable use is for the opening crawl of scrolling text in the *Star Wars* films.

From left. A selection of cover designs for classical, jazz and pop albums, showing News Gothic's versatility as a display sans and demonstrating that it is ideal for a variety of text applications.

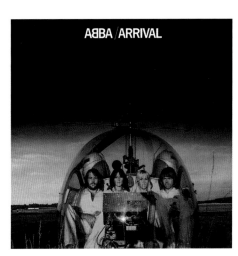

News Gothic No. 2

ABCDEFGHIJKLMNOPQRSTUVWXYZ
abcdefghijklmnopqrstuvwxyz
1234567890 !@#?:;"*&

Foundry: Stempel
Designer: Morris Fuller Benton / Stempel Design Studio
Designer Nationality: American / German
Date: 1908 / 1984

News Gothic No. 2 is an enhanced version of News Gothic created by German foundry Stempel in 1984. Stempel increased the number of weights to six, with matching italics, which is more than had previously been available, and helped encourage its use in contemporary design and communication.

Normal-Grotesk FSL

ABCDEFGHIJKLMNOPQRSTUVWXYZ
abcdefghijklmnopqrstuvwxyz
1234567890 !@#?:;"*&

Foundry: Forgotten Shapes
Designer: Haas Type Foundry / Stephan Müller
Designer Nationality: Swiss
Date: 1953 / 2008–18

Normal-Grotesk FSL is the digital reissue of Haas's Normal-Grotesk of 1953. Normal-Grotesk itself was based on Edel-Grotesk, released by the Ludwig Wagner foundry between c. 1912 and 1914. Haas redrew and substituted some of Edel-Grotesk's letters to give it a more modern appeal.

Oli Grotesk

ABCDEFGHIJKLMNOPQRSTUVWXYZ
abcdefghijklmnopqrstuvwxyz
1234567890 !#?:;"*&

Foundry: Typotheque
Designer: Shiva Nallaperumal / Aarya Purohit
Designer Nationality: Indian
Date: 2019

Oli by Shiva Nallaperumal and Aarya Purohit is available in Grotesk and Mono, with support for Latin, Cyrillic, Greek, Armenian and Devanagari. The first use of Oli Grotesk, an appealing modern grotesque, was the identity for the Design Fabric design conference in India in 2018.

Parmigiano Sans

ABCDEFGHIJKLMNOPQRSTUVWXYZ
abcdefghijklmnopqrstuvwxyz
1234567890 !@#?:;"*&

Foundry: Typotheque
Designer: Riccardo Olocco / Jonathan Pierini
Designer Nationality: Italian
Date: 2014

Parmigiano Sans is part of a larger family inspired by the work of 18th-century Italian typographer Giambattista Bodoni and raises questions of how his design sensibilities may have been applied to a sans serif. It comes in eight styles, recalling early grotesques thanks to its contrasting thicks and thins.

Patron

ABCDEFGHIJKLMNOPQRSTUVWXYZ
abcdefghijklmnopqrstuvwxyz
1234567890 !@#?:;"*&

Foundry: Milieu Grotesque
Designer: Timo Gaessner
Designer Nationality: German
Date: 2014

Patron's grotesque design is a tribute to the conflicting styles of type designers Günter Gerhard Lange and Roger Excoffon. The font combines the craftsmanship of Lange, seen in the precision of shape and form, with the subversive strokes that are characteristic of Excoffon.

PL Brazilia

ABCDEFGHIJKLMNOPQRSTUVWXYZ
abcdefghijklmnopqrstuvwxyz
1234567890 !#?:;"*&

Foundry: Photo-Lettering
Designer: Albert Boton
Designer Nationality: French
Date: 1960

French designer Albert Boton created the elegant Brazilia font family for US company Photo-Lettering in 1960. The distinctive extended sans serif comes in two weights, numbered Three and Seven. The wide lowercase 'r' is perhaps Brazilia's most characteristic letter.

Praxis

ABCDEFGHIJKLMNOPQRSTUVWXYZ
abcdefghijklmnopqrstuvwxyz
1234567890 !@#?:;"*&

Foundry: Hell
Designer: Gerard Unger
Designer Nationality: Dutch
Date: 1976

Dutch designer Gerard Unger created Praxis in 1976 for German company Hell. It is a legible, sans serif companion to his typeface Demos and both these early digital fonts have low contrast, a large x-height and fairly open counters. Praxis comes in five weights with matching obliques.

Praxis Next

ABCDEFGHIJKLMNOPQRSTUVWXYZ
abcdefghijklmnopqrstuvwxyz
1234567890 !@#?:;"*&

Foundry: Monotype
Designer: Gerard Unger / Linda Hintz
Designer Nationality: Dutch / Danish
Date: 2017

The German government adopted Praxis as an official typeface in the 1990s. In 2017, Linda Hintz at Monotype worked with its designer Gerard Unger on an update, Praxis Next, which added four new weights, as well as condensed versions, all with true italics rather than the original obliques.

Prima Sans

ABCDEFGHIJKLMNOPQRSTUVWXYZ
abcdefghijklmnopqrstuvwxyz
1234567890 !@#?:;"*&

Foundry: Bitstream
Designer: Jim Lyles
Designer Nationality: American
Date: 1998

Bitstream designer and font engineer Jim Lyles designed and released Prima Sans in 1998 as part of the Prima family, which also contained a serif and mono. Prima Sans was conceived to be easily read on-screen, even at lower resolutions. It is available in Roman and Bold with obliques.

Quitador Sans

ABCDEFGHIJKLMNOPQRSTUVWXYZ
abcdefghijklmnopqrstuvwxyz
1234567890 !@#?:;" * &

Foundry: Linotype
Designer: Arne Freytag
Designer Nationality: German
Date: 2016

Quitador Sans is a striking sibling of Arne Freytag's Quitador slab serif of 2014. It comes in seven weights with italics. Quitador Sans has many distinguishing features, such as the 'Q' in two parts, and many glyphs feature fine, pointed terminals that do not join stems, giving an almost stencil feel.

Rather

ABCDEFGHIJKLMNOPQRSTUVWXYZ
abcdefghijklmnopqrstuvwxyz
1234567890 !@#?:;"*&

Foundry: Or Type
Designer: Mads Freund Brunse / Guðmundur Úlfarsson (GUNMAD)
Designer Nationality: Danish / Icelandic
Date: 2015

Rather is an unconventional grotesque sans serif that is designed in nine weights with italics. The variation between the expansive shapes found in the rounded characters and the shorter horizontal strokes in the narrower forms yield an irregular, yet highly legible, typographic rhythm.

Reader

ABCDEFGHIJKLMNOPQRSTUVWXYZ
abcdefghijklmnopqrstuvwxyz
1234567890 !@#?:;"*&

Foundry: Colophon
Designer: The Entente
Designer Nationality: British
Date: 2018

Reader is a grotesque sans serif based on an unknown typeface found in a Royal Society for the Protection of Birds letter from 1972. The Entente's design features slight changes to the original, such as a rebalancing of the proportions and the addition of further stroke contrast for enhanced legibility.

Relative

ABCDEFGHIJKLMNOPQRSTUVWXYZ
abcdefghijklmnopqrstuvwxyz
1234567890 !@#?:;"*&

Foundry: Colophon
Designer: The Entente
Designer Nationality: British
Date: 2011

Relative is a grotesque sans serif that was originally designed for Stephen Gill's photo book *Outside In* (2010). Released in 2011, the font was expanded to include ten styles, made up of proportional weights and pitched monospaced versions, alongside a hybrid Faux monospace design.

Similar

ABCDEFGHIJKLMNOPQRSTUVWXYZ
abcdefghijklmnopqrstuvwxyz
1234567890 !@#?:;"*&

Foundry: Or Type
Designer: Guðmundur Úlfarsson
Designer Nationality: Icelandic
Date: 2015

Similar is a grotesque sans serif that combines a traditional structure with several idiosyncratic details. Curves that bridge the stroke and the stem are flattened to create an angled interior joint, while the vertical strokes feature a slight bend towards the foot.

Spartan

ABCDEFGHIJKLMNOPQRSTUVWXYZ
abcdefghijklmnopqrstuvwxyz
1234567890 !@#?:;"*&

Foundry: Monotype
Designer: John L. Renshaw
Designer Nationality: American
Date: 1939

The success of the Bauer foundry's geometric Futura inspired many copies, such as Spartan, which was designed by a team at Mergenthaler Linotype. John L. 'Bud' Renshaw later designed extra weights. Spartan is almost identical to Futura but has a flat-topped '1' and an alternate double-storey 'a'.

Surogat

ABCDEFGHIJKLMNOPQRSTUVWXYZ
abcdefghijklmnopqrstuvwxyz
1234567890 !@#?:;"*&

Foundry: Typotheque
Designer: Nikola Djurek
Designer Nationality: Croatian
Date: 2014

Nikola Djurek's Surogat is a versatile typeface family, comprised of three widths – Standard, Condensed and Compressed – in eight weights, all with italics. Dutch foundry Typotheque (see p. 90) markets it as a 'raw, sturdy, industrial sans serif typeface with dominant horizontal strokes'.

Swiss 721

ABCDEFGHIJKLMNOPQRSTUVWXYZ
abcdefghijklmnopqrstuvwxyz
1234567890 !@#?:;"*&

Foundry: Bitstream
Designer: Max Miedinger
Designer Nationality: Swiss
Date: 1957 / 1982

Swiss 721 is Bitstream's digitization of the legendary sans serif Helvetica, which it released in 1982. It comes in Roman and Italic in seven weights, Condensed in four weights with italics and extended in four weights without italics. There are outline versions of Bold, Black and Bold Condensed.

Swiss 721 Rounded

ABCDEFGHIJKLMNOPQRSTUVWXYZ
abcdefghijklmnopqrstuvwxyz
1234567890 !@#?:;"*&

Foundry: Bitstream
Designer: Max Miedinger
Designer Nationality: Swiss
Date: 1957 / 1982

Bitstream created Swiss 721 Rounded in 1982, when there was a trend for rounded fonts. Available in Bold and Black, it is a version of Helvetica Rounded, which is a softened redesign of the popular typeface Helvetica created by the Haas Type Foundry in 1957.

Syntax

ABCDEFGHIJKLMNOPQRSTUVWXYZ
abcdefghijklmnopqrstuvwxyz
1234567890 !@#?:;" *&

Foundry: Stempel
Designer: Hans Eduard Meier
Designer Nationality: German
Date: 1968

Syntax, designed by Hans Eduard Meier in 1968, was the last hot-metal type family produced by the foundry Stempel. It is a distinctive, optically monoline sans serif with a humanistic, double-storey 'a' and 'g'. The original cuts – four romans and an italic – were digitized in 1989.

Trade Gothic LT

ABCDEFGHIJKLMNOPQRSTUVWXYZ
abcdefghijklmnopqrstuvwxyz
1234567890 !@#?:;"*&

Foundry: Linotype
Designer: Jackson Burke
Designer Nationality: American
Date: 1948

Trade Gothic is an unorthodox, grotesque sans serif that was first cut in 1948 and then developed throughout Jackson Burke's time at Mergenthaler Linotype in the 1950s. Each of Trade Gothic's fourteen styles are designed with subtle variations in form and shape, unlike traditional font families. Originally released as 'Gothic' with a numeral suffix, the variants soon became popular for everyday work thanks to the condensed designs, and eventually the term 'Trade' was applied as they became the printers and typesetters' typeface of choice. Contemporary uses are in Amnesty International's logo and printed matter, and the branding of cycling-apparel company Rapha. The Bold Condensed weight is often chosen for impactful messaging and attention-grabbing designs.

Trade Gothic Next

ABCDEFGHIJKLMNOPQRSTUVWXYZ
abcdefghijklmnopqrstuvwxyz
1234567890 !@#?:;"*&

Foundry: Linotype
Designer: Jackson Burke /
Tom Grace / Akira Kobayashi
Designer Nationality: American /
American / Japanese
Date: 2008

Trade Gothic Next is both a revision and expansion of Jackson Burke's original design. Details such as the terminals, symbols and spacing were revised to remedy the inconsistency of the original, while extra widths and weights have been added to provide more versatility.

Trade Gothic Next Soft Rounded

ABCDEFGHIJKLMNOPQRSTUVWXYZ
abcdefghijklmnopqrstuvwxyz
1234567890 !@#?:;"*&

Foundry: Linotype
Designer: Jackson Burke /
Tom Grace / Akira Kobayashi
Designer Nationality: American /
American / Japanese
Date: 2008

In addition to revising details and expanding weights, Tom Grace and Akira Kobayashi updated Trade Gothic in 2008 to include Trade Gothic Next Soft Rounded. Unlike the font's other versions, this design favours circular forms, seen especially in the stroke endings.

Transcript

ABCDEFGHIJKLMNOPQRSTUVWXYZ
abcdefghijklmnopqrstuvwxyz
1234567890 !@#?:;"*&

Foundry: Colophon
Designer: The Entente
Designer Nationality: British
Date: 2017

Transcript is a grotesque sans serif that was originally designed in 2010 for issue 6 of *Centrefold Magazine* but was then released commercially as a single-weight font in 2011. In 2017, Transcript was expanded to include six weights and fourteen styles in proportional and monospaced versions.

Unitext

ABCDEFGHIJKLMNOPQRSTUVWXYZ
abcdefghijklmnopqrstuvwxyz
1234567890 !@#?:;"*&

Foundry: Monotype
Designer: Jan Hendrik Weber
Designer Nationality: German
Date: 2018

Unitext is a versatile grotesque sans serif designed for 21st-century branding. The result of detailed research into the requirements of brand typography, Jan Hendrik Weber's design includes fourteen styles, and combines narrow spacing with open shapes for legibility across all platforms.

Univers

ABCDEFGHIJKLMNOPQRSTUVWXYZ
abcdefghijklmnopqrstuvwxyz
1234567890 !@#?:;"*&

Foundry: Linotype
Designer: Adrian Frutiger
Designer Nationality: Swiss
Date: 1957

Univers is one of the most historically important typefaces to be designed in the 20th century. It possesses elegance, simplicity and purity within its modular forms, enabling it to become one of the most widely used typefaces of all time. Adrian Frutiger (see p. 290) designed the original twenty-one types that made up the family, which have a consistent and balanced structure throughout the differing weights. From the outset, a system was applied to the weights, widths and slopes through an innovative numbering system, akin to a periodic table. He later adopted this system for his eponymously titled Frutiger typeface (see p. 268). Other foundries also employed the system such as for Helvetica Neue (see p. 230). Based on a two-digit system, each typeface's weight was described by the first number. For example, '5' was

Roman and '7' was Black. The second number described the style; '3' for Extended, '5' for Regular, '6' for Italic, '7' for Condensed and so on.

Univers was based on Frutiger's earlier studies when he was a design student in Zurich, and from design principles and aesthetics established with the existing sans serif, Akzidenz Grotesk (see p. 248). He started designing Univers in 1954, when he was art director at the Parisian foundry Deberny & Peignot. The foundry required a linear sans serif as part of its offering. In 1957, the final design was released and was an instant success, and soon after Linotype produced it too. After Univers's launch, Frutiger worked on refinements and revisions to the design with the Linotype Design Studio and in 1997 released Linotype Univers, with a full revision to this family called Univers Next (see p. 250) in 2010.

Below. Konstantin Eremenko's award-winning packaging design for SRC Lab distinguishes their three product lines with a bold colour and numbering system.

Opposite. Otl Aicher's iconic Munich Olympic Games design from 1972 employs Univers across the entire range of printed and branded items.

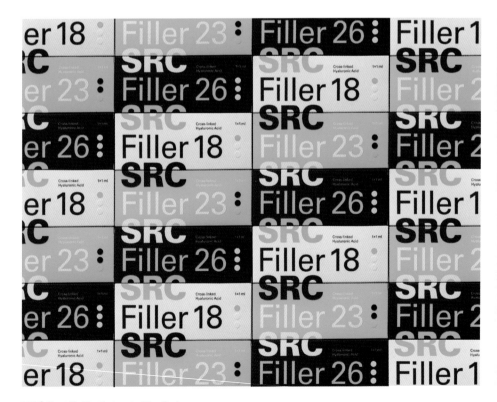

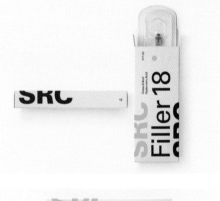

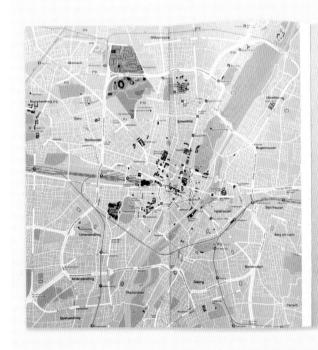

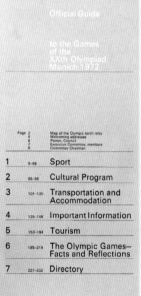

Univers Next

ABCDEFGHIJKLMNOPQRSTUVWXYZ
abcdefghijklmnopqrstuvwxyz
1234567890 !@#?:;"*&

Foundry: Linotype
Designer: Adrian Frutiger / Linotype Design Studio
Designer Nationality: Swiss
Date: 2010

Univers Next, originally titled Linotype Univers, is a detailed revision and expansion of the font family made in 1957 by Adrian Frutiger (see p. 290). Univers Next is collaboration between Frutiger and the design team at Linotype, and features redrawn strokes, revised weights and 35 new styles.

Right. The identity and branding for Solothurn Literary Days is formed employing Univers Next across all materials print and online. Its logotype is formed around four languages (German, French, Italian and Romansh). Design by Andrea Stebler, Thomas Berger and Thomas Hirter.

Vectora

ABCDEFGHIJKLMNOPQRSTUVWXYZ
abcdefghijklmnopqrstuvwxyz
1234567890 !@#?:;"*&

Foundry: Linotype
Designer: Adrian Frutiger
Designer Nationality: Swiss
Date: 1990

This grotesque sans serif was designed to enhance readability in small text sizes. Its design was influenced by the fonts of US type designer Morris Fuller Benton, such as News Gothic. Featuring tall x-heights and open counters, Vectora's precise forms are well suited to the demands of text typography.

Venus

ABCDEFGHIJKLMNOPQRSTUVWXYZ
abcdefghijklmnopqrstuvwxyz
1234567890 !@#?:;"*&

Foundry: Linotype
Designer: Bauersche Giesserei
Designer Nationality: German
Date: 1910

First produced by the Bauersche Giesserei foundry, but later digitized by Neufvill Digital and published by Linotype, Venus is a grotesque sans serif initially designed for use in German cartography. The family features distinctive left-leaning weights and a strict, taut frame.

Veto

ABCDEFGHIJKLMNOPQRSTUVWXYZ
abcdefghijklmnopqrstuvwxyz
1234567890 !@#?:;"*&

Foundry: Linotype
Designer: Marco Ganz
Designer Nationality: Swiss
Date: 1999

Veto is a functional, agile grotesque sans serif designed to reflect the dynamic mobility of the 21st century's digital culture. In each weight, from Light to Bold, letterforms are direct and utilitarian, seen in the single-sided cross-strokes and slanted stroke endings.

Vialog

ABCDEFGHIJKLMNOPQRSTUVWXYZ
abcdefghijklmnopqrstuvwxyz
1234567890 !@#?:;"*&

Foundry: Linotype
Designer: Werner Schneider / Helmut Ness
Designer Nationality: German
Date: 2002

Vialog is informed by Werner Schneider's previous work and extensive research on Euro Type, an unpublished design for the German Federal Transportation Ministry. It is a grotesque sans serif intended for transport information systems, which is legible at speed and distance.

Vialog 1450

ABCDEFGHIJKLMNOPQRSTUVWXYZ
abcdefghijklmnopqrstuvwxyz
1234567890 !@#?:;"*&

Foundry: Linotype
Designer: Werner Schneider / Helmut Ness
Designer Nationality: German
Date: 2016

Vialog 1450 is designed to conform to the German DIN 1450 regulations, a set of public standards issued by the Deutsches Institut für Normung that ensure readability in adverse conditions. Vialog 1450 features new proportions and stroke thicknesses, as well as redrawn characters that improve clarity.

Zurich

ABCDEFGHIJKLMNOPQRSTUVWXYZ
abcdefghijklmnopqrstuvwxyz
1234567890 !@#?:;"*&

Foundry: Bitstream
Designer: Adrian Frutiger
Designer Nationality: Swiss
Date: 1957

Zurich is Bitstream's digitization of the Univers grotesque sans serif. The font's title, Zurich, references the city in which designer Adrian Frutiger (see p. 290) made his first sketches for what would later become Univers, while a student at the School of Applied Arts.

Abadi

ABCDEFGHIJKLMNOPQRSTUVWXYZ
abcdefghijklmnopqrstuvwxyz
1234567890 !@#?:;"*&

Foundry: Monotype
Designer: Ong Chong Wah
Designer Nationality: Malaysian
Date: 1987

This friendly sans serif was inspired by Gill Sans and Helvetica, and blends humanist and Neo-grotesque styles. Its highly tapered strokes and generous x-height combine to give its curved letterforms an expanded look, and it is legible even at very small point sizes.

Adoquin

ABCDEFGHIJKLMNOPQRSTUVWXYZ
abcdefghijklmnopqrstuvwxyz
1234567890 !@#?:;"*&

Foundry: Huy!Fonts
Designer: Juanjo Lopez
Designer Nationality: Spanish
Date: 2013

Adoquin is described as a 'semi serif' and is a playful combination of an Old Style calligraphic typeface with a modern geometric sans serif. It is suitable for display and text use, and features seven weights, as well as small caps, ligatures, Old Style figures, fractions, numerators and denominators.

Adrianna

ABCDEFGHIJKLMNOPQRSTUVWXYZ
abcdefghijklmnopqrstuvwxyz
1234567890 !@#?:;"*&

Foundry: Chank
Designer: Chank Diesel
Designer Nationality: American
Date: 2015

Adrianna is a restrained sans serif with a sophisticated edge. It comes in five weights and three different widths: Regular (for general use), Extended (designed with HDTV and widescreens in mind), and Condensed, which is intended to look good on smartphones.

Aeris

ABCDEFGHIJKLMNOPQRSTUVWXYZ
abcdefghijklmnopqrstuvwxyz
1234567890 !@#?:;"*&

Foundry: Linotype
Designer: Tom Grace
Designer Nationality: American
Date: 2010

Aeris is a book face combining characteristics of both sans serif and script fonts, with open counters for optimal legibility. Each weight and style has two variants that should not be mixed. The A variant is for display use, while the B variant is best suited for use in text.

Agilita

ABCDEFGHIJKLMNOPQRSTUVWXYZ
abcdefghijklmnopqrstuvwxyz
1234567890 !@#?:;"*&

Foundry: Linotype
Designer: Jürgen Weltin
Designer Nationality: German
Date: 2006

Agilita is a humanist sans serif with classical proportions. It consists of thirty-two styles (including Italic and Condensed) and weights from Hairline to Black. With an emphasis on the horizontals, coupled with clear ascenders and descenders, the typeface looks solid and functional.

Antagométrica BT

ABCDEFGHIJKLMNOPQRSTUVWXYZ
abcdefghijklmnopqrstuvwxyz
1234567890 !@#?:;"*&

Foundry: Bitstream
Designer: Maximiliano Giungi
Designer Nationality: Argentinian
Date: 2006

Antagométrica is a condensed but curvy sans serif in the humanist tradition. It is the sole font available from Argentinian designer, Maximiliano Giungi, and is available in Light, Regular and Bold. The font has a very distinctive lowercase 'e', and is well suited for both display and text usage.

Antique Olive

ABCDEFGHIJKLMNOPQRSTUVWXYZ
abcdefghijklmnopqrstuvwxyz
1234567890 !@#?:;"*&

Foundry: Fonderie Olive
Designer: Roger Excoffon
Designer Nationality: French
Date: 1962

Antique Olive evolved from the lettering for the Air France logo, and is too eccentric to compete with Univers and Helvetica. Designer Roger Excoffon created the Nord and Nord italic versions, before completing the Bold, Compact, Black, Bold Condensed, Roman and Italic.

Aptifer Sans

ABCDEFGHIJKLMNOPQRSTUVWXYZ
abcdefghijklmnopqrstuvwxyz
1234567890 !@#?:;"*&

Foundry: Linotype
Designer: Mårten Thavenius
Designer Nationality: Swedish
Date: 2006

This sans serif channels two quite different influences: the robust American Gothic and the more open humanist traditions. It shares many similarities, such as stroke contrast and vertical stress, with its sister typeface, Aptifer Slab, which was also created by Mårten Thavenius.

Ayita Pro

ABCDEFGHIJKLMNOPQRSTUVWXYZ
abcdefghijklmnopqrstuvwxyz
1234567890 !@#?:;"*&

Foundry: Ascender
Designer: Jim Ford /
Steve Matteson
Designer Nationality: American
Date: 2010

Ayita Pro is a cheeky sans serif with a Cherokee name that means 'first in dance'. It is available in seven weights, from Thin to Fat. The typeface was conceived as an upright italic and has a distinctive bowed uppercase 'A'. It features a Latin character set and decorative patterns and ornaments.

Bariol

ABCDEFGHIJKLMNOPQRSTUVWXYZ
abcdefghijklmnopqrstuvwxyz
1234567890 !@#?:;"*&

Foundry: Atipo
Designer: Raul Garcia del Pomar / Ismael Gonzalez
Designer Nationality: Spanish
Date: 2010

This rounded, uncomplicated and slightly condensed sans serif is free to download for Regular and Italic or whatever a user can afford for the full set. The typeface's pricing policy and accessibility has meant it has proved very popular with students and anyone who prefers not to pay for typefaces.

Berling Nova Sans

ABCDEFGHIJKLMNOPQRSTUVWXYZ
abcdefghijklmnopqrstuvwxyz
1234567890 !@#?:;"*&

Foundry: Linotype
Designer: Karl-Erik Forsberg / Örjan Nordling / Fredrik Andersson
Designer Nationality: Swedish
Date: c. 1950s / 2004

This redesign of Karl-Erik Forsberg's classic newspaper font from the 1950s was created using much of his original source material from Linotype. It is available in four weights, from Light to Extra Bold. It has an increased x-height, as well as the addition of small caps and Old Style figures.

Big Vesta

ABCDEFGHIJKLMNOPQRSTUVWXYZ
abcdefghijklmnopqrstuvwxyz
1234567890 !@#?:;"*&

Foundry: Linotype
Designer: Gerard Unger
Designer Nationality: Dutch
Date: 2011

Gerard Unger designed this as a possible sans serif to mark the Jubilee of the Roman Catholic Church in 2000, then later expanded the family to create Big Vesta. A larger x-height than the original Vesta, shorter ascenders and descenders, and tighter letter spacing make it ideal for use at large sizes.

Bliss

ABCDEFGHIJKLMNOPQRSTUVWXYZ
abcdefghijklmnopqrstuvwxyz
1234567890 !@#?:;"*&

Acclaimed independent British type designer Jeremy Tankard drew from the ideas of one of the founding fathers of modern calligraphy, Edward Johnston, to develop the sans serif humanist face Bliss. A Uruguayan-British craftsman, Johnston is an important figure who taught the British sculptor, typeface designer and printmaker Eric Gill.

In 1906, Johnston published his seminal book *Writing & Illuminating & Lettering*, which helped to revive the interest in calligraphy. One of his key ideas was the belief that a block sans serif form could be made more harmonious if it were derived from the proportions of the Roman square capitals that are the basis for modern capital letters. Johnston's concept of the 'readableness, beauty and character' that constitute the 'essential virtues of good lettering' underpins the structure of Bliss.

Bliss was launched in 1996 and since then has grown to be one of the most popular humanist sans. It has been widely employed in everything from publishing applications to identities for international organizations.

Its minimal stroke contrast, angled cuts on extenders such as uppercase 'E' and 'F', large apertures and open counters all work towards creating a highly legible and flexible typeface with a softness that makes it accessible and friendly to the reader.

Bliss's humanist appearance also carries a certain 'Englishness' to it. This reflectis the influence of Johnston's own classic, the sans serif Johnston (see p. 278) that was first employed on the London Underground system in 1916, and to a degree, Gill's Gill Sans (see p. 276).

Name: Bliss
Foundry: Jeremy Tankard Typography
Designer: Jeremy Tankard
Designer Nationality: British
Date: 1996

Below, clockwise from top left.
The many faces of Bliss in use: identity for the Royal National Lifeboat Institution; wayfinding at Cape Town Airport, South Africa; corporate identity for the UK's Bank of England.

Bosis

ABCDEFGHIJKLMNOPQRSTUVWXYZ
abcdefghijklmnopqrstuvwxyz
1234567890 !@#?:;"*&

Foundry: Monotype
Designer: Bo Berndal
Designer Nationality: Swedish
Date: 1991

Swedish master typographer Bo Berndal created this no-nonsense sans serif in 1991. Bosis comes in four weights, from Light to Semibold. Subtle details such as the sloping verticals on the uppercase 'M' and the tail on the lowercase 'l' give it a softer, humanist look.

Calmetta

ABCDEFGHIJKLMNOPQRSTUVWXYZ
abcdefghijklmnopqrstuvwxyz
1234567890 !@#?:;"*&

Foundry: Dalton Maag
Designer: Elí Castellanos /
Marc Weymann
Designer Nationality: Mexican /
British
Date: 2017

Calmetta is Elí Castellanos's revision of Pantograph, a custom wayfinding font initially designed by Marc Weymann for the Manchester Metrolink. Castellanos added further versatility to the family by designing two extra weights and more than an additional 180 icons.

Camphor

ABCDEFGHIJKLMNOPQRSTUVWXYZ
abcdefghijklmnopqrstuvwxyz
1234567890 !@#?:;"*&

Foundry: Monotype
Designer: Nick Job
Designer Nationality: British
Date: 2009

Nick Job's economical font is modern, uncluttered and quintessentially English. Camphor has its roots in the typefaces of Eric Gill, Edward Johnston and, to some extent, Adrian Frutiger (see p. 290), yet is more subtle than Gill Sans and narrower than Johnston's typeface for the London Underground.

Carter Sans

ABCDEFGHIJKLMNOPQRSTUVWXYZ
abcdefghijklmnopqrstuvwxyz
1234567890 !@#?:;"*&

Foundry: Monotype
Designer: Matthew Carter /
Dan Reynolds
Designer Nationality: British /
American
Date: 2011

Matthew Carter (see p. 616) has described Carter Sans as 'a humanistic stressed sans'. This refined, chiselled sans serif takes inspiration from Berthold Wolpe's Albertus typeface of the 1930s. Its slightly flared strokes and solid baseline terminals give even its lightest weight a powerful presence.

Castle

ABCDEFGHIJKLMNOPQRSTUVWXYZ
abcdefghijklmnopqrstuvwxyz
1234567890 !@#?:;"*&

Foundry: Linotype
Designer: Steve Jackaman
Designer Nationality: British
Date: 1975

Castle is a humanist, sans serif typeface that comes in four weights, ranging from Light to Ultra. It has an unusually high stroke contrast, as well as a large x-height. Although Castle is best used at twelve point and above for this reason, it is still very legible when used in text.

Charlotte Sans

ABCDEFGHIJKLMNOPQRSTUVWXYZ
abcdefghijklmnopqrstuvwxyz
1234567890 !@#?:;"*&

Foundry: Letraset
Designer: Michael Gills
Designer Nationality: British
Date: 1992

Charlotte is a modern roman typeface inspired by the designs of 18th-century punch-cutter Pierre-Simon Fournier and shares characteristics with Gill Sans, FF Scala Sans and Syntax. It has a varied stroke width and its terminals on the vertical strokes are cut at an angle instead of parallel to the baseline.

Chiswick Sans

ABCDEFGHIJKLMNOPQRSTUVWXYZ
abcdefghijklmnopqrstuvwxyz
1234567890 !@#?:;"*&

Foundry: Commercial Type
Designer: Paul Barnes
Designer Nationality: British
Date: 2015

Chiswick Sans is a humanist typeface that integrates the utility of a sans serif with the formal flourishes of a serif. Intended primarily for headline use, it features seven weights which vary from Thin to Fat, each with an italic that enhances the font's distinctive details.

Chiswick Sans Poster

ABCDEFGHIJKLMNOPQRSTUVWXYZ
abcdefghijklmnopqrstuvwxyz
1234567890 !@#?:;"*&

Foundry: Commercial Type
Designer: Paul Barnes
Designer Nationality: British
Date: 2015

Chiswick Sans Poster is a high-contrast sans serif designed for the largest display sizes. It was first employed in *Document Journal*, a New York fashion and culture magazine. While sans serif in design, the letterforms have the elegance of a serif, seen in the expressive hooks and descenders.

Chiswick Sans Text

ABCDEFGHIJKLMNOPQRSTUVWXYZ
abcdefghijklmnopqrstuvwxyz
1234567890 !@#?:;"*&

Foundry: Commercial Type
Designer: Paul Barnes
Designer Nationality: British
Date: 2017

Unlike its siblings, Chiswick Sans and Chiswick Sans Poster, Chiswick Sans Text is designed to be most effective at smaller sizes. Its comparatively moderate stroke contrast allows the characters to provide legibility in denser texts while maintaining their expressive details.

Chong Modern

ABCDEFGHIJKLMNOPQRSTUVWXYZ
abcdefghijklmnopqrstuvwxyz
1234567890 !@#?:;"*&

Foundry: Monotype
Designer: Ong Chong Wah
Designer Nationality: Malaysian
Date: 2009

Along with its sister typeface Chong Old Style, this elegant Art Deco-inspired face mixes traditional and modern to great effect and has been likened to a Bodoni without serifs. Chong Modern has Light, Regular and Bold, Old Style figures, ligatures and small caps; Chong Old Style also has an Extra Bold.

Chong Old Style

ABCDEFGHIJKLMNOPQRSTUVWXYZ
abcdefghijklmnopqrstuvwxyz
1234567890 !@#?:;"*&

Foundry: Monotype
Designer: Ong Chong Wah
Designer Nationality: Malaysian
Date: 2011

Chong Old Style is the sister typeface to Chong Modern. It has similarities to traditional Old Style designs such as Goudy Old Style, while avoiding pastiche. It lacks the serifs and inclined stroke axis customarily seen in the traditional Old Style faces but still retains the colour and weight.

Clearface Gothic

ABCDEFGHIJKLMNOPQRSTUVWXYZ
abcdefghijklmnopqrstuvwxyz
1234567890 !@#?:;"*&

Foundry: ATF
Designer: Morris Fuller Benton / Linotype Studio
Designer Nationality: American
Date: 1910

Clearface Gothic is an informal sans serif by the designer of Franklin Gothic and Century Expanded, Morris Fuller Benton. It is notable for the upward-tilting horizontal stroke of its 'e', its arched 'k' and open forms. It is slightly condensed, making it legible when used at small sizes.

Daytona

ABCDEFGHIJKLMNOPQRSTUVWXYZ
abcdefghijklmnopqrstuvwxyz
1234567890 !@#?:;"*&

Foundry: Monotype
Designer: Jim Wasco
Designer Nationality: American
Date: 2015

Daytona was originally created to be used in televised sporting events but works well for any screen application. Its slightly condensed squared-off letterforms have humanist shapes and proportions. The typeface is available in seven weights from Thin to Fat.

Delvard

ABCDEFGHIJKLMNOPQRSTUVWXYZ
abcdefghijklmnopqrstuvwxyz
1234567890 !@#?:;"*&

Foundry: Typotheque
Designer: Nikola Djurek
Designer Nationality: Croatian
Date: 2010

Delvard is a low-contrast sans serif with four weights – Text, Condensed, Display and an unusual Gradient version – as well as small caps and swashes. Its graceful curves, angled segments and elevated crossbars are influenced by the lettering found on Art Nouveau posters.

Diurnal

ABCDEFGHIJKLMNOPQRSTUVWXYZ
abcdefghijklmnopqrstuvwxyz
1234567890 !@#?:;"*&

Foundry: Typotheque
Designer: Nikola Djurek
Designer Nationality: Croatian
Date: 2017

Diurnal is a companion font to Nocturno, which is available in both text and a more expressive display option. With a nod to Syntax and Legato, this humanist sans serif is designed for long, continuous reading, and its calligraphic rhythm and generous x-height both help legibility.

Diverda Sans

ABCDEFGHIJKLMNOPQRSTUVWXYZ
abcdefghijklmnopqrstuvwxyz
1234567890 !@#?:;"*&

Foundry: Linotype
Designer: Daniel Lanz
Designer Nationality: Swiss
Date: 2004

Diverda Sans stays true to the proportions of the Roman alphabet with its traditional round forms, low x-heights, heavier downward strokes and a clear contrast between its curved, square and triangular elements. It is available in five weights plus matching italics.

Echo

ABCDEFGHIJKLMNOPQRSTUVWXYZ
abcdefghijklmnopqrstuvwxyz
1234567890 !@#?:;"*&

Foundry: Typotheque
Designer: Ross Milne
Designer Nationality: Canadian
Date: 2015

Echo is Ross Milne's counterpart to his serif Charlie from 2010 and it too takes its name from the International Radiotelephony Spelling Alphabet.

This no-nonsense sans serif is clear and direct, and also displays subtle influences of the broad nib pen. It features five weights from Regular to Black.

Effra

ABCDEFGHIJKLMNOPQRSTUVWXYZ
abcdefghijklmnopqrstuvwxyz
1234567890 !@#?:;"*&

Foundry: Dalton Maag
Designer: Jonas Schudel / Azza Alameddine / Fabio Haag
Designer Nationality: Swiss / Lebanese / Brazilian
Date: 2008–16

Effra was inspired by one of the first commercial sans serif designs, Caslon Junior. It is a sans serif that utilizes grotesque and humanist features. Effra is available in five weights, each with their own italic, and includes the characters for Latin, Cyrillic, Greek and Arabic scripts.

Felbridge

ABCDEFGHIJKLMNOPQRSTUVWXYZ
abcdefghijklmnopqrstuvwxyz
1234567890 !@#?:;"*&

Foundry: Monotype
Designer: Robin Nicholas
Designer Nationality: British
Date: 2001

Felbridge is a clear, strong humanist sans serif with six weights from Light to Black. Created by British designer Robin Nicholas for on-screen use, it works equally well in print. It has distinctive italics that have lighter, 'hooked' strokes instead of the traditional 'sloped roman' style.

Fenland

ABCDEFGHIJKLMNOPQRSTUVWXYZ
abcdefghijklmnopqrstuvwxyz
1234567890 !@#?:;"*&

Foundry: Jeremy Tankard Typography
Designer: Jeremy Tankard
Designer Nationality: British
Date: 2012

Jeremy Tankard's bold design for Fenland evokes a modern, manufactured feel. Unlike most typefaces, it is not based on traditional handwritten forms; Tankard has shaped the letterforms according to their function, rather than how they would appear if created using a broad-nib pen.

Fedra Sans

ABCDEFGHIJKLMNOPQRSTUVWXYZ
abcdefghijklmnopqrstuvwxyz
1234567890 !@#?:;"*&

Foundry: Typotheque
Designer: Peter Biľak
Designer Nationality: Slovakian
Date: 2001

The creation of Fedra Sans came about as part of a rebrand of a German insurance company, Bayerische Rück. Paris-based studio Intégral Ruedi Baur was charged with the rebranding of the business and commissioned Dutch foundry Typotheque (see p. 90) to design a replacement for the company's existing typeface as a key component of the visual overhaul. The typeface in question was Univers, which had been employed since the 1970s when leading German graphic designer and typographer Otto 'Otl' Aicher designed the original corporate identity.

The brief was to humanize the message but also to create a typeface that would work across paper and screen internationally in multiple languages. However, nearing completion the insurance company was bought out and the need for a new identity vanished. Typotheque decided to complete the typeface because it was so far advanced in design and digitization. This delay was of benefit because it allowed Typotheque's founder Peter Biľak to review the design and improve upon it before its general release.

Fedra Sans is a type that balances the need to work within the structure of a computer screen and retain the 'handwritten', softer edge of a humanist sans. An OpenType Pro version was released in 2004 and Fedra Sans became Typotheque's most extensive offering with five weights, each accompanied by italics and small capitals. The font family supports Latin, Armenian, Bengali, Cyrillic, Devanagari, Greek, Hebrew, Inuktitut and Tamil writing scripts. Now in its fourth incarnation, Fedra Sans is a typeface that improves with age.

Below left. Award-winning wayfinding system employing Fedra Sans across Vienna Airport. Design by French studio Intégral Ruedi Baur Paris.

Below right. Typotheque's Fedra Sans family is available in a huge variety of languages, increasing its international suitability for global design solutions.

contemporary
качественные гарнитуры
SANS SERIF
for paper and screen
εταιρεία σχεδιασμού γραμματοσειρών
multilingual type family
функционировать самостоятельно
ГРАММАТΟΣΕΙΡΕΣ
versatile system
δημιουργώντας ποιοτικές γραμματοσειρές
шрифтовая фирма
διαφορετικών

FF Dax

ABCDEFGHIJKLMNOPQRSTUVWXYZ
abcdefghijklmnopqrstuvwxyz
1234567890 !@#?:;"*&

Foundry: FontFont
Designer: Hans Reichel
Designer Nationality: German
Date: 1995

A humanist sans serif that also comes with a compact version, FF Dax is very popular. It was modified to make United Parcel Service's corporate typeface UPS Sans in 2005. The same year, David Cameron used the font in his campaign for leadership of the British Conservative Party.

FF Fago

ABCDEFGHIJKLMNOPQRSTUVWXYZ
abcdefghijklmnopqrstuvwxyz
1234567890 !@#?:;"*&

Foundry: FontFont
Designer: Ole Schäfer / Andreas Eigendorf
Designer Nationality: German
Date: 2000

FF Fago is a straightforward sans serif that was created as a response to complex corporate design projects. It features thirty weights, including italics. It has an open structure and wide apertures that help legibility when viewed from a distance, making it suitable for information graphics and wayfinding.

FF Info Correspondence

ABCDEFGHIJKLMNOPQRSTUVWXYZ
abcdefghijklmnopqrstuvwxyz
1234567890 !@#?:;"*&

Foundry: FontFont
Designer: Erik Spiekermann / Ole Schäfer
Designer Nationality: German
Date: 1998

FF Info Correspondence is part of the FF Info super family, which also includes FF Info Display and FF Info Text. A well-crafted sans serif, it is available in six weights from Regular to Bold. As its name suggests, it is perfect for information-design projects where clarity is essential.

FF Info Text

ABCDEFGHIJKLMNOPQRSTUVWXYZ
abcdefghijklmnopqrstuvwxyz
1234567890 !@#?:;"*&

Foundry: FontFont
Designer: Erik Spiekermann / Ole Schäfer
Designer Nationality: German
Date: 1998

This finely tuned sans serif is part of the FF Info super family, which also includes FF Info Display and FF Info Correspondence. It was originally intended for use on traffic signage and is perfect for information-design projects where legibility is key and space is restricted.

FF Scala Sans

ABCDEFGHIJKLMNOPQRSTUVWXYZ
abcdefghijklmnopqrstuvwxyz
1234567890 !@#?:;"*&

Foundry: FontFont
Designer: Martin Majoor
Designer Nationality: Dutch
Date: 1993

This is a sister face to Martin Majoor's Old Style serif FF Scala from 1990. FF Scala Sans is a humanist sans serif typeface inspired by Gill Sans and Syntax. It was made for the Vredenburg music centre in Utrecht, the Netherlands and is used by the Los Angeles Metro Rail transportation system.

FF Unit

ABCDEFGHIJKLMNOPQRSTUVWXYZ
abcdefghijklmnopqrstuvwxyz
1234567890 !@#?:;"*&

Foundry: FontFont
Designer: Erik Spiekermann / Christian Schwartz
Designer Nationality: German / American
Date: 2003

FF Unit is more considered but equally as useable as its hugely popular predecessor, FF Meta. With greater contrast and simpler forms than Meta, it was first released in 2003, with the rounded version designed by New Zealand typeface designer Kris Sowersby. A slab serif was added later.

FF Unit Rounded

ABCDEFGHIJKLMNOPQRSTUVWXYZ
abcdefghijklmnopqrstuvwxyz
1234567890 !@#?:;"*&

Foundry: FontFont
Designer: Erik Spiekermann / Christian Schwartz
Designer Nationality: German / American
Date: 2008

FF Unit is a very considered typeface that irons out many of the idiosyncrasies of FF Meta by Erik Spiekermann (see p. 304). It was first released in 2003, with increased contrast and simplified forms. This rounded version was added in 2008, followed by a slab serif in 2009.

Foundry Sans

ABCDEFGHIJKLMNOPQRSTUVWXYZ
abcdefghijklmnopqrstuvwxyz
1234567890 !@#?:;"*&

Foundry: The Foundry
Designer: David Quay
Designer Nationality: British
Date: 1990

Foundry Sans is inspired by Hans Meier's design of the Syntax sans serif, which took its visual cues from the serif letterforms of Jan Tschichold's Sabon. Working in a similar manner, David Quay designed Foundry Sans by looking to the humanist serif characters of Stempel Garamond.

FF Meta

ABCDEFGHIJKLMNOPQRSTUVWXYZ
abcdefghijklmnopqrstuvwxyz
1234567890 !@#?:;"*&

Foundry: FontFont
Designer: Erik Spiekermann
Designer Nationality: German
Date: 1991

Renowned graphic and type designer Erik Spiekermann (see p. 304) created FF Meta typeface to be the 'antithesis' of Helvetica, which he described as 'boring and bland'. FF Meta has gone on to become a hugely influential typeface since its release in 1991.

FF Meta started out as a commission in 1985 for British design agency Sedley Place to rebrand the German post office, Deutsche Bundespost, and part of the brief was to create a new sans serif corporate typeface family. The need to work at relatively small sizes on low-quality paper stocks was key to the design. One reason for this was that a lot of the organization's printing was done at a local level on laser printers, so economy and legibility was paramount for efficiency and readability. However, Spiekermann's and Sedley Place's design, entitled PT55, was never used by Deutsche Bundespost, which shied away from using such an innovative design.

Fortunately, all was not lost: FontFont, the independent type foundry that had been launched in 1990 by Spiekermann, along with Neville Brody and Spiekermann's then wife, Joan, completed the design, rebranding it FF Meta. It was one of the foundry's earliest releases and was soon a critical and commercial success. FF Meta was digitized by Just van Rossum and Erik van Blokland at Spiekermann's Berlin design practice, MetaDesign, from the original outlines. Over the years there have been a number of revisions, refinements and expansions to the family. Most notable was an accompanying serif design, FF Meta Serif, which was released in 2007.

Below left. FF Meta employed on the night network map of ZVV (Zurich's public transport system).

Below right. FF Meta's creator Erik Spiekermann designed this poster as part of a submission from a number of international designers on the theme of 'public' for Public Bikes, Inc. The headline is set in the typeface Block, designed by Louis Oppenheim at the turn of the 20th century.

Opposite. The NYRB Classics series published by New York Review Books employs FF Meta consistently across its range of book covers.

INHUMAN LAND
SEARCHING FOR THE
TRUTH IN SOVIET RUSSIA,
1941–1942
JÓZEF CZAPSKI

INTRODUCTION BY
TIMOTHY SNYDER

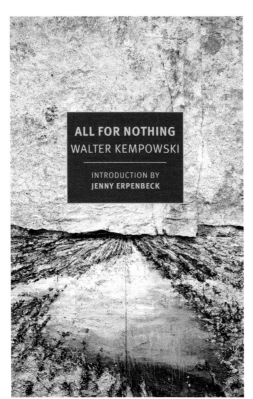

ALL FOR NOTHING
WALTER KEMPOWSKI

INTRODUCTION BY
JENNY ERPENBECK

ONCE AND FOREVER
THE TALES OF
KENJI MIYAZAWA

TRANSLATED BY
JOHN BESTER

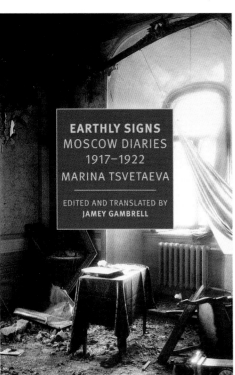

EARTHLY SIGNS
MOSCOW DIARIES
1917–1922
MARINA TSVETAEVA

EDITED AND TRANSLATED BY
JAMEY GAMBRELL

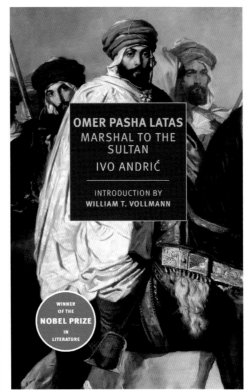

OMER PASHA LATAS
MARSHAL TO THE
SULTAN
IVO ANDRIĆ

INTRODUCTION BY
WILLIAM T. VOLLMANN

WINNER
OF THE
NOBEL PRIZE
IN
LITERATURE

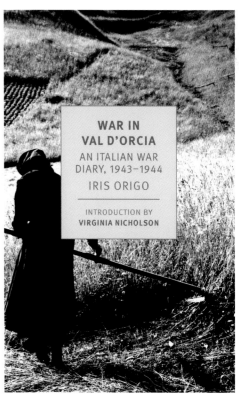

**WAR IN
VAL D'ORCIA**
AN ITALIAN WAR
DIARY, 1943–1944
IRIS ORIGO

INTRODUCTION BY
VIRGINIA NICHOLSON

Foundry Sterling

ABCDEFGHIJKLMNOPQRSTUVWXYZ
abcdefghijklmnopqrstuvwxyz
1234567890 !@#?:;"*&

Foundry: The Foundry
Designer: David Quay /
Freda Sack
Designer Nationality: British
Date: 2001

Foundry Sterling has been a consistently popular typeface since its inception and has gained the status of a modern classic. It also possesses a quintessentially English flavour for a modern sans serif type. Foundry Sterling's letterforms have been designed with particular attention to classical proportion and purity of form, yet its elegant and graceful appearance belies a flexibility and legibility that allow it to be incredibly versatile. It is a typeface that is as comfortable working in an editorial arena as in wayfinding and signage applications.

Designers David Quay and Freda Sack co-founded The Foundry (see p. 284) in 1989 and soon established an international reputation for original typefaces of a very high quality. The Foundry offers a diverse range of fonts, which combine traditional design approaches – thanks in great part to Quay and Sack's experience – and the latest digital OpenType technologies. Its typeface library includes collaborations with eminent designers such as Dutch typographer Wim Crouwel (see p. 540), and the Architype range of avant-garde typefaces derived mainly from the work of artists and designers of the interwar years.

Below. Foundry Sterling employed as wayfinding for the University of Applied Sciences Wildau, Germany where the type treatment also employed a cross-hatched infill for larger types describing building names.

←	↑
Foyer	Foyer
Hörsaal	Seminar
Seminar	Labor
Labor	
Besprechung	B001
Büro	B002
Aufzug	B008
WC	
A001–	
A234	
B001–	
B107	

Frisans

ABCDEFGHIJKLMNOPQRSTUVWXYZ
abcdefghijklmnopqrstuvwxyz
1234567890 !@#?:;"*&

Foundry: Monotype
Designer: Bo Berndal
Designer Nationality: Swedish
Date: 2005

Frisans was conceived as an experiment to combine the calligraphic forms of Warren Chappell's Lydian with 19th-century grotesque letterforms. Its regular weight shows similarities to Lydian's square-nib letters, while its slightly condensed proportions pay homage to faces like Franklin Gothic and Standard.

Frutiger Next

ABCDEFGHIJKLMNOPQRSTUVWXYZ
abcdefghijklmnopqrstuvwxyz
1234567890 !@#?:;"*&

Foundry: Linotype
Designer: Adrian Frutiger
Designer Nationality: Swiss
Date: 1976 / 1997

This is an updated cut of the sans designed in 1976. It was created for signage at Munich's Alte Pinakothek museum. Adrian Frutiger and the Linotype team optimized the forms of the original typeface to make them more consistent across the whole family, and created several sets of true italics.

FS Albert

ABCDEFGHIJKLMNOPQRSTUVWXYZ
abcdefghijklmnopqrstuvwxyz
1234567890 !@#?:;"*&

Foundry: Fontsmith
Designer: Jason Smith
Designer Nationality: British
Date: 2002

FS Albert features rounded edges to add warmth to its sans serif letterforms, helping make it solid and friendly, particularly in its heavier weights. The font is named after Jason Smith's son because of his chubbiness as a child, which is a dubious honour, although Smith says Albert has since forgiven him.

FS Aldrin

ABCDEFGHIJKLMNOPQRSTUVWXYZ
abcdefghijklmnopqrstuvwxyz
1234567890 !@#?:;"*&

Foundry: Fontsmith
Designer: Phil Garnham
Designer Nationality: British
Date: 2016

This approachable design by Fontsmith (see p. 272) includes an extensive icon set featuring symbols of space travel. Designer Phil Garnham felt its design was reminiscent of the space age, and gained approval from US astronaut Buzz Aldrin for the naming of the typeface.

Frutiger

ABCDEFGHIJKLMNOPQRSTUVWXYZ
abcdefghijklmnopqrstuvwxyz
1234567890 !@#?:;"*&

Foundry: Linotype /
D. Stempel AG
Designer: Adrian Frutiger
Designer Nationality: Swiss
Date: 1976

Renowned Swiss type and graphic designer Adrian Frutiger (see p. 290) was commissioned in 1968 to create a new typeface for the wayfinding system for the soon to be constructed Charles de Gaulle Airport in France. Rather than adapt any of his existing types, Frutiger set about creating a new design, one that would become an instant classic when completed and installed in 1975 and released to the public in 1976.

The typeface was originally called 'Roissy' and part of its design was to possess a modern yet friendly appearance, reflecting the architecture of its new home. Its success was also because of its outstanding ability to be read at varying distances, on the move at speed or at angles, and in low light – all of which helped recognition and navigation throughout the airport. The typeface's balanced letterforms and warm appearance also help to make it easily legible in distinguishing characters and understanding directions.

Although created as a display typeface, Frutiger is highly adept working as a text face and is employed in publishing, corporate identities and advertising applications across the globe. Its legibility has made it an incredibly versatile choice for designers and since its release a number of variations have been introduced, including Neue Frutiger World released by Monotype in 2018 and credited to Adrian Frutiger, Monotype type director Akira Kobayashi and the Monotype Studio. Neue Frutiger World covers more than 150 languages and scripts, providing a consistent voice and presentation to designs no matter where they are in the world.

Below left. Frutiger's wayfinding system in Charles de Gaulle Airport, Paris France, 1970.

Below right. Original drawing by Adrian Frutiger, showing his workings for the lowercase regular 'a' complete with annotation.

Opposite. Striking wayfinding design by Metapur AG for Kantonsschule Obwalden (High School Obwalden).

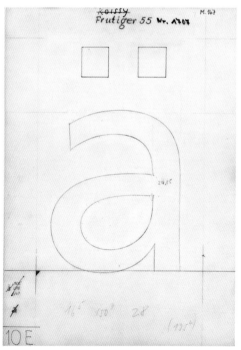

Sporthallen ↙

Abteilung Sport ↖

1—3 1—6

Judoraum
Gymnastikraum ↑

Foyer
Tribünen ↖

FS Blake

ABCDEFGHIJKLMNOPQRSTUVWXYZ
abcdefghijklmnopqrstuvwxyz
1234567890 !@#?:;"*&

Foundry: Fontsmith
Designer: Emanuela Conidi / Jason Smith
Designer Nationality: Italian / British
Date: 2010

Emanuela Conidi and Jason Smith's design for FS Blake wears its Art Deco influence lightly; the typeface's cool, contemporary appearance is tempered by a range of fine yet distinctive details within the design of each letterform. FS Blake is available in four weights, with corresponding italics.

FS Dillon

ABCDEFGHIJKLMNOPQRSTUVWXYZ
abcdefghijklmnopqrstuvwxyz
1234567890 !@#?:;"*&

Foundry: Fontsmith
Designer: Jason Smith
Designer Nationality: British
Date: 2009

FS Dillon was inspired by Bauhaus typography and features a strong vertical emphasis; its rounded, slightly condensed letterforms are built on a rectangular skeleton. The typeface was chosen for use on signage within the Queen Elizabeth Olympic Park in London for the Olympic Games in 2012.

FS Elliot

ABCDEFGHIJKLMNOPQRSTUVWXYZ
abcdefghijklmnopqrstuvwxyz
1234567890 !@#?:;"*&

Foundry: Fontsmith
Designer: Nick Job
Designer Nationality: British
Date: 2012

FS Elliot is the work of Nick Job, part of the team at Fontsmith (see p. 272). He designed it to follow in the footsteps of classic British Modernist typography, and it features clear, open letterforms with an even stroke weight throughout. The Pro edition also includes Greek and Cyrillic character sets.

FS Ingrid

ABCDEFGHIJKLMNOPQRSTUVWXYZ
abcdefghijklmnopqrstuvwxyz
1234567890 !@#?:;"*&

Foundry: Fontsmith
Designer: Jason Smith
Designer Nationality: British
Date: 2004

The sharp edges of this quietly authoritative sans serif by Jason Smith are softened by generous curves elsewhere within its letterforms. FS Ingrid was developed to perform well in screen-based contexts. The typeface is available in three weights plus italics.

FS Irwin

ABCDEFGHIJKLMNOPQRSTUVWXYZ
abcdefghijklmnopqrstuvwxyz
1234567890 !@#?:;"*&

Foundry: Fontsmith
Designer: Fernando Mello
Designer Nationality: Brazilian
Date: 2017

FS Irwin was developed from calligraphic sketches, and retains a sense of movement within its letterforms; this liveliness is particularly apparent within the italics. Brazilian designer Fernando Mello took inspiration for the font from his studies at the Cooper Union in New York.

FS Lola

ABCDEFGHIJKLMNOPQRSTUVWXYZ
abcdefghijklmnopqrstuvwxyz
1234567890 !@#?:;"*&

Foundry: Fontsmith
Designer: Phil Garnham
Designer Nationality: British
Date: 2005

This semi-serif design by Phil Garnham, type director at Fontsmith (see p. 272), features lively curved spurs, wide open counters and a generous x-height. Leftward-facing single slab serifs on certain letterforms balance the soft femininity of other details within the typeface.

FS Matthew

ABCDEFGHIJKLMNOPQRSTUVWXYZ
abcdefghijklmnopqrstuvwxyz
1234567890 !@#?:;"*&

Foundry: Fontsmith
Designer: Phil Garnham / Jason Smith
Designer Nationality: British
Date: 2013

Fontsmith (see p. 272) was commissioned to create FS Matthew for a UK terrestrial TV channel. The result is a curvaceous and legible sans serif typeface that features softened edges and slightly condensed letterforms, making it an economical choice for text typesetting.

FS Me

ABCDEFGHIJKLMNOPQRSTUVWXYZ
abcdefghijklmnopqrstuvwxyz
1234567890 !@#?:;"*&

Foundry: Fontsmith
Designer: Jason Smith
Designer Nationality: British
Date: 2008

FS Me began life as a commission from British charity Mencap to create a typeface with optimal legibility which would be accessible to readers with learning disabilities. A proportion of the proceeds from each FS Me licence is donated to Mencap, which works with people with learning disabilities.

Fontsmith

Offering a complete font design and production service, Fontsmith is a world-class boutique-type foundry. Established in 1997 by Jason Smith, Fontsmith has designed an award-winning portfolio of typefaces, and the commercial commissions it has created have established a reputation for designing fonts with a 'distinctively human character'. Based in London, Fontsmith is made up of a team of international designers who believe passionately in the craft of type and pride themselves on their deep understanding of form and detailing when creating precision designs.

As well as offering an extensive collection of retail fonts, with more than forty designs ranging from Modern / Didone serifs to humanist sans, Fontsmith spends a significant amount of studio time designing bespoke fonts for organizations across a variety of sectors. The foundry allows for technological innovation so its types can be adaptable and flexible, which has been necessary in a number of its private commissions for the design of typefaces for UK and internationally based brands across a variety of sectors, including finance, retail, automotive, FMCG, sport, telecommunications and luxury.

It designed the first-ever bespoke typeface for a digital television channel (E4) in 2001, and its credits also include the UK's BBC, Channel 4, ITV and Sky News, and Sweden's Kanal 5. Fontsmith aims to counter the challenges and limitations of television and similar platforms such as mobile media and computers, by designing typefaces that are consistently and clearly presented yet differentiate each brand, no matter the limitations of the presentation medium.

Founded: 1997
Country: Britain
Website: fontsmith.com
Notable typefaces:
FS Benjamin (see p. 66)
FS Industrie (see p. 225)
Lost & Foundry (see p. 368)

Below. Fontsmith founder Jason Smith and team often start any new design by sketching ideas before translating to digital.

Opposite top. Spreads from Fontsmith's Brandfont book, showcasing a number of corporate typefaces.

Opposite below. Revisiting ampersand designs and reworking letterform designs by hand.

FS Millbank

ABCDEFGHIJKLMNOPQRSTUVWXYZ
abcdefghijklmnopqrstuvwxyz
1234567890 !@#?:;"*&

FS Millbank was designed by Stuart de Rozario to be clear and legible and to encourage speedy comprehension when used within signage. It incorporates an extensive set of wayfinding-specific icons and a special optically tailored cut for use in lighter colours on dark backgrounds.

Foundry: Fontsmith
Designer: Stuart de Rozario
Designer Nationality: British
Date: 2014

FS Pimlico

ABCDEFGHIJKLMNOPQRSTUVWXYZ
abcdefghijklmnopqrstuvwxyz
1234567890 !@#?:;"*&

The 1970s flavour of FS Pimlico reflects designer Fernando Mello's personal fondness for the era – he created the voluptuous Black weight of the typeface first, before moving on to develop Light and Bold versions. A set of swash caps and alternate characters are also included.

Foundry: Fontsmith
Designer: Fernando Mello
Designer Nationality: Brazilian
Date: 2011

FS Siena

ABCDEFGHIJKLMNOPQRSTUVWXYZ
abcdefghijklmnopqrstuvwxyz
1234567890 !@#?:;"*&

Jason Smith drew his first sketches for FS Siena twenty-five years before its eventual release; its delicate and distinguished forms were developed into a fully functioning family by designer Krista Radoeva at Fontsmith (see p. 272). The original drawings were based on Optima by Hermann Zapf (see p. 574).

Foundry: Fontsmith
Designer: Krista Radoeva / Jason Smith
Designer Nationality: Bulgarian / British
Date: 2016

FS Silas Sans

ABCDEFGHIJKLMNOPQRSTUVWXYZ
abcdefghijklmnopqrstuvwxyz
1234567890 !@#?:;"*&

This sans serif member of the Silas type system was designed with subtle angled cuts to the ascenders of its letterforms, adding a sense of consistency within body text. The typeface offers a functional, businesslike feel with a subtle touch of warmth and movement.

Foundry: Fontsmith
Designer: Phil Garnham
Designer Nationality: British
Date: 2015

Generis Sans

ABCDEFGHIJKLMNOPQRSTUVWXYZ
abcdefghijklmnopqrstuvwxyz
1234567890 !@#?:;"*&

Foundry: Linotype
Designer: Erik Faulhaber
Designer Nationality: German
Date: 2006

Erik Faulhaber designed his extensive Generis type system to offer designers a cohesive family of styles that would serve a wide range of different typographic contexts and requirements. This slightly condensed sans serif version features wide open counters for maximum legibility.

Generis Simple

ABCDEFGHIJKLMNOPQRSTUVWXYZ
abcdefghijklmnopqrstuvwxyz
1234567890 !@#?:;"*&

Foundry: Linotype
Designer: Erik Faulhaber
Designer Nationality: German
Date: 2006

As its name suggests, this second sans serif member of the Generis family is a further refinement of Generis Sans. Working from the same formal skeleton, Erik Faulhaber removed the spurs from the original sans letterforms, simplifying their design for a more contemporary feel.

Gills Sans Nova

ABCDEFGHIJKLMNOPQRSTUVWXYZ
abcdefghijklmnopqrstuvwxyz
1234567890 !@#?:;"*&

Foundry: Monotype
Designer: Eric Gill / George Ryan
Designer Nationality: British / American
Date: 2015

Gill Sans Nova is part of Monotype's Eric Gill Series that builds upon the original Gill Sans (1931). Monotype designer George Ryan expanded its character set and added a range of weights, to create a fully fledged family that fulfils the diverse demands of contemporary typesetting.

Gordian

ABCDEFGHIJKLMNOPQRSTUVWXYZ
abcdefghijklmnopqrstuvwxyz
1234567890 !@#?:;"*&

Foundry: Typotheque
Designer: Nikola Djurek
Designer Nationality: Croatian
Date: 2018

Croatian type designer and winemaker Nikola Djurek has experience of stone-carving, which is evident within his design for Gordian, a Roman-influenced sans serif featuring subtle flared details. Alongside its four text weights are several handsome sets of display capitals.

Gill Sans

ABCDEFGHIJKLMNOPQRSTUVWXYZ
abcdefghijklmnopqrstuvwxyz
1234567890 !@#?:;'"*&

Foundry: Monotype
Designer: Eric Gill
Designer Nationality: British
Date: 1928

If any typeface offered itself as an English vernacular, then Gill Sans would take the crown. It was designed by engraver, calligrapher and sculptor Eric Gill as a commission from Monotype's Stanley Morison, and was Gill's first typeface. Monotype released Gill Sans in 1928 as metal type to compete with the German sans serifs appearing at the time, such as Futura. Gill served as an apprentice under British type designer and calligrapher Edward Johnston, and Gill Sans owes much of its appearance to Johnston's sans serif typeface designs for the London Underground in 1916.

Gill Sans is more than just an elegant, classic and distinctive sans serif. The typeface was adopted by numerous companies that were integral to the UK's infrastructure and it evolved to become a part of the national identity, leading to the face being dubbed the 'Helvetica of England'. The London North Eastern Railway (LNER) adopted Gill Sans soon after its release in 1929. The railway operator employed Gill Sans on everything from timetables to locomotive name plates. When LNER and the other 'Big Four' railways were nationalized in 1948 to form British Railways, Gill Sans was then used on all printed material and timetables. In addition, companies such as the Post Office, the BBC, Penguin Books and Monotype have used Gill Sans as part of their identity over the years, meaning that Gill Sans has never been out of the public eye.

Gill Sans was not drawn up mechanically from a single design and is known for possessing inconsistencies in design between the weights ranging from Light to the overinflated Ultra Bold. Yet this variation contributes to its charm and humanity.

Below, from left. Gill Sans featuring in the guidelines for LNER; appearing on the name plate for the Mallard, an A4 Pacific Class Locomotive, holder of the world speed record for a steam locomotive; and a galley set of Gill Sans woodblock types held at Typoretum, a letterpress and vintage printing studio in Colchester, UK.

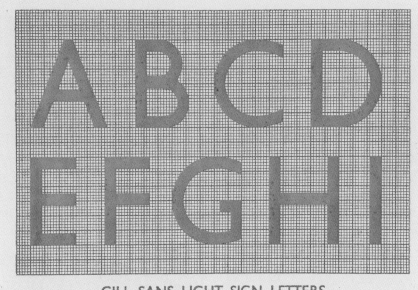

GILL SANS LIGHT SIGN LETTERS

Gill Sans Light Sign Letters and Figures (pages 6 to 10) are used only for
(i) notices requiring a considerable amount of lettering, where maximum legibility is not so important as economy in space
(ii) internally illuminated signs (anti-halation).

6

Greta Sans

ABCDEFGHIJKLMNOPQRSTUVWXYZ
abcdefghijklmnopqrstuvwxyz
1234567890 !@#?:;"*&

Foundry: Typotheque
Designer: Peter Biľak /
Nikola Djurek
Designer Nationality: Slovakian /
Croatian
Date: 2012

This sans serif member of Peter Biľak's innovative Greta type family was designed with the assistance of Nikola Djurek, his fellow designer at Typotheque (see p. 90). Its ten weights, four widths and distinctive, jaunty italics enable it to rise to even the most complex of editorial design challenges.

ITC Adderville

ABCDEFGHIJKLMNOPQRSTUVWXYZ
abcdefghijklmnopqrstuvwxyz
1234567890 !@#?:;"*&

Foundry: ITC
Designer: George Ryan
Designer Nationality: American
Date: 1999

When George Ryan of the Massachusetts-based Galapagos Design Group designed Adderville for ITC, he hoped to create a 'truly original' sans serif. The result is a typeface that has an appealing irregularity and flared details, which make it a lively choice for display type.

ITC Bailey Sans

ABCDEFGHIJKLMNOPQRSTUVWXYZ
abcdefghijklmnopqrstuvwxyz
1234567890 !@#?:;"*&

Foundry: ITC
Designer: Kevin Bailey
Designer Nationality: American
Date: 1996

Kevin Bailey's first typeface, ITC Bailey Sans, was created for a project that required a restrained style of typeface he was unable to find elsewhere. In addition to the four weights of this sans, he also designed an accompanying serif display style, Bailey Quad Bold.

ITC Eras

ABCDEFGHIJKLMNOPQRSTUVWXYZ
abcdefghijklmnopqrstuvwxyz
1234567890 !@#?:;"*&

Foundry: ITC
Designer: Albert Boton /
Albert Hollenstein
Designer Nationality: French /
Swiss
Date: 1976

French designer Albert Boton and Swiss designer Albert Hollenstein collaborated on Eras for ITC in 1976. It upholds the French tradition for sans serif styles that favour idiosyncrasy and character over brisk neutrality. Eras' forward-leaning letterforms provide a distinctive sense of energy and purpose.

ITC Johnston

ABCDEFGHIJKLMNOPQRSTUVWXYZ
abcdefghijklmnopqrstuvwxyz
1234567890 !@#?:;"*&

Foundry: ITC
Designer: Edward Johnston / Richard Dawson / Dave Farey
Designer Nationality: British
Date: 1916 / 1999

Edward Johnston's humanist sans serif was originally created in a single weight and never intended for body text typesetting. Richard Dawson and Dave Farey's version of the font for ITC in 1999 referred to Johnston's original letterforms, preserving their carefully constructed proportions.

ITC Legacy Sans

ABCDEFGHIJKLMNOPQRSTUVWXYZ
abcdefghijklmnopqrstuvwxyz
1234567890 !@#?:;"*&

Foundry: ITC
Designer: Ronald Arnholm
Designer Nationality: American
Date: 1992

Ronald Arnholm developed this sans serif from the skeleton of his Legacy Serif typeface. The latter was inspired by the lettering in an edition of Eusebius's *De praeparatione evangelica* (*Preparation for the Gospel*) by French type designer and printer Nicolas Jenson in 1470.

ITC Migration Sans

ABCDEFGHIJKLMNOPQRSTUVWXYZ
abcdefghijklmnopqrstuvwxyz
1234567890 !@#?:;"*&

Foundry: ITC
Designer: André Simard
Designer Nationality: Canadian
Date: 2008

Québécois designer André Simard founded his own studio in 1980, and brought his experience within graphic-design practice to bear in the design of his first typeface, ITC Migration Sans. Reflecting his experience in newspaper design, the font works well at small point sizes.

ITC Mixage

ABCDEFGHIJKLMNOPQRSTUVWXYZ
abcdefghijklmnopqrstuvwxyz
1234567890 !@#?:;"*&

Foundry: ITC
Designer: Aldo Novarese
Designer Nationality: Italian
Date: 1985

True to its name, ITC Mixage is a hybrid typeface created by Italian type designer Aldo Novarese, within which he blended certain characteristics of Antique Olive and Syntax to create an affable new sans serif design. It is available in four weights with corresponding italics.

ITC Obliqua

ABCDEFGHIJKLMNOPQRSTUVWXYZ
abcdefghijklmnopqrstuvwxyz
1234567890 !@#?:;"*&

Foundry: ITC
Designer: César Puertas
Designer Nationality: Colombian
Date: 2009

Colombian designer César Puertas, who is type director at the Bogota-based Typograma type-design studio, designed Obliqua for ITC in 2009.

Its utilitarian design blends characteristics of traditional, industrial grotesques with a subtle sense of movement inspired by handwriting.

ITC Officina Sans

ABCDEFGHIJKLMNOPQRSTUVWXYZ
abcdefghijklmnopqrstuvwxyz
1234567890 !@#?:;"*&

Foundry: ITC
Designer: Ole Schäfer / Erik Spiekermann
Designer Nationality: German
Date: 1990

ITC Officina Sans was originally designed as a functional font for business correspondence, tailored to reproduce well on low-quality office printers. Its popularity upon release prompted Ole Schäfer and Erik Spiekermann (see p. 304) to expand the typeface into an extensive font family.

ITC Panache

ABCDEFGHIJKLMNOPQRSTUVWXYZ
abcdefghijklmnopqrstuvwxyz
1234567890 !@#?:;"*&

Foundry: ITC
Designer: Ed Benguiat
Designer Nationality: American
Date: 1988

Although Ed Benguiat (see p. 514) stated that legibility was his principal concern when designing ITC Panache, he also incorporated a number of stylistic flourishes that elevate the font from this straightforward foundation. The resulting typeface is well suited for both headlines and body text.

ITC Pino

ABCDEFGHIJKLMNOPQRSTUVWXYZ
abcdefghijklmnopqrstuvwxyz
1234567890 !@#?:;"*&

Foundry: ITC
Designer: Slobodan Jelesijevic
Designer Nationality: Serbian
Date: 2008

Serbian designer and illustrator Slobodan Jelesijevic developed ITC Pino to accompany illustrations he was working on for a children's magazine; unable to find a typeface that fulfilled his requirements, he decided to design his own. The font was licensed by ITC in 2008.

ITC Quay Sans

ABCDEFGHIJKLMNOPQRSTUVWXYZ
abcdefghijklmnopqrstuvwxyz
1234567890 !@#?:;"*&

Foundry: ITC
Designer: David Quay
Designer Nationality: British
Date: 1990

Alongside his work as a co-founder of London-based type studio The Foundry (see p. 284), David Quay has designed a range of typefaces for other foundries over the course of his career. This design for ITC adds subtle visual interest to its sans serif letterforms with slightly flared stroke ends.

ITC Stone Humanist

ABCDEFGHIJKLMNOPQRSTUVWXYZ
abcdefghijklmnopqrstuvwxyz
1234567890 !@#?:;"*&

Foundry: ITC
Designer: Sumner Stone
Designer Nationality: American
Date: 2005

A member of Sumner Stone's extensive, eponymous type system, ITC Stone Humanist was designed to incorporate characteristics of both sans and serif type styles. The typeface is a subtle development of the design of its predecessor, Stone Sans, with which it shares its italics.

ITC Stone Sans

ABCDEFGHIJKLMNOPQRSTUVWXYZ
abcdefghijklmnopqrstuvwxyz
1234567890 !@#?:;"*&

Foundry: ITC
Designer: Sumner Stone /
Bob Ishi
Designer Nationality: American
Date: 1987

Designed by Sumner Stone with Adobe's Bob Ishi in 1987, Stone Sans is a humanist sans serif font that shares proportions with its Stone Serif counterpart. Alongside the Latin character set, a phonetic version by John Renner, and Cyrillic by Vladimir Yefimov, are also available.

ITC Stone Sans II

ABCDEFGHIJKLMNOPQRSTUVWXYZ
abcdefghijklmnopqrstuvwxyz
1234567890 !@#?:;"*&

Foundry: ITC
Designer: Sumner Stone /
Jim Wasco / Delve Withrington
Designer Nationality: American
Date: 2010

Sumner Stone's original aim when updating Stone Sans was to add further weights and condensed styles to the existing family; upon revisiting the font, however, he decided a more extensive reworking was in order. Stone Sans II builds upon the impressive legibility of its predecessor.

Jeunesse

ABCDEFGHIJKLMNOPQRSTUVWXYZ
abcdefghijklmnopqrstuvwxyz
1234567890 !@#?:;"*&

Foundry: Monotype
Designer: Johannes Birkenbach
Designer Nationality: German
Date: 1993

This semi-serif typeface was created by German type designer Johannes Birkenbach at Monotype UK, shortly before he established his own foundry, ABC Design. Together with its serif and sans counterparts, it forms part of the versatile Jeunesse superfamily of typefaces.

Jeunesse Sans

ABCDEFGHIJKLMNOPQRSTUVWXYZ
abcdefghijklmnopqrstuvwxyz
1234567890 !@#?:;"*&

Foundry: Monotype
Designer: Johannes Birkenbach
Designer Nationality: German
Date: 1993

With a slightly heavier stroke weight and fewer serif details than Jeunesse, this sans member of the superfamily offers a slightly more businesslike feel than its counterparts. The high waist of certain uppercase letterforms is reminiscent of Venus, the Bauer grotesque released in 1907.

Joanna Sans Nova

ABCDEFGHIJKLMNOPQRSTUVWXYZ
abcdefghijklmnopqrstuvwxyz
1234567890 !@#?:;"*&

Foundry: Monotype
Designer: Terrance Weinzierl
Designer Nationality: American
Date: 2015

This design by Terrance Weinzierl is a member of Monotype's Eric Gill Series and was developed from Eric Gill's serif Joanna (1931). Less diverse in character across its range of weights than Gill Sans, Joanna Sans Nova is particularly well suited to digital applications.

L10

ABCDEFGHIJKLMNOPQRSTUVWXYZ
abcdefghijklmnopqrstuvwxyz
1234567890 !@#?:;"*&

Foundry: Or Type
Designer: Guðmundur Úlfarsson
Designer Nationality: Icelandic
Date: 2013 / 2015

L10 is a font family developed to revitalize the traditional form of a humanist sans serif. Its characters, designed in four weights, feature vigorous strokes and dynamic counters and are ideally suited to multiplatform environments, editorial and identity projects.

L15

ABCDEFGHIJKLMNOPQRSTUVWXYZ
abcdefghijklmnopqrstuvwxyz
1234567890 !@#?:;"*&

Foundry: Or Type
Designer: Guðmundur Úlfarsson
Designer Nationality: Icelandic
Date: 2015

L15 is a revision of the earlier L10 sans serif design from Icelandic foundry Or Type. L15 maintains the nature of the original and introduces several distinctive features, such as the widening of characters and the lengthening of curved terminals, as is visible on the lowercase 'a'.

Legal

ABCDEFGHIJKLMNOPQRSTUVWXYZ
abcdefghijklmnopqrstuvwxyz
1234567890 !@#?:;"*&

Foundry: Linotype
Designer: Hellmut G. Bomm
Designer Nationality: German
Date: 2004

Hellmut G. Bomm developed the design of Legal from his earlier experiments in simplified, grotesque sans serif type design during the 1970s. The typeface offers a legible neutrality at smaller point sizes, but conveys a more pronounced sense of personality within headlines.

Lemance

ABCDEFGHIJKLMNOPQRSTUVWXYZ
abcdefghijklmnopqrstuvwxyz
1234567890 !@#?:;"*&

Foundry: Dalton Maag
Designer: Damien Collot
Designer Nationality: French
Date: 2016

Lemance is a functional sans serif designed in the humanist style. It takes its name from the river that runs through the French town of Monsempron-Libos, Nouvelle-Aquitaine, where designer Damien Collot was born. Like the river, Lemance's letterforms are governed by their lively and organic curves.

Letraset Arta

ABCDEFGHIJKLMNOPQRSTUVWXYZ
abcdefghijklmnopqrstuvwxyz
1234567890 !@#?:;"*&

Foundry: Letraset
Designer: David Quay
Designer Nationality: British
Date: 1991

The slight forward tilt of Letraset Arta adds a jaunty vitality to both body text and headlines; unusually, its italics are not tilted at a more exaggerated angle, but are instead considerably condensed, providing a sense of contrast with the openness of Arta's roman styles.

Ligurino

ABCDEFGHIJKLMNOPQRSTUVWXYZ
abcdefghijklmnopqrstuvwxyz
1234567890 !@#?:;"*&

Foundry: Typodermic
Designer: Ray Larabie
Designer Nationality: Canadian
Date: 2005

This straightforward sans serif design by Canadian Ray Larabie of Typodermic was created with a deliberate lack of ornamentation, in order to function first and foremost as a readable text typeface. It is available in an array of weights and widths, with an all-caps outline counterpart.

Linex Sans

ABCDEFGHIJKLMNOPQRSTUVWXYZ
abcdefghijklmnopqrstuvwxyz
1234567890 !@#?:;"*&

Foundry: Monotype
Designer: Albert Boton
Designer Nationality: French
Date: 2002

Carpenter turned type designer Albert Boton developed Linex Sans from his earlier typeface Linex Sweet (1996). He sharpened Sweet's rounded edges while preserving the calligraphic contrast within its letterforms, to create an amiable and slightly unconventional sans serif design.

Linotype Aperto

ABCDEFGHIJKLMNOPQRSTUVWXYZ
abcdefghijklmnopqrstuvwxyz
1234567890 !@#?:;"*&

Foundries: Calligraphics / Linotype
Designer: Paul Veres
Designer Nationality: American
Date: 1996

Paul Veres created this transitional sans serif featuring a generous x-height for his one-man foundry Calligraphics in 1995; it was licensed by Linotype the following year. Aperto was Veres's first typeface design and was influenced by his experience in calligraphy.

Linotype Aroma No. 2

ABCDEFGHIJKLMNOPQRSTUVWXYZ
abcdefghijklmnopqrstuvwxyz
1234567890 !@#?:;"*&

Foundry: Linotype
Designer: Tim Ahrens
Designer Nationality: German
Date: 2007

Type designer and architect Tim Ahrens hoped to preserve a formal elegance he felt was missing from many neutral sans serif designs with Linotype Aroma (1999). He refined the design of many of its letterforms for this OpenType update to the font, which was published in 2007.

The Foundry

The Foundry was co-founded in London in 1989 by David Quay and Freda Sack, with just two typefaces (Foundry Sans and Foundry Old Style), but its typeface library has now grown into a range of font styles, covering a range of languages and formats. The founders bring a combination of traditional and modern approaches to font design and implementation, having worked in every technological development of type design since hot metal, including the beginnings of digital font technology.

Sack is a British type designer and typographer. Since the late 1970s, she has worked for various font manufacturers in all aspects of type design and font development, including Stempel, Linotype, Berthold and the International Typeface Corporation (ITC), which still publishes many of her designs. Quay is a graphic designer, type designer, typographer and teacher from London, who now resides in the Netherlands. He has also designed fonts for Letraset, ITC and Berthold. He continues to work as a type and graphic designer, creating new typefaces for The Foundry as well as private commissions.

The Foundry's craft skills and predigital experience lend integrity and quality to its type design. Its involvement with design and typography gives the company a highly individual approach to its work as type designers. This is also motivated by personal dialogue with designers from all over the world. In 2013, the partners decided to work closely with Monotype towards a new era where all The Foundry typefaces would be available as web fonts and for use in e-publications, mobile apps, server-based applications, consumer devices and other products, all to be licensed through Monotype.

Founded: 1989
Country: Britain
Website: foundrytypes.co.uk
Notable typefaces:
Foundry Sterling (see p. 266)
Foundry Gridnik (see p. 426)

Below. From a visual identity and brand direction developed by Swedish agency Kurppa Hosk, London / Croatian studio Bunch implemented a wide range of information and promotional materials employing Foundry Gridnik as the brand's core type.

Above. *The New Sylva* book, designed by Grade Design in London, employs Foundry Wilson for titling and text setting across 400 pages. Foundry Wilson is a revival of a typeface originally cut in 1760 by Scottish type founder Alexander Wilson.

Below. Identity by designer and art director Patrick Myles for RIBA (Royal Institute of British Architects). The project employing Foundry Flek / Plek was applied online and in print, and as applied window graphics across London's Regent Street.

Linotype Authentic Sans

ABCDEFGHIJKLMNOPQRSTUVWXYZ
abcdefghijklmnopqrstuvwxyz
1234567890 !@#?:¡"*&

Foundry: Linotype
Designer: Karin Huschka
Designer Nationality: German
Date: 1999

This eccentric sans serif font is part of Linotype's TakeType Library, which was chosen from the entries of the International Digital Type Design Contest held in 1999. Slab serif, small serif and stencil versions of the typeface complete the Linotype Authentic family.

Linotype Projekt

ABCDEFGHIJKLMNOPQRSTUVWXYZ
abcdefghijklmnopqrstuvwxyz
1234567890 !@#?:;"*&

Foundry: Linotype
Designer: Andreas Koch
Designer Nationality: German
Date: 1999

Andreas Koch designed Linotype Projekt to capture some of the formal distortion that occurred from the process of printing metal type, which he felt resulted in a more robust and pleasing appearance. His humanist sans serif design also features slightly flared stroke ends.

Linotype Spitz

ABCDEFGHIJKLMNOPQRSTUVWXYZ
abcdefghijklmnopqrstuvwxyz
1234567890 !@#?:;"*&

Foundry: Linotype
Designer: Oliver Brentzel
Designer Nationality: German
Date: 1997

According to designer Oliver Brentzel, the pairing of pointed details and gentle semicircular curves within the letterforms of Linotype Spitz was inspired by the distinctive, decorative forms of the Chrysler Building in New York. The typeface is available in five weights.

Linotype Tetria

ABCDEFGHIJKLMNOPQRSTUVWXYZ
abcdefghijklmnopqrstuvwxyz
1234567890 !@#?:;"*&

Foundry: Linotype
Designer: Martin Jagodzinski
Designer Nationality: German
Date: 1999

Clear, legible and free from embellishment, Linotype Tetria shares some geometric characteristics with the German DIN typefaces, and its slightly condensed letterforms make it an economical choice for text typesetting. It was designed by Martin Jagodzinski for Linotype in 1999.

Linotype Textra

ABCDEFGHIJKLMNOPQRSTUVWXYZ
abcdefghijklmnopqrstuvwxyz
1234567890 !@#?:;"*&

Foundry: Linotype
Designer: Jörg Herz / Jochen Schuss
Designer Nationality: German
Date: 2002

Linotype Textra is a versatile font featuring subtle idiosyncrasies within the design of its letterforms, which are difficult to discern when used for body text, but become more evident at larger point sizes. Its name is a portmanteau of 'text' and 'extra', which reflects that duality.

Luba

ABCDEFGHIJKLMNOPQRSTUVWXYZ
abcdefghijklmnopqrstuvwxyz
1234567890 !@#?:;"*&

Foundry: Linotype
Designer: Hendrik Möller
Designer Nationality: German
Date: 2009

German designer Hendrik Möller designed this friendly sans serif in 2009. Luba is a multi-script font that comes in four weights with Latin and Cyrillic support. Möller created it as part of a university project aiming to develop a typeface for people learning Cyrillic-based languages.

Lumin Sans

ABCDEFGHIJKLMNOPQRSTUVWXYZ
abcdefghijklmnopqrstuvwxyz
1234567890 !@#?:;"*&

Foundry: Typotheque
Designer: Nikola Djurek
Designer Nationality: Croatian
Date: 2013

Nikola Djurek's legible but distinctive Lumin Sans is part of the Lumin family. It is available in Regular and Condensed in six weights with italics. Lumin Sans has many distinguishing features; on heavier weights the stroke connections are chiselled and the 'k' in the lighter weights is in two parts.

Mahsuri Sans

ABCDEFGHIJKLMNOPQRSTUVWXYZ
abcdefghijklmnopqrstuvwxyz
1234567890 !@#?:;"*&

Foundry: Monotype
Designer: Ong Chong Wah
Designer Nationality: Malaysian
Date: 2001

Mahsuri Sans is a legible, humanist sans serif available in four weights with italics. It was designed by Malaysian typographer Ong Chong Wah, who studied graphic design in England and worked in advertising before becoming a type designer and working in-house for Monotype in London.

Mallory

ABCDEFGHIJKLMNOPQRSTUVWXYZ
abcdefghijklmnopqrstuvwxyz
1234567890 !@#?:;"*&

Foundry: Frere-Jones Type
Designer: Tobias Frere-Jones
Designer Nationality: American
Date: 2015

Mallory was the first typeface released under Frere-Jones Type (see p. 80), the independent type design studio of Tobias Frere-Jones. It is a humanist design that combines British and US typographic traditions to fashion an unconventional, but novel, sans serif font family.

Mariposa Sans

ABCDEFGHIJKLMNOPQRSTUVWXYZ
abcdefghijklmnopqrstuvwxyz
1234567890 !@#?:;"*&

Foundry: ITC
Designer: Philip Bouwsma
Designer Nationality: American
Date: 1994

Mariposa Sans was released by ITC in 1994 as part of the Mariposa family. It is a distinctive, high-contrast sans serif with flared strokes. Philip Bouwsma's lifelong interest in calligraphy comes through in this face, which comes in four weights, of which only the book cut has an italic.

Massif

ABCDEFGHIJKLMNOPQRSTUVWXYZ
abcdefghijklmnopqrstuvwxyz
1234567890 !@#?:;"*&

Foundry: Monotype
Designer: Steve Matteson
Designer Nationality: American
Date: 2011

When Steve Matteson designed this rugged sans serif, he took inspiration from the many granite formations found in the Sierra Nevada mountains, particularly Yosemite National Park's Half Dome, which explains Massif's distinctive chiselled feel. It comes in six weights with italics.

Mentor Sans

ABCDEFGHIJKLMNOPQRSTUVWXYZ
abcdefghijklmnopqrstuvwxyz
1234567890 !@#?:;"*&

Foundry: Monotype
Designer: Michael Harvey
Designer Nationality: British
Date: 2005

British master typographer and book designer Michael Harvey designed Mentor Sans in 2005. It is a humanist sans serif with subtly flared strokes. The typeface is available from Monotype in four weights with italics. Harvey designed a serif partner, Mentor, the same year.

Metro Nova

ABCDEFGHIJKLMNOPQRSTUVWXYZ
abcdefghijklmnopqrstuvwxyz
1234567890 !@#?:;"*&

Foundry: Monotype
Designer: William A. Dwiggins / Toshi Omagari
Designer Nationality: American / Japanese
Date: 1928 / 2012

Metro is William A. Dwiggins's geometric, humanist sans; it came after he was critical of existing sans serifs in his book *Layout in Advertising* (1928), which lead to Mergenthaler Linotype asking him to create his own. Toshi Omagari's revival, Metro Nova, retains the spirit of the original in seven weights.

Metro Office

ABCDEFGHIJKLMNOPQRSTUVWXYZ
abcdefghijklmnopqrstuvwxyz
1234567890 !@#?:;"*&

Foundry: Linotype
Designer: William A. Dwiggins / Toshi Omagari
Designer Nationality: American / Japanese
Date: c. 1920s / 2006

Metro, which initially came in four weights, was William A. Dwiggins's first typeface, which he created at the age of forty-nine. Metro Office is an update by Linotype type director Akira Kobayashi which reinstates some lost features such as a double-storey 'a' and 'g' while enhancing legibility.

Metrolite #2

ABCDEFGHIJKLMNOPQRSTUVWXYZ
abcdefghijklmnopqrstuvwxyz
1234567890 !@#?:;"*&

Foundry: Linotype
Designer: William A. Dwiggins
Designer Nationality: American
Date: 1929–37

When William A. Dwiggins's geometric sans Metro was released in 1929, it was so successful that Mergenthaler Linotype was keen to expand it. The first addition was the heavier Metroblack, followed by Metromedium and Metrolite. They came in two styles: regular and #2. Only the latter has been digitized.

Metromedium #2

ABCDEFGHIJKLMNOPQRSTUVWXYZ
abcdefghijklmnopqrstuvwxyz
1234567890 !@#?:;"*&

Foundry: Linotype
Designer: William A. Dwiggins
Designer Nationality: American
Date: 1932–36

William A. Dwiggins updated Metro to Metro #2 in 1932, changing many glyphs to be more like its competitor Futura; characters such as 'M', 'N', 'A' and 'V' became sharp rather than flat. The additional weights added after 1932, such as Metromedium (1936), therefore had to be done in both versions.

Adrian Frutiger

Adrian Frutiger is considered to be the most important and influential type designers of the 20th century. His legacy pervades many aspects of everyday life, his craft being employed on everything from bus timetables to food packaging and airport wayfinding, shaping modern life.

Born in 1928, in Berne, Switzerland, Frutiger trained as a typesetter and then worked as a graphic designer before joining Paris-based type foundry Deberny & Peignot. In 1962, he formed his own design studio in Arcueil near Paris. His breakthrough typeface was Univers (see p. 248), which propelled him on to the world stage and became one of the most notable typeface designs of the 20th century. Univers had its roots in exercises Frutiger conducted at the age of twenty-one while studying at the School of Applied Arts, Zurich. Spending fifteen years to develop it, Frutiger devised a groundbreaking system in cataloguing the differing weights of type forms, making it an instant success upon release. Using a number system to indicate weight, width and slope, all set within a 'periodic table', allowed the user to visualize the differing weights of the font family instantly. In Frutiger's system, the first digit represents the weight, the second the width; odd numbers define roman variants and even numbers obliques.

Following Univers's success, Frutiger was commissioned to develop the signage for the soon to be built Charles de Gaulle Airport in Paris. Although Univers was originally considered, Frutiger revisited a seven-year-old sans serif design called Concorde, which he created in collaboration with Swiss typographer André Gürtler. The first bespoke airport alphabet was the result and upon the airport's inauguration, designers and typographers around the world clamoured to use it. Type foundries D. Stempel AG and Linotype eventually released the typeface renamed as Frutiger in 1976.

Frutiger designed more than twenty typeface families over sixty years. All of them were deemed revolutionary at the time of their release and the apex of perfection in legibility and form.

Date: 1928–2015
Nationality: Swiss
Notable typefaces:
Univers (see p. 248)
Frutiger (see p. 268)
Avenir (see p. 189)
Didot (see p. 96)

Below from left. Specimen card illustrating Univers's system of organizing weights and styles, 1955; promotional sample with Univers 53 highlighted from the Deberny et Peignot foundry, 1963; hand-lettered Univers bold '8' artwork, drawn for the Deberny et Peignot foundry, Paris, 1953.

Opposite, clockwise from left. Frutiger at work in his studio, 1996; presenting his Avenir typeface, September 1988; studying a type disc from a phototypesetting machine in his home studio, 1951.

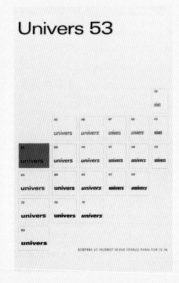

Univers 53

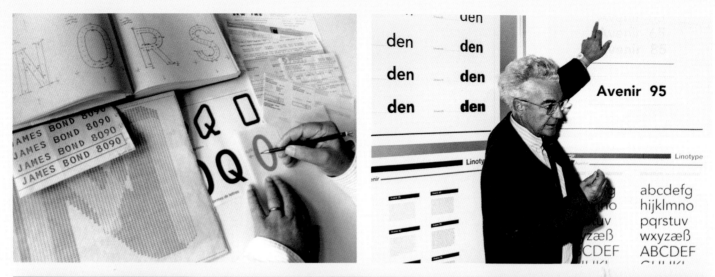

Miramonte

ABCDEFGHIJKLMNOPQRSTUVWXYZ
abcdefghijklmnopqrstuvwxyz
1234567890 !@#?:;"*&

Foundry: Ascender
Designer: Steve Matteson /
Stanislav Maršo
Designer Nationality: American /
Czech Republic
Date: 1960 / 2006

Miramonte by Steve Matteson, co-founder of the Chicago-based foundry Ascender, is based on the Maršuv Grotesk humanist sans designed by Stanislav Maršo and released by Czech foundry Grafotechna in 1960. Miramonte, which means 'behold the mountains' in Spanish, comes in two weights.

Morandi

ABCDEFGHIJKLMNOPQRSTUVWXYZ
abcdefghijklmnopqrstuvwxyz
1234567890 !@#?:;"*&

Foundry: Monotype
Designer: Jovica Veljović
Designer Nationality: Serbian
Date: 2018

Morandi was designed by Serbian typographer Jovica Veljović, a professor of type design at the Hamburg University of Applied Sciences, and was his first commercial sans serif release. It is a highly legible humanist sans serif available in three widths and eight weights with italics.

Mosquito

ABCDEFGHIJKLMNOPQRSTUVWXYZ
abcdefghijklmnopqrstuvwxyz
1234567890 !@#?:;"*&

Foundry: Linotype
Designer: Éric de Berranger
Designer Nationality: French
Date: 2002

Mosquito's designer is French typographer Éric de Berranger, who has created corporate fonts for Martini, Renault, Hermès and the French football governing body, Ligue de Football Professionnel. It is a jaunty but legible sans serif that comes in three weights – Regular, Bold and Black – with italics.

Mosquito Formal

ABCDEFGHIJKLMNOPQRSTUVWXYZ
abcdefghijklmnopqrstuvwxyz
1234567890 !@#?:;"*&

Foundry: Linotype
Designer: Éric de Berranger
Designer Nationality: French
Date: 2003

Mosquito Formal was released a year after Éric de Berranger's Mosquito (2002). He took the original design and removed a lot of the quirks, while maintaining the same base and proportions, to increase its sophistication. De Berranger describes it as 'Mosquito dressed in a tuxedo'.

Mr Eaves XL Modern

ABCDEFGHIJKLMNOPQRSTUVWXYZ
abcdefghijklmnopqrstuvwxyz
1234567890 !@#?:;"*&

Foundry: Emigre
Designer: Zuzana Licko
Designer Nationality: Slovakian
Date: 2009

Mr Eaves XL Modern is based on the frame of Mrs Eaves, a serif family designed by Licko in 1996. As with the XL Sans version, Mr Eaves XL Modern couples taller x-heights with shorter ascenders and descenders, but unlike its siblings, also features defining geometric tendencies.

Mundo Sans

ABCDEFGHIJKLMNOPQRSTUVWXYZ
abcdefghijklmnopqrstuvwxyz
1234567890 !@#?:;"*&

Foundry: Monotype
Designer: Carl Crossgrove
Designer Nationality: Mexican
Date: 2002

Mundo Sans was begun by Mexican-born typographer Carl Crossgrove in 1991 and released by his employer Monotype in 2002. Mundo forms a family of sans serifs in seven weights with italics. It is a humanist sans serif, partly inspired by Futura, and is unpretentious, legible and easy to use.

Myriad Pro

ABCDEFGHIJKLMNOPQRSTUVWXYZ
abcdefghijklmnopqrstuvwxyz
1234567890 !@#?:;"*&

Foundry: Adobe
Designer: Carol Twombly / Robert Slimbach / Fred Brady / Christopher Slye
Designer Nationality: American
Date: 2002

Robert Slimbach and Carol Twombly of Adobe designed Myriad in 1992. A neutral, humanist sans serif typeface, it is similar in appearance to Frutiger, so much so that Adrian Frutiger (see p. 290) commented that the similarities had gone 'a little bit too far'. Myriad is notable for being adopted as Apple's corporate font from 2002 until 2017, replacing Apple Garamond. It is now a part of Adobe software, and the software company's programs default to Myriad when typefaces are missing. In 2000, Adobe released an OpenType update of Myriad, Myriad Pro, which added Greek and Cyrillic, Old Style figures and better support for Latin-based languages. Myriad was discontinued at the release of Pro, which has Condensed, Normal, and Extended widths in five weights with italics.

Nara Sans

ABCDEFGHIJKLMNOPQRSTUVWXYZ
abcdefghijklmnopqrstuvwxyz
1234567890 !@#?:;"*&

Foundry: Typotheque
Designer: Andrej Krátky
Designer Nationality: Slovakian
Date: 2017

Nara Sans is a humanist sans partner to Andrej Krátky's serif face Nara (2017). It comes in five weights and like its serifed sibling has two types of italics – an upright cursive and a standard slanting italic. The cursive shares its uppercase with the regular, a reference to early Aldine italics.

Nautilus Monoline

ABCDEFGHIJKLMNOPQRSTUVWXYZ
abcdefghijklmnopqrstuvwxyz
1234567890 !@#?:;"*&

Foundry: Linotype
Designer: Hellmut G. Bomm
Designer Nationality: German
Date: 2008

German designer Hellmut G. Bomm released his sans serif typeface Linotype Nautilus in 1999. Less than ten years later, he added two new styles to the family, Nautilus Text and Nautilus Monoline. The monolinear Monoline shares the proportions of the text cut but lacks its calligraphic details.

Neue Frutiger

ABCDEFGHIJKLMNOPQRSTUVWXYZ
abcdefghijklmnopqrstuvwxyz
1234567890 !@#?:;"*&

Foundry: Linotype
Designer: Adrian Frutiger / Akira Kobayashi
Designer Nationality: Swiss / Japanese
Date: 1976 / 2009

Neue Frutiger is a revision and expansion of Frutiger (1976), made by Linotype type director Akira Kobayashi under the supervision of Adrian Frutiger (see p. 290). It comes in Regular and Condensed, in ten weights with italics. Frutiger was designed for wayfinding and is a highly legible face.

Neue Frutiger 1450

ABCDEFGHIJKLMNOPQRSTUVWXYZ
abcdefghijklmnopqrstuvwxyz
1234567890 !@#?:;"*&

Foundry: Linotype
Designer: Adrian Frutiger / Akira Kobayashi
Designer Nationality: Swiss / Japanese
Date: 1976 / 2013

Neue Frutiger 1450 is a slight update to Neue Frutiger. Akira Kobayashi designed it to be compliant with the German standard DIN 1450, a specification for barrier-free legibility. Neue Frutiger 1450 is a family of eight fonts in four weights – Book, Regular, Medium and Bold – with obliques.

Neutura

ABCDEFGHIJKLMNOPQRSTUVWXYZ
abcdefghijklmnopqrstuvwxyz
1234567890 !@#?:;"*&

Foundry: Neutura
Designer: Alexander McCracken
Designer Nationality: American
Date: 2004

Neutura is the eponymous typeface of the San Francisco foundry of the same name (see p. 472) founded by designer Alexander McCracken in 2003.

It is a clean but distinctive geometric sans serif that comes in four weights, ranging from Light to ExBold, without italics.

Noa

ABCDEFGHIJKLMNOPQRSTUVWXYZ
abcdefghijklmnopqrstuvwxyz
1234567890 !@#?:;"*&

Foundry: Linotype
Designer: Nina Lee Storm
Designer Nationality: Korean
Date: 2004

Noa was designed for TV and computer screen use during the late 1990s by Korean-born designer Nina Lee Storm, who is now based in Denmark. It

has short ascenders and descenders and a large x-height. It was released in three weights with obliques, and a condensed version followed in 2009.

Nota

ABCDEFGHIJKLMNOPQRSTUVWXYZ
abcdefghijklmnopqrstuvwxyz
1234567890 !@#?:;"*&

Foundry: Typotheque
Designer: Nikola Djurek
Designer Nationality: Croatian
Date: 2009

This low-contrast humanist text sans serif was designed by Nikola Djurek, with a Cyrillic designed by Ilya Ruderman. It comes in four weights with

italics, though the non-italic versions are at a 2° slant rather than upright, which mimics handwriting and enhances readability.

Ocean Sans

ABCDEFGHIJKLMNOPQRSTUVWXYZ
abcdefghijklmnopqrstuvwxyz
1234567890 !@#?:;"*&

Foundry: Monotype
Designer: Ong Chong Wah
Designer Nationality: Malaysian
Date: 1993

Ong Chong Wah designed Ocean Sans at Monotype London in 1993. It is a grotesque sans serif with contrast between thick and thin rather than a

monoline. The typeface comes in five weights and three widths – Regular, Condensed and Extended – all with cursive italics except for the Condensed.

Optima

ABCDEFGHIJKLMNOPQRSTUVWXYZ
abcdefghijklmnopqrstuvwxyz
1234567890 !@#?:;"*&

Optima is the most successful typeface created by Hermann Zapf (see p. 574). Inspired by the lettering at a church in Florence, it has the proportions of classical roman type but without serifs. Zapf designed the letterforms using the Golden Ratio, and its tapered stems were unique at the time.

Foundry: Stempel
Designer: Hermann Zapf
Designer Nationality: German
Date: 1958

Optima Nova

ABCDEFGHIJKLMNOPQRSTUVWXYZ
abcdefghijklmnopqrstuvwxyz
1234567890 !@#?:;"*&

Hermann Zapf (see p. 574) collaborated closely with Linotype type director Akira Kobayashi to create a digital expansion and redesign of Optima more than fifty years after his first sketches at a church in Florence. Nova gave Optima real italics and added new weights, creating a family of forty fonts.

Foundry: Linotype
Designer: Hermann Zapf / Akira Kobayashi
Designer Nationality: German / Japanese
Date: 2002

PL Westerveldt

ABCDEFGHIJKLMNOPQRSTUVWXYZ
abcdefghijklmnopqrstuvwxyz
1234567890 !©#?:;"*&

Westerveldt was designed in-house at the Photo-Lettering foundry and first appeared in 1965 in its catalogue, *Alphabet Thesaurus Vol. 2*. Westerveldt is a sans serif with subtly flared strokes which was once part of a large family, including casual variants. Only the light weight has been digitized.

Foundry: Photo-Lettering
Date: 1965

PMN Caecilia Sans

ABCDEFGHIJKLMNOPQRSTUVWXYZ
abcdefghijklmnopqrstuvwxyz
1234567890 !@#?:;"*&

Dutch designer Peter Matthias Noordzij released his slab serif PMN Caecilia in 1991 after more than seven years of development; later it was adopted as the default typeface for Kindle e-readers. In 2017, it finally received a sans serif sibling, explicitly designed with on-screen use in mind.

Foundry: Linotype
Designer: Peter Matthias Noordzij
Designer Nationality: Dutch
Date: 2017

Program

ABCDEFGHIJKLMNOPQRSTUVWXYZ
abcdefghijklmnopqrstuvwxyz
1234567890 !@#?:;"*&

Foundry: Emigre
Designer: Zuzana Licko
Designer Nationality: Slovakian
Date: 2013

Program is a sans serif designed to obscure traditional categorization, while maintaining the feel of a font family. The characters combine various structural features, terminals and proportions, alongside seemingly antithetical features, such as rounded edges and ink traps.

Quire Sans

ABCDEFGHIJKLMNOPQRSTUVWXYZ
abcdefghijklmnopqrstuvwxyz
1234567890 !@#?:;"*&

Foundry: Monotype
Designer: Jim Ford
Designer Nationality: American
Date: 2014

A type designer at Monotype USA, Jim Ford designed Quire Sans in 2014. It is a versatile, modern humanist sans serif with a double-storey 'a' and 'g', available in ten weights with italics. The name 'Quire' comes from a printing term for a signature of printed pages ready to be bound.

Retina Standard

ABCDEFGHIJKLMNOPQRSTUVWXYZ
abcdefghijklmnopqrstuvwxyz
1234567890 !@#?:;"*&

Foundry: Frere-Jones Type
Designer: Tobias Frere-Jones
Designer Nationality: American
Date: 2000–16

Retina Standard is a humanist, low-contrast sans serif designed for headlines and portions of larger text. The characters, which range in weight from Thin to Black, utilize conventional proportions and features to maintain clarity and efficacy across a variety of platforms.

Retina Microplus

ABCDEFGHIJKLMNOPQRSTUVWXYZ
abcdefghijklmnopqrstuvwxyz
1234567890 !@#?:;"*&

Foundry: Frere-Jones Type
Designer: Tobias Frere-Jones
Designer Nationality: American
Date: 2000–16

Retina Microplus was initially commissioned by *The Wall Street Journal*. The title's tables of financial data require a typeface that remains legible in small sizes and condensed spaces. The font maintains clarity in such conditions through the accentuation of its details and proportions.

Milieu Grotesque

Established in 2010 and run by Timo Gaessner and Maiko Gubler, Milieu Grotesque is an independent type foundry located on the west coast of Portugal. The foundry offers not only an exclusive library of digital typefaces but a number of type-related products. Milieu Grotesque's portfolio may not be as extensive as some other foundries, but their type designs are beautifully executed and have the craft and attention to detail required of them. They have a contemporary edge to their forms, which not only makes them highly flexible in usage but also provides a timeless and clean aesthetic to any design. Their inspirations come from a wide variety of sources, including a letter by singer Johnny Cash, addressed to a former US president, which went on to become their popular Chapeau typeface release.

Founded: 2010
Country: Portugal
Website: milieugrotesque.com
Notable typefaces:
Boutique (see p. 191)
Chapeau (see p. 192)
Maison (see p. 235)
Patron (see p. 242)

Right. Typeface library specimen, spreads showing Boutique (middle), which comes with an engraved version with hollow infill, and Maison, a monolined grotesque.

Opposite top. Chapeau specimen, loosely inspired by a letter that musician Johnny Cash wrote on an old IBM typewriter.

Opposite bottom. Detail from promotion for revised Maison typeface Maison Neue. Designed by Timo Gaessner and initially released in 2010, the new version is revised and extended and was published in April 2018.

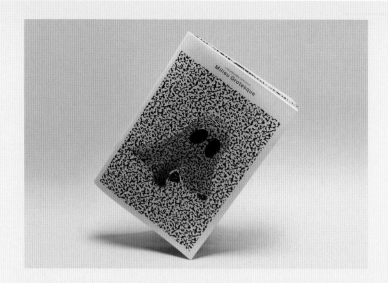

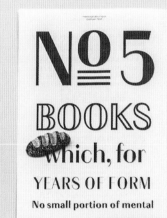

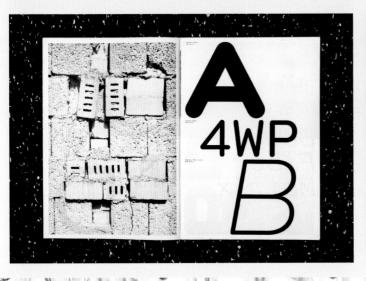

A
4WP
B

R
&
M

Maison ABCDE
FGHIJKLNOPQ
RSTUVWXYZ&
Maison ABCDE
MonoFFGHIJK
LMNOPQRSTUV

Robinson

ABCDEFGHIJKLMNOPQRSTUVWXYZ
abcdefghijklmnopqrstuvwxyz
1234567890 !@#?:;"*&

Foundry: Commercial Type
Designer: Greg Gazdowicz
Designer Nationality: American
Date: 2016

Robinson was Greg Gazdowicz's first release for Commercial Type (see p. 124). It is a humanist sans serif in the calligraphic style of typefaces such as Lydian and Samson. Grotesque frames combine with tapered stems, alongside the similarly calligraphic angling of the curves and stresses.

Saturday Sans

ABCDEFGHIJKLMNOPQRSTUVWXYZ
abcdefghijklmnopqrstuvwxyz
1234567890 !@#?:;"*&

Foundry: Image Club
Designer: Patricia Lillie
Designer Nationality: American
Date: 1996

Saturday Sans is an informal, rounded sans serif available in Regular and Bold weights. It was designed by US typographer and writer Patricia Lillie, a graduate of Parsons School of Design, in 1996 for the Image Club type library. Lillie has since drawn many dingbat fonts during her career.

Shaker

ABCDEFGHIJKLMNOPQRSTUVWXYZ
abcdefghijklmnopqrstuvwxyz
1234567890 !@#?:;"*&

Foundry: Jeremy Tankard Typography
Designer: Jeremy Tankard
Designer Nationality: British
Date: 2000

Jeremy Tankard, who worked at British brand consultancy Wolff Olins before leaving to start his type foundry in 1998, released Shaker in 2000. A companion to serif face Enigma, Shaker is a sans serif with small variations in stroke. It comes in three widths and five weights with italics.

Shannon

ABCDEFGHIJKLMNOPQRSTUVWXYZ
abcdefghijklmnopqrstuvwxyz
1234567890 !@#?:;"*&

Foundry: Compugraphic
Designer: Janice Prescott / Kris Holmes
Designer Nationality: American
Date: 1982

Janice Prescott and Kris Holmes designed Shannon for Compugraphic. It is a sans serif with slightly flared strokes that appear almost serif-like. It was inspired partly by 9th-century Irish calligraphy found in the *Book of Kells* illuminated manuscript and comes in Regular, Oblique, Bold and Extra Bold.

Sinova

ABCDEFGHIJKLMNOPQRSTUVWXYZ
abcdefghijklmnopqrstuvwxyz
1234567890 !@#?:;"*&

Foundry: Linotype
Designer: Christian Mengelt
Designer Nationality: Swiss
Date: 2011

Sinova is a functional and highly legible humanist sans serif designed by Christian Mengelt, who previously worked with Karl Gerstner and later the design team creating Haas Unica. He developed Sinova in co-operation with Linotype from 2010 to 2011. It comes in five weights with italics.

Slate

ABCDEFGHIJKLMNOPQRSTUVWXYZ
abcdefghijklmnopqrstuvwxyz
1234567890 !@#?:;"*&

Foundry: Monotype
Designer: Rod McDonald
Designer Nationality: Canadian
Date: 2006

Slate is a neutral and highly legible sans serif family, designed by Canadian typographer Rod McDonald. It comes in eight weights and two widths – Regular, which has an italic, and condensed, which does not. Smartphone company BlackBerry used Slate Pro as a user-interface font from 2013.

Stellar

ABCDEFGHIJKLMNOPQRSTUVWXYZ
abcdefghijklmnopqrstuvwxyz
1234567890 !□#?:;"*&

Foundry: Ludlow
Designer: Robert Hunter
Middleton / Dave Farey
Designer Nationality: British
Date: 1929 / c. 1990

Stellar is a sans serif with roman proportions designed by Scottish-born typographer Robert Hunter Middleton, who immigrated to the United States and studied in Chicago before working for the Ludlow foundry. Dave Farey digitized Stellar in the 1990s, doubling the number of weights.

Tanseek Sans

ABCDEFGHIJKLMNOPQRSTUVWXYZ
abcdefghijklmnopqrstuvwxyz
1234567890 !@#?:;"*&

Foundry: Monotype
Designer: Dave Farey /
Richard Dawson
Designer Nationality: British
Date: 2016

'Tanseek' is the Arabic word for 'harmony'. In keeping with its name, the Tanseek family of typefaces includes a serif and a sans that support Latin and Arabic. Tanseek Sans is a humanistic sans serif, which is based on the Latin typefaces in the family. It comes in five weights without italics.

TheMix

ABCDEFGHIJKLMNOPQRSTUVWXYZ
abcdefghijklmnopqrstuvwxyz
1234567890 !@#?:;"*&

Foundry: Lucas Fonts
Designer: Luc(as) de Groot
Designer Nationality: Dutch
Date: 1994

TheMix began life as an alphabet created by Luc(as) de Groot for the logotypes for Dutch governmental bodies while working at design agency BRS Premsela Vonk. TheMix is a sans with occasional asymmetric serifs and takes the middle ground between two other fonts, TheSans and TheSerif.

Tipperary eText

ABCDEFGHIJKLMNOPQRSTUVWXYZ
abcdefghijklmnopqrstuvwxyz
1234567890 !@#?:;"*&

Foundry: Monotype
Designer: Steve Matteson
Designer Nationality: American
Date: 2014

Tipperary eText is a humanist sans serif, designed to meet the demands of LCD and e-paper screens. The characters are spacious for legibility, and feature abrupt curves and keen corners, mimicking the routes on the Irish bike trail from which the font takes its name.

Trilogy Sans

ABCDEFGHIJKLMNOPQRSTUVWXYZ
abcdefghijklmnopqrstuvwxyz
1234567890 !@#?:;"*&

Foundry: Jeremy Tankard Typography
Designer: Jeremy Tankard
Designer Nationality: British
Date: 2009

Trilogy Sans is a humanist sans serif inspired by the early grotesques of the 17th century. Alongside the font's build and proportions, which reference the initial shapes of Caslon and Figgins, Trilogy Sans also features details such as shorter crossbars in the capital letters.

Typonine Sans

ABCDEFGHIJKLMNOPQRSTUVWXYZ
abcdefghijklmnopqrstuvwxyz
1234567890 !@#?:;"*&

Foundry: Typotheque
Designer: Nikola Djurek
Designer Nationality: Croatian
Date: 2008

Typonine Sans is a humanist sans serif with minimal contrast, which has been designed as a pragmatic and versatile font family. The letterforms combine spartan strokes with a slightly extended x-height, which maintains legibility in each weight and across both digital and printed surfaces.

Venn

ABCDEFGHIJKLMNOPQRSTUVWXYZ
abcdefghijklmnopqrstuvwxyz
1234567890 !@#?:;"*&

Foundry: Dalton Maag
Designer: Fernando Caro /
Deiverson Ribeiro
Designer Nationality: Brazilian
Date: 2018

Venn is a humanist sans serif designed to meet the various demands of multiplatform brands. It features twenty-five styles, from Condensed Light to Extended Extra Bold, and is the first face by Dalton Maag (see p. 594) to have a Variable Font version, which contains every weight in a single file.

Verdana

ABCDEFGHIJKLMNOPQRSTUVWXYZ
abcdefghijklmnopqrstuvwxyz
1234567890 !@#?:;"*&

Foundry: Microsoft
Designer: Matthew Carter
Nationality: British
Date: 1996

Created by Matthew Carter (see p. 616) for the Microsoft Corporation, Verdana was created specifically to address the issues of on-screen legibility and readability with hand-hinting by leading expert Tom Rickner. Verdana's larger width and character spacing contributes to increased legibility.

Vista Sans

ABCDEFGHIJKLMNOPQRSTUVWXYZ
abcdefghijklmnopqrstuvwxyz
1234567890 !@#?:;"*&

Foundry: Emigre
Designer: Xavier Dupré
Designer Nationality: French
Date: 2004

As with Vista Slab, the design of Vista Sans was inspired by hand-lettered shop signs on the island of Sumatra. Unable to introduce calligraphic curves without serifs, Vista Sans features a slight bounce to the stroke endings, which soften the sturdy verticals and sharp joints.

Whitney

ABCDEFGHIJKLMNOPQRSTUVWXYZ
abcdefghijklmnopqrstuvwxyz
1234567890 !@#?:;"*&

Foundry: Hoefler & Co.
Designer: Tobias Frere-Jones
Designer Nationality: American
Date: 1996–2004

Whitney was designed for the Whitney Museum in New York and developed to meet the distinct demands of editorial and signage typography. The design utilizes narrow forms and tall x-heights for compact spaces, while the vast counters maintain legibility at a distance.

Erik Spiekermann

German designer, author and professor Erik Spiekermann is one of the most prominent type designers and commentator on matters concerning typographic communications today. His work and contribution to the field have greatly influenced typeface and information design as well as how the industry operates. His impact in the arena of typography and communications is immeasurable.

In 1979, Spiekermann founded MetaDesign in Berlin, which became Germany's largest design company with overseas offices in London and San Francisco. It was at MetaDesign that Spiekermann's influence and reputation grew having designed corporate identity programmes for multinational organizations including Audi, Volkswagen and Bosch, along with wayfinding systems such as those at Dusseldorf Airport and BVG (Berlin Transport Company). In 1989, he founded an international manufacturer and distributor of digital typefaces, FontShop, with his then wife Joan Spiekermann and British designer Neville Brody. Soon after, they created FontFont, an independent type foundry to represent some of the most talented and interesting type designers in the world. Its first release was the FF Beowolf display serif font by Just Van Rossum and Erik Van Blokland. FontFont went on to become one of the largest libraries of contemporary fonts with more than 2,500 typefaces.

Spiekermann's own typefaces, such as FF Meta (see p. 264), ITC Officina, FF Info and Berliner Grotesk have been hugely popular, and are widely used in everything from print applications to wayfinding and online usage. He is a board member of the German Design Council and past president of both the International Society of Typographic Designers and the International Institute for Information Design. In 2001, he left MetaDesign to run Edenspiekermann, which has offices in Berlin, Amsterdam, Los Angeles, Singapore and San Francisco.

He has received numerous accolades in his career including an honorary professorship from the University of the Arts Bremen and an honorary doctorate from Pasadena Art Center. In 2007, the British Royal Society of Arts made him an Honorary Royal Designer for Industry and in 2009, the European Union made him Ambassador for the European Year of Creativity. In 2011, the German Design Council gave him the highest award in Germany, a Lifetime Achievement Award, and the same year he became the 25th recipient of the TDC Medal, awarded by the Type Directors Club New York.

Date: 1947–
Nationality: German
Notable typefaces:
ITC Officina Sans (see p. 279)
FF Meta (see pp. 264–65)
FF Meta Serif (see p. 264)

Below. Wayfinding system guidelines for BVG – *Berliner Verkehrsbetriebe* (Berlin Transport Company).

Opposite, clockwise from top left: Poster design by Spiekermann from his p98a experimental letterpress workshop in Berlin, dedicated to letters, printing and paper. where he is a founder-member; Cover design to Spiekermann's best-selling book *Hallo, ich bin Erik* (Hello, my name is Erik); Printing at p98a a sample sheet of his FF Real typeface design (with Ralph du Carrois); Nokia corporate typeface, one of the many corporate typefaces he has created.

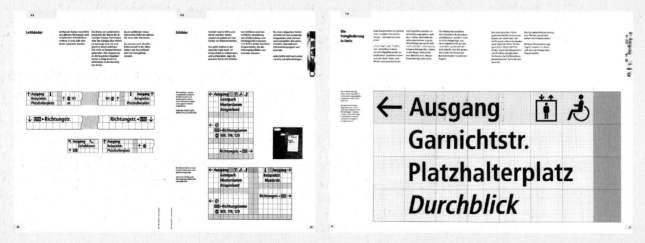

Don't work for assholes. Don't work with assholes.

Hallo ich bin Erik

Erik Spiekermann:
Schriftgestalter
Designer
Unternehmer

Von Johannes Erler

gestalten

A corporate type
A corporate typef
A corporate typefa
A corporate typefac
A corporate typeface
A corporate typeface f
A corporate typeface fo
A corporate typeface for
A corporate typeface for N
A corporate typeface for No
A corporate typeface for Nok
A corporate typeface for Noki

A corporate typeface for Nokia.

Xenois Sans

ABCDEFGHIJKLMNOPQRSTUVWXYZ
abcdefghijklmnopqrstuvwxyz
1234567890 !@#?:;"*&

Foundry: Linotype
Designer: Erik Faulhaber
Designer Nationality: German
Date: 2013

Xenois is a minimal humanist sans serif, designed to support the smooth rhythm of reading. Superfluous details, such as spurs or lengthy crossbars on the lowercase letters, are removed to maintain the reader's flow, while open counters and a tall x-height enhance legibility.

Xenois Semi

ABCDEFGHIJKLMNOPQRSTUVWXYZ
abcdefghijklmnopqrstuvwxyz
1234567890 !@#?:;"*&

Foundry: Linotype
Designer: Erik Faulhaber
Designer Nationality: German
Date: 2013

Much like Xenois Sans, Xenois Semi is a sans serif in the humanist style. The letterforms maintain the proportions and character of their siblings but feature a distinctly stronger stroke contrast, visible in both cases and especially in the shoulders, arcs and junctures.

Xenois Soft

ABCDEFGHIJKLMNOPQRSTUVWXYZ
abcdefghijklmnopqrstuvwxyz
1234567890 !@#?:;"*&

Foundry: Linotype
Designer: Erik Faulhaber
Designer Nationality: German
Date: 2013

Xenois Soft is distinguishable not only through its rounded terminals, but also its compliance with DIN 1450 requirements, a form of standardization that ensures readability in adverse conditions. This makes its design ideally suited to public signage and information systems.

Xenois Super

ABCDEFGHIJKLMNOPQRSTUVWXYZ
abcdefghijklmnopqrstuvwxyz
1234567890 !@#?:;"*&

Foundry: Linotype
Designer: Erik Faulhaber
Designer Nationality: German
Date: 2013

Xenois Super occupies the middle ground between its siblings Xenois Sans and Xenois Slab. Although designed with the characteristics of a humanist sans serif, Xenois Super introduces the occasional, muscular slab serif to several letters, spanning both upper- and lowercases.

Yalta Sans

ABCDEFGHIJKLMNOPQRSTUVWXYZ
abcdefghijklmnopqrstuvwxyz
1234567890 !@#?:;"*&

Foundry: Monotype
Designer: Stefan Claudius
Designer Nationality: German
Date: 2013

Yalta Sans is a humanist sans serif but draws on elements of both grotesque and square sans letterforms. It is also informed by the nature of Renaissance typefaces, designer Stefan Claudius combining calligraphic strokes with open counters, tapered verticals and gently squared curves.

Zapf Humanist 601

ABCDEFGHIJKLMNOPQRSTUVWXYZ
abcdefghijklmnopqrstuvwxyz
1234567890 !@#?:;"*&

Foundry: Bitstream
Designer: Hermann Zapf
Designer Nationality: German
Date: 1958

Zapf Humanist 601 is a humanist sans serif and Bitstream's digitization of the Optima typeface created in 1958 by Hermann Zapf (see p. 574). Bitstream's design mimics Optima's characteristically roman shapes and proportions, while also imitating the popular taper of its stems.

Zico Sans

ABCDEFGHIJKLMNOPQRSTUVWXYZ
abcdefghijklmnopqrstuvwxyz
1234567890 !@#?:;"*&

Foundry: Typotheque
Designer: Marko Hrastovec
Designer Nationality: Croatian
Date: 2017

Zico Sans was designed by Croatian type and graphic designer Marko Hrastovec and released by Dutch foundry Typotheque (see p. 90). It is a wide-set, humanist sans serif that was created to add versatility to the already established Zico typeface family, which has a beefy slab-serif version with a corresponding Display design and Sans Condensed.

Much like the initial slab version, Zico Sans is informed by the aesthetics of sport, in particular the robust letterforms typically used in sport jerseys. Hrastovec attempted to convey their feel of 'playful' boldness and warmth in his typeface. This is evident in the slightly squared shape of its curves and the low contrast of the strokes. Like all Typotheque fonts, Zico Sans includes small caps in all styles and possesses a wealth of OpenType features.

Ig Nobel Prize ceremony too

Since 1991, the Ig Nobel Prizes have been "honor achievements that first make pec and then make them think."

The Ig Nobels were created in 1991 by Marc Abrahams co-founder of the Annals of Improbable Research and ceremonies at all subsequent awards ceremonies. Av sented at that time for discoveries "that cannot, or sl produced". Ten prizes are awarded each year in many cluding the Nobel Prize categories of physics, chemist medicine, literature, and peace, but also other catego public health, engineering, biology, and interdisciplin The Ig Nobel Prizes recognize genuine achievements tion of three prizes awarded in the first year to fictitic Josiah S. Carberry, Paul DeFanti, and Thomas Kyle.

Rugby Championship: Australia and France draw as All Blacks retain title
ZICO SANS CONDENSED THIN

Fans injured as barrier collapses at Ligue 1 match
ZICO SANS BLACK

'I haven't actually retired yet!' France recall for Cantona?
ZICO SANS MEDIUM ITALIC

Scott apologises for missing match after being bitten by lion
ZICO SANS THIN

Lewis Hamilton: Could a vegan diet hamper his 'racing edge'?
ZICO SANS CONDENSED BOLD

Football is heading for trouble over brain injuries caused by the ball
ZICO SANS CONDENSED REGULAR ITALIC

Manchester City beat Arsenal in eleven-goal thriller
ZICO SANS MEDIUM

Italian Plate No. 1 Mono

ABCDEFGHIJKLMNOPQRSTUVWXYZ
abcdefghijklmnopqrstuvwxyz
1234567890 !@#?:;"'*&

Foundry: Playtype
Designer: Jonas Hecksher
Designer Nationality: Danish
Date: 1998

Italian Plate No. 1 Mono is a grotesque, monospaced sans serif inspired by research into the rounded and condensed letterforms of Italian vehicle number plates from the 1960s. The characters, which are designed in ten weights, are distinguished by their equal stems and straight terminals.

Monospace 821

ABCDEFGHIJKLMNOPQRSTUVWXYZ
abcdefghijklmnopqrstuvwxyz
1234567890 !@#?:;"*&

Foundry: Bitstream
Designer: Max Miedinger
Designer Nationality: Swiss
Date: c. 1980s

This is Bitstream's version of Helvetica Monospaced, which was created using the original design by Max Miedinger (see p. 229) revamped by the Linotype Design Studio in 1983. It is available in Bold, Bold Italic and WGL Roman, as well as a Hebrew version.

Monosten

ABCDEFGHIJKLMNOPQRSTUVWXYZ
abcdefghijklmnopqrstuvwxyz
1234567890 !@#?:;"*&

Foundry: Colophon
Designer: The Entente
Designer Nationality: British
Date: 2017

Monosten combines the styles of monospaced and stencil type and takes its name from a combination of the two. After its initial release in 2010, Monosten was expanded in 2011 to encompass three weights and six styles, and then again in 2017 to include further language support.

OCR A Tribute

ABCDEFGHIJKLMNOPQRSTUVWXYZ
abcdefghijklmnopqrstuvwxyz
1234567890 !@#?:;"*&

Foundry: Linotype
Designer: Miriam Röttgers
Designer Nationality: German
Date: 2007

OCR A was designed at American Type Founders in 1968 as a monospaced font that could be read by machines using optical-character recognition.

Miriam Röttgers designed OCR A Tribute to make a more versatile typeface that retained the spirit of the original, with mono and proportional spacing.

Olympia

ABCDEFGHIJKLMNOPQRSTUVWXYZ
abcdefghijklmnopqrstuvwxyz
1234567890 !@#?:;"*&

Foundry: Hell
Designer: Hell Design Studio
Date: *c.* 1960s

Olympia comes in one weight and is a monospaced typewriter font that shares its name with a now defunct typewriter brand. It was designed by the German foundry Hell, which merged with Linotype in 1990, and was available for the world's first digital typesetting system, Digiset, invented by Hell in 1965.

Orator

ABCDEFGHIJKLMNOPQRSTUVWXYZ
abcdefghijklmnopqrstuvwxyz
1234567890 !@#?:;"*&

Foundry: Adobe
Designer: John Scheppler
Designer Nationality: American
Date: 1962

Orator is a monospaced typewriter font that John Scheppler designed for technology company IBM in 1962. It comes in two styles, Medium and Slanted. The face features only capitals and small capitals because it was thought that uppercase was easier to read in typed-up speech notes, hence the name.

Prima Sans Mono

ABCDEFGHIJKLMNOPQRSTUVWXYZ
abcdefghijklmnopqrstuvwxyz
1234567890 !@#?:;"*&

Foundry: Bitstream
Designer: Sue Zafarana
Designer Nationality: American
Date: 1998

Jim Lyles tasked one of his colleagues at Bitstream, Sue Zafarana, with creating the monospace, fixed-width version of Prima, having designed the serif and sans himself. During her spare time, she also designs fonts with her husband Steve as Tail Spin Studio in Boston.

System85

ABCDEFGHIJKLMNOPQRSTUVWXYZ
abcdefghijklmnopqrstuvwxyz
1234567890 !@#?:;"*&

Foundry: Colophon
Designer: The Entente
Designer Nationality: British
Date: 2018

System85 is a monospaced sans serif that considers the vertical application of Latin type in Japan. Designed with uniform vertical-line spacing, irregular widths and short descenders, the design is also informed by the pan-Asian variants of Windows 3.1's grotesque system fonts.

Playtype

Created by Danish brand and design agency e-Types, Playtype is a foundry and online font shop that serves to showcase the e-Types type designs created over more than twenty years, from commissioned works to fonts created for pleasure. Typography has always been a focal point of e-Types' graphic design output. The decision to transform the e-Types typeface portfolio into an online foundry was taken so that others could benefit from its many years of crafting custom typefaces, as well as to promote Danish design.

Some of the fonts Playtype has released were custom-made for clients, and others come from sketches and doodles that gradually evolved into full-blown type families. There are others, such as Nouvel, which were inspired by a particular context – in this instance, the work of French architect Jean Nouvel for the Danish Broadcasting Corporation's Koncerthuset concert complex.

Playtype offers a comprehensive selection of differing styles with more than one hundred families and more than 1,000 different fonts. Playtype has over the years also been widely known for its concept store and use of type on design objects. These include limited-edition posters, notebooks, clothing and ceramics highlighting singular letters, words or phrases.

Founded: 2010
Country: Denmark
Website: playtype.com

Below and opposite. Playtype built a range of elegant and stylish products around typeface releases over the years, from fashion accessories to iconic and minimal posters featuring singular letterforms.

PLAYTYPE™
TYPE FOUNDRY and CONCEPT STORE
typed in NOIR TEXT Bold

Aeonis

ABCDEFGHIJKLMNOPQRSTUVWXYZ
abcdefghijklmnopqrstuvwxyz
1234567890 !@#?:;"*&

Foundry: Linotype
Designer: Erik Faulhaber
Designer Nationality: German
Date: 2009

Aeonis mixes ancient and modern, and references Ancient Greek inscriptions and a lamp created by industrial designer Wilhelm Wagenfeld in 1952. It has a distinctive open uppercase 'A' and all styles and weights share the same cap heights, x-heights, ascender heights and descender lengths.

Aguda

ABCDEFGHIJKLMNOPQRSTUVWXYZ
abcdefghijklmnopqrstuvwxyz
1234567890 !@#?:;"*&

Foundry: Graviton
Designer: Pablo Balcells
Designer Nationality: Argentinian
Date: 2014

Although Aguda is designed primarily to be used as a display face, this modular geometric typeface can also be used for short texts. Aguda is available in eight styles from Light to Bold, each containing small caps and several alternate characters, with Unicase and Stencil variants.

Akko

ABCDEFGHIJKLMNOPQRSTUVWXYZ
abcdefghijklmnopqrstuvwxyz
1234567890 !@#?:;"*&

Foundry: Linotype
Designer: Akira Kobayashi
Designer Nationality: Japanese
Date: 2011

Designer Akira Kobayashi describes Akko as a sans serif with a 'soft-focus effect' that references German Textura type, and comprises the full-bodied sans serif Akko and the playful Akko Rounded. It has six weights from Thin to Black, along with small caps, ligatures and alternate characters.

Arian

ABCDEFGHIJKLMNOPQRSTUVWXYZ
abcdefghijklmnopqrstuvwxyz
1234567890 !@#?:;"*&

Foundry: Linotype
Designer: Naghi Naghashian
Designer Nationality: Iranian
Date: 2012

Arian is the debut typeface of Iranian designer Naghi Naghashian, who is now based in Germany. This Arabic typeface is designed for screen and electronic use, and combines a contemporary sans serif with calligraphic tradition. Its forms can be artificially obliqued in InDesign without any loss in quality.

Azbuka

ABCDEFGHIJKLMNOPQRSTUVWXYZ
abcdefghijklmnopqrstuvwxyz
1234567890 !@#?:;"*&

Foundry: Monotype
Designer: Richard Dawson /
Dave Farey
Designer Nationality: British
Date: 2008

This workmanlike sans serif was inspired by street signage from London and Prague and named after the Russian word for 'alphabet'. It has eight weights, ranging from Extra Light to Extra Black, with complementary italics on the five mid-weights, as well as seven condensed weights.

Biome

ABCDEFGHIJKLMNOPQRSTUVWXYZ
abcdefghijklmnopqrstuvwxyz
1234567890 !@#?:;"*&

Foundry: Monotype
Designer: Carl Crossgrove
Designer Nationality: American
Date: 2009

'Biome' means 'ecosystem' and the Biome typeface reflects its name by being an amalgamation of many different influences. It has soft corners and a number of unusual character shapes, including a distinctive lowercase 'g' with its two semi-open counters. Biome comes in forty-two styles.

Burlingame

ABCDEFGHIJKLMNOPQRSTUVWXYZ
abcdefghijklmnopqrstuvwxyz
1234567890 !@#?:;"*&

Foundry: Monotype
Designer: Carl Crossgrove
Designer Nationality: American
Date: 2014

Burlingame was originally intended for a game identity. Designer Carl Crossgrove then developed it for use as a dashboard display font. He increased the x-height, slimmed down the corners and loosened the spacing, improving clarity and making it suitable for a wide range of applications.

Cachet

ABCDEFGHIJKLMNOPQRSTUVWXYZ
abcdefghijklmnopqrstuvwxyz
1234567890 !@#?:;"*&

Foundry: Panache / Agfa
Designer: Dave Farey
Designer Nationality: American
Date: 1997

Cachet appears to be based on geometric shapes but in reality it is slightly condensed, with flared terminals on some letters and rounded stroke terminals. It comes in weights ranging from Thin to Heavy, and is precise, space efficient and more legible than the monospaced fonts it resembles.

Citadina

ABCDEFGHIJKLMNOPQRSTUVWXYZ
abcdefghijklmnopqrstuvwxyz
1234567890 !@#?:;"*&

Foundry: Graviton
Designer: Pablo Balcells
Designer Nationality:
Argentinian
Date: 2016

Citadina is a geometric sans serif with a cool, neutral look that is available in six weights from Thin to Black with matching italics. Its condensed design makes it a good choice when setting large blocks of text, but its heavier weights are equally effective as display fonts.

DIN 1451

ABCDEFGHIJKLMNOPQRSTUVWXYZ
abcdefghijklmnopqrstuvwxyz
1234567890 !@#?:;"*&

Foundry: Linotype
Designer: DIN / Linotype Design Studio
Designer Nationality: German
Date: *c.* 1930 / 1990

'DIN' is an abbreviation of *Deutsches Institut für Normung* (German Institute for Industrial Standards) and DIN was the official typeface used on licence plates, trains and road signs across Germany from the 1930s. This is an updated version of the highly legible sans serif made by the Linotype Design Studio.

DIN Next

ABCDEFGHIJKLMNOPQRSTUVWXYZ
abcdefghijklmnopqrstuvwxyz
1234567890 !@#?:;"*&

Foundry: Linotype
Designer: Akira Kobayashi / Sandra Winter
Designer Nationality:
Japanese / German
Date: 2009

DIN Next is the sister font to DIN Next Slab and DIN Next Rounded, designed by Akira Kobayashi. He created this as a more humanistic take on the classic 1930s DIN typeface. It features eight weights, ranging from Light to Black, as well as italics and a condensed version.

DIN Next Rounded

ABCDEFGHIJKLMNOPQRSTUVWXYZ
abcdefghijklmnopqrstuvwxyz
1234567890 !@#?:;"*&

Foundry: Linotype
Designer: Akira Kobayashi
Designer Nationality: Japanese
Date: 2009

This is a rounded version of Akira Kobayashi's more humanistic take on the typeface introduced in Germany for use in official signage and traffic directional systems by the *Deutsches Institut für Normung* (German Institute for Industrial Standards) in the 1930s.

Eurostile

ABCDEFGHIJKLMNOPQRSTUVWXYZ
abcdefghijklmnopqrstuvwxyz
1234567890 !@#?:;"*&

Foundry: Linotype
Designer: Aldo Novarese
Designer Nationality: Italian
Date: 1962

Eurostile was designed for the 'future' in the early 1960s. Its release captured the zeitgeist of the science-fiction genre and intimated days to come through its clean lines, geometric square forms and rounded corners. The typeface is the creation of one of Italy's best-known and most prolific type designers, Aldo Novarese. He took his inspiration from Microgramma, an earlier design that he helped to create with his mentor Alessandro Butti, art director of the Nebiolo type foundry in Turin in 1952. A decade later, Novarese revisited the all-caps display face, designed a complementary lowercase – and Eurostile was born.

Ideally, Eurostile is best employed as a display face and its squared-up design appears to be influenced by old TV screens. Its distinctive appearance makes it stand out against many other sans serifs, thanks to its symmetry and the mathematical purity of its construction. It is used frequently in corporate identities and logos in everything from car to technology firms. The face is also highly visible in popular culture, appearing in film, video games and music applications as well as the science-fiction genre.

In 2016, Linotype type director Akira Kobayashi created Eurostile Next based on the specimens of the original metal fonts. This new release was an optically rescaled and redesigned version of the original font family containing fifty variants from Ultra Light to Extended and matching italics for all.

Below. Eurostile has become an ever-popular choice for use in science-fiction films, whether it's seen on user-interfaces (UI) or for the branding and title credits. Clockwise from top left: David Cronenberg's *The Fly*, *Starship Troopers*, Disney's *Wall-E* (both Eurostile Bold Extended) and *Johnny Mnemonic* (Eurostile Extended).

Estricta

ABCDEFGHIJKLMNOPQRSTUVWXYZ
abcdefghijklmnopqrstuvwxyz
1234567890 !@#?:;"*&

Foundry: Graviton
Designer: Pablo Balcells
Designer Nationality: Argentinian
Date: 2017

'Estricta' means 'strict' in Spanish and this geometric sans is a very constrained, mechanical-looking typeface with sharp angles and edges. It is most suitable for short- and middle-length text blocks, and is available in six weights, from Light to Black, with complementary italics and small caps.

Eurostile LT

ABCDEFGHIJKLMNOPQRSTUVWXYZ
abcdefghijklmnopqrstuvwxyz
1234567890 !@#?:;"*&

Foundry: Nebiolo / Linotype
Designer: Aldo Novarese / Linotype Studio
Designer Nationality: Italian
Date: 1962 / 2009

Following on from his Microgramma typeface of 1952, this is Linotype's version of Aldo Novarese's popular and quintessentially 1960s design. It combines square shapes with rounded corners to give a modern, technological feel, and comes in eleven weights, including an outline version.

Eurostile Next

ABCDEFGHIJKLMNOPQRSTUVWXYZ
abcdefghijklmnopqrstuvwxyz
1234567890 !@#?:;"*&

Foundry: Linotype
Designer: Aldo Novarese / Akira Kobayashi / Terrance Weinzierl
Designer Nationality: Italian / Japanese / American
Date: 2016

This is a redrawn and expanded version of Aldo Novarese's design which references the original metal types and reinstates the subtle curves lost in previous digital cuts. There are five weights from Ultra Light to Bold, and all weights also have Condensed and Extended versions.

Fluctuation

ABCDEFGHIJKLMNOPQRSTUVWXYZ
abcdefghijklmnopqrstuvwxyz
1234567890 !@#?:;"*&

Foundry: Typodermic
Designer: Ray Larabie
Designer Nationality: Canadian
Date: 2013

Fluctuation takes inspiration from technology such as remote control devices, game controllers and synthesizers. Once, its square 'M', 'N' and 'W' shapes were considered hard to read, but thanks to a generation raised on video games and low-res displays they now blend smoothly into a paragraph.

Foundry Monoline

ABCDEFGHIJKLMNOPQRSTUVWXYZ
abcdefghijklmnopqrstuvwxyz
1234567890 !@#?:;"*&

Foundry: The Foundry
Designer: David Quay
Designer Nationality: British
Date: 2000

Designed for the various requirements of editorial and advertising design, Foundry Monoline is a squared sans serif produced in seven weights.

Quay's design combines a structured grid system with optical adjustments to create the look of linear, single-thickness strokes.

Francker

ABCDEFGHIJKLMNOPQRSTUVWXYZ
abcdefghijklmnopqrstuvwxyz
1234567890 !@#?:;"*&

Foundry: Linotype
Designer: Anders Francker
Designer Nationality: Danish
Date: 2010

Francker's curves are based on the superellipse mathematical shape that is between an ellipse and a rectangle. The typeface is available in nine

weights and two widths. Its lowercase letterforms 'a', 'b', 'n' and 'u' have no spurs, which serves to emphasize the simplicity of their construction.

From the Internet

ABCDEFGHIJKLMNOPQRSTUVWXYZ
abcdefghijklmnopqrstuvwxyz
1234567890 !@#?:;"*&

Foundry: Typodermic
Designer: Ray Larabie
Designer Nationality: Canadian
Date: 2011

Canadian type designer Ray Larabie began his career in the video-game industry, and released freeware typefaces for several years before

establishing his foundry, Typodermic, which is now based in Japan. From the Internet is a rectangular sans with a distinctly futuristic feel.

From the Stars

ABCDEFGHIJKLMNOPQRSTUVWXYZ
abcdefghijklmnopqrstuvwxyz
1234567890 !@#?:;"*&

Foundry: Typodermic
Designer: Ray Larabie / Chikako Larabie
Designer Nationality: Canadian / Japanese
Date: 2010

From the Stars is a departure from the more decorative, stylized display typefaces for which Ray Larabie is best known and he designed it in

collaboration with his wife, Chikako. This square sans serif design is available in seven weights with corresponding italics.

FS Hackney

ABCDEFGHIJKLMNOPQRSTUVWXYZ
abcdefghijklmnopqrstuvwxyz
1234567890 !@#?:;"*&

Built upon a super-elliptical foundation, this no-nonsense design by Nick Job achieves an effective balance of legibility, neutrality and individuality.

The font was named not for the notorious East London borough, but for the city's stalwart 'Hackney Carriage' black cabs.

Foundry: Fontsmith
Designer: Nick Job / Jason Smith
Designer Nationality: British
Date: 2013

FS Joey

ABCDEFGHIJKLMNOPQRSTUVWXYZ
abcdefghijklmnopqrstuvwxyz
1234567890 !@#?:;"*&

FS Joey was designed for a TV streaming service from the BBC, ITV and Channel 4 which was never released. However, Fernando Mello completed the font design and Fontsmith released it as a retail typeface. Fittingly, the project for which it was originally designed was codenamed 'Kangaroo'.

Foundry: Fontsmith
Designer: Fernando Mello / Jason Smith
Designer Nationality: Brazilian / British
Date: 2009

FS Truman

ABCDEFGHIJKLMNOPQRSTUVWXYZ
abcdefghijklmnopqrstuvwxyz
1234567890 !@#?:;"*&

This firm but friendly sans serif is designed for display on TV screens but is equally at home in print and on the web. It shares certain formal traits with the FS Dillon typeface by Fontsmith (see p. 272), and features a blend of geometric and cursive details, and irregular diagonal cuts.

Foundry: Fontsmith
Designer: Fernando Mello / Jason Smith
Designer Nationality: Brazilian / British
Date: 2002

FS Untitled

ABCDEFGHIJKLMNOPQRSTUVWXYZ
abcdefghijklmnopqrstuvwxyz
1234567890 !@#?:;"*&

FS Untitled is based on a design created by Fontsmith (see p. 272) for Channel 4 in 2005. Jason Smith modelled its letterforms according to the pixel structure of digital screens and developed two versions of each weight, offering designers fine control over the font's eventual appearance.

Foundry: Fontsmith
Designer: Jason Smith
Designer Nationality: British
Date: 2016

Great Escape

ABCDEFGHIJKLMNOPQRSTUVWXYZ
abcdefghijklmnopqrstuvwxyz
1234567890 !@#?:;"*&

Foundry: Typodermic
Designer: Ray Larabie
Designer Nationality: Canadian
Date: 2010

Great Escape is a super-elliptical sans serif from Ray Larabie's Typodermic foundry based in Japan. It has a slightly futuristic, technical feel and is available in a staggering twenty-eight different styles, including narrow and regular widths ranging from Hairline to Ultrabold.

Isonorm

ABCDEFGHIJKLMNOPQRSTUVWXYZ
abcdefghijklmnopqrstuvwxyz
1234567890 !@#?:;"*&

Foundries: Linotype / URW++
Designer: International Standard Organization
Designer Nationality: Swiss
Date: 1980

This typeface was developed by the International Standard Organization as a proposal for a standard typeface to be used on architectural drafts and technical drawings. Its simple, geometric letterforms were designed to be legible to machine readers as well as people.

ITC Tabula

ABCDEFGHIJKLMNOPQRSTUVWXYZ
abcdefghijklmnopqrstuvwxyz
1234567890 !@#?:;"*&

Foundry: ITC
Designer: Julien Janiszewski
Designer Nationality: French
Date: 2001

ITC Tabula was developed for use in subtitles; its clear, squared forms are designed to be legible both on TV displays and cinema screens. Although readability was a key concern for designer Julien Janiszewski, he worked hard to ensure his design also maintains a sense of visual interest.

Kairos Sans

ABCDEFGHIJKLMNOPQRSTUVWXYZ
abcdefghijklmnopqrstuvwxyz
1234567890 !@#?:;"*&

Foundry: Monotype
Designer: Terrance Weinzierl
Designer Nationality: American
Date: 2016

Kairos Sans is a wood-type-influenced design with a sporty feel. The typeface shares the octagonal skeleton of its slab-serif predecessor published by Monotype in 2015. It is available in forty-eight styles, including three different widths, as well as Greek and Cyrillic character sets.

Klint

ABCDEFGHIJKLMNOPQRSTUVWXYZ
abcdefghijklmnopqrstuvwxyz
1234567890 !@#?:;"*&

Foundry: Linotype
Designer: Hannes von Döhren
Designer Nationality: German
Date: 2009

This versatile and assertive typeface from Linotype offers three different widths for each of its five weights. Hannes von Döhren's design features subtly curved details, and a comprehensive character set that caters to a broad range of typographic contexts.

Mensura

ABCDEFGHIJKLMNOPQRSTUVWXYZ
abcdefghijklmnopqrstuvwxyz
1234567890 !@#?:;"*&

Foundry: Graviton
Designer: Pablo Balcells
Designer Nationality: Argentinian
Date: 2012

Mensura was designed by Argentinian typographer Pablo Balcells, a graduate of the University of Buenos Aires. It is a modular, technical sans serif in eight styles, comprising four weights with italics. Balcells's foundry Graviton released Mensura in 2012 with a slab-serif version too.

Milibus

ABCDEFGHIJKLMNOPQRSTUVWXYZ
abcdefghijklmnopqrstuvwxyz
1234567890 !@#?:;"*&

Foundry: Typodermic
Designer: Ray Larabie
Designer Nationality: Canadian
Date: 2006

Milibus was created by the prolific Canadian type designer Ray Larabie, and released by his foundry Typodermic. It is a non-traditional sans serif face with a futuristic, technical feel. Milibus comes in three weights with real italics and has a distinctive capital 'A' with a low crossbar.

Order

ABCDEFGHIJKLMNOPQRSTUVWXYZ
abcdefghijklmnopqrstuvwxyz
1234567890 !@#?:;"*&

Foundry: Typodermic
Designer: Ray Larabie
Designer Nationality: Canadian
Date: 2006

Canadian Ray Larabie made this technical, angular sans serif in three weights. Larabie, who has drawn more than 1,000 fonts, once worked for Rockstar Games and his font Pricedown appears in the logo for the game *Grand Theft Auto*. In 2015, he devised a typeface, Canada 150, for Canada's 150th birthday.

Soho Gothic

ABCDEFGHIJKLMNOPQRSTUVWXYZ
abcdefghijklmnopqrstuvwxyz
1234567890 !@#?:;"*&

Foundry: Monotype
Designer: Seb Lester
Designer Nationality: British
Date: 2008

After the success of his Neo Sans and Neo Tech faces, Seb Lester worked for three years on the Soho family, which was released in 2008 and includes the slab serif Soho and sans Soho Gothic. The Gothic comes in nine weights and five widths with many alternate and semi-slab characters

Square 721

ABCDEFGHIJKLMNOPQRSTUVWXYZ
abcdefghijklmnopqrstuvwxyz
1234567890 !@#?:;"*&

Foundry: Bitstream
Designer: Aldo Novarese
Designer Nationality: Italian
Date: 1962

Square 721 is a Bitstream version of Aldo Novarese's sans serif Eurostile (1962), which was an upper- and lowercase update of Alessandro Butti's Microgramma of ten years earlier. Square 721 is available in two weights – Roman and Bold – and evokes science fiction of the 1960s and 1970s.

Vellvé

ABCDEFGHIJKLMNOPQRSTUVWXYZ
abcdefghijklmnopqrstuvwxyz
1234567890 !@#?:;"*&

Foundry: ITC
Designer: Tomás Vellvé
Designer Nationality: Spanish
Date: 2006

Initially designed in 1971, Vellvé is a squared sans serif with numerous calligraphic flourishes and is the only one of Tomás Vellvé's designs produced in digital form. Now published by ITC, the updated font family includes three further weights and an italic for the Light version.

Venacti

ABCDEFGHIJKLMNOPQRSTUVWXYZ
abcdefghijklmnopqrstuvwxyz
1234567890 !@#?:;"*&

Foundry: Typodermic
Designer: Ray Larabie
Designer Nationality: Canadian
Date: 2005

Venacti is a squared sans serif with rounded features, inspired by the aesthetics of science fiction. Its characters combine dynamic counter shapes with clinical, spurless forms and avoid retro periodization by drawing from the full visual canon of science fiction.

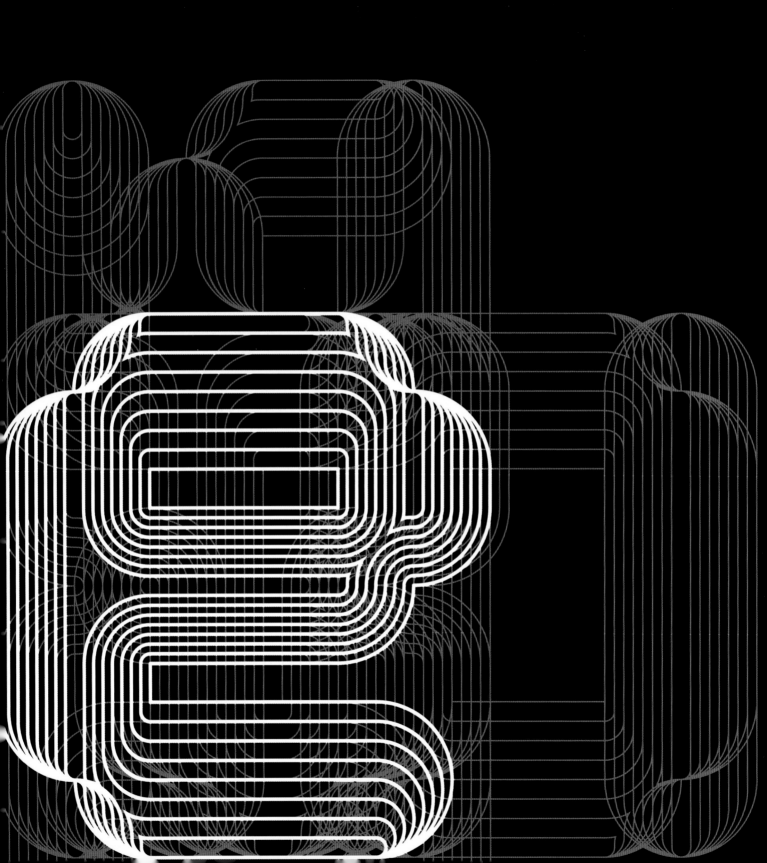

Display

Opposite. Detail showing the construction for the ThreeSix optical geomtretic type system by MuirMcNeil.

The very purpose of a display typeface is to catch the eye and provide an appropriate visual impact to a message, whether this be an advertisement in a magazine or a navigation sign by the side of a motorway. The distinguishing feature of display types over other typefaces is that they would never be appropriate to employ for lengthy pieces of text but are ideally suited for brief, attention-demanding titles or information that pull a reader's gaze towards their message, communicating in an instant. They not only help send a message but will evoke a mood or emotion. Display typefaces also intone historical reference points and styles in their presentation, providing all-important context quickly and clearly to a reader.

The earliest display types emerged in the early 19th century with an increasing use on posters, fliers (then known as handbills) and leaflets for commercial purposes as businesses sought to sell their goods and capture the attention of potential buyers. As such, and in order to aid distinction, mark themselves out from the competition and to deliver on the commercial demands required of their work, printers and typesetters looked for more innovative ways to present letterforms. Increasingly, they turned to elaborate and exaggerated type designs. With the advent and widespread use of woodblock types for printing, enlarged type styles such as heavy Clarendon serifs, emboldened grotesque sans serifs and serif Fat Face designs became more commonplace for display usage of the period.

When metal type was introduced in the late 19th century, so the use of exaggerated display types cooled off. This is because the production and usage of large-sized letterforms was difficult on the mechanical systems employed for commercial use.

The advent of phototypesetting in the 1950s triggered a resurgence in the design of display types. The new technology could be used to create oversized texts. However, it was the invention of dry-transfer lettering in the 1970s that caused a boom in the creation of display types. Letraset was the market leader and pioneer of this transformative way of working for graphic designers, and the company created nearly 500 typeface designs over four decades. When digital technology arrived in the 1980s, the Letraset collection was digitized, making a wealth of typeface designs for almost every conceivable application available to all. The ease of typesetting on a digital system signalled the end of dry-transfer instant lettering as a commercially viable way to produce design work. Letraset continued to design and commission display typefaces until the mid 1990s. The majority of them are available online to purchase today via font marketing companies and so they are still widely used across many genres.

The digital design revolution, combined with the arrival of software to allow fonts to be created on a desktop system, triggered a great amount of experimentation and further typeface releases. Many designers and foundries invested their energies in experimental and innovative designs that could be achieved only through using a computer-aided system. For example, in 1991 the FontShop network began releasing the FUSE fonts. The first, a limited-edition package of four experimental PostScript typeface designs, contained Phil Baines's F Can You (read me)?, Neville Brody's F State, Malcolm Garrett's F Stealth and Ian Swift's F Maze 91. All were highly experimental designs and all were achievable only with a computer. Around the same time, Zuzana Licko and Rudy VanderLans published their journal *Emigre*, which also acted as a catalyst for change. The title became a flagbearer for digital experimentation with adventurous layouts that employed digital typefaces from the duo's foundry for display and text purposes.

In recent years, the advancement and continuing sophistication of technology has allowed for increasingly complex designs with a number of display typefaces created as systems. These allow composite elements to be combined and integrated to create evermore interesting and exciting designs. Grid- and dot-based works, such as those envisaged and created by Dutch designer Wim Crouwel in the 1960s and 1970s with his *New Alphabet* manifesto, have provided inspiration and insight for contemporary designs as well as revivals by foundries including France's BB-Bureau, the United States' Neutura and the United Kingdom's MuirMcNeil. All of them challenge the boundaries of legibility and readability through their innovative and unique deconstructed types and provide the designer with exciting ways to capture a reader's attention.

Acroyear

ABCDEFGHIJKLMNOPQRSTUVWXYZ
1234567890 !@# ?:;""*&

Foundry: Typodermic
Designer: Ray Larabie
Designer Nationality: Canadian
Date: 2012

This distinctive display typeface, created by Nagoya-based Canadian type designer Ray Larabie, features an exaggerated forward slant that lends itself well to typesetting on an angled baseline. Irregular in form and irreverent in feel, it is available in uppercase only.

Adolescence

ABCDEFGHIJKLMNOPQRSTUVWXYZ
abcdefghijklmnopqrstUvwxyz
1234567890 !@*?:;"*&

Foundry: Lunchbox Studios
Designer: Adam Roe
Designer Nationality: American
Date: 1993

Type designer and former skateboarder Adam Roe established his Lunchbox Studios foundry in 1991, from which he created a range of postmodern and experimental typefaces. Adolescence, published in 1993, features distorted, grungy letterforms that vary wildly in weight and size.

Ammonia

ABCDEFGHIJKLMNOPQRSTUVWXYZ
a6cdefghijklmnopqrstuvwxyz.
1234S67890 !@#?:;"*&

Foundry: Chank Co.
Designer: Chank Diesel
Designer Nationality: American
Date: 1996

Chank Diesel established his Chank Co. foundry in 1996, and is renowned for his prolific output of playful, unpretentious display typefaces, influenced by his work in the music industry during the 1980s and 1990s. Available in one weight, Ammonia is a grungy, degraded sans serif.

Amorpheus

ABCDEFGHIJKLMNOPQRSTUVWXYZ
1234567890 !ATNº?:;""*&

Foundry: Device Type
Designer: Rian Hughes
Designer Nationality: British
Date: 1995

Multidisciplinary designer Rian Hughes has worked extensively in graphic design, illustration, type design and comic art; he established Device Fonts in 1997 to distribute his own range of typefaces. Amorpheus displays the influence of his work in comics and illustration.

F2F Madame Butterfly

ABCDEFGHIJKLMNOPQRSTUVWXYZ
abcdefghijklmnopqrstuvwxyz
1234567890 !@#?:;"*&

Foundry: Face2Face
Designer: Alessio Leonardi
Designer Nationality: Italian
Date: 1995

Madame Butterfly is a distressed-looking experimental typeface that embodies the grunge style popular in mid 1990s. It was created by Italian designer Alessio Leonardi, who relocated to Berlin in 1990, where he worked at MetaDesign for two years with Erik Spiekermann (see p. 304).

FF Blur

ABCDEFGHIJKLMNOPQRSTUVWXYZ
abcdefghijklmnopqrstuvwxyz
1234567890 !@#?:;''*&

Foundry: FontFont
Designer: Neville Brody
Nationality: British
Date: 1992

FF Blur was designed by British typographer Neville Brody, who was one of the world's best-known graphic designers during the 1980s and 1990s. It is a postmodern sans-serif typeface with contrast and irregular forms making it appear out of focus. It is available in light, medium and bold weights.

ITC Binary

ABCDEFGHIJKLMNOPQRSTUVWXYZ
abcdefghijklmnopqrstuvwxyz
1234567890 !@#?:;"*&

Foundry: ITC
Designer: Mauricio Reyes
Nationality: American
Date: 1997

This semi-serif type was designed by Mexican-born Mauricio Reyes in 1997 and devised as a mash-up of elements from both Helvetica and Times. ITC Binary is available in light and bold without italics. It was selected as the official font for the Sydney 2000 Olympic Games in Australia.

Johnstemp

ABCDEFGHIJKLMNOPQRSTUVWXYZ
abcdefghijklmnopqrstuvwxyz
1234567890 !@#?:;"*&

Foundry: Linotype
Designer: Georg John
Nationality: German
Date: 2008

Available in four weights, Johnstemp is a distressed sans serif with bumpy edges that give it a stamped appearance. It features many alternate glyphs that break the monotony to give a more realistic stamped feel. Johnstemp Mix is a version with inbuilt stylistic and weight variety.

Linotype Araby Rafique

ABCDEFGHIJKLMNOPQRSTUVWXYZ
abcdefghijklmnopqrstuvwxyz
1234567890 !@#?:;"*&

Foundry: Linotype
Designer: Tehmina Rauf
Designer Nationality: British
Date: 1997

Created by British designer Tehmina Rauf in 1997, Linotype Araby Rafique is part of the TakeType Library, compiled from winners of the Linotype International Digital Type Design Contest. Legibility was clearly not an aim; letters are constructed from flowing, contrasting, curving shapes.

Linotype BioPlasm

ABCDEFGHIJKLMNOPQRSTUVWXYZ
abcdefghijklmnopqrstuvwxyz
1234567890 !@#?:;"*&

Foundry: Linotype
Designer: Mauro Carichini
Designer Nationality: Italian
Date: 2002

Linotype BioPlasm was designed by Mauro Carichini in 2002. It is an experimental sans serif with rounded features, short descenders and ascenders, and a tall x-height. Its distinguishing feature is that some letters are missing pieces as if it is a living organism, growing and morphing.

Linotype Mineru

ABCDEFGHIJKLMNOPQRSTUVWXYZ
abcdefghijklmnopqrstuvwxyz
1234567890 !@#?:;"*&

Foundry: Linotype
Designer: Ronny Edelstein
Designer Nationality: German
Date: 1997

Linotype Mineru is an amorphous display face produced in two weights, alongside an Outline style. The design's stroke weight fluctuates throughout, imitating the variability of a pen's nib, while the letters are restless in shape, and convey an eerie, volatile character.

Nowwhat

ABCDEFGHIJKLMNOPQRSTUVWXYZ
abcdefghijklmnopqrstuvwxyz
1234567890 !@#?:;"*&

Foundry: Monotype
Designer: Adam Roe
Designer Nationality: American
Date: 1993

Nowwhat is an amorphous display font designed in a single weight. The characters, in both upper and lowercases, have no coherent baseline and vary in shape, stroke width and angle, as if the designer roughly cut the letterforms from a piece of paper by hand.

Orange

ABCDEFGHIJKLMNOPQRSTUVWXYZ
abcdefghijklmnopqrstuvwxyz
1234567890 !?:;"*&

Foundry: ITC
Designer: Timothy Donaldson
Designer Nationality: British
Date: 1995

Orange is an amorphous display font conceived by the type designer and calligrapher Timothy Donaldson. Unlike those of a traditional sans serif, Orange's letterforms favour fluid joints over angled junctures and combine both flat and rounded terminals for an unorthodox outline.

Overprint ICG

ABCDEFGHIJKLMNOPQRSTUVWXYZ
abcdefghijklmnopqrstuvwxyz
1234567890 !@#?:;"*&

Foundry: Image Club Graphics
Date: 1996

Overprint is an amorphous display font designed in three weights, from Light to Heavy. Unlike conventional type designs, in which the designer may adjust the proportions from style to style, Overprint's characters differ only in thickness, as if repeatedly overprinted.

Seven Sans ICG

ABCDEFGHIJKLMNOPQRSTUVWXYZ
abcdefghijklmnopqrstuvwxyz
1234567890 !@#?:;"*&

Foundry: Image Club Graphics
Date: 1997

Seven Sans is an amorphous display face designed as part of the larger Seven typeface family that also includes the Seven Serif font. The letterforms, ranging from Regular to Black, combine a fluid outline with an erratic stroke width for a grungy appearance.

Surrogate

ABCDEFGHIJKLMNOPQRSTUVWXYZ
abcdefghijklmnopqrstuvwxyz
1234567890 !@#?:;"*&

Foundry: Lunchbox
Designer: Adam Roe
Designer Nationality: American
Date: 1995

A laid-back, ripple-effect display face, Surrogate was designed by the former actor and pro-skateboarder Adam Roe. He set up the experimental type foundry Lunchbox (part of Lunchbox Studios) in 1991 and went on to found the Zero Labs Group in Los Angeles during 2015.

Algol

ABCDEFGHIJKLMNOPQRSTUVWXYZ
abcdefghijklmnopqrstuvwxyz
1234567890 !@#?;´´*&

Foundry: Typodermic
Designer: Ray Larabie
Designer Nationality: Canadian
Date: 2005

Another layered design by Typodermic founder Ray Larabie, Algol is a technologically influenced typeface, whose three styles can be combined to create a range of effects. Its core letterforms have a blocky, pixellated structure similar to lettering on early digital displays.

Arkeo BT

ABCDEFGHIJKLMNOPQRSTUVWXYZ
abcdefghijklmnopqrstuvwxyz
1234567890 !@#?;´´*&

Foundry: Bitstream
Designer: Brian Sooy
Designer Nationality: American
Date: 2003

Arkeo BT, a pixel-based bitmap font by US type designer Brian Sooy, was published by Bitstream in 2003 in Regular, Condensed and Extended styles. Despite its block-based skeleton, it remains legible at a range of sizes and is suitable for both print and screen-based use.

Bitmax

ABCDEFGHIJKLMNOPQRSTUVWXYZ
1234567890 !?;,"*&

Foundry: ITC
Designer: Alan Birch
Designer Nationality: British
Date: 1990

British typeface designer Alan Birch was inspired by the distortion created within fax-machine transmissions when creating Bitmax. Taking Helvetica Medium as his starting point, he developed an irregular, pixellated form for each character while preserving its essential shape.

Bubbledot ICG

ABCDEFGHIJKLMNOPQRSTUVWXYZ
abcdefghijklmnopqrstuvwxyz
1234567890 !@#?:;"*&

Foundry: Image Club Graphics
Designer: Noel Rubin
Designer Nationality: Canadian
Date: 1994

Noel Rubin designed Bubbledot for Image Club Graphics. It is offered in two styles: Coarse, which has its letterforms shrunk to the same overall height, and Fine, which features a more conventional range of ascenders and descenders. Negative versions of both styles are also available.

Elementar

ABCDEFGHIJKLMNOPQRSTUVWXYZ
abcdefghijklmnopqrstuvwxyz
1234567890 !@#?:;"*&

Foundry: Typotheque
Designer: Gustavo Ferreira
Designer Nationality: Brazilian
Date: 2011

A labour of love for its creator Gustavo Ferreira, Elementar is a parametric font system designed to bring flexibility to digital screens. Available in three styles – Sans A, Sans B and Serif – it consists of thousands of individual fonts in a continuum of different styles, sizes, weights and widths.

Facsimile

ABCDEFGHIJKLMNOPQRSTUVWXYZ
1234567890 !@#?:;"*&

Foundry: Linotype
Designer: Simon Wicker / Jenny Luigs
Designer Nationality: British
Date: 1994

One of the winners of Linotype's International Digital Type Design Contest, the bitmap face Facsimile is part of the TakeType Library. British designers Simon Wicker and Jenny Luigs created it in 1994, when the use of computers was increasing, to be used on electronic readers.

FF Moonbase Alpha

ABCDEFGHIJKLMNOPQRSTUVWXYZ
abcdefghijklmnopqrstuvwxyz
1234567890 !@#?:;"*+

Foundry: FontFont
Designer: Cornel Windlin
Designer Nationality: Swiss
Date: 1991

Swiss designer Cornel Windlin created this display sans serif. FF Moonbase Alpha is a futuristic font created from connected, rounded blob shapes. It was initially released in 1991 with the debut issue of *FUSE*, a magazine of experimental type started by Jon Wozencroft and Neville Brody.

Indoo BT

ABCDEFGHIJKLMNOPQRSTUVWXYZ
abcdefghijklmnopqrstuvwxyz
1234567890 !@#?:;"*&

Foundry: Bitstream
Designer: Julien Janiszewski
Designer Nationality: French
Date: 2004

French typographer Julien Janiszewski designed Indoo BT in 2004; it is a blocky, bitmap sans serif created from small squares. It features a built-in underline that connects with every letter except for 'o', 'c', 'O', 'C' and 'G'. The Indoo BT family includes regular, italic and ornaments.

Interact (02)

ABCDEFGHIJKLMNOPQRSTUVWXYZ
abcdefghijklmnopqrstuvwxyz
1234567890 !@#?;,""%&

ABCDEFGHIJKLMNOPQRSTUVWXYZ
abcdefghijklmnopqrstuvwxyz
1234567890 !@#?;,""%&

ABCDEFGHIJKLMNOPQRSTUVWXYZ
abcdefghijklmnopqrstuvwxyz
1234567890 !@#?;,""%&

Foundry: MuirMcNeil
Designer: Hamish Muir /
Paul McNeil
Designer Nationality: British
Date: 1994

Below. Promotional design by MuirMcNeil employing variable weights of Interact overlayed upon each other. The detail pictured shows the pixel junctions connecting the strokes.

British designer Hamish Muir created the Interact system of grid-based bitmap typefaces in 1994 as part of an invited submission to the *American Center for Design Journal* when he was a partner at London-based design studio 8vo. The design was originally created in lowercase only and purposed for screen use.

The starting point for the typeface was the optical characteristics of the stroke junctions in the lettering design used by Wim Crouwel (see p. 540) on his *Vormgevers* (*Designers*) poster for the Stedelijk Museum in Amsterdam in 1968. The lettering was built around horizontal and vertical strokes with 45° pixel steps forming the stroke junctions. By modulating these junctions, the effect was to round the letterforms. In Interact's grid system each weight follows a mathematical progression, which means the differing weights can be overlayed to create dynamic visual compositions.

MuirMcNeil (see p. 334) has expanded and revised Interact extensively to become a system of twenty-three typefaces in four scaleable groups or resolutions – 02 (left), 03, 04 and 06 – with a comprehensive range of twelve calibrated weights. MuirMcNeil has also added a complete set of capital letters, punctuation marks and accented characters for Western European languages.

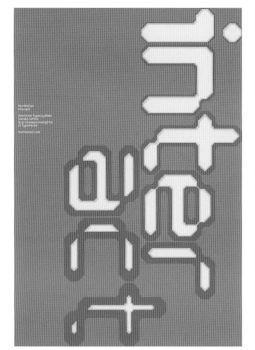

Intersect A

ABCDEFGHIJKLMNOPQRSTUVWXYZ
abcdefghijklmnopqrstuvwxyz
1234567890 !@#?:;'"*&

Foundry: MuirMcNeil
Designer: Hamish Muir /
Paul McNeil
Designer Nationality: British
Date: 2013

In MuirMcNeil's words Intersect is a 'type system which subverts typographic weight'. Its two styles come in fifteen versions each. A, the regular weight, is a low-resolution sans serif made variously from stripes, both horizontal and vertical, and rectangular blocks of different sizes.

Intersect B

ABCDEFGHIJKLMNOPQRSTUVWXYZ
abcdefghijklmnopqrstuvwxyz
1234567890 !@#?:;'"*&

Foundry: MuirMcNeil
Designer: Hamish Muir /
Paul McNeil
Designer Nationality: British
Date: 2013

Intersect B, which is of a far heavier weight than Intersect A, comes in fifteen numbered styles constructed using gridlike screen patterns. A and B are intended to be used in tandem and overlaid in their 256 possible combinations, and enhanced by the use of colour, tint and opacity.

Joystix

ABCDEFGHIJKLMNOPQRSTUVWXYZ
1234567890 /@#?:;"*&

Foundry: Typodermic
Designer: Ray Larabie
Designer Nationality: Canadian
Date: 2011

Designed by the prolific Canadian-born type designer Ray Larabie, who is based in Japan, Joystix is a single style, bold bitmap sans-serif font. Its jagged look, the result of being constructed from large squares, mimics the early digital type found mainly in arcade games.

Linotype Leggodt

ABCDEFGHIJKLMNOPQRSTUVWXYZ
abcdefghijklmnopqrstuvwxyz
1234567890 !@#?:;'"*&

Foundry: Linotype
Designer: Gunter Schwarzmaier
Designer Nationality: German
Date: 1997

Linotype Leggodt is a bitmap display face based on early multimedia-inspired designs, such as OCR-B (1968) by Adrian Frutiger (see p. 290). The font's characters were designed in three styles, titled One, Two, and Three, and each proposes an alternative version of pixel-built letterforms.

Lomo

ABCDEFGHIJKLMNOPQRSTUV
abcdefghijklmnopqrstuvwxyz
1234567890 !@#?:;"*&

Foundry: Linotype
Designer: Fidel Peugeot
Designer Nationality: Swiss
Date: 2002

Designed by Fidel Peugeot, a Swiss designer based in Vienna, the Lomo family is named after an old Russian camera brand and was created for Lomography, a company selling modern reproductions of these fun cameras. Lomo, a lo-fi pixellated sans serif, comes in thirty-seven varied styles.

Nerdropol

ABCDEFGHIJKLMNOPQRSTUVWXY
abcdefghijklmnopqrstuvwxyz
1234567890 !@#?:;"*&

Foundry: Typodermic
Designer: Ray Larabie
Designer Nationality: Canadian
Date: 2012

Nerdropol, released by Typodermic in 2012, is a bitmap version of Neuropol X, a typeface designed by Larabie in 1997. It is a wide, low-resolution sans serif that comes in eight varied styles, including Nerdropol Screen, which mimics the distortions of an old cathode-ray tube monitor.

New Geneva Nine

ABCDEFGHIJKLMNOPQRSTUVWXYZ
abcdefghijklmnopqrstuvwxyz
1234567890 !@#?:;"*&

Foundry: Image Club Graphics
Designer: Grant Hutchinson
Designer Nationality: Canadian
Date: 1991

Canadian designer Grant Hutchinson created the New Geneva Nine pixellated typeface in 1991. In 2009, Hutchinson co-founded Veer, which sold stock photos, illustrations and fonts until the company closed in 2016. New Geneva Nine comes in two styles, Regular and Point, which is condensed.

Pistol Shot

ABCDEFGHIJKLMNOPQRSTUVWXYZ
abcdefghijklmnopqrstuvwxyz
1234567890 !@#?:;"*&

Foundry: Linotype
Designer: Roselyne Besnard / Michel Besnard
Designer Nationality: French
Date: 2003

French couple Michel and Roselyne Besnard designed Pistol Shot, in 2003. The pixellated, blocky Western-style font was included in Linotype's TakeType 5 library, which comprised entries from the Linotype International Type Design Contest. It comes in two weights, Light and Normal.

Pixelar

ABCDEFGHIJKLMNOPQRSTUVWXYZ

abcdefghijklmnopqrstuvwxyz

1234567890 !@#?:;"*&

Foundry: Graviton
Designer: Pablo Balcells
Designer Nationality: Argentinian
Date: 2014

Pablo Balcells designed Pixelar for Graviton in 2014. The pixellated typeface comes in four styles; Regular, Outline, Textured (made from diagonal lines) and Textured Outline. An animated version, made in collaboration with Jeroen Krielaars, is available from Animography.

Rukyltronic

ABCDEFGHIJKLMNOPQRSTUVWXYZ

abcdefghijklmnopqrstuvwxyz

1234567890 !@#?:;"*&

Foundry: Typodermic
Designer: Ray Larabie
Designer Nationality: Canadian
Date: 2012

Ray Larabie designed Rukyltronic in 2012. The typeface is an angular, simulated bitmap typeface that comes in eight different styles. It was inspired by the Sinclair ZX Spectrum, an early computer produced in Britain which was popular for video games.

Zeitgeist

ABCDEFGHIJKLMNOPQRSTUVWXYZ

abcdefghijklmnopqrstuvwxyz

1234567890 !@#?:;"*&

Foundry: Monotype
Designer: Michael Johnson
Designer Nationality: British
Date: 1990

Michael Johnson's only font, Zeitgeist is a low-resolution, pixellated condensed slab serif. It features alternate swashed letters and comes in six styles: Regular, Italic, Condensed, Bold, Cameo (white letters on black rectangles), and Crazy Paving, which has an eccentric lowercase.

Zerbydoo

ABCDEFGHIJKLMNOPQRSTUVWXYZ

abcdefghijklmnopqrstuvwxyz

1234567890 !@#?:;"*&

Foundry: Typodermic
Designer: Ray Larabie
Designer Nationality: Canadian
Date: 2012

This eccentrically named face by Ray Larabie is a heavy, pixellated sans serif that is available in many styles; one is solid, one is constructed from circles, another from stars and three are made from different sized squares. Its kerning is restricted to full pixel increments.

Foundry Profile

MuirMcNeil

Founded in 2010, MuirMcNeil focuses its activities on 'exploring parametric design systems to generate appropriate solutions to visual communication problems'. The founding partners are Paul McNeil and Hamish Muir. McNeil is a typographic designer with experience in brand and corporate communications. He is also a senior lecturer in typography at the London College of Communication, where he was course leader on the masters in contemporary typographic media from 2010–15. Muir co-founded the London-based graphic design studio 8vo in 1985 and was co-editor of *Octavo, International Journal of Typography* from 1986 to 1992. Since 2001, Muir has worked as a senior lecturer on the graphic and media design programme at the London College of Communication.

The duo's unusual typefaces can be seen as challenging the notion of legibility and questioning letterforms in the traditional sense of the word. However, Muir and McNeil rigorously employ mathematics, grids and systems in their work to maintain readability. Their portfolio includes typefaces that are stunning – more pattern than texts – and their constructed appearance via overlays, alignments, contrasting stroke weights and dot sizes communicate the beauty of the mathematics within. The intrinsic aesthetic beauty in the structure of their typefaces comes to the fore when using the fonts with a spirit of experimentation and exploration.

Founded: 2010
Country: Britain
Website: muirmcneil.com
Notable typefaces:
ThreeSix (see p. 442)
TwoPoint (see p. 413)
TwoPlus (see p. 445)
TwoBit (see p. 444)
Cut (see p. 549)

Right. Limited-edition promotional poster of 100 for the TwoPoint typeface (top). Poster design for multi-disciplinary artist Russell Haswell's three-day festival held at Cafe Oto, London. The design is set in TwoPoint C in two weights (middle). Bisect poster typeface system (bottom).

Opposite. Detail from MuirMcNeil's limited-edition poster for their modular Intersect typeface system. All designs by MuirMcNeil.

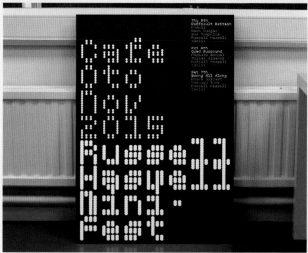

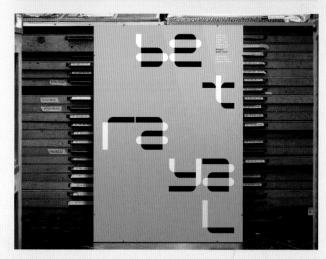

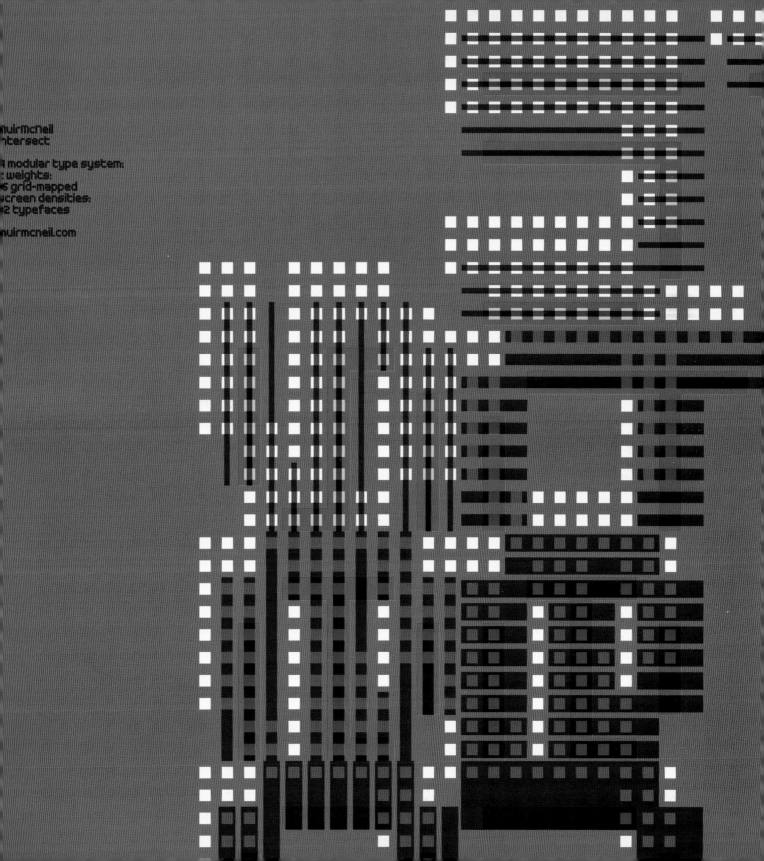

MuirMcNeil
Intersect

A modular type system:
weights:
grid-mapped
screen densities:
2 typefaces

muirmcneil.com

Ad Lib

ABCDEFGHIJKLMNOPQRSTUVWXYZ
abcdefghijklmnopqrstuvwxyz
1234567890 !@#?:;"'"*&

Foundry: American Type Founders
Designer: Freeman Craw
Designer Nationality: American
Date: 1961

Ad Lib's chunky forms and squared counters will be instantly recognizable to cartoon fans, thanks to its use in the credits of the *Looney Tunes* series and *The Pink Panther* films. Designer Freeman Craw went on to win the Type Director's Club Medal in 1988 for his contributions to typography.

Ambrose

ABCDEFGHIJKLMNOPQRSTUVWXYZ
1234567890 !?:;"'"*&

Foundry: ITC
Designer: Rudolf Koch / Alan Meeks
Designer Nationality: German / British
Date: 1914 / 1985

Designed by Alan Meeks shortly after he left Letraset to go freelance, Ambrose is based on Rudolf Koch's typeface Maximilian Antiqua, which was first published by the Klingspor foundry in Germany in 1914. Ambrose is a bold and characterful all-caps serif featuring engraved details.

Amherst

ABCDEFGHIJKLMNOPQRSTUVWXYZ
abcdefghijklmnopqrstuvwxyz
1234567890 !@#?:;"'"*&

Foundry: Linotype
Designer: Richard Yeend
Designer Nationality: British
Date: 2002

A member of Linotype's TakeType 5 Library, Amherst cleverly combines key formal features of Blackletter type with Art Deco details, to create a unique and contemporary sans serif. The family includes additional ornamental Gothic and Split styles alongside three standard weights.

Ampacity

ABCDEFGHIJKLMNOPQRSTUVWXYZ
1234567890 !@#?:;"'"*&

Foundry: Typodermic
Designer: Ray Larabie
Designer Nationality: Canadian
Date: 2012

Ampacity is a condensed display typeface available in uppercase only. Best set in larger point sizes to maximize legibility, each letterform within the font is made up of a single line of unwavering weight, folded and manipulated in much the same manner as neon lighting tubes.

Angle Bold

ABCDEFGHIJKLMNOPQRSTUVWXYZ
abcdefghijklmnopqrstuvwxyz
1234567890 !@#?:;"'*&

Foundry: Monotype
Designer: Zavier Leslie Cabarga
Designer Nationality: American
Date: 2000

Illustrator, type designer and comic artist Zavier Cabarga started his career early – he sold his first comics at age fourteen and three years later he was developing his first font for phototypesetting. Angle, which is available in Bold and Inline styles, was first published in 2000.

Aquitaine Initials

ABCDEFGHIJKLMNOPQRSTUVWXYZ
ABCDEFGHIJKLMNOPQRSTUVWXYZ
1234567890 !@#?:;"'*&

Foundry: Letraset
Designer: Steven Albert
Designer Nationality: American
Date: 1987

Displaying a distinctive Celtic influence throughout its letterforms, Aquitaine Initials was designed with two character sets: a basic uppercase alphabet, and a set of more decorative alternates that work particularly well at larger sizes. Both sets feature fine engraved details.

Arcadia

ABCDEFGHIJKLMNOPQRSTUVWXYZ
abcdefghijklmnopqrstuvwxyz
1234567890 !@#?:;"'*&

Foundry: Linotype
Designer: Neville Brody
Designer Nationality: British
Date: 1990

This condensed, didone-influenced display font was designed by Neville Brody in 1986 for headline type within *Arena* magazine, which at the time was the first men's lifestyle title to be launched in Britain in two decades. Linotype published a retail version of the font in 1990.

Arnold Boecklin

ABCDEFGHIJKLMNOPQRSTUVWXYZ
abcdefghijklmnopqrstuvwxyz
1234567890 !@#?:;"'*&

Foundry: Otto Weisert
Designer: Otto Weisert
Designer Nationality: German
Date: 1904

This archetypal Jungendstil font was designed in Stuttgart by Otto Weisert at the turn of the 20th century. Its swooping forms experienced a renaissance during the 1960s and 1970s, and it remains a popular if predictable choice to this day when an Art Nouveau look is required.

Artistik

ABCDEFGHIJKLMNOPQRSTUVWXYZ
abcdefghijklmnopqrstuvwxyz
1234567890 !@#?:;"*&

Foundry: Monotype
Designer: Monotype Studio
Date: 1897

Artistik was first published at the end of the 19th century. It features an irregularity influenced by brush-drawn calligraphy and Asian hand-lettering styles, and comes with a range of decorative alternate caps. Monotype published a digitization of the typeface in 1992.

Atomic

ABCDEFGHIJKLMNOPQRSTUVWXYZ
abcdefghijklmnopqrstuvwxyz
1234567890 !@#?:;"*¿

Foundry: Image Club Graphics
Designer: Lorne Maclean
Designer Nationality: Canadian
Date: 1997

Canadian typographer Lorne Maclean designed Atomic in 1997. It is available in both serif and sans-serif styles and forms part of Linotype's NicePrice font collection, an array of decorative display typefaces intended for use outside of professional graphic design contexts.

Auriol

ABCDEFGHIJKLMNOPQRSTUVWXYZ
abcdefghijklmnopqrstuvwxyz
1234567890 !@#?:;"*&

Foundry: G. Peignot et Fils
Designer: George Auriol
Designer Nationality: French
Date: 1901

This stencilled typeface is based on the handwriting of Art Nouveau designer George Auriol, and displays the influence of brush-drawn calligraphy. It was used as the basis for the Paris Métro entrance signage. Linotype rereleased it with an additional bold cut in 1979.

Balega

ABCDEFGHIJKLMNOPQRSTUVWXYZ
abcdefghijklmnopqrstuvwxyz
1234567890 !@#?:;"*&

Foundry: Linotype
Designer: Jürgen Weltin
Designer Nationality: German
Date: 2003

German type designer Jürgen Weltin drew this stencil typeface, featuring a slight forward slant, for Linotype in 2003. It is based on Resolut, a font designed by H. Brünnel for the Turin-based foundry Nebiolo in 1937. It includes a range of new characters that were missing within the original.

Beluga LT

ABCDEFGHIJKLMNOPQRSTUVWXY
abcdefghijklmnopqrstuvwxyz
1234567890 !@#?:;"*&

Foundry: Linotype
Designer: Hans-Jürgen Ellenberger
Designer Nationality: German
Date: 1994

The German illustrator, type designer and former science teacher Hans-Jürgen Ellenberger developed the medieval feel of this display typeface without direct reference to specific historic examples of calligraphy. Its forms nonetheless reflect the movement of the quill on the page.

Billsville

ABCDEFGHIJKLMNOPQRSTUVWXYZ
abcdefghijklmnopqrstuvwxyz
1234567890 !@#?:;"*&

Foundry: Chank Co.
Designer: Chank Diesel
Designer Nationality: American
Date: 1997

This display typeface was commissioned by the Tripod web-hosting company, one of the pioneers of user-generated content online. It is named for the town in which Tripod is based, Williamstown, Massachusetts. The font features irregular forms and star-shaped tittles.

Bomr

ABCDEFGHIJKLMNOPQRSTUVWXYZ
ABCDEFGHIJKLMNOPQRSTUVWXYZ
1234567890 !@#?:;"*&

Foundry: Typodermic
Designer: Ray Larabie
Designer Nationality: Canadian
Date: 2002

Ray Larabie's Bomr display typeface features exaggerated top serifs and an irreverent feel; its design was inspired by the graffiti tags seen on the side of freight trains. The typeface includes OpenType features that automatically substitute custom letter pairs for a remixed effect.

Bonehead

ABCDEFGHIJKLMNOPQRSTUVWXYZ
abcdefghijklmnopqrstuvwxyz
1234567890 !@#?:;"*&

Foundry: Chank Co.
Designer: Chank Diesel
Designer Nationality: American
Date: 1995

Chank Diesel designed this typeface for *Cake* magazine. It is one of a trio of typefaces created by Diesel as an experiment in type design without the use of curved lines, and is available in a package with its companion styles, Buckethead and Brainhead.

Boogie

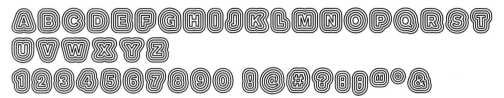

Foundry: Linotype
Designer: Ralf Weissmantel
Designer Nationality: German
Date: 2003

Ralf Weissmantel's playful and retro Boogie typeface was a winner in the Linotype International Digital Type Design Contest in 2003. It comprises several different styles intended to be layered over one another, allowing designers to control the impact and legibility of its appearance.

Boogie School Sans

ABCDEFGHIJKLMNOPQRSTUVWXYZ
abcdefghijklmnopqrstuvwxyz
1234567890 !@#?:;"*&

Foundry: Or Type
Designer: Mads Freund Brunse
Designer Nationality: Danish
Date: 2016

Or Type (see p. 498) was founded in 2013 by Guðmundur Úlfarsson and Mads Freund Brunse, who work between Reykjavik and London. They began development of this reverse contrast font in 2011, for use on a series of posters for a club night held in Freetown Christiania, Copenhagen.

Boogie School Serif

ABCDEFGHIJKLMNOPQRSTUVWXYZ
abcdefghijklmnopqrstuvwxyz
1234567890 !@#?:;"*&

Foundry: Or Type
Designer: Mads Freund Brunse
Designer Nationality: Danish
Date: 2016

This counterpart to Boogie School Sans features the addition of bulbous, rounded serifs, which heighten the appealing oddity of its predecessor – according to the foundry, its appearance was influenced by type found on old soul and funk record covers. It was published in 2016.

Breeze

ABCDEFGHIJKLMNOPQRSTUVWXYZ
abcdefghijklmnopqrstuvwxyz
1234567890)@#?:;"*&

Foundry: Linotype
Designer: Frank Marciuliano
Designer Nationality: American
Date: 1997

US type designer Frank Marciuliano developed Breeze's letterforms to look like sails. Two versions of the typeface are available, each with its 'sails' facing a different direction; the two can be combined to add a further sense of movement to display type.

Broadband

ABCDEFGHIJKLMNOPQRSTUVWXYZ
abcdefghijklmnopqrstuvwxyz
1234567890 !@#?.;"*&

Foundry: Image Club Graphics
Designer: Grant Hutchinson
Designer Nationality: Canadian
Date: 1991

This design by Veer co-founder Grant Hutchinson features rounded forms and geometric details. It remains legible even when set at smaller sizes – a somewhat unusual characteristic within display typefaces. First published by Image Club Graphics, it has since been licensed by Linotype.

Broadstreet

ABCDEFGHIJKLWNOPQRSTUVWXYZ
abcdefghijklmnopqrstuvwxyz
1234567890 !@#?.;"*&

Foundry: Monotype
Designer: Richard Yeend
Designer Nationality: British
Date: 2001

Designer and cartoonist Richard Yeend has worked extensively in the editorial world, undertaking redesigns for newspapers including the *International Herald Tribune* and *Die Welt* over the course of his career. This stylized display serif design of his was published in 2001.

Broadway

ABCDEFGHIJKLMNOPQRSTUVWXYZ
abcdefghijklmnopqrstuvwxyz
1234567890 !@#?:;""*&

Foundry: American Type Founders
Designer: Morris Fuller Benton / Sol Hess
Designer Nationality: American
Date: 1927 / 1928

First designed by Morris Fuller Benton in uppercase only, this distinctive Art Deco font was quickly developed into a full typeface by Sol Hess following its release in 1928. He contributed an engraved cut the following year, alongside a condensed version designed by Fuller Benton.

Buckethead

ABCDEFGHIJKLMNOPQRSTUVWXYZ
abcdefghijklmnopqrstuvwxyz
1234567890 !@#?:;"*&

Foundry: Chank Co.
Designer: Chank Diesel
Designer Nationality: American
Date: 1995

The third of Chank Diesel's angular and jovial experiments in type design without the use of curves, Buckethead was designed for use in *Cake* magazine, which Diesel founded and worked on as creative director. The typeface has since been licensed for sale by Linotype.

Budmo

ABCDEFGHIJKLMNOPQRSTUVWXYZ
1234567890 !@#?:;''*&

Foundry: Typodermic
Designer: Ray Larabie
Designer Nationality: Canadian
Date: 1998

Budmo is a marquee signage-style typeface built on a geometric skeleton, and is available in a number of different variants that are designed to be layered to achieve a range of effects. Ray Larabie designed the typeface, which was published by his Typodermic foundry in 1998.

Burweed ICG

ABCDEFGHIJKLMNOPQRSTUVWXYZ
abcdefghijklmnopqrstuvwxyz
1234567890 !@#?:;"*&

Foundry: Image Club Graphics
Designer: Patricia Lillie
Designer Nationality: American
Date: 1996

Perhaps best known as a prolific producer of dingbat typefaces, US designer Patricia Lillie has also created a number of display typefaces, among them Burweed, which was published by Image Club Graphics in 1996. Tapered towards the bottom, it offers a jaunty and informal feel for headlines.

Buster

ABCDEFGHIJKLMNOPQRSTUVWXYZ
1234567890 !@#?:;"*&

Foundry: Letraset
Designer: Tony Wenman
Designer Nationality: British
Date: 1972

The letterforms of this shadowed display typeface by Letraset's Tony Wenman share similarities with those of traditional, industrial grotesques, but are presented here to appear three-dimensional. Buster, which has since been licensed by Linotype, is available in uppercase only.

Buxotic

ABCDEFGHIJKLMNOPQRSTUVWXYZ
1234567890 ?:;"*&

Foundry: Typodermic
Designer: Ray Larabie
Designer Nationality: Canadian
Date: 2006

The highly decorative and occasionally anthropomorphized forms of this display font by Ray Larabie feature a number of inclusions and embellishments. While legibility might not be its strength, the unconventional appearance of Buxotic rarely fails to make an impression.

Buzzer Three

ABCDEFGHIJKLMNOPQRSTUVWXYZ
1234567890 !?:;"*&

Foundry: Letraset
Designer: Paul Crome /
Tony Lyons
Designer Nationality: British
Date: 1993

Designed by Paul Crome and Tony Lyons at Letraset, this typeface is based on the appearance of early optical character recognition fonts, which were developed to be readable by the human eye and by computers. It features irregularly placed serif details and occasional curved forms throughout.

Candice

ABCDEFGHIJKLMNOPQRSTUV
abcdefghijklmnopqrstuvwxyz
1234567890 !@#?:;"*&

Foundry: Letraset
Designer: Alan Meeks
Designer Nationality: British
Date: 1976

Curvaceous and exuberant, Candice has become synonymous with the 1970s – instantly recognizable, it can be seen everywhere from The Carpenters' record covers to the logotype for the TV series *Cheers*. It shares similarities with Benguiat Charisma, published the previous decade.

Carouselambra

ABCDEFGHIJKLMNOPQRSTUVWXYZ
1234567890 !@#?:;"*&

Foundry: Typodermic
Designer: Ray Larabie
Nationality: Canadian
Date: 2008

Carouselambra was created in tribute to the type on the cover of Led Zeppelin's LP *Houses of the Holy* (1973). It shares certain similarities with ITC Willow (1990), including double crossbars and lifted letters, which were themselves influenced by the work of Scottish architect Charles Rennie Mackintosh.

Carver

ABCDEFGHIJKLMNOPQRSTUVWXYZ
abcdefghijklmnopqrstuvwxyz
1234567890 !@#?:;"*&

Foundry: Image Club Graphics
Designer: Grant Hutchinson /
Noel Rubin
Designer Nationality: Canadian
Date: 1994

Designed for Image Club Graphics in 1994, Carver is a blocky, angular sans-serif font embellished with engraved strokes that provide both a slight sense of movement and the impression of crude tool marks. The details within its letterforms are best appreciated at larger point sizes.

Chic

ABCDEFGHIJKLMNOPQRSTUVWXYZ
1234567890 !@#?‚°°°'' * &

Foundry: American Type Founders
Designer: Morris Fuller Benton
Designer Nationality: American
Date: 1928

Morris Fuller Benton designed the Art Deco-influenced Chic typeface for American Type Founders in 1928. Linotype offers the font in digital form, and Nick Curtis's Odalisque NF (2008) is another contemporary interpretation, although this latter version lacks the striped details of the original.

Chilada ICG Uno

ABCDEFGHIJKLMNOPQRSTUVWXYZ
abcdefghijklmnopqrstuvwxyz
1234567890 !@#?:,"*&

Foundry: Image Club Graphics
Designer: Patricia Lillie
Designer Nationality: American
Date: 1994

Chilada is an angular font featuring zigzag emblems within the engraved outlines of its letterforms. It is unmistakably 1990s in style, its lowercase including some letters elevated from the baseline, encouraging playful typesetting. It was designed by Patricia Lillie for Image Club Graphics.

Chromium One

ABCDEFGHIJKLMNOPQRSTUVWXYZ
1234567890 !?:;"*&

Foundry: Letraset
Designer: David Harris
Designer Nationality: British
Date: 1983

This highly decorative font was designed by lettering artist and calligrapher David Harris for Letraset in 1983, and was later licensed by ITC and Linotype. Resembling hyper-glossy raised chrome type thanks to its intricate shaded details, it is available in uppercase only.

Chwast Buffalo

ABCDEFGHIJKLMNOPQRSTUVWXYZ
abcdefghijklmnopqrstuvwxyz
1234567890 !@#?:;"°&

Foundry: Linotype
Designer: Seymour Chwast
Designer Nationality: American
Date: 1978

Chwast Buffalo is a chunky semi-serif display typeface with rounded terminals and small counters, created by US designer Seymour Chwast in 1978 and published by Linotype three years later. Due to the font's heavy stroke weight, it is best used at large point sizes to maximize its legibility.

Clipwave

ABCDEFGHIJKLMNOPQRSTUVWXYZ
ABCDEFGHIJKLMNOPQRSTUVWXYZ
1234567890 !@#?:;"*&

Foundry: Typodermic
Designer: Ray Larabie
Nationality: Canadian
Date: 2011

Clipwave is a sans-serif display typeface with an informal character; the design of its letterforms is angular but with rounded corners for added friendliness. As is characteristic of many Typodermic fonts, it offers a range of OpenType-enabled features and alternates.

Cosmic

ABCDEFGHIJKLMNOPQRSTUVWXYZ
abcdefghijklmnopqrstuvwxyz
1234567890 !@#?:;"*&

Foundry: Chank Co.
Designer: Chank Diesel
Designer Nationality: American
Date: 1995

Cosmic, designed by Chank Diesel for his Chank Co. foundry, is an ultra-heavy sans-serif typeface with slim, open counters and a condensed appearance. In 1997, Swedish designer Claes Källarsson created an exaggerated version of the font, even bolder and more condensed than the original.

Creepy

ABCDEFGHIJKLMNOPQRSTUVWXYZ
ABCDEFGHIJKLMNOPQRSTUVWXYZ
1234567890 !@#?:;"*&

Foundry: Ascender
Designer: Carl Crossgrove / Steve Matteson
Designer Nationality: American
Date: 2001

Co-founder of the Ascender foundry and creative type director at Monotype, Steve Matteson designed the Creepy cartoonish typeface with its dripping details that suit a range of spooky scenarios. He created the font in collaboration with fellow US type designer Carl Crossgrove.

Croissant

ABCDEFGHIJKLMNOPQRSTUVWXYZ
abcdefghijklmnopqrstuvwxyz
1234567890 !@#?:;"*&

Foundry: Letraset
Designer: Philip Kelly
Designer Nationality: British
Date: 1978

Croissant is a pleasingly plump display typeface that appears to be formed from stylized and simplified brushstrokes. It was designed in 1978 by Philip Kelly, a prolific British type designer who worked at Letraset for twenty-five years. Croissant has since been licensed for sale by Linotype.

Curlz

ABCDEFGHIJKLMNOPQRSTUVWXYZ
abcdefghijklmnopqrstuvwxyz
1234567890 !@#?:,"*&

Foundry: Monotype
Designer: Carl Crossgrove /
Steve Matteson
Designer Nationality: American
Date: 1995

Curlz is ubiquitous thanks to its inclusion within a range of Microsoft programmes and has been a popular choice for vernacular typesetting since its release by Agfa Monotype in 1995. It features a playful mix of straight serifs and curled stroke ends, with an uneven stress throughout.

Davida

ABCDEFGHIJKLMNOPQRSTUVWXYZ
1234567890 !@#?:,"*&

Foundry: VGC
Designer: Louis Minott
Designer Nationality: American
Date: 1965

Davida is a bold and highly decorative typeface, probably inspired by Victorian designs such as Central Type Foundry's Hogarth (1887). Also released as Silva and Darling, the original phototype font offered various alternates for 'A', 'E' and 'F' and numbers 1 to 9, which digital versions lack.

Debusen

ABCDEFGHIJKLMNOPQRSTUVWXYZ
abcdefghijklmnopqrstuvwxyz
1234567890 !@#?:,"*&

Foundry: Typodermic
Designer: Ray Larabie
Nationality: Canadian
Date: 2008

Creator Ray Larabie has said the secret of this typeface is that it is 'Soft like a kitten soaked in butter. That's what makes Debusen so friendly'. The bulbous display typeface is completely devoid of any straight lines or angles, and in many ways it is similar to children's bubble writing.

Decorated 035

ABCDEFGHIJKLMNOP
QRSTUVWXYZ
1234567890 !@#?:,""*&

Foundry: Bitstream
Designer: Eugen Lenz /
Max Lenz
Designer Nationality: Swiss
Date: 1946 / c. 1980s

Formed from inclined rimmed capitals and numbers, Decorated 035 is Bitstream's version of Profil, which was designed by brothers Eugen and Max Lenz for the Swiss foundry Haas in 1946. Upright and Contour (without a shadow) versions were added by Photo-Lettering.

Desperate

ABCDEFGHIJKLMNOPQRSTUVWXYZ
1234567890 !@#?:;"*&

Foundry: Typodermic
Designer: Ray Larabie
Designer Nationality: Canadian
Date: 2009

Creator Ray Larabie has described Desperate as being 'a punk, post-punk, new wave, Reagan-punk font.' It is a visual cacophony of sharp points and angles – there are a few verticals to be found among the jagged edges, but not many, making it suitable for display purposes only.

Diamond Bodoni

Foundry: Monotype
Designer: Monotype Studio
Date: Unknown

Diamond comes in three styles: Bodoni, Negative and Positive. Bodoni has condensed Bodoni-style capitals and figures reversed on to the background. Positive and Negative offer capitals and figures in positive and negative form respectively. It is useful in labelling on certificates and advertising.

Digital

ABCDEFGHIJKLMNOPQRSTUVWXYZ
ABCDEFGHIJKLMNOPQRSTUVWXYZ
1234567890 !@#?:;"*&

Foundry: Image Club Graphics
Designer: Greg Kolodziejzyk
Designer Nationality: Canadian
Date: 1994

Canadian designer Greg Kolodziejzyk's typeface Digital was inspired by the very basic modular typefaces that first appeared on calculators and digital watches during the 1960s and 1970s. It scores very low on the legibility scale and is available in one uppercase weight.

DR Lineart

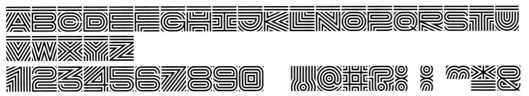

Foundry: Dmitry Rastvortsev
Designer: Dmitry Rastvortsev
Designer Nationality: Ukrainian
Date: 2017

This striking Op art display face by self-taught type designer Dmitry Rastvortsev can be tiled to create a grid format. In 2016, it won an award for the Best of Ukrainian Design in Typestyle and Typography. It contains five styles: Regular, Regular Alt, Skeleton, Background and Ornament.

Ecliptica BT

ABCDEFGHIJKLMNOPQRSTUVWXYZ
abcdefghijklmnopqrstuvwxyz
1234567890 !@#?:;"*&

Foundry: Bitstream
Designer: Robert Bell
Designer Nationality: Australian
Date: 2004

An extended family of very condensed typefaces in a single bold weight, Ecliptica BT is available in Sans, Semi-Serif, Serif, Cursive and Blackletter, all of which are designed to work well together. Both the Sans and Cursive versions contain some cap and lowercase alternatives.

Eirinn

ABCDEFGHIJKLMNOPQRSTUVWXYZ
abcdefghijklmnopqnrtuvwxyz
1234567890 !@#?:;"*&

Foundry: Linotype
Designer: Norbert Reiners
Designer Nationality: German
Date: 1994

Eirinn's Celtic forms are based on Irish scripts of the 7th to 9th centuries, such as the *Book of Kells*. The typeface is characterized by its lowercase 'f' with its short cross-stroke on baseline and long cross-stroke above, and the unusual form of the 'g', and the 't', whose form is almost like that of a letter 'c'.

Eon Age ATT

ABCDEFGHIJKLMNOPQRSTUVWXYZ
1234567890 !@#?:;"*&

Foundry: ITC
Designer: Paul Prue
Designer Nationality: British
Date: 1994

Paul Prue designed this futuristic display typeface for the Agfa Compugraphic Creative Alliance in 1994. Eon Age features unusual characters with blocks that balance on the baseline. Prue also designed the similarly science-fiction influenced System X3, Galaxy Run and Logan in the same year.

F2F Haakonsen

Foundry: Face2Face
Designer: Stefan Hauser
Designer Nationality: German
Date: 2003

An outline-based layered, experimental typeface, Haakonsen is part of the Face2Face series. It was created by German designer and educator Stefan Hauser. Many of Face2Face's typefaces featured in layouts for the leading 1990s German techno music magazine *Frontpage*.

F2F HogRoach

ABCDEFGHIJKLMNOPQRSTUVWXYZ
abcdefghijklmnopqrstuvwxyz
1234567890 !@#?;"*&

Foundry: Face2Face
Designer: Thomas Nagel
Designer Nationality: German
Date: 1995

HogRoach is an experimental typeface that challenges conventional notions of legibility. It is part of the Face2Face series of unusual designs created by the collective formed by German designer and typographer Thomas Nagel and his friends. Many of Face2Face's typefaces featured in *Frontpage*.

F2F Monako Stoned

ABCDEFGHIJKLMNOPQRSTUVWXYZ
abcdefghijklmnopqrstuvwxyz
1234567890 !@#?;:;"*&

Foundry: Face2Face
Designer: Alexander Branczyk / Heike Nehl
Designer Nationality: German
Date: 1995

An Op art-inspired typeface created from half-tone textures, Monako Stoned is part of the Face2Face series that explored the design potential of type with experimental fonts and unconventional interfaces. Monako Stoned was created by German designers Alexander Branczyk and Heike Nehl.

Fajita Mild

ABCDEFGHIJKLMNOPQRSTUVWXYZ
ABCDEFGHIJKLMNOPQRSTUVWXYZ
1234567890 !@#?;"*&

Foundry: Image Club Graphics
Designer: Noel Rubin
Designer Nationality: Canadian
Date: 1994

Fajita is named after the Tex-Mex dish. It is a woodcut-style display face with small caps for its lowercase and rough, textured random shapes around each glyph. The typeface is available in two styles, Mild and Picante, and the latter features accent lines above or below its small caps.

Fat Albert BT

ABCDEFGHIJKLMNOPQRSTUVWXYZ
abcdefghijklmnopqrstuvwxyz
1234567890 !@#?;:"*&

Foundry: Bitstream
Designer: Ray Cruz
Designer Nationality: American
Date: 2004

Fat Albert BT was inspired by 1970s pop-culture fonts and named after an animated cartoon starring Bill Cosby which debuted in 1972. It is a heavy display sans serif with circular- and oval-shaped counters and flat tops and bottoms. It comes in three styles: Solid, Outline and Shadow.

Farset / Feirste

ABCDEFGHIJKLMNOPQRSTUVWXYZ
ABCDEFGHIJKLMNOPQRSTUVWXYZ
1234567890 !@#?:;"*&

ABCDEFSHIJKLMNOPQRSTUVWXYZ
AbcdefSHIJKLMNOPQRSTUVWXYZ
1234567890 !@#?:;"*&

Foundry: MuirMcNeil
Designer: John McMillan
Designer Nationality: British / Irish
Date: 2019

From the streets of Northern Ireland's Belfast (literally) comes the typeface Farset (named after the river that flows to Belfast from the surrounding hills) and its Gaelic equivalent Feirste (from the city's Irish name Béal Feirste). The design of Farset / Feirste is based on Belfast's historic tiled street signage. These striking tiled signs were handmade during the late 19th and early 20th centuries and their distinctive white capital lettering on black tiles are familiar to residents and visitors alike.

The development of Latin and Gaelic typefaces was the brainchild of Belfast resident John McMillan, Emeritus Professor of Graphic Design at Ulster University. The project began in 2015 and was realized only in 2018, when McMillan approached foundry and design studio MuirMcNeil for help with the digitization. They interpreted his designs in both Latin and Gaelic variants with each available in the cameo format of the signs and in normal font format.

Below. The distinctive tiled street signage of Belfast was the inspiration behind Farset / Feirste. Its distinctive capital lettering has striking 'G', 'R' and 'S' designs that provide a unique character to the letterforms.

Opposite. Examples and character sets of both typefaces.

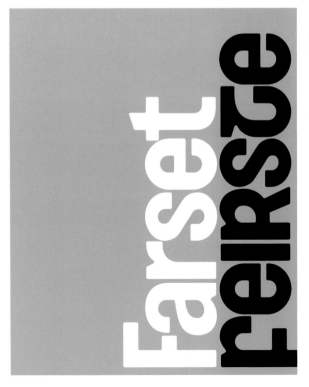

SHANKILL ROAD
BURREN WAY
BROOMHILL PARK
FALLS ROAD
STRANMILLIS
CASTLEREACH
LEGONIEL
SKEGONEIL
MALONE

BÓTHAR NA SEANCHILLE
BEALACH NA BOIRNE
PÁIRC CHNOC NA SCUAB
BÓTHAR NA BHFÁL
AN SRUTHÁN MILIS
AN CAISLEÁN RIABHACH
LAS AN AOIL
SCEACHÓS AN IARLA
MASH LÓIN

ABCDEFGGHHIIJKLMM
NOPQRRSTTUVWWXYZ
abcdefgghijklm
nopqrstuvwxyz

0123456789

ÄÅÀÃÂÁÉÊÊÈÍÎÍÎÌÖÕÓÔ
ÒØŒÚÛÙÜÇÑ¥Æáàâä
ãåæéèêëíîíïíóòôöõø
œúùûüçñµÿ$&£§ß
ƒ@®©™ªºo₀º₀₀†‡
•*¶(){}/!?¿¡
'„""„,'
.,,,,….;;
-–—‹›÷±¬~ ^°

ABCDEFShIJKLM
NOPQRSCUVWXYZ
Abcdefʃhɪjklmn
opqɒʀsɾɕuvɯxyz

0123456789

ÄÅÀÃÂÁẞĊĊÈÉÊÊÈʄŚÍÍÌ̀ṁ
ÖÕÓÒÔP̦ŜČÚÛÙÜÛ̀Ẁ̀ẂẄ
ÄÅÀÃÂÁẞbċ̇Ḋ́é̋êêël̯ʄśííì̀ṁ
öõóòôṗṣɾ̦ṫúûùüû̀ẁ̀ẃ
ØøŒœÇÑ¥Æñµÿ

$&7£§ßƒ@®©™ªº
º₀º₀₀†‡•*¶(){}/!?¿¡
'„""„,'
.,,,,….;;
-–—‹›÷±¬~ ^°

Faux Occident & Orient

ABCDEFGHIJKLMNOPQRSTUVWXYZ
1234567890 !(A)#?:;"*&

Foundry: Playtype
Designer: Jess Andersen / Andreas Peitersen / Stefan Friedli
Designer Nationality: Danish
Date: 2013

Developed by a team of Danish designers and published by Playtype (see p. 310), Faux is a three-dimensional, uppercase, sans serif display face.

It achieves an illusion of dimensionality through shadows; Faux Orient appears embossed while Faux Occident looks debossed.

FF CrashBangWallop

ABCDEFGHIJKLMNOPQRSTU
abcdefghijklmnopqrstuvwxy
1234567890 !@@@?:;"*&

Foundry: FontFont
Designer: Rian Hughes
Designer Nationality: British
Date: 1994

British graphic designer, illustrator and comic artist Rian Hughes designed FF CrashBangWallop. It is a quirky, angular display sans serif available in light

and medium with italics, as well as in two decorative styles – Highlight, a three-dimensional version, and Contour, which features an outline.

FF Dolores

ABCDEFGHIJKLMNOPQRSTUVWXYZ
abcdefghijklmnopqrstuvwxyz
1234567890 !@#?:;"*&

Foundry: FontFont
Designer: Tobias Frere-Jones
Designer Nationality: American
Date: 1991

An early font from the leading US typeface designer Tobias Frere-Jones, FF Dolores is a childlike, informal slab serif with many curls and quirks. It is

available in five weights and has Cyrillic support. FF Dolores is the only typeface that Frere-Jones released with FontFont.

FF Dynamoe

ABCDEFGHIJKLMNOPQRSTUVWXYZ
1234567890 ! ?:;"*&

Foundry: FontFont
Designer: Just van Rossum
Designer Nationality: Dutch
Date: 1992

FF Dynamoe is a distressed, sans serif which is reversed out of a thick black band. It is based on the look of labels created with old Dymo handheld

label makers that embossed letters into tape – a technique invented in 1958 which has been replaced by battery-powered printing.

FF Harlem

ABCDEFGHIJKLMNOPQRSTUVWXYZ
abcdefghijklmnopqrstuvwxyz
1234567890 !@#?:.,"*&

Foundry: FontFont
Designer: Neville Brody
Designer Nationality: British
Date: 1993

Neville Brody's FF Harlem is named after the traditionally African-American neighbourhood of Harlem at the north end of Manhattan. It is a heavy, energetic sans serif with irregular counters that give it a vibrant feel. The typeface is available in two styles: Regular and a distressed version, Slang.

FF Klunder

ABCDEFGHIJKLMNOPQRSTUVWXYZ
abcdefghijkLMNopqrstuvwxyz
1234567890 !@# ?:.,"*&

Foundry: FontFont
Designer: Barbara Klunder
Designer Nationality: Canadian
Date: 1994

This eponymous typeface by Canadian designer Barbara Klunder comes in regular and bold and was released by FontFont in 1994. Klunder Script is a quirky, irregular sans serif with a cheerful, festive mood. Letters alternate randomly between tilting left, upright and tilting right.

Fiesta

ABCDEFGHIJKLMNOPQRSTUVWXYZ
abcdefghijklmnopqrstuvwxyz
1234567890 !@#?:;"*&

Foundry: Aerotype
Designer: Stephen Miggas
Designer Nationality: American
Date: 1995

Fiesta is a decorative, display font in a woodcutlike style. It was released by Aerotype in 1995, the year that the foundry was established by Los Angeles-based graphic designer Stephen Miggas. Each letter features triangular inlaid details as well as small angular accenting just outside their outline.

Follies

ABCDEFGHIJKLMNOPQRSTUVWXYZ
1234567890 !?:;"**&

Foundry: Letraset
Designer: Alan Meeks
Designer Nationality: British
Date: 1991

Alan Meeks's Follies, released by Letraset in 1991, is a distinctive, display sans serif inspired by the 1940s and featuring a thin inline. The inline has small slab serifs on many letters. Follies is uppercase only and comes in a single style, which is heavy to allow for the inline.

Fruitygreen

ABCDEFGHIJKLMNOPQRSTUVWXYZ
abcdefghijklmnopqrstuvwxyz
1234567890 !@#?:;"*&

Foundry: Linotype
Designer: Andi AW. Masry
Designer Nationality: Indonesian
Date: 2012

Indonesian designer Andi AW. Masry created Fruitygreen, a distinctive soft sans serif inspired by the unique shapes of various fruits, in 2012. It is available in Regular, Bold and Black weights with italics. Fruitygreen was Masry's second font release after his debut Coomeec the same year.

FS Erskine

ABCDEFGHIJKLMNOPQRSTUVWXYZ
1234567890 !@#?:;"*&

Foundry: Fontsmith
Designer: Jimmy Turrell
Designer Nationality: British
Date: 2017

FS Erskine by illustrator Jimmy Turrell was part of Local Characters, a collaboration between Fontsmith (see p. 272) and agency It's Nice That. The brief was to make a font inspired by a place. They chose the Byker Wall estate in Newcastle, his hometown, and used primary colours and geometric shapes.

FS Kitty

ABCDEFGHIJKLMNOPQRSTUVWXYZ
1234567890 !@#?:;''*&

Foundry: Fontsmith
Designer: Jason Smith / Phil Garnham
Designer Nationality: British
Date: 2009

FS Kitty, designed by Jason Smith and Phil Garnham, is a chunky, curvy, uppercase display sans serif. It comes in five styles: Light and Regular, which are outlined; Solid, which features hairline interior details; Headline, which is solid with a keyline; and Shadow, which has a 3D effect.

FS Sally Triestina

ABCDEFGHIJKLMNOPQRSTUVWXYZ
abcdefghijklmnopqrstuvwxyz
1234567890 !@#?:;"*&

Foundry: Fontsmith
Designer: Astrid Stavro
Designer Nationality: Italian
Date: 2017

Designed by Astrid Stavro and Fontsmith (see p. 272), Sally Triestina was inspired by Trieste, Italy, where Stavro was born. It is a splicing of a bold and regular serif, with the lower half heavier and offset. Stavro, then creative director of Atlas, is a partner at the international design studio, Pentagram.

Glowworm

ABCDEFGHIJKLMNOPQRSTUVWXYZ
abcdefghijklmnopqrstuvwxyz
1234567890 !@#?:;"*&

Foundry: Mecanorma
Designer: Bogdan Żochowski
Designer Nationality: Polish
Date: 1975

Glowworm was released by French dry-transfer lettering company Mecanorma in 1975 and designed by Polish typographer Bogdan Żochowski. It is a bold, round sans serif with small highlights that give it a shiny, 3D look. It is available in Regular and Compressed versions.

Goudy Ornate MT

ABCDEFGHIJKLMNOPQRSTUVWXY
1234567890 !@#?:;"*&

Foundry: Monotype
Designer: Frederic W. Goudy
Designer Nationality: American
Date: 1931

This decorative, titling serif display face by Frederic W. Goudy comes in a single weight with uppercase letters only. It is open and features many small curly details. Goudy described it as a 'simple, decorative face that has been used by some good presses for use on title pages'.

Gurkner

ABCDEFGHIJKLMNOPQRSTUVWXYZ
1234567890 !@#?:;"*&

Foundry: Typodermic
Designer: Ray Larabie
Nationality: Canadian
Date: 2007

Ray Larabie's typeface Gurkner is a rounded, top-heavy display sans serif. Its heavy, spooky forms bulge at the top. Released by Larabie's Typodermic foundry in 2007, Gurkner has capitals only. It is available in two styles, Regular and Jump, and the latter does not conform to a consistent baseline.

Harlow

ABCDEFGHIJKLMNOPQRSTUVWX
abcdefghijklmnopqrstuvwxyz
1234567890 !?:;"*&

Foundry: ITC / Letraset
Designer: Colin Brignall
Designer Nationality: British
Date: 1977

Colin Brignall's Harlow, released by both ITC and Letraset in 1977, is a retro, inclined display sans serif with exuberant swashed capitals and long ascenders. Harlow is available in two styles, Solid and Regular, and the latter is outlined with an offset shadow built-in to give a 3D look.

Hemi Head 426

ABCDEFGHIJKLMNOPQRSTUVWXYZ
abcdefghijklmnopqrstuvwxyz
1234567890 !@#?:;" *&

Foundry: Typodermic
Designer: Ray Larabie
Nationality: Canadian
Date: 1998

Hemi Head 426, named after an engine part, is a square, industrial sans serif available in a single heavy italic style. As with many of Ray Larabie's early fonts, it was available for free online. Larabie was inspired by the lettering on 1960s' Dodge cars and other muscle-car insignia.

Hobo

ABCDEFGHIJKLMNOPQRSTUVWXYZ
abcdefghijklmnopqrstuvwxyz
1234567890 !@#?:;"*&

Foundry: American Type Founders
Designer: Morris Fuller Benton
Designer Nationality: American
Date: 1910

Hobo, an oft-derided sans serif, shares its name with the US term for a homeless drifter. It was designed by Morris Fuller Benton and released by American Type Founders in 1910 in one weight; a light cut followed in 1915. Inspired by Art Nouveau, it has no descenders and almost no straight lines.

Horndon

ABCDEFGHIJKLMNOPQRSTUVWXYZ
1234567890 !@#?:;"*&

Foundry: Letraset
Designer: Martin Wait
Designer Nationality: British
Date: 1984

Martin Wait designed Horndon for Letraset in 1984, and named it after Horndon-on-the-Hill, the Essex village where he lives. It is an all uppercase display face with small serifs, high crossbars and a built-in drop shadow with uniform gaps between the shadow and type giving a 3D effect.

Ignatius

ABCDEFGHIJKLMNOPQRSTUVWXYZ
abcdefghijklmnopqrstuvwxyz
1234567890 !?:;"*&

Foundry: Letraset
Designer: Freda Sack
Designer Nationality: British
Date: 1987

Freda Sack designed this elegant, two-line display serif face for Letraset in 1987. Ignatius comes in a single style with upper and lowercase. The two-line effect is extended even to the punctuation and tittles. Sack began her career at Letraset and then co-founded The Foundry in London.

ITC Aftershock

ABCDEFGHIJKLMNOPQRSTUVWXYZ
abcdefghijklmnopqrstuvwxyz
1234567890 !@#?:;"*&

Foundry: ITC
Designer: Bob Alonso
Designer Nationality: American
Date: 1996

US designer Bob Alonso worked at Photo-Lettering for many years and created Aftershock for the International Typeface Corporation (ITC) in 1996.

It is a robust and heavy display face whose irregular, square forms were intended to resemble lettering created through woodcut or linocut printing.

ITC Arecibo

ABCDEFGHIJKLMNOPQRSTUVWXYZ
ABCDEFGHIJKLMNOPQRSTUVWXYZ
1234567890 !@#?:;"*&

Foundry: ITC
Designer: Luis Siquot
Designer Nationality: Argentinian
Date: 2002

Luis Siquot designed ITC Arecibo for ITC in 2004. This typeface is a condensed display sans serif with a hairline shadow and high crossbars.

Available in one weight and two styles, Arecibo has uppercase and small caps only, and achieves an Art Deco feel.

ITC Batak

ABCDEFGHIJKLMNOPQRSTUVWXYZ
abcdefghijklmnopqrstuvwxyz
1234567890 !@#?:;"*&

Foundry: ITC
Designer: Charles Nix
Designer Nationality: American
Date: 2002

Charles Nix, US type designer and type director at Monotype, created ITC Batak in 2002 based on hand-painted lettering he saw in Northern Sumatra.

With the skeleton of a grotesque and hexagonal serifs, Batak is distinctive and comes in condensed and bold condensed versions.

ITC Belter

ABCDEFGHIJKLMNOPQRSTUVWXYZ
abcdefghijklmnopqrstuvwxyz
1234567890 !@#?:;"*&

Foundry: ITC
Designer: Andreu Balius
Designer Nationality: Spanish
Date: 1996

Barcelona-based Andreu Balius designed Belter in 1996. It is a distinctive, monoline display typeface with crosses at the ends of many of its strokes,

which act almost like serifs. It is available in two styles, Regular and Mega Outline, and the latter has dual outer keylines.

ITC Bottleneck

ABCDEFGHIJKLMNOPQRSTUVWXYZ
abcdefghijklmnopqrstuvwxyz
1234567890 !@#?:;"*&

Foundry: ITC
Designer: Tony Wenman
Designer Nationality: British
Date: 1972

ITC Bottleneck is a retro decorative serif that is characteristic of the groovy mood of the early 1970s. It has very thick and heavy lower serifs, which recall the platform shoes that were fashionable at the time. Bottleneck was also available as dry-transfer lettering from Letraset.

ITC Digital Woodcuts

ABCDEFGHIJKLMNOPQRSTUVWXYZ
1234567890 !@#?:;"*&

Foundry: ITC
Designer: Timothy Donaldson
Designer Nationality: British
Date: 1995

As its name implies, Timothy Donaldson's ITC Digital Woodcuts is inspired by traditional printing techniques but recreated on a computer. It is all caps and each letter is reversed out of a black, rough-edged square. An alternate with the squares outlined and black letters is also included.

ITC Einhorn

ABCDEFGHIJKLMNOPQRSTUVWXYZ
abcdefghijklmnopqrstuvwxyz
1234567890 !@#?:;"*&

Foundry: ITC
Designer: Alan Meeks
Designer Nationality: British
Date: 1980

Available in a single weight, which is very bold, ITC Einhorn is a distinctive semi-serif font by British designer Alan Meek. Many of its capital letters and all of the lowercase alphabet feature small upward flicks at their base which join them to the next letter, much like a connecting script.

ITC Florinda

ABCDEFGHIJKLMNOPQRSTUVWXYZ
ABCDEFGHIJKLMNOPQRSTUVWXYZ
1234567890 !@#?:;"*&

Foundry: ITC
Designer: Luis Siquot
Designer Nationality: Argentinian
Date: 1997

An interesting display face, Florinda by Luis Siquot has the basic form of an uppercase grotesque sans serif; however, it features rounded, ornamental knobs that jut out of the letters horizontally and vertically. It is available in one heavy weight, and has caps and small caps only.

ITC Jellybaby

ABCDEFGHIJKLMNOPQRSTUVWXYZ
abcdefghijklmnopqrstuvwxyz
1234567890 !@#?:;"*&

Foundry: ITC
Designer: Timothy Donaldson
Designer Nationality: British
Date: 1997

Available in a single style, and published in 1997, Timothy Donaldson's ITC Jellybaby is a curvy, fun, retro display sans serif with oval-shaped counters that are not placed centrally in the letters and ball terminals. It began life as a pumped-up version of another Donaldson font, Pink, published in 2001.

ITC Liverpool

ABCDEFGHIJKLMNOPQRSTUVWXYZ
abcdefghijklmnopqrstuvwxyz
1234567890 !@#?:;"*&

Foundry: ITC
Designer: Kevin Bailey
Designer Nationality: American
Date: 1999

ITC Liverpool, created by US typeface designer Kevin Bailey for the International Typeface Corporation (ITC) in 1999, is a bulbous, bold, display sans serif that brings to mind exuberant type from the 1960s and 1970s. It has wide letters and undersized counters that are not centrally placed.

ITC Magnifico

ABCDEFGHIJKLMNOPQ
RSTUVWXYZ
1234567890 !@#?:;"*&

Foundry: ITC
Designer: Akira Kobayashi
Designer Nationality: Japanese
Date: 1999

Inspired by 19th-century display types, Magnifico is an all-caps italic slab serif with built-in outlines and shadows. It comes in two styles: Daytime with white type and black shadows, and Nighttime with black type and white shadows. Akira Kobayashi was a freelance type designer in Japan at the time.

ITC Masquerade

ABCDEFGHIJKLMNOPQRSTUVWXYZ
ABCDEFGHIJKLMNOPQRSTUVWXYZ
1234567890 !@#?:;"*&

Foundry: ITC
Designer: Martin Wait
Designer Nationality: British
Date: 2009

Designed by Martin Wait, a British designer who worked in font production at Letraset for twenty-five years, ITC Masquerade is an all-caps, highly ornamented serif display face with a double outline and drop shadows. Included in the font are decorative capitals with elaborate curlicues.

ITC Minska

ΛBCƊEFGHIJKLMNOPQRSTUUVIXYZ
ɑBCƊEFGHIJKLMNOPQRSTUVѱXYŽ
1234567890 !@⚕?:;"*ʊ

ITC Minska is a highly distinctive and unconventional typeface that blends upper and lowercase as well as curves and angles. Although legible, many of its characters do not conform to expected archetypes. It is available in three weights: Light, Medium and Bold, without italics.

Foundry: ITC
Designer: Carl Crossgrove
Designer Nationality: American
Date: 1996

ITC Motter Sparta

ABCƊEFGHIJKLMNOPQRSTUVWXYZ
abcdefghijklmnopqrstuvwxyz
1234567890 !@#?:;"*&

Austrian type designer Othmar Motter created ITC Motter Sparta in 1997. It is a heavy sans serif that mixes dynamic curves, points and sharp angles in a unique way. The most distinctive characters are the pointy 'o' and the 'a', which is almost an upside-down 'v' but still reads as an 'a'.

Foundry: ITC
Designer: Othmar Motter
Designer Nationality: Austrian
Date: 1997

ITC Pioneer

ABCDEFGHIJKLMNOPQRSTUVWXYZ
1234567890 !@#?:;"*&

Pioneer is one of a number of fonts designed for ITC by Ronne Bonder and Tom Carnase in 1970. It is an experimental, uppercase sans serif with angular forms, no curves and a drop shadow. It was used on the film poster for *Shaft* (1971), the blaxploitation film with a soundtrack composed by Isaac Hayes.

Foundry: ITC
Designer: Ronne Bonder / Tom Carnase
Designer Nationality: American
Date: 1970

ITC Snap

ABCDEFGHIJKLMNOPQRSTUVWXY
abcdefghijklmnopqrstuvwxyz
1234567890 !@#?:;"*&

ITC Snap is the work of US designer David Sagorski, who created fonts for Letraset and the International Typeface Corporation (ITC) after changing his career as a worker in the oil industry. It is a curvy, bulbous font with small sharp serifs and a jaunty, humorous feel that evokes cartoons.

Foundry: ITC
Designer: David Sagorski
Designer Nationality: American
Date: 1995

ITC Talking Drum

ABCDEFGHIJKLMNOPQRStUVWXYZ
abcdefghijklmnopqrstuvwxyz
1234567890 !@#?:;"*G

Foundry: ITC
Designer: Timothy Donaldson
Designer Nationality: British
Date: 1999

ITC Talking Drum is a distinctive, angular, heavy sans-serif font. Many elements – such as the crossbars of 'F' and 'H', the tail of 'Q' and the arm of 'r' – are constructed from a single square diamond. It reappears in unexpected places, such as the bottom of the 'Y' and 'L'.

ITC Willow

ABCDEFGHIJKLMNOPQRSTUVWXYZ
1234567890 !@#?:;"*&

Foundry: ITC
Designer: Tony Forster
Designer Nationality: British
Date: 1990

ITC Willow was designed by Tony Forster, a British lettering artist and designer who was based near Manchester and taught at Bolton College of Art. It is a condensed display sans serif inspired by Charles Rennie Mackintosh's style and features many decorative alternates and ligatures.

ITC Ziggy

ABCDEFGHIJKLMNOPQRSTUVWXYZ
abcdefghijklmnopqrstuvwxyz
1234567890 !@#?:;"*&

Foundry: ITC
Designer: Bob Alonso
Designer Nationality: American
Date: 1997

Ziggy began as doodles made by Bob Alonso during the 1970s. When he later rediscovered some of these sketches, he was inspired to revive it as a full font. ITC Ziggy is a wild and curly display serif with bottom-heavy letters which is typical of the groovy, 1970s era in type design.

ITC Zinzinnati

ABCDEFGHIJKLMNOPQRSTUVWX
abcdefghijklmnopqrstuvwxyz
1234567890 !@#?:;"*&

Foundry: ITC
Designer: Schriftguss Foundry / Nick Curtis
Designer Nationality: American
Date: 1924 / 2002

Nick Curtis based Zinzinnati on Ohio, an old German typeface released by the Schriftguss Foundry in Dresden in 1924. Ohio was a playful, curvy serif typical of the *Plakatstil* (poster style) type popular in Germany at the time. Curtis cleaned up its rough edges but kept Ohio's original spirit.

ITC Zipper

ABCDEFGHIJKLMNOPQRSTUVWXYZ
abcdefghijklmnopqrstuvwxyz
1234567890 !@#?:;"*&

Foundry: ITC
Designer: Phillip Kelly
Designer Nationality: British
Date: 1970

ITC Zipper, designed by Letraset staff member Phillip Kelly, is a distinctive and heavy reverse-contrast condensed sans-serif font available in a single weight. It has very wide horizontal strokes and thin verticals. It was used on the cover of David Bowie's album *Hunky Dory* (1971).

JMC Engraver

ABCDEFGHIJKLMNOPQRSTUVWXYZ
abcdefghijklmnopqrstuvwxyz
1234567890 !@#?:;"*&

Foundry: Monotype
Designer: Terrance Weinzierl
Designer Nationality: American
Date: 2012

JMC Engraver was designed by Terrance Weinzierl, a US type designer and lettering artist who has worked at Monotype since 2008. It is a distinctive monoline sans serif that features an abundance of curls and kinks. It comes in a single style with upper and lowercases.

Jokerman

ABCDEFGHIJKLMNOPQRSTUVWXYZ
abcdefghijklmnopqrstuvwxyz
1234567890 !@#?:;"*&

Foundry: ITC
Designer: Andrew Smith
Designer Nationality: British
Date: 1995

Jokerman is a jaunty decorative font, ornamented with dots, dashes and curls that stick out of its letters, float nearby, or are inlaid as negative space. It was once highly popular thanks to inclusion in many Microsoft programs, notably as one of the fonts bundled with Office.

Kalligraphia

ABCDEFGHIJKLMNOPQRSTUVWXYZ
abcdefghijklmnopqrstuvwxyz
1234567890 !@#?:;"*&

Foundry: Berthold
Designer: Otto Weisert
Designer Nationality: German
Date: 1902

Kalligraphia was first cast in 1902 by Carl August Kloberg's eponymous type foundry that was acquired by Berthold in 1922. It is an exuberant, curvy Art Nouveau script in a single fairly heavy style. It was revived by Photo-Lettering in the 1960s when its style was suddenly back in fashion.

Karloff Negative

ABCDEFGHIJKLMNOPQRSTUVWXYZ
abcdefghijklmnopqrstuvwxyz
1234567890 !@#?:;"'*&

Foundry: Typotheque
Designer: Peter Biľak / Pieter van Rosmalen / Nikola Djurek
Designer Nationality: Slovakian / Dutch / Croatian
Date: 2015

The Karloff family explores extreme contrast. It was conceived by Peter Biľak but designed by Pieter van Rosmalen with Nikola Djurek. Karloff Negative is a reverse-contrast serif inspired by the Italian styles of the 19th century which pioneered the switching of contrast, designed to attract readers' attention.

Kelso

ABCDEFGHIJKLMNOPQRSTUVWXYZ
abcdefghijklmnopqrstuvwxyz
1234567890 !@#?:;"'*&

Foundry: Talbot Type
Designer: Adrian Talbot
Designer Nationality: British
Date: 2014

Kelso is a distinctive geometric sans serif where each letter is made from a continuous monoline, giving an outlined look. It was designed by British designer Adrian Talbot in 2014 and released by his independent foundry Talbot Type. Kelso comes in three weights: Light, Regular and Bold.

Kino

ABCDEFGHIJKLMNOPQRSTUVWXYZ
abcdefghijklmnopqrstuvwxyz
1234567890 !@#?:;"'*&

Foundry: Monotype
Designer: Martin Dovey
Designer Nationality: British
Date: 1930

Kino is an angular display sans serif with completely flat tops and bottoms that look to have been cleanly cut, leaving behind triangles in places such as the arm of the 'r'. Triangles are also found as the crossbars of 'A', 'E' and 'H', and as the full point. The tittles are diamond shaped.

La Pontaise Poster

ABCDEFGHIJKLMNOPQRSTUVWXYZ
abcdefghijklmnopqrstuvwxyz
1234567890 !@#?:;"'*&

Foundry: Or Type
Designer: Mads Freund Brunse
Designer Nationality: Danish
Date: 2013

La Pontaise Poster is a version of La Pontaise, a grotesque sans by Or Type (see p. 498), but with extreme contrast and more exaggerated forms. Danish designer Mads Freund Brunse has been the head of the typography design programme at La Cambre art school in Brussels since 2017.

Lazybones

ABCDEFGHIJKLMNOPQRSTUVWXYZ
abcdefghijklmnopqrstuvwxyz
1234567890 !@#?:;"*&

Foundry: URW
Designer: Letraset Design Studio
Date: 1972

Designed in 1972 at the Letraset design studio, and also available from ITC, Lazybones is a chunky, curvy and slightly inclined heavy display face with many exuberant swashed capitals, small counters and an Art Nouveau feel, which became popular during the early 1970s.

LCD

ABCDEFGHIJKLMNOPQRSTUVWXYZ
1234567890!@#?:;"*&

Foundry: Letraset
Designer: Alan Birch
Designer Nationality: British
Date: 1981

An LCD (liquid crystal display) is a type of electronic screen and was first used on items such as digital watches and clock radios during the 1970s. These basic LCD screens led to a particular style of type, which British designer Alan Birch's LCD font replicates. It is an italic, all-caps stencil sans serif.

Linotype Albafire

ABCDEFGHIJKLMNOPQRSTUVWXYZ
abcdefghijklmnopqrstuvwxyz
1234567890 !@#?:;"*&

Foundry: Linotype
Designer: Hans-Jürgen Ellenberger
Designer Nationality: German
Date: 2002

Hans-Jürgen Ellenberger's Albafire is part of Linotype's Alba family, which also includes Albatross and Albawing, all from 2002. It is a decorative sans serif that features small jagged flame shapes sticking out of the right side of each letter like speed-lines, giving it a flaming, dynamic feel.

Linotype Albatross

ABCDEFGHIJKLMNOPQRSTUVWXYZ
abcdefghijklmnopqrstuvwxyz
1234567890 !@#?:;"*&

Foundry: Linotype
Designer: Hans-Jürgen Ellenberger
Designer Nationality: German
Date: 2002

Part of Linotype's Alba family, which also includes Albafire and Albawing, Albatross by German designer Hans-Jürgen Ellenberger is a decorative display font. Whereas Albafire has a standard base with flames jutting out, Albatross is made entirely from right-pointing flame shapes.

Linotype Alphabat

ABCDEFGHIJKLMNOPQRSTUVWXYZ
1234567890 !?;;"&

Foundry: Linotype
Designer: Jan Tomás
Designer Nationality: Czech
Date: 1999

The Czech designer Jan Tomás, a graduate of the University of the Arts in Berlin's Visual Communication course, created Linotype Alphabat, a strange all-caps font that features distinctive batwing shapes and double counters. Many letters look doubled as if seen cross-eyed.

Linotype Atomatic

ABCDEFGHIJKLMNOPQRSTUVW
abcdefghijklmnopqrstuvwxyz
1234567890 !@#?:;"*¢

Foundry: Linotype
Designer: Johannes Plass
Designer Nationality: German
Date: 1997

Johannes Plass, a graduate of the Muthesius University of Fine Arts and Design in Kiel, Germany, designed Linotype Atomatic, a winner of the Linotype International Digital Type Design Contest. It comes in a single, wide and bold style and leans to the right, giving a sense of dynamism and speed.

Linotype Barock

ABCDEFGHIJKLMNOPQRSTUVWXYZ
abcdefghijklmnopqrstuvwxyz
1234567890 !@#?:;"*&

Foundry: Linotype
Designer: Jean-Jacques Tachdjian
Designer Nationality: French
Date: 1999

Jean-Jacques Tachdjian's Barock is an experimental, postmodern font that challenges legibility. All of its characters are constructed from multiple versions of the same letter overlapping each other, some of which are smaller or reversed, or cause shapes to cut out of the black.

Linotype BlackWhite

Foundry: Linotype
Designer: Ferdinay Duman
Designer Nationality: German
Date: 1989

Linotype BlackWhite, the work of Ferdinay Duman, is an all-caps display sans in five styles. Its regular cut has no counters, a solid black lower half and an outline. Other styles include entirely solid and outlined versions and Laser, which has a horizontal break in every capital.

Linotype Dharma

ABCDEFGHIJKLMNOPQRSTUD
abcdefghijklmnopqrstuvwxyz
1234567890 !@#?:;"*&

Foundry: Linotype
Designer: Gerd Sebastian Jakob /
Joerg Ewald Meissner
Designer Nationality: German
Date: 1997

Linotype Dharma is a decorative display font, designed in a stand-alone Regular weight. The character set includes multiple ornamental details, such as the angled slashes that replace standard dots, the wedged serifs and the sicklelike curves found on vertical strokes.

Linotype Flamingo

ABCDEFGHIJKLMNOPQRSTUVWXYZ
abcdefghijklmnopqrstuvwxyz
1234567890 !@#?:;"*&

Foundry: Linotype
Designer: Michael Leonhard
Designer Nationality: German
Date: 1999

Linotype Flamingo is a decorative display face that tests the boundaries of reductionism. German font designer Michael Leonhard removed elements from each character, such as a curve, stroke ending or joint, thus forcing the reader to fill in the gaps for full legibility.

Linotype Funny Bones

ABCDEFGHIJKLMNOPQRSTUVWXYZ
abcdefghijklmnopqrstuvwxyz
1234567890 !@#?:;"*&

Foundry: Linotype
Designer: Ingo Preuss
Designer Nationality: German
Date: 1997

Linotype Funny Bones is a decorative display face, produced in two distinct weights. The first, Linotype Funny Bones One, comprises a combination of eccentric all-capital letterforms. Alternatively, Linotype Funny Bones Two contains restrained, condensed lowercase characters.

Linotype Gotharda

ABCDEFGHIJKLMNOPQRSTUVWXYZ
abcdefghijklmnopqrstuvwxyz
1234567890 !@#?:;"*et

Foundry: Linotype
Designer: Milo Dominik Ivir
Designer Nationality: Croatian
Date: 1997

Linotype Gotharda is a display font that combines the features of both gothic and sans-serif type styles. The bullish characters exhibit the narrow width and bulky strokes, typical of gothic faces, alongside the clarity, standardization and economy of sans-serif designs.

Linotype Konflikt

ABCDEFGHIJKLMNOPQRSTUVWXYZ
abcdefghijklmnopqrstuvwxyz
1234567890 !@#?:;"'&*

Foundry: Linotype
Designer: Stefan Pott
Designer Nationality: German
Date: 1997

Linotype Konflikt is a decorative display face that addresses the aesthetic clash between print and digital type design. To bridge the gap, Linotype Konflikt blends calligraphic strokes, reminiscent of early print faces, and the pixellated forms of the computer screen.

Linotype Labyrinth

ABCDEFGHIJKLMNOPQRSTUVWXYZ
ABCDEFGHIJKLMNOPQRSTUVWXYZ
1234567890

Foundry: Linotype
Designer: Frank Marciuliano
Designer Nationality: American
Date: 2002

Linotype Labyrinth is a display face designed in a single style and is modelled on the complex blueprint of a maze. The characters share a single height, with no ascenders or descenders, and consist of concentric shapes that feature a single gap, or gateway, in their outer stroke.

Linotype Lindy

ABCDEFGHIJKLMNOPQRSTUVWXYZ
abcdefghijklmnopqrstuvwxyz
1234567890 !@#?;,"'*&

Foundry: Linotype
Designer: Frank Marciuliano
Designer Nationality: American
Date: 1997

Frank Marciuliano's Linotype Lindy is a decorative display face designed for use at headline sizes, which is reminiscent of early digital lettering. The characters feature high-contrast, boxy outer strokes, and these in turn define the inner strokes through their creation of negative space.

Linotype MhaiThaipe

ABCDEFGHIJKLMNOPQRSTUVWXYZ
abcdefghijklmnopqrstuvwxyz
1234567890 !@#?:;"'*&

Foundry: Linotype
Designer: Markus Remscheid
Designer Nationality: German
Date: 1997

Markus Remscheid's Linotype MhaiThaipe is a display font inspired by Arabic and Sanskrit letterforms. Features, such as the small circles that embellish the terminals and the calligraphic stroke styles, provide the design with a decorative approach similar to that of non-Latin alphabets.

Lost & Foundry

FS Berwick
ABCDEFGHIJKLMNOPQRSTUVWXYZ
1234567890 !@#?:;"*&

FS Cattle
ABCDEFGHIJKLMNOPQRSTUVWXYZ
1234567890 !@#?:;"*&

FS Century
ABCDEFGHIJKLMNOPQRSTUVWXYZ
1234567890 !@#?:;"*&

FS Charity
ABCDEFGHIJKLMNOPQRSTUVWXYZ
ABCDŁF GHIJKLMNOPQRSTUVWXYZ
1234567890 !@#?:;"*&

FS Malborough
ABCDEFGHIJKLMNOPQRSTUVWXYZ
1234567890 !@#?:;"*&

FS Portland
ABCDEFGHIJKLMNOPQRSTUVWXYZ
1234567890 !@#?:;"&*

FS St James
ABCDEFGHIJKLMNOPQRSTUVWXYZ
ABCDEFGHIJKLMNOPQRSTUVWXYZ
1234567890 !@#?:;"*&

Lost & Foundry is a unique collection of seven typefaces that was created based on historic signage found within London's Soho, an area that is slowly disappearing because of the constant development of the city. London-based foundry Fontsmith (see p. 272) partnered with the House of St Barnabas, a private members' club in Soho Square to launch this innovative project in an effort to save the visual history of an area that is being redeveloped. Each sale of the fonts as a family pack comes with a month's membership to the club.

In addition, the project is helping break the cycle of homelessness in London. The House also works to tackle this social issue as charity, and its efforts have helped many individuals get off the streets. All the proceeds of the sale of the font family packs go towards the charity.

Each typeface has a remarkable story concerning its original source and is a document of times long past. Fontsmith's efforts have ensured that these characteristic and historical types are preserved for future use and admiration.

Foundry: Fontsmith
Designer: Jason Smith / Stuart de Rozario / Pedro Arilla
Designer Nationality: British / British / Spanish
Date: 2018

Opposite. Samples of the Lost & Foundry collection in use. A sign in an archway on Portland Mews (centre) served as the inspiration for FS Cattle.

LOST&FOUNDRY

TYPEFACES INSPIRED BY THE DISAPPEARING **SIGNS OF SOHO**

ABCDEFGHIJK LOST&FO-
UNDRYMARLBOROUGH
NOPQRSTUVWXYZ?£!

TWENTIE
CENTUR
– HOUSE – SP
*CHISELL
†INSPIRE

R.N.CATTLE & S
PORTLAND WO

PORTLA
ESTMINS
*LONDO
D'ARB
STREE

ABCHARITYDE
FGHIJKLOST&
FOUNDRYMNO
PQRSTUVWX
YZ123456789»

EXPRES
QUIRK
REDISCOV
¡BERW
†STRE

— 1864
– & 2018
*St JAMES
SOHO CL
ONDONES

Linotype Mindline

Foundry: Linotype
Designer: Critzla
Designer Nationality: German
Date: 1997

Linotype Mindline was inspired by the aesthetics of 1920s advertising typefaces and Constructivist posters. It is a geometric display font, designed in two styles, Inside and Outside. The characters are comprised of rectangular frames, which each house a thin, inconspicuous letterform.

Linotype Minos

Foundry: Linotype
Designer: Christian Goetz
Designer Nationality: Swiss
Date: 1997

Linotype Minos is a decorative display font inspired by early Greek scripts and named after Crete's legendary King Minos. The design is informed by typical scripts found in the ornamental borders around the characters that embellished Cretan palaces such as Knossos, Phaistos and Malia.

Linotype Paint It

Foundry: Linotype
Designer: Jochen Schuss
Designer Nationality: German
Date: 1997

Linotype Paint It is a playful face, designed in capitals and two styles. In the Empty style, the characters, which are at the centre of a labyrinthine block, are visible only through dots on each stroke, whereas the letters in the Black style are discernible by colour.

Linotype Tiger

Foundry: Linotype
Designer: Gerd Sebastian Jakob / Joerg Ewald Meissner
Designer Nationality: German
Date: 1997

Linotype Tiger is a display face designed entirely without curves, leaving the splintered strokes to meet at sharp angles. The font family consists of five weights, which range from Brave One, a heavy, outlined version, to Tame, comprised of light, single-stroke characters.

Logan

ABCDEFGHIJKLMNOPQRSTUVWXYZ
abcdefghijklmnopqrstuvwxyz
1234567890 !@#?:;"*&

Foundry: Monotype
Designer: Paul Prue
Designer Nationality: British
Date: 1994

Logan is a decorative display face designed to imitate the high-tech aesthetic of computing. The letterforms, released in a single Regular style, are high in contrast and squared in shape, while the strokes are reminiscent of the dynamic patterns found on computer chips.

Luncheonette

ABCDEFGHIJKLMNOPQRSTUVWXYZ
abcdefghijklmnopqrstuvwxyz
1234567890 !@#?:;"*&

Foundry: Chank Co.
Designer: Chank Diesel
Designer Nationality: American
Date: 2002

Luncheonette is a retro display face and is a horizontally scaled version of Laundrette, both of which, along with Lambrettista, comprise Chank's Laundry Fonts family. Unlike its sibling fonts, Luncheonette features slim strokes and narrow spacing for tighter compositions.

Macbeth

ABCDEFGHIJKLMNOPQRSTUVWXYZ
abcdefghijklmnopqrstuvwxyz
1234567890 !@#?:;"*&

Foundry: Linotype
Designer: Linotype Design Studio
Designer Nationality: American
Date: 1994

Macbeth is a burly, condensed display font that was inspired by posters for *Frankenstein* (1931) and other early films. Like much cinematic poster design at the start of the 20th century, Macbeth combines the sloping strokes of Art Deco with the gothic features of early horror films.

MAD Sans

ABCDEFGHIJKLMNOPQRSTUVWXYZ
abcdefghijklmnopqrstuvwxyz
1234567890 !@#?:;"*&

Foundry: Colophon
Designer: Dries Wiewauters
Designer Nationality: Belgian
Date: 2017

MAD Sans was designed by Dries Wiewauters, a Belgian graduate of the Werkplaats Typografie, a Dutch university in Arnhem. It is a distinctive sans serif inspired by computer-aided design and constructed without curves. It comes in four weights – Light to Black – with italics.

MAD Serif

ABCDEFGHIJKLMNOPQRSTUVWXYZ
abcdefghijklmnopqrstuvwxyz
1234567890 !@#?.,""*&

Foundry: Colophon
Designer: Dries Wiewauters
Designer Nationality: Belgian
Date: 2017

MAD Serif is an angular typeface with no curves, drawn using a plotter machine. It comes in roman and italic, and two styles, Fill and Outline, in four weights. With each higher weight, the Outline style gains a line, starting with the monoline Light. MAD stands for Machine Aided Design.

Maximus BT

ABCDEFGHIJKLMNOPQRSTUVWXYZ
1234567890 !@#?::"*&

Foundry: Bitstream
Designer: Lou Scolnik
Designer Nationality: American
Date: 1973

Maximus BT is a decorative display face and is Bitstream's digital version of Lou Scolnik's Maximus font family, designed in 1973 for the Visual Graphics Corporation font foundry. The letterforms, produced in a single capitalized style, are characterized by their repeated horizontal strikethroughs.

Metropolitaines

ABCDEFGHIJKLMNOPQRSTUVWXYZ
1234567890 !@#?.;""*&

Foundry: URW
Designer: Hector Guimard
Designer Nationality: French
Date: c. 1905

Metropolitaines is a decorative display font that was produced by French architect Hector Guimard as signage lettering for Paris Métro stations, and then later published by German foundry URW. Like much of Guimard's architecture, Metropolitaines is designed in the Art Nouveau style.

Mexcellent

ABCDEFGHIJKLMNOPQRSTUVWXYZ
1234567890 !@#?::"☆&

Foundry: Typodermic
Designer: Ray Larabie
Nationality: Canadian
Date: 2000

Mexcellent is a trilinear display face inspired by Lance Wyman's font for the Mexico City 1968 Olympic Games. Unlike traditional font families, Mexcellent's supporting styles are available as layers, as opposed to weights, which enables users to draft their own combinations.

Modern 735

ABCDEFGHIJKLMNOPQRSTUVWXYZ
abcdefghijklmnopqrstuvwxyz
1234567890 !@#?:;"*&

Foundry: Bitstream
Designer: Robert Hunter Middleton
Designer Nationality: British
Date: 1936

Modern 735 is Bitstream's version of Bodoni Campanile, a typeface originally designed by Robert Hunter Middleton for the US foundry Ludlow in 1936. Modern 735 is a heavy and compressed interpretation of the high-contrast serif face Bodoni and is available in a single weight.

Modernique

ABCDEFGHIJKLMNOPQRSTUVWXYZ
abcdefghijklmnopqrstuvwxyz
1234567890 !@#?:;""*&

Foundry: American Type Founders
Designer: Morris Fuller Benton
Designer Nationality: American
Date: 1928

Modernique is a decorative display face designed in the style of the early 20th century. The letterforms feature extreme contrasts, with the verticals often much thicker than the horizontal strokes, while smaller details, such as the lowercase tittles, are distinctive in shape.

Monotype Gallia

ABCDEFGHIJKLMNOPQRSTUVWXYZ
1234567890 !@#?:;""*&

Foundry: Monotype
Designer: Wadsworth A. Parker
Designer Nationality: American
Date: 1927 / 1928

Monotype Gallia is a decorative display face, initially designed by Wadsworth A. Parker for the American Type Founders foundry in 1927, before being republished by Monotype in 1928. The characters, with their high-contrast strokes and curled terminals, are typical of 1920s Art Deco lettering.

Mustang Sally

ABCDEFGHIJKLMNOPQRSTUVWXYZ
abcdefghijklmnopqrstuvwxyz
1234567890 !@#?:;"*&

Foundry: Monotype
Designer: Bo Berndal
Designer Nationality: Swedish
Date: 2001

Mustang Sally is a decorative display face that combines strict strokes with liberal outlines. The characters, designed in a single style, feature several quirks, such as the striped interiors and tittles, alongside the expressive ear of the lowercase 'g'.

Netherlands Dirty Numbers

Foundry: Typo Graphic Design
Designer: Manuel Viergutz
Designer Nationality: German
Date: 2017

Netherlands Dirty Numbers is a display face inspired by numeric forms, such as house numbers and graffiti, found by the designer in the Netherlands.

These numbers provided the basis for an alphabet, including upper- and lowercase characters alongside more than forty decorative glyphs.

Newtron ICG

Foundry: Image Club Graphics
Date: 1995

Newtron is an outlined sans-serif display font comprising three distinct styles. While each design maintains a similar shape and character, certain features express their slight variation, such as the alternative letterforms of Newtron Alt, or the open joints of Newtron Open.

Novecento Carved

Foundry: Synthview
Designer: Jan Tonellato
Designer Nationality: Polish
Date: 2016

Novecento Carved is a decorative display face designed as a complementary layer for Synthview's font of 2013, Novecento Sans. The minimal letterforms, which imitate the shadowing of carved typography, were each manually adjusted to match the existing framework of Novecento Sans.

Nyxali

Foundry: Typodermic
Designer: Ray Larabie
Nationality: Canadian
Date: 2007

Nyxali is a decorative display font produced exclusively in capitals. Individual sans-serif characters sit centrally within a squared, textured oval which, along with the recess at the top of each outline, conjure a stamped design similar to that of military dog tags.

Odin

ABCDEFGHIJKLMNOPQRSTUVWXYZ
abcdefghijklmnopqrstuvwxyz
1234567890 !@#?:;"*&

Foundry: ITC
Designer: Bob Newman
Designer Nationality: British
Date: 1972

Odin is a decorative display face intended exclusively for headlines. Taking its name from the Norse god of war, Odin, the font features strong strokes and weighty serifs, while in the uppercase characters, the shoulder of each letterform is extended, forming a roof over the body.

Old Glory

ABCDEFGHIJKLMNOPQRSTUVWXYZ
ABCDEFGHIJKLMNOPQRSTUVWXYZ

Foundry: Monotype
Designer: Monotype Studio
Date: 2001

Old Glory is a display face designed in upper- and lowercase figures and inspired by the flag of the United States. Unlike conventional type designs, however, the cases of Old Glory are distinguished by pattern, the former being furnished with stars and the latter with stripes.

Owned

ABCDEFGHIJKLMNOPQRSTUVWXYZ
ABCDEFGHIJKLMNOPQRSTUVWXYZ
1234567890 !@#?:;"*&

Foundry: Typodermic
Designer: Ray Larabie
Nationality: Canadian
Date: 2005

Owned is a decorative display font designed to imitate the fast-paced scrawl of graffiti, hence its anti-authoritarian urgency. The font is comprised of two styles, Owned and Owned Concrete, the latter featuring a worn texture typical of fading spray paint.

Permanence

ABCDEFGHIJKLMNOPQRSTUVWXYZ
abcdefghijklmnopqrstuvwxyz
1234567890 !@#?:;"*&

Foundry: Typodermic
Designer: Ray Larabie
Nationality: Canadian
Date: 2012

Permanence is a decorative display font inspired by the lettering of S. Neil Fujita's cover for the book *Future Shock* (1970) written by sociologist and futurologist Alvin Toffler. The narrow shapes and liquid counters are, like Fujita's lettering, modelled on Stanley Davis's Amelia font designed in c. 1965.

Philco

ABCDEFGHIJKLMNOPQRSTUVWXYZ
1234567890 !@#?:¨*&

Foundry: Monotype
Designer: Jasper Manchipp
Designer Nationality: British
Date: 1994

The Philco decorative display face was inspired by the Art Deco movement. It comes in capitals only, in two distinct styles: Philco Regular is high in contrast with solid, angular strokes, while Philco Deco features a series of overlapping shapes that emphasize the font's geometry.

Phoebus

ABCDEFGHIJKLMNOPQRSTUVWXYZ
1234567890 !@#?:¨*&

Foundry: Linotype
Designer: Adrian Frutiger
Designer Nationality: Swiss
Date: 1953

Phoebus is a serif display face and one of the first designed by Adrian Frutiger (see p. 290) for the Deberny & Peignot foundry. Sharing its name with the Greek god of light, Phoebus is a shadowed font designed in italicized capitals, the style of which is emphasized by the sharp serifs.

Phosphor

ABCDEFGHIJKLMNOPQRSTUVWXYZ
1234567890 !@#?:;"*8

Foundry: Ludwig & Mayer
Designer: Jakob Erbar
Designer Nationality: German
Date: 1923

Phosphor is a display face based on the glowing letterforms of neon signage, which were first exhibited in 1910 at the Paris Motor Show. As with neon sign characters, Phosphor features a hairline stroke inside a bolder form, mimicking the appearance of the light tube inside its case.

Piercing

ABCDEFGHIJKLMNOPQRSTUVWXYZ
abcdefghijklmnopqrstuvwxyz
1234567890 !@#?:; *♪

Foundry: Linotype
Designer: Michael Parson
Designer Nationality: Swiss
Date: 2003

Michael Parson's Piercing is a decorative display face constructed of single weight strokes and ball terminals that imitate the basic forms of a piercing bar. The font features three weights, including Regular, Bold and an abstracted Code version with deconstructed letterforms.

Pierrot

ABCDEFGHIJKLMNOPQRSTUVWXYZ
abcdefghijklmnopqrstuvwxyz
1234567890 !@#?:;"*a

Foundry: Linotype
Designer: Günter Jäntsch
Designer Nationality: German
Date: 1973

Inspired by the fluid designs of the 1960s and early 1970s, Pierrot is a decorative display face conceived for editorial headlines and posters. Unlike similar fonts, Pierrot is notable for its precise outlines and sharp stroke endings. Designer Günter Jäntsch also worked as an illustrator and sculptor.

Plotter Wave

ABCDEFGHIJKLMNOPQRSTUVWXYZ
1234567890 \.@#?:;"×&

Foundry: Typotheque
Designer: Nikola Djurek / Gustavo Ferreira
Designer Nationality: Croatian / Brazilian
Date: 2017

Plotter Wave is a sans-serif display face inspired by the aesthetic of architectural drawings. The monolinear design utilizes a series of OpenType substitutions, specifically devised by designer Gustavo Ferreira, to order typed letterforms according to the angle of their sloping.

Porkshop

ABCDEFGHIJKLMNOPQRSTUVWXYZ
abcdefghijklmnopqrstuvwxyz
1234567890 !@#?:;"*&

Foundry: Chank Co.
Designer: Chank Diesel
Designer Nationality: American
Date: 2011

First designed in 1997, and expanded in 2011 to include Bold and Italic styles, Porkshop is a serif display face inspired by a vintage 'Pork Shop' sign in New York. Mimicking a hand-rendered style, the letterforms combine upper- and lowercase letters into a single character set.

Promdate

ABCDEFGHIJKLMNOPQRSTUVWXYZ
ABCDEFGHIJKLMNOPQRSTUVWXYZ
1234567890 !@&?:;"*&

Foundry: Lunchbox
Designer: Adam Roe
Designer Nationality: American
Date: 1993

Promdate is a decorative display font designed in two styles, including a slightly heightened Tall version. The capitalized letterforms feature flat bases, even in the circular characters, and boast sharp angles in both the strokes and the serifs. The font's name evokes Americana, as does its styling.

Quartz

ABCDEFGHIJKLMNOPQRSTUVWXYZ
1234567890 !@#?:;"*&

Foundry: Letraset
Designer: Letraset Design Studio
Designer Nationality: British
Date: 1970

Quartz is a capitalized typeface based on the digital displays that began to proliferate in the 1960s and 1970s. The electronic letterforms, like those found on the faces of digital clocks, feature segmented strokes that imitate the construction of liquid-crystal display lettering.

Ragtime

ABCDEFGHIJKLMNOPQRSTUVWXYZ
1234567890 !?:;"*&

Foundry: ITC
Designer: Alan Meeks
Designer Nationality: British
Date: 1987

Ragtime is a sans-serif display face designed in capitals for elegant yet eccentric headline use. Featuring both subtle shifts in stroke weight, seen particularly in the joints, and fine line shadowing, the letterforms are reminiscent of magazine headline styles from the 1940s.

Refracta

ABCDEFGHIJKLMNOPQRSTUVWXYZ
1234567890 !?:;"*&

Foundry: ITC
Designer: Martin Wait
Designer Nationality: British
Date: 1988

Designed in all caps, Refracta is a condensed display face intended for a variety of uses, from posters to editorials. The italicized sans-serif characters, whose hairline strokes initially seem rather timid, are emboldened by a heavy shadow that adds an aesthetic authority.

Retro Bold

ABCDEFGHIJKLMNOPQRSTUVWXYZ
1234567890 !?:;"*&

Foundry: Letraset
Designer: Colin Brignall / Andrew Smith
Designer Nationality: British
Date: 1992

The Retro family, an uppercase slab serif in two weights – Bold and Bold Condensed – was designed for Letraset by Colin Brignall and Andrew Smith in 1992. As its name implies, it was inspired by old design movements, such as Constructivism, the Bauhaus, Art Deco and Streamline.

Rundfunk

ABCDEFGHIJKLMNOPQRSTUVWXYZ

abcdefghijklmnopqrstuvwxyz

1234567890 !?.:;”*&

Foundry: Berthold
Designer: Adolf Behrmann
Designer Nationality: Latvian
Date: 1928

Rundfunk was designed for the Berthold foundry in 1928 by Latvian-born designer Adolf Behrmann. It is a distinctive, heavy sans serif with a low x-height, short descenders and large, exaggerated ascenders. It was revived by Letraset in 1987 and comes in a single bold, roman style.

Salut

ABCDEFGHIJKLMNOPQRSTUVWXYZ

abcdefghijklmnopqrstuvwxyz

1234567890 !@#?:;”*&

Foundry: Klingspor
Designer: Heinrich Johannes Maehler
Designer Nationality: German
Date: 1931

Released by the Offenbach-based foundry Klingspor in 1931, Heinrich Johannes Maehler's Salut is an upright, calligraphic font that connects in a script-style. It is almost a sans serif but for a few of the capitals that have slabs, and comes in a single heavy style.

Samba

ABCDEFGHIJKLMNOPQRSTUVWXYZ

ABCDEFGHIJKLMNOPQRSTUVWXYZ

1234567890 !@#?:;”*&

Foundry: Linotype
Designer: Tony de Marco / Caio de Marco
Designer Nationality: Brazilian
Date: 2003

Samba comes in three styles: Regular, Expert and Bold. It was designed by brothers Tony and Caio de Marco and inspired by the lettering of José Carlos de Brito e Cunha, a Brazilian illustrator working in the early 20th century. Samba is an exuberant, curly all-caps face with a monolinear regular cut.

Saphir

ABCDEFGHIJKLMNOPQRST

UVWXYZ

1234567890 !@#?:;”*&

Foundry: Stempel
Designer: Hermann Zapf
Designer Nationality: German
Date: 1952

Saphir, known as Sapphire in English-speaking countries, is an all-caps display serif with high-contrast and decorative patterns, made from a central diamond between flourishes, reversed out of the black. It was created by the prolific German designer Hermann Zapf (see p. 574).

Sarcophagus

ABCDEFGHIJKLMNOPQRSTUVWXYZ
abcdefghijklmnopqrstuvwxyz
1234567890 !@#?;:"*&

Foundry: T-26
Designer: Alexander McCracken
Designer Nationality: American
Date: 2004

Sarcophagus was designed by Alexander McCracken for the T-26 foundry and named after decorative stone coffins used in ancient Egypt. It is an intricate, Blackletter-inspired typeface with a spiky, gothic feel. It comes in Regular and Bold weights and has a monolinear construction.

Shaman

ABCDEFGHIJKLMNOPQRSTUVWXYZ
1234567890 !?;:""*&

Foundry: Letraset
Designer: Phill Grimshaw
Designer Nationality: British
Date: 1994

The work of British designer Phill Grimshaw, and released by Letraset and ITC, Shaman is an all-caps display font with a jagged inline. Grimshaw was aiming for a primitive feel, and the font also includes decorative borders and illustrative dingbats inspired by cave paintings.

Sharquefin

ABCDEFGHIJKLMNOPQRSTUVWXYZ
abcdefghijklmnopqrstuvwxyz
1234567890 !@#?;:"*&

Foundry: Linotype
Designer: Gary Tennant
Designer Nationality: British
Date: 2004

Sharquefin, by British type designer Gary Tennant, is one of two fonts he designed for Linotype. It is a postmodern display typeface that comes in two styles, Regular and Oblique. It features shapes that stick out of most of the letters like a shark's fin and was designed for fun use.

Shatter

ABCDEFGHIJKLMNOPQRSTUVWXYZ
abcdefghijklmnopqrstuvwxyz
1234567890 !?;:""*&

Foundry: Letraset
Designer: Vic Carless
Designer Nationality: British
Date: 1973

Shatter font was one of twenty winners of an international competition held by Letraset in 1973 and judged by leading designers Herb Lubalin (see p. 62), Derek Birdsall, Roger Excoffon, Colin Forbes, Armin Hofmann and Marcello Minale. Shatter is a diagonally fractured, bold sans serif.

Siesta

ABCDEFGHIJKLMNOPQRSTUVWXYZ
abcdefghijklmnopqrstuvwxyz
1234567890 !@#?:;"*&

Foundry: Aerotype
Designer: Steve Miggas
Designer Nationality: American
Date: 1995

US type designer Steve Miggas created Siesta for Aerotype in 1995. It is a single-style display font that is bold and inspired by lettering made using traditional printing techniques such as woodcut and linocut. It has upper- and lowercase letters, and rough, imperfect edges.

Sinah

ABCDEFGHIJKLMNOPQRSTUV
abcdefghijklmnopqrstuvwxyz
1234567890 !@#?:;"*&

Foundry: Linotype
Designer: Peter Huschka
Designer Nationality: German
Date: 1994

A rounded ornamental font, created by artist Peter Huschka, Sinah has an Asian feel. Many of its strokes end in teardrop forms and none of its characters share a common baseline, meaning that it should be used with generous line spacing, and at sizes of 12 point or above.

Slipstream

ABCDEFGHIJKLMNOPQRSTUVWXYZ
1234567890 !?:;"*&

Foundry: Letraset
Designer: Letraset Type Studio
Designer Nationality: British
Date: 1985

Slipstream, developed in-house by the Letraset Type Studio, is based on an italic sans serif. As the name suggests, its horizontal lines look like streaks left behind as the letters speed off to the right of the page. Characters can be slightly overlapped without losing the impression of movement.

Sprint

ABCDEFGHIJKLMNOPQRSTUVWXYZ
abcdefghijklmnopqrstuvwxyz
1234567890 !@#?:;"*&

Foundry: VGC
Designer: Aldo Novarese
Designer Nationality: Italian
Date: 1974

A stylized forward-leaning display face created by the noted Italian type designer Aldo Novarese, Sprint was also the inspiration for the fonts Starlet and Star, both released in 2007 by Gestalten and created by the Berlin-based designer and VJ (video jockey) Critzla.

Syllogon

ABCDEFGHIJKLMNOPQRSTUVWXYZ
abcdefghijklmnopqrstuvwxyz
1234567890 !@#?:;"*&

Foundry: Image Club Graphics
Designer: Patricia Lillie
Designer Nationality: American
Date: 1995

Syllogon is just one of the many mainly display faces created by the prolific Ohio-based writer and type designer Patricia Lillie. This quirky, rectangular-based design is available in two weights: the very angular Syllogon Hard, and Syllogon Soft, which has more curves.

Syrup

abcdefghijklmnopqrstuvwxyz
1234567890 !@#?:;"*&

Foundry: Neutura
Designer: Alexander McCracken
Designer Nationality: American
Date: 2001

Syrup was created by the founder of Neutura (see p. 472), the San Francisco-based designer Alexander McCracken. The typeface is available in a single weight. Its very stylized and playful display face is based on the semi-abstract forms generated by bending paperclips.

System X3

ABCDEFGHIJKLMNOPQRSTUVWXYZ
1234567890 !@#?:;"*&

Foundry: Monotype
Designer: Paul Prue
Designer Nationality: British
Date: 1994

System X3 is a highly futuristic display typeface designed for the Agfa Type Creative Alliance by Paul Prue. He also designed the similarly science-fiction influenced Eon Age, Galaxy, Run and Logan in the same year. System X3 is available in a single weight and as uppercase only.

Tangerine

ABCDEFGHIJKLMNOPQRST
UVWXYZ
1234567890 !@#?:;"*&

Foundry: ITC
Designer: Tomi Haaparanta
Designer Nationality: Finnish
Date: 2001

A bulbous display face with many top-heavy characters, Tangerine is one of a number of display faces created by Finnish designer Tomi Haaparant. He began designing typefaces in 1990, founded the Suomi Type Foundry in 2005 and teaches type design at the University of Industrial Arts in Helsinki.

Tango

ABCDEFGHIJKLMNOPQRSTUVWXYZ
abcdefghijklmnopqrstuvwxyz
1234567890 !@#?:;"'*&

Tango was probably inspired by Joe Caroff's logo for the movie *Last Tango in Paris* (1972). Tango's playful curves and swashes made it a popular choice for many dance music LP covers from the 1970s. URW released a version that includes a second set of unswashed caps and is called Theia.

Foundry: Letraset
Designer: Colin Brignall
Designer Nationality: British
Date: 1974

Tropica Script

ABCDEFGHIJKLMNOPQRSTUVWXYZ
abcdefghijklmnopqrstuvwxyz
1234567890 !?:;"'*&

Tropica Script, created by British type designer Vince Whitlock for his employers Letraset in 1988, is an outlined italic connecting-script available in a single style. The thick outlines give Tropica Script the look of a retro neon sign. It was published by both Letraset and ITC.

Foundry: Letraset
Designer: Vince Whitlock
Designer Nationality: British
Date: 1988

Tugboat Annie

ABCDEFGHIJKLMNOPQRSTUVWXYZ
abcdefghijklmnopqrstuvwxyz
1234567890 !@#?:;"'*&

Tugboat Annie, named after a black and white comedy film released in 1933, was designed by Nick Curtis in 2001. It comes in a single heavy style and is a high-contrast, wide serif font with many quirky features, such as the small vertical strokes that stick out of some letters.

Foundry: Monotype
Designer: Nick Curtis
Designer Nationality: American
Date: 2001

Umbra

ABCDEFGHIJKLMNOPQRSTUVWXYZ
1234567890 !@#?:;"'*&

Umbra, designed for Ludlow in 1935, is an uppercase only sans serif whose letters were taken from an earlier Robert Hunter Middleton typeface, Tempo (1930), and are defined only by the existence of a drop shadow. Berthold released a shadow-only sans serif also called Umbra the same year.

Foundry: Ludlow
Designer: Robert Hunter Middleton
Designer Nationality: British
Date: 1935

University Roman

ABCDEFGHIJKLMNOPQRSTUVWXYZ
abcdefghijklmnopqrstuvwxyz
1234567890 !@#?:;"*&

Foundry: Letraset
Designer: Mike Daines /
Phillip Kelly / Freda Sack
Designer Nationality: British
Date: 1972

University Roman, designed by Mike Daines in 1972, was inspired by Speedball-lettering. In 1984, it was updated by two Letraset staff; Phillip Kelly added swash alternatives and Freda Sack drew an italic. Available in regular, italic and bold, it has small sharp serifs and a large x-height.

Vegas

ABCDEFGHIJKLMNOPQRSTUVWXYZ
abcdefghijklmnopqrstuvwxyz
1234567890 !?:;"*&

Foundry: Letraset
Designer: David Quay
Designer Nationality: British
Date: 1984

By the British designer David Quay, co-founder with Freda Sack of The Foundry (see p. 284), Vegas is a decorative italic script with a 3D effect created by outlines, highlights and shadows. Vegas, which suits its glitzy name, is non-connecting but its lowercase can be tightly set.

Victorian

ABCDEFGHIJKLMNOPQRSTUVWXYZ
abcdefghijklmnopqrstuvwxyz
1234567890 !@#?:;"*&

Foundry: Letraset
Designer: Freda Sack /
Nick Belshaw
Designer Nationality: British
Date: 1976

Victorian, developed by Letraset designer Freda Sack and directed by Colin Brignall, is a decorative, ornate serif inspired by the 19th-century font Victoria, which was released by the German foundry Schriftgiesserei Flinsch. Nick Belshaw later added an Inline Shaded display version.

Warmer

ABCDEFGHIJKLMNOPQRSTUVWXYZ
ABCDEFGHIJKLMNOPQRSTUVWXYZ
1234567890 !@#?:;"*&

Foundry: Typodermic
Designer: Ray Larabie
Designer Nationality: Canadian
Date: 2010

Ray Larabie's Warmer is a chunky, counter-less, all uppercase, sans-serif display face, which looks like it was constructed by cutting paper with scissors. The family includes three fonts: a solid base version plus Check and Cross, both of which can be layered on top to give a plaid look.

Wavy Rounded BT

ABCDEFGHIJKLMNOPQRSTUVWXYZ
abcdefghijklmnopqrstuvwxyz
1234567890 !@#?:;"*&

Foundry: Bitstream
Designer: Hajime Kawakami
Designer Nationality: Japan
Date: 2004

Japanese industrial designer turned graphic designer Hajime Kawakami created Wavy Rounded BT for Bitstream in 2004. It is an eccentric, rounded sans serif available in a single, extra-bold weight. Many letters feature small notches or steps that gives the font its wavy appearance.

Westwood

ABCDEFGHIJKLMNOPQRSTUVWXYZ
abcdefghijklmnopqrstuvwxyz
1234567890 !?:;"*&

Foundry: Letraset
Designer: David Westwood
Designer Nationality: American
Date: 1991

David Westwood, a US designer based on the West Coast, designed this eponymous typeface for Letraset in 1991. Westwood is a bold, linocut-style display sans serif and is available in a single style. It features highlights and rough edges, which give it a hand-hewn look.

Whassis

ABCDEFGHIJKLMN©PQRSTUVWXYZ
abcdefghijklmn©pqrstuvwxyz
1234567890 !@#?:;"*&

Foundry: Image Club Graphics
Designer: Patricia Lillie
Designer Nationality: American
Date: 1995

Designed in 1995 for Image Club Graphics by Patricia Lillie, a US designer best known for her dingbat fonts, Whassis is a distinctive serif typeface with jagged edges and a spiral 'O' and 'o'. It comes in two styles, Calm and Frantic, and the latter has dots and triangles floating around glyphs.

Wind

Foundry: Typotheque
Designer: Hansje van Halem / Peter Biľak
Designer Nationality: Dutch / Slovakian
Date: 2017

Wind, by Amsterdam-based designer Hansje van Halem, is an experimental typeface created from lines facing the same direction. Its four styles – NE, NW, SE and SW – equate to the direction the strokes point. A variable font version allows the user total control over the angle the lines face.

BB-Bureau

The BB-Bureau foundry, based in Nantes, France, was established by the independent graphic and type designer Benoît Bodhuin, and offers an eclectic and highly innovative range of display types that challenge the conventions of legibility yet which are enthused with great wit and a dynamic playfulness.

Each is a typographical experiment, yet all have a high degree of mathematical integrity thanks to Bodhuin's passion for geometrical patterns developed from his earlier studies in mathematics at university. He was subsequently able to channel these interests in a new direction at design school. His typefaces are developed from a range of ideas, from hand-drawn sketches to geometric shapes, and his rigour and experimentation lead to typefaces of great distinction and integrity.

Typefaces of note include Elastik, a grotesk with elastic punctuation and diacritical mark in four styles: A (small), B (normal), C (big) and D (very too big). Other notable typefaces are Standard and Pickle Standard (see p. 436), both grid-inspired designs, and Brutal, a stencil calligraphic typeface designed in light, regular and bold.

Founded: 2004
Country: France
Website: bb-bureau.fr
Notable typefaces:
Brutal (see p. 547)
Pickle Standard (see p. 436)
Standard (see p. 440)

Below. *Toulouse en vue[s]* exhibition branding, employing an extruded Mineral designed by Vif Design, Toulouse, France.

Below. bb-book B typeface specimen designed by Benoît Bodhuin.

Below. Marianne poster, a multi-layered titling typeface by BB-Bureau. Available in three styles (Inline, Solid and Outline).

Above. Large format BB-Bureau font catalogue, limited edition of 200 numbered copies. Design by Benoît Bodhuin.

Woodkit Print

ABCDEFGHIJKLMNOPQRSTUVWXYZ
1234567890 !@#?:;"*&

Foundry: Typotheque
Designer: Ondrej Jób
Designer Nationality: Slovakian
Date: 2014

Ondrej Jób's Woodkit Print is a worn version of Woodkit and collects four eclectic wood-type inspired fonts. Letterpress, the primary style, combines Tuscan, slab serif, reverse-contrast and other type genres in the same font. There is also the more distressed Woodkit Reprint.

Zaragoza

ABCDEFGHIJKLMNOPQRSTUVW
abcdefghijklmnopqrstuvwxyz
1234567890 !?:;"*&

Foundry: Letraset
Designer: Phill Grimshaw
Designer Nationality: British
Date: 1995

Phill Grimshaw's font Zaragoza is named after the city in the Aragon region of Spain, and was designed for Letraset in 1995. It is a decorative, non-connecting serif script with inlaid zigzag decorations reversed out of the black. It has wide, swashed capitals and is best used at large sizes.

Zigzag

ABCDEFGHIJKLMNOPQRSTUVWXYZ
1234567890 !@#?:;"*&

Foundry: BB-Bureau
Designer: Benoît Bodhuin
Designer Nationality: French
Date: 2012

Benoît Bodhuin designed Zigzag for Le Vivat theatre near Lille in a single Rounded style. In 2012, it was originally published by Volcano Type with an additional Not Rounded version. Both fonts come with four forms of each letter; a simple uppercase sans serif, and three alternate distorted versions.

Zinjaro

ABCDEFGHIJKLMNOPQRSTUVWXYZ
1234567890 !?:;"*&

Foundry: Letraset
Designer: Carol Kemp
Designer Nationality: British
Date: 1994

Zinjaro, which was available from both Letraset and ITC, was created by British designer Carol Kemp in 1994. It is an uppercase display face with an exotic feel thanks to its inlaid patterns and ornaments. Zinjaro has slightly rough, bumpy edges and comes in a single heavy style.

Addlethorpe

ABCDEFGHIJKLMNOPQRSTUVWXYZ
abcdefghijklmnopqrstuvwxyz
1234567890 !@#?:;"'*&

Foundry: Typodermic
Designer: Ray Larabie
Designer Nationality: Canadian
Date: 2008

Addlethorpe is a layered typeface that allows designers to tailor its appearance in use. It is based on the physical appearance of metal type letters.

The letterforms themselves are based on Winthorpe, a more conventional design by Ray Larabie which he published the previous year.

Badoni

ABCDEFGHIJKLMNOPQRSTUVWXYZ
abcdefghijklmnopqrstuvwxyz
1234567890 !@#?:;"'*&

Foundry: Chank Co.
Designer: Chank Diesel
Designer Nationality: American
Date: 1993

Badoni was designed by Chank Diesel for *Cake*, a grunge music fanzine of which he was creative director at the time. As implied by its name, Badoni

is a heavily distorted and distressed typeface based on the forms of modern serifs such as Bodoni but set on an irregular baseline.

Blockade

ABCDEFGHIJKLMNOPQRSTUVWXYZ
1234567890 !@#?:;"'*&

Foundry: Monotype
Designer: Hans Bacher
Designer Nationality: American
Date: 2001

Blockade was designed by Hans Bacher, a German animator based in California, who works for Disney and is a member of the Academy of Motion Picture

Arts and Sciences. This grungy display sans is one of several decorative typefaces produced by Bacher for Monotype.

Burnaby

ABCDEFGHIJKLMNOPQRSTUVWXYZ
abcdefghijklmnopqrstuvwxyz
1234567890 !@#?:;"'*&

Foundry: Typodermic
Designer: Ray Larabie
Designer Nationality: Canadian
Date: 2007

This graffiti-inspired stencil typeface by Typodermic founder Ray Larabie features irregularities and imperfections reminiscent of the spray painting

process. An OpenType font, it offers a range of custom letter pairings to create a convincingly uneven and informal effect.

Ceroxa

ABCDEFGHIJKLMNOPQRSTUVWXYZ
abcdefghijklmnopqrstuvwxyz
1234567890 !@#?:;"*&

Another stencil design by Typodermic founder Ray Larabie, Ceroxa features degraded details. The typeface makes use of OpenType features that allow for automatic ligatures, inserting custom letter pairings within text set in Ceroxa for a more random and irregular effect.

Foundry: Typodermic
Designer: Ray Larabie
Designer Nationality: Canadian
Date: 2006

Chandler 42

ABCDEFGHIJKLMNOPQRSTUVWXYZ
abcdefghijklmnopqrstuvwxyz
1234567890 !@#?:;"*&

This typewriter font was developed by US designer Steve Mehallo, and is based on the letters created by a portable typewriter from 1942. Mehallo's meticulous approach to the reproduction of its type resulted in a convincingly irregular font that is available in several weights.

Foundry: Psy/Ops
Designer: Steve Mehallo
Designer Nationality: American
Date: 1994

Chinese Rocks

ABCDEFGHIJKLMNOPQRSTUVWXYZ
ABCDEFGHIJKLMNOPQRSTUVWXYZ
1234567890 !@#?:;"★+

The design of this rough-hewn display typeface was based on the hand-cut lettering seen on shipping containers from China. Purposefully irregular, Chinese Rocks is available in a range of weights and styles, from Fine to Bold and Condensed to Fat, plus two shaded versions.

Foundry: Typodermic
Designer: Ray Larabie
Designer Nationality: Canadian
Date: 1999

Chrysotile

ABCDEFGHIJKLMNOPQRSTUVWXYZ
ABCDEFGHIJKLMNOPQRSTUVWXYZ
1234567890 !@#?:;"*&

Featuring sans-serif uppercase letterforms reversed out of blocky tiles, this display font by Ray Larabie provides a tactile hand-printed effect for headlines. As with many Typodermic designs, it exploits OpenType functionality to swap in alternate characters as required.

Foundry: Typodermic
Designer: Ray Larabie
Designer Nationality: Canadian
Date: 2008

Croteau

ABCDEFGHIJKLMNOPQRSTUVWXYZ
ABCDEFGHIJKLMNOPQRSTUVWXYZ
1234567890 !@#?:;"*&

Foundry: Typodermic
Designer: Ray Larabie
Designer Nationality: Canadian
Date: 1995

Reportedly based on old film posters, Croteau by Ray Larabie is a slightly distressed sans serif with a subtle forward incline. It features a range of ligatures, allowing letters to stack and sit closely within each other's space, adding a decorative element to headlines.

Crusti

ABCDEFGHIJKLMNOPQRSTUVWXYZ
abcdefghijklmnopqrstuvwxyz
1234567890 !@#?:;"*&

Foundry: Chank Co.
Designer: Chank Diesel
Designer Nationality: American
Date: 1993

Designed by Chank Diesel, the thoroughly distressed letterforms of Crusti were created by distorting type through a repeated process of photocopying. Diesel created two additional similar fonts, Crustier and Crustiest, with each providing an increase in weight and distortion.

Crustier

ABCDEFGHIJKLMNOPQRSTUVWXYZ
abcdefghijklmnopqrstuvwxyz
1234567890 !@#?:;"*&

Foundry: Chank Co.
Designer: Chank Diesel
Designer Nationality: American
Date: 1993

Chank Diesel's Crustier is part of a family that also contains Crusti, Crustiest and Crusti Wacky. It is a grungy, display serif with a large x-height and a distressed effect. It is bolder than Crusti, but lighter than Crustiest, and was made using a photocopier machine at a Kinko's store.

Crustiest

ABCDEFGHIJKLMNOPQRSTUVWXYZ
abcdefghijklmnopqrstuvwxyz
1234567890 !@#?:;"*&

Foundry: Chank Co.
Designer: Chank Diesel
Designer Nationality: American
Date: 1993

The Crusti family, of which Crustiest is the heaviest weight, was designed by Chank Diesel in 1993 for *Cake*, a fanzine celebrating grunge music. It was inspired by the rough DIY ethos that surrounded the grunge scene. Crustiest features lots of fine dirt and grime around its glyphs.

Dirtstorm

ABCDEFGHIJKLMNOPQRSTUVWXYZ
ABCDEFGHIJKLMNOPQRSTUVWXYZ
1234567890 !@#?:;"★&

Foundry: Typodermic
Designer: Ray Larabie
Designer Nationality: Canadian
Date: 2007

A grungy, uneven spraypainted stencil font, and one of a number of stencil fonts designed by Typodermic's Ray Larabie, Dirtstorm is available in one weight and in uppercase. The font's legibility is deliberately low, making it suitable for display purposes only.

Ebenezer

ABCDEFGHIJKLMNOPQRSTUVWXYZ
ABCDEFGHIJKLMNOPQRSTUVWXYZ
1234567890 !@#?:;"*&

Foundry: Typodermic
Designer: Ray Larabie
Designer Nationality: Canadian
Date: 2008

Ray Larabie has described Ebenezer as 'an eerie, detailed font'. Its letterforms are based on another Typodermic font, Goldburg, which was inspired by the lettering found on Idaho's historical roadside markers. The marker scheme was launched in 1956, with lettering designed by George Bowditch.

Edifact

ABCDEFGHIJKLMNOPQRSTUVWXYZ
abcdefghijklmnopqrstuvwxyz
1234567890 !@#?:;"*&

Foundry: Typodermic
Designer: Ray Larabie
Designer Nationality: Canadian
Date: 2007

Edifact is a scratchy computer font that looks like it should belong on an obsolete computer from the 1960s. Its creator, Typodermic's Ray Larabie, has described it as being 'a severely damaged 1960s style techno font'. The font's poor legibility means it is suitable for display purposes only.

Emory

ABCDEFGHIJKLMNOPQRSTUVWXYZ
abcdefghijklmnopqrstuvwxyz
1234567890 !@#?:;"*&

Foundry: Typodermic
Designer: Ray Larabie
Designer Nationality: Canadian
Date: 2005

Emory is a typeface that looks like it has been torn from scraps of paper – there are no clean edges or right angles. Ray Larabie says his creation is 'easy to grip and rather rough'. The OpenType version offers class-based kerning and auto-ligatures. It is suitable for display purposes only.

Eroxion BT

ABCDEFGHIJKLMNOPQRSTUVWXYZ
abcdefghijklmnopqrstuvwxyz
1234567890 !@#?:;"'*&

Foundry: Bitstream
Designer: Eduardo Manso
Designer Nationality:
Argentinian
Date: 1997

This grunge font was created by Argentinian-born designer Eduardo Manso, who runs the EmType foundry in Barcelona. Eroxion channels degenerative typographic design, inspired by techniques first explored by designers such as Neville Brody and Erik van Blokland aka LettError.

F2F El Dee Cons

ABCDEFGHIJKLMNOPQRSTUVWX
abcdefghijklmnopqrstuvwxyz
1234567890 !@#?:;"'*&

Foundry: Face2Face
Designer: Thomas Nagel
Designer Nationality: German
Date: 1993

A layered, disjointed and primarily experimental typeface, El Dee Cons is part of the Face2Face series created by the collective formed by Thomas Nagel and his friends. Many of the foundry's typefaces featured in layouts for *Frontpage*, the leading 1990s German techno magazine.

F2F Entebbe

aBCDEFGHIJKLMNOPQrSTUVWX
aBCDefg#ijKLMNOPQrsTUVWXYZ
1234567890 /\#?:;"'*&

Foundry: Face2Face
Designer: Alexander Branczyk
Designer Nationality: German
Date: 1995

Alexander Branczyk has designed a distressed ransom-note-style typeface, comprised of juxtaposed characters from different typefaces. Operation Entebbe was a successful counterterrorist hostage-rescue mission carried out by the Israel Defense Forces at Entebbe Airport, Uganda in 1976.

F2F OCRAlexczyk

ABCDEFGHIJKLMNOPQRSTUVWXYZ
abcdefghijklmnopqrstuvwxyz
1234567890 !@#?:;"'*&

Foundry: Face2Face
Designer: Alexander Branczyk
Designer Nationality: German
Date: 1995

This is Face2Face co-founder Alexander Branczyk's take on the classic OCR-A, designed by American Type Founders for the US National Bureau of Standards in 1968. OCRAlexczyk also has a sister typeface by the same designer for Face2Face, OCRAlexczyk Shake.

F2F Screen Scream

ABCDEFGHIJKLMNOPQRSTUVWXYZ
abcdefghijklmnopqrstuvwxyz
1234567890 !@#?:;"*&

Foundry: Face2Face
Designer: Thomas Nagel
Designer Nationality: German
Date: 1997

Screen Scream is an experimental typeface that is based on a textured screen aesthetic. It is part of the Face2Face series created by the collective formed by Thomas Nagel and his friends. Many of the foundry's typefaces featured in layouts for *Frontpage*, the leading German techno magazine.

F2F Tyrell Corp

ABCDEFGHIJKLMNOPQRSTUVWXY
abcdefghijklmnopqrstuvwxyz
1234567890 ! ?:;"*&

Foundry: Face2Face
Designer: Thomas Nagel
Designer Nationality: German
Date: 1997

This mechanical, layered font by Face2Face founder Thomas Nagel is named after a fictional biotechnology firm, Tyrell Corporation, which features in Ridley Scott's science-fiction epic *Blade Runner* (1982). In the film, the company manufactures androids, known as replicants.

FF Confidential

ABCDEFGHIJKLMNOPQRSTUVWXYZ
ABCDEFGHIJKLMNOPQRSTUVWXYZ
1234567890 !@#?:;"*&

Foundry: FontFont
Designer: Just van Rossum
Designer Nationality: Dutch
Date: 1992

FF Confidential is the work of Dutch designer and educator Just van Rossum. It is an uppercase, distressed sans serif available in a single style. The lowercase glyphs provide an alternate, rougher alphabet. The ghostly, thin lettering evokes the feel of documentation in spy films and thrillers.

Flyswim

ABCDEFGHIJKLMNOPQRSTUVWXYZ
abcdefghijklmnopqrstuvwxyz
1234567890 !@#?:;"*&

Foundry: Typodermic
Designer: Ray Larabie
Designer Nationality: Canadian
Date: 2007

Flyswim was created by prolific Canadian typeface designer Ray Larabie in 2007, and released by his foundry Typodermic. It is a single style, distressed san serif with built-in drop shadows. Its 3D effect and sketchy roughness means that Flyswim does not work well at smaller point sizes.

Gnuolane Grind

ABCDEFGHIJKLMNOPQRSTUVWXYZ
abcdefghijklmnopqrstuvwxyz
1234567890 !@#?:,"*&

Foundry: Typodermic
Designer: Ray Larabie
Designer Nationality: Canadian
Date: 2007

Gnuolane Grind is a distressed, rough-edged version of Ray Larabie's Gnuolane, a headline sans-serif inspired by 19th-century grotesques but described by its creator as having a 'superelliptical sixties sneer'. Gnuolane Grind is available in two weights: Regular and Bold.

Goodies

ABCDEFGHIJKLMNOPQRSTUVWXYZ
ABCDEFGHIJKLMNOPQRSTUVWXYZ
1234567890 ! "?:,"*&

Foundry: Linotype
Designer: Anne Boskamp
Designer Nationality: German
Date: 2003

Goodies is a unique, illustrative typeface inspired by the work of Spanish artist Joan Miró. It comes in two styles: A and B. The typeface was the second font released by designer Anne Boskamp and her first, Merlin, had been a winner in the Linotype International Digital Type Design Contest in 1994.

Green

ABCDEFGHIJKLMNOPQRSTUVWXYZ
abcdefghijklmnopqrstuvwxyz
1234567890 !?:,"*G

Foundry: ITC / Letraset
Designer: Timothy Donaldson
Designer Nationality: British
Date: 1995

Timothy Donaldson's Green was released in 1995 by both ITC and Letraset. It is a single-weight postmodern, display sans serif with angular features and irregular contrast, which makes it better used at large sizes. Green is similar to Pink, another Donaldson font from a year earlier.

Hit

ABCDEFGHIJKLMNOPQRSTUVWXYZ
abcdefghijklmnopqrstuvwxyz
1234567890 !@#?:,'"*&

Foundry: Typodermic
Designer: Ray Larabie
Designer Nationality: Canadian
Date: 2008

Described by its creator, the prolific Canadian type designer Ray Larabie, as 'crunchy and primed for fun', Hit is a single-style, rough-edged informal sans serif. Its idiosyncratic forms are heavy, and its edges are bumpy. The legs of the 'R', 'K', 'f' and 'h' hang below the baseline.

Hot Plate

ABCDEFGHIJ-KLMNOPQRSTUVWXYZ
abcdefghi-jklmnopqrstuvwxyz
1234567890 !@ ?:; *&

Foundry: Linotype
Designer: Nico Hensel /
Timo Brauchle
Designer Nationality: German
Date: 2002

German designers Nico Hensel and Timo Brauchle created Hot Plate in 2002. It comes in ten variants and also includes a dingbat symbol font in the same style. Hot Plate is a distinctive, distressed typeface whose many versions can be mixed to create a effect akin to a ransom note.

ITC Coventry

ABCDEFGHIJKLMNOPQRSTUVWXYZ
abcdefghijklmnopqrstuvwxyz
1234567890 !@#?:;"'*&

Foundry: ITC
Designer: Brian Sooy
Designer Nationality: American
Date: 1998

Brian Sooy's ITC Coventry is a distressed sans serif with the appearance of cheaply photocopied text. It comes in three weights and was named in honour of fliers found in Coventry Village, a bohemian suburb of Cleveland Heights, Ohio. Sooy now works under the name Altered Ego Fonts.

ITC Don't Panic

ABCDEFGHIJKLMNOPQRSTUVWXYZ
ABCDEFGHIJKLMNOPQRSTUVWXYZ
1234567890 !@#?:;"'*&

Foundry: ITC
Designer: Wayne Thompson
Designer Nationality: Australian
Date: 1995

Wayne Thompson, an Australian designer, teacher and typographer, got the inspiration for ITC Don't Panic from the lettering stamped on envelopes. It is an uppercase, outlined and distressed sans serif that also features random square shapes alongside some letters, adding texture.

ITC Outback

ABCDEFGHIJKLMNOPQRSTUVWXYZ
abcdefghijklmnopqrstuvwxyz
1234567890 !@#?:;"'*&

Foundry: ITC
Designer: Bob Alonso
Designer Nationality: American
Date: 1997

Bob Alonso's ITC Outback is a heavy, compact sans serif along the lines of Rudolph Koch's Neuland of 1923, yet with the rough, distressed-looking edges that were common during the 1990s. Alonso, who died in 2007, was a graduate of New York's School of Visual Arts, where he studied font design.

ITC Panic

ABCDEFGHIJKLMNOPQRSTUVWXYZ
ABCDEFGHIJKLMNOPQRSTUVWXYZ
1234567890 !@#?:;"*&

Foundry: ITC
Designer: Wayne Thompson
Designer Nationality: Australian
Date: 2000

Five years after Wayne Thompson designed ITC Don't Panic he decided to create ITC Panic, an even rougher and more distressed version of the uppercase outlined sans serif. He went on to found the Australian Type Foundry in 2002. Panic has alternate characters on a shifted baseline.

ITC Pious Henry

ABCDEFGHIJKLMNOPQRSTUVWXYZ
abcdefghijklmnopqrstuvwxyz
1234567890 !@#?:;"*&

Foundry: ITC
Designer: Eric Stevens
Designer Nationality: American
Date: 1997

ITC Pious Henry is a single-style distressed sans-serif font whose letters have a random energy thanks to an inconsistent baseline and subtly different angles throughout. Its designer, the South Carolina-born Eric Stevens, describes it as evoking 'a feeling of the rural South'.

ITC Schizoid

ABCDEFGHIJKLMNOPQRSTUVWXYZ
abcdefghijklmnopqrstuvwxyz
1234567890 !@#?:;"*&

Foundry: ITC
Designer: Frank Marciuliano
Designer Nationality: American
Date: 1997

As the name implies, Frank Marciuliano's font ITC Schizoid is an eccentric, unbalanced and unconventional typeface. It is rough and angular with high contrast; its thin, fine strokes suddenly become wide and blocky, and small, spindly spikes that appear hand-drawn jut out at random.

Lavaman

ABCDEFGHIJKLMNOPQRSTUVWXYZ
abcdefghijklmnopqrstuvwxyz
1234567890 !@#?:;"*&

Foundry: Chank Co.
Designer: Chank Diesel
Designer Nationality: American
Date: 1995

Available in a single style, and published by Chank Diesel's foundry Chank Co., Lavaman is a craggy, rough-edged display sans serif. The single weight available is bold, and it has a high x-height, short ascenders and capitals that are barely taller than the lowercase letters.

Linotype Compendio

ABCDEFGHIJKLMNOPQRSTUVWXYZ
abcdefghijklmnopqrstuvwxyz
1234567890 !@#?:;"*&

Foundry: Linotype
Designer: Christian Bauer
Designer Nationality: German
Date: 1997

Linotype Compendio, by German designer Christian Bauer, is based on the forms of transitional serif faces of the 17th century and has rough, imperfect edges that give it an aged look. Available in regular and italic, it has Old Style numerals and large tittles, or dots, for 'i' and 'j'.

Linotype Fluxus

ABCDEFGHIJKLMNOPQRSTUVWXYZ
abcdefghijklmnopqrstuvwxyz
1234567890 !@#?:;"*&

Foundry: Linotype
Designer: Andreas Karl
Designer Nationality: German
Date: 1997

Linotype Fluxus is a distressed display face, which was initially submitted by designer Andreas Karl for Linotype's International Digital Type Design Contest. Intended for headlines, Linotype Fluxus features erratic strokes, reminiscent of the inconsistency of ink, within a solid yet irregular structure.

Linotype Fresh Ewka

ABCDEFGHIJKLMNOPQRSTUVWXYZ
abcdefghijklmnopqrstuvwxyz
1234567890 !?:;"&

Foundry: Linotype
Designer: Dariusz Nowak-Nova
Designer Nationality: Polish
Date: 1997

Linotype Fresh Ewka is a display typeface designed to balance a variety of distinct stroke styles. The characters, in both Dry and Hot weights, feature a harmony of single hairlines, or triple hairlines in the thicker Hot version, squares and brushlike strokes. The typeface is part of Linotype's TakeType Library.

Linotype Invasion

ABCDEFGHIJKLMNOPQRSTUVWXYZ
ABCDEFGHIJKLMNOPQRSTUVWXYZ
1234567890 !@#?:;"*ET

Foundry: Linotype
Designer: Hellmut G. Bomm
Designer Nationality: German
Date: 2002

Linotype Invasion is a display typeface inspired by the letterforms found on Britain's Bayeux Tapestry, which recounts the Norman invasion of England in the 11th century. The font family comprises three versions – Harold, Wilhelm and Rex – alongside a heraldic Animals style.

Linotype Laika

ABCDEFGHIJKLMNOPQRSTUVWXYZ
abcdefghijklmnopqrstuvwxyz
1234567890 !@?:;"'*&

Foundry: Linotype
Designer: Mark van Wageningen
Designer Nationality: Dutch
Date: 1997

Linotype Laika is a display font that is informed by the design of a sans serif but with misshapen, wavy strokes. The undulation of the characters mimics the movement of water while the letters seem to drift independently in their own space when placed next to one another.

Linotype MMistel

ABCDEFGHIJKLMNOPQRSTUVWXYZ
1234567890 !#?:;"'*&

Foundry: Linotype
Designer: Kerstin Fritsche
Designer Nationality: German
Date: 1997

Linotype MMistel is a display font that imitates the forms of the mistletoe plant and was acquired by Linotype after its entry into the company's International Digital Type Design Contest in 1999. Its letterforms combine separate, tapering stems with decorative dots like berries.

Linotype Not Painted

ABCDEFGHIJKLMNOPQRSTUVWXYZ
ABCDEFGHIJKLMNOPQRSTUVWXYZ
1234567890 !?:;" *&

Foundry: Linotype
Designer: Robert Bucan
Designer Nationality: American
Date: 1997

Linotype Not Painted is an energetic display font that combines multiple typographic layers. For the capitals, two uppercase styles sit on top of one another. The lowercase letters, alternately, layer one uppercase and one lowercase letterform in the same style.

Linotype Red Babe

ABCDEFGHIJKLMNOPQRSTUVWXYZ
abcdefghijklmnopqrstuvwxyz
1234567890 !@?:;"

Foundry: Linotype
Designer: Moritz Majce
Designer Nationality: Austrian
Date: 1997

Linotype Red Babe is a distressed display face, designed in a single weight for larger point sizes. Its letterforms are a composite of restless, jagged fragments, as if captured in the continual motion of a videotape playing on fast forward. The typeface is part of the Linotype TakeType Library.

Linotype Russisch Brot

ABCDEFGHIJKLMNOPQRSTUVWXYZ
abcdefghijklmnopqrstuvwxyz
1234567890 !@#?:;"*&

Foundry: Linotype
Designer: Markus Remscheid / Helmut Ness
Designer Nationality: German
Date: 1997

As its name suggests, Linotype Russisch Brot is modelled on the brittle form of *Russisch Brot*, (Russian bread), the dry biscuits produced in the style of letters. The font comprises six weights, each more eaten than the last, with the final weight mostly formed of crumbs.

Linotype Transis

ABCDEFGHIJKLMNOPQRSTUVWXYZ
abcdefghijpqrstuvwxyz
1234567890 !?:;"&

Foundry: Linotype
Designer: Kelvin Tan Tec Loong
Designer Nationality: American
Date: 1999

Linotype Transis is a distressed, restless display face that combines two stroke widths in a single character. Although using a similar vernacular of a painterly brushstroke, the letterforms feature a distinct contrast, with the right side a fuller, stronger version of the left.

Linotype Wildfont

ABCDEFGHIJKLMNOPQRSTUVWXYZ
1234567890 !?:;"*&

Foundry: Linotype
Designer: Meike Sander
Designer Nationality: German
Date: 1997

Linotype Wildfont is an unconventional display face, designed in all capitals, and constructed from the contorted figures of animals. The font features cats, alligators and snakes, which are all rendered in the coarse texture of monoprint to enhance the design's animalistic character.

Linotype Zensur

ABCDEFGHIJKLMNOPQRSTUVWXYZ
abcdefghijklmnopqrstuvwxyz
1234567890 !@#?:;"*&

Foundry: Linotype
Designer: Gérald Alexandre
Designer Nationality: French
Date: 1997

Linotype Zensur takes its name from the German word for 'censorship'. It is a distressed display font designed in a single weight. The rounded letterforms are sans serif in character, but the strokes are only partially complete, as if to abstract the true nature of each letter.

Mallorca Dirty Numbers

Foundry: Typo Graphic Design
Designer: Manuel Viergutz
Designer Nationality: German
Date: 2017

Mallorca Dirty Numbers is a display typeface inspired by numeric forms, such as house numbers and graffiti, found by the designer while in Mallorca.

These numbers provided the basis for an alphabet, including upper- and lowercase characters alongside more than ninety-nine decorative glyphs.

Maychurch

Foundry: Typodermic
Designer: Ray Larabie
Nationality: Canadian
Date: 2005

Maychurch is an architectural display face inspired by the drawings of a drafting technician. Its serif letterforms, which combine regular and small capitals in a single font, are complemented by extended rules, which overrun the regular stroke length in each character.

Merlin

Foundry: Linotype
Designer: Anne Boskamp
Designer Nationality: German
Date: 1994

Designed solely in capitals, Merlin is a distressed, historical display face. The strokes are trembling and irregular as if carved into paper with ink, or stone with flint. Meanwhile, the characters comprise several references to Stone Age pictograms, as seen in the 'I' and 'M'.

Moonshine

Foundry: Chank Co.
Designer: Chank Diesel
Designer Nationality: American
Date: 1993

Moonshine is a distressed display face, initially conceived for *Cake* magazine in the early 1990s. The unruly design, produced in a single Regular style, features distorted strokes and irregular shapes, and takes its name from the distilled spirit popularized in the southern United States.

Murkshine

ABCDEFGHIJKLMNOPQRSTUVWXYZ
abcdefghijklmnopqrstuvwxyz
1234567890 !@#?:;"'*&

Foundry: Chank Co.
Designer: Chank Diesel
Designer Nationality: American
Date: 1993

Like its quirky sibling typeface Moonshine, Murkshine is a distressed, grunge-serif display face. Chank Diesel designed Murkshine to complement Moonshine, and it features bolder versions of the initially disfigured letterforms to accentuate their buckled shapes.

Octin Spraypaint

ABCDEFGHIJKLMNOPQRSTUVWXYZ
ABCDEFGHIJKLMNOPQRSTUVWXYZ
1234567890 !@#?:;"'*&

Foundry: Typodermic
Designer: Ray Larabie
Designer Nationality: Canadian
Date: 2007

Octin Spraypaint is a stencil display font family designed in serif and sans-serif styles and comprising three weights, from Regular to Black. The distressed letterforms imitate the visual effect of paint sprayed through a stencil and are reminiscent of military or institutional aesthetics.

Octin Vintage

ABCDEFGHIJKLMNOPQRSTUVWXYZ
ABCDEFGHIJKLMNOPQRSTUVWXYZ
1234567890 !@#?:;"'*&

Foundry: Typodermic
Designer: Ray Larabie
Designer Nationality: Canadian
Date: 2007

Ray Larabie's Octin Vintage is a distressed display font family designed in serif and sans serif styles. It consists of three weights, from Regular to Black. The font's forms exhibit inconsistencies in their surface and are reminiscent of analogue printing methods such as stamps.

Octynaz

ABCDEFGHIJKLMNOPQRSTUVWXYZ
ABCDEFGHIJKLMNOPQRSTUVWXYZ
1234567890 !@#?:;"'*&

Foundry: Typodermic
Designer: Ray Larabie
Designer Nationality: Canadian
Date: 2006

Designed in a single style and all in capitals, Octynaz is a distressed display face intended for large headline sizes. The sans-serif design includes several distinctions, such as filled counters, irregular alignment, and a textured surface that simulates the appearance of smudged ink.

Oxeran

ABCDEFGHIJKLMNOPQRSTUVWXYZ
abcdefghijklmnopqrstuvwxyz
1234567890 !@#?:;"*&

Foundry: Typodermic
Designer: Ray Larabie
Designer Nationality: Canadian
Date: 2007

Oxeran is a distressed display font comprised of two styles, Oxeran and Oxeran Z. While both character sets utilize worn slab serif letterforms set on an irregular baseline and feature upper and lowercases, Oxeran Z also includes a textured outline that encircles each letter.

Pitchfork

ABCDEFGHIJKLMNOPQRSTUVWXYZ
1234567890 !@#?:;"*&

Foundry: Monotype
Designer: Stephen Miggas
Designer Nationality: American
Date: 1995

Pitchfork is a distressed display face produced in all capitals and a single weight. The characters, modelled on the forms of an Old Style serif, feature a series of angular gouges and are reminiscent of those displayed in the publicity materials for early horror films such as *Frankenstein* (1931).

PRINTF

ABCDEFGHIJKLMNOPQRSTUVWXYZ
ABCDEFGHIJKLMNOPQRSTUVWXYZ
1234567890 !@#?:;"*&

Foundry: Typodermic
Designer: Ray Larabie
Designer Nationality: Canadian
Date: 2007

PRINTF is a distressed display face designed to mimic the appearance of typewriter characters. Although available in only a single style, PRINTF includes variable OpenType letter pairs, so that each form can be replaced by another to create more diverse and authentic combinations.

Raclette

ABCDEFGHIJKLMNOPQRSTUVWXYZ
abcdefghijklmnopqrstuvwxyz
1234567890 !@ ?:; &

Foundry: Linotype
Designer: Michael Parson
Designer Nationality: Swiss
Date: 2002

Raclette is a distressed display face inspired by a traditional Swiss grill designed to cook (and melt) raclette cheese. Its sans-serif letterforms are irregular in shape and are similar in appearance to a raclette grill from which the individual cooking trays have been removed or replaced.

Raw Street Wall

ABCDEFGHIJKLMnoPQRStuvwXYZ
abcdefghijklmhoPqrStuvwHyz
1234567890 !@#?:; *&

Foundry: Volcano Type
Designer: Manuel Viergutz
Designer Nationality: German
Date: 2016

Inspired by the playful lettering of graffiti art, Raw Street Wall is an eclectic display face comprised of a single style, more than 567 glyphs and contextual alternates. For authenticity, the blockish characters also imitate the texture of letters painted on a rough surface. It is best used in headlines.

Reagan

ABCDEFGHIJKLMNOPQRSTUVWXYZ
abcdefghijklmnopqrstuvwxyz
1234567890 !@#?:;"*&

Foundry: Typodermic
Designer: Ray Larabie
Designer Nationality: Canadian
Date: 2007

Reagan is designed to symbolize the 1980s. It is based on a revival font, Pretorian, from the early 20th century which became an icon of T-shirt design in the 1980s. Reagan maintains the flamboyant style, but adds a layer of wear, as if the letters have been put repeatedly through the wash.

Rina BT

ABCDEFGHIJKLMNOPQRSTUVWXYZ
abcdefghijklmnopqrstuvwxyz
1234567890 !@#?:;"*&

Foundry: Bitstream
Designer: Eduardo Manso
Designer Nationality: Argentinian
Date: 2001

Rina BT is a distressed display font featuring two styles, Rina Regular and Rina Linea, the outline version. The serif figures, which designer Eduardo Manso inverted, cut and contorted at random, are chaotic yet refined and remain legible even at smaller display sizes.

Sabotage

ABCDEFGHIJKLMNOPQRSTUVWXYZ
abcdefghijklmnopqrstuvwxyz
1234567890 !@#?:;"*&

Foundry: PintassilgoPrints
Designer: Ricardo Marcin / Erica Jung
Designer Nationality: Brazilian
Date: 2013

Sabotage is a distressed display face inspired by the all-caps lettering of Saul Bass's seminal poster for the film *Vertigo* (1958). The design also includes a Sabotage Pictures version, which unlike Sabotage and Sabotage Solid, takes inspiration from the minimalist illustrations of Dutch artist Dick Bruna.

Schmutz

ABCDEFGHIJKLMNOPQRSTUVWXYZ
abcdefghijklmnopqrstuvwxyz
1234567890 !@#?:;"*&

Foundry: Image Club Graphics
Designer: Grant Hutchinson
Nationality: Canadian
Date: 1995

Schmutz is a distressed display font produced in three versions. The characters, modelled on those of a typewriter, vary in clarity throughout the family, from the articulate appearance of the Cleansed face to the smudged and worn designs of the Clogged and Corroded styles.

Shatterday

ABCDEFGHIJKLMNOPQRSTUVWXYZ
abcdefghijklmnopqrstuvwxyz
1234567890 !@#?:;"*&

Foundry: Image Club Graphics
Designer: Patricia Lillie
Designer Nationality: American
Date: 1996

Shatterday comprises three options – Shatterday Slice, Shatterday Dice and Shatterday Shred – all of which appear to be based on chopping up things. These are just a handful of mainly display faces created by the prolific US writer and type designer Patricia Lillie.

Shnixgun

ABCDEFGHIJKLMNOPQRSTUVWXYZ
ABCDEFGHIJKLMNOPQRSTUVWXYZ
1234567890 !@Nº?:;"*&

Foundry: Typodermic
Designer: Ray Larabie
Designer Nationality: Canadian
Date: 2007

Ray Larabie's Shnixgun is an all-caps copperplate-style serif font based on a an old metal type called Franklin Card Gothic. It has a distressed, grungy finish that looks like it has been printed from under-inked metal type. Some letters are slightly skewed or off the baseline.

Spooky

ABCDEFGHIJKLMNOPQRSTUVWXYZ
abcdefghijklmnopqrstuvwxyz
1234567890 !@#?:;"*&

Foundry: ITC
Designer: Timothy Donaldson
Designer Nationality: British
Date: 1995

Spooky, by British educator and lettering artist Timothy Donaldson, is in the vampire-style genre of typefaces thanks to its eerie, tattered-looking letterforms, and 'x' and 'X' even resemble bats in flight. It is perfect for use in anything goth or related to Halloween.

Teeshirt

ABCDEFGHIJKLMNOPQRSTUVWXYZ
ABCDEFGHIJKLMNOPQRSTUVWXYZ
1234567890 !@#?:;"'*&

Foundry: Typodermic
Designer: Ray Larabie
Designer Nationality: Canadian
Date: 2008

Teeshirt is Ray Larabie's homage to ITC's typeface American Typewriter of 1974. Teeshirt is a heavier display face inspired by type found on vintage 1980s T-shirts. It is available in two weights: Teeshirt Regular has unevenly spaced characters and Teeshirt Pressed has letters sitting on the baseline.

Thumtax

ABCDEFGHIJKLMNOPQRS
TUVWXYZ
1234567890 !@#?:;"'*&

Foundry: Image Club Graphics
Designer: Jeff Prybolsky
Designer Nationality: American
Date: 1996

Jeff Prybolsky designed Thumtax for Image Club Graphics. It comes in a single all-caps style and is a rough display typeface that has the appearance of being quickly scrawled with a heavy marker. Prybolsky designed type for various foundries as Disappearing Inc., from 1994–2000.

Wolfsblood

ABCDEFGHIJKLMNOPQRSTUVWXYZ
ABCDEFGHIJKLMNOPQRSTUVWXYZ
1234567890 !@#?:;"'*&

Foundry: Monotype
Designer: Jim Ford
Designer Nationality: American
Date: 2013

Jim Ford's Wolfsblood, an all-caps sans serif, is as its name suggests, horror-inspired, with rough wobbly edges. Wolfsblood's lowercase capitals are slightly smaller, and it also features a variety of ligatures and context-sensitive OpenType functions that help vary the style.

Woodcut Alpha

ABCDEFGHIJKLMNOPQRSTUVWXYZ
abcdefghijklmnopqrstuvwxyz
1234567890 !@#?:;"'*&

Foundry: Monotype
Designer: Hans Bacher
Designer Nationality: American
Date: 2001

Woodcut Alpha is a rough, chaotic woodcut style sans serif, available in a single style, with imperfect shapes and textures that give a printed look. Its designer Hans Bacher was born in Germany but works in animation for Disney in California on films such as *The Lion King* (1994) and *Mulan* (1998).

DIN Next Shapes

ABCDEFGHIJKLMNOPQRSTUVWXYZ
abcdefghijklmnopqrstuvwxyz
1234567890 !@#?:;"*&

Foundry: Monotype
Designer: Sabina Chipară /
Akira Kobayashi
Designer Nationality: Romanian /
Japanese
Date: 2018

Designed to work in harmony with its sister typeface DIN Next (2009), Sabina Chipară has taken the outline of the German industrial classic and created four new and much more expressive versions using various shapes – dots, hearts, snowflakes and stars – to replace solid lines. Light Dots is shown here.

Foundry Flek/Plek

ABCDEFGHIJKLMNOPQRSTUVWXYZ
abcdefghijklmnopqrstuvwxyz
1234567890 !@#?:;""&

ABCDEFGHIJKLMNOPQRSTUVWXYZ
abcdefghijklmnopqrstuvwxyz
1234567890 !@#?:;""&

Foundry: The Foundry
Designer: Freda Sack /
David Quay
Designer Nationality: British
Date: 2002

Below. Logo for online and print, leaflet, screen and window graphics by Patrick Myles for RIBA (Royal Institute of British Architects).

Foundry Flek was designed by David Quay and Freda Sack, the co-founders of The Foundry (see p. 284). It is a typeface created from circular forms on a consistent dot-matrix grid, which is visible in the background. It is available in four weights – Light, Regular, Medium and Bold – and includes a version with just the dot grid and no letters.

The sister type to Flek, Plek is built on the same dot-matrix grid. However, it just includes the letters without the gridded dot background. As with Flek, Plek is available in four weights and includes a font with only the dot-matrix grid that can then be built into a continuous background. With varying weights and the opportunity to overlay these weights, dynamic and involving designs can be created, with the resultant radiating circles forming letterforms as well as contrasting surrounding textures. This opportunity for experimentation allows for endless configurations and varying effects.

FourPoint (03)

Foundry: MuirMcNeil
Designer: Hamish Muir /
Paul McNeil
Designer Nationality: British
Date: 2014

MuirMcNeil (see p. 334) created this geometric typeface system as a playful response to the everyday lettering that can be seen on transportation light-emitting diode (LED) displays such as on train and road networks. The typeface system is formed around a varying dot size, stroke width and grid.

Designers Hamish Muir and Paul McNeil intended the FourPoint system to explore two specific typographic conditions. The first is resolution – 'the proportionate relationship between scale and visual information'. The second is weight – 'the proportionate relationship between filled and negative space elements of letters and word forms'. The resultant design has been built on a fixed grid at four resolutions. FourPoint 04 has a consistent stroke width of four dots; FourPoint 03, three dots (left); FourPoint 02, two dots and FourPoint 01, one dot. Every dot aligns consistently on the same grid and their weights are incremented without the dots altering position. The grid therefore dictates the letterform shapes, spacing, kerning and suchlike.

As with other MuirMcNeil typefaces, individual characters vary within the system. FourPoint is designed in four scaleable groups of five weights each. The five weights (or tonal densities) in each scale group are identified both by name – Light, Regular, Bold, Black and Fat – and numerically. The number codes describe dot diameters in units as fractions of the 1,000-unit PostScript em square. 'FourPoint 03 054 Regular', for example, indicates stroke width (3 dots) and dot diameter (54/1,000 units). Consequently, size and weight ratios can be accurately calculated in setting typographic compositions and overlays.

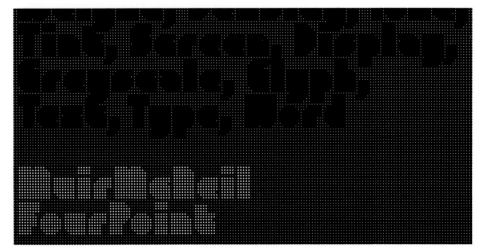

Left. FourPoint poster designed by MuirMcNeil (detail).

Led

ABCDEFGHIJKLMNOPQRSTUVWXYZ
abcdefghijklmnopqrstuvwxyz
1234567890 !@#?;,""*&

Foundry: Graviton
Designer: Pablo Balcells
Designer Nationality:
Argentinian
Date: 2012

Designed by Pablo Balcells, an Argentinian designer and a graduate of the University of Buenos Aires, Led is a display sans serif created from unconnected dots. It comes in two styles, Regular and Outline (whose dots are outlined rather than solid), and is published by Graviton.

Linotype Dot

ABCDEFGHIJKLMNOPQRSTUVWXYZ
abcdefghijklmnopqrstuvwxyz
1234567890 !?;"";

Foundry: Linotype
Designer: Lucy Davies
Designer Nationality: British
Date: 1997

Dot, by British designer Lucy Davies, was one of the winners in the display category of Linotype's second International Type Design Contest in 1997. It comes in two styles – Regular and Oblique – and is an intricate, ornamental display face made from interconnected white and black dots.

Linotype Punkt

abcdefghijklmnopqrstuvwxyz
1234567890 !@#?;,""*&

Foundry: Linotype
Designer: Mischa Leiner
Designer Nationality: Swiss
Date: 1999

Swiss typographer Mischa Leiner designed Linotype Punkt in 1999. It is an extended sans serif created from dots and is named after the German word for 'dot', *punkt*. The font is available in three styles: Light, Regular and Bold. Leiner is a lecturer at the Basel School of Design.

Nebulae

ABCDEFGHIJKLMNOPQRSTUVWXYZ
abcdefghijklmnopqrstuvwxyz
1234567890 !@#?;,""&

Foundry: Lucas Fonts
Designer: Lucas de Groot
Designer Nationality: Dutch
Date: 1994

Nebulae is the work of Dutch designer Lucas de Groot and was released by his Lucas Fonts foundry in 1994. It is an experimental sans serif that comes in four styles; One, Two, Three, Three Dee and Four. Each font is made from clouds of different-sized dots, and they can be layered together.

Perfin

A B C D E F G H I J K L M N O P Q R S T U V W X Y Z
1 2 3 4 5 6 7 8 9 0 ! @ # ? : ; " * &

Foundry: Colophon
Designer: Alison Haigh
Designer Nationality: British
Date: 2009

Created by Alison Haigh, a designer who has worked at DesignStudio and Wolff Olins, Perfin is short for 'Perforated Initials', an old system whereby companies stamped letters or symbols into postage stamps as a protection against theft. It is an uppercase sans serif made from dots.

PIN

A B C D E F G H I J K L M N O P Q R S T U V W X Y Z
a b c d e f g h i j k l m n o p q r s t u v w x y z
1 2 3 4 5 6 7 8 9 0 ! @ # ? : ; " * &

Foundry: Colophon
Designer: Hoon Kim
Designer Nationality: Korean
Date: 2015

New York-based Korean designer Hoon Kim created PIN in three styles – Solid, Dot and Stencil – and three roman weights – Light, Regular and Medium. It is a friendly, geometric sans serif that is almost monoline and was initially constructed in its Dot style using a gridded dot matrix.

Synchro

A B C D E F G H I J K L M N O P Q R S T U V W X Y Z
1 2 3 4 5 6 7 8 9 0 ! @ # ? : ; " * &

Foundry: Letraset
Designer: Alan Birch
Designer Nationality: British
Date: 1984

British designer Alan Birch created this pixellated typeface that simulates electronic display systems. Synchro is also available as Synchro Reversed, and in the non-pixellated versions as Synchro No. 1 and Synchro No. 2. It is suitable for instances where a high-tech appearance is required.

Telidon

A B C D E F G H I J K L M N O P Q R S T U V W X Y Z
a b c d e f g h i j k l m n o p q r s t u v w x y z
1 2 3 4 5 6 7 8 9 0 ! @ # ? : ; " * &

Foundry: Typodermic
Designer: Ray Larabie
Nationality: Canadian
Date: 2004

An adaptable dot-matrix display face, Telidon is available in a surprisingly wide range of weights: Regular, Bold, Heavy, Condensed, Condensed Bold, Condensed Heavy, Expanded, Expanded Bold and Expanded Heavy. All of the weights come with matching italics.

TenPoint (08)

ABCDEFGHIJKLMNOPQRSTUVWXYZ
abcdefghijklmnopqrstuvwxyz
1234567890 !&#?:;""+&

TenPoint, by MuirMcNeil (see p. 334), is a modular type system built around a repeating single cell – a circular disc with an open counterform – all fixed to a consistent circular-based geometric grid. This experimental typeface pushes the barriers of legibility to the limit of what can be interpreted as a recognizable set of characters as well as creating a system of construction for the letterforms.

There are seven sizes of TenPoint: 01, 02, 03, 04, 05, 06 and 08 (above and below right). The numerical index refers to the vertical cell count repetitions that define the overall body height of each size. For example, TenPoint 08 is constructed from eight precisely positioned, partially overlapping circles on its vertical axis, allowing for ascenders and descenders.

Because of the nature of TenPoint's construction, it is challenging to identify individual characters when set at smaller sizes and readability is reduced, to the point of even disappearring. As such, it takes on a more geometric texture and the typeface creates rhythmic patterns. At larger settings, the letterforms' readability and shape become much clearer, allowing for legibility and communication.

Foundry: MuirMcNeil
Designer: Hamish Muir / Paul McNeil
Designer Nationality: British
Date: 2014

Below. A modular geometric type system in seven sizes. The repeating single cell construction is at the core of the typeface's design, with all points fixed to a geometric grid.

ThreePoint (A)

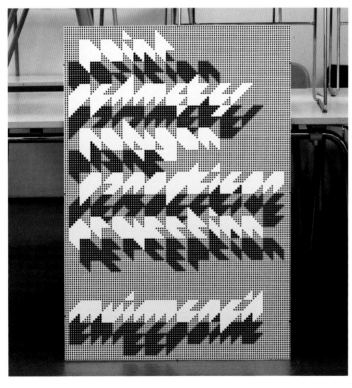

ThreePoint by MuirMcNeil (see p. 334) is based around four differing orthographic projections. It is a 3D display typeface formed of precisely placed and sized dots set on a standardized grid and is a development of MuirMcNeil's Panopticon typeface system (see p. 434). The four views making up ThreePoint are categorized as A: top right view (above), B: bottom left view, C: top left view and D: bottom right view.

The four viewpoints are each provided as four differing typefaces and with differing size dot patterns built on a consistent grid. They provide the illusion of three dimensions and depth to the letterforms. The variants for each of the projections are 01: Comp H, a two-tone composite that is darker in the horizontal plane; 02: Comp V, a two-tone composite that is darker in the vertical plane

(above); 03: Light, an even screen pattern of light dots; and 04: Bold, an even screen pattern of dark dots. Letterforms abut to each other with no interspacing between characters; so all dots may be aligned vertically and horizontally and therefore provide an evenly set placing for the dots making up the letterforms. The family comes in a Latin lowercase only and, for ease of use, the lowercase is duplicated in the uppercase family.

There are also a further four sub-variants for each projection, with variations supplied for Light and Bold weights in horizontal and vertical planes all designed to interact and link together as sharing the same grid construction. These additional types can be used to create textured patterns, overlays and offset types, and are intended for use for complex designs built around layered constructions.

Foundry: MuirMcNeil
Designer: Hamish Muir / Paul McNeil
Designer Nationality: British
Date: 2014

Below. A 3D type system in four orthographic projections. As such, the possibilities when combining the differing views are near infinite, when also adding in to the mix colour, transparency, outlining and the designers' experimentation and creativity.

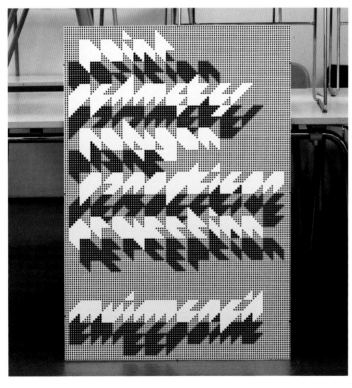

TwoPoint (A)

ABCDEFGHIJKLMNOPQRSTUVWXYZ
abcdefghijklmnopqrstuvwxyz
1234567890 !&#*?:;"'+$

TwoPoint was inspired by the earliest dot-matrix and light-emitting diode (LED) display letterforms. It is a monospaced geometric type system that explores how differing permutations can generate letterforms while maintaining legibility and readability. TwoPoint has been created around a consistent grid wherein placement of the centres of the dots that make up the letterform are always consistent at the intersections of horizontal and vertical lines of the grid behind the construction and placement of the dots.

TwoPoint has been created in four variant styles. A (above) is a two-dot stroke form that is consistent in both dimensions. B is a two-dot stroke form where alternate dot rows have been removed in order to emphasize the horizontal. C is a two-dot stroke form where alternate dot columns have been removed in

order to emphasize the vertical. D is a two-dot stroke form where alternate diagonal rows have been removed, thus creating a chequerboard effect.

Each of the four TwoPoint styles come in six weights, ranging from Light to Black. They are identified both by name and numerically in dot diameters. Their weight increases as the dot diameters increase in size in units as fractions of the 1,000-unit PostScript em square, while all the time never moving from their placed position on the grid. For example, the numerical value in 'TwoPoint A 044 Regular' indicates the dot component diameter (44/1,000 units). Eventually, these dots scale up in size to touch and then overlap each other. This creates denser and bolder weights, and provides contrast and texture to longer set extents of text.

Foundry: MuirMcNeil
Designer: Hamish Muir / Paul McNeil
Designer Nationality: British
Date: 2014

Below. For the design, Paul McNeil and Hamish Muir of MuirMcNeil generated 8,000 uniquely different pieces of artwork using conditional design methods. The front cover of *Eye 94* employs their coordinated TwoPoint and TwoPlus typefaces.

Blenny

ABCDEFGHIJKLMNOPQRSTUVWXYZ
abcdefghijklmnopqrstuvwxyz
1234567890 !@#?:;""*&

The curvaceous forms of this Fat Face display font are voluptuous and glorious, creating a truly individual and eye-catching display type. Blenny's dynamic character make it ideal for branding or product label applications or anywhere where a message needs to shout out. It is the work of US-born font developer Spike Spondike of Dalton Maag (see p. 594).

Spondike has created a number of ligatures with elegant hairlines and ball terminals to ensure the letter spacing is kept tight throughout and guarantee its solid appeal. A number of design features such as the ball terminals of the 'A' provide letterforms that turn in to wrap itself up.

Unusually, the Blenny family is available in Thai as well as Latin. Indeed, the Latin design of Blenny was heavily influenced by Thai script and its diversity of character shapes. During the development of the Thai variant, refinements were made to the design of the Latin version, which brought the two language types closer together in appearance, and they share design characteristics. Bruno Maag, founder and chairman of Dalton Maag, loved the retro-feel design so much he said he was considering having a tattoo done in it. When the design was launched, a Blenny gin cocktail was invented to honour its arrival, which like its namesake is 'bold, punchy and has a touch of class'.

Foundry: Dalton Maag
Designer: Spike Spondike
Designer Nationality: American
Date: 2014

Below. Examples and workings for Dalton Maag's single weight Fat Face typeface Blenny, where the influence of Thai scripts can clearly be seen in the Latin version and vice versa.

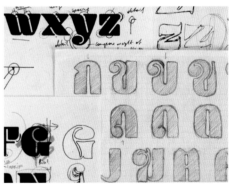

Bodoni Poster

ABCDEFGHIJKLMNOPQRSTUVWXYZ
abcdefghijklmnopqrstuvwxyz
1234567890 !@#?:;""*&

The archetypal 'fat face', although not really a variant of Giambattista's eponymous typeface, this extreme cut was designed by Chauncey H. Griffith for Linotype in 1929 and resembles more of the fat face types that could be found in the 19th century. It was a popular choice for posters and advertisements in the mid 20th century and its generous presence, extremely heavy weighted strokes and curvaceous forms (as seen in the rounded ball terminals of letters such as 'a', 'c' and 'r') still make it a popular choice today. Available in black, black italic and compressed, it can be seen used in film, musc and packaging applications. The logotype of American rock band Nirvana closely resembles the compressed cut of Bodoni Poster were it not for subtle differences in the terminals of the R and the shape of the serif on the V marking it as a revised variant.

Foundry: Linotype
Designer: Giambattista Bodoni / Chauncey H. Griffith
Designer Nationality: Italian / American
Date: 1929

Right. The cover for *123* by Màrius Sampere, one of a series of poetry titles published by Edicions del Buc and designed by Dídac Ballester.

Carousel

ABCDEFGHIJKLMNOPQRSTUVWXYZ
abcdefghijklmnopqrstuvwxyz
1234567890 !@#?:;"'*&

Foundry: Letraset
Designer: Gary Gillot
Designer Nationality: British
Date: 1966

Carousel, by British type designer Gary Gillot, is a classic example of the Fat Face type style, which developed from earlier modern serifs such as Didot and Bodoni. It is a high-contrast typeface featuring generous curves and fine serifs, which is well-suited for display use.

Caslon Graphique

ABCDEFGHIJKLMNOPQRSTUVWXYZ
abcdefghijklmnopqrstuvwxyz
1234567890 !@#?:;"'*&

Foundry: ITC
Designer: William Caslon / Leslie Usherwood
Designer Nationality: British
Date: 1980

Caslon Graphique was designed by the British-born and Toronto-based advertising designer, typographer and type designer Leslie Usherwood. This elegant display serif closely resembles the forms of the original Caslon yet possesses greatly contrasting stroke weights, from hairline to fat, along with incisor-like serifs, giving it an approachable appearance overall with precise, razor-sharp finishing details, making it ideal for headlines and titles in larger sizes.

Usherwood was a prolific type designer, who created 211 typefaces during his career. He created his first font design, Melure, in 1965 for Headliners International in New York and in 1968 he co-founded Typesettra in Toronto.

Right. Website interface for http://lesliink.com

Falstaff

ABCDEFGHIJKLMNOPQRSTUV
abcdefghijklmnopqrstuvwxyz
1234567890 !@#?:;"'*&

Foundry: Monotype
Designer: Monotype Studio
Date: 1931

Falstaff is named after the fictional character Sir John Falstaff, who appears in four plays by William Shakespeare. Monotype released the wide, bold, ultra-high-contrast antiqua serif in 1931, which was created in-house by an uncredited designer who took inspiration from 19th-century poster types.

ITC Scram Gravy

ABCDEFGHIJKLMNOPQRST
abcdefghijklmnopqrstuv
1234567890 !@#?:;"*&

Foundry: ITC
Designer: Nick Curtis
Designer Nationality: American
Date: 2002

ITC Scram Gravy has extreme contrast, its thick strokes are broad, taking up two thirds or more of the width of most capitals, and its lowercase counters are very thin. Nick Curtis, who designed it in 2002, began this font after being inspired by the 1928 logotype for Sertal Toiletries.

Maisalle

ABCDEFGHIJKLMNOPQRSTUVWXYZ
abcdefghijklmnopqrstuvwxyz
1234567890 !@#?:;"*&

Foundry: Neutura
Designer: Alexander McCracken
Designer Nationality: American
Date: 2012

US foundry Neutura (see p. 472) was inspired by the Fat Faces that were popular during the 1960s – especially in the fashion world – to create Maisalle. The foundry's faithful homage to this style of type design nevertheless possesses a refinement and sharpness that is its own. The high contrast between stroke weights and the near circular forms for its ball endings and exaggerated, incisor-like serifs combine to create a voluptous and flamboyant presentation to the design. Neutura has also created an accompanying italic.

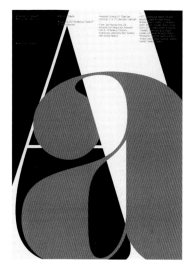

Right. Poster designs by Neutura.

Normande

ABCDEFGHIJKLMNOPQRSTUVW
abcdefghijklmnopqrstuvwxyz
1234567890 !@#?:;"*&

Foundry: Bitstream
Designer: Unknown
Date: 1860

Normande is Bitstream's digitization of a French Fat Face font, initially produced in 1860 and later acquired by the Berthold foundry in Berlin. As with the original design, Bitstream's Normande features two styles, Roman and Italic, and there are family-package options.

Royale

ABCDEFGHIJKLMNOPQRSTUVWXYZ
abcdefghijklmnopqrstuvwxyz
1234567890 !@#?:;"*&

Foundry: Neutura
Designer: Alexander McCracken
Designer Nationality: American
Date: 2009

Royale is an ultra-high-contrast didone serif typeface created by San Francisco-based designer Alexander McCracken and released by Neutura (see p. 472). It comes in a single style, Roman, and has a large x-height, chunky ball terminals and two attractive ampersands to choose between.

Stilla

ABCDEFGHIJKLMNOPQRSTUVWX
abcdefghijklmnopqrstuvwxyz
1234567890 !@#?:;"*&

Foundry: Letraset
Designer: François Boltana
Designer Nationality: French
Date: 1973

The prolific 20th-century French lettering artist François Boltana designed this voluptuous cursive Fat Face. It was inspired by the first large advertising and display faces that were produced following the successful launches of Bodoni, Didot and Walbaum in the 19th century.

Thorowgood

ABCDEFGHIJKLMNOPQRSTUVWXYZ
abcdefghijklmnopqrstuvwxyz
1234567890 !@#?:;"*&

Foundry: Linotype
Designer: Robert Thorne
Designer Nationality: British
Date: 1836

This didone-style display face was created by English typefounder Robert Thorne, and named after his predecessor, the punch-cutter and typefounder William Thorowgood, who worked at the Fann Street foundry in London. Stephenson, Blake & Co. revived it in 1953. It is available in Regular and Italic weights.

Trilogy Fatface

ABCDEFGHIJKLMNOPQRSTUVWXYZ
abcdefghijklmnopqrstuvwxyz
1234567890 !@#?:;"*&

Foundry: Jeremy Tankard Typography
Designer: Jeremy Tankard
Designer Nationality: British
Date: 2009

Part of the Trilogy type family, Jeremy Tankard's Trilogy Fatface is a high-contrast serif that comes in a heavy weight in five widths: regular, wide, expanded, extra-expanded and ultra-expanded. It is italic only and was inspired by the Fat Face poster types of the 19th century.

Amelia

ABCDEFGHIJKLMNOPQRSTUVWXYZ
abcdefghijklmnopqrstuvwxyz
1234567890 !@#?:;"'*&

Foundry: Visual Graphics Corporation
Designer: Stan Davis
Designer Nationality: American
Date: 1964

Stan Davis designed Amelia for Visual Graphics Corporation in 1964. It was used in the titles artwork for the Beatles' film *Yellow Submarine* (1968).

Controversy surrounds the various digitizations of the font because Davis maintains they were created without his consent.

Anlinear

ABCDEFGHIJKLMNOPQRSTUVWXYZ
abcdefghijklmnopqrstuvwxyz
1234567890 !@#?:;•'3

Foundry: Linotype
Designer: Michael Parson
Designer Nationality: Swiss
Date: 2003

Anlinear is one of ten different designs by Michael Parson to be included in Linotype's TakeType 5 library. It is an experimental display typeface whose

forms are composed of arrangements of straight lines set at right angles to one another. It is available in three weights.

Architype Stedelijk

abcdefghijklmnopqrstuvwxyz
1234567890!   ?:' +

Foundry: The Foundry
Designer: Wim Crouwel / Freda Sack / David Quay
Designer Nationality: Dutch / British / British
Date: 1996

In 1996, The Foundry, run by Freda Sack and David Quay, struck an agreement with Wim Crouwel (see p. 540) to create digital fonts based on lettering he

had created. Stedelijk is based on his posters for the Stedelijk Museum in Amsterdam. It is a low-resolution sans serif created with a strict grid.

Armadura

ABCDEFGHIJKLMNOPQRSTUV
ƆBCDEFGHIJKLMNOPQRSTUV
1234567890 !@#?:;"'*&

Foundry: Graviton
Designer: Pablo Balcells
Designer Nationality: Argentinian
Date: 2012

This geometric sans by Pablo Balcells features a distinctive diagonal tilt to its crossbars. It is available in a wide range of variants, including Inline, Outline,

Stencil and Double Line styles, with alternate lowercase characters to incorporate into its uppercase alphabet.

Belfast

ABCDEFGHIJKLMNOPQRSTUVWXYZ
1234567890 [A]#!'"*&

An early pre-Neutura (see p. 472) project, this collaboration with designer Grant Dickson and Neutura founder Alexander McCracken was produced while the latter worked at the renowned British design studio, Attik. Dickson had created letterforms but was struggling to work with them because they were still individual artworks. McCracken offered to make a working font from the design. Together, they revisited the characters that had been designed and went on to make them into a full working typeface with the addition of numbers, punctuation and alternate characters. The typeface gained its name after Dickson's home town in Northern Ireland, Belfast.

Belfast's minimal character forms use chamfered corners to create shape. Combined with its pared-back indentation for counters, this helps to create an aggressive and imposing font with high impact. An alternative set of characters features bold diagonal lines forming the characters, where shortening of the strokes and angled endings provide the shape of the characters.

Foundry: Neutura
Designer: Alexander McCracken / Grant Dickson
Designer Nationality: American / British
Date: 2007

Below and opposite. The octagonal-based Belfast typeface is available not only in solid form but also comes as a diagonal infill version. Designs by Neutura.

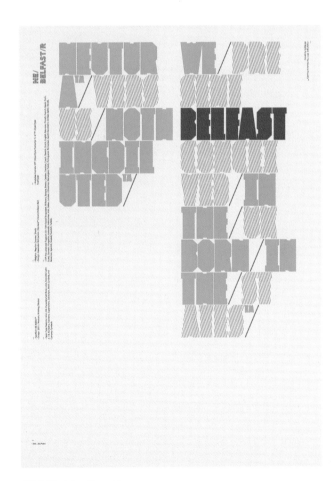

Betaphid

ABCDEFGHIJKLMNOP
abcdefghijklmnopqrstuvwx
1234567890 !@#?:;"•&

Foundry: Typodermic
Designer: Ray Larabie
Designer Nationality: Canadian
Date: 2006

A futuristic font from prolific display typeface designer Ray Larabie, this sans serif features squat, extended square forms with floating details, and a distinctive diagonal slant to certain stroke ends. Betaphid is available in a single weight, in both upper and lowercase.

Bisect A

ABCDEFGHIJKLMNOPQRST
abcdefghijklmnopqrst
1234567890 !@#?:;"✲+

Foundry: MuirMcNeil
Designer: Natasha Lucas / Paul McNeil / Hamish Muir
Designer Nationality: British
Date: 2018

The Bisect type system was begun by designer Natasha Lucas during her undergraduate studies, as a typographic response to the central conceit of Harold Pinter's so-called 'memory plays'. This modular typeface is built from sliced circular forms and rectangles, set on a geometric grid.

Bisect B

Foundry: MuirMcNeil
Designer: Natasha Lucas / Paul McNeil / Hamish Muir
Designer Nationality: British
Date: 2018

Natasha Lucas created this geometric modular font when she was a student at the London College of Communication, with help from her tutors Hamish Muir and Paul McNeil. Bisect B is made from the vertical elements of Bisect A and is illegible without being used in combination with Bisect C.

Bisect C

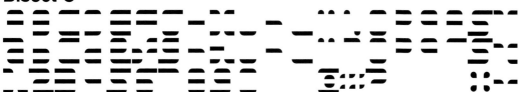

Foundry: MuirMcNeil
Designer: Natasha Lucas / Paul McNeil / Hamish Muir
Designer Nationality: British
Date: 2018

Natasha Lucas designed Bisect, an experimental type family, as an exploration into Harold Pinter's 'memory plays', which feature the recollections of unreliable narrators. Bisect A is fully legible, while Bisect C features the horizontal strokes only and needs to be combined with Bisect B to be read.

Black Boton

ABCDEFGHIJKLMNOPQRSTUVWXYZ
1234567890 ● !@#?:;"*&

Foundry: Hollenstein
Designer: Albert Boton
Designer Nationality: French
Date: 1970

This solid geometric display face was originally created when Albert Boton was a director at the Delpire agency in Paris. Black Boton featured in a catalogue from the Hollenstein foundry in 1974 with Solid and Outline styles, and with lowercase. Monotype reissued this caps-only version in 1997.

Blippo

ABCDEFGHIJKLMNOPQRSTUVWXYZ
abcdefghijklmnopqrstuvwxyz
1234567890 !@#?::"*&

Foundry: Fotostar
Designer: Joe Taylor / Robert Trogman
Designer Nationality: American
Date: 1969

Joe Taylor designed Blippo as a photolettering font for FotoStar as part of its Facsimile Fonts range. It was inspired by a thinner, unfinished design developed by the Bauhaus. Blippo is available as a family that includes various Black, Stencil, Poster and Outline versions.

Blocks

ABCDEFGHIJKLMNOPQRSTUVWXYZ
abcdefghijklmnopqrstuvwxyz
1234567890 !@#?:;"*&

Foundry: Keystrokes
Designer: Douglas Olena
Designer Nationality: American
Date: 1995

Blocks is a very black geometric face from Douglas Olena's Keystrokes foundry, which is similar in style to Albert Boton's display face Black Boton (1970). Blocks differs in that it has a lowercase option, but this scores relatively low on the legibility scale, even when used at large sizes.

Calcula

ABCDEFGHIJKLMNOPQRSTUVWXYZ
abcdefghijklmnopqrstuvwxyz
1234567890 !@#?:;"*&

Foundry: Typotheque
Designer: Shiva Nallaperumal
Designer Nationality: Indian
Date: 2017

Shiva Nallaperumal began Calcula during the final year of his Master of Fine Arts. This experimental font family was inspired by geometric Kufic lettering, a form of Arabic calligraphy. Exploiting OpenType functionality, its letters can stack, layer and tessellate to create myriad fascinating forms.

Children

abcdefghijklmnopqrstuvwxyz
1234567890 !@#?:;"*$

Foundry: Neutura / T-26
Designer: Alexander McCracken
Designer Nationality: American
Date: 2000

US designer Alexander McCracken constructed Children on a square skeleton. The typeface features letterforms built from a single folded line, as if bent into shape from a paper clip. It is available in two weights, and is published by McCracken's Neutura foundry (see p. 472) and the T-26 foundry.

Chilopod

ABCDEFGHIJKLMNOPQRSTUVWXYZ
1234567890 !@#?:;"*&

Foundry: Typodermic
Designer: Ray Larabie
Designer Nationality: Canadian
Date: 2006

This rounded linear design by Ray Larabie was inspired by the lettering within the logo of the arcade game Centipede, which was released by Atari in 1981. It deviates slightly from its source material, with forms such as the 'E' opened up, and fewer letter ligatures throughout.

Circle

ABCDEFGHIJKLMNOPQRSTUVWXYZ
1234567890 !@№?:;"*&

Foundry: Neutura
Designer: Alexander McCracken
Designer Nationality: American
Date: 2006

Circle is an airy, sans-serif display font featuring a blend of tall, narrow letterforms and open, circular forms, as its name implies. The typeface, which is available in four weights, includes a range of alternate characters and ligatures, and its numerals are particularly distinctive.

Cirkulus

abcdefghijklmnopqrstuvwxyz
1234567890 !@#?:;"*&

Foundry: Letraset
Designer: Michael Neugebauer
Designer Nationality: Austrian
Date: 1970

This fine and airy typeface by Michael Neugebauer is composed of interconnected and bisected circles and straight strokes in a uniform hairline weight. Cirkulus is available in lowercase only. Originally published by Letraset, the typeface has since been licensed by Linotype.

Computechnodigitronic

ABCDEFGHIJKLMNOPQRSTUVWXYZ
1234567890 !@#?:;"*&

Foundry: Typodermic
Designer: Ray Larabie
Designer Nationality: Canadian
Date: 2010

The notched letterforms of Computechnodigitronic are designed to resemble those of simple light-emitting diode (LED) displays, but designer Ray Larabie has made them more solid by to aid legibility. The typeface is available in Regular and Oblique styles, and in uppercase only.

Countdown

ABCDEFGHIJKLMNOPQRSTUVWXYZ
abcdefghijklmnopqrstuvwxyz
1234567890 !@#?:;"*&

Foundry: Letraset
Designer: Colin Brignall
Designer Nationality: British
Date: 1965

The design of this early original Letraset font was influenced by digital displays, and it was frequently used in the initial years after its release to convey a science-fiction feel in display contexts. A Cyrillic version of the typeface was developed by Alexey Kustov in 1993.

Covent BT

ABCDEFGHIJKLMNOPQRSTUVWXYZ
abcdefghijklmnopqrstuvwxyz
1234567890 !@#?:;"*&

Foundry: Bitstream
Designer: Jochen Hasinger
Designer Nationality: German
Date: 2003

German type designer Jochen Hasinger studied under Wolfgang Weingart in Switzerland during the early 1990s, and has since started his own foundry, Typeimage, where he specializes in pictogram fonts. Hasinger designed Covent BT, a monolinear sans serif, for Bitstream in 2003.

Cuantica

ABCDEFGHIJKLMNOPQRSTUVWXYZ
ABCDEFGHIJKLMNOPQRSTUVWXYZ
1234567890 !@#?:;"*&

Foundry: Graviton
Designer: Pablo Balcells
Designer Nationality: Argentinian
Date: 2012

Pablo Balcells designed Cuantica for his Buenos Aires-based foundry Graviton. Geometric and monolinear, it features distinctive numerals and includes a slightly shorter set of small caps in place of lowercase characters. It comprises four styles – two solid and two outline.

Data 70

ABCDEFGHIJKLMNOPQRSTUVWXYZ
abcdefghijklmnopqrstuvwxyz
1234567890 !@#?:;"*&

Foundry: Letraset
Designer: Bob Newman
Designer Nationality: British
Date: 1970

Data 70, by British designer Bob Newman, and published by Letraset and ITC in 1970, is a sans serif with contrast inspired by early computer-readable type, specifically the MICR E13B font for bank cheques, which had caps only. It was popular throughout the 1970s for giving a futuristic look.

Deuce

ABCDEFGHIJKLMNOPQRSTUVWXYZ
1234567890 !@#?:;"*&

Foundry: T-26
Designer: Alexander McCracken
Designer Nationality: American
Date: 2005

Alexander McCracken's Deuce is an uppercase, blocky sans-serif typeface without counters and with characters that are all the same width. It comes in three styles: Solid, Outline and Gradient. The Gradient style is made from horizontal stripes that get thicker as they travel up the letters.

Dujour

ABCDEFGHIJKLMNOPQRSTUVWXYZ
1234567890 !@#?:;"*&

Foundry: Ascender
Designer: Steve Matteson
Designer Nationality: American
Date: 2005

Dujour is an ultra-bold display sans serif with tiny circular counters and an Art Deco feel. It is a revival of Indépendant, a font designed by Jos Dufour and Joan Collette for the Belgian branch of the Amsterdam Foundry in 1931 to celebrate one hundred years of Belgian independence.

Frankfurter

ABCDEFGHIJKLMNOPQRSTUVWXYZ
1234567890 !@#?:;"*&

Foundry: Letraset
Designer: Bob Newman / Alan Meeks / Nick Belshaw
Designer Nationality: British
Date: 1970 / 1978 / 1981

The chunky, round sans serif Frankfurter typeface was named after a sausage and created by Bob Newman in 1970. In 1978, Letraset released a Medium version, designed by Alan Meeks, and a Highlight version, designed by Nick Belshaw. The uncredited Inline version followed in 1981.

Foundry Gridnik

ABCDEFGHIJKLMNOPQRSTUVWXYZ
abcdefghijklmnopqrstuvwxyz
1234567890 !@#?:;"*&

Foundry: The Foundry
Designer: Wim Crouwel /
Freda Sack / David Quay
Designer Nationality: Dutch /
British / British
Date: 1960s / 1996

London type designers The Foundry (see p. 284) have a close working relationship with legendary Dutch designer Wim Crouwel (see p. 540). As part of this initiative, the company has worked to realize a digital version of his 1970s design of a single weight monospaced typewriter typeface, and Foundry Gridnik is the result.

Crouwel's original design was from a commission in 1974 by typewriter maker Olivetti, to create a typeface that could be used on its new electronic typewriters. The original design was called Politene, but the rapid decline in the use of typewriters with the advent of PC technology meant it was never used in the manner for which it was intended. However, it gained a new lease of life in 1976, when Crouwel used it on his range of postage stamps for the Dutch Post Office, PTT, where it was employed up to 2002.

Foundry Gridnik's geometric form, monoline stroke weight and 45°-angled corners give a highly engineered appearance to its design, evoking a technical theme. Despite the consistent underlying grid approach to the typeface's creation, it has a humanist quality, so it is not entirely mechanical in tone. This reflects Crouwel's thoughts about his work; he once said: 'I am a functionalist troubled by aesthetics.' The typeface was named after Crouwel's nickname 'Mr Gridnik', a reference to his passion for grids and systems in his work. It extends Crouwel's single-weight design into a five-weight family, ranging from Light to Extra Bold plus italics.

Right. *5054* automative magazine employing Foundry Gridnik for its masthead and title typography. Design and art direction by Patrick Myles.

FS Conrad

ABCDEFGHIJKLMNOPQRSTUVWXYZ
abcdefghijklmnopqrstuvwxyz
1234567890 !@?:;"×+

FS Conrad is a display sans serif made from thin lines. The Regular weight is constructed from five lines, while Headline uses seven and is subsequently harder to use at small sizes. Conrad began as a commission to design a typeface to complement the sculptures of Conrad Shawcross.

Foundry: Fontsmith
Designer: Phil Garnham
Designer Nationality: British
Date: 2012

FS Pele

ABCDEFGHIJKLMNOPQRSTUVWXYZ
abcdefghijklmnopqrstuvwxyz
1234567890 !@?:;"*&

FS Pele is named after the legendary Brazilian footballer. Phil Garnham from Fontsmith (see p. 272) created the dynamic, retro typeface in 2009, inspired by 'chunky typefaces from the late 1960s and early 1970s'. It comes in two weights with italics and is best used at large headline sizes.

Foundry: Fontsmith
Designer: Phil Garnham
Designer Nationality: British
Date: 2009

Geometric 885

ABCDEFGHIJKLMNOPQRSTUVWXYZ
abcdefghijklmnopqrstuvwxyz
1234567890 !@#?:;"*&

Geometric 885 is Bitstream's version of Aldo Novarese's typeface Bloc (1974), which was originally released by Visual Graphics Corporation after Novarese left Italian foundry Nebiolo. Available in a single style, Geometric 885 is a heavy, outlined, geometric sans serif best used at large sizes.

Foundry: Bitstream
Designer: Aldo Novarese
Designer Nationality: Italian
Date: 1974

History 01

ABCDEFGHIJKLMNOPQRSTUVWXYZ
1234567890 !@#?:;"×&

History 01 is one of the twenty-one styles of Peter Biľak's History typeface. It is an elegant, hairline, geometric sans-serif font. History's eclectic fonts are all inspired by the evolution of typography and can be layered together to create exciting and unexpected combinations.

Foundry: Typotheque
Designer: Peter Biľak
Designer Nationality: Slovakian
Date: 2008

Horatio

ABCDEFGHIJKLMNOPQRSTUVWXYZ
abcdefghijklmnopqrstuvwxyz
1234567890 !@#?:;"*&

Foundry: Letraset
Designer: Bob Newman
Designer Nationality: British
Date: 1971

Letraset typeface Horatio was created by British designer Bob Newman in 1971. It is a geometric sans serif inspired by the typographic experiments of early 20th-century modernist designers such as Herbert Bayer and Joost Schmidt. Horatio comes in three weights: Light, Medium and Bold.

Industria

ABCDEFGHIJKLMNOPQRSTUVWXYZ
abcdefghijklmnopqrstuvwxyz
1234567890 !@#?:;"*&

Foundry: Linotype
Designer: Neville Brody
Designer Nationality: British
Date: 1990

Industria, by British designer Neville Brody, is a condensed geometric sans serif that mixes right-angles and curves. Linotype released it with three other fonts by Brody in 1990. It comes in two styles: Solid and Inline. *The X-Files* science-fiction TV series features Industria for intro titles.

Interpol

ABCDEFGHIJKLMNOPQRSTUVWXYZ
1234567890 !@#?:;"*&

Foundry: Neutura
Designer: Alexander McCracken
Designer Nationality: American
Date: 2008

Designed by Alexander McCracken and released by Neutura (see p. 472) in 2008, Interpol is an all-caps, geometric display sans serif that comes in eight styles, some of which are textured or include backgrounds. Interpol shares its name with a Fundición Tipográfica Nacional typeface from 1950.

ITC Ronda

ABCDEFGHIJKLMNOPQRSTUVWXYZ
abcdefghijklmnopqrstuvwxyz
1234567890 !@#?:;"*&

Foundry: ITC
Designer: Ronne Bonder /
Tom Carnase
Designer Nationality: American
Date: 1970

Ronne Bonder and Tom Carnase created this modernist-inspired geometric, monoline sans serif in 1970. ITC Ronda is built around the forms of the circle, triangle and rectangle, clearly visible in the distinctive uppercase 'Q'. Originally, it was available in three weights, but ITC has digitized only one.

Julien

abcdefghijkl mnopqrstuvwxyz
abcdefghijklmnopqrstuvwxyz
1234567890 !@#?:;"*&

Foundry: Typotheque
Designer: Peter Biľak
Designer Nationality: Slovakian
Date: 2010–11

This wonderfully playful geometric typeface comes from Dutch foundry Typotheque (see p. 90) and its founder, Slovakian designer Peter Biľak. It was inspired by the simple, geometric forms of the 20th century avant-garde, in particular by art movements such as Dada and Futurism, as well as the Bauhaus school.

Key Bauhaus figures such as László Moholy-Nagy and Herbert Bayer considered typography primarily to be a medium of communication. They embraced 20th-century machine culture and favoured a highly functional approach to type, opting to employ simplified forms without ornamentation. As such, each of Julien's characters is formed from elementary geometric shapes, which simultaneously evoke and pay homage to this innovative period in the history of design.

Each of Julien's characters contain multiple glyphs so variation can be introduced when letters repeat themselves within words or in lengths of text. When the glyphs are partnered with intelligent OpenType scripts, they enhance the design process, since the user can choose the glyphs that make the best word shapes. Using software that is adept at handling OpenType substitutions, allows the Contextual Alternates feature to alter the characters and achieve a unique flow of letterforms. These can be overwritten and altered by replacing characters selected from the Glyphs palette.

Julien is a unicase typeface, which means upper- and lowercase letters are mixed together, giving the designer the opportunity to experiment. It is available in two weights; a light, thin-stroked version and a heavy black version.

Below left. Example setting of Julien showing variants.

Below right. With the Contextual Alternates feature switched on, Julien possesses a wide range of alternate characters. Here it is shown in Light and Bold, both lower and uppercase.

Jillican

ABCDEFGHIJKLMNOPQRSTUVWXYZ
abcdefghijklmnopqrstuvwxyz
1234567890 !@#?:;"*&

Foundry: Typodermic
Designer: Ray Larabie
Designer Nationality: Canadian
Date: 2001

Inspired by a trip to London, Canadian designer Ray Larabie designed Jillican in 2001. He followed the proportions of Gill Sans to create an angular sans serif made from straight lines, not curves. It comes in eighteen styles, some of which are italic, stencilled, 3D or distressed.

Kairos

ABCDEFGHIJKLMNOPQRSTUVWXYZ
abcdefghijklmnopqrstuvwxyz
1234567890 !@#?:;"*&

Foundry: Monotype
Designer: Terrance Weinzierl
Designer Nationality: American
Date: 2015

Terrance Weinzierl of Monotype took inspiration from the forms and bevelled corners of 19th-century US wood types known as Grecians to design the Kairos geometric slab serif. It is available in regular, condensed and extended, in eight weights, plus a display version with shadows and highlights.

Laundrette

ABCDEFGHIJKLMNOPQRSTUVWXYZ
abcdefghijklmnopqrstuvwxyz
1234567890 !@#?:;"*&

Foundry: Chank Co.
Designer: Chank Diesel
Designer Nationality: American
Date: 1993

Laundrette is the work of prolific US type designer Chank Diesel. It is an extended, angular, squat slab serif, which is constructed entirely without the use of curves. It has a particularly idiosyncratic lowercase 'g'. Laundrette has a low x-height and thin, rectangular tittles.

Linotype Carmen

ABCDEFGHIJKLMNOPQRSTUVWXYZ
abcdefghijklmnopqrstuvwxyz
1234567890 !@#?:;"&

Foundry: Linotype
Designer: Lutz Günther
Designer Nationality: German
Date: 2002

Lutz Günther's Carmen is part of the TakeType 4 library of winners from the Linotype International Digital Type Design Contest of 2002. It is a distinctive geometric stencil sans serif created from overlapping shapes in places. It has undersized, offset titles in the manner of Gill Kayo.

Linotype Fehrle Display

ABCDEFGHIJKCMNOPQRSTUVWXYZ
abcdefghijklmnopqrstuvwxyz
1234567890 !@#?:;"'*&

Foundry: Linotype
Designer: Erich Fehrle
Designer Nationality: German
Date: 1976

Erich Fehrle's Linotype Fehrle Display is a geometric display face designed exclusively for headlines, which utilizes the structural forms of the rectangle.

The bold letterforms embrace a combination of sharp angles, rounded corners, slablike serifs and narrowly opened joints.

Linotype Isilda

ABCDEFGHIJKLMNOPQRSTUVWXYZ
abcdefghijklmnopqrstuvwxyz
1234567890 !@#?:;"'*&

Foundry: Linotype
Designer: Frank Marciuliano
Designer Nationality: American
Date: 1997

Linotype Isilda is a geometric display face with a focus on narrow vertical strokes. The characters are reminiscent of a sprawling skyline, a feature that

is emphasized by the slanted descender on the 'y', which appears as a shadow extending beyond the letter's architectural stem.

Linotype Renee Display

ABCDEFGHIJKLMNOPQRSTUVWXY
abcdefghijklmnopqrstuvwxy
1234567890 !@#?:;"'*&

Foundry: Linotype
Designer: Renee Ramsey-Passmore
Designer Nationality: American
Date: 1997

Linotype Renee Display is a geometric face designed on a strict, mathematical grid, which is made visible in the font's Lines weight. The

characters are seen more clearly in the Types weight, and are constructed from a combination of circles, triangles and rectangles.

Linotype Vision

ABCDEFGHIJKLMNOPQRSTUVWXYZ
abcdefghijklmnopqrstuvwxyz
1234567890 !@#?:;"'*&

Foundry: Linotype
Designer: Dan-André Niemeyer
Designer Nationality: German
Date: 1997

The Linotype Vision geometric display font was originally an entrant into the Linotype International Digital Type Design Contest, and Linotype published

it in 1997 as part of its TakeType Library. The letterforms, designed in five styles, are comprised of a single line, akin to an electrical circuit.

Matra

ABCDEFGHIJKLMNOPQRSTUVWXYZ
1234567890 !@#P:;"*&

Foundry: Monotype
Designer: Cassandre
Designer Nationality: French
Date: 1930

Matra is a modern, geometric display type, designed entirely in capitals and informed by the Art Deco style. Unlike similar designs, Matra tends to separate the thicker cross-strokes from the hairline verticals, as seen in the 'E', 'F' and 'B'. 'Cassandre' was the pseudonym of Adolphe Jean-Marie Mouron.

Mineral

ABCDEFGHIJKLMNOPQRSTUVWXYZ
abcdefghijklmnopqrstuvwxyz
1234567890 !@#?:;"*&

Foundry: BB-Bureau
Designer: Benoît Bodhuin
Designer Nationality: French
Date: 2013

Mineral is the work of French type designer Benoît Bodhuin, who studied maths at university before switching to graphic design. He releases typefaces through his foundry BB-Bureau (see p. 386). It is a modular, experimental stencil sans serif in five varied styles: Solid, Blunt, Smooth, Outline and Border.

Ned

ABCDEFGHIJKLMNOPQRSTUVWXY
abcdefghijklmnopqrstuvwxyz
1234567890 !@#?., *&

Foundry: Linotype
Designer: Michael Parson
Designer Nationality: Swiss
Date: 2002

Michael Parsons's Ned is a geometric display font designed using a broad hexagonal grid, similar in shape to the cells of a honeycomb. In both upper and lowercases, the characters are carefully regimented and employ interchangeable shapes alongside a uniform stroke width.

Neutrino

ABCDEFGHIJKLMNOPQRSTUVWXYZ
abcdefghijklmnopqrstuvwxyz
1234567890 !@#?:;"*&

Foundry: Neutura
Designer: Alexander McCracken
Designer Nationality: American
Date: 2004

Neutrino is a geometric display face designed in both Regular and Alternate styles. Unlike many heavy types, Neutrino's letterforms feature no counters and are a combination of shapely curves and sharp angles, evidenced in both the lower- and uppercase characters.

Nine Metric

ABCDEFGHIJKLMNOPQRSTUVWXYZ
abcdefghijklmnopqrstuvwxyz
1234567890 !@#?:;"*&

Foundry: MuirMcNeil
Designer: Hamish Muir / Paul McNeil
Designer Nationality: British
Date: 2013

MuirMcNeil's Nine Metric, designed in 2013, is a rounded geometric sans serif constructed using a dot-matrix grid. It comes in nine weights – hence its name – each of which increase incrementally by eighteen units on the base grid. Weights go from the ultra-light 018 to extra-black 162.

Nine Mono

ABCDEFGHIJKLMNOPQRSTUVWXYZ
abcdefghijklmnopqrstuvwxyz
1234567890 !@#?:;"*&

Foundry: MuirMcNeil
Designer: Hamish Muir / Paul McNeil
Designer Nationality: British
Date: 2013

Nine Mono is designed by Hamish Muir and Paul McNeil. It is a monospaced version of Nine Metric which is also more angular, including right angles as well as added serifs in places to equalize letter widths. Muir and McNeil both teach at the London College of Communication.

Oblong

ABCDEFGHIJKLMNOPQRSTUVWXYZ
abcdefghijklmnopqrstuvwxyz
1234567890 !@#?:;"*&

Foundry: Emigré
Designer: Rudy VanderLans / Zuzana Licko
Designer Nationality: Dutch / Slovakian
Date: 1988

Oblong was designed by US-based couple Rudy VanderLans and Zuzana Licko, who also founded the digital type foundry and publisher Emigré (see p. 106) in 1984. Oblong is a square, monoline slab serif that comes in two roman weights. Its square forms point towards its construction from pixels.

Oboe

ABCDEFGHIJKLMNOPQRSTU
VWXYZ
1234567890 ! ?:;""*&

Foundry: Graviton
Designer: Pablo Balcells
Designer Nationality: Argentinian
Date: 2012

Pablo Balcells designed Oboe for the Graviton foundry in 2012. It is a chunky, blocky, uppercase sans serif with rounded corners, fixed width and small counters. The typeface comes in six styles: Solid, Solid Wide, Solid Framed, Outline, Outline Wide and Outline Framed.

Odessa

ABCDEFGHIJKLMNOPQRSTUVWXYZ
abcdefghijklmnopqrstuvwxyz
1234567890 !?:;"*&

Foundry: Letraset
Designer: Peter O'Donnell
Designer Nationality: British
Date: 1988

Odessa is a geometric sans serif with an inline that creates a fine line on the edge of the characters. Its forms, which come in a single roman style, are heavily influenced by Futura. Peter O'Donnell, Odessa's British designer, created a handful of other fonts for Letraset.

Panopticon

Panopticon A: 010 Perimeter

Panopticon A: 020 Interior

Panopticon A: 030 Horizontal

Panopticon A: 040 Vertical

Foundry: MuirMcNeil
Designer: Hamish Muir /
Paul McNeil
Designer Nationality: British
Date: 2014

Right. Panopticon poster employing differing orthographic projections of the 3D display typeface. Design by MuirMcNeil.

Panopticon (left, Variation A) is a system of 3D display typefaces built in four orthographic projections by MuirMcNeil (see p. 334). It is named after a form of polygonal building developed in the 18th century by English philosopher and social reformer Jeremy Bentham to facilitate controlled and concealed viewpoints.

The Panopticon system challenges convention and legibility and has been implemented in four alternative viewpoints, or projections. A: is the top right view, B: is the bottom left view, C: is the top left view and D: is the bottom right view. Each of the four Panopticon projections is subdivided into four separate typeface layers: 10: Perimeter, 20: Interior, 30: Horizontal and 40: Vertical.

Pump

ABCDEFGHIJKLMNOPQRSTUVWXYZ
abcdefghijklmnopqrstuvwxyz
1234567890 !@#?:;"*&

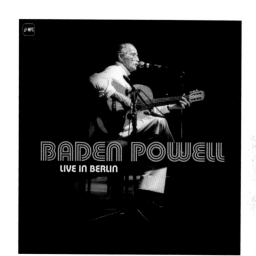

Foundry: ITC
Designer: Philip Kelly
Designer Nationality: British
Date: 1975

British designer Philip Kelly created Pump in 1975 while he was working at Letraset. The fun typeface is retro enough to create nostalgia for the 1970s, but can also look contemporary in the appropriate design setting. Its geometric curves and rounded forms share similar aesthetics to typefaces such as ITC Bauhaus, which was based around Herbert Bayer's designs of 1925 and revived by Ed Benguiat (see p. 514) and Victor Caruso for ITC in 1975, ITC Ronda designed in 1970 by Herb Lubalin (see p. 63) and Linotype's Blippo from 1992. Pump is available in Light, Medium, Demi, Bold and Triline versions. Triline is a bold design formed of three strokes in parallel, which is ideal for sport graphic applications.

Right. Album cover design for celebrated Brazilian guitarist and composer Baden Powell de Aquino, employing Pump and Pump Triline in its typography.

Rabbit

ABCDEFGHIJKLMNOPQRSTUVWXYZ
1234567890 !@#?:;"*&

Foundry: Neutura
Designer: Alexander McCracken
Designer Nationality: American
Date: 2000

Rabbit is one of Alexander McCracken's earliest font designs and was created three years before he founded the Neutura foundry (see p. 472). It is an all uppercase, geometric sans serif with a monoline construction, and rounded corners. It comes in four weights: Light, Regular, Bold and Heavy.

Rimouski

ABCDEFGHIJKLMNOPQRSTUVWXYZ
abcdefghijklmnopqrstuvwxyz
1234567890 !@#?:;"*&

Foundry: Typodermic
Designer: Ray Larabie
Designer Nationality: Canadian
Date: 2005

Ray Larabie designed Rimouski in 2005. It is a rounded geometric type family that contains five weights, from ultra-light to bold. It has a large x-height and OpenType features such as automatic ligatures, class-based kerning and stylistic alternate slanted letters for 'A', 'V' and 'W'.

Pickle Standard

ABCDEFGHIJKLMNOPQRSTUVWXYZ
abcdefghijklmnopqrstuvwxyz
1234567890 !@#?.,"'*&

Foundry: BB-Bureau
Designer: Benoît Bodhuin
Designer Nationality: French
Date: 2018

The Pickle Standard typeface is a grid-based design by French type and graphic designer Benoît Bodhuin (see p. 386). Its convoluted forms possess a logic and a simplicity as only a highly geometric typeface design can. Nevertheless, its resultant aesthetic is organic. On first impressions the typeface appears somewhat anarchic, with an almost runic quality to its forms. The letterform strokes kick back in 90° corners after flowing curves. Its deep-cut inset horizontal and vertical counters are even more exaggerated in the italic versions. Despite the abstract-shaped letterforms, this distinctive typeface is still highly legible.

Pickle Standard is based on Bodhuin's Standard typeface, which comes in six weights: 20, 40, 60, 80, 100 and 120. The Pickle Standard design comes in one weight and three styles: Regular, Italic and a Reverse Italic.

Below and right. Launch material and specimen samples for the Pickle Standard grid-inspired typeface by BB-Bureau.

before touching
the ground

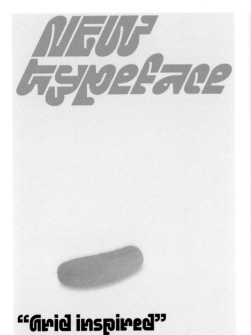

NEW
typeface

"Grid inspired"

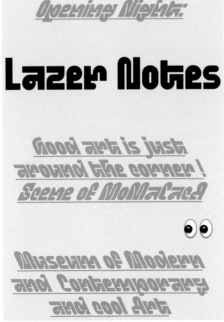

Opening Night:

Lazer Notes

Good art is just around the corner! Scene of MoMaCaca

Museum of Modern and Contemporary and cool Art

We're very excited, there is a danger in choice, in making decisions and sticking to them!

Separat

ABCDEFGHIJKLMNOPQRSTUVWXYZ
abcdefghijklmnopqrstuvwxyz
1234567890 !@#?:;"*&

The Separat typeface comes from Or Type (see p. 498), the online type foundry of GUNMAD, the Iceland and Brussels-based design studio. It is based on the concept of separating the shapes of the letterforms. This gives the geometric sans serif display type an industrial feel. Built around short curves and straight lines, the design principle creates a number of striking letterforms. It is available in four styles: Regular, Medium, Bold and Black. The lighter uppercase weights show the separate elements of the character construction, especially in letters such as 'B', 'K' and 'R'. Separat has fast become a popular choice for designers to use in branding and packaging applications. It has also been employed as display type for the British Council's *Ice Lab: New Architecture and Science in Antarctica* touring exhibition and the Europarque exhibition and conference centre in Portugal.

Foundry: Or Type
Designer: Mads Freund Brunse / Guðmundur Úlfarsson (GUNMAD)
Designer Nationality: Danish / Icelandic
Date: 2013

Below from left. Poster for *Learning from Japan* exhibition at the Designmuseum Denmark, design by Studio Claus Due; identity and branding for the London-based Redchurch Brewery (top), design by Bibliothèque; publication design *BAT: Bridging Art + Text* (bottom), design by Daniel Siim; poster design for British Council international touring exhibition *Ice Lab*, design by OK-RM.

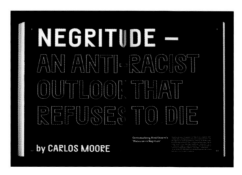

Sabre

ABCDEFGHIJKLMNOPQRSTUVWXYZ
1234567890 !@#?:;"*&

Foundry: Neutura
Designer: Alexander McCracken
Designer Nationality: American
Date: 2002

San Francisco-based designer Alexander McCracken created Sabre in 2002. It is a geometric sans serif with a monoline construction and rounded forms and corners. It comes in four weights: Thin, Light, Regular and Bold. Sabre has uppercase roman letters only.

Shotgun

ABCDEFGHIJKLMNOPQRSTUVWXYZ
1234567890 !@#?:;""*&

Foundry: Bitstream
Designer: J. Looney
Designer Nationality: American
Date: 1972

Bitstream's version of J. Looney's geometric Art Deco was originally designed for Visual Graphics Corporation in 1972, and comprises two options, the solid black Shotgun and the inline Shotgun Blanks. A Cyrillic version called Target was designed in 1997 by the Russian foundry Diai JS.

Sinaloa

ABCDEFGHIJKLMNOPQRSTUVWXYZ
1234567890 !?:;"*&

Foundry: Letraset
Designer: Rosemarie Tissi
Designer Nationality: Swiss
Date: 1974

This very decorative display face with strong geometric forms and characters with distinctive striped strokes was one of a handful created by Swiss designer Rosemarie Tissi. She set up the renowned Zurich graphic design studio Odermatt & Tissi with Siegfried Odermatt in 1968.

Solida

ABCDEFGHIJKLMNOPQRSTUVWXYZ
1234567890 !@#?:;"*&

Foundry: Graviton
Designer: Pablo Balcells
Designer Nationality: Argentinian
Date: 2012

As its name suggests, Solida is a very solid, display-only block-based typeface with a geometric angular look and science-fiction overtones. Argentinian designer Pablo Balcells released Solida through Graviton, the small type foundry he established in Buenos Aires in 2013.

Slayer

ABCDEFGHIJKLMNOPQRSTUVWXYZ
1234567890 !@#?:;"'*£

Never has a typeface been more appropriate for a Scandinavian death-metal record label in its appearance or by its name than the Slayer font family from Neutura (see p. 472). Slayer had its beginnings as a side project when Neutura's founder Alexander McCracken was working for Oslo design studio Bleed. Originally called Magma, Slayer comes in three weights: Regular, Bold and Heavy. Its heavy, aggressive, angular strokes, combined with its dark and bold appearance, and diagonally slashed end strokes mark it out as one attention-seeking rocker of typeface.

Foundry: Neutura
Designer: Alexander McCracken
Designer Nationality: American
Date: 2005

Below and right. Promotional posters for Slayer. Design by Neutura.

Standard

ABCDEFGHIJKLMNNOPQRSTUVWXYZ
abcdefghijklmnopqrstuvwxyz
1234567890 !@#?:;"‌‌&

Foundry: BB-Bureau
Designer: Benoît Bodhuin
Designer Nationality: French
Date: 2018

Standard is a grid-based geometric display typeface from French type and graphic design guru Benoît Bodhuin and his foundry, BB-Bureau (see p. 386). It is available in six weights, described as 20, 40, 60, 80, 100 and 120, and the numbers denote percentage increases in stroke weight dictated by the underlying grid structure used for each weight. As with its accompanying typeface cousin, Pickle Standard, the letterforms are built over a grid structure. Bodhuin studied mathematics at university before starting design school, and his imagination, passion for mathematics and love of geometrical patterns has been let loose with the aid of the grid. He has used the grid to create exaggerated character shapes employing semicircular forms married with horizontal and vertical strokes. The resultant design possesses an industrial consistency to its letterforms, while distinctive and strikingly playful patterns run through extended lengths of text.

Far left. Identity and poster for French jazz festival *Sur le Grill*. Design by Brest Brest Brest, using both Standard and Pickle Standard along with Laurenz Brunner's Circular sans serif.

Left. Promotion designs for Standard by BB-Bureau. Design by Benoît Bodhuin.

Spade

ABCDEFGHIJKLMNOPQRSTUVWXYZ
abcdefghijklmnopqrstuvwxyz
1234567890 !@#?;:"*&

Foundry: Neutura
Designer: Alexander McCracken
Designer Nationality: American
Date: 2008

Spade arrived on the scene during the early 21st century, when there was a trend in graphic design for contemporary, geometric, Fat Face typefaces. It struck first because Alexander McCracken, founder of Neutura (see p. 472), designed it as an all lowercase to accompany the uppercase.

Spade is an extremely heavy geometric display face that is available in three different styles. Ultralight possesses the thinnest of strokes tracing its outline, Regular is completely solid and is infilled, and Counter (above) possesses the smallest of counters.

Below. Posters for Spade display font by Neutura, designed by Alexander McCracken.

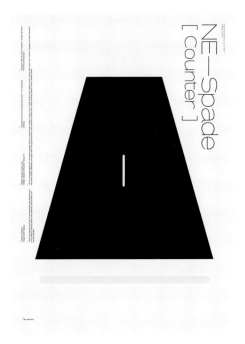
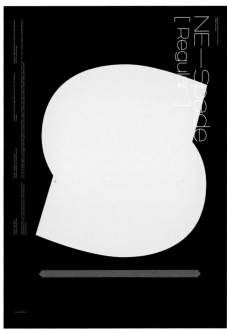
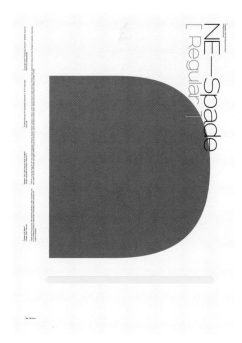

Ténica Slab

ABCDEFGHIJKLMNOPQRSTUVWXYZ
abcdefghijklmnopqrstuvwxyz
1234567890 !@#?;:"*&

Foundry: Graviton
Designer: Pablo Balcells
Designer Nationality: Argentinian
Date: 2014

A slightly condensed, modular, geometric slab serif with subtle rounded angles, Pablo Balcells's Ténica Slab is available in Regular and Bold weights that give text a classic look. It is also available in Regular Alternate and Bold Alternate versions for text that requires a more playful appearance.

ThreeSix Typeface System

ABCDEFGHIJKLMNOPQRSTUVWXYZ
abcdefghijklmnopqrstuvwxyz
1234567890 !@#?:;"*&

Foundry: FontFont
Designer: Hamish Muir /
Paul McNeil
Designer Nationality: British
Date: 2011

The ThreeSix Typeface System from MuirMcNeil (see p. 334) is an optical / geometric type system consisting of six typefaces in eight weights. The system is the result of an exploration of the legibility and readability of geometric typeface design. MuirMcNeil researched issues relating to the design of geometric typefaces that could be used for extended lengths of text as opposed to display applications.

The ThreeSix system operates to a rigid grid system and works within strict geometric constraints. All of its typefaces are based on a grid of 36-unit squares subdivided into 9 units. All of the typefaces are constructed from a set of modules using vertical or horizontal straight lines and circular arcs. In each typeface group, the vertical strokes of all weights align on a central axis and weight is applied as an increase or decrease on the stroke axis in 18-unit steps. In this way, all the letterform contours within each typeface group map on to each other exactly. This allows the designer to overlay differing weights precisely for varying effects because the cap-height, x-height, ascent and descent measurements are identical across all ThreeSix typefaces.

The optical and structural elements of ThreeSix operate on five key typographic functions: contour – the shape of individual letterforms; stroke modulation – the optical balance between horizontal strokes and vertical strokes; junctions – the optical effects at the intersections of strokes; weight – the progressive increase in density on the underlying structure of the letterforms; and spacing – the fit of the forms in sequences. Each typeface group has eight weights: 018 Ultra Light, 036 Extra Light, 054 Light, 072 Regular, 090 Medium, 108 Bold, 124 Heavy and 144 Black.

Below from left. Design process workings for testing of weights; *Inside Out* poster design showing overlaying of decreasing weights in register to each other; *Wim Crouwel: A Graphic Odyssey* show poster by MuirMcNeil.

Opposite. 36 poster, design by MuirMcNeil.

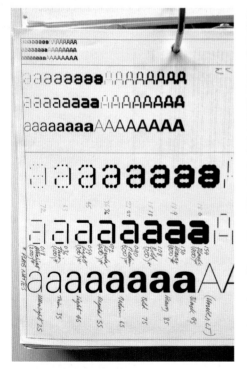
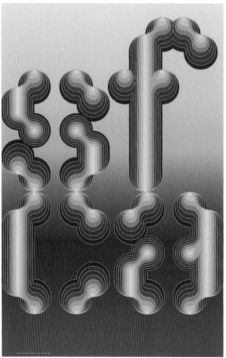

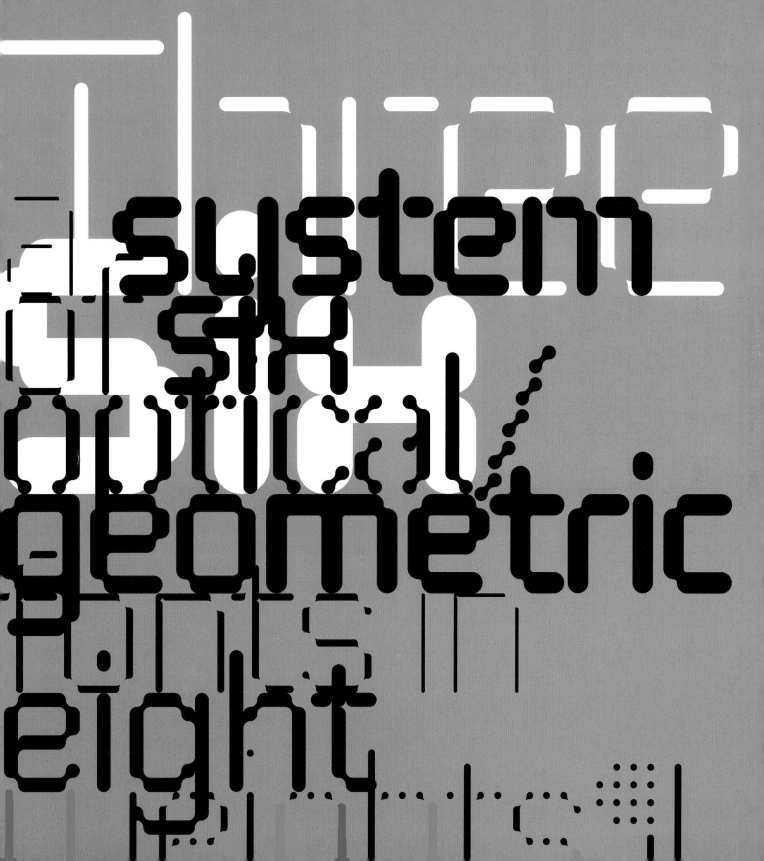

TwoBit

ABCDEFGHIJKLMNOPQRSTUVWXYZ
abcdefghijklmnopqrstuvwxyz
1234567890 !⊡#?:;"+&

Foundry: MuirMcNeil
Designer: Hamish Muir /
Paul McNeil
Designer Nationality: British
Date: 2018

TwoBit shares the same underlying grid as two other typefaces from MuirMcNeil (see p. 334), TwoPoint and TwoPlus. Also, as with a number of other typeface families from the foundry, individual characters are provided as segmented elements, which allows the designer free rein to experiment and build customized letterforms. The TwoBit family comes in five styles, each with seven weights. TwoBit A is a composite design. TwoBit B, C, D and E are segmented elements of partial strokes and points. They can be combined in multiple overlays because they share the same underlying grid position so that matching, spacing and interlocking can be exact. When combined, the effect is reminiscent of electrical circuits and components linked together, with a visual connectivity linking the letterforms in a striking and dynamic presentation.

The ability for designers to create custom characters is not the only feature that makes TwoBit appealing. Overlaid in pairs, TwoBit's thirty-five fonts allow for 1,225 combinations and, when paired with any of the seventy-six MuirMcNeil TwoPoint and TwoPlus collections – a combined total of 111 fonts – a possible 12,321 combinations can be achieved. The designer's creative options are further increased as they can also use software to outline, tint and colour type as well as apply textures, patterns and transparencies.

Below left. In TwoBit, one core (A) and four partial typefaces (B–E) comprise thirty-five fonts in matched ranges of seven numerically calibrated weights, all interlocking precisely when overlayed.

Below. Poster design for TwoBit by MuirMcNeil.

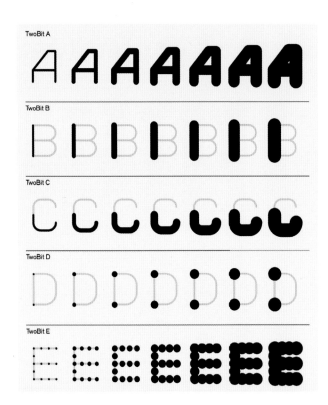

TwoBit A

TwoBit B

TwoBit C

TwoBit D

TwoBit E

TwoPlus

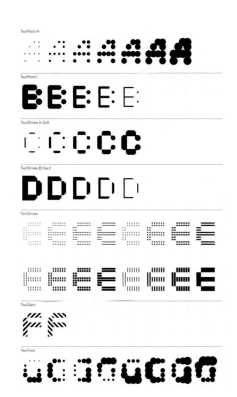

ABCDEFGHIJKLMNOPQRSTUVWXYZ
abcdefghijklmnopqrstuvwxyz
1234567890 !&#?:;"'+&

Foundry: MuirMcNeil
Designer: Hamish Muir /
Paul McNeil
Designer Nationality: British
Date: 2016

TwoPlus began life in 2015 as a custom type design for the London College of Communication summer and postgraduate shows. MuirMcNeil (see p. 334) then refined, expanded and completed it to create a full typeface collection for TypeCon 2016, an annual convention of the American Society of Typographic Aficionados. TwoPlus was used as the identity for the event and in the supporting print and media.

The TwoPlus type system comprises seven monospaced type collections with a total of forty-eight typefaces. Each collection comes in matched ranges of calibrated weights and has a set of rectangular background panels in corresponding grid patterns to the letters. As with other MuirMcNeil designs, characters are supplied as component elements to allow the designer to combine and vary letterforms. All the elements

match to an exact grid to permit precise layering, interlocking or even offsetting of the typeface components as well as inter-character spacing. It is possible to achieve 5,776 combinations when the seventy-six fonts across TwoPoint and TwoPlus are overlaid and used in pairs. The underlying precise grid structure means that the arrangement of characters and letter components can be set to exact positions. This makes TwoPlus and TwoPoint ideal for use in motion graphics, where precise placement of forms is vital when transitioning and animating, and in helping to create movement.

Below from left. Based on TwoPoint, TwoPlus is built around seven monospaced type groups, each font having a set of matching rectangular background panels with corresponding grid patterns; TwoPlus displayed at the LCC, London; TypeCon 2016 identity designed by MuirMcNeil.

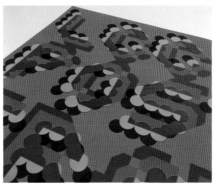

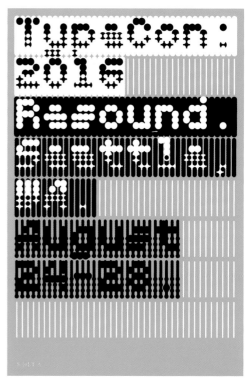

Cowhand

ABCDEFGHIJKLMNOPQRSTUVWXYZ
ABCDEFGHIJKLMNOPQRSTUVWXYZ
1234567890

Foundry: Monotype
Designer: Toshi Omagari
Designer Nationality: Japanese
Date: 2015

Toshi Omagari designed Cowhand as part of Monotype's first-ever Font Marathon, in which the foundry challenged designers to create a typeface from scratch in three days. Cowhand is a variable Western-style font, which allows all words set within it to share a single width.

DesperadoFLF

ABCDEFGHIJKLMNOPQRSTUVWXYZ
1234567890 !@#?:;"*&

Foundry: Casady & Greene
Designer: Richard Ware / Mike Wright
Designer Nationality: American
Date: 1993

The 'FLF' in Desperado FLF stands for 'Fluent Laser Fonts'. It was published in 1993 by Casady & Greene, a software publisher started by Robin Casady and Mike Greene which released the world's first PostScript fonts and closed in 2003. Desperado is an all-caps, Western-style slab serif.

Figaro

ABCDEFGHIJKLMNOPQRSTUVWXYZ
abcdefghijklmnopqrstuvwxyz
1234567890 !@#?:;"*&

Foundry: Monotype
Designer: Monotype Studio
Date: 1940

Monotype developed Figaro in-house and it was initially released as Figaro 536. This heavy, condensed, slab serif font has thick horizontals that make it almost a reverse-contrast face. It is inspired by 19th-century advertising types, and was released as Showboat in the United States.

IFC Boothill

ABCDEFGHIJKLMNOPQRSTUVWXYZ
ABCDEFGHIJKLMNOPQRSTUVWXYZ
1234567890

Foundry: Ink Font Customs
Designer: Anton Krylov
Designer Nationality: Russian
Date: 2012

Ink Font Customs released IFC Boothill as a free font for personal use in 2012. It was created by Anton Krylov, a designer based in Chelyabinsk, Russia, close to the Ural Mountains. It is a wobbly, condensed, Western-style display font with fat slab serifs and uppercase and small caps only.

Italienne

ABCDEFGHIJKLMNOPQRSTUVWXYZ
abcdefghijklmnopqrstuvwxyz
1234567890 ! @ #?:;"'*&

Foundry: Linotype
Designer: Richard Yeend
Designer Nationality: British
Date: 2002

Italienne is a heavy, condensed display font with extreme contrast and thick serifs. British designer Richard Yeend created it for Linotype in 2002. The typeface was inspired by US wood type of the Wild West era and the reverse-contrast Italienne (or Italian) type style popular in the 19th century.

Old Towne No 536

ABCDEFGHIJKLMNOPQRSTUVWXYZ
abcdefghijklmnopqrstuvwxyz
1234567890 !@#?:;"*&

Foundry: Elsner+Flake
Designer: Elsner+Flake
Designer Nationality: German
Date: 1990

Old Towne No 356 is a robust, historical display face. It was inspired by old wood types, popularized in the United States through cinematic visions of the Wild West. The letterforms are notable for having serifs thicker than their strokes, which is a feature of Italienne-style reverse-contrast types.

Playbill

ABCDEFGHIJKLMNOPQRSTUVWXYZ
abcdefghijklmnopqrstuvwxyz
1234567890 !@#?:;"*&

Foundry: Stephenson, Blake & Co.
Designer: Robert Harling
Designer Nationality: British
Date: 1938

Playbill is an Italienne display font inspired by 19th-century wood types, later popularized in Hollywood westerns. The font contains a single style, which features bold, condensed shapes alongside serifs that are greater in weight than their corresponding strokes.

Rio Oro

ABCDEFGHIJKLMNOPQRSTUVWXYZ
ABCDEFGHIJKLMNOPQRSTUVWXYZ
1234567890 !@#?:;"*&

Foundry: Pixel Sagas
Designer: Neale Davidson
Designer Nationality: American
Date: 2012

Released in 2012, and later updated in 2015, Rio Oro is a Tuscan, Western-style, display slab serif with uppercase and small caps only. It was designed by Neale Davidson of Pixel Sagas and is available free for personal use. Rio Oro comes in Regular and Bold weights with italics.

Wainwright

ABCDEFGHIJKLMNOPQRSTUVWXYZ
1234567890 !@#?.;,"*&

Foundry: Image Club Graphics
Designer: Noel Rubin
Designer Nationality: Canadian
Date: 1995

Wainwright is an extremely condensed, uppercase slab serif with thick serifs. It comes in a single style, which is heavy with a Wild West feel. Noel Rubin designed many fonts for Image Club Graphics and later created interfaces shown in *Star Wars: Episode I* (1999) and *Star Wars: Episode III* (2005).

Wanted

ABCDEFGHIJKLMNOPQRSTUVWXYZ
abcdefghijklmnopqrstuvwxyz
1234567890 !@#?.;,"*&

Foundry: Letraset
Designer: Letraset Design Studio
Date: 1995

Designed by an unnamed staffer at Letraset in 1996, Wanted is a distressed, condensed slab serif in the Italienne style that emerged in the 19th century. As the name suggests, it would suit a wanted poster in the old West, thanks to its thick serifs and under-inked appearance.

Westside

ABCDEFGHIJKLMNOPQRSTUVWXYZ
abcdefghijklmnopqrstuvwxyz
1234567890 !@#?.;,"*&

Foundry: Linotype
Designer: Adrian Frutiger
Designer Nationality: Swiss
Date: 1989

Westside, which is perhaps one of the most surprising of the typeface designs by Adrian Frutiger (see p. 290), is a wood-type-inspired Italienne slab serif with thick serifs and reverse-contrast. Westside is best used at large sizes and comes in one style. As the name implies, it has a Wild West feel.

Winslett

ABCDEFGHIJKLMNOPQRSTUVWXYZ
ABCDEFGHIJKLMNOPQRSTUVWXYZ
1234567890 !@#?.;,"*&

Foundry: Pixel Sagas
Designer: Neale Davidson
Designer Nationality: American
Date: 2012

Winslett is a decorative Western-style typeface with thick slab serifs and central diamond ornaments on most letters. It was designed by Neale Davidson and has caps and small caps only. It comes in two weights, with a further outline version, all of which have matching italics.

Academy Engraved

ABCDEFGHIJKLMNOPQRSTUVWXYZ
abcdefghijklmnopqrstuvwxyz
1234567890 !@#?:;"'*&

Foundry: Letraset
Designer: Vince Whitlock
Designer Nationality: British
Date: 1989

Vince Whitlock designed this distinguished serif typeface for Esselte Letraset in 1989. It was based on the forms of 18th-century Roman fonts such as Caslon, which were a popular source of inspiration for designers of similar engraved typefaces in the early 20th century.

Augustea Open

ABCDEFGHIJKLMNOPQRSTUVWXYZ
1234567890 !@#9:;"'*&

Foundry: Nebiolo
Designer: Alessandro Butti / Aldo Novarese
Designer Nationality: Italian
Date: 1951

Augustea Open is a classical uppercase serif typeface with distinctive details influenced by Roman stone carved type. It was originally published under the name Augustea Filettato, and digital versions of the font were later developed by Letraset, ITC and Elsner+Flake.

Boca Raton

ABCDEFGHIJKLMNOPQRSTUVWXYZ
abcdefghijklmnopqrstuvwxyz
1234567890 !@#?:;"'*&

Foundry: Image Club Graphics
Designer: Grant Hutchinson
Designer Nationality: Canadian
Date: 1993

Grant Hutchinson designed Boca Raton during his years working the night shift at Image Club, which he worked around his day job as a high school assistant. Hutchinson and his co-workers went on to found the visual-content library Veer, which has since been bought by Getty Images.

Burlington

ABCDEFGHIJKLMNOPQRSTUVWXYZ
abcdefghijklmnopqrstuvwxyz
1234567890 !@#?:;"'*&

Foundry: ITC
Designer: Alan Meeks
Designer Nationality: British
Date: 1985

Burlington is an engraved typeface designed by Alan Meeks in 1985, shortly after he departed from his role at Letraset to go freelance. Its tall ascenders and sharp serifs lend it a delicate, retro feel, and elongated tittles on the lowercase 'i' and 'j' add further interest.

Cabaret

ABCDEFGHIJKLMNOPQRSTUVWXYZ
abcdefghijklmnopqrstuvwxyz
1234567890 !?:;"*&

Foundry: Letraset
Designer: Alan Meeks
Designer Nationality: British
Date: 1980

This typeface shares certain similarities with the rounded letterforms of George Auriol's Robur Noir, which was published by Peignot in 1909 and in turn is said to have influenced the design of Cooper Black. Cabaret features additional engraved details and shaded embellishments.

Caslon OpenFace

ABCDEFGHIJKLMNOPQRSTUVWXYZ
abcdefghijklmnopqrstuvwxyz
1234567890 !@#?:;"*&

Foundry: Bitstream
Designer: William Caslon / Unknown
Designer Nationality: British
Date: 1915

The first engraved typeface to be published under the name 'Caslon Open Face' was released by Barnhart Brothers & Spindler in 1915; it features a lower x-height than many other Caslon-style fonts. This later digitization, created by Bitstream, is slightly heavier than its predecessor.

Castellar

ABCDEFGHIJKLMNOPQRSTUVWXYZ
1234567890 !@#?:;"*&

Foundry: Monotype
Designer: John Peters
Designer Nationality: British
Date: 1957

British type designer John Peters based his design of Castellar on ancient Roman square capitals; the typeface was first published by Monotype in 1957, relatively early in the phototypesetting era. Its finely chiselled serifs and engraved details suit larger point sizes.

Chevalier

ABCDEFGHIJKLMNOPQRSTUV
ABCDEFGHIJKLMNOPQRSTUVWXY
1234567890 !@#?:;"*&

Foundry: Haas
Designer: Emil A. Neukomm
Designer Nationality: Swiss
Date: 1946

Chevalier is an all-caps serif typeface with distinctive striped engraving, and was first released by Haas as metal type in 1946. Based on a style of lettering popular within 19th-century stationery and documents, it has since been expanded to include a full set of small caps.

Chisel

ABCDEFGHIJKLMNOPQRSTUVWXYZ
abcdefghijklmnopqrstuvwxyz
1234567890 !@#?:;"*&

Foundry: Stephenson, Blake & Co.
Designer: Robert Harling
Designer Nationality: British
Date: 1939

Robert Harling created this inline font for Stephenson, Blake & Co. based on the earlier Latin Bold Condensed. Harling was an interesting figure in the type world; he co-founded the journal *Typography* and the Shenval Press, and was also typographic advisor to London Transport.

Citation

ABCDEFGHIJKLMNOPQRSTUVWXYZ
1234567890 !@#?:;"*&

Foundry: Letraset
Designer: Trevor Loane
Designer Nationality: British
Date: 1990

Citation is a Copperplate-influenced display font designed by Trevor Loane for Letraset; it was one of the company's later releases and was published in 1990. The typeface features engraving, adding dimension and lending a sense of quiet authority to its uppercase letterforms.

Cloister Open Face

ABCDEFGHIJKLMNOPQRSTUVWXYZ
abcdefghijklmnopqrstuvwxyz
1234567890 !@#?:;"*&

Foundry: American Type Founders
Designer: Morris Fuller Benton
Designer Nationality: American
Date: 1929

Originally part of the Cloister Old Style family, this engraved Open Face version was first designed by Morris Fuller Benton for American Type Founders, and would later be revived for digital type by Bitstream. Benton's original design was heavily influenced by the work of Nicolas Jenson.

Commerce Gothic

ABCDEFGHIJKLMNOPQRSTUVWXYZ
1234567890 !@#?:;"*&

Foundry: Monotype
Designer: Jim Parkinson
Designer Nationality: American
Date: 1998

Type and logo designer Jim Parkinson developed this shadowed headline font in 1998 for the AgfaType Creative Alliance, one year after Monotype joined forces with Agfa to expand the Alliance's growing library of typefaces. Commerce Gothic is available in uppercase only.

Fashion

ABCDEFGHIJKLMNOPQRSTUVWXYZ
abcdefghijklmnopqrstuvwxyz
1234567890 !?:;"*&

Foundry: Letraset
Designer: Alan Meeks
Designer Nationality: British
Date: 1986 / 1991

This font was first released as Fashion Compressed No. 3 in 1986. Alan Meeks updated it in 1991, when he added an extra style, Fashion Engraved. Fashion is a condensed but elegant high-contrast modern, roman, serif typeface with fine serifs, ball terminals and hairline contrast in places.

Festival

ABCDEFGHIJKLMNOPQRSTUVWXYZ
1234567890 !@#?:;"*&

Foundry: Monotype
Designer: Phillip Boydell
Designer Nationality: British
Date: 1950

Festival, cut by Monotype in 1950 and used as the official type of the Festival of Britain in 1951, then released to the public in 1952, comes in a single Titling style. Festival Titling, designed by Phillip Boydell, is a distinctive uppercase, angular, shaded display sans serif.

ITC Abaton

ABCDEFGHIJKLMNOPQRSTUVWXYZ
ABCDEFGHIJKLMNOPQRSTUVWXYZ
1234567890 !@#?:;"*&

Foundry: ITC
Designer: Luis Siquot
Designer Nationality: Argentinian
Date: 1997

The work of Argentine designer Luis Siquot, ITC Abaton is a shaded display typeface with a thick outline, horizontal stripes within and small wedge-shaped serifs. It includes only uppercase and small-cap letters. Siquot studied in Germany, worked in Spain and then moved back to Argentina.

Jazz

ABCDEFGHIJKLMNOPQRSTUVWXYZ
abcdefghijklmnopqrstuvwxyz
1234567890 !?:;"*&

Foundry: Letraset
Designer: Alan Meeks
Designer Nationality: British
Date: 1992

Alan Meeks's Jazz, designed for Letraset and ITC in 1992, is a bold, wide headline font that has an Art Deco look thanks to thin stripes inlaid into its characters. These black and white horizontals also give it an elegant energy, much like the music from which it takes its name.

Modernistic

ABCDEFGHIJKLMNOPQRSTUVWXYZ
1234567890 !@#?:,""*&

Foundry: Monotype
Designer: Wadsworth A. Parker
Designer Nationality: American
Date: 1928

Wadsworth A. Parker's Modernistic is an open-face display font designed in the Art Deco style. The characters, which were drawn solely in uppercase, are defined by their high contrast, ornamental patterned interiors and short, keen serifs. It is ideal for posters and packaging.

PL Torino

ABCDEFGHIJKLMNOPQRSTUVWXYZ
abcdefghijklmnopqrstuvwxyz
1234567890 !©#?:,""*&

Foundry: Photo-Lettering
Designer: Ed Benguiat
Designer Nationality: American
Date: 1960

PL Torino is an open display typeface based on Alessandro Butti's Torino font, designed in 1908 for the Nebiolo foundry in Turin. While preserving the modern style of Butti's design, PL Torino introduces hollow, outlined strokes, which are accommodated by wider character widths.

Princetown

ABCDEFGHIJKLMNOPQRSTUVWXYZ
1234567890 !@#?:,""*&

Foundry: ITC
Designer: Richard Jones
Designer Nationality: British
Date: 1981

Princetown is an open display typeface based on the lettering commonly found on college and university sports garments. The geometric characters, designed in all-capitals, utilize squared curves, monoweight strokes and muscular slab serifs to convey an athletic style.

Smaragd

ABCDEFGHIJKLMNOPQRSTU
VWXYZ
1234567890 !@#?:;"*&

Foundry: Stempel
Designer: Gudrun Zapf von Hesse
Designer Nationality: German
Date: 1952

Smaragd is named after the German word for 'emerald'. A light and elegant font, it is ideally suited for formal situations, and is Gudrun Zapf von Hesse's interpretation of Baroque adornment engravings. Originally produced as metal type, it was later digitized by Linotype.

Advertisers Gothic

ABCDEFGHIJKLMNOPQRSTUVWXYZ
abcdefghijklmnopqrstuvwxyz
1234567890 !@#?:;"*&

Foundry: Western Type
Designer: Robert Wiebking
Designer Nationality: German
Date: 1917

German-born type designer Robert Wiebking built an impressive career as a type cutter in Chicago at the turn of the 20th century, using a pantographic punch-cutting device he designed himself. This assertive sans serif design of his from 1917 proved very popular upon its release.

AG Book Rounded

ABCDEFGHIJKLMNOPQRSTUVWXYZ
abcdefghijklmnopqrstuvwxyz
1234567890 ! ?:;"*&

Foundry: Berthold
Designer: Günter Gerhard Lange
Designer Nationality: German
Date: 1980

A friendlier counterpart to Berthold's Book font family, designed by Günter Gerhard Lange, this rounded typeface is well-suited to a wide range of informal display contexts. AG Book Rounded is available in six weights, with accompanying italics and an outline version.

Aldous

ABCDEFGHIJKLMNOPQRSTUVWXYZ
1234567890 !@#?:;"*&

Foundry: American Type Founders / Monotype
Designer: Walter Huxley
Designer Nationality: American
Date: 1935

Walter Huxley created this condensed monoline typeface in 1935, and it was originally published by American Type Founders as Huxley Vertical. Subject to several subsequent digitizations, the typeface is now also known as Aldous Vertical, and is published by Monotype.

Alternate Gothic

ABCDEFGHIJKLMNOPQRSTUVWXYZ
abcdefghijklmnopqrstuvwxyz
1234567890 !@#?:;"*&

Foundry: American Type Founders
Designer: Morris Fuller Benton
Designer Nationality: American
Date: 1903

Alternate Gothic shares several formal traits with Franklin Gothic and News Gothic, both of which it was designed to pair with well. The typeface was expanded in 2015, when it was republished as American Type Founders Alternate Gothic, to include a much wider range of weights and widths.

Anzeigen Grotesk

ABCDEFGHIJKLMNOPQRSTUVWXYZ
abcdefghijklmnopqrstuvwxyz
1234567890 !@#?:;"*&

Foundry: Haas Type Foundry
Designer: Haas Studio
Designer Nationality: Swiss
Date: 1943

A heavy sans serif typeface featuring an extremely large x-height, Anzeigen Grotesk was developed by the Swiss foundry Haas in 1943 for display use in advertising. Its influence can be seen in the design of later heavyweight condensed display typefaces such as Impact (1965).

Aura

ABCDEFGHIJKLMNOPQRSTUVWXYZ
abcdefghijklmnopqrstuvwxyz
1234567890 !@#?:;"*&

Foundry: Linotype
Designer: Jackson Burke
Designer Nationality: American
Date: 1960

This authoritative display sans was designed by Jackson Burke, then director of typographic development at Linotype, who was also responsible for the design of the popular Trade Gothic typeface. Aura remains a steadfast choice for headline type in an array of contexts.

Aurora

ABCDEFGHIJKLMNOPQRSTUVWXYZ
abcdefghijklmnopqrstuvwxyz
1234567890 !@#?:;"*&

Foundry: Linotype
Designer: Jackson Burke
Designer Nationality: American
Date: 1960

Based on the earlier heavy sans serif Corona and designed by Jackson Burke for newspaper use, Aurora is a German-influenced grotesque typeface, with distinctive curved diagonal details within certain uppercase letterforms. It has been the subject of numerous digitizations.

Avenida

ABCDEFGHIJKLMNOPQRSTUVWXYZ
ABCDEFGHIJKLMNOPQRSTUVWXYZ
1234567890 !@#?:;"*&

Foundry: ITC
Designer: John Chippindale
Designer Nationality: American
Date: 1994

John Chippindale designed Avenida in 1994, influenced by the type styles found on buildings in Andalusia around the time of World War II. Available in uppercase only, it features a mix of low-slung and raised crossbars, and high vertices within the 'M' and 'N'.

Balkan

ABCDEFGHIJKLMNOPQRSTUVWXYZ
АБЦДЕФГХИЈКЛМНОПQРСТУВWXYЗ

ABCDEFGHIJKLMNOPQRSTUVWXYZ
АБЦДЕФГХИЈКЛМНОПQРСТУВWXYЗ

1234567890 !@#?:;"'"&

Foundry: Typotheque
Design: Nikola Djurek /
Marija Juza
Designer Nationality: Croatian
Date: 2012

Created by Croatian designers Nikola Djurek and Mrija Juza, this bi-script display typeface features Cyrillic and Latin characters in tandem. Highlighting the letterforms shared between alphabets frequently used within the Balkan states, it is intended to promote unity and communication.

Bernhard Fashion

ABCDEFGHIJKLMNOPQRSTUVWXYZ
abcdefghijklmnopqrstuvwxyz
1234567890 !@#?:;"*&

Foundry: American Type
Founders
Designer: Lucian Bernhard
Designer Nationality: German
Date: 1929

Developed by the German-born designer Lucian Bernhard for American Type Founders, this fine and airy typeface captures the blithe spirit of the 1920s, with its balance of exaggerated capitals, low x-height and comparatively short descenders. It has since been digitized by URW and Bitstream.

Bigband

ABCDEFGHIJKLMNOPQRSTUVWXYZ
abcdefghijklmnopqrstuvwxyz
1234567890 !@#?:;"*&

Foundry: Ludwig & Mayer
Designer: Karlgeorg Hoefer
Designer Nationality: German
Date: 1974

This heavyweight sans serif typeface was originally issued by German foundry Ludwig & Mayer in 1974, featuring open and shaded styles; its later reissue by Linotype did away with the open Light cut and replaced it with Bigband Terrazo, a fractured version of the typeface.

Biondi Sans

ABCDEFGHIJKLMNOPQRSTUVWXYZ
ABCDEFGHIJKLMNOPQRSTUVWXYZ
1234567890 !@#?:;"*&

Foundry: Typodermic
Designer: Ray Larabie /
Chikako Larabie
Designer Nationality: Canadian /
Japanese
Date: 2010

Biondi Sans is a Copperplate-influenced uppercase sans serif with a subtly extended feel; it is also more formally restrained than many of Ray Larabie's other display typeface designs. It is available in a range of six weights, from Ultra Fine to Bold, with corresponding italics for each.

Brda

ABCDEFGHIJKLMNOPQRSTUVWXYZ
abcdefghijklmnopqrstuvwxyz
1234567890 !@#?:;"'*&

Foundry: Linotype
Designer: Franciszek Otto
Designer Nationality: Polish
Date: 2003

Brda was a winner of Linotype's International Type Design Contest in 2003. The heavy grotesque typeface features distinctive notched details. It was originally designed by Franciszek Otto for the Polish weekly newspaper *Powiat*, and is available in three weights, plus italics.

Camulogen

ABCDEFGHIJKLMNOPQRSTUVWXYZ
1234567890 !@#?:;"'*&

Foundry: Typodermic
Designer: Ray Larabie
Designer Nationality: Canadian
Date: 2012

This condensed sans serif typeface features geometric details and a subtly irregular stress within its stroke weight, making it an impactful yet distinctive choice for typesetting at a larger scale. Inspired by 19th-century poster type, Camulogen is available in uppercase only.

Carbon

ABCDEFGHIJKLMNOPQRSTUVWXYZ
1234567890 !@#?:;"'*&

Foundry: Typodermic
Designer: Ray Larabie
Designer Nationality: Canadian
Date: 1999

Carbon, designed by Ray Larabie in 1999, is a unicase, rounded geometric sans serif that comes in seven weights with italics. There are also two textured display versions: Fence which has a diagonal grid cut into it, and Phyber, with a hexagonal pattern inspired by carbon fibre.

Central Avenue

ABCDEFGHIJKLMNOPQRSTUVWXYZ
ABCDEFGHIJKLMNOPQRSTUVWXYZ
1234567890 !@#?:;"'*&

Foundry: Colophon
Designer: Studio Makgill
Designer Nationality: British
Date: 2011

Central Avenue was created for the identity of a show *Made in Birmingham: The Exhibition of Local Manufactures and Natural History 1886*. It is based on the exhibition's Victorian hand-painted type. This simple sans serif also has a superscripted alternative that enables users to create their own word logos.

Conductor

ABCDEFGHIJKLMNOPQRSTUVWXYZ
abcdefghijklmnopqrstuvwxyz
1234567890 !@#?:;"*&

Conductor was inspired by the blocky numerals appearing on vintage Bulgarian lottery tickets. The imposing sans serif display is a release from the foundry of esteemed US typeface designer Tobias Frere-Jones. As with many of Frere-Jones's type designs, there are a myriad of influences at play in the structure of these elegant letterforms. The chance for Bulgarians to become millionaires was not the only influence to play a part in the design; vernacular shopfront lettering and mid-century type designs, such as Eurostile, all contributed to the aesthetic.

Frere-Jones designed Conductor with Nina Stössinger, aided by contributions from colleague Fred Shallcrass. The intention was always that Conductor would be a display typeface, a change from the foundry's previous releases of text typefaces Exchange, Mallory and Retina. Conductor is available in four widths – wide, normal, narrow and condensed – with just bold and bold italic variants of each. Its roman construction is based around rectangular forms whereas the italic style is triangular forms, which is evident in the dramatic three-sided bowls and counters, and the vibrant movement and rhythm of its lowercase.

Foundry: Frere-Jones Type
Designer: Tobias Frere-Jones / Nina Stössinger
Designer Nationality: American / Swiss
Date: 2017

Below and opposite. Conductor is a commanding display family, which references among its various sources of inspiration delicate, blocky numerals from vintage Bulgarian lottery tickets.

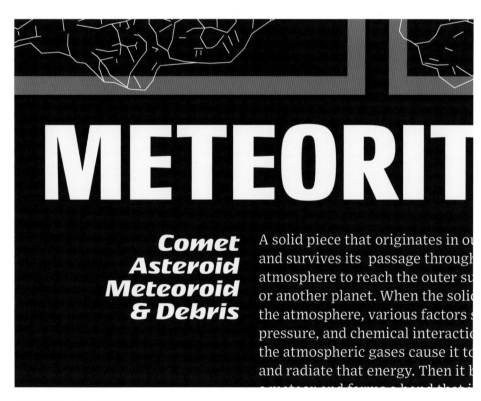

METEORIT

Comet
Asteroid
Meteoroid
& Debris

A solid piece that originates in ou and survives its passage through atmosphere to reach the outer su or another planet. When the solic the atmosphere, various factors s pressure, and chemical interactic the atmospheric gases cause it to and radiate that energy. Then it k

№2 Standard Brand

GAP
FILLE

Chelsea Clock Co.

03 25 cCc

SHOCKPROOF

Conductor
Conductor
Conductor
Conductor
Conductor
Conductor
Conductor
Conductor

Cable
Inertia
23 Volts
Semitone

CUBS
GLOVE
DINKUM
PALISADE

CONDUCTOR

Wide	***Wide Italic***
Normal	***Normal Italic***
Narrow	***Narrow Italic***
Condensed	***Condensed Italic***

CONDUCTOR

Chervonec Uzkj BT

ABCDEFGHIJKLMNOPQRSTUVWXYZ
abcdefghijklmnopqrstuvwxyz
1234567890 !@#?:,"*&

Foundry: Bitstream
Designer: Oleg Karpinsky
Designer Nationality: Ukrainian
Date: 2002

A hybrid semi-serif design, this condensed typeface with irregular serif details was created by Ukrainian type designer Oleg Karpinsky in three weights, each with a corresponding italic. A versatile and legible display typeface, it was published by Bitstream in 2002.

Compacta

ABCDEFGHIJKLMNOPQRSTUVWXYZ
abcdefghijklmnopqrstuvwxyz
1234567890 !@#?:,"*&

Foundry: Letraset
Designer: Fred Lambert
Designer Nationality: British
Date: 1963

Letraset's first original typeface design, Compacta was published in 1963 and went on to become widely used throughout the 1960s and beyond. Heavy and condensed, its rectangular forms are softened by rounded corners; two outline versions and a black cut are also available.

Conference

ABCDEFGHIJKLMNOPQRSTUVWXYZ
abcdefghijklmnopqrstuvwxyz
1234567890 !@#?:,"*&

Foundry: Letraset
Designer: Martin Wait
Designer Nationality: British
Date: 1978

British designer Martin Wait created Conference for Letraset. Wait is also known for the logos he designed for household brands, including Tetley Tea and the *Radio Times* TV listings magazine. Conference is a friendly and bold display font featuring a minuscule flare on some stroke ends.

Cruz Cantera BT

ABCDEFGHIJKLMNOPQRSTUVWXYZ
abcdefghijklmnopqrstuvwxyz
1234567890 !@#?:,"*&

Foundry: Bitstream
Designer: Ray Cruz
Designer Nationality: American
Date: 2002

Cruz Cantera is a narrow font featuring rounded stroke ends and a high contrast within its letterforms. It was designed by US type designer Ray Cruz, who founded his own Cruz Fonts foundry in New Jersey in 2004 and has created typefaces for a range of other distributors.

Decotura

ABCDEFGHIJKLMNOPQRSTUVWXYZ
ABCDEFGHIJKLMNOPQRSTUVWXYZ
1234567890 !@#?:;"*&

Foundry: Image Club Graphics
Designer: Greg Kolodziejzyk
Designer Nationality: Canadian
Date: 1995

Also available as an inline version, Decotura is an uppercase-only, geometric, Art Deco-inspired display typeface designed by Greg Kolodziejzyk, who was the founder of Image Club Graphics. A successful Canadian type foundry and distributor, Image Club Graphics was sold to Adobe in 1994.

Diablo

ABCDEFGHIJKLMNOPQRSTUVWXYZ
ABCDEFGHIJKLMNOPQRSTUVWXYZ
1234567890 !@#?:;"*&

Foundry: Monotype
Designer: Jim Parkinson
Designer Nationality: American
Date: 2002

Diablo is named after the Spanish word for 'devil'. The chunky geometric display font was inspired by the type found in early 20th-century sample books and hand-drawn poster lettering, and the aesthetic of the Arts and Craft movement. It has no lowercase, but there is a set of alternative characters.

Doric

ABCDEFGHIJKLMNOPQRST
abcdefghijklmnopqrstuvwxyz
1234567890 !@#?:;" *&

Foundry: Linotype
Designer: Walter Tracy
Designer Nationality: British
Date: 1973

Doric was originally released by the Stephenson, Blake & Co. foundry. It is modelled on one of William Caslon IV's popular sans serifs and was designed by Walter Tracy, who was head of the type development department at Linotype for thirty years, as well as typographic advisor to *The Times*.

Dynamo

ABCDEFGHIJKLMNOPQRSTUVWXYZ
abcdefghijklmnopqrstuvwxyz
1234567890 !@#?:;"*&

Foundry: Ludwig & Mayer
Designer: Karl Sommer
Designer Nationality: German
Date: 1930

Karl Sommer designed Dynamo in 1930 for Ludwig & Mayer. It is a bold typeface with the structure of a sans serif but with small angular notches and serifs. Letraset updated the typeface in the 1970s, with Colin Brignall creating a Medium weight and Alan Meeks adding a shadow version.

Druk

Druk

ABCDEFGHIJKLMNOPQRSTUVWXYZ
abcdefghijklmnopqrstuvwxyz
1234567890 !@#?:;"*&

Druk Text

ABCDEFGHIJKLMNOPQRSTUVWXYZ
abcdefghijklmnopqrstuvwxyz
1234567890 !@#?:;"*&

Druk Text Wide

ABCDEFGHIJKLMNOPQRSTUVWX
abcdefghijklmnopqrstuvwxyz
1234567890 !@#?:;"*&

Druk Wide

ABCDEFGHIJKLMNOPQRSTUVW
abcdefghijklmnopqrstuvwxyz
1234567890 !@#?:;"*&

Druk Cond

ABCDEFGHIJKLMNOPQRSTUVWXYZ
abcdefghijklmnopqrstuvwxyz
1234567890 !@#?:;"*&

Druk XCond

ABCDEFGHIJKLMNOPQRSTU
abcdefghijklmnopqrstuvwxyz
1234567890 !@#?:;"*&

Druk XXCond

ABCDEFGHIJKLMNOPQRSTU
abcdefghijklmnopqrstuvwxyz
1234567890 !@#?:;"*&

The extensive and uncompromising Druk typeface family by Independent US type designer Berton Hasebe is influenced by the sans serif types created in the 19th century for display purposes. The condensed styles established in Britain in the 1830s were soon widespread across Europe; their condensed and expanded forms with flat sides allowed for tight letter spacing, which made them ideal for eye-catching headline typography.

The Druk typeface came about in response to a commission in 2013 from Richard Turley, when he was creative director at *Bloomberg Businessweek*, to create a typeface for use in the style and culture section of the journal. Hasebe's research led him to investigate titles such as *Twen*, a 1960s German style magazine designed and art directed by influential post-war German graphic designer Willy Fleckhaus. Hasebe also examined the work of Dutch typographer Willem Sandberg and his catalogue designs for the Stedelijk Museum in Amsterdam. Druk contemporizes the historic condensed sans serifs that Hasebe researched.

It possesses no regular width and aims to be heavy and condensed or heavy and wide. Mixing the differing styles together, the designer can achieve the effect of woodblock compositions as contrasting lettershapes interlock with each other for dramatic effect.

Druk is available in twenty-two styles in four distinct families: Text, Text Wide, Wide and Condensed. Both Text and Text Wide are ideal for using the texts at smaller sizes. Condensed is the most extreme in design ranging from a Condensed Super, which is recommended for 40 point and above, to a Condensed XX Super, which is ideal for 72 point and above.

Foundry: Commercial Type
Designer: Berton Hasebe
Designer Nationality: American
Date: 2014 / 2015

Below left. *Bloomberg Businessweek* cover. Illustration by Tracy Ma, creative director Richard Turley.

Below right. Promotional print for Skate Agora, a stand-out typography system for the largest skate park in Europe in Barcelona. Design by Solo design studio, Madrid. Druk's variable styles employed to create design reminiscent of woodblock composition.

Eagle

ABCDEFGHIJKLMNOPQRSTUVWXYZ
1234567890 !@#?:;" * &

Foundry: American Type Founders
Designer: Morris Fuller Benton
Designer Nationality: American
Date: 1933

Morris Fuller Benton designed Eagle in 1933 for the National Recovery Administration established by President Franklin D. Roosevelt, and it was released by American Type Founders. It is an uppercase only, geometric sans serif in a single bold weight. The 'G' and 'Q' have angular spurs.

Engravers Gothic BT

ABCDEFGHIJKLMNOPQRSTUVWXYZ
ABCDEFGHIJKLMNOPQRSTUVWXYZ
1234567890 !@#?:;" * &

Foundry: Bitstream
Designer: Frederic W. Goudy
Designer Nationality: American
Date: 1990

Engravers Gothic BT is an extended sans serif font that has caps and small caps only. It is essentially Frederic W. Goudy's Copperplate Gothic but with the sharp little serifs removed, and comes in a regular weight only. Isabella Chaeva added a bold weight and Cyrillic for ParaType in 2003.

F2F Czykago

ABCDEFGHIJKLMNOPQRSTUVWXYZ
abcdefghijklmnopqrstuvwxyz
1234567890 !@#?:;"*&

Foundry: Linotype
Designer: Alexander Branczyk
Designer Nationality: German
Date: 1995

F2F Czykago was inspired by the Apple font Chicago. It comes in three distinct styles; a light sans serif, a bolder semi serif and the extended, experimental Trans. Its designer Alexander Branczyk worked at MetaDesign in Berlin and teaches typography at the Bauhaus-Universität Weimar.

FF Info Display

ABCDEFGHIJKLMNOPQRSTUVWXYZ
abcdefghijklmnopqrstuvwxyz
1234567890 !@#?:;"*&

Foundry: FontFont
Design: Erik Spiekermann / Ole Schäfer
Designer Nationality: German
Date: 2000

Erik Spiekermann (see p. 304) and Ole Schäfer began FF Info Display at agency Meta in 1996. The soft, highly legible sans serif typeface is part of a superfamily that also includes Info Correspondence and Info Text. It comes in eighteen styles and nine weights with italics.

FF Marten

ABCDEFGHIJKLMNOPQRSTUVWXYZ
abcdefghijklmnopqrstuvwxyz
1234567890 !@#?:;"'*&

Foundry: FontFont
Designer: Martin Wenzel
Designer Nationality: German
Date: 1991

FF Marten is a condensed display sans in two styles: Regular and the less-rounded Grotesque. Its creator, German designer Martin Wenzel, releases fonts with the Supertype foundry he co-founded with Jürgen Huber, a fellow typography teacher at the HTW Berlin.

Francis

ABCDEFGHIJKLMNOPQRSTUVWXYZ
abcdefghijklmnopqrstuvwxyz
1234567890 !@#?:;"'*&

Foundry: Typotheque
Designer: Nikola Djurek
Designer Nationality: Croatian
Date: 2016

Francis is a narrow sans serif in five weights with italics, and as the weight increases so does overall width. There is also Francis Gradient, four capital-only display versions, which each contain 2,690 glyphs that are selected automatically using OpenType's contextual alternates feature.

Gill Display Compressed

ABCDEFGHIJKLMNOPQRSTUVWXYZ
abcdefghijklmnopqrstuvwxyz
1234567890 !?:;"'*&

Foundry: ITC / Letraset
Designer: Eric Gill / Alan Meeks
Designer Nationality: British
Date: 1987

Alan Meeks designed this additional version of Gill Sans in 1987. Meeks stuck firmly to Eric Gill's design vision, creating a new cut that was heavy and compressed, filling a gap in Gill's initial range of weights and styles. It was released by International Typeface Corporation (ITC) and Letraset.

Gill Kayo Condensed

ABCDEFGHIJKLMNOPQRSTUVWXYZ
abcdefghijklmnopqrstuvwxyz
1234567890 !?:;"'*&

Foundry: Letraset
Designer: Eric Gill
Designer Nationality: British
Date: 1980

Gill Kayo, the ultra-bold version of Gill Sans drawn in 1932, received a condensed version from Letraset in 1980. Its extreme forms are far removed from the regular cut of Gill Sans. Eric Gill originally wanted to call Kayo (derived from 'KO', boxing slang for 'knockout') Double Elefans.

Good Times

ABCDEFGHIJKLMNOPQRSTU
VWXYZ
1234567890 !@#?:;"*&

Foundry: Typodermic
Designer: Ray Larabie
Designer Nationality: Canadian
Date: 2005

Good Times is a futuristic, extended, uppercase display sans serif created by Canadian designer Ray Larabie. It is available in seven weights with italics. Also included in the family is Bad Times, which is a distressed version of the heavy cut. Larabie was inspired by lettering on Pontiac cars.

Gothic 13

ABCDEFGHIJKLMNOPQRSTUVWXYZ
abcdefghijklmnopqrstuvwxyz
1234567890 !@#?:;"*&

Foundry: Adobe
Designer: Unknown
Date: c. 1800s

Gothic 13 is a single-style Bitstream sans serif. It is a digitization of an anonymous grotesque typeface called simply 'Gothic Condensed', which dates to the 19th century. It is heavy, compact and utilitarian, and is well-suited to use at large sizes such as headlines and poster type.

Gothic 821

ABCDEFGHIJKLMNOPQRSTUVWXYZ
abcdefghijklmnopqrstuvwxyz
1234567890 !@#?:;"*&

Foundry: Bitstream
Designer: Heinz Hoffmann
Designer Nationality: German
Date: 1921

Gothic 821 is a Bitstream version of Block, the heavy, rough sans serif released by Berthold in 1908. Block was first released in Bold only, but many weights followed in the two following decades. Gothic 821 is based on Block Condensed, known in German as *Schmale Block*.

Graphik XCond

ABCDEFGHIJKLMNOPQRSTUVWXYZ
abcdefghijklmnopqrstuvwxyz
1234567890 !@#?:;"*&

Foundry: Commercial Type
Designer: Christian Schwartz
Designer Nationality: American
Date: 2017

Christian Schwartz designed Graphik XCond with production assistance from Croatian type designer Hrvoje Živčić. It is an extra-condensed version of the earlier typeface Graphik, released in 2009 by Commercial Type (see p. 124). It comes in nine weights with italics and has been used by *Esquire*.

Graphik XXCond

ABCDEFGHIJKLMNOPQRSTUVWXYZ
abcdefghijklmnopqrstuvwxyz
1234567890 !@#?:;"*&

Foundry: Commercial Type
Designer: Christian Schwartz
Designer Nationality: American
Date: 2017

Christian Schwartz, the US co-founder of Commercial Type (see p. 124) who runs the foundry's New York office, designed Graphik XXCond in 2017. It is a very condensed grotesque sans serif type family that contains a large range of styles and comes in nine weights – Thin to Super – with matching italics.

Graphik XXXCond

ABCDEFGHIJKLMNOPQRSTUVWXYZ
abcdefghijklmnopqrstuvwxyz
1234567890 !@#?:;"*&

Foundry: Commercial Type
Designer: Christian Schwartz
Designer Nationality: American
Date: 2017

Graphik XXXCond, the third most condensed version of Schwartz's Graphik, has a large x-height and small ascenders and descenders. Commercial Type (see p. 124) explains that its open terminals create 'breathing room in the white spaces within the characters' and 'an inviting openness in the text'.

Graphik XXXXCond

ABCDEFGHIJKLMNOPQRSTUVWXYZ
abcdefghijklmnopqrstuvwxyz
1234567890 !@#?:;"*&

Foundry: Commercial Type
Designer: Christian Schwartz
Designer Nationality: American
Date: 2017

This is the most extreme of the Graphik condensed family and comes in eighteen styles. It was created while Christian Schwartz was working on what he thought would be the narrowest possible variant of Graphik when fellow designer Abi Huynh challenged him to try making it twice as narrow.

Halte

ABCDEFGHIJKLMNOPQRSTUVWXYZ
abcdefghijklmnopqrstuvwxyz
1234567890 !@#?:;"*&

Foundry: Typotheque
Designer: Hrvoje Živčić
Designer Nationality: Croatian
Date: 2018

Hrvoje Živčić's Halte is a distinctive and blocky condensed sans serif that was inspired by type used on transport signage in the streets of Zagreb. It is available in five weights with italics and small caps, and includes many alternate letters and transport-related pictograms.

Headline

ABCDEFGHIJKLMNOPQRSTUVWXYZ
abcdefghijklmnopqrstuvwxyz
1234567890 !@#?:;"'*&

Foundry: Monotype
Designer: Eleisha Pechey
Designer Nationality: British
Date: 1906

Headline is a compact grotesque sans serif available in bold only. It is a Monotype copy of Grotesque No. 9, which was designed by Eleisha Pechey for the Stephenson, Blake & Co. foundry in 1906 but based on 19th-century type styles. Headline, as the name implies, is best used large.

Helvetica Compressed

ABCDEFGHIJKLMNOPQRSTUVWXYZ
abcdefghijklmnopqrstuvwxyz
1234567890 !@#?:;"'*&

Foundry: Linotype
Designer: Matthew Carter
Designer Nationality: British
Date: 1966

Matthew Carter (see p. 616) designed Helvetica Compressed, a heavy condensed sans serif, for the Linofilm phototypesetter in 1966. Although by name it is part of the Helvetica family, this was mainly for marketing reasons; it has more in common with an earlier sans serif, Schmalfette Grotesk.

Horizon

ABCDEFGHIJKLMNOPQRSTUVWXYZ
abcdefghijklmnopqrstuvwxyz
1234567890 !@#?:;"'*&

Foundry: Bitstream
Designer: Bitstream Design Studio
Designer Nationality: American
Date: 1992

Horizon is an uncredited font designed in-house at digital foundry Bitstream in 1992. It was supposedly inspired by lettering used in the early series of the science-fiction TV show *Star Trek*. Available in one style, it is a heavy, sharp sans serif with angled crossbars and diamond tittles.

Huxley Vertical

ABCDEFGHIJKLMNOPQRSTUVWXYZ
1234567890 !@ #?:;"'*&

Foundry: American Type Founders
Designer: Walter Huxley
Designer Nationality: American
Date: 1935

An uppercase, monoline condensed sans serif released in 1935, Walter Huxley's Huxley Vertical has an Art Deco feel. It originally came in one style, which is fairly thin, with alternate versions of 'A', 'K', 'M', 'N', 'W' and 'Y'. There have been many digitizations, some of which added weights.

Impact

ABCDEFGHIJKLMNOPQRSTUVWXYZ
abcdefghijklmnopqrstuvwxyz
1234567890 !@#?:;"'*&

Foundry: Stephenson, Blake & Co.
Designer: Geoffrey Lee
Designer Nationality: British
Date: 1965

This compact heavy sans serif is ubiquitous thanks to its inclusion in Microsoft software. It was originally designed by Geoffrey Lee for Stephenson, Blake & Co. in 1965. Two extra styles, Condensed and Outline, were added in 1967. It has a large x-height and short ascenders and descenders.

Impacta

ABCDEFGHIJKLMNOPQRSTUVWXYZ
abcdefghijklmnopqrstuvwxyz
1234567890 !@#?:;"'*➊

Foundry: Linotype
Designer: Marc Lubbers
Designer Nationality: Dutch
Date: 1994

Impacta was created by Dutch typographer Marc Lubbers of GraphicMix in 1994 and was a winner in Linotype's first International Digital Type Design Contest. It is a heavy sans serif with angular details and sloped strokes. The typeface is available in a single style, which is very black.

Industrial Gothic

ABCDEFGHIJKLMNOPQRSTUVWXYZ
ABCDEFGHIJKLMNOPQRSTUVWXYZ
1234567890 !@#?:;"'*&

Foundry: Agfa
Designer: Jim Parkinson
Designer Nationality: American
Date: 1997

Industrial Gothic is a heavy, condensed all-caps sans serif. It comes in three styles, each of which has different lowercases. In Single Line, these letters are smaller and float above a line; Double Line has lines above and below; and Banner has lines and a gap through the middle.

Ingram BT

ABCDEFGHIJKLMNOPQRSTUVWXYZ
abcdefghijklmnopqrstuvwxyz
1234567890 !@#?:;"'*&

Foundry: Bitstream
Designer: Alexander Marshall
Designer Nationality: Scottish
Date: 2004

Ingram BT was created by Scottish-born designer Alexander Marshall, who trained in London before moving to California in 1980. The typeface is a tall, thin, decorative sans with Arts and Crafts details such as the dots on 'A', 'E', 'F', 'H' and 'Q', which replace crossbars. It has a slightly rough finish.

Insignia

ABCDEFGHIJKLMNOPQRSTUVWXYZ
abcdefghijklmnopqrstuvwxyz
1234567890 !@#?:;"*&

Foundry: Linotype
Designer: Neville Brody
Designer Nationality: British
Date: 1989

Linotype released Insignia under the name 'Stadia' in 1989. Insignia began life as lettering used by Neville Brody on *Arena*, the British men's magazine, for which he designed the debut issue in 1986. It is a geometric sans serif with eye-catching, extended strokes on many capitals.

Integral

ABCDEFGHIJKLMNOPQRSTUVWXYZ
abcdefghijklmnopqrstuvwxyz
1234567890 !®#?:;"*&

Foundry: Monotype
Designer: Jim Marcus
Designer Nationality: American
Date: Unknown

Integral was designed by Jim Marcus, a US designer who created many fonts while working in-house at the T-26 foundry. It is a distinctive, rounded sans serif with letters that look like they have been squeezed horizontally. Available in a single weight, it has a large x-height.

ITC Blair

ABCDEFGHIJKLMNOPQRSTUV
ABCDEFGHIJKLMNOPQRSTUVWXYZ
1234567890 !@#?:;"*&

Foundry: ITC
Designer: Jim Spiece
Designer Nationality: American
Date: 1997

ITC Blair is a revival made by Jim Spiece in 1997 of Blair, an extended serif-less take on the Copperplate style released in 1900 by the St Louis-based Inland Type Foundry. ITC Blair originally came in three styles, but after input from Monotype in 2016, this was expanded to twelve.

ITC Flatiron

ABCDEFGHIJKLMNO
PQRSTUVWXYZ
1234567890 !@#?:;"*&

Foundry: ITC
Designer: Unknown
Date: 1997

Flatiron is an extremely wide, monoline, uppercase only sans serif typeface, which the International Typeface Corporation (ITC) released in 1997. It was based on an earlier design from Photo-Lettering, whose co-founder Ed Rondthaler also co-founded ITC, so the two foundries shared many fonts.

ITC Freddo

ABCDEFGHIJKLMNOPQRSTUV
abcdefghijklmnopqrstuvw
1234567890 !@#?:;"'"*&

Foundry: ITC
Designer: James Montalbano
Designer Nationality: American
Date: 1996

US type designer James Montalbano trained under Ed Benguiat (see p. 514). He designed Freddo for the International Typeface Corporation (ITC) in 1996.

It is a wide sans serif with rounded forms and an informal feel. Available in one style with upper and lowercase, it is suited to large use only.

ITC Grapefruit

ABCDEFGHIJKLMNOPQRSTUVWXYZ
abcdefghijklmnopqrstuvwxyz
1234567890 !@#?:;"'*&

Foundry: ITC
Designer: Györi Attila
Designer Nationality: Hungarian
Date: 1997

ITC Grapefruit is the only font release from Hungarian designer Györi Attila. Informal and energetic, this angular geometric sans serif has a slightly retro feel. The typeface is available in a single weight – Bold, with upper and lowercases – and is suitable for a wide variety of uses.

ITC Migrate

ABCDEFGHIJKLMNOPQRSTUVWXYZ
abcdefghijklmnopqrstuvwxyz
1234567890 !@#?:;"'*&

Foundry: ITC
Designer: George Ryan
Designer Nationality: American
Date: 1999

ITC Migrate is a condensed display sans serif. It is an update of the Oz Handicraft typeface George Ryan designed for Bitstream in 1991, based on drawing samples found by type designer Oswald Bruce Cooper in the *Book of Oz Cooper* (1949), published by the Society of Typographic Arts in Chicago.

ITC New Rennie Mackintosh

ABCDEFGHIJKLMNOPQRSTUVWXYZ
abcdefghijklmnopqrstuvwxyz
1234567890 !@#?:;"'*&

Foundry: ITC
Designer: Phill Grimshaw
Designer Nationality: British
Date: 2017

ITC Rennie Mackintosh was the result of a collaboration between the International Typeface Corporation (ITC) and the Glasgow School of Art in 1996 based on the work of architect Charles Rennie Mackintosh. The update improved on the original two styles, expanding it to four weights with italics.

Neutura

Neutura, the San Francisco-based foundry and design studio established by Alexander McCracken in 2003, offers a concise portfolio of fine display typefaces. Design styles include modern, antique and classical, as well as a range of illustrative, contemporary block and stencil types. Neutura offers bespoke font-design services as well as customization of its existing types, and its types can be seen in commissions for high-profile clients including Nike, Electronic Arts and *Wired* magazine. In addition, the studio specializes in producing visual identities and print design for creative, design-led clients. A number of typefaces in the Neutura portfolio were created specifically for design commissions and later developed to be available to the public.

Founded: 2003
Country: America
Website: neutura.org
Notable typefaces:
Maisalle (see p. 417)
Spade (see p. 441)

Below and right. Neutura promotional designs for a selection of its crafted display types – from left, Royale (ampersand detail), Royale, Neutrino and Interpol (top).

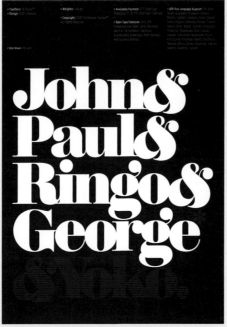

Below. Geometric sans serif
Orange Round.

Bottom. Decorative display type
Cérie available in Regular and
Outline styles.

Below. A sans serif design
with humanist traits, Aperture
is available in thin, regular and
heavy weights.

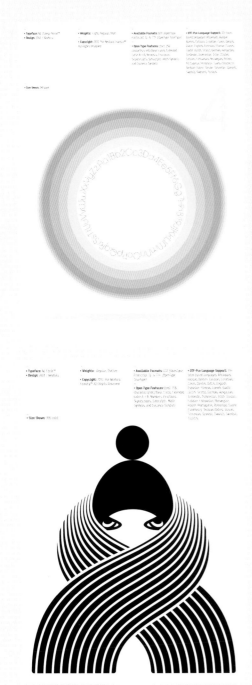

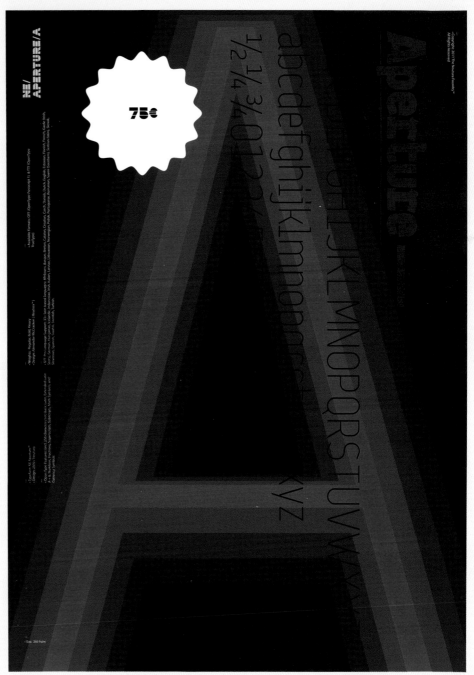

ITC Odyssée

ABCDEFGHIJKLMNOPQRSTUVWXYZ
abcdefghijklmnopqrstuvwxyz
1234567890 !@#?:;"*&

Foundry: ITC
Designer: Roselyne Besnard / Michel Besnard
Designer Nationality: French
Date: 1996

ITC Odyssée is a sans serif display typeface, inspired by the illusionary aesthetics of digital media. The font, designed in four weights from Light to Ultra, replicates the dynamic lines created by a TV screen's optical residue to fashion a series of electric letterforms.

ITC Verkehr

ABCDEFGHIJKLMNOPQRSTUVWXYZ
abcdefghijklmnopqrstuvwxyz
1234567890 !@#?:,"&

Foundry: ITC
Designer: Mott Jordan
Designer Nationality: American
Date: 1996

Available in one bold weight, ITC Verkehr is a heavy, condensed grotesque sans serif. It was created by Mott Jordan, a freelance designer from California, who reversed the usual convention of a grotesque by making the top halves of letters slightly heavier than their bottoms.

Kadeworth

ABCDEFGHIJKLMNOPQRSTUVWXYZ
abcdefghijklmnopqrstuvwxyz
1234567890 !@#?:,"*&

Foundry: Typodermic
Designer: Ray Larabie
Designer Nationality: Canadian
Date: 2010

Kadeworth is a bold, rounded condensed sans serif in a single style designed with headline usage in mind. It manages to achieve an authoritative feel while remaining friendly. According to its designer, Ray Larabie, Kadeworth was 'specifically designed for use on the web'.

Kleptocracy

ABCDEFGHIJKLMNOPQRSTUVWXYZ
abcdefghijklmnopqrstuvwxyz
1234567890 !@#?:,"*&

Foundry: Larabie Fonts
Designer: Ray Larabie
Designer Nationality: Canadian
Date: 1999

Before he started commercial foundry Typodermic in 2001, Canadian designer Ray Larabie released fonts on his Larabie Fonts website, publishing some 250 free fonts from 1996 to 2001. Kleptocracy is a curvy sans serif that comes in three weights and three widths – Condensed, Regular and Extended.

Koala

ABCDEFGHIJKLMNOPQRSTUVWXYZ
abcdefghijklmnopqrstuvwxyz
1234567890 !@#?:;"'*&

Foundry: Linotype
Designer: Éric de Berranger
Designer Nationality: French
Date: 2003

Koala was created by French type designer Éric de Berranger, a former student of Jean-François Porchez and co-founder of La Fonderie. The display sans serif was first published by Linotype in three weights. It has a large x-height, short descenders and broad strokes.

Kobalt

ABCDEFGHIJKLMNOPQRSTUVWXYZ
abcdefghijklmnopqrstuvwxyz
1234567890 !@#?:;"'*&

Foundry: ITC
Designer: Leslie Cabarga
Designer Nationality: American
Date: 1998

US illustrator, writer and designer Leslie Cabarga created Kobalt for the International Typeface Corporation (ITC). It is a heavy geometric sans serif that pays homage to fonts of the 1920s and 1930s. Kobalt is available in two weights – Bold and Black – and has an all-caps, shadowed version, Kartoon.

Koloss

ABCDEFGHIJKLMNOPQRSTUVWXYZ
abcdefghijklmnopqrstuvwxyz
1234567890 !@#?:;"'*&

Foundry: Ludwig & Mayer
Designer: Jakob Erbar
Designer Nationality: German
Date: 1923

German foundry Ludwig & Mayer released Koloss in 1923 as an extra-bold companion to Feder-Grotesk, a sans serif family designed by Jakob Erbar in 1909. Koloss is a heavy and wide upright sans serif with broad strokes, small counters, a large x-height and short descenders.

La Pontaise

ABCDEFGHIJKLMNOPQRSTUVWXYZ
abcdefghijklmnopqrstuvwxyz
1234567890 !@#?:;"'*&

Foundry: Or Type
Designer: Mads Freund Brunse
Designer Nationality: Danish
Date: 2013

La Pontaise is a high-contrast, elegant grotesque sans serif designed by Mads Freund Brunse, the Danish co-founder of foundry Or Type (see p. 498). It was first used on opening invitations to the Saint-Valentin gallery in Lausanne, Switzerland. It comes in four roman weights from Light to Semibold.

Lexikos

ABCDEFGHIJKLMNOPQRSTUVWXYZ
abcdefghijklmnopqrstuvwxyz
1234567890 !?:;"*&

Foundry: ITC
Designer: Vince Whitlock
Designer Nationality: British
Date: 1990

British designer Vince Whitlock designed Lexikos for the International Typeface Corporation (ITC) in 1990. It is a condensed sans serif, which seems squished thanks to narrow letters and horizontal strokes heavier than the vertical. Colin Brignall's typeface Corinthian provided Whitlock's base.

Linotype Freytag

ABCDEFGHIJKLMNOPQRSTUVWXYZ
abcdefghijklmnopqrstuvwxyz
1234567890 !@#?:;"*&

Foundry: Linotype
Designer: Arne Freytag
Designer Nationality: German
Date: 2012

Linotype Freytag is a geometric display typeface comprised of four weights and corresponding italics. The condensed sans serif characters combine rounded strokes with spur-less stems, as seen in the 'a' or 'n', alongside distinguishing stroke endings, notable in the uppercase 'T'.

Linotype Rory

ABCDEFGHIJKLMNOPQRSTUVWXYZ
abcdefghijklmnopqrstuvwxyz
1234567890 !@#?:;"*&

Foundry: Linotype
Designer: Tad Biernot
Designer Nationality: Canadian
Date: 1997

Linotype Rory is a dynamic display typeface, initially submitted to Linotype's International Digital Type Design Contest and later published as part of Linotype's TakeType Library. The font's oblique forms are reminiscent of mechanical precision, strength and speed.

Loft

ABCDEFGHIJKLMNOPQRSTUVWXYZ
abcdefghijklmnopqrstuvwxyz
1234567890 !@#?:;"*&

Foundry: Monotype
Designer: Julien Janiszewski
Designer Nationality: French
Date: 2007

Loft is a sans serif display typeface inspired by 19th-century wood types and *défense d'afficher* (post no bills) signs, commonly found across France. The font features seven weights, which expand only in stroke thickness, with counter size remaining the same throughout.

Marché Super

ABCDEFGHIJKLMNOPQRSTUVWXYZ
abcdefghijklmnopqrstuvwxyz
1234567890 !@#?:;"*&

Foundry: Colophon
Designer: The Entente
Designer Nationality: British
Date: 2014

Marché Super was designed by The Entente – the graphic design agency linked to the independent London-based foundry Colophon (see p. 210) – for issue 186 of the photography magazine *Hotshoe*. It is a heavy, utilitarian sans serif inspired by Eurostile, which is available in a single bold, roman style.

Metroblack 2

ABCDEFGHIJKLMNOPQRSTUVWXYZ
abcdefghijklmnopqrstuvwxyz
1234567890 !@#?:;"*&

Foundry: Linotype
Designer: William A. Dwiggins
Designer Nationality: American
Date: 1932

In 1929, pioneering US graphic designer William A. Dwiggins was commissioned to create a sans serif, which he named Metro. Linotype wanted a competitor to Bauer's Futura, so in 1932 Dwiggins made revisions, creating the more geometric Metro No. 2 starting with the black weight.

Modified Gothic

ABCDEFGHIJKLMNOPQRSTUVWXYZ
ABCDEFGHIJKLMNOPQRSTUVWXYZ
1234567890 !@#?:;"*&

Foundry: Linotype
Designer: Linotype Design Studio
Date: 2002

Modified Gothic is a 1920's style Art Deco-inspired titling sans serif typeface designed in-house by Linotype. It has uppercase and small caps only and a monoline geometric construction. It comes in a single weight and was included in Linotype's TakeType 4 Library released in 2002.

Monotype Clearface Gothic

ABCDEFGHIJKLMNOPQRSTUVWXYZ
abcdefghijklmnopqrstuvwxyz
1234567890 !@#?:;"*&

Foundry: Monotype
Designer: Morris Fuller Benton
Designer Nationality: American
Date: 1910

US type designer Morris Fuller Benton created Clearface Gothic, a slightly flared sans serif companion to his serifed Clearface, for the American Type Founders in 1910. Monotype's digitization, one of many foundries' versions, comes in two roman weights, Bold and Demi Bold.

Montefiore

ABCDEFGHIJKLMNOPQRSTUVWXYZ
abcdefghijklmnopqrstuvwxyz
1234567890 !@#?:;"*&

Foundry: Colophon
Designer: The Entente
Designer Nationality: British
Date: 2009

Montefiore, a condensed utilitarian sans serif, was initially released by Colophon (see p. 210) in 2009 in two weights. In 2017, it was revamped and comes in six condensed weights – Thin to Extra Bold. It was inspired by lettering on a Victorian street nameplate on Montefiore Road in Hove, East Sussex, England.

Moon Cresta

ABCDEFGHIJKLMNOPQRSTUVWXYZ
abcdefghijklmnopqrstuvwxyz
1234567890 !@#?:;"*&

Foundry: Typodermic
Designer: Ray Larabie
Designer Nationality: Canadian
Date: 2010

Ray Larabie, the prolific Canadian type designer based in Japan, designed Moon Cresta in 2010. It is a friendly, bold rounded sans serif font that was built using the same proportions as Goudy Sans. Moon Cresta comes in a single roman weight and is intended for contemporary headline usage.

Neographik

ABCDEFGHIJKLMNOPQRSTUVWXYZ
abcdefghijklmnopqrstuvwxyz
1234567890 !@#?:;"*&

Foundry: Monotype
Designer: Robert Barbour
Designer Nationality: British
Date: 1970

Neographik by British designer Robert Barbour was one of Monotype's first photolettering fonts. It is a heavy sans serif with a large x-height and short ascenders and descenders. It was released in 1970 and appeared on the cover of *Monotype Newsletter 88* in February 1971.

Pantograph

ABCDEFGHIJKLMNOPQRSTUVWXYZ
abcdefghijklmnopqrstuvwxyz
1234567890 !@#?:;"*&

Foundry: Colophon
Designer: Studio Makgill
Designer Nationality: British
Date: 2009

Designed by the Brighton-based creative agency Studio Makgill in 2009, Pantograph is a quirky, narrow, rounded sans serif typeface that replicates the lettering used in the British pantograph etching process, mostly for technical signs on buildings and streets. It is available in a single roman style.

PDU

ABCDEFGHIJKLMNOPQRSTUVWXYZ
abcdefghijklmnopqrstuvwxyz
1234567890 !αт#?:;"'*ᕿ

Foundry: Colophon
Designer: Dries Wiewauters
Designer Nationality: Belgian
Date: 2011

Dries Wiewauters designed PDU; its name refers to the *Plaque Découpée Universelle* stencil-based signwriting system patented by Joseph A. David in 1876. It is a bold sans serif and comes in Solid, Stencil and Outline versions, with many ornament glyphs for making patterns.

Peignot

ABCDEFGHIJKLMNOPQRSTUVWXYZ
abcdefghijklmnopqrstuvwxyz
1234567890 !@#?:;"*&

Foundry: Deberny & Peignot
Designer: Cassandre / Charles Peignot
Designer Nationality: French
Date: 1937

Peignot was created in 1937 by leading French designer Cassandre and Charles Peignot of the foundry Deberny & Peignot. It is a sans serif with contrast, which mixes the styles of upper- and lowercase letters. It was released in two weights, with a third – the bold – added in 1938.

Placard

ABCDEFGHIJKLMNOPQRSTUVWXYZ
abcdefghijklmnopqrstuvwxyz
1234567890 !@#?:;"*&

Foundry: Monotype
Designer: Monotype Studio
Date: 1937

Placard is a heavy, condensed poster sans serif designed by an unnamed staff member at Monotype. It was released in a single weight in 1937 and four extra styles followed in 1939. In 2018, Monotype's Malou Verlomme designed Placard Next, expanding the family to four widths with six weights each.

Plaza

ABCDEFGHIJKLMNOPQRSTUVWXYZ
1234567890 !@#?:;"*&

Foundry: Letraset
Designer: Alan Meeks
Designer Nationality: British
Date: 1975

Plaza – originally named Playboy until magazine publisher Hugh Hefner threatened legal action – was designed by Letraset type designer Alan Meeks in 1975. It was released in three styles – Plaza, Plaza Ultra and Plaza Inline – and is an uppercase, geometric sans serif with swashed alternates.

Posterama

ABCDEFGHIJKLMNOPQRSTUVWXYZ
abcdefghijklmnopqrstuvwxyz
1234567890 !@#?:;"*&

Foundry: Monotype
Designer: Jim Ford
Designer Nationality: American
Date: 2016

The Posterama typeface has been described as 'a journey through space and type'. Its creator Jim Ford, a US visual artist and type designer for Monotype, has said it is 'the typeface of the future…only yesterday'. Posterama's subtle but distinctive varying styles have been influenced by reference points in art, typography, science fiction, architecture, science and culture of the 20th century.

Each year referred to in the Posterama typeface names has a variation in its construction reflecting the time period after which it is named as well as themes from the time and 20th-century depictions of the future. At its core is Posterama 1927, referring to the year Paul Renner created the Futura typeface. However, 1927 is also the year that the groundbreaking science-fiction drama *Metropolis* by Expressionist film director Fritz Lang was released.

Other typefaces in the family include Posterama 1901, which pays homage to the Art Nouveau and Art and Crafts movement that arose at the turn of the 20th century. Posterama 1913 is a tribute to the 'International Exhibition of Modern Art' (aka 'Armory Show') of 1913, where the work of revolutionary artists such as Pablo Picasso, Marcel Duchamp and Wassily Kandinsky were first shown in the United States. Posterama 1919 recalls the founding of the Bauhaus and its ensuing influence on the design of European typography. Posterama 1933 includes Art Deco elements. Posterama 1945's Cyrillic characters signify the end of World War II, and the start of the Cold War and the nuclear arms race. Posterama 1984 alludes to George Orwell's novel and the science-fiction movies of the 1980s such as *Blade Runner* (1982) and *Terminator* (1984), along with the

advent of arcades games such as Pac-Man. Finally, Posterama 2001 was inspired by director Stanley Kubrick's space epic *2001: A Space Odyssey* (1968) as well as influences from the National Aeronautics and Space Administration's logotype. Each of the eight typefaces in the Posterama collection are available in seven weights, ranging from Thin through to Ultra.

Below. With multiple cultural reference points from the 20th century, Posterama is a comprehensive and diverse portfolio of display types.

Railroad Gothic

ABCDEFGHIJKLMNOPQRSTUVWXYZ
1234567890 !@#P:;"*&

Foundry: American Type Founders
Date: 1906

Railroad Gothic – a heavy, condensed, uppercase grotesque sans serif – was released by the American Type Founders in 1906 and was a popular choice for headline use thanks to its no-nonsense, industrial feel. Derek Birdsall used it on his series of book covers for Penguin Education.

Regatta Condensed

ABCDEFGHIJKLMNOPQRSTUVWXYZ
abcdefghijklmnopqrstuvwxyz
1234567890 !?:;"*&

Foundry: Letraset
Designer: Alan Meeks
Designer Nationality: British
Date: 1987

Regatta Condensed was designed by former Letraset in-house type designer Alan Meeks in 1987. It comes in a single roman weight, which is black and narrow. The typeface is a quirky sans serif with diamond-shaped dots, a large x-height and angled terminals.

Republik Sans

ABCDEFGHIJKLMNOPQRSTUVWXYZ
1234567890 !@#?:;"*&

Foundry: Image Club Graphics
Designer: Jackson Mahr / Noel Rubin
Designer Nationality: British / Canadian
Date: 1994

British designer Jackson Mahr and US designer Noel Rubin created Republik Sans for Image Club Graphics in 1994. It is an angular all-caps sans serif that comes in four styles: 01, which is the regular weight; 02, which is bold; 03, which is outlined; and 03 Alt, which is inlined.

Revue

ABCDEFGHIJKLMNOPQRSTUVWXYZ
abcdefghijklmnopqrstuvwxyz
1234567890 !@#?:;"*&

Foundry: Letraset
Designer: Colin Brignall
Designer Nationality: British
Date: 1968

Letraset designer Colin Brignall created Revue in 1968, inspired by poster lettering from the early 20th century. It is a heavy, quirky sans serif font with many distinguishing features, such as the angled lower terminals of 'F', 'H' and 'Y' which hang below the baseline.

Rubino Sans

ABCDEFGHIJKLMNOPQRSTUVWXYZ
abcdefghijklmnopqrstuvwxyz
1234567890 !@#?:;"'*&

Foundry: Image Club Graphics
Designer: Noel Rubin
Designer Nationality: Canadian
Date: 1994

Noel Rubin created Rubino Sans for Image Club Graphics in 1994. It is a humanist sans serif with contrast. The typeface comes in five styles that are the same weight: the conventional Fill and Outline, as well as three versions – Regular, Solid and Guides – which features construction lines and grids.

Rumori

ABCDEFGHIJKLMNOPQRSTUVWXYZ
abcdefghijklmnopqrstuvwxyz
1234567890 !@#?:;"'*&

Foundry: Type Brut
Designer: Paul McNeil
Designer Nationality: British
Date: 2014

Rumori was designed for a reprint of Luigi Russolo's Futurist manifesto *L'Arte dei rumori* (*The Art of Noise*, 1913). Paul McNeil found inspiration for the heavy grotesque sans serif from lettering on the cover of a 1916 edition. It comes in one weight in two versions: Chiari (sharp) and Morbidi (soft).

Sackers Gothic

ABCDEFGHIJKLMNOPQRSTUVWX
ABCDEFGHIJKLMNOPQRSTUVWXYZ
1234567890 !@#?:;"*&

Foundry: Compugraphic
Designer: Gary Sackers
Designer Nationality: American
Date: 1975

Sackers Gothic is part of a series of typefaces designed by Gary Sackers for Compugraphic in 1974 and 1975 based on old engraving types. It is an uppercase and small caps-only extended sans serif which comes in three roman weights: Light, Medium and Heavy. A square version is also available.

Smart Sans

ABCDEFGHIJKLMNOPQRSTUVWXYZ
abcdefghijklmnopqrstuvwxyz
1234567890 !@#?:;"*&

Foundry: Monotype
Designer: Rod McDonald
Designer Nationality: Canadian
Date: 2000

Smart Sans is a tribute to Canada's design pioneer Leslie 'Sam' Smart, and this is Rod McDonald's second typeface. He was inspired by Fred Lambert's Compacta designed in 1963 for Letraset and the Helvetica Compressed series designed by Matthew Carter (see p. 616) for Linotype in 1966.

Shire Types

ABCDEFGHIJKLMNOPQRSTUVWXYZ
ABCDEFGHIJKLMNOPQRSTUVWXYZ
1234567890 !@#?:;"*&

Foundry: Jeremy Tankard Typography
Designer: Jeremy Tankard
Designer Nationality: British
Date: 1998

Shire Types, by British type designer Jeremy Tankard, is a heavy, Blackletter design that was inspired by idiosyncratic 19th-century grotesque and Egyptian-style vernacular lettering from around the British Isles. The playful and characterful family is designed in an Ultra Heavy style, with a mix of eye-catching sans and serif characters whose chunky and rounded forms make an impact.

Shire Types is available in six fonts, each named after English counties grouped around the Black Country, which formed the industrial heartland of the UK. The fonts have design variations to create variety when used separately, yet have a unified appearance when mixed together. The block sans of Derbyshire and Staffordshire are capitals only and reflect the industrial strength of the areas. The Cheshire and Shropshire designs have a more uncial feel to their appearance, based on historical ideas of mixing uppercase and lowercase letters. The fonts named after the counties of Warwickshire and Worcestershire possess a more rounded, scriptlike design to reflect the rolling hills of the English countryside.

The Shire Types family features a number of highly crafted design details. For example, there are no ascenders or descenders so all the characters fit to the same height, allowing lowercase and capital letters to be mixed with a uniform setting. Some letters are constant across the designs – for instance, the 'O' and 'S'. Cyrillic and Greek variants were released in 2011 in addition to the Roman. In 2012, Mourad Boutros, one of the world's leading Arabic calligraphers, designers and typographers, helped to create an Arabic version, Shire Arabic.

Below. From snappy hairdresser store fronts to bicycle liveries, Shire Types' mix of upper and lowercase, sans and serif letterforms make for playful and impactful designs.

Steelfish

ABCDEFGHIJKLMNOPQRSTUVWXYZ
abcdefghijklmnopqrstuvwxyz
1234567890 !@#?:;"*&

Foundry: Typodermic
Designer: Ray Larabie
Designer Nationality: Canadian
Date: 2005

Steelfish is a gritty display typeface with an authoritative tone that was inspired by newspaper headlines from the mid 20th century. It has been updated and expanded since its release in 2001 and comprises fifteen weights, from ExtraLight to ExtraBold, with matching italics and an inline version.

Storm Sans

ABCDEFGHIJKLMNOPQRSTUVWXYZ
abcdefghijklmnopqrstuvwxyz
1234567890 !@#?:;"*&

Foundry: Agfa / Monotype
Designer: Nina Lee Storm
Designer Nationality: Danish
Date: 1999

Storm Sans was the first commercially available typeface from Korean-born, Denmark-based designer Nina Lee Storm. A neutral, fairly condensed sans serif display typeface, it is available in two weights, Regular and Bold. Storm's next creation was for Linotype in 2004, Noa.

Swiss 911

ABCDEFGHIJKLMNOPQRSTUVWXYZ
abcdefghijklmnopqrstuvwxyz
1234567890 !@#?:;"*&

Foundry: Bitstream
Designer: Max Miedinger / Hans-Jörg Hunziker / Matthew Carter
Designer Nationality: Swiss / Swiss / British
Date: 1957 / 1966

Bitstream's version of Helvetica Compressed was developed in 1966 by Hans-Jörg Hunziker and Matthew Carter (see p. 616) from the original Neue Haas Grotesk design created for the Haas foundry in Switzerland by Max Miedinger (see p. 229) in 1957 and renamed Helvetica in 1960.

Swiss 921

ABCDEFGHIJKLMNOPQRSTUVWXYZ
abcdefghijklmnopqrstuvwxyz
1234567890 !@#?:;"*&

Foundry: Bitstream
Designer: Max Miedinger
Designer Nationality: Swiss
Date: 1957

Swiss 921 is Bitstream's version of Helvetica Inserat (1957) by Max Miedinger (see p. 229), renamed to avoid copyright infringement. It is a grotesque sans serif with short ascenders and descenders and comes in a bold condensed roman style that is well suited to advertising and headline use.

Tempo

ABCDEFGHIJKLMNOPQRSTUVWXYZ
abcdefghijklmnopqrstuvwxyz
1234567890 !@#?:;"'*&

Foundry: Ludlow Typograph
Designer: R. Hunter Middleton
Designer Nationality: British
Date: 1930–31

This headline typeface was created for use in newspapers and produced as a response to the instant success of Paul Renner's Futura. Tempo is a heavy, condensed font that is also based on a geometric design, but with a number of more humanistic traits.

THD Sentient

ABCDEFGHIJKLMNOPQRSTUVWXYZ
1234567890 !@#?:;"'*&

Foundry: MuirMcNeil
Designer: Tim Hutchinson / Hamish Muir / Paul McNeil
Designer Nationality: British
Date: 2017

THD Sentient is an all-caps monolinear sans serif designed for the *Beyond 2001: New Horizons* exhibition at the London College of Communication to celebrate ten years of the Stanley Kubrick Archive. It was inspired by type used on the screen of HAL 9000 in *2001: A Space Odyssey* (1968).

Trotzkopf

ABCDEFGHIJKLMNOPQRSTUVWXYZ
abcdefghijklmnopqrstuvwxyz
1234567890 !@#?:;"'*&

Foundry: Agfa
Designer: Bo Berndal
Designer Nationality: Swedish
Date: 1997

Bo Berndal designed Trotzkopf in 1997 for Agfa and was one of Sweden's leading graphic designers and typographers up until his death in 2013. It is a decorative sans serif that comes in two weights, Regular and Bold. Trotzkopf blends rounded corners with wider, swooping curves.

Valter

ABCDEFGHIJKLMNOPQRSTUVWXYZ
abcdefghijklmnopqrstuvwxyz
1234567890 !@#?:;"*&

Foundry: Typotheque
Designer: Nikola Djurek
Designer Nationality: Croatian
Date: 2014

Nikola Djurek's Valter is a distinctive, elegant high-contrast sans serif that comes in seven weights – Hairline to Bold – with matching cursive italics. It was published by Typotheque (see p. 90) in 2014 and the Type Directors Club awarded it a Certificate of Typographic Excellence a year later.

Vendela

ABCDEFGHIJKLMNOPQRSTUVWXYZ
1234567890 !@#?:;"*&

Neutura, the San Francisco-based foundry and studio of Alexander McCracken, published the Vendela heavy rounded sans serif in 2011. It is available in a single weight, without italics or lowercase, and has a futuristic, technical feel thanks to its geometric construction.

Foundry: Neutura
Designer: Alexander McCracken
Designer Nationality: American
Date: 2011

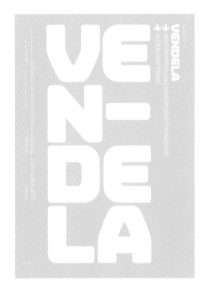

Vienna Extended

ABCDEFGHIJKLMN
PQRSTUVWXYZ
1234567890 !@#?:;"*&

Foundry: Letraset
Designer: Anthony De Meester
Designer Nationality: Canadian
Date: 1989

The work of Canadian designer Anthony De Meester, Vienna Extended is a very wide, monoline uppercase sans serif that was released by Letraset in 1989. It is available in a single weight, which is light, and it has high crossbars. Vienna is most effective where a look of regal elegance is desired.

Windpower

ABCDEFGHIJKLMNOPQRSTUVWXYZ
ABCDEFGHIJKLMNOPQRSTUVWXYZ
1234567890 !@#?:;"&*

Foundry: Typodermic
Designer: Ray Larabie
Designer Nationality: Canadian
Date: 2005

Windpower, released by Typodermic in 2005, is a heavy sans serif display font in a single style. Both its upper and lowercase are capitals only, but the uppercase capitals feature triangular wings facing left – which, according to designer Ray Larabie, 'give them extra aerodynamic thrust'.

Algerian

ABCDEFGHIJKLMNOPQRSTUVWXYZ
1234567890 !@#?:;"*&

Foundry: Stephenson, Blake & Co.
Designer: Alan Carr / Philip Kelly / Alan Meeks
Designer Nationality: British
Date: 1907

Algerian was first released in *c.* 1907 by Stephenson, Blake & Co. and then experienced a revival during the 1980s when several digitizations of the typeface were developed. Algerian has been included with Microsoft Office products since 1993, and has earned a certain notoriety as a result.

Arsis

ABCDEFGHIJKLMNOPQRSTUVWXYZ
abcdefghijklmnopqrstuvwxyz
1234567890 !@#?:;"*&

Foundry: American Type Founders / Amsterdam Type
Designer: Gerry Powell
Designer Nationality: American
Date: 1937

Credited to former American Type Founders director Gerry Powell, this neoclassical typeface is said to have been released by two foundries simultaneously – as Arsis in the Netherlands and as Onyx in the United States. Whatever its origin, it remains an elegant and robust choice for display typesetting.

BB-book A

ABCDEFGHIJKLMNOPQRSTUVWXYZ
abcdefghijklmnopqrstuvwxyz
1234567890 !@#?:;"*&

Foundry: BB-Bureau
Designer: Benoît Bodhuin
Designer Nationality: French
Date: 2016

BB-book A is part of Benoît Bodhuin's playful BB-book font family. It is a characterful display typeface featuring a mix of jaunty curves, diagonal forms and triangular semi-serif details. It is available in four distinctive styles, from an ultra-extended Bold to a super-condensed Light.

BB-book B

ABCDEFGHIJKLMNOPQRSTUVWXYZ
abcdefghijklmnopqrstuvwxyz
1234567890 !@#?:;"*&

Foundry: BB-Bureau
Designer: Benoît Bodhuin
Designer Nationality: French
Date: 2016

BB-book B continues the ideas Benoît Bodhuin explored within BB-book A (2016), and features increased contrast and more open characters throughout. Its distinctive wedge details are more pronounced than in the previous version, and its line weight grows finer within its expanded weights.

BB-book Contrasted

ABCDEFGHIJKLMNOP
abcdefghijklmnopqrs
1234567890 !@#?:;"*&

Foundry: BB-Bureau
Designer: Benoît Bodhuin
Designer Nationality: French
Date: 2016

This font is based on the bold cut of Bodhuin's earlier typeface BB-book A (2016). It was developed with increased contrast and a deliberate sense of awkwardness within its characters. The extended forms and exaggerated curves offer a distinctly contemporary feel within display contexts.

BB-book Monospaced

ABCDEFGHIJKLMNOPQRSTUVWXYZ
abcdefghijklmnopqrstuvwxyz
1234567890 !@#?:;"*&

Foundry: BB-Bureau
Designer: Benoît Bodhuin
Designer Nationality: French
Date: 2018

This addition to the BB-book family features monospaced characters based on those of its predecessors, BB-book A and BB-book B (both 2016). Unifying the widths of the entire alphabet means the unconventional proportions and irregular details of Bodhuin's earlier designs are amplified.

BB-book Text

ABCDEFGHIJKLMNOPQRSTUVWX
abcdefghijklmnopqrstuvwxyz
1234567890 !@#?:;"*&

Foundry: BB-Bureau
Designer: Benoît Bodhuin
Designer Nationality: French
Date: 2018

Bodhuin developed BB-book Text from his earlier designs for BB-book A and BB-book B (both 2016), translating their unexpected angular details and reversed contrast into a typeface more suitable for the setting of longer passages of text. BB-book Text retains the distinctiveness of its predecessors.

Belshaw

ABCDEFGHIJKLMNOPQRSTUVWXYZ
abcdefghijklmnopqrstuvwxyz
1234567890 !@#?:;"*&

Foundry: ITC
Designer: Nick Belshaw
Designer Nationality: British
Date: 1980

Nick Belshaw's eponymous display font exhibits the influence of Art Nouveau typefaces, featuring generous curves and rounded corners throughout. A heavy typeface with comparatively small counters, it is best used at larger point sizes for headline type to remain legible.

Bernhard Modern

ABCDEFGHIJKLMNOPQRSTUVWXYZ
abcdefghijklmnopqrstuvwxyz
1234567890 !@#?:;"*&

Foundry: American Type Founders
Designer: Lucian Bernhard
Designer Nationality: German
Date: 1937

German typographer and creative polymath Lucian Bernhard designed this high-contrast modern serif font for American Type Founders in 1937. A versatile design with a low x-height, it features a subtle softness and slight irregularity within its fine serifs, appearing crisp yet approachable.

Bodebeck

ABCDEFGHIJKLMNOPQRSTUVWXYZ
abcdefghijklmnopqrstuvwxyz
1234567890 !@#?:;"*&

Foundry: Linotype
Designer: Anders Bodebeck
Designer Nationality: Swedish
Date: 2002

This neo-transitional roman type family by Swedish designer Anders Bodebeck is a clean, elegant choice for display typesetting, featuring sinuous curves and wide open counters. Published by Linotype in 2002, it is available in three weights with two accompanying italics.

Bodoni Unique

ABCDEFGHIJKLMNOPQRSTUVWXYZ
ABCDEFGHIJKLMNOPQRSTUVWXYZ
1234567890 !@#?:;"*&

Foundry: Panache Typography
Designer: Giambattista Bodoni / David Farey
Designer Nationality: Italian / British
Date: 1995

Based on Giambattista Bodoni's eponymous design, this contemporary interpretation by British type designer David Farey is extreme in terms of distortion and is the result of an experiment to see how far the original Bodoni could be condensed. It is available in uppercase only.

Bordeaux

ABCDEFGHIJKLMNOPQRSTUVWXYZ
abcdefghijklmnopqrstuvwxyz
1234567890 !@#?:;"*&

Foundry: Letraset
Designer: David Quay
Designer Nationality: British
Date: 1987

David Quay, the co-founder of The Foundry (see p. 284), designed this didone display typeface for Letraset in 1987. Condensed and romantic in style, it has subsequently been licensed by several other distributors, and both script and shadowed counterparts to the original are also available.

Brothers

ABCDEFGHIJKLMNOPQRSTUVWXYZ
abcdefghijklmnopqrstuvwxyz
1234567890 !@#?:;"*&

Foundry: Emigre
Designer: John Downer
Designer Nationality: American
Date: 1999

Brothers was inspired by lettering found on the stationery of a travelling-circus company from the turn of the 20th century. It is a robust and angular display typeface featuring flared serifs and octagonal forms, which is available in Regular and Bold styles with a Super Slant oblique.

Burgstaedt Antiqua

ABCDEFGHIJKLMNOPQRSTUVWXYZ
abcdefghijklmnopqrstuvwxyz
1234567890 !@#?:;"*&

Foundry: Linotype
Designer: Richard Yeend
Designer Nationality: British
Date: 2002

Burgstaedt Antiqua is part of Linotype's TakeType 5 collection. It features a mix of different serif styles within its character set. Irregularities and asymmetric forms appear throughout the design, creating a sense of character that becomes more pronounced upon closer inspection.

Burin

ABCDEFGHIJKLMNOPQRSTUVWXYZ
abcdefghijklmnopqrstuvwxyz
1234567890 !@#?:;"*&

Foundry: Monotype
Designer: Monotype Studio
Date: 1994

Burin is a quirky serif designed in 1994 by an unnamed member of Monotype's type design team. It is part of a two-font family that contains its sans serif sibling Burin Sans. Burin, which comes in one regular roman weight, is a Clarendon-esque serif with contrast and ball terminals.

Cajoun

ABCDEFGHIJKLMNOPQRSTUVWXYZ
abcdefghijklmnopqrstuvwxyz
1234567890 !@#?:;"*&

Foundry: Linotype
Designer: Hans-Jürgen Ellenberger
Designer Nationality: German
Date: 2002

The curves of Cajoun's distinctive letterforms have a distribution of weight similar to Old Style typefaces. This, coupled with a low x-height, causes the letterforms to pull the eye in a downward direction, meaning that the typeface is most effective when used at larger sizes.

Canela

ABCDEFGHIJKLMNOPQRSTUVWXYZ
abcdefghijklmnopqrstuvwxyz
1234567890 !@#?:;"*&

Foundry: Commercial Type
Designer: Miguel Reyes
Designer Nationality: Mexican
Date: 2016

Miguel Reyes took Caslon as his starting point for the design of Canela, developing an elegant font with a contemporary feel that offers a new perspective on this traditional type style. Canela made its debut in Issue No. 5 of the US arts and fashion magazine *Document Journal*.

Canela Condensed

ABCDEFGHIJKLMNOPQRSTUVWXYZ
abcdefghijklmnopqrstuvwxyz
1234567890 !@#?:;"*&

Foundry: Commercial Type
Designer: Miguel Reyes
Designer Nationality: Mexican
Date: 2018

This condensed cut of Canela was created by Mexican designer Miguel Reyes. It was developed to emphasize the verticality of the original, while preserving the fluid balance of its forms. Like its predecessor, its details are best appreciated within large-scale display and headline applications.

Carlton

ABCDEFGHIJKLMNOPQRSTUVWXYZ
abcdefghijklmnopqrstuvwxyz
1234567890 !@#?:;"*&

Foundry: Letraset
Designer: Letraset Design Studio
Date: 1983

Digitized by Letraset in 1983, this graceful and refined serif font was based on an earlier Stephenson, Blake & Co. typeface of the same name, which itself was copied from Fritz Helmuth Ehmcke's Ehmcke Antiqua from 1909. It has since been licensed by ITC and Linotype.

Caslon Antique

ABCDEFGHIJKLMNOPQRSTUVWXYZ
abcdefghijklmnopqrstuvwxyz
1234567890 !@#?:;"*&

Foundry: Barnhart Brothers & Spindler / American Type Founders
Designer: Berne Nadall
Designer Nationality: American
Date: 1898

Originally called Fifteenth Century, this was acquired by American Type Founders and renamed Caslon Antique. However, it is not a true Caslon type, having been designed to imitate 15th-century types created for the Venetian master printers. The first digital version was made by URW in 1990.

Caslon Black

ABCDEFGHIJKLMNOPQRSTUVWXYZ
abcdefghijklmnopqrstuvwxyz
1234567890 !@#?:;"*&

Foundry: ITC
Designer: William Caslon / Dave Farey
Designer Nationality: British
Date: 1725 / 1982

Caslon Black is one of the many variations of William Caslon's 18th-century original and is intended exclusively for display use. It retains a hint of the original design but has taken on its own robust character. Designer Dave Farey has described his work as being that of a 'letter repairer'.

Caslon Titling

ABCDEFGHIJKLMNOPQRSTUVWXYZ
1234567890 !@#?:;"*&

Foundry: Monotype
Designer: William Caslon / Monotype Studio
Designer Nationality: British
Date: 1932

This is one of many versions of William Caslon's 18th-century classic and one of three revivals by the British Monotype company. Caslon Titling's letters were based on those from the British foundry Stephenson, Blake & Co., giving it a distinctive style, with generous proportions.

Central Station

ABCDEFGHIJKLMNOPQRSTUVWXYZ
abcdefghijklmnopqrstuvwxyz
1234567890 !@#?:;"*&

Foundry: Monotype
Designer: Leslie Cabarga
Designer Nationality: American
Date: 1999

The multitalented US author, illustrator, cartoonist, animator, publication and typeface designer Leslie Cabarga took part in the underground comix movement in the early 1970s. His refined Central Station font is available in Standard Regular and Bold, as well as Pro Regular and Bold.

Chesterfield

ABCDEFGHIJKLMNOPQRSTUVWXYZ
abcdefghijklmnopqrstuvwxyz
1234567890 !@#?:;"*&

Foundry: Linotype
Designer: Alan Meeks
Designer Nationality: British
Date: 2004

Chesterfield is a retro-inspired type referencing decorative design from the turn of the 19th century, with many subtle Art Nouveau traits and curves, and a nod to Frederic W. Goudy. It is available in two styles, Chesterfield and Chesterfield Antique; the latter has characters that appear corroded.

Chiswick Headline

ABCDEFGHIJKLMNOPQRSTUVWXYZ
abcdefghijklmnopqrstuvwxyz
1234567890 !@#?:;"*&

Foundry: Commercial Type
Designer: Paul Barnes
Designer Nationality: British
Date: 2010

This is part of Paul Barnes's Chiswick family and was designed for situations where Chiswick Deck is too heavy and Chiswick Poster is too delicate. Chiswick Headline is perfect for use at sizes from 30 to 60 point and is available in five weights from Extralight to Bold with matching italics, plus small caps.

Chiswick Poster

ABCDEFGHIJKLMNOPQRSTUVWXYZ
abcdefghijklmnopqrstuvwxyz
1234567890 !@#?:;"*&

Foundry: Commercial Type
Designer: Paul Barnes
Designer Nationality: British
Date: 2010

Chiswick Poster is designed to be used at 80 point and above. Paul Barnes's expertly crafted design was the primary display typeface in the redesign of *O, The Oprah Magazine* in 2010 and is available in five weights from Extralight to Bold with matching italics, plus small caps and swashes.

Classic Roman

ABCDEFGHIJKLMNOPQRSTUVWXYZ
ABCDEFGHIJKLMNOPQRSTUVWXYZ
1234567890 !@#?:;"*&

Foundry: Monotype
Designer: Monotype Studio
Date: 1998

Classic Roman is an elegant all-caps headline typeface that was created in-house at Monotype. It shares similarities with Carol Twombly's font Trajan of 1989, which is one of many typefaces inspired by the letterforms used on the inscription on the base of Trajan's Column in Rome.

Cocaine

ABCDEFGHIJKLMNOPQRSTUVWXYZ
abcdefghijklmnopqrstuvwxyz
1234567890 !@#?:;"*&

Foundry: Chank Co.
Designer: Chank Diesel / Josh Eshbach
Designer Nationality: American
Date: 2000

Cocaine was created by prolific US typeface designer Chank Diesel in 2000 with help from Josh Eshbach, an intern from the Minneapolis College of Art and Design. It is a single-style, informal display typeface inspired by Speedball type designs of the 1920s and 1930s.

Columna

ABCDEFGHIJKLMNOPQRSTUVWXYZ
1234567890 !@#?.;"'*&

Foundry: Bauer
Designer: Max Caflisch
Designer Nationality: Swiss
Date: 1952

Columna by Swiss typographer Max Caflisch is an uppercase titling serif inspired by classical Roman inscriptions. The original type of 1952 was outlined, a solid version was created decades later, and it is this that has been variously digitized by Linotype, URW and Elsner+Flake.

Cooper BT

ABCDEFGHIJKLMNOPQRSTUVWXYZ
abcdefghijklmnopqrstuvwxyz
1234567890 !@#?:;"'*&

Foundry: Bitstream
Designer: Oswald Cooper
Designer Nationality: American
Date: 1922

Oswald Cooper's famous chunky display serif Cooper Black was released by US foundry Barnhart Brothers & Spindler in 1922. Cooper Black originally came in a single weight, but an italic soon followed. Bitstream's expansion and update, Cooper BT, added three weights with italics.

Delphian

ABCDEFGHIJKLMNOPQRSTUVWXYZ
1234567890 !©?.;"'*&

Foundry: Ludlow
Designer: Robert Hunter Middleton
Designer Nationality: Scottish
Date: 1928

Robert Hunter Middleton's Delphian, designed for Ludlow Typograph in 1928, is an elegant uppercase titling serif with classical proportions. Known on its release as Delphian Open Titling, it features small serifs and a fine inline. Middleton worked at Ludlow from 1923 to 1971.

Edwardian

ABCDEFGHIJKLMNOPQRSTUVWXYZ
abcdefghijklmnopqrstuvwxyz
1234567890 !@#?:;"'*&

Foundry: Letraset
Designer: Colin Brignall
Designer Nationality: British
Date: 1983

British designer Colin Brignall made use of Letraset's Ikarus font-design software to create this playful, rather decorative serif with early 20th-century charm, which proved to be very popular on release. Edwardian features a true italic as opposed to a sloped Roman.

Engravers

ABCDEFGHIJKLMNOPQRSTUVWXYZ
ABCDEFGHIJKLMNOPQRSTUVWXYZ
1234567890 !@#?:;"*&

Foundry: Barnhart Brothers & Spindler
Designer: Robert Wiebking
Designer Nationality: German
Date: 1899

Engravers was designed by Robert Wiebking for the Chicago-based type foundry Barnhart Brothers & Spindler in 1899. An elegant, extended high-contrast serif typeface with small caps, it was based on lettering used by copperplate engravers of the time for luxury applications.

Engravers 2

ABCDEFGHIJKLMNOPQRSTUV
ABCDEFGHIJKLMNOPQRSTUVWXYZ
1234567890 !@#?:;"*&

Foundry: Barnhart Brothers & Spindler
Designer: Robert Wiebking
Designer Nationality: German
Date: 1899

Engravers 2 is one of the types made by Robert Wiebking in 1899 based on traditional engraving alphabets. It is available in Regular and Bold, with uppercase and small caps only. The '2' is in the name because American Type Founders' Engravers Roman came in three numbered styles.

Engravers Roman BT

ABCDEFGHIJKLMNOPQRSTUVWXYZ
ABCDEFGHIJKLMNOPQRSTUVWXYZ
1234567890 !@#?:;"*&

Foundry: Bitstream
Designer: Robert Wiebking
Designer Nationality: German
Date: 1899

This is Bitstream's version of Engravers Roman, which was originally designed by Robert Wiebking for US foundry Barnhart Brothers & Spindler in 1899. It is available in two styles, Regular and Bold. An extended copperplate-style serif, it features small caps rather than a lowercase.

Engravure

ABCDEFGHIJKLMNOPQRSTUVWX
ABCDEFGHIJKLMNOPQRSTUVWXYZ
1234567890 !@#?:;" * &

Foundry: American Type Founders
Designer: Robert Wiebking
Designer Nationality: German
Date: 1903

Engravure is one of Robert Wiebking's typefaces based on traditional engraving lettering designed for American Type Founders at the turn of the 19th century. It is an elegant extended, high-contrast serif typeface with uppercase and small caps in a single weight. The 'R' is distinctive with a notched leg.

Façade

ABCDEFGHIJKLMNOPQRSTUVWXYZ
abcdefghijklmnopqrstuvwxyz
1234567890 !@#?:."*&

Foundry: Boston Type Foundry / Monotype
Designer: Steve Matteson
Designer Nationality: American
Date: c. 1890 / 2001

Façade is a revival, by Monotype's American typeface designer Steve Matteson, of display type Facade No. 2 created by the Boston Type Foundry in the late 19th century. It is a tall, condensed display font with small serifs, a very high x-height and short ascenders and descenders.

Felix Titling

ABCDEFGHIJKLMNOPQRSTUVWXYZ
1234567890 !@#?:."*&

Foundry: Monotype
Designer: Felice Feliciano
Designer Nationality: Italian
Date: 1463

Felix Titling is based on an alphabet included in a treatise on Roman inscriptions by the Italian calligrapher Felice Feliciano, written in 1463. It is a single-style, uppercase serif in the tradition of inscriptional lettering. The typeface has small angular serifs, wide curves and high contrast.

FF Trixie

ABCDEFGHIJKLMNOPQRSTUVWXYZ
abcdefghijklmnopqrstuvwxyz
1234567890 ! #?:;"*&

Foundry: FontFont
Designer: Erik van Blokland
Designer Nationality: Dutch
Date: 1991

Dutch designer Erik van Blokland, who works under the name 'LettError', designed Trixie for FontFont in 1991. It is a grungy typewriter face initially available in five styles: Light, Plain, Text, Extra and Cameo. In 200, Van Blokland released an update with additional styles and features.

FS Rome

ABCDEFGHIJKLMNOPQRSTUVWXYZ

Foundry: Fontsmith
Designer: Jason Smith
Designer Nationality: British
Date: 1996

FS Rome was created by Jason Smith, the British typeface designer and founder of Fontsmith (see p. 272). It is a classical, titling serif in uppercase only. It was inspired by the lettering inscribed on Trajan's Column (AD 106–113). FS Rome is available in a single style only.

Gill Facia

ABCDEFGHIJKLMNOPQRSTUVWXYZ
abcdefghijklmnopqrstuvwxyz
1234567890 !@#?:;"*&

Foundry: Monotype
Designer: Eric Gill / Colin Banks
Designer Nationality: British
Date: 1996

Colin Banks's Gill Facia is a typeface based on lettering created by Eric Gill for the British book retailer WHSmith, and first used in 1903 for its Paris branch. It is a distinctive typeface with small, sharp serifs and a double storey 'a' and 'g'. It is available in regular, italic and titling styles.

Ginkgo

ABCDEFGHIJKLMNOPQRSTUVWXYZ
abcdefghijklmnopqrstuvwxyz
1234567890 !@#?:;"*&

Foundry: Linotype
Designer: Alex Rütten
Designer Nationality: German
Date: 2008

Ginkgo was the first published font by German type designer Alex Rütten, and it won him a Certificate of Excellence in Type Design at the Type Directors Club Awards in 2009. It is designed for use in long passages of text, and its open counters offer enhanced legibility at smaller point sizes.

Goudy Handtooled

ABCDEFGHIJKLMNOPQRSTUVWXYZ
abcdefghijklmnopqrstuvwxyz
1234567890 !@#?:;"*&

Foundry: American Type Founders
Designer: Frederic W. Goudy / Morris Fuller Benton
Designer Nationality: American
Date: c. 1915

Goudy Handtooled is a decorative, display version of Frederic W. Goudy's serif typeface Goudy; it has thin white lines on the left side of every letter which look like highlights, creating a 3D effect. Unlike the standard Goudy, it comes in only one weight without italics.

GT Super

ABCDEFGHIJKLMNOPQRSTUVWXYZ
abcdefghijklmnopqrstuvwxyz
1234567890 !@#?:;"*&

Foundry: Grilli Type
Designer: Noël Leu
Designer Nationality: Swiss
Date: 2018

Grilli Type's GT Super is a versatile typeface family inspired by various high-contrast titling serifs that were popular in the 1970s and 1908s, such as Times Modern, Trooper Roman and Perpetua Bold. It is available in text and display styles, each in five weights with italics.

Or Type

Or Type is an Icelandic type foundry established by Guðmundur Úlfarsson and Mads Freund Brunse in 2013 to publish typefaces designed by the Reykjavík / Brussels-based design studio GUNMAD, whose primary work is typographically focused.

Or Type's works aim to challenge the conventions found in typographic traditions and contemporary values. The company placed the typefaces it developed as research or designed for specific projects on its online type foundry to display and sell. It works with local references and from intrinsic ideas, designing its typefaces to have their own reason for being, rather than filling a gap in the font market. Through its growing library of alphabets, new ideas are being developed and existing typefaces are refined and revised in order to 'create a new take on previous ideas'.

The foundry offers ten typefaces. These include Lemmen, a decorative serif reminiscent of Victorian period; Separat (see p. 437); L10, a geometric sans serif; Boogie School Sans, a contrasting stroke sans serif display face; and Landnáma and variant Landnáma Nýja (see p. 506) an elegant display serif that incorporates a number of quirks within its strokes and counters, such as missing serifs or incomplete strokes.

Founded: 2013
Countries: Iceland / Belgium
Website: ortype.is
Notable typefaces:
Landnáma / Landnáma Nýja
(see p. 506)
Separat (see p. 437)

Below. Various exhibitions featuring Or Type's creations on show.

Right. Various type specimens.

Below. Poster for the Most Beautiful Swiss Books exhibition in Copenhagen in 2011. Design by GUNMAD.

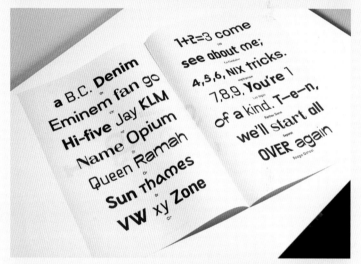

Handle Oldstyle

ABCDEFGHIJKLMNOPQRSTUVWXYZ
ABCDEFGHIJKLMNOPQRSTUVWXYZ
1234567890 !@#?:;”*&

Foundry: Monotype
Designer: Monotype Studio
Date: Unknown

Handle Oldstyle is one of Monotype's Engravers series of types released at the turn of the 20th century based on lettering styles traditionally used by engravers for stationery. It is an uppercase and small caps only, broad serif typeface that comes in a relatively heavy, single style.

Hawthorn

ABCDEFGHIJKLMNOPQRSTUVWXYZ
abcdefghijklmnopqrstuvwxyz
1234567890 !@#?:;”*&

Foundry: Letraset
Designer: Mike Daines
Designer Nationality: British
Date: 1968

Based on DeVinne, which originated at the Central Type Foundry (St Louis) *c.* 1892 (and was hugely popular at the time), Hawthorn was revived by Mike Daines and is a heavy compact serif, often used for book covers in the 1970s. It has a mixture of features, both sharp and bulbous, and has a slightly gothic feel.

Homeland BT

ABCDEFGHIJKLMNOPQRSTUVWXYZ
abcdefghijklmnopqrstuvwxyz
1234567890 !@#?:;”*&

Foundry: Bitstream
Designer: Ray Cruz
Designer Nationality: American
Date: 2004

Ray Cruz began his career in the phototypesetting industry, and has since worked extensively on custom lettering and type design for corporate clients, advertising agencies and publishers. Open counters and bracketed serifs make his Homeland BT font family characterful and readable.

Isis

ABCDEFGHIJKLMNOPQRSTUVWXYZ
1234567890 !?:;”*&

Foundry: Letraset
Designer: Michael Gills
Designer Nationality: British
Date: 1990

Named after the ancient Egyptian goddess, Isis is an uppercase, classical titling roman-style serif font with an open engraved effect. Michael Gills, who designed Isis in 1990, worked at the Letraset Type Studio under Colin Brignall after studying design at Suffolk College, Ipswich.

Italia

ABCDEFGHIJKLMNOPQRSTUVWXYZ
abcdefghijklmnopqrstuvwxyz
1234567890 !@#?:;"*&

British type designer and photographer Colin Brignall joined Letraset in 1964, and was promoted to UK type director at the foundry in 1980. Italia is his revival of Joseph W. Phinney's Jenson Oldstyle released by American Type Founders in 1893, which was based on William Morris's Golden Type of 1890.

Foundry: Letraset
Designer: Colin Brignall
Designer Nationality: British
Date: 1974

ITC Benguiat

ABCDEFGHIJKLMNOPQRSTUVWXYZ
abcdefghijklmnopqrstuvwxyz
1234567890 !@#?:;"*&

This robust, Art Nouveau-influenced font was a popular choice for display type in the decades following its release; it is particularly well known for its appearance on the covers of novels by Stephen King and those of the *Choose Your Own Adventure* children's book series (1979–98).

Foundry: ITC
Designer: Ed Benguiat
Designer Nationality: American
Date: 1977

ITC Cheltenham Handtooled

ABCDEFGHIJKLMNOPQRSTUVWXYZ
abcdefghijklmnopqrstuvwxyz
1234567890 !@#?:;"*&

ITC Cheltenham was designed in 1975 by Tony Stan, and based on the typeface first designed by architect Bertram Goodhue and later expanded by Morris Fuller Benton. In 1993 Ed Benguiat (see p. 514) created a Handtooled style, adding a highlight to the Bold and Bold Italic cuts.

Foundry: ITC
Designer: Ed Benguiat
Designer Nationality: American
Date: 1993

ITC Clearface

ABCDEFGHIJKLMNOPQRSTUVWXYZ
abcdefghijklmnopqrstuvwxyz
1234567890 !@#?:;"*&

Clearface was designed by Morris Fuller Benton in 1907 with assistance from his father, Victor Caruso updated it for the International Typeface Corporation (ITC) in 1978, removing some of the more unusual details from within the font's letterforms, achieving a more consistent feel across four weights.

Foundry: ITC
Designer: Linton Boyd Benton / Morris Fuller Benton / Victor Caruso
Designer Nationality: American
Date: 1978

ITC Elan

ABCDEFGHIJKLMNOPQRSTUVWXYZ
abcdefghijklmnopqrstuvwxyz
1234567890 !@#?:;"*&

The low contrast and open counters of Albert Boton's design for Elan create a stable, legible impression in both body text and display contexts.

Boton worked under Adrian Frutiger (see p. 290) at Deberny & Peignot during the 1950s, and has taught type design since the late 1960s.

Foundry: ITC
Designer: Albert Boton
Designer Nationality: French
Date: 1985

ITC Garamond Handtooled

ABCDEFGHIJKLMNOPQRSTUVWXYZ
abcdefghijklmnopqrstuvwxyz
1234567890 !@#?:;"*&

ITC's Garamond was developed in 1977 by Tony Stan, and based on the serif type designed by Claude Garamond in the 16th century, but with tighter spacing and a taller x-height. In 1993, Ed Benguiat (see p. 514) created a Handtooled style, adding a highlight to the Bold and Bold Italic cuts.

Foundry: ITC
Designer: Ed Benguiat
Designer Nationality: American
Date: 1993

ITC Golden Type

ABCDEFGHIJKLMNOPQRSTUVWXYZ
abcdefghijklmnopqrstuvwxyz
1234567890 !@#?:;"*&

Sigrid Engelmann, Helga Jörgenson and Andrew Newton designed ITC Golden Type. It is a revival of a classical serif by British designer William Morris which was used by the Kelmscott Press to print its edition of *The Golden Legend* (1846) in 1892 and was itself based on type designs by Nicolas Jenson.

Foundry: ITC
Designer: Sigrid Engelmann / Helga Jörgenson / Andrew Newton
Designer Nationality: German / German / British
Date: 1989

ITC Isbell

ABCDEFGHIJKLMNOPQRSTUVWXYZ
abcdefghijklmnopqrstuvwxyz
1234567890 !@#?:;"*&

Designed in 1981 by Jerry Campbell and Richard Isbell, ITC Isbell is a distinctive, stylized roman serif typeface with a large x-height, stencil-style gaps in the joins of many lowercase letters and short ascenders and descenders. It comes in four styles – Book and Bold with italics.

Foundry: ITC
Designer: Jerry Campbell / Richard Isbell
Designer Nationality: American
Date: 1981

ITC Korinna

ABCDEFGHIJKLMNOPQRSTUVWXYZ
abcdefghijklmnopqrstuvwxyz
1234567890 !@#?:;"*&

Foundry: Berthold / ITC
Designer: Ed Benguiat / Victor Caruso
Designer Nationality: American
Date: 1904 / 1974

The contemporary redrawing by Ed Benguiat (see p. 514) and Victor Caruso of this German Art Nouveau design made its debut for the International Typeface Corporation (ITC) in the second issue of *U&lc*, the foundry's free quarterly type magazine, art directed by Herb Lubalin (see p. 62).

ITC Newtext

ABCDEFGHIJKLMNOPQRSTUVWXYZ
abcdefghijklmnopqrstuvwxyz
1234567890 !@#?:;"*&

Foundry: ITC
Designer: Ray Baker
Designer Nationality: American
Date: 1974

Ray Baker designed the extended letterforms of ITC Newtext, with their flared serifs and consistent stroke weight, for optimal legibility when used for body text. Its squat proportions permit more lines of type to be set on a page, which is useful where economy is a key concern.

ITC Quorum

ABCDEFGHIJKLMNOPQRSTUVWXYZ
abcdefghijklmnopqrstuvwxyz
1234567890 !@#?:;"*&

Foundry: ITC
Designer: Ray Baker
Designer Nationality: American
Date: 1977

Ray Baker's design for ITC Quorum borrows several formal characteristics from sans serif type design, with its subtle flared serifs adding a sense of historic detail. The slightly condensed letterforms of this ovoid typeface make it an economical choice for text typesetting.

ITC Serif Gothic

ABCDEFGHIJKLMNOPQRSTUVWXYZ
abcdefghijklmnopqrstuvwxyz
1234567890 !@#?:;"*&

Foundry: ITC
Designer: Antonio DiSpigna / Herb Lubalin
Designer Nationality: Italian / American
Date: 1972

Herb Lubalin (see p. 62) and Antonio DiSpigna collaborated on the design of ITC Serif Gothic, resulting in an unusual, display-friendly font, which was widely used on film posters, album artwork and book covers following its release. Its tiny serifs give it the appearance of a sans at smaller sizes.

ITC Stepp

ABCDEFGHIJKLMNOPQRSTUVWXYZ
abcdefghijklmnopqrstuvwxyz
1234567890 !@#?:;,"*&

Foundry: ITC
Designer: Hal Taylor
Designer Nationality: American
Date: 2005

Hand-lettering artist and illustrator Hal Taylor began his career in phototypesetting, and went on to design typefaces. He developed his design for ITC Stepp from uppercase lettering found within an Art Deco logo for the Stetson Shoe Company of Weymouth, Massachusetts from 1930.

ITC Tiffany

ABCDEFGHIJKLMNOPQRSTUVWXYZ
abcdefghijklmnopqrstuvwxyz
1234567890 !@#?:;,"*&

Foundry: ITC
Designer: Ed Benguiat
Designer Nationality: American
Date: 1974

An early release from the International Typeface Corporation (ITC), Tiffany has a sturdy, voluptuous design incorporating formal details taken by Ed Benguiat (see p. 514) from two earlier typefaces, Caxton and Ronaldson. ITC published a true italic version of the typeface, also cut by Benguiat, in 1981.

Jenson Old Style

ABCDEFGHIJKLMNOPQRSTUVWXYZ
abcdefghijklmnopqrstuvwxyz
1234567890 !@#?:;,"*&

Foundry: Letraset
Designer: Freda Sack /
Colin Brignall
Designer Nationality: British
Date: 1982

Jenson Old Style is a display serif based on the work of Nicolas Jenson, a French printer who made his name in 13th-century Italy. While many have optimized Jenson's designs for text purposes, the broad characters of Jenson Old Style are better suited to headline typography.

Juliana Text

ABCDEFGHIJKLMNOPQRSTUVWXYZ
ABCDEFGHIJKLMNOPQRSTUVWXYZ
1234567890 !@#?:;,"*&

Foundry: Linotype
Designer: Sem Hartz /
Sam Berlow
Designer Nationality: Dutch /
American
Date: 1958 / 2009

Dutch typographer Sem Hartz was commissioned by Walter Tracy at Linotype to design Juliana, which is a classical serif reminiscent of the Roman typefaces designed in 16th-century Italy. Juliana has diamond-shaped dots and is available in roman, italic and small capitals.

Kelvingrove

ABCDEFGHIJKLMNOPQRSTUVWXYZ

ABCDEFGHIJKLMNOPQRSTUVWXYZ

1234567890 !@#?:;"*&

Foundry: Typodermic
Designer: Ray Larabie
Designer Nationality: Canadian
Date: 2007

Kelvingrove is a copperplate display typeface designed in regular and small capitals, including alternative swash characters for the 'k', 'q' and 'r'. Intended for headlines and short runs of text, Kelvingrove features two sets of balanced numerals to match both capital styles.

Latin

ABCDEFGHIJKLMNOPQRSTUVWXYZ

abcdefghijklmnopqrstuvwxyz

1234567890 !@#?:,"*&

Foundry: Monotype
Designer: Monotype Studio
Date: 1890

Latin is a condensed serif display typeface design in the Latin type style popularized in the 19th century. Like those that preceded it, Monotype's Latin font features structured strokes, glyphic serifs and keen terminals. The foundry was set up in Philadelphia in 1887 and this was one of its first fonts.

Latin #2

ABCDEFGHIJKLMNOPQRSTUVWXYZ

1234567890 !@#?:;"*&

Foundry: Stephenson, Blake & Co.
Designer: Stephenson, Blake & Co.
Date: 1884

Similar to Monotype's Latin, the Latin #2 font is a structured, glyphic serif designed for headline purposes. Unlike the former, Stephenson, Blake & Co.'s Latin #2 offers two styles, Compressed and Wide, both in a single weight, to cater for a variety of layouts and compositions.

Latin Extra Condensed

ABCDEFGHIJKLMNOPQRSTUVWXYZ

1234567890 !@ #?:,"*&

Foundry: Bitstream
Designer: M. Jean Rochaix
Designer Nationality: French
Date: 1873

Latin Extra Condensed is a Bitstream revival of M. Jean Rochaix's Elongated Latin, a typeface released by Stephenson, Blake & Co. in 1873. A tall, stout, triangular-serifed typeface, Latin Extra Condensed is available in one weight and, unlike Monotype's version Latin Condensed, has only an uppercase.

Landnáma / Landnáma Nýja

ABCDEFGHIJKLMNOPQRSTUVWXYZ
abcdefghijklmnopqrstuvwxyz
1234567890 !@#?:;”*&

ABCDEFGHIJKLMNOPQRSTUVWXYZ
abcdefghijklmnopqrstuvwxyz
1234567890 !@#?:;”*&

Foundry: Or Type
Designer: Guðmundur Úlfarsson
Designer Nationality: Icelandic
Date: 2015

Landnáma and Landnáma Nýja were designed by Guðmundur Úlfarsson of the Danish / Icelandic foundry Or Type (see p. 498). He based his design on embossed lettering on a plaque on a public sculpture in Reykjavik. The tightly set letterforms have partially melted counters and strokes, as is visible in the 'a', which has a ball ending on a part of the bowl beneath. There are also omissions to certain strokes, which aim to reflect the inaccuracies created when lettering has been blind-embossed through a metal surface. Available in the one weight with no italic, the Landnáma pairing is ideal when looking for a serif display type with a part-weathered appearance or unusual, distressed quirk.

Below. *Competing Temporalities* and *The World For Less* are artist publications by Lloyd Corporation (artists Ali Eisa and Sebastian Lloyd Rees). Design by GUNMAD.

Lemmen

ABCDEFGHIJKLMNOPQRSTUVWXYZ
abcdefghijklmnopqrstuvwxyz
1234567890 !@#?:;"*&

Lemmen is modelled on the typeface Antiqua, designed by the Belgian painter Georges Lemmen in the early 20th century. It is a serif display font comprised of six styles. Informed by the original specimen, the characters feature incised junctures alongside high-contrast strokes.

Foundry: Or Type
Designer: Mads Freund Brunse / Guðmundur Úlfarsson (GUNMAD)
Designer Nationality: Danish / Icelandic
Date: 2018

Letraset Romic

ABCDEFGHIJKLMNOPQRSTUVWXYZ
abcdefghijklmnopqrstuvwxyz
1234567890 !@#?:;"*&

Letraset Romic is a quirky, chunky calligraphic serif created by Colin Brignall, an in-house designer at Letraset. It features distinctive notches cut out of various letters, which leave the dots of the 'i' and 'j' shaped like speech bubbles, as are the counters of the 'e', 'P', 'R' and 'B'.

Foundry: Letraset
Designer: Colin Brignall
Designer Nationality: British
Date: 1979

Light Roman

ABCDEFGHIJKLMNOPQRSTUVWX
ABCDEFGHIJKLMNOPQRSTUVWXYZ
1234567890 !@#?:;"*&

Light Roman is an all-capitals serif display typeface intended to bestow a delicate elegance to printed materials, such as invitations and stationery. Inspired by classical engraved lettering, Light Roman utilizes both high-contrast strokes and its angled joints and brackets.

Foundry: Monotype
Designer: Monotype Studio
Date: 1998

Linotype Venezia

ABCDEFGHIJKLMNOPQRSTUVWXYZ

Linotype Venezia is modelled on the classical style of Roman writing, found in the architecture of the 1st and 2nd centuries. It is a historical serif display face that combines positive and negative space to imitate the chiselled aesthetic of carved letterforms. Linotype Venezia is part of the TakeType Library.

Foundry: Linotype
Designer: Robert Kolben
Designer Nationality: German
Date: 1997

Lucian

ABCDEFGHIJKLMNOPQRSTUVWXYZ
abcdefghijklmnopqrstuvwxyz
1234567890 !@#?:;"*&

Foundry: Bitstream
Designer: Lucian Bernhard
Designer Nationality: German
Date: 1928 / 1990

Lucian was drawn by the leading German designer of the early 20th century for the Bauer foundry. Bitstream digitized it in two weights – Bold and Roman – and initially renamed it 'Kuenstler 185'. A chunky serif, Lucian has large dots and ball terminals, most obvious on top of the quirky 'g'.

LuMarc

ABCDEFGHIJKLMNOPQRSTUVWXYZ
abcdefghijklmnopqrstuvwxyz
1234567890 !@#?:;"*&

Foundry: Monotype
Designer: Marc Lubbers
Designer Nationality: Dutch
Date: 1994

With squat, wide letters and tiny angular serifs, LuMarc is almost a sans serif. It is available in Roman and Bold. Utrecht-based designer Marc Lubbers began many of his fonts while still a student and switched his focus to web design by the late 1990s.

Marco Polo

ABCDEFGHIJKLMNOPQRSTUVWXYZ
abcdefghijklmnopqrstuvwxyz
1234567890 !@#?:;"*&

Foundry: Omnibus Typografi
Designer: Franko Luin
Designer Nationality: Swedish
Date: 1993

Franko Luin of Omnibus Typografi designed Marco Polo and named it after the famous Venetian explorer. It is an Old Style serif with fairly rounded serifs that has been designed with imperfect rough edges to give an antique, old world feel; it comes in roman, italic and small caps.

Maximus

ABCDEFGHIJKLMNOPQRST
abcdefghijklmnopqrstuvwxyz
1234567890 !@#?:;" *&

Foundry: Linotype
Designer: Walter Tracy
Designer Nationality: American
Date: 1967

Maximus was designed for the Linotype foundry in 1967 by Walter Tracy, the renowned English type designer, typographer and writer. It is a horizontally striped, all-caps sans serif, with bold, condensed forms and was specifically designed for use at very small sizes on newsprint.

Medium Roman

ABCDEFGHIJKLMNOPQRSTUVWX
ABCDEFGHIJKLMNOPQRSTUVWXYZ
1234567890 !@#?:;"*&

Foundry: Monotype
Designer: Monotype Studio
Date: Unknown

Monotype's Medium Roman is one of many fonts based on lettering used historically by engravers. It is an extended, high-contrast serif in a single weight and style with caps and small caps. The font has many quirks, such as the spurs on 'J' and 'U', the tail of the 'Q' and the unconnected leg of 'R'.

Monotype Clearface

ABCDEFGHIJKLMNOPQRSTUVWXYZ
abcdefghijklmnopqrstuvwxyz
1234567890 !@#?:;"*&

Foundry: Monotype
Designer: Morris Fuller Benton
Designer Nationality: American
Date: 1907

As its name implies, Morris Benton designed Clearface for American Type Founders to be easy to read, even at smaller sizes. Letters are relatively condensed and heavy, with short ascenders and descenders. Monotype's version, one of many, comes in the original Bold.

Monotype Engravers

ABCDEFGHIJKLMNOPQRSTUV
WXYZ
1234567890 !@#?:;"*&

Foundry: Monotype
Designer: Robert Wiebking / Morris Fuller Benton / Monotype Studio
Designer Nationality: German / American
Date: 1902

Monotype Engravers is an all-caps display typeface inspired by the copper- and steel-plate designs of the 19th century. Robert Wiebking designed the initial Regular version, while Morris Fuller Benton added the Bold style in 1902 before they were both packaged by Monotype.

Monotype Modern Display

ABCDEFGHIJKLMNOPQRSTUVWXYZ
abcdefghijklmnopqrstuvwxyz
1234567890 !@#?:;"*&

Foundry: Monotype
Designer: Dan Rhatigan
Designer Nationality: American
Date: 2013

US typographer Dan Rhatigan designed Modern Display when he was UK type director at Monotype. It is a single-weight headline font intended to supplement the Monotype Modern family. A beautiful serif, with extreme contrast, it was initially a custom font for fashion title *Centrefold Magazine*.

Musketeer

ABCDEFGHIJKLMNOPQRSTUVWXYZ
abcdefghijklmnopqrstuvwxyz
1234567890 !@#?:;"*&

Foundry: Compugraphic
Designer: Tony Geddes
Designer Nationality: British
Date: 1968

Musketeer was designed for Quick Brown Fox by Tony Geddes, who later co-founded the Panache Graphics foundry. It is a quirky, Art Nouveau-inspired display serif now available from Monotype in four weights: Light, Regular, Demi Bold and Extra Bold. The lowercase has large, open counters.

Onyx

ABCDEFGHIJKLMNOPQRSTUVWXYZ
abcdefghijklmnopqrstuvwxyz
1234567890 !@#?:;"*&

Foundry: American Type Founders
Designer: Gerry Powell
Designer Nationality: American
Date: 1937

Onyx is a serif display typeface created by Gerry Powell, former director of typographic design for the American Type Founders. It was designed in the style of a modern serif but optimized for display, and the refined impact of its characters made Onyx a popular choice for advertising in the 1940s.

Origami

ABCDEFGHIJKLMNOPQRSTUVWXYZ
abcdefghijklmnopqrstuvwxyz
1234567890 !@#?:;"*&

Foundry: Monotype
Designer: Carl Crossgrove
Designer Nationality: American
Date: 1998

The Origami typeface is named after the ancient Japanese art of paper folding. It is a low-contrast, angular typeface with virtually no curves and fairly minimal serifs, especially on the regular cut. Origami is available in four weights, with a chancery italic, and is best suited to headline use.

Paddington

ABCDEFGHIJKLMNOPQRSTUVWXYZ
abcdefghijklmnopqrstuvwxyz
1234567890 !@#?:;"*&

Foundry: Letraset
Designer: Freda Sack
Designer Nationality: British
Date: 1977

Adrian Williams commissioned Freda Sack, the co-founder of The Foundry (see p. 284), to design Paddington. Sack also designed the popular types Proteus, Stratford and Victorian. Paddington is a soft-serifed roman in the classic style, which is reminiscent of Frederic W Goudy's types.

PL Latin

ABCDEFGHIJKLMNOPQRSTUVWXYZ
abcdefghijklmnopqrstuvwxyz
1234567890 !©#?:;”*&

Foundry: Monotype
Designer: David Quay
Designer Nationality: British
Date: 1988

With enunciated details found in the serifs and terminals, PL Latin is a glyphic style typeface intended for headline typography. The PL Latin font family features only two styles, Elongated and Bold, which were both designed for maximum impact at larger sizes.

PL Modern

ABCDEFGHIJKLMNOPQRSTUVWXYZ
abcdefghijklmnopqrstuvwxyz
1234567890 !©#?:;”*&

Foundry: Photo-Lettering
Designer: Robert Hunter Middleton
Designer Nationality: British
Date: 1936

PL Modern (also known as PL Modern Heavy Condensed) is based on a design done in 1936 by Robert Hunter Middleton, the Scottish book designer, painter and type designer. Created at Photo-Lettering in New York, it has classic Bodoni-style letterforms, typical of modern serif faces.

Plate Gothic

ABCDEFGHIJKLMNOPQRSTUVWXYZ
ABCDEFGHIJKLMNOPQRSTUVWXYZ
1234567890 !@#?:;”*&

Foundry: Monotype
Designer: Monotype Studio
Date: 1921

Plate Gothic, which was designed by the Monotype team in 1921 and inspired by Goudy's Copperplate, is an extended, engraving-style typeface. It is essentially a sans serif with added thin, straight serifs, and it comes in fifteen styles. Five of these are italic, with caps and small caps.

Pompeii

ABCDEFGHIJKLMNOPQRSTUVWXYZ
ABCDEFGHIJKLMNOPQRSTUVWXYZ
1234567890 !@#?:;"*&

Foundry: ITC
Designer: Philip Bouwsma
Designer Nationality: American
Date: 1994

Philip Bouwsma designed Pompeii Capitals for the International Typeface Corporation (ITC) in 1994. It is a calligraphic titling serif typeface with uppercase and small caps only. It takes its name from the Roman city outside Naples destroyed by the eruption of the Mount Vesuvius volcano in AD 79.

Portrait Inline

ABCDEFGHIJKLMNOPQRSTUVWXYZ
ABCDEFGHIJKLMNOPQRSTUVWXYZ
1234567890 !@#?:;"'*&

Foundry: Commercial Type
Designer: Berton Hasebe
Designer Nationality: American
Date: 2013

Portrait Inline was designed by Hawaiian-born designer Berton Hasebe, who worked in the New York office of Commercial Type (see p. 124) from 2008 to 2013 before starting his own studio. It is a classical, inlined titling serif with capitals and small caps only. A sans serif version is also available.

President

ABCDEFGHIJKLMNOPQRSTUVWXY
ABCDEFGHIJKLMNOPQRSTUVWXYZ
1234567890 !@#?:;"'*&

Foundry: Deberny & Peignot
Designer: Adrian Frutiger
Designer Nationality: Swiss
Date: 1954

President (also known as Initiales Président) is one of the first typefaces produced by legendary Swiss designer Adrian Frutiger (see p. 290) for Deberny & Peignot. It is an uppercase, Latin titling font with low contrast and small, sharp serifs. The addition of small caps came after its initial release in 1954.

Ragnar

ABCDEFGHIJKLMNOPQRSTUVWXYZ
abcdefghijklmnopqrstuvwxyz
1234567890 !@#?:;"'*&

Foundry: Omnibus Typografi
Designer: Franko Luin
Designer Nationality: Swedish
Date: 1993

Swedish type designer Franko Luin named the Ragnar typeface after 'Ragnarök', which is an apocalyptic event predicted in Norse mythology. Ragnar is an angular text serif with a large x-height; it comes in three weights with italics and one weight of small caps.

Rameau

ABCDEFGHIJKLMNOPQRSTUVWXYZ
abcdefghijklmnopqrstuvwxyz
1234567890 !@#?:;"'*&

Foundry: Linotype
Designer: Sarah Lazarevic
Designer Nationality: French
Date: 2011

French typographer, teacher, designer and engraver Sarah Lazarevic designed Rameau in 2011. It began as an italic font inspired by engraved text found on a manuscript of music composed by Jean-Philippe Rameau in 1747 for an opera. It is a sharp text serif in three weights with italics.

Rosella

ABCDEFGHIJKLMNOPQRSTU VWXYZ
1234567890 !@#?:;"*&

Foundry: Monotype
Designer: Sabina Chipară
Designer Nationality: Romanian
Date: 2017

Sabina Chipară, a Romanian designer based in the Netherlands, designed Rosella in 2017. It is an uppercase and small caps only high-contrast serif inspired by majuscule engraving fonts. Rosella comes in a single weight with five display versions: Inline, Engraved, Hatched, Deco and Flourish.

Rundfunk Antiqua

ABCDEFGHIJKLMNOPQRSTUVWXYZ
abcdefghijklmnopqrstuvwxyz
1234567890 !@#?:;"*&

Foundry: Linotype
Designer: Linotype Design Studio
Date: 1933–35

An unknown member of Linotype's studio drew Rundfunk Antiqua in the 1930s. It is a text serif with a large x-height, and short ascenders and descenders. Rundfunk Antiqua comes in a single roman weight and was designed with a sans serif, Rundfunk Grotesk, but neither evolved beyond one style.

Sackers Classic Roman

ABCDEFGHIJKLMNOPQRSTUVWXYZ
ABCDEFGHIJKLMNOPQRSTUVWXYZ
1234567890 !@#?:;"*&

Foundry: Agfa Compugraphic
Designer: Gary Sackers
Designer Nationality: American
Date: 1975

Sackers Classic Roman was one of a series of fonts designed by Gary Sackers between 1974 and 1975, based on old engraving masterplates for Agfa Compugraphic. It is a thin, classical titling serif with caps and small caps only, and it is available from Monotype in a single light weight.

Sackers Roman

ABCDEFGHIJKLMNOPQRSTUV
ABCDEFGHIJKLMNOPQRSTUVWX
1234567890 !@#?:;"*&

Foundry: Agfa Compugraphic
Designer: Gary Sackers
Designer Nationality: American
Date: 1975

Between 1974 and 1975, Gary Sackers created a range of fonts for Agfa Compugraphic based on historic engraving masterplates, including Sackers Roman, a wide high-contrast serif available in light and heavy weights with caps and small caps only. It has an especially distinctive 'U'.

Ed Benguiat

Typographer and lettering artist Ed Benguiat is one of the most prolific US type designers of all time and a legendary character. He has crafted and been involved in the creation of more than 600 typefaces, and is recognized as one of the leading logotype designers, who has created a wealth of iconic marques.

Born in New York in the 1920s, Benguiat's first job was as a jazz percussionist – and as an accomplished one, playing in several big bands and with some of the jazz greats of the day. With a young family, he became concerned that his musical career did not have long-term work prospects and having drawn since a boy, he decided to become an illustrator. After his change in direction, he studied at the Workshop School of Advertising Art, New York, where he experimented with his first typeface. In 1962, he joined Photo-Lettering Inc (PLINC) as a type designer. The company was one of the first and most successful foundries to utilize photo technology in the production of typography and lettering. From 1936 to 1997, it served the design and advertising studios of New York, providing typesetting and designs.

In 1971, he joined fellow designers Aaron Burns, Herb Lubalin and Edward Rondthaler, who had founded International Typeface Corporation (ITC) as the first independent licensing company for type designers. He also worked on ITC's typographic in-house magazine *U&lc* with his contemporary and great collaborator Lubalin (see pp. 62–63). Benguiat has created many notable fonts over his long and incredibly productive career, including ITC Bookman, ITC Souvenir, ITC Tiffany and the eponymously titled ITC Benguiat.

He has also produced logotypes for institutions such as *The New York Times*, *Playboy*, *Sports Illustrated* and *Esquire*, and for brands such as Coca-Cola, Ford, AT&T and Estée Lauder, as well as film titles including the original *Planet of the Apes* (1968) and *The Guns of Navarone* (1961). Benguiat was lauded in 1989, when he was awarded the New York Type Directors Club Medal, citing for those 'who have made significant contributions to the life, art and craft of typography'.

In 2002, US foundry House Industries released the Ed Benguiat Font Collection. House Industries type designer Ken Barber collaborated with Benguiat to redraw a collection of five of Benguiat's PLINC display typefaces along with a fun dingbats font entitled Bengbats. As further tribute, House Industries made a documentary film about him, honouring his contribution and influence on US type design and craft. ITC Benguiat has enjoyed a resurgence in the 21st century and is used for the main titles on the Netflix hit show *Stranger Things* (2016).

Date: 1927–
Nationality: American
Notable typefaces:
ITC Bookman (see p. 42)
ITC Benguiat (see p. 501)
ITC Edwardian Script (see p. 611)
ITC Souvenir (see p. 129)
ITC Tiffany (see p. 501)

Below. Benguiat's iconic logotypes for *Esquire* magazine and *Planet of the Apes*. In recent years his ITC Benguiat typeface was modified and employed for the main logo on hit Netflix show *Stranger Things*, design by Jacob Boghosian.

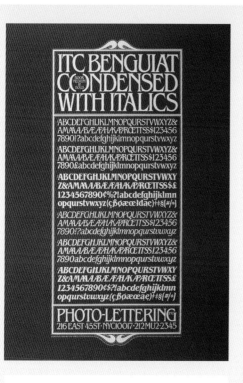

abcdefghijklmnopqrstuvwxyz
ABCDEFGHIJKLMNOPQRSTUVWXYZ
1234567890&$$¢£%
AMAÆBÆÆAKÆPRÆSSTT
ÇØÆŒßçøãèòèfi
(:;.!?-ˆˇ˜·/#@*')(†‡§«»1234567890)

COMPLETE ITC DISPLAY ALPHABET

Left. Promotion for ITC Benguiat Condensed by Photo-Lettering Inc. (top) and specimen page for ITC Benguiat Book (bottom). An Art Nouveau-influenced design, it was a popular choice for display type for many years after its release, being particularly well known for its use on the covers of novels by Stephen King.

Above. Hand-lettered and coloured artwork by Ed Benguiat for a New York television network.

Below left. Legendary type designer and lettering artist Ed Benguiat at work.

Below. Cover for Photo-Lettering Inc's catalogue of *Psychedelitypes*. A collection of typeface designs built around the visual properties of Psychedelia sub-culture. The ornate circular typographic kaleidoscope motif and design were created by Ed Benguiat, employing Dave Davison's Arabesque typeface for the headlines.

26
good
reasons
to use
ITC Benguiat
Book

Schnyder M

ABCDEFGHIJKLMNOPQRSTUVWXYZ
abcdefghijklmnopqrstuvwxyz
1234567890 !@#?:;"*&

Foundry: Commercial Type
Designer: Berton Hasebe / Christian Schwartz
Designer Nationality: American
Date: 2018

Schnyder is a vast family by Christian Schwartz and Berton Hasebe of Commercial Type (see p. 124). It was released in 2018 but designed in 2013 for *T: The New York Times Style Magazine*. Schnyder, the regular width, comes in four optical sizes: Schnyder M, the medium is available in three weights with italics.

Schnyder Cond M

ABCDEFGHIJKLMNOPQRSTUVWXYZ
abcdefghijklmnopqrstuvwxyz
1234567890 !@#?:;"*&

Foundry: Commercial Type
Designer: Berton Hasebe / Christian Schwartz
Designer Nationality: American
Date: 2018

Schnyder was inspired by Beaux Arts serifs from the late 19th century and the lettering of Swiss artist Jean-Frédéric Schnyder (from whom it got its name). It comes in four widths. The condensed style comes in four optical sizes and three weights: Light, Demi and Bold (without italics).

Schnyder Wide M

ABCDEFGHIJKLMNOPQRSTUVWXYZ
abcdefghijklmnopqrstuvwxyz
1234567890 !@#?:;"*&

Foundry: Commercial Type
Designer: Berton Hasebe / Christian Schwartz
Designer Nationality: American
Date: 2018

Schnyder has one expanded style, Schnyder Wide. It was first created in 2014 when *T: The New York Times Style Magazine* wanted more versatility from the serif it had commissioned a year earlier. Schnyder Wide comes in four optical sizes and three weights: Light, Demi and Bold.

Schnyder Xcond XL

ABCDEFGHIJKLMNOPQRSTUVWXYZ
abcdefghijklmnopqrstuvwxyz
1234567890 !@#?:;"*&

Foundry: Commercial Type
Designer: Berton Hasebe / Christian Schwartz
Designer Nationality: American
Date: 2018

The creative director of *T: The New York Times Style Magazine*, Patrick Li, often worked with Christian Schwartz and Berton Hasebe. Apart from Schnyder, they also created Pialat, Karl and Graphik Titling for the magazine. Schnyder Xcond comes in only two optical sizes, L and XL.

Schnyder XL

ABCDEFGHIJKLMNOPQRSTUVWXYZ
abcdefghijklmnopqrstuvwxyz
1234567890 !@#?:;"*&

Foundry: Commercial Type
Designer: Berton Hasebe /
Christian Schwartz
Designer Nationality: American
Date: 2018

Schnyder is an elegant, high-contrast display serif; the XL cut is the version optically optimized for larger use such as headlines. It comes in three weights with italics drawn by Miguel Reyes which are unique to the regular width. Hrvoje Živčić provided production assistance.

Serlio

ABCDEFGHIJKLMNOPQRSTUVWXYZ
ABCDEFGHIJKLMNOPQRSTUVWXYZ
1234567890 !@#?:;"*&

Foundry: Linotype
Designer: Sebastiano Serlio
Designer Nationality: Italian
Date: 1990

Linotype's font Serlio, designed in-house in 1990, is based on lettering created by the 16th-century Italian architect, engraver and painter Sebastiano Serlio. It is an uppercase and small caps only inscriptional titling typeface, with classical proportions and small, fine serifs.

SG Cheltenham Old Style SB

ABCDEFGHIJKLMNOPQRSTUVWXYZ
abcdefghijklmnopqrstuvwxyz
1234567890 !@#?:;"*&

Foundry: Scangraphic
Designer: Bertram Grosvenor
Goodhue / Morris Fuller Benton
Designer Nationality: American
Date: 1902

Cheltenham Old Style SB is a Scangraphic version of Cheltenham Old Style, the quirky serif designed by architect Bertram Grosvenor Goodhue and refined by Morris Fuller Benton in 1902. The 'SB' in the name references a Scangraphic convention and indicates it was created to set text or body type.

SG Copperplate SB

ABCDEFGHIJKLMNOPQRSTUVWXYZ
ABCDEFGHIJKLMNOPQRSTUVWXYZ
1234567890 !@#?:;"*&

Foundry: Scangraphic
Designer: Frederic W. Goudy
Designer Nationality: American
Date: 1901

Copperplate SB is Scangraphic's version of Copperplate, an extended uppercase and small caps only typeface designed by Frederic W. Goudy. It comes in Light, Regular and Bold weights in two widths and has blunt, straight serifs on otherwise sans serif-style letters.

SPQR

ABCDEFGHIJKLMNOPQRSTUVWXYZ
ABCDEFGHIJKLMNOPQRSTUVWXYZ
1234567890 !@#?:;"*&

Foundry: Munch Fonts
Designer: Gary Munch
Designer Nationality: American
Date: 1993

SPQR is named after the Latin abbreviation of *Senatus Populusque Romanus* (the Roman Senate and People). US font designer Gary Munch created the classical, uppercase titling serif for his foundry Munch Fonts. It is heavy and comes in roman and italic styles.

Stevens Titling

ABCDEFGHIJKLMNOPQRSTUVWXYZ
ABCDEFGHIJKLMNOPQRSTUVWXYZ
1234567890 !@#?:;"*&

Foundry: Linotype
Designer: John Stevens / Ryuichi Tateno
Designer Nationality: American / Japanese
Date: 2011

Calligraphers John Stevens and Ryuichi Tateno created Stevens Titling in 2011. It is a collection of four classical uppercase serif fonts. Three variants – Badger Brush, Boar Brush and Wolf Brush – have visible brushstroke textures, while Sable Brush is solid and also has small caps.

Throhand

ABCDEFGHIJKLMNOPQRSTUVWXYZ
abcdefghijklmnopqrstuvwxyz
1234567890 !@#?:;"*&

Foundry: Font Bureau
Designer: David Berlow
Designer Nationality: American
Date: 1995

David Berlow worked at Linotype and Bitstream before co-founding the Font Bureau in 1989. His design for Throhand was inspired by the 16th-century types of Claude Garamond and Hendrik van den Keere. It is a sharp, elegant high-contrast serif in three weights with italics.

Titus

ABCDEFGHIJKLMNOPQRSTUVWXYZ
abcdefghijklmnopqrstuvwxyz
1234567890 !@#?:;"*&

Foundry: Linotype
Designer: David Quay
Designer Nationality: British
Date: 1984

Titus is a serif text typeface with subtly calligraphic features, a tall x-height and large counters. It comes in Light Roman only. British type designer David Quay created Titus for Linotype in 1984. He went on to co-found The Foundry (see p. 284) in 1990 with fellow British type designer Freda Sack.

Trajan

ABCDEFGHIJKLMNOPQRSTUVWXYZ
1234567890 ! ?:;"*&

Foundry: Adobe
Designer: Carol Twombly
Designer Nationality: American
Date: 1989

Carol Twombly designed Trajan in 1989. It is a classical, inscriptional titling serif typeface with uppercase and small caps only in Regular and Bold roman weights. It was based on the lettering inscribed on Trajan's Column (106–113 AD) in Rome and is a popular choice for film-poster text.

Ultramarina

ABCDEFGHIJKLMNOPQRSTUVWXYZ
abcdefghijklmnopqrstuvwxyz
1234567890 !@#?:;"*&

Foundry: Huy!Fonts
Designer: Juanjo Lopez
Designer Nationality: Spanish
Date: 2011

Huy!Fonts, the Madrid-based foundry of Spanish designer Juanjo Lopez, released Ultramarina in 2011. It is a quirky, condensed bold serif in a single style with ball terminals and a large x-height. Lopez is also involved in lettering, letterpress printing, calligraphy and teaching.

Value Serif

ABCDEFGHIJKLMNOPQRSTUVWXYZ
abcdefghijklmnopqrstuvwxyz
1234567890 !@#?:;"*&

Foundry: Colophon
Designer: Benjamin Critton
Designer Nationality: American
Date: 2013

Benjamin Critton's Value Serif, which comes in a single style, was designed in 2013 to pair with the Value Sans font designed by The Entente's Edd Harrington and Anthony Sheret. Value Serif is a chunky, quirky typeface with a tall x-height. Plantin Infant was an influence on Value Serif.

VeraCruz BT

ABCDEFGHIJKLMNOPQRSTUVWXYZ
abcdefghijklmnopqrstuvwxyz
1234567890 !@#?:;"*&

Foundry: Bitstream
Designer: Ray Cruz
Designer Nationality: American
Date: 2003

US lettering artist and typeface designer Ray Cruz began his career at the Headliners photolettering firm in New York. His VeraCruz is a sharp, angular flared serif font in a bold weight. It features contextual alternates that sit off the baseline, thus giving any text a bouncy feel.

Volta

ABCDEFGHIJKLMNOPQRSTUVWXY
abcdefghijklmnopqrstuvwxyz
1234567890 !@#?:;"*&

Foundry: Bauer
Designer: Konrad F. Bauer / Walter Baum
Designer Nationality: German
Date: 1956

Volta is a Clarendon-esque slab serif released by the Bauer foundry in 1956, and designed by Konrad F. Bauer and Walter Baum. It comes in three weights: Regular, Medium and Bold. In the United States, Volta was renamed Fortune and it is sometimes known as Fortuna.

Windsor

ABCDEFGHIJKLMNOPQRSTUVWXYZ
abcdefghijklmnopqrstuvwxyz
1234567890 !@#?:;"*&

Foundry: Stephenson, Blake & Co.
Designer: Eleisha Pechey
Designer Nationality: British
Date: 1905

Eleisha Pechey designed Windsor for Stephenson, Blake & Co., and the typeface was released three years after his death. It is a quirky, Old Style serif with many distinctive features. It is Woody Allen's favourite typeface; the director has used it on his film titles and credits since *Annie Hall* (1977).

Woodblock

ABCDEFGHIJKLMNOPQRSTUVWXYZ
1234567890 !@#?:;"*&

Foundry: Monotype
Designer: Monotype Studio
Date: 1999

Woodblock was designed in 1999 by Monotype's in-house design team, inspired by old, wood type styles. It is an uppercase only, heavy condensed font with small, sharp triangular serifs, angled terminals and mainly diagonal crossbars. Woodblock is constructed from exclusively straight lines.

Woodley Park

ABCDEFGHIJKLMNOPQRSTUVWXYZ
abcdefghijklmnopqrstuvwxyz
1234567890 !@#?:;"*&

Foundry: Monotype
Designer: Nick Curtis
Designer Nationality: American
Date: 2001

Nick Curtis's Woodley Park was a winner in the Type Directors Club's Typeface Design competition in 2002. It is a double-stroked, medieval-style display serif inspired by the Naudin Champlevé uppercase serif released by Deberny & Peignot in 1924, which was known as Sylvan in the United States.

Affichen-Schriften FSL

ABCDEFGHIJKLMNOPQRSTUVWXYZ
abcdefghijklmnopqrstuvwxyz
1234567890 !@#?:;"'*&

In the 1830s, German typefounder Eduard Haenel was inspired by the new, large, eye-catching type designs found in England and France, and he became one of the first to introduce such types to the German printing trade. The Affichen-Schriften series revives four distinctive and brutal display styles, covering a spectrum of the peculiar shapes common to that era.

Doppel-Mittel Egyptienne is based on an Egyptian that Haenel imported and advertised in 1833. British typographer William Thorowgood orginally showed it as Two Lines English Egyptian No. 1, in London in 1821. Schmale Egyptienne No. 12 is another reissue of a Haenel typeface. With a cap height of 11.7 cm (4⅝ in.), it is the largest font shown in his specimen from 1841. Antiques originated at E. Tarbé & Cie in Paris and hints at

the splendour found in French poster typefaces. Advertised in 1839, it represents an early sans serif adaption of a condensed Egyptian. Breite-Fette Antiqua FSL is the digital reissue of an unidentified display typeface that was part of the type case in Oskar Leiner's printing workshop in Leipzig from c. 1850. It is unknown whether it was a custom-made design or if the typeface was distributed commercially by a foundry.

Type designer Pierre Pané-Farré, the co-founder of Forgotten Shapes, translated the historical shapes into digital fonts for contemporary use. Pané-Farré extended the language support and added subscript and superscript figures. He also included various font-specific OpenType features like a second set of numerals, alternate glyphs and case-sensitive punctuation.

Foundry: Forgotten Shapes
Designer: William Thorowgood / Eduard Haenel / E. Tarbé & Cie / Pierre Pané-Farré
Designer Nationality: British / German / French
Date: c. 1821–50 / 2011–17

Below from left. Overview of the different styles within the Affichen-Schriften family; *Soirée Fantastique* book design using Schmale Egyptienne FSL for the headline; posters from 1848 and 1849 from two Leipzig printing houses.

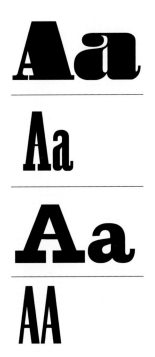

Aachen

ABCDEFGHIJKLMNOPQRSTUVWXYZ
abcdefghijklmnopqrstuvwxyz
1234567890 !@#?:;"*&

Foundry: Letraset
Designer: Colin Brignall
Designer Nationality: British
Date: 1969

Aachen was originally designed in a Bold weight by Colin Brignall in 1969, and another British Letraset designer Alan Meeks created a Medium weight eight years later. Aachen is a strong, heavy slab serif ideally suited to use at large point sizes, such as posters and headlines.

Claire News

ABCDEFGHIJKLMNOPQRSTUVW
abcdefghijklmnopqrstuvwxyz
1234567890 !@#?:;"*&

Foundry: Monotype
Designer: Unknown
Date: Unknown

Claire News is a robust and slightly extended slab serif typeface that shares certain proportions and design details with Clarendon and its ilk, though it displays a higher contrast within its letterforms. Its tall x-height and pronounced serifs make it a legible choice for headlines.

Epokha

ABCDEFGHIJKLMNOPQRSTUVWXYZ
1234567890 !@#?:;"*&

Foundry: Letraset
Designer: Colin Brignall
Designer Nationality: British
Date: 1992

Letraset and the International Typeface Corporation (ITC) released Colin Brignall's Ephoka in 1992. It is a very heavy, uppercase only slab serif font that comes in a single weight. It features many alternate letters that add variety and was inspired by early 20th-century geometric poster typefaces.

Goudy Heavyface

ABCDEFGHIJKLMNOPQRSTUVWXYZ
abcdefghijklmnopqrstuvwxyz
1234567890 !@#?:;"*&

Foundry: Monotype
Designer: Frederic W. Goudy
Designer Nationality: American
Date: 1925

Following the success of Cooper Black from a rival foundry, Lanston Monotype had Frederic W. Goudy design a heavy, rounder serif typeface of his own. The result, Goudy Heavyface, was released in 1925 in roman and italic styles. Sol Hess added condensed and outlined versions in 1926 and 1927.

Impakt

ABCDEFGHIJKLMNOPQRSTUVWXYZ
abcdefghijklmnopqrstuvwxyz
1234567890 !?:;"*&

Foundry: Linotype
Designer: Leonard Currie
Designer Nationality: British
Date: 1995

Created by British designer Leonard Currie for Letraset in 1995, and also sold by the International Typeface Corporation (ITC), Impakt is a quirky, bold slab serif available in a single weight. The Russian Constructivist movement of the 1920s inspired its condensed, geometric forms.

ITC Bailey Quad

ABCDEFGHIJKLMNOPQRSTUVWXYZ
abcdefghijklmnopqrstuvwxyz
1234567890 !@#?:;"*&

Foundry: ITC
Designer: Kevin Bailey
Designer Nationality: American
Date: 1994

ITC Bailey Quad, an eponymous typeface by Texas-born graphic designer Kevin Bailey, is a semi-serif font; it has slab-style serifs on some letters but not others and does not always follow the conventions of serif placement, giving a modern look. It is available in Bold only.

Kegger

ABCDEFGHIJKLMNOPQRSTUVWXYZ
abcdefghijklmnopqrstuvwxyz
1234567890 !@#?:;"*&

Foundry: Chank Co.
Designer: Chank Diesel
Designer Nationality: American
Date: 2007

Kegger is named after a US college term for a party with kegs of beer. It was designed in 2007 by Canadian-born, Florida-based type designer Chank Diesel. It is a bold slab serif that comes in two styles, a solid Regular and alternate Collegiate, which is outlined and shadowed.

Kengwin

ABCDEFGHIJKLMNOPQRSTUVWXYZ
abcdefghijklmnopqrstuvwxyz
1234567890 !@#?:;"*&

Foundry: Typodermic Fonts
Designer: Ray Larabie
Designer Nationality: Canadian
Date: 2010

The Kengwin typeface was created by prolific type designer Ray Larabie and published by his foundry Typodermic Fonts in 2010. It is a display slab serif that is available in a single style, which is bold and softly rounded, giving it a friendly, childish appeal despite its overall heaviness.

Letraset Bramley

ABCDEFGHIJKLMNOPQRSTUVWXYZ
abcdefghijklmnopqrstuvwxyz
1234567890 !@#?:;"*&

Foundry: Letraset
Designer: Alan Meeks
Designer Nationality: British
Date: 1979

Bramley was created by Alan Meeks, a type designer at the British dry-transfer lettering company Letraset, whose fonts are all now held by Monotype. A key feature is a gap between the base of the bowl and stem on 'a', 'd' and 'q'. It recalls Morris Fuller Benton's Souvenir designed in 1914.

Linotype Authentic Serif

ABCDEFGHIJKLMNOPQRSTUVWXYZ
abcdefghijklmnopqrstuvwxyz
1234567890 !@#?:;"*&

Foundry: Linotype
Designer: Karin Huschka
Designer Nationality: German
Date: 1999

The Authentic type family was acquired by Linotype when it was chosen from the entries of the foundry's International Digital Type Design Contest in 1999. Authentic Serif is a quirky, distinctive text typeface with many distinctive shapes and is typical of the postmodern, experimental fonts of the era.

Linotype Authentic Small Serif

ABCDEFGHIJKLMNOPQRSTUVWXYZ
abcdefghijklmnopqrstuvwxyz
1234567890 !@#?:;"*&

Foundry: Linotype
Designer: Karin Huschka
Designer Nationality: German
Date: 1999

German designer Karin Huschka's widely spaced Authentic family is a member of the TakeType Library, which was created from the winners of Linotype's International Type Design Contest. Small Serif has thinner serifs than Authentic Serif, making it even more idiosyncratic.

Magnus

ABCDEFGHIJKLMNOPQRSTUVWXYZ
abcdefghijklmnopqrstuvwxyz
1234567890 !@#?:;"*&

Foundry: ITC
Designer: Bruno Grasswill
Designer Nationality: American
Date: 1981

Magnus is a titling display font designed in the style of a slab serif. Its characters are narrow but sturdy, with low-contrast strokes and serifs that swap between rectangular blocks and curved stroke endings, which are often combined, as seen in several lowercase figures.

Melina BT

ABCDEFGHIJKLMNOPQRSTUVWXYZ
abcdefghijklmnopqrstuvwxyz
1234567890 !@#?:;"*&

Foundry: Bitstream
Designer: Nick Curtis
Designer Nationality: American
Date: 2003

Melina BT is an eloquent display serif designed in two styles, Plain and Fancy. It is modelled on two typefaces, Greco Adornado and Greco Bold, which were produced by the Imprenta y Fundición Tipográfica Richard Gans type foundry in Madrid during the 1920s.

Mensura Slab

ABCDEFGHIJKLMNOPQRSTUVWXYZ
abcdefghijklmnopqrstuvwxyz
1234567890 !@#?:;"*&

Foundry: Graviton Font Foundry
Designer: Pablo Balcells
Designer Nationality: Argentinian
Date: 2013

A modular, geometric slab serif, Mensura Slab has a technical feel and is versatile thanks to many alternate letters, which are curved rather than angular. Argentinian typographer Pablo Balcells also designed a sans version, called Mensura; both come in four weights with italics.

Monotype Bernard

ABCDEFGHIJKLMNOPQRSTUVWXYZ
abcdefghijklmnopqrstuvwxyz
1234567890 !@#?:;"*&

Foundry: Monotype
Designer: Monotype Studio
Date: 1926

Monotype Bernard is a serif display font, closely associated with the Art Nouveau movement of the early 20th century. The design's trademarks include bold strokes, moderate contrast, rounded edges and bulbous terminals. It is typical of romans evolving at the time with a soft, scriptlike quality.

Monotype Egyptian 72 Extended

ABCDEFGHIJKLMNOPQRSTUVWXYZ
abcdefghijklmnopqrstuvwxyz
1234567890 !@#?:;"*&

Foundry: Monotype
Designer: Monotype Studio
Date: c. 1930s

Available in one weight, Egyptian 72 Extended is a characterful slab serif that was designed in-house by the Monotype Studio, and is a revival of a French style from the late 19th century, adapted by Monotype before World War II. It has large, square serifs and is suited to display use only.

Foundry Profile

Forgotten Shapes

Forgotten Shapes was formed in 2018 by Stephan Müller (founding partner of Lineto), Pierre Pané-Farré and Reymund Schröder to publish digital reconstructions of typefaces that have vanished from existence. The foundry revives such typefaces according to its guiding principle of *werktreue* – meaning in a form as faithful to the original as possible. To do this, they extensively research from archive material, sketches and drawings and, in several instances, have worked with the original type designers such as Karl Gerstner and Gert Wunderlich. As most of the source designs were created post-war, in the 1950s and 1960s, they were never digitized and so remain in predigital formats. Through the efforts of Forgotten Shapes, past design processes can be examined and explored, providing insight into current methodologies.

The first of the four releases are an unpublished design for a Clarendon-type serif Kleukens-Egyptienne, created in 1929 by German designer Friedrich Wilhelm Kleukens. The source material was part of a collection of digital materials by Hans Reichardt, a former Stempel employee who had been maintaining the archives of the D. Stempel AG foundry since its dissolution in 1985. The second family, Affichen-Schriften, is a collection of woodblock poster types used in German-speaking countries in the mid 19th century. Third in the suite is Gerstner-Programm, a sans serif Grotesque by Gerstner, who was one of the key figures in Swiss graphic design. Finally, Lector is an elegant serif type design Wunderlich created in the 1960s in East Germany.

To create an 'historical' atmosphere and more general associations in regards to each typeface published, every individual type specimen by Forgotten Shapes introduces the typeface with a specific and curated image collage. In order for the *Type Directory* to represent the approach of the Forgotten Shapes foundry and its collection, the foundry created this bespoke collage based on the different photographs they have used so far, with each image representing one typeface.

Founded: 2018
Country: Germany
Website: forgotten-shapes.com
Notable typefaces:
Affichen-Schriften
FSL (see p. 521)
Gerstner-Programm
FSL (see p. 226)
Kleukens-Egyptienne
FSL (see p. 46)
Lector FSL (see p. 167)
Normal-Grotesk FSL (see p. 242)

Above. Stonehenge. Inger Schulstad, 1963.

Left. Ether Dome Daguerreotype No. 1. A. Southworth & J. Hawes, c. 1847.

Right top. Painters Jindrich Štyrský a Toyen in masks during work with 'Deka' colours. n/a, before 4 May 1929.

Right middle. Maclyn McCarty with Francis Crick and James D. Watson. Marjorie McCarty, 1953.

Right below. People on the steps of Konserthuset, Stockholm. Andy Eick, 1965.

Neo Contact

ABCDEFGHIJKLMNOPQRSTUVWXYZ
abcdefghijklmnopqrstuvwxyz
1234567890 !@#?:;"*&

Foundry: American Type Founders / Linotype
Designer: Frank H. Riley
Designer Nationality: American
Date: 1948 / 1955

Originally called Contact when released by ATF, this bold, condensed Egyptian display typeface is recognizable as being used on Marlboro cigarette packs. The design combines strong, moderately contrasted strokes, as seen in the stems and curves, alongside thinner, sharper serifs and crossbars.

Octin Sports

ABCDEFGHIJKLMNOPQRSTUVWXYZ
1234567890 !@#?:;"*&

Foundry: Typodermic
Designer: Ray Larabie
Designer Nationality: Canadian
Date: 2007

Octin Sports is a slab serif display font and comprises seven weights, including Light, Semibold and Black. Like the letterforms often found on the back of sporting jerseys, Octin Sports is designed entirely in capitals, and features squared curves and mono-weighted strokes.

PL Barnum Block

ABCDEFGHIJKLMNOPQRSTUVWXYZ
abcdefghijklmnopqrstuvwxyz
1234567890 !© #?:;"*&

Foundry: Monotype
Designer: Dave West
Designer Nationality: American
Date: 1960

Named after P. T. Barnum, the US travelling showman, PL Barnum Block is a slab serif display typeface inspired by 19th-century woodcut lettering. Intended for posters, signage and packaging, the heavy strokes and minimal apertures ensure impact in both upper and lowercases.

PL Behemoth

ABCDEFGHIJKLMNOPQRSTUVWXYZ
abcdefghijklmnopqrstuvwxyz
1234567890 !© #?:;"*&

Foundry: Photo-Lettering
Designer: Dave West
Designer Nationality: American
Date: 1960

PL Behemoth is a slab serif display typeface inspired by 19th-century woodcut lettering. In comparison to similar typefaces designed by Dave West for Photo-Lettering in the 1960s, such as PL Barnum Block, PL Behemoth features narrower forms as well as stricter strokes and serifs.

PL Tower Condensed

ABCDEFGHIJKLMNOPQRSTUVWXYZ
abcdefghijklmnopqrstuvwxyz
1234567890 ! © #?:;"*&

Foundry: Photo-Lettering / Monotype
Designer: Morris Fuller Benton
Designer Nationality: American
Date: 1934

PL Tower is a light slab serif display font based around an earlier, heavier design by Morris Fuller Benton. Published originally by the Photo-Lettering type foundry, the condensed characters contain a wealth of white space and pronounced serifs, and are intended for use in narrow headlines.

Pokerface

abcdeFGHIJKLMNOPqrstuvwxyz
abcDEFghijklmnopqrstuvwxyz
1234567890 !@#?:;"*&

Foundry: Ascender
Designer: Jim Ford
Designer Nationality: American
Date: 2009

Jim Ford's Pokerface is a slab serif display font inspired by the randomness of drawing playing cards. The letterforms are grouped in either pairs or fours, similar to traditional poker hands, and are shuffled upon their use to generate serendipitous style combinations.

P.T. Barnum

ABCDEFGHIJKLMNOPQRSTUVWXYZ
abcdefghijklmnopqrstuvwxyz
1234567890 !@#?:;"*&

Foundry: Bitstream
Designer: Unknown
Date: Unknown

P.T. Barnum is Bitstream's revival of a 19th-century type produced at the Barnhart Brothers & Spindler foundry in *c.* 1880 and subsequently published by the American Type Founders. In contrast to the majority of wood type designs, P.T. Barnum includes a number of bracketed serifs.

Pueblo

ABCDEFGHIJKLMNOPQRSTUVWXYZ
abcdefghijklmnopqrstuvwxyz
1234567890 !@#?:;"*&

Foundry: Monotype
Designer: Jim Parkinson
Designer Nationality: American
Date: 1998

Pueblo is a display typeface that draws upon a variety of influences, from Speedball lettering to *fin-de-siècle* sign painting. The distinctive forms feature bold strokes and gently rounded stroke endings, which reference the softness of the Speedball pen while retaining legibility.

Robotik

ABCDEFGHIJKLMNOPQRSTUVWXYZ
abcdefghijklmnopqrstuvwxyz
1234567890 !?:;"*&

Foundry: ITC
Designer: David Quay
Designer Nationality: British
Date: 1989

David Quay's Robotik is a slab serif display font informed by the mechanic precision of Russian Constructivism after World War I. The font, designed in regular and italic styles, features condensed, squared letterforms. Robotik is best used for headlines in large point sizes.

Scriptek

ABCDEFGHIJKLMNOPQRSTUVWXYZ
abcdefghijklmnopqrstuvwxyz
1234567890 !?:;"*&

Foundry: Letraset / ITC
Designer: David Quay
Designer Nationality: British
Date: 1992

British type designer David Quay designed Scriptek for Letraset; it was also released by the International Typeface Corporation. It is a compact, angular slab serif that comes in a single bold weight in roman and italic styles. It was inspired by early Constructivist typefaces popular in interwar Europe.

Special Forces

ABCDEFGHIJKLMNOPQRSTUVWXYZ
abcdefghijklmnopqrstuvwxyz
1234567890 !@#?:;"*&

Foundry: Typodermic
Designer: Ray Larabie
Designer Nationality: Canadian
Date: 2010

Special Forces is a robust, slab serif headline font designed especially for screen use by the Typodermic founder, Canadian designer Ray Larabie. It is available in upper and lowercase, and in two styles, Special Forces Regular and Special Forces Italic. Its name and appearance evoke the military.

Stratford

ABCDEFGHIJKLMNOPQRSTUVWXYZ
abcdefghijklmnopqrstuvwxyz
1234567890 !@#?:;"*&

Foundry: Fonts
Designer: Freda Sack
Designer Nationality: British
Date: 1977

Stratford is an idiosyncratic slab serif display font, with an Arts and Crafts overtone, skilfully crafted to facilitate the close letterspacing in 1970s fashion. Its creator Freda Sack co-founded The Foundry (see p. 284) and together with Colin Brignall designed popular faces such as Proteus and Paddington.

Teknik

ABCDEFGHIJKLMNOPQRSTUVWXYZ
abcdefghijklmnopqrstuvwxyz
1234567890 !@#?:;"*&

Foundry: Letraset
Designer: David Quay
Designer Nationality: British
Date: 1990

David Quay's Teknik is an impactful and stylized display typeface that is often categorized as an Egyptian due to its slab serifs. It is similar to his Robotik design of 1989, and both typefaces are inspired by the geometric designs of the 1920s Soviet Constructivist movement.

Tesla Caps

ABCDEFGHIJKLMNOPQRSTUVWXYZ
1234567890 !@#?:;"*&

Foundry: Typotheque
Designer: Nikola Djurek
Designer Nationality: Croatian
Date: 2015

The Tesla family is named after the inventor, physicist and engineer Nikola Tesla. It consists of Tesla Slab, Stencil, Caps and Mono. Tesla Caps is a constructed slab serif typeface with monolinear and inverted contrast, which is available in three weights from the lightweight A, to the super black weight C.

Waterloo Bold

ABCDEFGHIJKLMNOPQRSTUVWXYZ
abcdefghijklmnopqrstuvwxyz
1234567890 !?:;"*&

Foundry: Letraset
Designer: Alan Meeks
Designer Nationality: British
Date: 1987

British designer Alan Meeks joined the studio at Letraset in 1975. He created Waterloo Bold in 1987. It is a heavy slab serif with a large x-height, high crossbars and a subtle slant. It comes in a single bold weight only and is suited best to display and headline usage.

Yearbook

ABCDEFGHIJKLMNOPQRSTUVWXYZ
1234567890 !@#?:;"*&

Foundry: Monotype
Designer: Monotype Studio
Date: Unknown

Yearbook is an uppercase, angular, heavy slab serif constructed without curves. It comes in three styles, which are all the same weight: Filler, Outline and Solid. The first two of these faces are designed to be superimposed. Yearbook has a US collegiate feel, reminiscent of the type on letterman jackets.

Aerion

ABCDEFGHIJKLMNOPQRSTUVWXYZ
1234567890 !@#?:;"*&

In 2003, US designer Alexander McCracken established his San Francisco-based foundry Neutura, which specializes in display typeface design. Aerion is a square sans serif typeface with extended letterforms and a slightly futuristic feel, and is available in four weights.

Foundry: Neutura
Designer: Alexander McCracken
Designer Nationality: American
Date: 2012

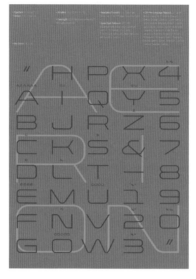
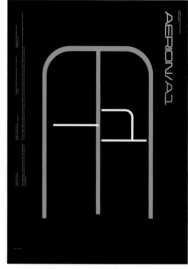

Ambule BT

ABCDEFGHIJKLMNOPQRSTUVWXYZ
abcdefghijklmnopqrstuvwxyz
1234567890 !@#?:;"※&

Foundry: Bitstream
Designer: Julien Janiszewski
Designer Nationality: French
Date: 2002

Julien Janiszewski designed Ambule BT for Bitstream in 2002. It is a hybrid typeface featuring letterforms from both upper and lowercase within its single character set. The font combines several stylistic flourishes found within Huxley Vertical (1935) and Peignot (1937).

Board of Directors

ABCDEFGHIJKLMNOPQRSTUVWXYZ
abcdefghijklmnopqrstuvwxyz
1234567890 !@#?:;"*&

Foundry: Typodermic
Designer: Ray Larabie
Designer Nationality: Canadian
Date: 2010

Board of Directors was influenced by early plotter typefaces and has a distinct science-fiction feel. It is a display sans serif typeface available in a broad range of weights, from fine Ultralight through to Black. It was designed by Ray Larabie for his foundry Typodermic in 2010.

Bank Gothic

ABCDEFGHIJKLMNOPQRSTUVWXYZ
ABCDEFGHIJKLMNOPQRSTUVWXYZ
1234567890 !@#?:;"*&

Foundry: Bitstream
Designer: Morris Fuller Benton
Nationality: American
Date: 1930–33

Despite being widely used to reflect technological and science-fiction themed genres, Bank Gothic has lasted the test of time. It remains as popular in the 21st century as when it was created in the early 1930s by the esteemed and influential type designer Morris Fuller Benton. Bank Gothic has become firmly established as the typeface *de rigueur* for science-fiction film posters, while films such as *I, Robot* (2004), *Source Code* (2011) and *The Hunger Games* (2012) have all employed its geometric, squared-up forms that are indicative of technology.

Bank Gothic's monoline stroke weight and rectilinear construction provide a no-nonsense appearance. The typeface's slightly extended character width makes it ideal for titling purposes where a sense of gravitas is required. Benton designed Bank Gothic in capitals only, and the suite of characters comes in uppercase and small caps. There have been a number of versions since the original cut by Benton for American Type Founders, with the most popular being offered by Linotype and Bitstream. Fonthaus created an extended family in 2010 with Bank Gothic Pro, which included lowercase and three weights – Light, Medium and Bold.

Below. Bank Gothic features heavily in and around Arsenal Football Club's Emirates Stadium in North London. Here it is seen set in concrete at the start of one of the pedestrian approaches.

Bullet

ABCDEFGHIJKLMNOPQRSTUVWXYZ

abcdefghijklmnopqrstuvwxyz

1234567890 !@#?:;"*&

Tal Leming designed Bullet for House Industries before he started his own foundry in 2005, Type Supply. It began as lettering by Ken Barber on House Industries' *Pop Art* catalogue. Bullet is a heavy, italic sans serif and also comes in a script style with a joined, underlined lowercase.

Foundry: House Industries
Designer: Tal Leming
Designer Nationality: American
Date: 2000

Cintra

ABCDEFGHIJKLMNOPQRSTUVWXYZ

ABCDEFGHIJKLMNOPQRSTUVWXYZ

1234567890 !@#?:;"*&

Pablo Balcells's Graviton foundry published Cintra in 2014. It is a square sans serif font with a friendly appearance. The font includes two character sets of uppercase letterforms, one featuring a range of rounded details. A slab serif counterpart, Cintra Slab, is also available.

Foundry: Graviton
Designer: Pablo Balcells
Designer Nationality: Argentinian
Date: 2014

Conthrax

ABCDEFGHIJKLMNOPQRSTUVW

abcdefghijklmnopqrstuvwxyz

1234567890 !@#?:;"*&

This futuristic and slightly extended display font by Typodermic's Ray Larabie offers an extensive character set, and supports languages including Greek, Cyrillic and Vietnamese alongside the Latin. The foundry offers a desktop licence for the semibold cut free of charge.

Foundry: Typodermic
Designer: Ray Larabie
Designer Nationality: Canadian
Date: 2016

Eurostile Candy

ABCDEFGHIJKLMNOPQRSTUV

abcdefghijklmnopqrstuvwxyz

1234567890 !@#?:;"*&

Eurostile Candy is based on Akira Kobayashi's Eurostile Next, which is part of the Eurostile Next superfamily. Eurostile Candy's extra strokes have been removed and its corners and joints have been rounded off, giving a friendlier, softer feel than the original Eurostile created by Aldo Novarese in 1962.

Foundry: Linotype
Designer: Aldo Novarese / Akira Kobayashi
Designer Nationality: Italian / Japanese
Date: 2008

Eurostile Unicase

ABCDEFGHIJKLMNOPQRSTU
abcdefghijklmnopqrstu
1234567890 !@#?:;"*&

Foundry: Linotype
Designer: Aldo Novarese / Akira Kobayashi
Designer Nationality: Italian / Japanese
Date: 2008

Eurostile Unicase is an adaption of Akira Kobayashi's Eurostile Next design. Here, Kobayashi has created a quirky unicase version that does away with ascenders and descenders to create letters which are the same height, such as a raised lowercase 'y', and modified lowercase 'a' and 'e'.

Hemi Head

ABCDEFGHIJKLMNOPQRSTUVWXYZ
abcdefghijklmnopqrstuvwxyz
1234567890 !@#?:;"*&

Foundry: Typodermic
Designer: Ray Larabie
Designer Nationality: Canadian
Date: 2009

In 1998, Canadian designer Ray Larabie created the original Hemi Head 426, inspired by the old Dodge logo. The square, industrial sans serif came in one bold, italic style. Eleven years later, he released an extensive update that included eight weights with italics.

Injekuta

ABCDEFGHIJKLNOPQRSTUV
WXYZ
1234567890 !@#?:;"*6

Foundry: Typodermic
Designer: Ray Larabie
Designer Nationality: Canadian
Date: 2007

Ray Larabie designed Injekuta for Typodermic in 2007. It is an extended, uppercase only, geometric sans serif. Like many of Ray Larabie's fonts, the overall feel is technical, futuristic and sleek. Injekuta comes in four weights – Light to Black – without italics or lowercase.

ITC Black Tulip

ABCDEFGHIJKLMNOPQRSTUVWXYZ
abcdefghijklmnopqrstuvwxyz
1234567890 !@#?:;"*6

Foundry: ITC
Designer: Dudley Rees
Designer Nationality: British
Date: 1997

Black Tulip is a heavy, compact sans serif with distinctive open counters on many lowercase glyphs. Designer Dudley Rees was inspired by the Greek fret band, which is a repeating pattern formed by tracing a line at right angles between two horizontal rules to form an interlocking motif.

ITC Bolt

ABCDEFGHIJKLMNOPQRSTUVWXYZ
abcdefghijklmnopqrstuvwxyz
1234567890 !☐☐?:;"*&

Foundry: ITC
Designer: Ronne Bonder /
Tom Carnase
Designer Nationality: American
Date: 1970

ITC Bolt is a heavy, squat modular sans serif font designed by Ronne Bonder and Tom Carnase. The US duo had worked together as the Bonder & Carnase studio in New York during the 1960s before Carnase left to join Herb Lubalin and Ernie Smith as a partner in Lubalin, Smith, Carnase (see p. 62).

ITC CuppaJoe

ABCDEFGHIJKLMNOPQRSTUVWXYZ
ABCDEFGHIJKLMNOPQRSTUVWXYZ
1234567890 !@#?:;"*&

Foundry: ITC
Designer: Nick Curtis
Designer Nationality: American
Date: 2001

Nick Curtis's ITC CuppaJoe is a bold, Art Deco-inspired sans serif. It gained its name because it was based on lettering found on Bokar Coffee packaging from the 1930s. Curtis also released fonts from his own foundry, Nick's Fonts, and most of its designs were based on authentic historical sources.

ITC Deli

ABCDEFGHIJKLMNOPQRSTUVWXYZ
ABCDEFGHIJKLMNOPQRSTUVWXYZ
1234567890 !@#?:;"*&

Foundry: ITC
Designer: Jim Spiece
Designer Nationality: American
Date: 1999

ITC Deli is a retro, extended sans serif designed by Jim Spiece in 1999. It is evocative of mid-century ideas of futuristic type. ITC Deli comes in two styles: Deluxe is square with rounded corners and small caps, while Supreme has a lowercase that joins together as a script style.

ITC Machine

ABCDEFGHIJKLMNOPQRSTUVWXYZ
1234567890 !@#?:;"*&

Foundry: ITC
Designer: Ronne Bonder /
Tom Carnase
Designer Nationality: American
Date: 1970

ITC Machine is a dense, all-caps sans serif available in Bold and Medium. It has a very utilitarian feel, achieved through the lack of curves; letters are constructed using straight lines alone and often 45° angles. The Blockbuster video-rental service used the face for its company logo.

ITC Stenberg

ABCDEFGHIJKLMNOPQRSTUVWXYZ
ABCDEFGHIJKLMNOPQRSTUVWXYZ
1234567890 !@#?:;"*&

Foundry: ITC
Designer: Tagir Safayev
Designer Nationality: Russian
Date: 1997

Moscow-based designer Tagir Safayev drew inspiration from the Constructivist movement, especially the work of the brothers Vladimir and Georgii Stenberg, to create this typeface. Available in regular and inline, Stenberg is a heavy, curveless, geometric sans serif with caps and small caps only.

ITC Tetra

ABCDEFGHIJKLMNOPQRSTUVWXYZ
abcdefghijklmnopqrstuvwxyz
1234567890 !@№?:;"*&

Foundry: ITC
Designer: Tomi Haaparanta
Designer Nationality: Finnish
Date: 2005

ITC Tetra is the work of Finnish designer Tomi Haaparanta, who studied graphic design at the University of Industrial Arts in Helsinki and founded the Suomi Type Foundry in 2004. It is a simple geometric sans serif with mostly square letters and rounded corners. ITC Tetra comes in three weights.

Just Square

ABCDEFGHIJKLMNOPQRSTUVWXYZ
abcdefghijklmnopqrstuvwxyz
1234567890 !@#?:;"*&

Foundry: Linotype
Designer: Zoran Kostic
Designer Nationality: Serbian
Date: 2004

Zoran Kostic began Just Square during the Kosovo War in 1999; he based it on a logo drawn by his son. It is a part of a family that started with Why Square (2004), and both are sans serifs constructed from squares. Just Square comes in eight weights with Latin and Cyrillic support.

Korataki

ABCDEFGHIJKLMNOPQ
abcdefghijklmnopqrstuvwxyz
1234567890 !@#?:;"*&

Foundry: Typodermic
Designer: Ray Larabie
Designer Nationality: Canadian
Date: 2006

Typodermic published Korataki in 2006. It was inspired by China, a futuristic font designed by M. Mitchell in 1975. Korataki is an extended sans serif typeface available in fourteen styles – seven weights with italics – and features alternate versions of 'A', 'G', 'Q' and '4'.

Las Vegas

ABCDEFGHIJKLMNOPQRSTUVWXYZ
abcdefghijklmnopqrstuvwxyz
1234567890 !@#?:;"'*&

Las Vegas is an unreleased design by Guðmundur Úlfarsson of Or Type (see p. 498), which debuted in *Conveyor* magazine in 2015. It is an angular sans serif with multiple alternate letters, some of which were inspired by New Alphabet (1967) by Wim Crouwel (see p. 540).

Foundry: Or Type
Designer: Guðmundur Úlfarsson
Designer Nationality: Icelandic
Date: 2015

Lineavec

ABCDEFGHIJKLMNOPQRST
abcdefghijklmnopqrstuvwxyz
1234567890 !@#?:;"'*&

Ray Larabie's Lineavec, designed in 2006, is a wide, monoline, futuristic sans serif available from Typodermic in a single style, Light. As with many of Larabie's fonts it achieves a science-fiction, high-tech feel thanks to its angular construction and subtly rounded corners.

Foundry: Typodermic
Designer: Ray Larabie
Designer Nationality: Canadian
Date: 2006

Linotype Kaliber

ABCDEFGHIJKLMNOPQRSTUVWXYZ
abcdefghijklmnopqrstuvwxyz
1234567890 !@#?:;"'*&

Linotype Kaliber is an exacting display font designed in four styles, including Regular, Italic, Bold and Black. The rigid, monoline strokes and stiff curves characterizing the letterforms give the impression of steel pipes that have been carefully bent into shape.

Foundry: Linotype
Designer: Lutz Baar
Designer Nationality: German
Date: 1999

Linotype Lichtwerk

ABCDEFGHIJKLMNOPQRSTUVWXYZ
abcdefghijklmnopqrstuvwxyz
1234567890 !@#?:;"'*&

Linotype Lichtwerk is a headline typeface designed in three styles – Regular, Italic and Bold – and inspired by the mechanical forms of 1920s Constructivism. The characters contain extended x-heights, narrow forms and rounded strokes, and convey both precision and approachability.

Foundry: Linotype
Designer: Bernd Pfannkuchen
Designer Nationality: German
Date: 1999

Linotype Spacera

ABCDEFGHIJKLMNOPQRSTUVW
ABCDEFGHIJKLMNOPQRSTUVW
1234567890 !@#?:;"*&

Foundry: Linotype
Designer: Louis Lemoine
Designer Nationality: American
Date: 2002

Linotype Spacera is a squared display font, conceived to embody a futuristic sensibility. The characters, which are designed exclusively in capitals, feature several distinguishing details, such as cubic serifs, extended cross-strokes and central dots in the 'c' and the 'd'.

Liquorstore

ABCDEFGHIJKLMNOPQRSTUVWXYZ
abcdefghijklmnopqrstuvwxyz
1234567890 !@#?:;"*&

Foundry: Chank Co.
Designer: Chank Diesel
Designer Nationality: American
Date: 1997

Liquorstore is a sans serif display font informed by the hand-rendered liquor-store signage around Minneapolis, Minnesota. The squared letterforms, also inspired by Constructivist posters and vintage magazine logos, were designed in four weights, including Jazz and 3D.

Mesotone BT

ABCDEFGHIJKLMNOPQRSTUVWXYZ
abcdefghijklmnopqrstuvwxyz
1234567890 !@#?:;"*&

Foundry: Bitstream
Designer: Matt Desmond
Designer Nationality: American
Date: 2006

Matt Desmond's Mesotone BT is a computer-style display typeface, conceived in a single weight. The font's unicase characters feature monoweight strokes, a relatively standardized width, and an accompanying glyph set that incorporates Baltic, Turkish and European languages.

Morris Sans

ABCDEFGHIJKLMNOPQRSTU
abcdefghijklmnopqrstuvwxyz
1234567890 !@#?:;"*&

Foundry: Linotype
Designer: Morris Fuller Benton / Dan Reynolds
Designer Nationality: American
Date: 2006

Designed by Dan Reynolds, Morris Sans is a revision and extension of Bank Gothic designed by Morris Fuller Benton for the American Type Founders in 1930. In addition to redrawing the uppercase characters, Reynolds also introduced a lowercase character set and six new figure styles.

Wim Crouwel

Designer Wim Crouwel was a leading exponent of the International Style that came to prominence in the 1950s and 1960s. His underlying use of grids in all aspects of his work signified a distinctive and revolutionary approach to type development as well as his own graphic design output.

In the late 1940s, Crouwel studied Fine Art at Academie Minerva in Groningen, the Netherlands and typography at what is now the Gerrit Rietveld Academie in Amsterdam. In 1963, he co-founded the design studio Total Design (now Total Identity). He earned an international reputation for brilliance and radical design just a year later, when he created the designs for the posters, catalogues and exhibitions of the Stedelijk Museum, Amsterdam. This was a relationship that would last over two decades, Crouwel the sole-appointed designer. His grid-based design systems offered flexibility and creativity, all the while providing the museum with a recognizable visual language. The wealth of work created during this period stands up to be some of the most innovative and striking designs created.

In 1967, he wrote and designed a short book presenting his experimental *New Alphabet* design. A personal project, it was a typeface design that adopted the limitations of the cathode-ray tube technology of the time, being constructed in grid form with only horizontal and vertical strokes making up its characters. Other significant designs were his Fodor and Gridnik types. The latter was originally called Politene and was commissioned by Olivetti in 1974 as a typewriter typeface but was later renamed after a nickname given to Crouwel by his friends. Digital versions of these highly constructed and experimental types were created by London-based The Foundry (see p. 284) in close collaboration with Crouwel as part of its Architype 3 Crouwel Collection in 1996.

In later life, Crouwel was active in education, teaching at a number of top design schools. In 1985, he was appointed a director at the Museum Boijmans van Beuningen in Rotterdam, commissioning London design studio 8vo to meet the design requirements for the site. He retired from the museum in 1993. Crouwel continues to design on a range of print and exhibition projects.

In July 2019, Wim Crouwel was given the highest honour from the internationally renowned Type Directors Club, the award of its 32nd TDC Medal. This is only given out to the 'most influential and inspiring practitioners and thinkers in typography'.

Date: 1928–
Nationality: Dutch
Notable typefaces:
Foundry Gridnik (see p. 426)
Foundry Stedelijk (see p. 419)

Below. Crouwel's book *New Alphabet*, released in 1967, documenting his proposals for 'programmed typography'.

Opposite top. Wim Crouwel, not only designing, but dressing for the future, 1969 (left). *Visuele Communicatie Nederland*, Stedelijk Museum, 1969 (right).

Opposite bottom. A selection of Crouwel's iconic designs for the Stedelijk Museum. From left: Poster *Elmar Berkovich*, Stedelijk van Abbemuseum, 1962; Poster *Vormgevers*, Stedelijk Museum Amsterdam, 1968; Catalogue cover *Werkgroep Plakat Prag politieke affiches uit Tsjechoslowakije*, Stedelijk Museum Amsterdam, 1966.

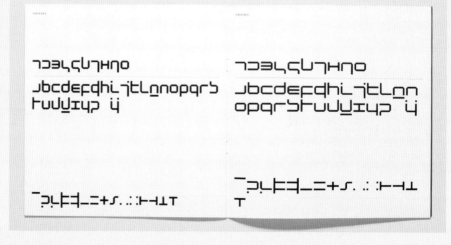

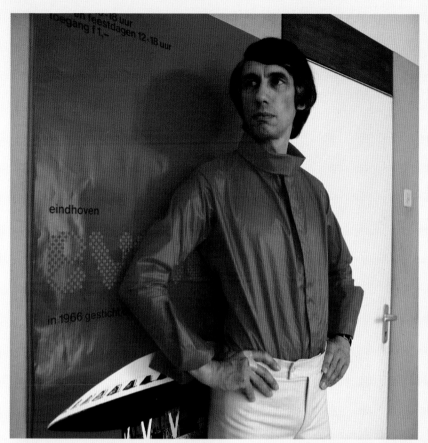

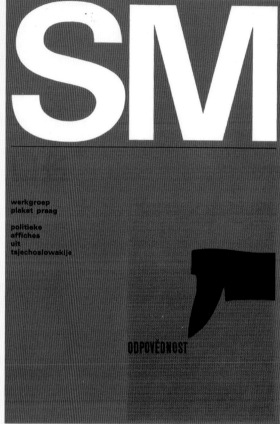

werkgroep
plakat praag

politieke
affiches
uit
tsjechoslowakije

ODPOVĔDNOST

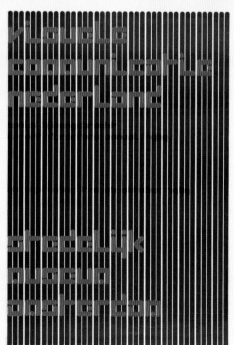

stedelijk museum amsterdam
5 april t/m 23 juni 68

vorm
gevers

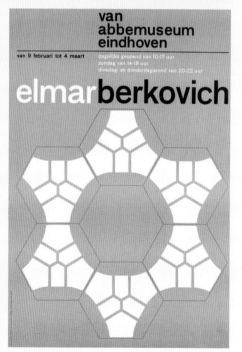

van
abbemuseum
eindhoven

van 9 februari tot 4 maart

dagelijks geopend van 10-17 uur
zondag van 14-18 uur
dinsdag- en donderdagavond van 20-22 uur

elmar berkovich

Necia

ABCDEFGHIJKLMNOPQRSTUVWXYZ
abcdefghijklmnopqrstuvwxyz
1234567890 !@#?:;"*&

Necia is a geometric display typeface that combines sharply angled joints and terminals with softly rounded corners. Designed in the style of a squared sans serif, the Necia font family includes four weights, from Light to Black, each with corresponding unicase versions.

Foundry: Graviton
Designer: Pablo Balcells
Designer Nationality: Argentinian
Date: 2014

Nicotine

ABCDEFGHIJKLMNOPQRSTUVWXYZ
abcdefghijklmnopqrstuvwxyz
1234567890 !@#?:;"*¢

Nicotine is a squared sans serif display font comprising five styles, including the unicase Nicotine Jazz. The condensed characters, most notably the 'I', which takes the silhouette of a filtered cigarette, were designed to exert a strong influence in tight compositions.

Foundry: Chank Co.
Designer: Chank Diesel
Designer Nationality: American
Date: 1998

Pacifica

ABCDEFGHIJKLMNOPQRSTUVWXYZ
1234567890 !@#?:;"*&

Pacifica is a display typeface designed in a single style. It was based on the Congo font produced by the US foundry Barnhart Brothers & Spindler c. 1895 and is almost identical to the original. Solotype conceived Pacifica in an effort to smooth Congo's curves and refine the font's shape.

Foundry: Solotype
Designer: Dan X. Solo
Designer Nationality: American
Date: 2005

PL Fiedler Gothic

ABCDEFGHIJKLMNOPQRSTUVWXYZ
abcdefghijklmnopqrstuvwxyz
1234567890 !©#?:;"*&

Hal Fiedler's PL Fiedler Gothic is a sans serif display typeface designed in a single style. The squared letterforms, which are in many ways typical of a gothic sans, feature several quirks, such as the short tail on the lowercase 'q' or the dented stem on the 't'.

Foundry: Monotype
Designer: Hal Fiedler
Designer Nationality: American
Date: Unknown

Quartan

ABCDEFGHIJKLMNOPQRSTUVWXYZ
abcdefghijklmnopqrstuvwxyz
1234567890 !@#?:;"*&

Foundry: Linotype
Designer: Maria Martina Schmitt
Designer Nationality: Austrian
Date: 2004

Maria Martina Schmitt's Quartan is a display font comprised of three weights, from Light to Bold. The industrial characters, which feature unicase forms that resist the use of ascenders and descenders, act like building blocks that allow the designer to render the text in stylish stacks.

Sackers Square Gothic

ABCDEFGHIJKLMNOPQRSTUVWXY
ABCDEFGHIJKLMNOPQRSTUVWXYZ
1234567890 !@#?:;"*&

Foundry: Compugraphic
Designer: Gary Sackers
Designer Nationality: American
Date: 1975

Sackers Square Gothic is part of a collection of faces designed by Gary Sackers for Compugraphic between 1974 and 1975, based on old engraving type masterplates. It is a caps and small caps only extended sans serif with square edges that comes in three roman weights: Light, Medium and Heavy.

Serpentine

ABCDEFGHIJKLMNOPQRSTUVWXYZ
abcdefghijklmnopqrstuvwxyz
1234567890 !@#?:;"*&

Foundry: VGC
Designer: Dick Jensen
Designer Nationality: American
Date: 1972

Dick Jensen's Serpentine is a wide, slightly flared semi serif with a blocky feel and large x-height. The Visual Graphics Corporation released it in 1972 in Light, Medium, Bold and Bold Italic styles. The typeface was used in the posters and titles for the James Bond film *Tomorrow Never Dies* (1997).

Superstar

ABCDEFGHIJKLMNOPQRSTUVWXYZ
1234567890 !@#?:;"*&

Foundry: Letraset
Designer: Colin Brignall
Designer Nationality: British
Date: 1970

Letraset type director Colin Brignall was inspired by US sportswear graphics – in particular the lettering found on baseball and soccer shirts – when he designed Superstar. It is an inline sans serif with wedgelike cutouts taking the place of curves, and is the perfect choice for sports-related designs.

Tank

ABCDEFGHIJKLMNOPQRSTUVWXYZ
1234567890 !@#?:;"*&

Foundry: Typodermic
Designer: Ray Larabie
Designer Nationality: Canadian
Date: 2004

Available in two weights, Tank and Tank Lite, this sturdy display typeface has a heavy mechanical look and tight spacing. Tank is supplied with a set of alternate characters with no counters, whereas Tank Lite is designed for smaller spaces and sizes, when Tank Regular's narrow counters are likely to vanish.

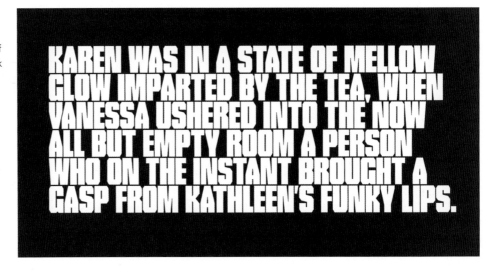

KAREN WAS IN A STATE OF MELLOW GLOW IMPARTED BY THE TEA, WHEN VANESSA USHERED INTO THE NOW ALL BUT EMPTY ROOM A PERSON WHO ON THE INSTANT BROUGHT A GASP FROM KATHLEEN'S FUNKY LIPS.

Titanium

ABCDEFGHIJKLMNOPQRSTUVWXYZ
abcdefghijklmnopqrstuvwxyz
1234567890 !@#?:;"*&

Foundry: Ascender
Designer: Steve Matteson
Designer Nationality: American
Date: 2006

Titanium is a rounded monoline sans serif with a futuristic feel available in a single weight. Steve Matteson designed it for the Chicago-based Ascender foundry in 2006. Matteson co-founded Ascender in 2004, and it was purchased by his former employer, Monotype, in 2010.

Titanium Motors

ABCDEFGHIJKLMNOPQRSTUVW XYZ
1234567890 !@#?:;"*&

Foundry: Monotype
Designer: Steve Matteson
Designer Nationality: American
Date: 2012

Steve Matteson became Monotype's creative type director when the company subsumed his foundry Ascender in 2010. He designed Titanium Motors two years later; this bold, rounded all-caps sans serif is available in regular and italic, conveying a dynamic sense of speed, especially when used in italic.

Violenta

ABCDEFGHIJKLMNOPQRSTUVWXYZ
ABCDEFGHIJKLMNOPQRSTUVWXYZ
1234567890 !@#?.,"'*&

Foundry: Graviton
Designer: Pablo Balcells
Designer Nationality: Argentinian
Date: 2015

Pablo Balcells, the Argentinian designer and graduate of the University of Buenos Aires, created this condensed, bold, geometric sans serif. Violenta comes in uppercase and unicase in four styles: Solid, Outline, Inline and Stencil. The Graviton type foundry published Violenta in 2015.

Why Square

abcdefghijklmnopqrstuvwxyz
1234567890 !@#?.:"'*&

Foundry: Linotype
Designer: Zoran Kostic
Designer Nationality: Serbian
Date: 1999

Zoran Kostic drew Why Square in 1999 during the Kosovo War; it was the start of a type family that also includes Just Square and began as lettering by Kostic's son. It is a narrow, square sans serif and comes in five weights with Cyrillic support and alternate ultra-wide capitals.

Zekton

ABCDEFGHIJKLMNOPQRSTUVWXYZ
abcdefghijklmnopqrstuvwxyz
1234567890 !@#?.;"'*&

Foundry: Typodermic
Designer: Ray Larabie
Designer Nationality: Canadian
Date: 1998

Zekton, designed by the prolific font maker Ray Larabie, is a geometric sans serif with round corners and even line widths. It comes in many styles, with three widths and seven weights, all of which have matching italics. Like many of Larabie's fonts, it has a futuristic atmosphere.

Zosma

ABCDEFGHIJKLMNOPQRSTUV
WXYZ
1234567890 !@#?.;"'*&

Foundry: Typodermic
Designer: Ray Larabie
Designer Nationality: Canadian
Date: 2005

Zosma, designed by Ray Larabie and released by his foundry Typodermic in 2005, is an uppercase, geometric sans serif that is constructed with straight lines and subtle curves. Zosma conveys a technical feel and comes in three weights – Light to Bold – with matching italics.

AG Book Stencil

ABCDEFGHIJKLMNOPQRSTUVWXYZ
abcdefghijklmnopqrstuvwxyz
1234567890 ! ?:;"*&

Günter Gerhard Lange added this stencil design to his AG Book family in 1985. It is sold by Berthold as part of a package with several other display typefaces, including AG Old Face Shaded, Barmeno Extra Bold and Formata Outline, offering designers a range of impactful fonts from which to choose.

Foundry: Berthold
Designer: Günter Gerhard Lange
Designer Nationality: German
Date: 1985

Aguda Stencil

ABCDEFGHIJKLMNOPQRSTUVWXYZ
ABCDEFGHIJKLMNOPQRSTUVWXYZ
1234567890 !@#?:;"*&

Aguda Stencil is published by Graviton, a foundry established by Pablo Balcells in 2013 to focus on the design of geometric fonts suitable for technical and digital use. Two versions of the typeface are available, with one tailored for display use and the other for smaller text.

Foundry: Graviton
Designer: Pablo Balcells
Designer Nationality: Argentinian
Date: 2014

Ammo

ABCDEFGHIJKLMNOPQRSTUVWXYZ
1234567890 !@#?:;""*&

This extremely heavyweight sans serif typeface was designed by Alexander McCracken, founder of the independent foundry Neutura (see p. 546), who also publishes typefaces through T26. A stencil design, the font features an unconventional approach to divisions within its letterforms.

Foundry: Neutura
Designer: Alexander McCracken
Designer Nationality: American
Date: 2010

Audree

ABCDEFGHIJKLMNOPQRSTUVWXYZ
abcdefghijklmnopqrstuvwxyz
1234567890 !@#?:;"'*&

Published in 2013 by Typotheque (see p. 90), this comprehensive type system is staggering in its scope, offering designers the ability to create hundreds of potential type styles from its selection of components. *Typographica* review featured Audree as one of the best releases of 2013.

Foundry: Typotheque
Designer: Nikola Djurek / Marko Hrastovec
Designer Nationality: Croatian
Date: 2013

Brutal

ABCDEFGHIJKLMNOPQRSTUVWXYZ
abcdefghijklmnopqrstuvwxyz
1234567890 !¢£#?:;"*&

Foundry: BB-Bureau
Designer: Benoît Bodhuin
Designer Nationality: French
Date: 2017

Brutal's distinctive features and highly deconstructed look mark it out as truly unique. An anarchic and fun stencil design from the furtive imagination of French designer Benoît Bodhuin and his foundry BB-Bureau (see p. 386), the typeface is available in Light, Regular and Bold weights.

With a varying contrast in stroke weight, Brutal possesses a calligraphic quality. Its non-aligning characters provide fluidity and rhythm as the letters bounce to one another. The use of verticals and horizontal-only strokes, with the curved connections made in a broad-nib manner, help make for a striking appearance.

A mathematical design principle underpins all the characters, which share the same construction. This rigour is visible in the separated strokes, 90° angles and consistently matching bowls.

Below left. *Oripeau* by Benoît Bodhuin.

Below. Art directed by Yu Qiongjie and designed by Transwhite Studio, an exhibition catalogue celebrating the first decade of the Inna Art Space, based in New York and Huangzhou, China, which features the work of thirteen contemporary artists.

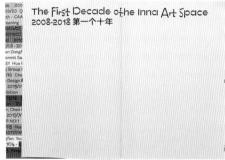

Braggadocio

ABCDEFGHIJKLMNOPQRSTUV
abcdefghijklmnopqrstuvwxyz
1234567890 !@#?:;"*&

Foundry: Monotype
Designer: William A. Woolley
Designer Nationality: American
Date: 1930

Influenced by the design of Futura Black, this geometric stencil font was created by US type designer William A. Woolley for Monotype in 1930.

Its heavy letterforms offer relatively poor legibility, but give a strong and characterful impression in display contexts.

Campaign

ABCDEFGHIJKLMNOPQRSTUVWXYZ
1234567890 !@#?:;"*&

Foundry: ITC
Designer: Alan Meeks
Designer Nationality: British
Date: 1987

Campaign is a stencil typeface designed by Alan Meeks in 1987, featuring a uniform stroke weight and distinctive diagonal details within its uppercase only letterforms. It is available in a single weight, and works best when set at larger point sizes and in headline contexts.

Densmore

ABCDEFGHIJKLMNOPQRSTUV
abcdefghijklmnopqrstuvwxyz
1234567890 !@#?:;"*&

Foundry: Typodermic
Designer: Ray Larabie
Designer Nationality: Canadian
Date: 2009

A solidly built and blocky stencil typeface, Densmore consists of three styles: Regular, Blue and Pink. Blue and Pink are designed to be used together to create a layered effect by using different colours, with the double lowercase 'o' combination automatically replaced by a mirrored 'o o'.

DIN Next Stencil

ABCDEFGHIJKLMNOPQRSTUVWXYZ
abcdefghijklmnopqrstuvwxyz
1234567890 !@#?:;"*&

Foundry: Linotype
Designer: Akira Kobayashi / Sabina Chipară
Designer Nationality: Romanian / Japanese
Date: 2017

DIN Next Stencil is based on DIN Next, Akira Kobayshi's 2009 version of the classic 1930s typeface DIN by Deutsches Institut für Normung (German Institute for Standardization). The commanding stencil font was customized by Romanian designer Sabina Chipară. It is available in seven weights.

Cut

ABCDEFGHIJKLMNOPQRSTUVWXYZ
abcdefghijklmnopqrstuvwxyz
1234567890 !@#?:;"*&

Foundry: MuirMcNeil
Designer: Hamish Muir /
Paul McNeil
Designer Nationality: British
Date: 2016

The Cut typeface was inspired by two distinct typographical periods from history, and draws its design and proportions from the work of leading designers who shaped type design and construction. It is available in three weights.

Cut's proportions are based on those of neoclassical typefaces from the early 19th century, created by innovative type designers such as Firmin Didot and Giambattista Bodoni. Cut takes the contrast seen in the strokes of their typefaces to such an extreme that the hairline strokes connecting the components of the letterforms disappear, leaving just geometric shapes.

Cut also refers to the early 20th century and typographers such as Herbert Bayer, Josef Albers and Jan Tschichold, who worked with type elements often as simple geometric elements. Their work informs the system construction behind Cut.

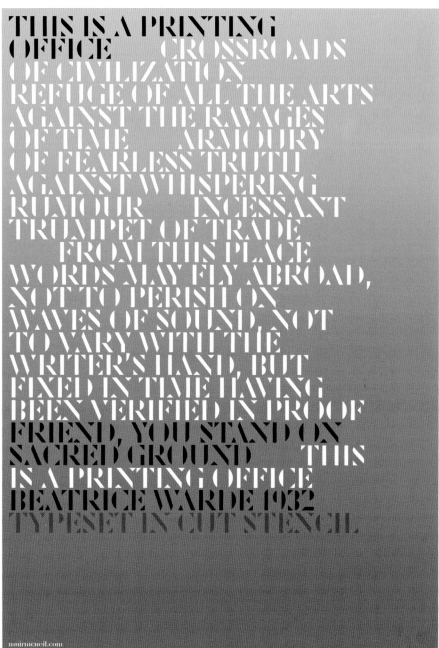

Dirty Baker's Dozen

ABCDEFGHIJKLMNOPQRSTUVWXYZ
1234567890 !@#?:;"★&

Foundry: Typodermic
Designer: Ray Larabie
Designer Nationality: Canadian
Date: 1998

A solid stencil font with lots of deliberate imperfections, Dirty Baker's Dozen by Ray Larabie comes with plenty of symbols, fractions and accents. Two new styles were introduced in 2009: Scorch, which has a burnt-out effect, and Spraypaint, which has a rough-edged look.

DR Zhek

ABCDEFGHIJKLMNOPQRSTUVWXYZ
ABCDEFGHIJKLMNOPQRSTUVWXYZ
1234567890 !@#?:;"*&

Foundry: Dmitry Rastvortsev
Designer: Dmitry Rastvortsev
Designer Nationality: Ukrainian
Date: 2017

Ukrainian designer Dmitry Rastvortsev released DR Zhek through his eponymous foundry in 2017. It is a single-style, condensed stencil sans serif with a utilitarian feel and uppercase and small caps only. DR Zhek is a multilingual font with support for Cyrillic, Greek and Latin alphabets.

Five 01

ABCDEFGHIJKLMNOPQRSTUVWXYZ
abcdefghijklmnopqrstuvwxyz
1234567890 !@#?:;"*&

Foundry: MuirMcNeil
Designer: Hamish Muir / Paul McNeil
Designer Nationality: British
Date: 2017

The Five geometric stencil family was designed and released by the MuirMcNeil foundry (see p. 334) in 2017. It comes in three styles. The first, Five 01, is angular and curve-less and has four weights: the counter-less 330; and 290, 250 and 210, each of which has progressively wider counters.

Five 02

ABCDEFGHIJKLMNOPQRSTUVWXYZ
abcdefghijklmnopqrstuvwxyz
1234567890 !@#?:;"*&

Foundry: MuirMcNeil
Designer: Hamish Muir / Paul McNeil
Designer Nationality: British
Date: 2017

The Five family was inspired by a variety of typefaces such as Schmalfette Grotesk, Compacta and Josef Albers's Kombinations-Schrift, as well as Walter Ballmer's lettering for Olivetti. Five 02 has soft rounded corners and comes in four numbered weights: 330, 290, 250 and 210.

Five 03

ABCDEFGHIJKLMNOPQRSTUVWXYZ
abcdefghijklmnopqrstuvwxyz
1234567890 !@#?:;"*&

Foundry: MuirMcNeil
Designer: Hamish Muir /
Paul McNeil
Designer Nationality: British
Date: 2017

Five 03 is the most geometric and curved of the Five family from MuirMcNeil (see p. 334), and has many details constructed from half or quarter circles. It comes in four, bold, numbered weights: the totally solid 330; and 290, 250 and 210, each of which has progressively wider counters and more white space.

Foundry Fabriek

ABCDEFGHIJKLMNOPQRSTUVWXYZ
abcdefghijklmnopqrstuvwxyz
1234567890 !@#?:;"*&

Foundry: The Foundry
Designer: David Quay /
Wim Crouwel
Designer Nationality: British /
Dutch
Date: 2016

Foundry Fabriek began as a commission when Dutch designer Wim Crouwel (see p. 540) recommended The Foundry (see p. 284) to interior-design consultant Kho Liang Ie, who wanted a stencil version of the Gridnik typeface to laser cut in steel for a building-signage project.

Frank

ABCDEFGHIJKLMNOPQRSTUVW
XYZ
1234567890 !@#?:;"*&

Foundry: Neutura
Designer: Alexander McCracken
Designer Nationality: American
Date: 2005

Alexander McCracken released his typeface Frank through Neutura, the foundry he runs in San Francisco. It is a heavy slab serif in three numbered styles: 1 and 2 are solid and counter-less, while 3 is a stencil version with extremely fine gaps. All three styles are the same weight.

Gendouki

ABCDEFGHIJKLMN
abcdefghijklmnopqrst
1234567890 !@#?:;"*&

Foundry: Typodermic
Designer: Ray Larabie
Designer Nationality: Canadian
Date: 2006

A wide, geometric stencil sans serif typeface, Gendouki was designed by prolific Canadian type designer Ray Larabie in 2006 and released by his foundry Typodermic. Gendouki has a futuristic feel and is angular, with 'filament stencil lines inspired by spaceship access panels'.

Glaser Stencil

ABCDEFGHIJKLMNOPQRSTUVWXYZ
123-4567890 !@#?:;"*&

Foundry: Photo-Lettering
Designer: Milton Glaser
Designer Nationality: American
Date: 1969

Glaser Stencil was first used as lettering on a Carnegie Hall poster by the legendary illustrator and designer Milton Glaser in 1967. Photo-Lettering debuted Glaser Stencil in its yearbook for 1969. It was available in three weights – Light, Regular and Bold – but many digital versions only include Bold.

Gunplay

ABCDEFGHIJKLMNOPQRSTUVWXYZ
abcdefghijklmnopqrstuvwxyz
1234567890 !@#?:;" &

Foundry: Typodermic
Designer: Ray Larabie
Designer Nationality: Canadian
Date: 2000

Gunplay was inspired by lettering on posters for the Steve McQueen film *The Getaway* (1972). It is a bold, no-nonsense stencil sans serif available in four styles: Regular; 3D, which has drop shadows; Damage, which is distressed but mostly solid edged; and Spraypaint, which is rough edged.

Interrogator Stencil

ABCDEFGHIJKLMNOPQRSTUVWXYZ
1234567890 !@#?:;"*&

Foundry: Typodermic
Designer: Ray Larabie
Designer Nationality: Canadian
Date: 2014

Interrogator Stencil was created by the prolific Japan-based designer Ray Larabie. It is a tall, condensed sans serif stencil typeface from the Typodermic foundry. The stencilling details include a thin horizontal gap that runs through the centre of all letters. It is available in one weight.

ITC Portago

ABCDEFGHIJKLMNOPQRSTUVWXYZ
ABCDEFGHIJKLMNOPQRSTUVWXYZ
1234567890 !@#?:;"*&

Foundry: ITC
Designer: Luis Siquot
Designer Nationality: Argentinian
Date: 1997

Luis Siquot's ITC Portago, published in 1997, is a heavy, uppercase only, stencil sans serif with rough edges and small caps. It was inspired by the lettering spray-painted on crates and luggage. Siquot was born in Argentina and educated at the University of Fine Arts Hamburg.

Iwan Stencil

ABCDEFGHIJKLMNOPQRSTUVWXYZ
abcdefghijklmnopqrstuvwxyz
1234567890 !@#?:;"*&

Foundry: Linotype
Designer: Klaus Sutter
Designer Nationality: German
Date: 2007

German designer Klaus Sutter, a former Linotype employee, specializes in creating digital revivals of metal type. For Iwan Stencil he focused on a font created by German designer Jan Tschichold in 1929, adding new characters and language support to this high-contrast, stencilled semi serif.

Jigsaw Stencil

ABCDEFGHIJKLMNOPQRSTUVWXYZ
abcdefghijklmnopqrstuvwxyz
1234567890 !@#?:;"*&

Foundry: Typotheque
Designer: Johanna Biľak
Designer Nationality: Slovakian
Date: 1999

Johanna Biľak designed the Jigsaw type family for Typotheque (see p. 90), the foundry she runs with Peter Biľak and Nikola Djurek. Jigsaw is a geometric sans serif and was neatly turned into an attractive stencil version. Both faces are available in twelve styles, six weights with italics.

Linotype Authentic Stencil

ABCDEFGHIJKLMNOPQRSTUVWXYZ
abcdefghijklmnopqrstuvwxyz
1234567890 !@#?:;"*&

Foundry: Linotype
Designer: Karin Huschka
Designer Nationality: German
Date: 1999

Linotype Authentic Stencil is a stencil display font and is part of the Linotype Authentic typeface family, which also includes Sans, Serif and Small Serif versions. The characters feature small slab serifs, gently squared curves and three weights with corresponding italics.

Linotype Element

ABCDEFGHIJKLMNOPQRSTUVWXY
abcdefghijklmnopqrstuvwxyz
1234567890 !!??:;"&

Foundry: Linotype
Designer: Jan Tomáš
Designer Nationality: Czech
Date: 1999

Linotype Element is an abstract display typeface inspired by the emergent technology of the 1990s. Its characters blur the typical structure of letterforms by introducing concentric forms, which generate an aesthetic of hypnotic motion when displayed in large point sizes.

Lisbon

ABCDEFGHIJKLMNOPQRSTUVWXYZ
abcdefghijklmnopqrstuvwxyz
1234567890 !@#?:;"*&

Foundry: Colophon
Designer: Anthony Burrill
Designer Nationality: British
Date: 2013

Lisbon is a geometric stencil typeface from acclaimed graphic artist, printmaker and designer Anthony Burrill, developed and marketed by the Colophon foundry (see p. 210). The typeface's source of inspiration was a metal stencil that Burrill discovered in a signmaker's shop in Lisbon, Portugal. Digitized by Colophon, Lisbon was first used in a series of Burrill's posters commissioned by the British Council for the ExperimentaDesign cultural biennale in the Portuguese capital in 2010. Lisbon was originally an all-caps design, and a lowercase set and punctuation has been added using the same geometric elements as the original.

Below. Global design group Pentagram created the identity, signage and website design for Mediterranean restaurant Gato in New York. Burrill's stencil design is perfectly suited for the architecture of the site as well as for being printed. It is also stencilled on its restroom walls.

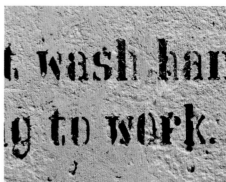

Octin Prison

ABCDEFGHIJKLMNOPQRSTUVWXYZ
1234567890 !@#?:;"*&

Foundry: Typodermic
Designer: Ray Larabie
Designer Nationality: Canadian
Date: 2007

Octin Prison is part of Typodermic's Octin type family, which also contains Octin College, Octin Sports, Octin Stencil, Octin Spraypaint and Octin Vintage. It is a tough, uppercase, stencil slab serif that comes in seven roman weights: Light, Book, Regular, Semi-bold, Heavy and Black.

Octin Stencil

ABCDEFGHIJKLMNOPQRSTUVWXYZ
1234567890 !@#?:;"*&

Foundry: Typodermic
Designer: Ray Larabie
Designer Nationality: Canadian
Date: 2007

Octin Stencil was created by Canadian type designer Ray Larabie. It is an angular, curve-less, authoritative, stencil sans serif typeface with uppercase letters only. Octin Stencil comes in seven weights: Light, Book, Regular, Semi-bold, Heavy and Black.

Plotter Display

ABCDEFGHIJKLMNOPQRSTUVWXYZ
abcdefghijklmnopqrstuvwxyz
1234567890 !@#?:;"*&

Foundry: Typotheque
Designer: Nikola Djurek
Designer Nationality: Croatian
Date: 2017

According to Typotheque (see p. 90), Plotter 'explores the world of technical drawings and architectural plans'. Plotter Display is the most experimental of the family. It comes in five styles of the same weight which can be layered: Bold, Layer A, Layer B, Layer C and Layer D.

Rubber Stamp

ABCDEFGHIJKLMNOPQRSTUVWXYZ
1234567890 !@#?:;"*&

Foundry: Letraset
Designer: Alan Birch
Designer Nationality: British
Date: 1983

Created by Alan Birch for Letraset in 1983, and also released by the International Typeface Corporation, Rubber Stamp is a bold, uppercase only, stencil serif font with corroded, imperfect edges and a distressed texture that mimics the effect of text printed with a worn rubber stamp and ink.

Rumori Stencil

ABCDEFGHIJKLMNOPQRSTUVWXYZ
abcdefghijklmnopqrstuvwxyz
1234567890 !@#?:;"'*&

Foundry: MuirMcNeil
Designer: Hamish Muir /
Paul McNeil
Designer Nationality: British
Date: 2017

Three years after designing Rumori, Paul McNeil refined it, adding a stencil version and releasing the updated family through MuirMcNeil, the foundry and studio he runs with Hamish Muir. The stencil cut comes in roman and italic, in two styles: the rounded Morbidi and angular Chiari.

Stem

ABCDEFGHIJKLMNOPQRSTUVWXYZ
abcdefghijklmnopqrstuvwxyz
1234567890 !@#?:;"'*&

Foundry: MuirMcNeil
Designer: Hamish Muir /
Paul McNeil
Designer Nationality: British
Date: 2016

MuirMcNeil (see p. 334) designed Stem, a stencil typeface with contrast, in 2016 as an evolution of its earlier typeface, Cut. In 2018, MuirMcNeil expanded it to include two styles in five weights. Style A is squarer with hairline flat serifs, while B is more rounded with floating circular terminals.

Stencil

ABCDEFGHIJKLMNOPQRSTUVWXYZ
1234567890 !@#?:;"'*&

Foundry: Linotype
Designer: Gerry Powell
Designer Nationality: American
Date: 1938

Gerry Powell designed Stencil for American Type Founders in 1938. It has rounded edges and thick strokes and is inspired by the traditional stencilled letters found on packaging and crates. It is used in the TV series *M*A*S*H*. Alexei Chekulaev designed a Cyrillic version of Stencil in 1997.

Stencil Moonlight

ABCDEFGHIJKLMNOPQRSTUVWXYZ
ABCDEFGHIJKLMNOPQRSTUVWXYZ
1234567890 !@#?:;"'*&

Foundry: Linotype
Designer: Gustav Andrejs
Grinbergs
Designer Nationality: Latvian
Date: 2003

Gustav Andrejs Grinbergs's Stencil Moonlight was a runner-up in the Display category in Linotype's International Type Design Contest in 2003. It is a fresh take on Gerry Powell's classic Stencil typeface and shares many of its characteristics, but has an added lowercase.

Stop

ABCDEFGHJKLMNOPQRSTUVWXYZ
1234567890 !@#?:;"*&

Foundry: URW
Designer: Aldo Novarese
Designer Nationality: Italian
Date: 1971

This stylized and very heavy display typeface with a number of abstract characters is one of Aldo Novarese's many futuristic-looking fonts. Stop's strong horizontal lines give it a distinct look, and its influence can clearly be seen on the font used for the *Blade Runner* (1982) film poster.

Ténica Slab Stencil

ABCDEFGHIJKLMNOPQRSTUVWXYZ
abcdefghijklmnopqrstuvwxyz
1234567890 !@#?:;"*&

Foundry: Graviton
Designer: Pablo Balcells
Designer Nationality: Argentinian
Date: 2014

The stencil version of Ténica Slab is available in eight styles. Stencil 1 consists of four styles with a narrow stem, suitable for larger-sized text and printing on rigid materials. Stencil 2 consists of four styles with a wider stem, suitable for larger-sized text and printing on lighter materials.

Ténica Stencil

ABCDEFGHIJKLMNOPQRSTUVWXYZ
abcdefghijklmnopqrstuvwxyz
1234567890 !@#?:;"*&

Foundry: Graviton
Designer: Pablo Balcells
Designer Nationality: Argentinian
Date: 2014

Designed for the Graviton Font Foundry by Pablo Balcells in 2014, the stencil version of the Ténica font family is available in eight styles. With two stem widths (Stencil 1 and Stencil 2), each variant consists of four styles, each with Regular and Bold weights and each having an alternate variant.

Threefortysixbarrel

ABCDEFGHIJKLMNOPQRSTUVWXYZ
ABCDEFGHIJKLMNOPQRSTUVWXYZ
1234567890 !@#?:;"*&

Foundry: Typodermic
Designer: Ray Larabie
Designer Nationality: Canadian
Date: 2004

Ray Larabie's Threefortysixbarrel is a slightly condensed stencil font inspired by lettering found sprayed on to the air filter of a 1970 Plymouth Barracuda, and which he describes as 'the ultimate, barely street legal font'. It is available in three weights: Regular, Intake and Exhaust.

Buffalo Gal

ABCDEFGHIJKLMNOPQRSTUVWXYZ
abcdefghijklmnopqrstuvwxyz
1234567890 !@#?:;"'*&

Foundry: Rickner Type
Designer: Tom Rickner
Designer Nationality: American
Date: 1994

This Wild West-inspired font was designed by Tom Rickner following his two-year tenure as lead typographer for Apple, where he supervised the production of the company's first TrueType releases. Buffalo Gal is one of the first of a generation of variable GX fonts released during the 1990s.

Circus Poster Shadow

ABCDEFGHIJKLMNOPQRSTUVWXYZ
abcdefghijklmnopqrstuvwxyz
1234567890 !@#?:;"'*&

Foundry: Ascender
Designer: Tom Rickner
Designer Nationality: American
Date: 2005

Ascender co-founder Tom Rickner designed Circus Poster. The typeface was influenced by the forms of wood type used within 19th-century advertising, which have become synonymous with depictions of the Wild West in popular culture. It features shadow details for further weight and impact.

ITC Buckeroo

ABCDEFGHIJKLMNOPQRSTUV
ABCDEFGHIJKLMNOPQRSTUVWXYZ
1234567890 !@#?:;"'*&

Foundry: ITC
Designer: Richard William Mueller
Designer Nationality: American
Date: 1997

Buckeroo is credited to US type designer Richard William Mueller. It is a heavy, Wild West-inspired display typeface with distinctive notched slab serifs. Mueller digitized an earlier typeface Frontier, which was released by Photo-Lettering, and then improved it by adding small caps.

Madame

ABCDEFGHIJKLMNOPQRSTUVWXYZ
1234567890 !@#?:;"'*&

Foundry: Fonderie Typographique Française
Designer: Joseph Gillé
Designer Nationality: French
Date: 1820

Madame is a display typeface designed to add flamboyance to titles, headlines or initials, and initially appeared in a sample with a variety of other similar types. Its letterforms are defined by their expressive Tuscan aesthetic, seen in the ornate serifs and embellished strokes.

PL Davison Americana

ABCDEFGHIJKLMNOPQRSTUVW
abcdefghijklmnopqrstuvwxyz
1234567890 !©#?::,"*&

Foundry: Photo-Lettering
Designer: M. M. Davison
Designer Nationality: American
Date: 1965

Designer M. M. Davison created fonts for Photo-Lettering during the 1950s and 1960s, often based on historical models. Monotype has digitized two of these fonts: PL Davison Americana, a bold, spurred, Wild West-style titling slab serif; and PL Davison Zip, a chunky uppercase handwritten script.

Rosewood

ABCDEFGHIJKLMNOPQRSTUVWXYZ
1234567890 !@#?::,"*&

Foundry: Adobe
Designer: William Page / Carl Crossgrove / Carol Twombly / Kim Buker Chansler
Nationality: American
Date: 1874 / 1994

Rosewood is a Tuscan display typeface based on a chromatic design by William Page dating to 1874. Rosewood includes two styles, Regular and Fill, with the latter designed to overlay the first. Like original overprinting methods, it uses layers to add multiple colours to a single character.

Thunderbird Extra Condensed

ABCDEFGHIJKLMNOPQRSTUVWXYZ
1234567890 !@#?::,"*&

Foundry: Linotype
Designer: American Type Founders Studio
Date: 1920

Thunderbird is an ornate Tuscan serif in all caps, which was released by the American Type Founders in 1920. Its anonymous designer was clearly inspired by Wild West-era wood type. Many foundries have digitized Thunderbird; Linotype's version includes the extra-condensed style.

Zebrawood

ABCDEFGHIJKLMNOPQRSTUVWXYZ
1234567890 !@#?::,"*&

Foundry: Adobe
Designer: Carl Crossgrove / Carol Twombly / Kim Buker Chansler
Designer Nationality: American
Date: 1994

The Zebrawood uppercase Tuscan serif was created by a team of designers at Adobe. It is based on lettering found in a Wells & Webb type catalogue dating to 1854, which was often used in circus posters and advertisements. Zebrawood comes in two styles: the decorated Regular and solid Fill.

ABCDEFGHIJKLMNOPQRSTUVWXYZ · abcdefghijklmnopqrstuvwxyz

DALTON MAAG LTD.
SINCE 1991 · LONDON

Script

Opposite. Design detail showing Volina typeface by London type-face design studio Dalton Maag.

Based on the principles of handwriting, Script typefaces possess fluid forms, varying strokes and a rhythm to their appearance when set as if they were drawn by hand. Script typefaces can be categorized into two main areas: 'Formal' are predominantly based around actual writing, often nibbed or quill-penned from the 17th and 18th centuries, and did not actually become typefaces until the 18th / 19th centuries; and 'Casual' scripts, whose style is much looser, more brushlike in appearance, mostly emerged from the early 20th century. To aid visual comparison and construction, the two groupings have been divided further with the addition of Calligraphic and Handwriting. There are inevitably always many shared design elements across the styles.

The earliest form of script is Blackletter, also referred to as Gothic Script. Blackletter types were developed and predominantly used across Europe in the Middle Ages, starting from around the 1100s until around the 17th century. The generic term *blackletter* comes from their heavy and dominant presence on the page, with condensed letterforms, tightly spaced setting and heavy, evenly spaced vertical strokes. There are, however, a number of variations in construction and appearance for these Gothic types. Textualis (Textura) is a style associated with northern parts of Europe, and was used by German printer and pioneer Johannes Gutenberg when he printed his 42-line Bible (one of the first books printed using metal movable type in the 1450s); it is the most calligraphic in terms of appearance. By contrast, the Italian Rotunda from Europe used a less angular approach. Further variations appeared around the 15th century, such as Bastarda from France (an amalgamation of differing styles), and in the 16th century came Fraktur from Germany, which was widely used there until the middle of the 20th century.

Calligraphic scripts connect closely to a cursive process, with their classical, angular appearance informing their creation from a broad-edged nib or brush and their inclined letterforms denoting a rhythm and movement from the writer that provides a dynamism to the letterforms. Decorative elements are often employed, such as extended descenders with flourishes and swashes to provide a more extrovert and flamboyant tone. Casual scripts are increasingly playful and relaxed in appearance, as if rendered by an active and impatient hand. Their immediacy, whether seemingly created by brush or marker pen or more precisely drawn, brings a softer appearance and their informal aesthetic invariably commands less authority.

Often seen as the perfect typeface for a wedding invitation or similar, Formal script typefaces have in recent years been enjoying a comeback as their usage increases and diversifies. Even so, not many smaller contemporary foundries take on the challenge of creating new formal scripts. This is probably based on commercial and financial considerations when creating any new typeface but also on the designer's preference and interest (or lack of interest). A number of the formal typefaces that have been created owe much to the hand-drawn letters from English writing masters such as George Bickham and George Shelley. These fluid and elegant letterforms often have connecting strokes so that they appear joined when typeset. They are a demanding technical challenge to replicate when many historical reference points were originally created as Copperplate engravings (letters incised into copper plates using the intaglio method of printing). This progressed into hot-metal type in later years, and with the advent of phototypesetting; the process became easier as technological advances such as OpenType meant that the letter pairing permutations were realized with less effort.

To conclude; from childish playfulness to anarchic and quirky scribblings, the digital technologies today allow any Handwriting styles to be captured. What is more, they can convey not only any individual's handwriting but also the personality that lay behind them, for others to use and enjoy.

Agincourt

𝔄𝔅𝔒𝔇𝔈𝔉𝔊𝔥𝔦𝔧𝔨𝔩𝔪𝔫𝔬𝔭𝔮𝔯𝔰𝔱𝔲𝔳𝔴𝔵𝔶𝔷
abcdefghijklmnopqrstuvwxyz
1234567890 !@#?:;"*&

Foundry: ITC
Designer: David Quay
Designer Nationality: British
Date: 1983

Agincourt is a beautifully crafted Old English script featuring intricate capitals and a more reserved, condensed lowercase. It was inspired by the age of chivalry and King Henry V, who was the first English monarch to send a letter (announcing his victory at Agincourt in 1415) written in the English language.

Beneta

ABCDEFGHIJKLMNOPQRSTUVWXYZ
abcdefghijklmnopqrstuvwxyz
1234567890 !@#?:;"*&

Foundry: Linotype
Designer: Karlgeorg Hoefer
Designer Nationality: German
Date: 1995

Beneta is a French bastarda, which is a blackletter script that was used in France, Germany and the Burgundian Netherlands during the 14th and 15th centuries. It was inspired by the *littera Beneventana* (Beneventan script) Latin script used by Benedictine scribes from the 8th to the 16th centuries.

Blackletter 686 BT

𝔄𝔅𝔒𝔇𝔈𝔉𝔊𝔥𝔦𝔧𝔨𝔩𝔪𝔫𝔬𝔭𝔮𝔯𝔰𝔱𝔲𝔳𝔴𝔵𝔶𝔷
abcdefghijklmnopqrstuvwxyz
1234567890 !?:;"*&

Foundry: Bitstream
Designer: Unknown
Date: 1998

Bitstream's version of a classic blackletter is based on Linotype's London Text, which emulates scripts created using a quill pen in the Middle Ages, and its clean, traditional letterforms give it an engraved appearance. Blackletter 686 is available in a single regular weight.

Blackmoor

𝔄𝔅𝔒𝔇𝔈𝔉𝔊𝔥𝔦𝔧𝔨𝔩𝔪𝔫𝔬𝔭𝔮𝔯𝔰𝔱𝔲𝔳𝔴𝔵𝔶𝔷
abcdefghijklmnopqrstuvwxyz
1234567890 !@#?:;"*&

Foundry: ITC
Designer: David Quay
Designer Nationality: British
Date: 1983

Blackmoor is a textura-style blackletter based on an Old English letter style. It is unusual in that it mixes gothic lowercase with Lombardic capitals. Its rough, distressed features and medieval influences give it a very distinctive character, making it perfect for anything related to horror.

Bollatica

ABCDEFGHIJKLMNOPQRSTUVWXYZ
abcdefghijklmnopqrstuvwxyz
1234567890 !@#?:;"*&

Bollatica is one of Philip Bouwsma's many fonts based on broad pen calligraphy. It is a modern interpretation of the *scrittura bollatica* historical script, which was used from the 16th to 19th centuries for papal bulls and had no punctuation, and was virtually indecipherable by ordinary readers.

Foundry: Monotype
Designer: Philip Bouwsma
Designer Nationality: American
Date: 2012

Clairvaux

ABCDEFGHIJKLMNOPQRSTUVWXYZ
abcdefghijklmnopqrstuvwxyz
1234567890 !@#?:;"*&

Clairvaux is named after Clairvaux Abbey, a Cistercian monastery in northeastern France. It is based on the early gothic typefaces used by Cistercian monks. Available in a single weight, it is closer than any other bastarda to the forms of the Caroline minuscule, making it more legible.

Foundry: Linotype
Designer: Herbert Maring
Designer Nationality: German
Date: 1990

Clemente Rotunda

ABCDEFGHIJKLMNOPQRSTUVWXY
abcdefghijklmnopqrstuvwryz
1234567890 !@#?:;"*&

One of Philip Bouwsma's many fonts based on broad pen calligraphy and inspired by classic manuscripts, this robust typeface is a rotunda – the medieval Italian version of blackletter type, less angular than those created in northern Europe and characterized by several unique abbreviations.

Foundry: Monotype
Designer: Philip Bouwsma
Designer Nationality: American
Date: 1997

Cloister Black

ABCDEFGHIJKLMNOPQRSTUVWXYZ
abcdefghijklmnopqrstubwxyz
1234567890 !@#?:;"*&

Bitstream's version of American Type Founders' original version, Cloister Black was an adaptation of Priory Text, itself a version of Caslon Text from the 1870s. Morris Fuller Benton and Joseph Warren Phinney streamlined it, making it a popular version of Old English.

Foundry: Bitstream
Designer: Morris Fuller Benton / Joseph Warren Phinney
Designer Nationality: American
Date: 1904

Duc De Berry

ABCDEFGHIJKLMNOPQRSTUVWXYZ
abcdefghijklmnopqrstuvwxyz
1234567890 !@#?:;"*&

Foundry: Linotype
Designer: Gottfried Pott
Designer Nationality: German
Date: 1990

German designer Gottfried Pott created Duc De Berry as part of the Type Before Gutenberg programme, for which Linotype invited lettering artists to create typefaces based on historical handwriting styles. It is a decorative, blackletter font in the style of medieval bastarda scripts.

Engravers Old English BT

ABCDEFGHIJKLMNOPQRSTUVWXYZ
abcdefghijklmnopqrstuvwxyz
1234567890 !@#?:;"*&

Foundry: Bitstream
Designer: Morris Fuller Benton
Designer Nationality: American
Date: 1901

Morris Fuller Benton created this archetypal blackletter typeface for American Type Founders at the turn of the 20th century; it was designed as a development upon his earlier Wedding Text font, which is very similar in style. This version is a contemporary digitization by Bitstream.

Fette Fraktur

ABCDEFGHIJKLMNOPQRSTUVWXYZ
abcdefghijklmnopqrstuvwxyz
1234567890 !@#?:;"*&

Foundry: Weber
Designer: Johann Christian Bauer
Designer Nationality: German
Date: 1850

Johann Christian Bauer designed this heavy blackletter typeface in 1850. Fette Fraktur was first published by the Weber foundry in 1875; many subsequent versions have since been released by numerous foundries worldwide. Its bold weight and complex letterforms are best suited for display use.

Fette Gotisch

ABCDEFGHIJKLMNOPQRSTUVWXYZ
abcdefghijklmnopqrstuvwxyz
1234567890 !@#?:;"*&

Foundry: Bauer
Designer: Friedrich Wilhelm Bauer
Designer Nationality: German
Date: c. 875

Published by a variety of foundries since its creation, Fette Gotisch was first cut in c. 1975 by Friedrich Wilhelm Bauer. Son of the founder of the Bauer type foundry, he went on to establish Bauer & Co in 1880 and designed several other blackletter fonts during his career.

Frakto

ABCDEFGHIJKLMNOPQRSTUVWXYZ
abcdefghijklmnopqrstuvwxyz
1234567890 !@#?:,"*&

Foundry: Linotype
Designer: Julius de Goede
Designer Nationality: Dutch
Date: 2003

This contemporary interpretation of the Fraktur type tradition, which originated in 16th-century Germany, was created by Dutch designer Julius de Goede for Linotype in 2003. Featuring slightly condensed and upright letterforms, Frakto displays a clear calligraphic influence throughout.

Fraktur

ABCDEFGHIJKLMNOPQRSTUVWXYZ
abcdefghijklmnopqrstuvwxyz
1234567890 !@#?:,"*&

Foundry: Bitstream
Designer: Unknown
Date: 1708 / 1990–93

This Bitstream interpretation of Fraktur is based on Linotype Luthersche Fraktur, probably created in the design studio at Stempel, Germany, which was itself a revival of a typeface designed by Erasmus Luther in 1708. It is more legible than other examples of Fraktur but is still best suited for display use.

Goudy Text

ABCDEFGHIJKLMNOPQRSTUVWXYZ
abcdefghijklmnopqrstuvwxyz
1234567890 !@#?:,"*&

Foundry: Monotype
Designer: Frederic W. Goudy
Designer Nationality: American
Date: 1928

Goudy Text is based on the forty-two-line Gutenberg Bible. Frederic W. Goudy first employed the blackletter type in 1928 in a Christmas card, using type cast at his foundry. It was originally known as Goudy Black, but Monotype sought permission to copy the face and to change its name to Goudy Text.

ITC Honda

ABCDEFGHIJKLMNOPQRSTUVWXYZ
abcdefghijklmnopqrstuvwxyz
1234567890 !?:,"*&

Foundry: ITC
Designer: Ronne Bonder /
Tom Carnase
Designer Nationality: American
Date: 1970

US typeface designers Ronne Bonder and Tom Carnase designed this distinctive, Fraktur-inspired sans serif blackletter face in 1970. Carnase often worked closely with Herb Lubalin (see p. 62), one of the founders of the International Typeface Corporation (ITC). ITC Honda has a single weight.

Linotext

ABCDEFGHIJKLMNOPQRSTUVWXYZ
abcdefghijklmnopqrstuvwxyz
1234567890 !@#?:;"*&

Foundry: American Type Founders
Designer: Morris Fuller Benton
Designer Nationality: American
Date: 1901 / 1924

American Type Founders initially released this heavy, ornamental blackletter script font in 1901 under the name 'Wedding Text'. It was renamed 'Linotext' when it was adapted to work with Linotype machines; many other foundries also released metal versions copied from the original designs.

Linotype Dala

ABCDEFGHIJKLMNOPQRSTUVWXYZ
abcdefghijklmnopqrstuvwxyz
1234567890 !@#?:;"*&

Foundry: Linotype
Designer: Bo Berndal
Designer Nationality: Swedish
Date: 1999

Swedish designer Bo Berndal created this quirky, Fraktur-inspired blackletter script influenced by Scandinavian folktales in 1999. Many of Dala's letters feature distinctive double kinks, such as the 'T', 'w', 'z' and 'y'. It comes with an ornamental frame typeface and dingbats.

Linotype Richmond

ABCDEFGHIJKLMNOPQRSTUVWXY
abcdefghijklmnopqrstuvwxyz
1234567890 !@#?:;"*&

Foundry: Linotype
Designer: Richard Yeend
Designer Nationality: British
Date: 2002

The newspaper art director, type designer and caricaturist Richard Yeend has designed more than twenty typefaces – mostly for Linotype – including this gothic, medieval-style blackletter. Richmond is available in two styles: a solid version, Fraktur, and an inlaid version, Zierschrift.

Linotype Textur

ABCDEFGHIJKLMNOPQRSTUVWXYZ
abcdefghijklmnopqrstuvwxyz
1234567890 !@#?:;"*&

Foundry: Linotype
Designer: Roland John Goulsbra
Designer Nationality: British
Date: 2002

Textur is an extremely heavy ornate and intricate blackletter typeface by British designer Roland John Goulsbra. It comes in two styles: Gotisch, the regular, and Lombardisch, which has wider, more decorative capitals, including a 'J' whose tail more than doubles the standard cap height.

Luthersche Fraktur

ABCDEFGHIJKLMNOPQRSTUVWXYZ
abcdefghijklmnopqrstuvwxyz
1234567890 !@#?:;"*&

Foundry: Linotype
Designer: Erasmus Luther / Linotype Design Studio
Designer Nationality: German
Date: 1708 / 1996

Luthersche Fraktur is an ornate blackletter designed by the Linotype Design Studio and based on type drawn by Erasmus Luther in 1708. Linotype's version is lighter and crisper than Luther's original and is available in a single weight. Many other foundries have their own versions.

Mariage

ABCDEFGHIJKLMNOPQRSTUVWXYZ
abcdefghijklmnopqrstuvwxyz
1234567890 !@#?:;"*&

Foundry: American Type Founders
Designer: Morris Fuller Benton
Designer Nationality: American
Date: 1907

Mariage, Morris Fuller Benton's Old English blackletter typeface designed for American Type Founders in 1901, was also released under the name 'Wedding Text'. The Old English style, which dates to the work of Wynken de Worde in 1498, was a popular choice for 20th-century newspaper mastheads.

Monotype Engravers Old English

ABCDEFGHIJKLMNOPQRSTUVWXYZ
abcdefghijklmnopqrstuvwxyz
1234567890 !@#?:;"*&

Foundry: Monotype
Designer: Morris Fuller Benton / Monotype Studio
Designer Nationality: American
Date: 1901 / c. 1910

Part of Monotype's Engravers collection, this Old English was first designed by Morris Fuller Benton in 1901 for American Type Founders and was based on steel plate engravers lettering. It is a heavy blackletter font, available in a single weight, and evocative of gothic, medieval writing styles.

Monotype Old English Text

ABCDEFGHIJKLMNOPQRSTUVWXYZ
abcdefghijklmnopqrstuvwxyz
1234567890 !@#?:;"*&

Foundry: Monotype
Designer: William Caslon / Monotype Studio
Designer Nationality: British
Date: c. 1760 / 1935

Caslon Black, a blackletter designed by William Caslon c. 1760, was the source material for Monotype's Old English, which was first released in 1935 and digitized in the 1990s. American Type Founders' Cloister Black (1904) was an earlier interpretation of the same Caslon face, one of many.

Neudoerffer Fraktur

ABCDEFGHIJKLMNOPQRSTUVWXYZ
abcdefghijklmnopqrstuvwxyz
1234567890 !@#?:;"* &

Foundry: Linotype
Designer: Hellmut G. Bomm
Designer Nationality: German
Date: 2009

Neudoerffer Fraktur is a blackletter script based on Johan Neudörffer the Elder's writing manual of 1538 and his design of the Fraktur type style he created with Albrecht Dürer and Hieronymus Andreä. Hellmut G. Bomm's adaptation includes four versions, which each feature a variation on the initial flourish.

Notre Dame

ABCDEFGHIJKLMNOPQRSTUVWXYZ
abcdefghijklmnopqrstuvwxyz
1234567890 !@#?:;"* &

Foundry: Linotype
Designer: Karlgeorg Hoefer
Designer Nationality: German
Date: 1993

Notre Dame is a blackletter script informed by the shapes found in traditional liturgical writings. It was designed as part of Linotype's Type Before Gutenberg programme, which invited contemporary calligraphers to revise historical handwriting styles for digital publication.

Old English

ABCDEFGHIJKLMNOPQRSTUVWXYZ
abcdefghijklmnopqrstuvwxyz
1234567890 !@#?:;"* &

Foundry: Monotype
Designer: Monotype Studio
Date: 1935

Old English is a blackletter script inspired by the textura forms of Europe's early printed manuscripts. Unlike most blackletter revivals, Old English features a long 's', a prominent vertical figure that fell out of favour at the start of the 18th century. It is ideal for use in certificates and diplomas.

Old English (Let)

ABCDEFGHIJKLMNOPQRSTUVWXYZ
abcdefghijklmnopqrstuvwxyz
1234567890 !@#?:;"* &

Foundry: Monotype
Designer: Monotype Studio
Date: c. 1990

Old English (Let) is a digital revival of Caslon Black, a blackletter font cast by William Caslon's foundry in the middle of the 18th century, which remained popular for centuries. The letterforms, designed in the textura style, feature spacious counters and high-contrast strokes for optimum readability.

Rockner

ABCDEFGHIJKLMNOPQRSTUVWXYZ
abcdefghijklmnopqrstuvwxyz
1234567890 !@5?:;ßäß

Rockner is a script designed in the Fraktur style, the most popular blackletter style that emerged from the manuscript traditions of northern Europe in the medieval period. The blackletter lines are broken up. Unlike the majority of Fraktur fonts, Rockner includes Regular, Medium and Bold weights.

Foundry: Linotype
Designer: Julius de Goede
Designer Nationality: Dutch
Date: 2003

Rudolph

ABCDEFGHIJKLMNOPQRSTUVWYZ
abcdefghijklmnopqrstuvwxyz
1234567890 !@#?:;"'*ß

Rudolph is a blackletter script inspired by the Fraktur style of the 16th and 17th centuries. The structured lowercase forms feature thick, calligraphic terminals and high-contrast joints, while the uppercase characters exhibit embellishment typical of manuscript initials.

Foundry: Monotype
Designer: Julius de Goede
Designer Nationality: Dutch
Date: 1999

Sachsenwald

ABCDEFGHIJKLMNOPQRSTUVWXYZ
abcdefghijklmnopqrstuvwxyz
1234567890 !@#?:;"'*&

Monotype's Sachsenwald is a revival and digitization of Berthold Wolpe's 20th-century decorative blackletter script of the same name. Revised by Toshi Omagari, as part of Monotype's Wolpe Collection, the updated design includes the addition of both Regular and Light weights.

Foundry: Monotype
Designer: Berthold Wolpe / Toshi Omagari
Designer Nationality: German / Japanese
Date: 1937 / 2017

San Marco

ABCDEFGHIJKLMNOPQRSTUVWXYZ
abcdefghijklmnopqrstuvwxyz
1234567890 !@#?:;"'*&

San Marco is a blackletter script designed for Linotype's Type Before Gutenberg programme, for which a series of designers revived historical type styles. San Marco's gothic letterforms were inspired by those found on the facade of St Mark's Basilica in Venice, Italy.

Foundry: Linotype
Designer: Karlgeorg Hoefer
Designer Nationality: German
Date: 1990

Walbaum Fraktur

𝔄𝔅𝔆𝔇𝔈𝔉𝔊𝔥𝔍𝔎𝔏𝔐𝔑𝔒𝔓𝔔𝔕𝔖𝔗𝔘𝔙𝔚𝔛𝔜𝔷
abcdefghijklmnopqrstuvwxyz
1234567890 !@ß?:;"*&

Foundry: Berthold
Designer: Justus Erich Walbaum
Designer Nationality: German
Date: *c.* 1800 / 1918

Walbaum Fraktur is a blackletter script designed by prominent punch-cutter Justus Erich Walbaum at the start of the 19th century. The font, cast by Berthold more than a century later, features the extreme stroke contrasts and decorative capitals typical of the Fraktur style.

Wedding Text

ABCDEFGHIJKLMNOPQRSTUVWXYZ
abcdefghijklmnopqrstuvwxyz
1234567890 !@#?:;"*&

Foundry: American Type Founders
Designer: Morris Fuller Benton
Designer Nationality: American
Date: 1901

Wedding Text is a blackletter script designed in a single style and intended, as its name suggests, for formal occasions. Intensely popular and widely imitated, Morris Fuller Benton's letterforms combine formal structure in the lowercase with decorative flourishes in the capitals.

Wilhelm Klingspor Gotisch

𝔄𝔅𝔆𝔇𝔈𝔉𝔊𝔥𝔍𝔎𝔏𝔐𝔑𝔒𝔓𝔔𝔕𝔖𝔗𝔘𝔙𝔚𝔛𝔜𝔷
abcdefghijklmnopqrstuvwxyz
1234567890 !@#?:;"*&

Foundry: Klingspor
Designer: Rudolf Koch
Designer Nationality: German
Date: 1925

Wilhelm Klingspor Gotisch is a blackletter script designed in the textura style. It is named after the co-owner of the type foundry for which Rudolph Koch produced the font. The design, one of the most significant of its kind, is notable for its refined forms and meticulous spacing.

Wittenberger Fraktur

𝔄𝔅𝔆𝔇𝔈𝔉𝔊𝔥𝔍𝔎𝔏𝔐𝔑𝔒𝔓𝔔𝔕𝔖𝔗𝔘𝔙𝔚𝔛𝔜𝔷
abcdefghijklmnopqrstuvwxyz
1234567890 !@#?:;"*&

Foundry: Monotype
Designer: Monotype Studio
Date: 1906

An adaptation of Schul-Fraktur, released by the Schelter & Giesecke foundry in the late 19th century, Wittenberger Fraktur is a blackletter script designed in two weights, Regular and Semibold, and is one of the earliest typefaces Monotype produced. There are two 's' versions: a long 's' and a round, or final, 's'.

Alfie

ABCDEFGHIJKLMNOPQRSTUVWXYZ
abcdefghijklmnopqrstuvwxyz
1234567890 !@#?:;"*&

Foundry: Monotype
Designer: Jim Ford
Designer Nationality: American
Date: 2018

Alfie is a jaunty, curvaceous face with a decidedly 1950s' vibe, which takes inspiration from Emil J. Klumpp's font Murray Hill (1956). Alfie is a connecting script that is available in four variations: Casual (regular and small caps), Script (regular) and Informal (regular).

Amanda

ABCDEFGHIJKLMNOPQRSTUVWXYZ
abcdefghijklmnopqrstuvwxyz
1234567890 !@#?:;"*&

Foundry: Monotype
Designer: Tom Rickner
Designer Nationality: American
Date: 1996

Amanda is a well-crafted calligraphic script that is one of a handful of fonts designed by Tom Rickner. A co-founder of Ascender, he oversaw the development of the first TrueType fonts that were shipped with Apple Computer's System 7 operating system in 1991. Amanda is available in two weights.

Angeletta

ABCDEFGHIJKLMNOPQRSTUV
abcdefghijklmnopqrstuvwxyz
1234567890 !@#?:;"*&

Foundry: Monotype
Designer: Robert E. Leuschke
Designer Nationality: American
Date: 2018

The former Hallmark Cards lettering artist and prolific designer Robert E. Leuschke created Angeletta. It is an exuberant semi-connecting script available in a single weight with briskly drawn loops and dashes reminiscent of hand-lettered forms, and is ideal for greeting cards, menus, packaging or posters.

Arioso

ABCDEFGHIJKLMNOPQRSTUVWXYZ
abcdefghijklmnopqrstuvwxyz
1234567890 !@#?:;"*&

Foundry: Linotype
Designer: Gottfried Pott
Designer Nationality: German
Date: 1995

Arioso's combination of Roman square capitals and Carolingian lowercase make it similar to other Italic Chancery typefaces, such as ITC Zapf Chancery by Hermann Zapf (see p. 574). Its calligraphic style originates from an early form of old face developed in Italy during the 14th and 15th centuries.

Augusta

ABCDEFGHIJKLMNOPQRSTUVWXYZ
abcdefghijklmnopqrstuvwxyz
1234567890 !@#?.;'*&

Foundry: Monotype
Designer: Julius de Goede
Designer Nationality: Dutch
Date: 1999

Augusta is based on the chancery style, which is a cursive Italian hand originating from 15th- and 16th-century Italian writing masters such as Giambattista Palatino and Giovanantonio Tagliente. It is available in three variations: Augusta Regular, Augusta Cancellaresca and Augusta Schnurkl.

Basilica

ABCDEFGHIJKLMNOPQRSTUVWXYZ
abcdefghijklmnopqrstuvwxyz
1234567890 !@#?.;'*&

Foundry: Monotype
Designer: Monotype Studio
Date: 1990

This calligraphic script with ecclesiastical influences bridges the gap between historical and contemporary. Basilica takes its name from a rectangular building with double colonnades and a semicircular apse. St Peter's Basilica in Rome is often considered to be the largest church in the world.

Belltrap

ABCDEFGHIJKLMNOPQRSTUVWXYZ
abcdefghijklmnopqrstuvwxyz
1234567890 !@#?.;'*&

Foundry: ITC
Designer: Bo Berndal
Designer Nationality: Swedish
Date: 2006

Belltrap is one of the lesser known designs by Bo Berndal, Sweden's master typographer and founder of the design and advertising agency Berndal, Ingemarsson, Günther & Günther (BIGG). It is a low-key but beautifully crafted calligraphic script available in a single weight.

Bendigo

ABCDEFGHIJKLMNOPQRSTUVWXYZ
abcdefghijklmnopqrstu uwxyz
1234567890 !@#?.;'*&

Foundry: Letraset
Designer: Phill Grimshaw
Designer Nationality: British
Date: 1993

Bendigo is an energetic script font with generous uppercase characters that fit well with the more reserved lowercase characters, both of which slant to the right, emphasizing its dynamic nature. The typeface is best suited to headline use, and it is advisable to use it at a size of 14 point or more.

Bernhard Tango

ABCDEFGHIJKLMNOPQRSTUVWXYZ
abcdefghijklmnopqrstuvwxyz
1234567890 !@#?:;"*&

Foundry: American Type Founders
Designer: Lucian Bernhard
Designer Nationality: German
Date: 1931

Bernhard Tango is a very open and delicate non-connected script face that is available in a single regular weight. It was designed in 1931 but not cut until c. 1933. The typeface has a companion set of swash capitals that was issued in 1939 by Lettergieterij Amsterdam as the font Aigrette.

Bernhardt Standard

ABCDEFGHIJKLMNOPQRSTUVWXYZ
abcdefghijklmnopqrstuvwxyz
1234567890 !@#?:;"*&

Foundry: Linotype
Designer: Julius de Goede
Designer Nationality: Dutch
Date: 2003

One of the subcategories of blackletter, this is a flowing Bastarda script face with elements of the wide-nibbed pen stroke within its forms. Bernhardt Standard is available in two weights – its highly calligraphic style makes it most suitable for formal applications.

Bible Script

ABCDEFGHIJKLMNOPQRSTUVWXYZ
abcdefghijklmnopqrstuvwxyz
1234567890 !@#?:;"*&

Foundry: Letraset
Designer: Richard Bradley
Designer Nationality: British
Date: 1979

Richard Bradley created Bible Script in close conjunction with Letraset's Colin Brignall. It is a modest, no-frills calligraphic script face that is enhanced by a textured edge, swash alternate characters and additional flourishes. The typeface is available in a single regular weight.

Bickley Script

ABCDEFGHIJKLMNOPQRSTUVW
abcdefghijklmnopqrstuvwxyz
1234567890 !@#?:;"*&

Foundry: Letraset
Designer: Alan Meeks
Designer Nationality: British
Date: 1986

Bickley Script is a poised and elegant, flowing script that resembles handwriting. It combines expressive uppercase characters with a more reserved lowercase. The font was created by ex-Letraset senior designer Alan Meeks, and was released by the new company formed when Letraset and ITC merged.

Hermann Zapf

The prolific career of German type designer and calligrapher Hermann Zapf spanned more than five decades and the creation of more than 200 typefaces, including classics such as Palatino, Optima, Zapf Chancery and Zapfino.

Zapf started designing typefaces in the 1930s, creating his first printed font – a fraktur type called Gilgengart – at the age of twenty. During World War II, he served as a cartographer in the German army. Afterwards he joined the esteemed D. Stempel AG type foundry, and as art director there he gained international attention for the first time for his Palatino typeface released in 1950. Published within a limited-edition journal *Feder und Stichel* (*Pen and Graver*), it had an immediate impact and because of demand was soon reprinted in German and English, impressing the typographic community in his native Germany and overseas. An exhibition of his work was held soon after Palatino's release at the Cooper Union in New York in 1951, where his outstanding skills were celebrated.

Zapf continued to work at Stempel, where he also created the elegant sans serif Optima (see p. 296). Released in 1958, this refined humanist sans serif with elegant flared details is widely used and was inspired by etched grave plates he saw on the floor of Florence's Santa Croce church while on a trip to Italy.

In the 1950s, Zapf turned his skills to book design, working on several titles that enhanced his reputation even further. In the 1960s, he was one of the first designers to explore the nature of computerized typefaces and typesetting. Although the norm today, this was then in its infancy and seen as radical. In the early 1970s, he designed one of the first typefaces for computer-based typesetting. In 1976, Zapf took up a professorship at the Rochester Institute of Technology, New York to teach the principles of the subject. In later life, he created digital typefaces for computer programs for companies such as IBM and Xerox, and worked with Aaron Burns and Herb Lubalin in the mid 1970s creating typographical computer software.

Date: 1928–2015
Nationality: German
Notable typefaces:
Palatino (see p. 138)
Optima (see p. 296)
Zapf Chancery (see p. 581)
Zapfino Extra (see p. 586)

Below. Sketched on the back of bank notes, Zapf's initial designs of letterforms from etched graved plates in Florence's Santa Croce church would lead to the creation of his hugely successful Optima sans serif typeface.

Opposite, middle left. Optima employed on a German Deutsche Bundepost stamp, 1976.

Opposite, bottom left. Hermann Zapf, designer of more than 200 typefaces including the ever popular Palatino and Optima designs.

abcdefghijklmnopqrstuvwxyz
abcdefghijklmnopqrstuvwxyz
abcdefghijklmnopqrstuvwxyz

abc

yz

ABCDEFGHIJKLMNOPQRSTUVWXYZ
ABCDEFGHIJKLMNOPQRSTUVWXYZ
ABCDEFGHIJKLMNOPQRSTUVWXYZ

Printed in Germany. Our type designs are fully protected by international copyright

ABCDE FG HI JK LM NO PQ RS TU VWXYZ

Galileo Galilei Ma sopra tutte le invenzioni stupende, qual eminenza di mente fu quella di colui che s'immaginò di trovar modo di comunicare i suoi più reconditi pensieri a qualsivoglia altra persona, benchè distante per lunghissimo intervallo di luogo e di tempo ? parlare con quelli che son nell'Indie, parlare a quelli che non sono ancora nati nè saranno se non di qua a mille e dieci mila anni ? e con qual facilità ? con i vari accozzamenti di venti caratteruzzi sopra una carta.

Above. Specimen page for Hermann Zapf's Palatino Old Style serif by the Stempel Foundry, *c.* 1960, named after the 16th-century Italian calligrapher Giovanni Battista Palatino.

Below. Advert by Herb Lubalin for Zapf's iconic ITC Zapf Dingbats typeface appearing in volume 5 of *U&lc journal*, 1978.

Above. Page detail from Hermann Zapf's 1968 book *Manuale Typographicum*, consisting of 100 typographical arrangements by Zapf and essays on type, typography and printing.

Blado

ABCDEFGHIJKLMNOPQRSTUVWXYZ
abcdefghijklmnopqrstuvwxyz
1234567890 !@#?:;"*&

Foundry: Monotype
Designer: Ludovico degli Arrighi / Stanley Morison
Designer Nationality: Italian / British
Date: 1539 / 1923

The italic companion to Poliphilus (1499), Blado is based on the italic created by the calligrapher Ludovico degli Arrighi for Aldus Manutius in 1526.

Despite not being considered good enough at the time, the well-crafted Old Style italic was revived by Stanley Morison for Monotype in 1923.

Boscribe

ABCDEFGHIJKLMNOPQRSTUVWXYZ
abcdefghijklmnopqrstuvwxyz
1234567890 !@#?:;"*&

Foundry: Monotype
Designer: Bo Berndal
Designer Nationality: Swedish
Date: 1989

When Bo Berndal worked as an apprentice in a printing shop, he spent time copying Garamond Italic to improve his terrible handwriting. Later, he created Boscribe inspired by Paul Standard, the US calligrapher, and Alfred Fairbank, the British calligrapher and advocate of handwriting reform.

Brigida

ABCDEFGHIJKLMNOPQRSTUVWXYZ
abcdefghijklmnopqrstuvwxyz
1234567890 !@?:;"*&

Foundry: Monotype
Designer: Bo Berndal
Designer Nationality: Swedish
Date: 1995

Brigida is named after one of the six patron saints of Europe, St Bridget of Sweden, who was famed for her visions. Swedish designer Bo Berndal's modest, single-weight calligraphic script was influenced by a European letterform that was commonly used in Sweden between 1350 and 1500.

Cancellaresca Script

ABCDEFGHIJKLMNOPQRSTUVWXYZ
abcdefghijklmnopqrstuvwxyz
1234567890 !@#?:;" *&

Foundry: ITC
Designer: Alan Meeks
Designer Nationality: British
Date: 1982

Letraset stalwart Alan Meeks designed this graceful, finely crafted and rather decorative calligraphic script face. Cancellaresca Script has some unusual detailing, along with flowing uppercase letterforms that are combined with a more reserved lowercase.

Captain Quill

ABCD EFGHIJKLMNOPQRSTUVWXYZ
abcdefghijklmnopqrstuvwxyz
1234567890 !@#?:;"*&

Foundry: Ascender
Designer: Jim Ford
Designer Nationality: American
Date: 2008

This jaunty calligraphic script font is based on the handwriting of a fictional pirate figure Paul Pierce – aka Captain Quill, the forgotten son of Blackbeard and his 12th wife – as dreamed up by Ascender's Jim Ford. Suitably swashbuckling, it has an authentic rough texture and an old-world feel.

Carmela

ABCDEFGHIJKLMNOPQRSTUVWXYZ
abcdefghijklmnopqrstuvwxyz
1234567890 !@#?:;"*&

Foundry: Monotype
Designer: Philip Bouwsma
Designer Nationality: American
Date: 2006

The US type designer and calligrapher Philip Bouwsma has an enduring love of traditional broad-pen calligraphy found in historic scripts. This inspired Carmela, a calligraphic low-key connecting script with very open counters, which is available in a single weight.

Cataneo BT

ABCDEFGHIJKLMNOPQRSTUVWXYZ
abcdefghijklmnopqrstuvwxyz
1234567890 !@#?:;"*&

Foundry: Bitstream
Designer: Richard Lipton / Jacqueline Sakwa
Designer Nationality: American
Date: 1993

This elegant cursive serif was inspired by the work of 16th-century Italian writing master Bennardino Cataneo, who is best known for his single manuscript copybook of twenty leaves. It has three weights – Light, Regular and Bold – as well as complimentary swash characters and extensions.

Codex

ABCDEFGHIJKLMNOPQRSTUVWXYZ
abcdefghijklmnopqrstuvwxyz
1234567890 !@#?:;"*&

Foundry: Weber
Designer: Georg Trump
Designer Nationality: German
Date: 1954

The Codex handwriting font is based on 13th-century German gothic script and its uppercase letters are extremely large compared to the lowercase characters, making it ideal for contrast in short pieces of text. Bitstream released a digitized version in the 1990s called Calligraphic 421.

Coptek

ABCDEFGHIJKLMNOPQRSTUVWXYZ
abcdefghijklmnopqrstuvwxyz
1234567890 !?:; "*&

Foundry: Letraset
Designer: David Quay
Designer Nationality: British
Date: 1992

Coptek derives its name from its combination of a high-tech, computer-generated look and the flowing lines of a traditional copperplate script. The uppercase characters fit well with its lowercase characters, whose letters are joined together in the style of handwriting.

Delphin

ABCDEFGHIJKLMNOPQRSTUVWXYZ
abcdefghijklmnopqrstuvwxyz
1234567890 !@#?:; "*&

Foundry: Weber
Designer: Georg Trump
Designer Nationality: German
Date: 1951

The German type designer and educator Georg Trump designed Delphin for Weber in 1951. It is unusual in its pairing of upright capitals with slanted calligraphic lowercase letterforms. The typeface was originally developed for hot-metal typesetting, and has since been digitized.

Diskus

ABCDEFGHIJKLMNOPQRSTUV
abcdefghijklmnopqrstuvwxyz
1234567890 !@#?:; "*&

Foundry: Stempel
Designer: Martin Wilke
Designer Nationality: German
Date: 1938

Diskus is a high-contrast, ribbon-style script typeface available in two weights, Mager (lean) and Halbfett (medium-fat). Its creator, German type designer Martin Wilke, created a varied range of attractive script fonts for several foundries during his long career.

Elegy

ABCDEFGHIJKLMNOPQRST
abcdefghijklmnopqrstuvwxyz
1234567890 !@#?:; "*&

Foundry: Monotype
Designer: Ed Benguiat / Jim Wasco
Designer Nationality: American
Date: 2010

This elaborate typeface is based on a hand-lettered logotype created for ITC by Ed Benguiat (see p. 514). It was requested regularly by the foundry's customers as a usable typeface, and Jim Wasco of Monotype worked for two years to develop its complex design into a fully functioning font.

Fairbank

ABCDEFGHIJKLMNOPQRSTUVWXYZ
abcdefghijklmnopqrstuvwxyz
1234567890 !@#?:;”*℧

Fairbank is a revival of a font commissioned by Stanley Morison from Alfred Fairbank in the early 20th century – it was intended as an italic for Bembo, but was never used. Robin Nicholas and Carl Crossgrove breathed new life into its letterforms with this respectful digitization.

Foundry: Monotype
Designer: Alfred Fairbank / Carl Crossgrove / Robin Nicholas
Designer Nationality: British
Date: 2004

Gravura

ABCDEFGHIJKLMNOPQRSTUV
abcdefghijklmnopqrstuvwxyz
1234567890 !@# ?.:;”*&

Gravura is a classic copperplate script with perfect strokes and proportions. It has intricate capitals and an elegant and perfectly linked lowercase. Gravura is one of many typefaces created for Letraset by Phill Grimshaw under the watchful eye of the foundry's type director Colin Brignall.

Foundry: Letraset
Designer: Phill Grimshaw
Designer Nationality: British
Date: 1995

Hamada

ABCDEFGHIJKLMNOPQRSTUV
abcdefghijklmnopqrstuvwxyz
1234567890 ! @# ? .; ”*&

An elegant script typeface based on the work of English calligrapher Gaynor Goffe, Hamada captures the unmistakable irregularities of the pen marks on the page, allowing the ink to edge out from the contours. Most of the characters have alternate versions, including ligatures and ending swashes.

Foundry: Linotype
Designer: Gaynor Goffe
Designer Nationality: British
Date: 2007

ITC Braganza

ABCDEFGHIJKLMNOPQRSTUVWXYZ
abcdefghijklmnopqrstuvwxyz
1234567890 !@#?:;”*℧

This refined, upright script is inspired by handwritten manuscript styles of the 16th century, and is available in Light and Regular weights. ITC Braganza takes its name from Catherine, Duchess of Braganza, who was a prominent figure in Portuguese society and wife of King Charles II of England.

Foundry: ITC
Designer: Phill Grimshaw
Designer Nationality: British
Date: 1995

ITC Cali

ABCDEFGHIJKLMNOPQRSTUVWXYZ
abcdefghijklmnopqrstuvwxyz
1234567890 !@#?:;"*&

Foundry: ITC
Designer: Luis Siquot
Designer Nationality: Argentinian
Date: 2004

Luis Siquot based ITC Cali on his own handwriting using a pen designed for left-handed calligraphers, and decided to leave in some of the imperfections to avoid an overtly mechanical look. The unusual notches in the strokes are intended to imitate the texture of writing on a rough cotton paper stock.

ITC Chivalry

ABCDEFGHIJKLMNOPQRSTUVWXYZ
abcdefghijklmnopqrstuvwxyz
1234567890 !@#?:;"*&

Foundry: ITC
Designer: Rob Leuschke
Designer Nationality: American
Date: 2003

ITC Chivalry is a very legible calligraphic hybrid combining roman capitals with italic lowercase letters. It was created by digitizing drawings made using a flat-nib pen on textured watercolour paper. Designer Rob Leuschke added a companion set of more decorative blackletter caps for display use.

ITC Freemouse

ABCDEFGHIJKLMNOPQRSTUVWXYZ
abcdefghijklmnopqrstuvwxyz
1234567890 !@#?:;"*&

Foundry: ITC
Designer: Slobodan Miladinov
Designer Nationality: Serbian
Date: 1998

Serbian font designer Slobodan Miladinov captures the expressiveness of calligraphic writing with ITC Freemouse, which is named after the freehand technique he used to create it. The result is a lively script with a contrast of stroke and curve similar to that of a chancery italic.

ITC Grimshaw Hand

ABCDEFGHIJKLMNOPQRSTUVWXYZ
abcdefghijklmnopqrstuvwxyz
1234567890 !@#?:;"*&

Foundry: ITC
Designer: Phill Grimshaw
Designer Nationality: British
Date: 1995

This lively script typeface has lots of personality and is based on Phill Grimshaw's own handwriting. Grimshaw designed it at a time when he was playing the guitar and mandolin, and it is easy to detect the musical influences in the typeface's enthusiastic strokes.

ITC Hedera

ABCDEFGHIJKLMNOPQRSTUVWXYZ
abcdefghijklmnopqrstuvwxyz
1234567890 !@#?:;"*&

Foundry: ITC
Designer: Olivera Stojadinovic
Designer Nationality: Serbian
Date: 2002

ITC Hedera by Serbian designer Olivera Stojadinovic began as a set of initials drawn with a makeshift pen (a pair of flexible metal strips tied to some wood) as part of a book design project. The finished font, a rough exuberant calligraphic script, is available in one weight.

ITC Rastko

ABCDEFGHIJKLMNOPQRSTUVWXYZ
abcdefghijklmnopqrstuvwxyz
1234567890 !@#?:;"*&

Foundry: ITC
Designer: Olivera Stojadinovic
Designer Nationality: Serbian
Date: 2001

Named after the Serbian poet Rastko Petrović, ITC Rastko started out as capital letters drawn for a book. An elegant, calligraphic script, it features wide capitals with flourishes and many fine details that give a spontaneous feel and are the result of forms drawn with a pointed pen.

ITC Regallia

ABCDEFGHIJKLMNOPQRSTUVWXY
abcdefghijklmnopqrstuvwxyz
1234567890 !@#?:;"*&

Foundry: ITC
Designer: Phill Grimshaw
Designer Nationality: British
Date: 1998

ITC Regallia is a calligraphic script drawn by the British designer Phill Grimshaw, a graduate of the Royal College of Art. It features many ligatures, decorative capitals and more reserved, yet elegant lowercase letters. Available in a single regular weight, Regallia is graceful and legible.

ITC Zapf Chancery

ABCDEFGHIJKLMNOPQRSTUVWXYZ
abcdefghijklmnopqrstuvwxyz
1234567890 !@#?:;"*&

Foundry: ITC
Designer: Hermann Zapf
Designer Nationality: German
Date: 1979

Zapf Chancery comes in four weights with italics and debuted in the June 1979 issue of ITC's publication *U&lc*. For Zapf Chancery, Hermann Zapf (see p. 574) put his calligraphy skills to use and took inspiration from Renaissance scripts. The Medium Italic is a system font on most computers.

Klang

ABCDEFGHIJKLMNOPQRSTUVWXYZ
abcdefghijklmnopqrstuvwxyz
1234567890 !@#?:;"*&

Foundry: Monotype
Designer: Will Carter
Designer Nationality: British
Date: 1955

British typographer and printer Will Carter designed Klang for Monotype in 1955. It is a slightly inclined, heavy calligraphic sans serif available in a single weight. In 1960, British type foundry Stephenson, Blake & Co. released a bold cut, but unlike the regular, it has not been digitized.

Laser

ABCDEFGHIJKLMNOPQRSTUVWXYZ
abcdefghijklmnopqrstuvwxyz
1234567890 !?:;"*&

Foundry: Letraset
Designer: Martin Wait
Designer Nationality: British
Date: 1987

Martin Wait designed Laser for Letraset in 1987. It is an energetic, inclined connecting script in a single, fairly heavy weight. Wait, who was born in Forest Gate, London in 1942, designed many typefaces for Letraset, including a decorative, display version of Laser called Laser Chrome.

Le Griffe

ABCDEFGHIJKLMNOPQRSTUVWXYZ
abcdefghijklmnopqrstuvwxyz
1234567890 !?:;"*&

Foundry: Letraset
Designer: André-Michel Lubac
Designer Nationality: French
Date: 1973

French designer André-Michel Lubac created Le Griffe for Letraset in 1973. It is a classical, angular calligraphic script in a single weight. Digital versions are available from ITC and Elsner+Flake. Le Griffe has many alternate swash letters and is Lubac's sole font credit.

Lightnin'

ABCDEFGHIJKLMNOPQRSTUVWXYZ
abcdefghijklmnopqrstuvwxyz
1234567890 !?:;"*&

Foundry: ITC
Designer: Alan Meeks
Designer Nationality: British
Date: 1994

Lightnin' is an angular, heavy script designed by former Letraset designer Alan Meeks. It is slightly inclined and features diagonal terminals, which give it a dynamic, energetic feel that is in keeping its name. Available in one weight, Lightnin' is best suited to display and headline usage.

Linotype Gaius

ABCDEFGHIJKLMNOPQRSTUVWXYZ
abcdefghijklmnopqrstuvwxyz
1234567890 !@#?:,"'*&

Foundry: Linotype
Designer: Julius de Goede
Designer Nationality: Dutch
Date: 2002

Julius de Goede's Gaius is a versatile typeface. This attractive, calligraphic script offers the contrast that comes from being drawn with a broad-edged pen nib. It comes in two weights – Regular and Bold – each of which have alternate versions with beginning and ending swashes, and ligatures.

Linotype Gneisenauette

ABCDEFGHIJKLMNOPQRSTUVWXYZ
abcdefghijklmnopqrstuvwxyz
1234567890 !@#?:,"'*&

Foundry: Linotype
Designer: Gustavs Andrejs Grinbergs
Designer Nationality: Latvian
Date: 1997

Heavy, angular and condensed, Gneisenautte is a distinctive, connecting sans serif script available in four weights, from Light to Black, although the Light is of a colour that would be considered Bold in most scripts. Each weight has an alternate cut with more exuberant letterforms.

Ludovico

ABCDEFGHIJKLMNOPQRSTUVWXYZ
abcdefghijklmnopqrstuvwxyz
1234567890 !@#?:,"'*&

Foundry: Linotype
Designer: Philip Bouwsma
Designer Nationality: American
Date: 2007

US designer Philip Bouwsma's Ludovico is an angular, old-fashioned calligraphic script, which features elongated ascenders and descenders, a high x-height and capitals that are predominantly swashed. Ludovico comes in two styles: Smooth and the much rougher Woodcut.

Mantegna

ABCDEFGHIJKLMNOPQRSTUVWXYZ
abcdefghijklmnopqrstuvwxyz
1234567890 !@#?:,"'*&

Foundry: Agfa
Designer: Philip Bouwsma
Designer Nationality: American
Date: 1994

Philip Bouwsma designed the single-weight, spiky calligraphic script Mantegna in 1994. It is available in italic only; however, it is an almost upright italic. The 'e' features a distinctive horizontal line under its bowl. Since 2005, Bouwsma has released exclusively with Toronto-based Canada Type studio.

Medici Script

ABCDEFGHIJKLMNOPQRSTUVWXYZ
abcdefghijklmnopqrstuvwxyz
1234567890 !@#?:;"*&

Foundry: Linotype
Designer: Hermann Zapf
Designer Nationality: German
Date: 1971

Medici is a calligraphic script that takes its name from the prominent Medici family of Renaissance Florence. The refined letterforms, designed in a single style, imitate the strokes of a broad-edged pen and exhibit many of the details later featured in ITC Zapf Chancery.

Nuptial Script

ABCDEFGHIJKLMNOPQRSTUVWXYZ
abcdefghijklmnopqrstuvwxyz
1234567890 !@#?:;"*&

Foundry: Linotype
Designer: Edwin W. Shaar
Designer Nationality: American
Date: 1952

Nuptial Script is, as its name suggests, a calligraphic script designed exclusively for wedding invitations. Combining the shape of English copperplate types with Italian swash capitals, Edwin W. Shaar's design conveys opulence while maintaining maximum legibility in all sizes.

Ondine

ABCDEFGHIJKLMNOPQRSTUVWXYZ
abcdefghijklmnopqrstuvwxyz
1234567890 !@#?:;"*&

Foundry: Linotype
Designer: Adrian Frutiger
Designer Nationality: Swiss
Date: 1954

Ondine is a calligraphic script designed primarily for use in headlines, and is evocative of the humanist letterforms of 15th-century Florence. It is seemingly drawn with the broad nib of a pen, though Swiss designer Adrian Frutiger (see p. 290) actually cut the distinctive letterforms from paper with scissors.

Pristina

ABCDEFGHIJKLMNOPQRSTUVWXYZ
abcdefghijklmnopqrstuvwxyz
1234567890 !@#?:;"*&

Foundry: ITC
Designer: Phill Grimshaw
Designer Nationality: British
Date: 1994

Pristina is a calligraphic script designed to imitate the refined characteristics of calligraphic artistry. The font features expressive terminals and exaggerated strokes in upper- and lowercase forms and is designed to meet the demands of both text and display sizes.

Pyes Pa

ABCDEFGHIJKLMNOPQRSTUVWXYZ
abcdefghijklmnopqrstuvwxyz
1234567890 !@#?.:˝*&

Foundry: The Suburbs
Designer: Tim Donaldson
Designer Nationality: New Zealander
Date: 2010

Pyes Pa is a script font that combines the dynamic stroke contrast of late 19th-century modern faces, such as Bodoni or Modern Didot, with the eloquent forms of calligraphy. Designed for display use, the Pyes Pa font family includes Headline, Poster and Billboard styles.

Quill

ABCDEFGHIJKLMNOPQRSTUVWXYZ
abcdefghijklmnopqrstuvwxyz
1234567890 !@#?:;"*&

Foundry: Monotype
Designer: Monotype Design Studio
Date: 2005

Quill is a script face informed by the practice of broad-pen calligraphy during the Renaissance. The figures feature strong strokes, high-contrast junctures, sharp terminals and angled stresses, mimicking the visual quality of forms drawn with the nib of a quill.

Sho

ABCDEFGHIJKLMNOPQRSTUVWXYZ
abcdefghijklmnopqrstuvwxyz
1234567890 !@#?:;"*&

Foundry: Linotype
Designer: Karlgeorg Hoefer
Designer Nationality: German
Date: 1992

Released as part of Linotype's Calligraphy for Print package, Sho is a script face designed in a single style and reminiscent of the thick, rounded brushstrokes of Japanese calligraphy. Its distinctive characters are intended for display uses, such as posters and headlines.

Supernova

ABCDEFGHIJKLMNOPQRSTUVWXYZ
abcdefghijklmnopqrstuvwxyz
1234567890 !@#?:;"*&

Foundry: Typotheque
Designer: Martina Flor
Designer Nationality: Argentinian
Date: 2013

Supernova is a script font family comprised of five weights, from Light to Black, alongside an expressive Poster version. The design, partly inspired by brush calligraphy, was conceived to combine the energy of a script with the adaptability and legibility of a Roman text face.

Tiranti Solid

ABCDEFGHIJKLMNOPQRSTUVWXYZ
abcdefghijklmnopqrstuvwxyz
1234567890 !@#?.;"&*

Foundry: ITC
Designer: Tony Forster
Designer Nationality: British
Date: 1993

Tiranti Solid is a calligraphic script and Tony Forster's revision of his earlier Tiranti font. Unlike the original design, in which the strokes were gently textured, Tiranti Solid is more substantial in its structure, and thus better suited to the demands of digital displays.

Veljovic Script

ABCDEFGHIJKLMNOPQRSTUVWXYZ
abcdefghijklmnopqrstuvwxyz
1234567890 !@#?.;"&*

Foundry: Linotype
Designer: Jovica Veljović
Designer Nationality: Serbian
Date: 2009

Veljovic Script is a brush-style calligraphic font family that includes four weights, from Light to Bold, in both Latin and Cyrillic alphabets. Alongside its multiple styles, the font also includes a variety of alternates and more than 2,000 glyphs in each character set.

Vivaldi

ABCDEFGHIJKLMNOPQR
abcdefghijklmnopqrstuvwxyz
1234567890 !@#?.;"&*

Foundry: VGC
Designer: Friedrich Peter
Designer Nationality: German
Date: 1966

Vivaldi is a calligraphic script conceived for formal applications, such as invitations or certificates. The font's characters combine traditional calligraphic details, seen in the rhythmic strokes and flourishes, with the keen terminals that are commonly found in copperplate types.

Zapfino Extra

ABCDEFGHIJKLMNOPQRSTUVWXYZ
abcdefghijklmnopqrstuvwxyz
1234567890 !@#?.;"&*

Foundry: Linotype
Designer: Hermann Zapf / Akira Kobayashi
Designer Nationality: German / Japanese
Date: 1998 / 2003

Zapfino Extra is an expansion of the Zapfino script created by Hermann Zapf (see p. 574) in 1998. Designed in collaboration with Akira Kobayashi, Zapfino Extra is comprised of eleven styles, in contrast to the original four, and features a range of alternative characters ligatures, and flourishes.

Volina

ABCDEFGHIJKLMNOPQRST
abcdefghijklmnopqrstuvwxyz
1234567890 !@#?;;"*&

Volina is a contemporary interpretation of 19th-century pointed pen calligraphy by Francesca Bolognini and Sebastian Losch. The face draws its inspiration from Bolognini's childhood ambition to become an Olympic gymnast. She played for hours twirling a ribbon wand, fascinated by the patterns it created in the air. The flowing forms of a ribbon in movement are echoed throughout Volina's exquisite forms, and its many detailed design features mark it as a remarkably innovative and highly crafted script.

The three-dimensional effect of an undulating ribbon is ingeniously built into the character strokes. An ever-changing stroke direction varies the line thickness, while the designers' passion for flowing copperplate calligraphy and the stroke modulation of a nib under pressure are reflected in the lines broken by negative space like a ribbon turning over. Bolognini photographed moving ribbons to understand how light plays upon them, and then translated these transitions between light and dark into various copperplate styles. Extensive development went into each character and some of them, such as the lowercase 'f', had more than fifty exploratory versions. This helped ensure a correct rhythm was maintained across the characters when set. The diagonal emphasis to the character forms also reflect that of handwriting and provide further flourishes to this most elegant of typefaces.

Volina is available in a single weight. Like most classically proportioned script fonts, it possesses extended ascenders and descenders, and oversized flowing capitals. It includes a wide range of playful symbols and dingbats, from pointing hands and arrows to ribbons and flying birds.

Foundry: Dalton Maag
Designer: Francesca Bolognini / Sebastian Losch
Designer Nationality: Italian / German
Date: 2017

Below. Drawing inspiration from flowing ribbons and copperplate calligraphy, Volina's elegant forms are also accompanied by a range of illustrated symbols and dingbats.

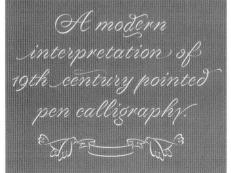

Amazone

$ABCDEFGHIJKLMNOPQRSTUV$
abcdefghijklmnopqrstuvwxyz
1234567890 !@#?:;"*&

Foundry: Lettergieterij Amsterdam
Designer: Leonard H. D. Smit
Designer Nationality: Dutch
Date: 1958

Leonard H. D. Smit's first typeface was created to compete with Günter Gerhard Lange's font Boulevard (1955). It is a graceful script designed to be connected without kerning. This made it much easier to cast and handle than other connected scripts, with no effect on how the characters joined.

Amienne

ABCDEFGHIJKLMNOPQRSTUVWXYZ
abcdefghijklmnopqrstuvwxyz
1234567890 !@#?:;"*&

Foundry: Typodermic
Designer: Ray Larabie
Designer Nationality: Canadian
Date: 2004

Ray Larabie's Amienne is a lively and very informal brush script font with an open, airy feel and a distinctive rhythm. It is available in Regular and Bold weights in full upper and lowercase, with regular numerals, accents and punctuation as well as a set of arrows.

Arriba

ABCDEFGHIJKLMNOPQRSTUVWXYZ
abcdefghijklmnopqrstuvwxyz
1234567890 !@#?:;"*&

Foundry: Letraset
Designer: Phill Grimshaw
Designer Nationality: British
Date: 1993

Arriba is an energetic Latin-American influenced font with angular forms and a simulated broad-brush style, which works best when its characters are set close together. It has two variants: Arriba Plain and Arriba Arriba, an even more decorative version of the original.

Banco

ABCDEFGHIJKLMNOPQRSTUVWXYZ
abcdefghijklmnopqrstuvwxyz
1234567890 !@#?:;"*&

Foundry: Fonderie Olive
Designer: Roger Excoffon / Phill Grimshaw
Designer Nationality: French / British
Date: 1951

Roger Excoffon's first typeface, Banco, was designed as an uppercase font with strong forms and upright, tapering strokes; lowercase and Light versions were added in 1997 by Phill Grimshaw. Banco is often associated with musician Bob Marley and the skateboarding magazine *Thrasher*.

Barrista

ABCDEFGHIJKLMNOPQRSTUVWXYZ
abcdefghijklmnopqrstuvwxyz
1234567890 !@#?:;"*&

Foundry: Typodermic
Designer: Ray Larabie
Designer Nationality: Canadian
Date: 2005

This casual, retro-inspired curly script, reminiscent of the swirling curls of steam from a hot cup of coffee, is available in a single weight. Barrista is not the only caffeine-inspired font from Ray Larabie. In 1999 he designed the seven-weight, sans serif typeface Kenyan Coffee.

Becka Script

ABCDEFGHIJKLMNOPQRSTUVWXY
abcdefghijklmnopqrstuvwxyz
1234567890 !@#?:;"*&

Foundry: ITC
Designer: David Harris
Designer Nationality: British
Date: 1985

Becka Script is a bold, single-weight font that looks like it could have been created with a marker pen. It is one of only a handful of typefaces created by British lettering artist David Harris, who specializes in cadels, which are the large, patterned capitals used in medieval manuscripts.

Brody

ABCDEFGHIJKLMNOPQRSTUVWXYZ
abcdefghijklmnopqrstuvwxyz
1234567890 !@#?:;"*&

Foundry: American Type Founders
Designer: Harold Broderson
Designer Nationality: American
Date: 1953

This nostalgic-looking, cursive-style brush script echoes the showcard style of lettering popular in the United States during the first half of the 20th century. Its characters look like they were drawn with a wide, flat brush, giving it a feeling of fun and spontaneity.

Bronx

ABCDEFGHIJKLMNOPQRSTUVWXYZ
abcdefghijklmnopqrstuvwxyz
1234567890 !@#?:;"*&

Foundry: Letraset
Designer: David Quay
Designer Nationality: British
Date: 1986

With its deliberate imperfections and rough edges, this very stylized and dynamic script resembles quickly rendered (but very neat) brush lettering. Quintessentially 1980s, Bronx has uppercase letters that can be joined with the lowercase to look like handwriting.

Brophy Script

ABCDEFGHJJKLMNOPQRSTUVWXYZ
abcdefghijklmnopqrstuvwxyz
1234567890 !@#?:;"*&

Foundry: Monotype
Designer: Harold Broderson / Carolyn Gibbs
Designer Nationality: American
Date: 1953

Brophy Script is a very close interpretation of Harold Broderson's nostalgic, showcard-influenced Brody typeface from 1953 but with more handwritten letters. It features different versions of the uppercase characters 'Y', 'E', 'I' and 'J', as well as a new, double-storey lowercase 'z'.

Brush 455

ABCDEFGHIJKLMNOPQRSTUVWX
abcdefghijklmnopqrstuvwxyz
1234567890 !@#?:;"*&

Foundry: Bitstream
Designer: Martin Wilke
Designer Nationality: German
Date: 1950 / 1990

This is Bitstream's digitized version of Palette, a lively, single-weight brush script that was originally created by German designer Martin Wilke for the Berthold type foundry in 1950. Wilke's other typefaces of note are Diskus, New Berolina and the eponymous Wilke.

Brush 738

ABCDEFGHIJKLMNOPQRSTUVWXYZ
abcdefghijklmnopqrstuvwxyz
1234567890 !@#?:;"*&

Foundry: Bitstream
Designer: Julius Kirn
Designer Nationality: German
Date: 1938 / 1990

This is Bitstream's version of Bison, the font designed by Julius Kirn in 1938 for the Stuttgart-based foundry, Weber. The foundry shared some designs with Altona-based J. D. Trennert, which released Bison as Blizzard. URW++'s digitized version is more tightly spaced than Brush 738.

Brush Script

ABCDEFGHIJKLMNOP2RSTUVWXYZ
abcdefghijklmnopqrstuvwxyz
1234567890 !@#?:;"*&

Foundry: American Type Founders
Designer: Robert E. Smith
Designer Nationality: American
Date: 1942

The classic and much-copied Brush Script was designed by Robert E. Smith for the American Type Founders with the intention of replacing similar designs from the early part of the 20th century. It has a pleasing hand-lettered look and carefully joined letters that give it a seamless appearance.

Cascade Script

ABCDEFGHIJKLMNOPQRSTUVWXYZ
abcdefghijklmnopqrstuvwxyz
1234567890 !@#?:;"*&

Foundry: Mergenthaler
Designer: Matthew Carter
Designer Nationality: British
Date: 1965

Matthew Carter (see p. 616) designed this reserved but very balanced calligraphic script face when he was in his twenties. Cascade Script evokes the fonts used in the advertising agencies of the 1940s, with its angular outlines and appearance as if drawn using a broad-tipped pen.

Challenge

ABCDEFGHIJKLMNOPQRSTUVWXYZ
abcdefghijklmnopqrstuvwxyz
1234567890 !@#?:;"*&

Foundry: Letraset
Designer: Martin Wait
Designer Nationality: British
Date: 1982

Challenge is a jaunty, non-connecting, brush-lettering face that looks like it was created with a marker pen. It is one of more than thirty typefaces created for Letraset by British type designer Martin Wait. Challenge is available in two weights – Bold and Extra Bold.

Challenger

ABCDEFGHIJKLMNOPQRSTUVW
abcdefghijklmnopqrstuvwxyz
1234567890 !@#?:;"*&

Foundry: Linotype
Designer: Manfred Kloppert
Designer Nationality: German
Date: 2011

This dynamic and expressive single weight handwriting font was the first digital typeface developed by German graphic designer and calligrapher Manfred Kloppert. It is well suited for use in advertisement texts, on packaging, invitations and greetings cards.

Chaplin

ABCDEFGHIJKLMNOPQRSTUVWXYZ
abcdefghijklmnopqrstuvwxyz
1234567890 !@#?:;"*&

Foundry: Monotype
Designer: Monotype Studio
Date: Unknown

Chaplin is a light-hearted script created for display purposes. It leans slightly to the right, evoking the Tramp, the silent film character made famous by actor Charlie Chaplin. Available as a single regular weight, the script has a relaxed charm that makes it ideal for everything from packaging to posters.

Choc

ABCDEFGHIJKLMNOPQRSTUVWXYZ
abcdefghijklmnopqrstuvwxyz
1234567890 !@?:;"*&

Foundry: Fonderie Olive
Designer: Roger Excoffon
Designer Nationality: French
Date: 1955

This brush script was created as a result of Roger Excoffon's repeated efforts to make a bold version of his typeface Mistral of 1953, which is based on his own handwriting. It is supplied with CorelDraw as Bitstream's Staccato 555, and is very popular with Asian-themed restaurants in New York.

Chunder

ABCDEFGHIJKLMNOPQRSTUVWXYZ
abcdefghijklmnopqrstuvwxyz
1234567890 !@#?:;"*&

Foundry: Chank Co.
Designer: Chank Diesel
Designer Nationality: American
Date: 1996

Chunder was inspired by hand-painted vernacular signage where the sign writing is less than perfect. US designer Chank Diesel said of his clunky yet flowery script: 'It's not pretty, but it's mine.' The quirky looking – and named – Chunder is available in a single weight.

Comedia

ABCDEFGHIJKLMNOPQRSTUVWXYZ
abcdefghijklmnopqrstuvwxyz
1234567890 !@#?:;" *&

Foundry: Monotype
Designer: Olivier Nineuil
Designer Nationality: French
Date: 1996

A simplified single-weight typeface with some unexpected angles and quirky additions, Comedia was created by the self-taught French designer, lecturer and 'magician of letters' Olivier Nineuil. He is also co-founder of the Paris-based foundry and publisher Typofacto.

Coomeec

ABCDEFGHIJKLMNOPQRSTUVWXYZ
abcdefghijklmnopqrstuvwxyz
1234567890 !@#?:;"*&

Foundry: Linotype
Designer: Andi AW. Masry
Designer Nationality: Indonesian
Date: 2012

Although Indonesian designer Andi AW. Masry is a big fan of comics, Coomeec has more in common with a calligraphic brush typeface than a conventional cartoon font. It has several distinct characters, such as the lowercase 'g' and 's' and uppercase 'Y. It is available in regular and bold with matching italics.

Crestwood

ABCDEFGHIJKLMNOPQRSTUVWXYZ
abcdefghijklmnopqrstuvwxyz
1234567890 !@#?.:; ""*&

Foundry: Ascender
Designer: Robert Hunter Middleton / Steve Matteson
Designer Nationality: American
Date: 1937 / 2006

Crestwood is an elegant semiformal script typeface that was first released by the US foundry Ludlow Typograph in 1937 and titled Coronet. The typeface is best used at larger sizes, and it is often found on greeting cards and invitations. Matteson, who created the revival, is now type director at Monotype.

Demian

ABCDEFGHIJKLMNOPQRSTUVWXYZ
abcdefghijklmnopqrstuvwxyz
1234567890 !?.:; ""*&

Foundry: Letraset
Designer: Peter O'Donnell / Jan van Dijk
Designer Nationality: British / Dutch
Date: 1984 / 1987

This informal script font features narrow letterforms with a pronounced forward slant, angular details and horizontal tittles on the lowercase 'i' and 'j'. It was designed for Letraset by Jan van Dijk in 1984, with Peter O'Donnell contributing the bold cut three years later.

DR Agu Script

ABCDEFGHIJKLMNOPQRSTUVWXYZ
abcdefghijklmnopqrstuvwxyz
1234567890 !@#?:;"*&

Foundry: Dmitry Rastvortsev
Designer: Dmitry Rastvortsev
Designer Nationality: Ukrainian
Date: 2016

This font is part of Dmitry Rastvortsev's DR Agu family. It supports a wide range of languages, including Latin and Cyrillic alphabets with stylistic subsets for Baltic and Serbian Cyrillic. It features an extensive set of contextual ligatures, alternate letterforms and numerals.

Éclat

ABCDEFGHIJKLMNOPQRST
abcdefghijklmnopqrstuvwxyz
1234567890 !@#?:;"*&

Foundry: Letraset
Designer: Doyald Young
Designer Nationality: American
Date: 1984

Doyald Young, an ccomplished logo designer once mentored by Hermann Zapf (see p. 574), created this highly decorative fat face font replete with loops, curls and flourishes. It was initially published by Letraset and subsequently digitized by ICG; Monotype released its own version in 2015.

Dalton Maag

Dalton Maag is a London-based typeface design studio founded in 1991 by Swiss designer Bruno Maag. The studio works with designers, advertising agencies and brands in their visual communications. With an international team of over forty staff, spanning twenty nationalities and twelve languages, it is truly an international studio, working with clients from around the world.

As well as the creation of small to large custom font families, Dalton Maag works on any number of type-related projects, including type modifications and logotype refinements. It is this level of assistance and broad range of services that have endeared it to global organizations such as Amazon, Intel, Nokia, Airbnb, Ubuntu and the USA Today network, which all require multilingual typeface systems that can communicate in separate languages across platforms, often in completely different writing systems.

Dalton Maag has a library of almost forty retail fonts and a number of these have been recognized in awards by the New York Type Directors Club, London's Design Museum and D&AD. Its portfolio crosses a wide array of styles, from its best-selling fonts Effra and Aktiv Grotesk (see p. 215) to its elegant ribbon-inspired script design Volina (see p. 587).

Founded: 1991
Country: Britain
Website: daltonmaag.com
Notable typefaces:
Aktiv Grotesk (see p. 215)
Blenny (see p. 414)
Volina (see p. 587)

Below. Lush Handwritten for Lush Cosmetics and AT&T Aleck for communications giant.

Opposite. Typefaces for Airbnb (Airbnb Cereal), the BBC (BBC Reith) and branding for cyclist Sir Bradley Wiggins in conjunction with cycling brand Rapha.

Airbnb Cereal · **Welcon**
community · Sans serif
ide · **playful & friendly**
Six styles · Superhost ·
belong anywhere · com

BBC Reith

The new face of the BBC

Inform, educate & entertain

fit for all Audiences

LEGIBLE & FUNCTIONAL

Broadcasting

Enamel Brush

ABCDEFGHIJKLMNOPQRSTUVWXYZ
abcdefghijklmnopqrstuvwxyz3
1234567890 !@#?:;"*&

Foundry: Typodermic
Designer: Emil J. Klumpp /
Ray Larabie
Designer Nationality: American /
Canadian
Date: 1955 / 2009

Enamel Brush is a contemporary digitization of Catalina, an earlier typeface published in 1955 and created by Emil J. Klumpp, the former American Type Founders type design director. It is a jaunty brush script font, its appearance characteristic of the more informal type styles popular during that decade.

Excritura

ABCDEFGHIJKLMNOPQRSTUVWXYZ
abcdefghijklmnopqrstuvwxyz
1234567890 !@#?:;"*&

Foundry: Linotype
Designer: Alex Camacho
Designer Nationality: Spanish
Date: 2013

This calligraphic typeface by Spanish designer Alex Camacho features connected letterforms and a characterful irregularity in its stroke weight. Slightly condensed and upright, Excritura captures a dynamic sense of the movement of the pen within its forms and flourishes.

Expectation

ABCDEFGHIJKLMNOPQRSTUVWXYZ
abcdefghijklmnopqrstuvwxyz
1234567890 !@#?:;"*&

Foundry: Linotype
Designer: Guido Bittner
Designer Nationality: German
Date: 2003

Expectation is a script typeface based on the handwriting of German type designer Guido Bittner, who developed the font from scans of his own lettering. Its irregular forms, available in a single weight, capture the texture of the paper on which the originals were written.

Flash

ABCDEFGHIJKLMNOPQRSTUVWXYZ
abcdefghijklmnopqrstuvwxyz
1234567890 !@#?:;"*&

Foundry: Monotype
Designer: Edwin W. Shaar
Designer Nationality: American
Date: 1939

US type designer Edwin W. Shaar designed this cartoonish typeface for Monotype in 1939; a bold cut, also by Shaar, was published the following year. Flash was a popular choice for title typesetting on the pulp-fiction novels popular during that era, and is still widely used to this day.

Forte

ABCDEFGHIJKLMNOPQRSTUVWXYZ
abcdefghijklmnopqrstuvwxyz
1234567890 !@#?:;"*&

Foundry: Monotype
Designer: Carl Reissberger
Designer Nationality: Austrian
Date: 1962

Bold yet soft, Forte was created by Austrian type designer Carl Reissberger for Monotype and published in 1962. Its rounded letterforms and heavy appearance make this script typeface well-suited to large-scale display use, as its legibility is rather limited at smaller point sizes.

Freestyle Script

ABCDEFGHIJKLMNOPQRSTUVWXYZ
abcdefghijklmnopqrstuvwxyz
1234567890 !@# ?:;"*&

Foundry: Letraset
Designer: Martin Wait
Designer Nationality: British
Date: 1981

The even stroke weight and linked letterforms of Freestyle Script make it an elegant yet informal choice for typesetting where a handwritten look is required. The typeface was created by British designer Martin Wait for Letraset in 1981; he added a bold weight five years later.

FS Shepton

ABCDEFGHIJKLMNOPQRSTUVWXYZ
abcdefghijklmnopqrstuvwxyz
1234567890 !@#?:;"*&

Foundry: Fontsmith
Designer: Andy Lethbridge
Designer Nationality: British
Date: 2015

The three versions of FS Shepton were created as a collection of alphabets with similar characters but different styles and textures. Inspired by the organic shapes and textures of market stall signs, Regular was drawn with a wet brush pen, Light with a dry brush and Bold with a wider, looser dry brush pen.

Glastonbury

ABCDEFGHIJKLMNOPQRSTUVWXYZ
abcdefghijklmnopqrstuvwxyz
1234567890 !?:;" *&

Foundry: Letraset
Designer: Alan Meeks
Designer Nationality: British
Date: 1979

Glastonbury is a soft, monolinear script typeface with an intricate set of free-flowing initial capitals. It is one of more than forty typefaces developed by British font designer Alan Meeks during his time as senior type designer and studio manager at Letraset from 1975 to 1984.

Greyhound

ABCDEFGHIJKLMNOPQRSTUVWXYZ
abcdefghijklmnopqrstuvwxyz
1234567890 !$#?.:;"*&

Foundry: Panache Typography
Designer: Dave Farey
Designer Nationality: British
Date: 1998

Greyhound is a delicate single-weight script with connecting lowercase and plenty of pleasing curls. It is published by British foundry Panache Typography, which is run by Richard Dawson and self-confessed 'letter-repairer' Dave Farey. Panache has issued many revivals of the classics.

Impuls

ABCDEFGHIJKLMNOPQRSTUVWXYZ
abcdefghijklmnopqrstuvwxyz
1234567890 !@#?.:;"*&

Foundry: Ludwig Wagner
Designer: Paul Zimmermann
Designer Nationality: German
Date: 1945

German designer Paul Zimmermann's vigorous brush-stroke font Impuls was originally released in 1945. Bitstream revived and digitized it in 1993 (where it also appears as Brush 439). Leading German type designer Ralph M. Unger revived it in 2010 as Impuls Pro.

ITC Arid

ABCDEFGHIJKLMNOPQRSTUVW
abcdefghijklmnopqrstuvwxyz
1234567890 !@#?.:;"*&

Foundry: ITC
Designer: Rob Leuschke
Designer Nationality: American
Date: 1997

This sparky calligraphy font looks as though it was drawn with a piece of charcoal but was actually drawn using a camel-hair bristle brush on cold-press Strathmore Watercolor paper. ITC Arid's forward slanting letterforms give it a dynamic feel. It is best used at sizes of 12 point and above.

ITC Blaze

ABCDEFGHIJKLMNOPQRSTUVWXYZ
abcdefghijklmnopqrstuvwxyz
1234567890 !@#?.:;"*&

Foundry: ITC
Designer: Patty King
Designer Nationality: American
Date: 1995

The ITC Blaze script font looks as though it were written by hand with a broad-tipped pen on rough paper. It has a dynamic feel, thanks to the pointed ends of its characters and their leaning to the right. Blaze is influenced by the typography of the late 1940s and is best suited for headlines.

ITC Kick

ABCDEFGHIJKLMNOPQRSTUVWXYZ
abcdefghijklmnopqrstuvwxyz
1234567890 !@#?:;"*&

Foundry: ITC
Designer: Patty King
Designer Nationality: American
Date: 1995

Available in a single italic weight, ITC Kick by Californian designer Patty King is a rough, bold and dynamic brush script. King designed five calligraphic faces for ITC before her death in 2002, including her final font ITC Bette, which was completed in 2002 and released posthumously.

ITC True Grit

ABCDEFGHIJKLMNOPQRSTUVWXYZ
abcdefghijklmnopqrstuvwxyz
1234567890 !@#?:;"*&

Foundry: ITC
Designer: Michael Stacey
Designer Nationality: American
Date: 1995

US designer Michael Stacey is a keen collector of vintage graphics and ephemera. His single-weight ITC True Grit was inspired by lettering from the 1930s and he describes the typeface as 'a hybrid design, a cross between German Blackletter and brush script with a hint of Jugendstil thrown in'.

ITC Wisteria

ABCDEFGHIJKLMNOPQRSTUVWXYZ
abcdefghijklmnopqrstuvwxyz
1234567890 !@#?:;"*&

Foundry: ITC
Designer: Michael Stacey
Designer Nationality: American
Date: 1995

Michael Stacey's ITC Wisteria is a distinctive, heavy double-stroke script font that mimics the effects of drawing with a broad split-tip pen. The energetic and robust typeface entered into the ITC library in 1995. Stacey based it on an alphabet by the inventor of the Speedball pen, type designer Ross F. George.

Jiffy

ABCDEFGHIJKLMNOPQR
abcdefghijklmnopqrstuvwxyz
1234567890 !@#?:;"*&

Foundry: Linotype
Designer: Unknown / Linotype Design Studio
Date: c. 1960 / 2003

An exuberant, wispy connecting script, Jiffy is available in one weight and was digitized by the Linotype Design Studio in 2003, based on a phototype released by Filmotype in the 1960s. Garrett Boge's Wendy (1998) from LetterPerfect is based on the same source and has two extra weights.

Kaufmann

ABCDEFGHIJKLMNOP2RSTUVWXYZ
abcdefghijklmnopqrstuvwxyz
1234567890 !@#?:; "*&

Foundry: American Type Founders
Designer: Max R. Kaufmann
Designer Nationality: American
Date: 1936

Max R. Kaufmann, US typographer and art director of *McCall's* magazine, drew the Kaufmann monoline connecting script for American Type Founders in 1936. It comes in a single bold weight and has relatively short descenders. Many different foundries have digitized Kaufmann.

Limehouse Script

ABCDEFGHIJKLMNOPQRSTUVWXYZ
abcdefghijklmnopqrstuvwxyz
1234567890 !@#?:;"*&

Foundry: ITC
Designer: Alan Meeks
Designer Nationality: British
Date: 1986

Limehouse Script is an informal, upright monoline handwriting font designed by Alan Meeks for ITC in 1986. It is named after a neighbourhood in the East End of London. The lowercase 'o', the most distinctive character, features a horizontal terminal above its bowl.

Mantika Informal

ABCDEFGHIJKLMNOPQRSTUVWXYZ
abcdefghijklmnopqrstuvwxyz
1234567890 !@#?:;"*&

Foundry: Linotype
Designer: Jürgen Weltin
Designer Nationality: German
Date: 2010

Mantika Informal is part of the Mantika superfamily, which also includes another sans serif and two serifs. It is a soft, slightly cursive sans serif with humanist influences, and German designer Jürgen Weltin created it with children's books in mind. It is available in two weights – Regular and Bold.

Marnie

ABCDEFGHIJKLMNOPQRSTUVWXYZ
abcdefghijklmnopqrstuvwxyz
1234567890 !@#?:;"*&

Foundry: Agfa
Designer: Gérard Mariscalchi
Designer Nationality: Canadian
Date: 1997

Marnie, Gérard Mariscalchi's elegant connecting script, was inspired by early 20th-century Art Nouveau calligraphic hand-lettering. It is highly legible, thanks to a high x-height and low contrast, and features large curlicued capitals that often wrap around the next letter.

Mercurius Script

ABCDEFGHIJKLMNOPQRSTUVWXYZ
abcdefghijklmnopqrstuvwxyz
1234567890 !@#?:;"*&

Foundry: Monotype
Designer: Imre Reiner
Designer Nationality: Hungarian
Date: 1957

Hungarian-born graphic artist and typographer Imre Reiner designed Mercurius in 1957, when he was living in the Swiss town of Ruvigliana near Lugano. It is a bold, inclined script font with angular features. Reiner achieved its distinct look through the use of a bamboo pen.

Monoline Script

ABCDEFGHIJKLMNOPQRSTUVWXYZ
abcdefghijklmnopqrstuvwxyz
1234567890 !@#?:;"*&

Foundry: Monotype
Designer: Monotype Studio
Date: 1933

A fun, optimistic connecting script with a consistent stroke width, Monoline Script is available in a single weight (roughly a medium). It was designed in-house at Monotype in 1933 and is slightly inclined with many curling, looping features, especially on capitals and ascenders.

Monterey BT

ABCDEFGHIJKLMNOPQRSTUVWXYZ
abcdefghijklmnopqrstuvwxyz
1234567890 !@#?:;"*&

Foundry: Bitstream
Designer: Rand Holub
Designer Nationality: American
Date: 1958 / 1987

Monterey BT is a Bitstream digitization of Monterey Script, designed by Rand Holub for Intertype in 1958 as a response to Emil J. Klumpp's Murray Hill font published by American Type Founders two years earlier. The casual characters feature a moderate contrast and include a single, regular style.

Morris Freestyle

ABCDEFGHIJKLMNOPQRSTUVWXYZ
abcdefghijklmnopqrstuvwxyz
1234567890 !@#?:;"*&

Foundry: Monotype
Designer: Keith Morris
Designer Nationality: Australian
Date: 2006

Morris Freestyle is a casual script designed in a single style. The font, which features upper- and lowercase forms, combines spacious character widths, broad strokes and open counters with shortened ascenders and descenders for an approachable and articulate appearance.

New Berolina

ABCDEFGHIJKLMNOPQRSTUVWXY
abcdefghijklmnopqrstuvwxyz
1234567890 !@#?:;"*&

Foundry: Monotype
Designer: Martin Wilke
Designer Nationality: German
Date: 1965

New Berolina is a casual script designed in a single weight and intended for careful use in body text. The lowercase letterforms feature sharp, calligraphic strokes, which, combined with a relatively low x-height and expressive capitals, comprise a dynamic, spirited typeface.

Okay

ABCDEFGHIJKLMNOPQRSTUVWXYZ
abcdefghijklmnopqrstuvwxyz
1234567890 !@#?:;"*&

Foundry: Linotype
Designer: Edwin W. Shaar
Designer Nationality: American
Date: 1939

Okay is a casual script designed in a single style. Like other script faces designed by Edwin W. Shaar in this period, such as Flash, Okay's characters are narrow, italicized and comprised of thick, brushlike strokes with irregular terminals that render them both soft and dynamic.

Park Avenue

ABCDEFGHIJKLMNOPQRSTUVWXYZ
abcdefghijklmnopqrstuvwxyz
1234567890 !@#?:;"*&

Foundry: American Type Founders
Designer: Robert E. Smith
Designer Nationality: American
Date: 1933

Park Avenue is a casual script, designed in a single style, which combines decoration and readability. The calligraphic letterforms feature a low x-height and long, swirling strokes, alongside brushlike terminals that provide the sturdy shapes with a formal elegance.

Pendry Script

ABCDEFGHIJKLMNOPQRSTUVWXYZ
abcdefghijklmnopqrstuvwxyz
1234567890 !?:;"*&

Foundry: ITC
Designer: Martin Wait
Designer Nationality: British
Date: 1981

Pendry Script is a casual script that imitates the idiosyncrasies of calligraphic lettering. Alongside the organic and high-contrast strokes, the design also features a smeared outline that mimics the effect of ink smudging, as if a hand is dragging across the page as it writes.

Pepita

ABCDEFGHIJKLMNOPQRSTUVWXY
abcdefghijklmnopqrstuvwxyz
1234567890 ! @ #?.;"*&

Foundry: Monotype
Designer: Imre Reiner
Designer Nationality: Hungarian
Date: 1959

Inspired by the stylish sweep of the artist's brush stroke, Pepita is a casual script designed for display purposes, such as advertising, menus or book covers. The characters, with their oblique forms and irregular baseline, combine elegance with a measured flamboyance.

Rapier

ABCDEFGHIJKLMNOPQRSTUVWXYZ
abcdefghijklmnopqrstuvwxyz
1234567890 ! @# ?.; "*&

Foundry: ITC
Designer: Martin Wait
Designer Nationality: British
Date: 1989

Rapier is a casual script designed in a single style and inspired by the brush-style fonts found in advertising of the 1940s. The cursive characters, which assert their energy through vigorous adjoining strokes and sweeping terminals, were conceived for dynamic headline texts.

Reporter No. 2

ABCDEFGHIJKLMNOPQRSTUVWXYZ
abcdefghijklmnopqrstuvwxyz
1234567890 !@#?.;"*&

Foundry: Linotype
Designer: Carlos Winkow
Designer Nationality: Spanish
Date: 1938

Reporter No. 2 is a casual script and a revision by German type designer Carlos Winkow of his own Reporter font, initially designed for the Wagner foundry in 1938. In an effort to simplify the design, Reporter No. 2 includes fewer aesthetic details, while also removing various alternative characters.

Ribjoint

ABCDEFGHIJKLMNOPQRSTUVWXYZ
abcdefghijklmnopqrstuvwxyz
1234567890 !@#?.;"*&

Foundry: Chank Co.
Designer: Chank Diesel
Designer Nationality: American
Date: 1992

Ribjoint is a casual script designed in the Egyptian style. The font's lowercase letterforms, in which the rigid curves and robust strokes combine to induce a distinctly muscular character, represent Chank Diesel's first experiment in the design of computerized cursive.

Romany

ABCDEFGHIJKLMNOPQRSTUVWXYZ
abcdefghijklmnopqrstuvwxyz
1234567890 !@#?:;"*&

Foundry: Ascender
Designer: A. R. Bosco / Terrance Weinzierl
Designer Nationality: American
Date: 1934 / 2009

Romany is a digitization of A. R. Bosco's design of 1934 with the same name, produced in a single weight for American Type Founders. Terrance Weinzierl's revival, and expansion into a family of four styles, was conceived to revitalize Romany as a flexible script across all platforms.

Sagrantino

ABCDEFGHIJKLMNOPQRSTUVWXYZ
abcdefghijklmnopqrstuvwxyz
1234567890 !@#?:;"*&

Foundry: Monotype
Designer: Carl Crossgrove / Karl Leuthold / Juan Villanueva
Designer Nationality: American
Date: 2017

Sagrantino is a vivacious, casual script designed for use at large sizes, from packaging to banners. The font comprises three styles, including Regular, Highlight and Shadow, alongside a variety of OpenType features, such as decorative ligatures and alternate characters.

Salsbury

ABCDEFGHIJKLMNOPQRSTUVWXYZ
abcdefghijklmnopqrstuvwxyz
1234567890 !@#?:;"*&

Foundry: Typodermic
Designer: Ray Larabie
Designer Nationality: Canadian
Date: 2006

Salsbury is a casual script inspired by the 20th-century brush fonts Dom Casual and Flash, by Peter Dom and Edwin W. Shaar respectively. The letterforms, which feature rounded strokes and terminals, were optimized for television graphics such as DVD menus and video games.

Santa Fe

ABCDEFGHIJKLMNOPQRSTUVWXYZ
abcdefghijklmnopqrstuvwxyz
1234567890 !@#?:;"*&

Foundry: Letraset
Designer: David Quay
Designer Nationality: British
Date: 1983

David Quay's Santa Fe is a casual script font that is evocative of lettering found in American popular culture of the 1960s. The font combines rodlike verticals with inflated curves and rounded terminals and features several distinctive forms in both the upper- and lowercases.

Saussa

ABCDEFGHIJKLMNOPQRSTUVWXYZ
abcdefghijklmnopqrstuvwxyz
1234567890 !@#?:;"*&

Foundry: Linotype
Designer: Patricia Roesch-Pothin
Designer Nationality: French
Date: 2009

Saussa is a casual script initially designed for the packaging of a French brand of fruit salad. The brushlike strokes, which were first painted by hand before being refined digitally, and the lowercase styling of the capitals ensure an informality throughout the font.

Shamrock

ABCDEFGHIJKLMNOPQRSTUVWXYZ
abcdefghijklmnopqrstuvwxyz
1234567890 !@#?:;"*&

Foundry: Letraset
Designer: Alan Withers
Designer Nationality: British
Date: 1978

Shamrock is a casual, hand-drawn script designed in a single style. It takes its name from the three-leafed clover that serves as the symbol for Ireland.

The letterforms share many characteristics with traditional Irish type, such as the angled stress and looping strokes.

Stempel Elan

ABCDEFGHIJKLMNOPQRSTUVWX
abcdefghijklmnopqrstuvwxyz
1234567890 !@#?:;"*&

Foundry: Linotype
Designer: Hans Karl Gustav Möhring / Frank Griesshammer
Designer Nationality: German
Date: 2010

Stempel Elan is a casual script and Frank Griesshammer's digital revival of Stempel's Elan font, designed by Hans Möhring in 1937. While remaining faithful to the original, Stempel Elan increases flexibility with a variety of OpenType features, such as alternative characters.

Sunetta

ABCDEFGHIJKLMNOPQRSTUVWXYZ
abcdefghijklmnopqrstuvwxyz
1234567890 !@#?:;"*&

Foundry: Linotype
Designer: Werner Schneider
Designer Nationality: German
Date: 2005

Sunetta is a casual script drawn using an inkstone, ink, a brush and paper, known in the Chinese calligraphic tradition as the Four Treasures of the Study. The font's three styles – Sunetta Flair, Sunetta Charme and Sunetta Magic – range from relatively moderate to expressive.

Swing

ABCDEFGHIJKLMNOPQRSTUVWXYZ
abcdefghijklmnopqrstuvwxyz
1234567890 !@#?:;"*&

Foundry: Monotype
Designer: Max R. Kaufmann / Monotype Studio
Designer Nationality: American
Date: 1936

Swing is a casual script and Monotype's revival of Kaufmann, a rhythmic script originally created by US font designer Max R. Kaufmann for American Type Founders in 1936. Unlike the majority of cursive script designs, Swing's characters feature minimal stroke contrast.

Time Script

ABCDEFGHIJKLMNOPQRSTUVWXYZ
abcdefghijklmnopqrstuvwxyz
1234567890 !@#?:;"*&

Foundry: Weber
Designer: Georg Trump
Designer Nationality: German
Date: 1956

Time Script is a casual script designed in three weights, including Light, Medium and Bold. The characters are distinctive in their blending of calligraphic detail with the zealous strokes of handwriting, notable in both the capital and lowercase letterforms.

WilliamLucas

ABCDEFGHIJKLMNOPQRSTUVWXYZ
abcdefghijklmnopqrstuvwxyz
1234567890 !@#?.;"*&

Foundry: ITC
Designer: Martin Wait
Designer Nationality: British
Date: 2010

WilliamLucas is a casual script designed to replicate the versatility of hand-lettering. The font utilizes OpenType software to provide a variety of alternative characters and glyphs, such as initials, swashes, capitals, and terminals, which add both flexibility and balance.

Zennor

ABCDEFGHIJKLMNOPQRSTUVWXYZ
abcdefghijklmnopqrstuvwxyz
1234567890 !?:;"*&

Foundry: ITC
Designer: Phill Grimshaw
Designer Nationality: British
Date: 1935

Zennor is a casual script designed for display uses in a single bold style. The brushlike figures, which appear to have been painted at speed, provide a muscular dynamism in the lowercase, while the capitals, which can also serve as initials, exhibit a more placid authority.

Aristocrat

ABCDEFGHIJKLMNOPQRSTUVWX
abcdefghijklmnopqrstuvwxyz
1234567890 !@#?.:; "*&

Foundry: Letraset
Designer: Donald Stevens
Designer Nationality: British
Date: 1978

Aristocrat, the typeface by British designer Donald Stevens, combines intricately crafted uppercase characters with a more reserved lowercase. It is a very refined single-weight script face, which makes a good choice for use on certificates, greeting cards and invitations.

Balmoral

ABCDEFGHIJKLMNOPQRS
abcdefghijklmnopqrstuvwxyz
1234567890 !@#?.:; "*&

Foundry: Letraset
Designer: Martin Wait
Designer Nationality: British
Date: 1978

Available as a single weight, Martin Wait's Balmoral is an elegant and free-flowing copperplate-script style typeface. It has elaborate initial capitals that complement the more restrained lowercase characters, which join for more balanced letter spacing in word settings.

Carl Beck

ABCDEFGHIJKLMNOPQRSTUVWXYZ
abcdefghijklmnopqrstuvwxyz
1234567890 !@ ?.:;"*&

Foundry: Monotype
Designer: Carolyn Gibbs
Designer Nationality: American
Date: 1992

This modest script was inspired by the cartographer Carl Beckman. He published an instruction and pattern book showing four different styles (including Cursiv Skriften No. 1, upon which this font is based) in Stockholm in 1794, as a response to the poor standard of lettering in Sweden at the time.

Carmine Tango

ABCDEFGHIJKLMNOPQRSTUVWXYZ
abcdefghijklmnopqrstuvwxyz
1234567890 !#?.:; "*&

Foundry: Bitstream
Designer: Lucian Bernhard
Designer Nationality: American
Date: 1931

This is Bitstream's version of Lucian Bernhard's original script face Bernhard Tango of 1931, an open and delicate non-connected script face. A companion set of swash capitals to Bernhard's design was issued in 1939 by Lettergieterij Amsterdam as the font Aigrette.

Citadel Script

ABCDEFGHIJKLMNOPQRSTUV
abcdefghijklmnopqrstuvwxyz
1234567890 !@#?.:; " &*

This delicate, flowing script is based on the handwriting and engraving traditionally found in formal announcements and invitations. While Flemish Script, Florentine Script and Old Fashion Script have similar lowercase letters, Citadel Script has unique flourished capitals.

Foundry: Monotype
Designer: Monotype Studio
Date: 1994

Commercial Script

ABCDEFGHIJKLMNOPQRSTUVWXYZ
abcdefghijklmnopqrstuvwxyz
1234567890 !@#?.:; " &*

Also known as Spencerian, this very popular copperplate connected script is similar to Bank Script but slightly heavier and without so many flourishes. It was influenced by a similar face by Barnhart Brothers & Spindler from 1895. Digitized versions have been released by Letraset, Bitstream and ITC.

Foundry: American Type Founders
Designer: Morris Fuller Benton
Designer Nationality: American
Date: 1906

Coronet

ABCDEFGHIJKLMNOPQRSTUVWXYZ
abcdefghijklmnopqrstuvwxyz
1234567890 !@# ?.:; " &*

Coronet is a stylized retro-looking script originally designed for the Ludlow hot-metal typesetting system used in letterpress printing. It was digitized by Bitstream (as Ribbon 131) and later by Steve Jackaman. The script is used on the cover of the LP *The Velvet Underground & Nico* (1967).

Foundry: Ludlow Typograph
Designer: Robert Hunter Middleton
Designer Nationality: American
Date: 1937

Dorchester Script

ABCDEFGHIJKLMNOPQRSTUVWXYZ
abcdefghijklmnopqrstuvwxyz
1234567890 !@# ?.:;" &*

This elegant typeface with a slight forward slant was widely used to provide a high-society feel within correspondence and invitations following its release by Monotype in 1939. No specific designer is credited for the font, which was probably created by the foundry's in-house team.

Foundry: Monotype
Designer: Monotype Studio
Date: 1939

Embassy

ABCDEFGHIJKLMNOPQRSTUVWXYZ
abcdefghijklmnopqrstuvwxyz
1234567890 !@#?.:; "*&

Foundry: Bitstream
Designer: Studio of H. W. Caslon
Designer Nationality: British
Date: 1923 / c. 1955

Embassy is based on the rounded script styles popular with engravers at the turn of the 20th century. It was designed at the Caslon works in London in 1923 as a rival to Stephenson, Blake & Co.'s Palace Script (1923). It was converted for phototypesetting c. 1955; Bitstream's version was likely published in the 1990s.

English 111

ABCDEFGHIJKLMNOPQRSTU
abcdefghijklmnopqrstuvwxyz
1234567890 !@#?.:; "*&

Foundry: Bitstream
Designer: George Shelley
Designer Nationality: British
Date: c. 1990s

This Bitstream digitization stems from the work of the 18th-century British writing master George Shelley. It is based on the Shelley Script typeface developed by British designer Matthew Carter (see p. 616) for Linotype in 1972, in reference to Shelley's distinctive lettering style.

English 157

ABCDEFGHIJKLMNOPQRSTUVWXYZ
abcdefghijklmnopqrstuvwxyz
1234567890 !@#?.:; "*&

Foundry: Bitstream
Designer: Günther Gerhard Lange
Designer Nationality: German
Date: c. 1990s

English 157 is a digital revival of Englische Schreibschrift, originally published by Berthold. It is an example of the Spencerian style popular in the United States in the latter half of the 19th century. English 157 features unlinked letterforms, which is unusual for script fonts of its kind.

English Script

ABCDEFGHIJKLMNOPQRSTUVWXYZ
abcdefghijklmnopqrstuvwxyz
1234567890 !@#?.:; "*&

Foundry: Linotype
Designer: Günther Gerhard Lange
Designer Nationality: German
Date: 2006

This is Linotype's version of Englische Schreibschrift. It is available in three weights, including an appealingly robust bold cut. The typeface features a heavy slant to its letterforms, and its distinctive horizontal stroke ends are emphasized within the Demi and Bold styles.

Flemish Script

ABCDEFGHIJKLMNOPQRSTUVWXYZ
abcdefghijklmnopqrstuvwxyz
1234567890 !@#.?.;" * &

Foundry: Bitstream
Date: 1998

The origins of this ornamental Roundhand script typeface are difficult to discern; it is said to have originated at the Photon foundry in Wilmington, as a font for phototypesetting, and was subsequently digitized by Bitstream. Featuring complex curlicues, it is best used at larger point sizes.

Fluidum

ABCDEFGHIJKLMNOPQRSTUVWXYZ
abcdefghijklmnopqrstuvwxyz
1234567890 !@#?:;"*&

Foundry: Nebiolo
Designer: Alessandro Butti / Aldo Novarese
Designer Nationality: Italian
Date: 1951

Fluidum is a high-contrast script font, whose uniformity provides a linear and regular appearance. It was originally published in two weights, though only the heavier was digitized by Monotype. In 2011, Ralph Unger's foundry RMU released an alternative revival of Fluidum, Butti, which also includes the lighter cut.

French Script

ABCDEFGHIJKLMNOPQRSTUVWXYZ
abcdefghijklmnopqrstuvwxyz
1234567890 !@#?:;"*&

Foundry: Monotype
Designer: Morris Fuller Benton / Monotype Studio
Designer Nationality: American
Date: 1905 / 1989

French Script is based on script handwriting and engraving used for invitations and announcements and on the Typo Upright script created by Morris Fuller Benton for American Type Founders in 1905. It is an elegant, upright script with flourished capitals and joining lowercase characters.

Gavotte

ABCDEFGHIJKLMNOPQRSTUVWXYZ
abcdefghijklmnopqrstuvwxyz
1234567890 !@#?:;"*&

Foundry: Klingspor
Designer: Rudo Spemann
Designer Nationality: German
Date: 1940

Rudo Spemann's decorative script is named after an 18th-century French dance. The script shows off his expert calligraphic skills. Spemann was much respected as an educator and since 1954 the city of Offenbach has awarded the Rudo Spemann Prize every two years in memory of his work.

ITC Edwardian Script

ABCDEFGHIJKLMNOPQRSTUVWXY

abcdefghijklmnopqrstuvwxyz

1234567890 !@#?:;"*©

Foundry: ITC
Designer: Ed Benguiat
Designer Nationality: American
Date: 1994

ITC Edwardian Script is one of more than 600 typefaces created by US type designer Ed Benguiat (see p. 514). It is a sophisticated, connected script with delicate letterforms, inspired by the strong stroke contrasts created when writing with a steel pointed pen.

ITC Isadora

ABCDEFGHIJKLMNOPQRSTUVWXYZ

abcdefghijklmnopqrstuvwxyz

1234567890 !@#?:;"*&

Foundry: ITC
Designer: Kris Holmes
Designer Nationality: American
Date: 1989

US type designer Kris Holmes founded the Bigelow & Holmes studio with Charles Bigelow in 1976. She designed the ITC Isadora elegant calligraphic script, which is available in Regular and Bold weights. The US ballet dancer Isadora Duncan inspired the type's forms and its name.

ITC Redonda

ABCDEFGHIJKLMNOPQRSTUVWX

abcdefghijklmnopqrstuvwxyz

1234567890 !@#?:;"*&

Foundry: ITC
Designer: Gérard Mariscalchi
Designer Nationality: French
Date: 1998

French-born designer Gérard Mariscalchi created this elegant single-weight script inspired by 19th-century French handwriting in 1998. ITC Redonda has two sets of flourished, swashed capitals to add variety. Mariscalchi lives in Canada and has designed everything from fonts to stamps.

Kuenstler Script

ABCDEFGHIJKLMNOPQRSTUVWXYZ

abcdefghijklmnopqrstuvwxyz

1234567890 !@#?:;"*&

Foundry: Linotype
Designer: Stempel Studio / Hans Bohn
Designer Nationality: German
Date: 1902 / 1957

Hans Bohn designed Kuenstler Script for Linotype in 1957. It is based on Künstlerschreibschrift, an elegant script released by Stempel in 1902. Kuenstler Script comes in three weights; the Medium and Bold are based on the two original Stempel weights and the Black was Bohn's addition in 1957.

Libelle

ABCDEFGHIJKLMNOPQRSTUVWXYZ
abcdefghijklmnopqrstuvwxyz
1234567890 !@#?:;"*&

Foundry: Linotype
Designer: Jovica Veljović
Designer Nationality: Serbian
Date: 2009

Experienced Serbian calligrapher and designer Jovica Veljović created Libelle. It is an elegant, modern take on the copperplate script style.

Although only available in a single weight, Libelle is highly versatile with many ligatures, ornaments, alternates and swash options.

Liberty Script

ABCDEFGHIJKLMNOPQRSTUVWXYZ
abcdefghijklmnopqrstuvwxyz
1234567890 !@#?:;"*&

Foundry: American Type Founders
Designer: Willard T. Sniffin
Designer Nationality: American
Date: 1927

Willard T. Sniffin designed this delicate, non-connecting script released by American Type Founders. Sniffin designed many typefaces for the trust from 1927 to 1933. Liberty Script features large, flourish-heavy capitals and a slightly more understated lowercase with a very small x-height.

Linoscript

ABCDEFGHIJKLMNOPQRSTUVWXYZ
abcdefghijklmnopqrstuvwxyz
1234567890 !@#?:;"*&

Foundry: American Type Founders
Designer: Morris Fuller Benton
Designer Nationality: American
Date: 1905 / 1926

American Type Founders released this upright, connecting script as Typo Upright in 1905. It was renamed 'Linoscript' in 1926 when it was launched on the Linotype machine. It was inspired by the French script style and features large, flourished capitals. Many lowercase letters have flourishes too.

Lucia

ABCDEFGHIJKLMNOPQRSTUVWXYZ
abcdefghijklmnopqrstuvwxyz
1234567890 !@#?:;"*&

Foundry: Bitstream
Date: c. 1990

Bitstream's Lucia is an elegant, delicate roundhand script with a small x-height and swashed capitals. It is a digitization of a font that was first transferred from an engravers' master plate (where it was named Italian Script) to the Intertype Fotosetter system by Compugraphic in 1955.

Old Fashion Script

ABCDEFGHIJKLMNOPQRSTUVWXYZ
abcdefghijklmnopqrstuvwxyz
1234567890 !@#?.:; "* &

Foundry: Monotype
Designer: Monotype Studio
Date: 1920

Old Fashion Script is a formal script inspired by antiquated handwriting styles. The decorous letterforms, while featuring extravagant flourishes and high-contrast strokes, alongside cursive characters in the lowercase, are suitable for both text and headline sizes.

Original Script

ABCDEFGHIJKLMNOPQRSTUVWXYZ
abcdefghijklmnopqrstuvwxyz
1234567890 !@#?.:; "* &

Foundry: Monotype
Designer: Monotype Studio
Date: 1999

Original Script is a hand-lettered font designed as part of Monotype's script collection. The elegant characters, which are linked together through a series of cursive strokes, are intended for formal occasions, such as wedding invitations, and for items such as certificates and stationery.

Palace Script

ABCDEFGHIJKLMNOPQRSTUVWXYZ
abcdefghijklmnopqrstuvwxyz
1234567890 !@#?.:; "* &

Foundry: Monotype
Designer: Monotype Studio
Date: 1936

Palace Script is a formal script inspired by English copperplate engravings from the 18th and 19th centuries. The font, designed in both Regular and Semibold weights, features high-contrast, cursive strokes, alongside a low x-height for optimum legibility.

Phyllis

ABCDEFGHIJKLMNOPQRSTUVWXYZ
abcdefghijklmnopqrstuvwxyz
1234567890 !@#?.:; "* &

Foundry: Linotype
Designer: Heinrich Wieynck
Designer Nationality: German
Date: 1911

Linotype's Phyllis, which was also released by the Schriftgiesserei Bauer foundry under the name of Wieynck Cursive, is a formal script that merges calligraphic strokes, seen in the flourished uppercase, with sturdy serifs, demonstrated in the reserved lowercase.

Sackers Script

ABCDEFGHIJKLMNOPQRSTUVWXYZ
abcdefghijklmnopqrstuvwxyz
*1234567890 !@#?:,.;" *&*

Foundry: Monotype
Designer: Monotype Studio
Date: 1900

Sackers Script is a formal script designed in two styles, Sackers English Script and Sackers Italian Script, both conceived primarily for invitations and stationery. The two styles are discernible in weight, the English font being slightly heavier, as well as stroke detail.

Shelley Script

ABCDEFGHIJKLMNOPQRSTUVWXYZ
abcdefghijklmnopqrstuvwxyz
*1234567890 !@#?:,.;" *&*

Foundry: Linotype
Designer: George Shelley / Matthew Carter
Designer Nationality: British
Date: 1972

Shelley Script is a formal script face and a revival of the handwriting style of the 18th-century writing master George Shelley. This design from Matthew Carter (see p. 616) includes three versions – Allegro, Andante and Volante – in which only the flourishes of the capitals differ.

Snell Roundhand

ABCDEFGHIJKLMNOPQRSTUVWXYZ
abcdefghijklmnopqrstuvwxyz
*1234567890 !@#?:,.;" *&*

Foundry: Linotype
Designer: Charles Snell / Matthew Carter
Designer Nationality: British
Date: 1966

Snell Roundhand is a formal script and a revival of a 17th-century roundhand by English writing master Charles Snell, who avoided all flourishes in keeping with Puritan tradition. While retaining the distinctive details of the original, Snell Roundhand includes the addition of two new weights, Bold and Black.

Young Baroque

ABCDEFGHIJKLMNOPQRSTU
abcdefghijklmnopqrstuvwxyz
*1234567890 !@#?:,.;" *&*

Foundry: ITC
Designer: Doyald Young
Designer Nationality: American
Date: 1984

Young Baroque is a formal script inspired by the decorative forms of 17th-century baroque lettering. The font integrates gentle cursive strokes in the lowercase with ostentatious flourishes in the capitals and is intended for formal correspondence, such as invitations.

Amadeo

ABCDEFGHIJKLMNOPQRSTUVWXYZ
abcdefghijklmnopqrstuvwxyz
1234567890 !@#?:;"*&

Foundry: Monotype
Designer: Julius de Goede
Designer Nationality: Dutch
Date: 1999

This informal handwriting script is by Dutch designer, typographer and teacher Julius de Goede. He is the author of several books on type and calligraphy including *Kalligraphie Lehrbuch* (*Calligraphy Manual*, 2003). Amadeo is available in Regular and Bold weights, both with small caps.

Ambiance BT

ABCDEFGHIJKLMNOPQRSTUVWXYZ
abcdefghijklmnopqrstuvwxyz
1234567890 !@#?:;"*&

Foundry: Bitstream
Designer: Rob Leuschke
Designer Nationality: American
Date: 2004

This fine, expressive calligraphic script is the first typeface created for Bitstream by US designer Rob Leuschke, a former lettering artist at Hallmark Cards. Ambiance BT is available in a single weight. It also includes a swash alternate for each upper- and lowercase letter.

Andy

ABCDEFGHIJKLMNOPQRSTUVWXYZ
abcdefghijklmnopqrstuvwxyz
1234567890 !@#?:;"*&

Foundry: Monotype
Designer: Steve Matteson
Designer Nationality: American
Date: 1993

Andy was originally known as 'Mead' because designer Steve Matteson loosely based the font on the handwriting of his friend Andy Mead. It is a childish looking, slightly slanted handwriting script that is available in Regular and Bold weights, with corresponding italics.

Ashley Script

ABCDEFGHIJKLMNOPQRSTUVWXYZ
abcdefghijklmnopqrstuvwxyz
1234567890 !@#?:;"*&

Foundry: Monotype
Designer: Ashley Havinden
Designer Nationality: British
Date: 1955

A relatively plain brush script, Ashley Script is based on Ashley Havinden's own handwriting. He was a key figure in the British design industry during the post-war years, and worked at the top British advertising agency W. S. Crawford. In 1947, he was appointed a Royal Designer for Industry.

Matthew Carter

British designer Matthew Carter is one of the foremost type creatives of the last sixty years. His contribution to type design is inestimable: his typefaces are employed across the globe every day.

He was born in London in 1937, the son of Harry Carter, a book designer and in later years a print historian. His early forays in the world of print and type began with an apprenticeship at the esteemed Joh. Enschedé type foundry and printers in the Netherlands. There he studied the craft of traditional punch-cutting, the process of creating the physical designs to cast hot-metal type. Inspired, he moved into a graphic design and printing career.

Returning to London, Carter set up as a freelance type designer and was soon a consultant to Crosfield Electronics, a British electronic-imaging company. In 1965, he moved to New York and began a long relationship designing typefaces for Mergenthaler Linotype. Among them are his well-known script designs Snell Roundhand (see p. 614) and Bell Centennial (see p. 217), the revolutionary design commissioned by the US Bell Telephone Company for its telephone directories to mark the company's centenary. In 1971, he moved back to England, where he continued to work for Mergenthaler Linotype. Later for the International Typeface Corporation he created among others, the serif ITC Galliard as a tribute to 16th-century master letter-cutter Robert Granjon, and ITC Charter.

In 1981, Carter and Mike Parker, a former director of Mergenthaler Linotype, co-founded Bitstream, a digital type design studio, in Marlborough, Massachusetts. A highly successful and well-timed venture, Bitstream developed a library of digital type where anyone could license a font. As the advancement of desktop publishing and personal computer use became widespread, so did the distribution of their typefaces.

In 1991, Carter left Bitstream and a year later he founded the Carter & Cone Type foundry with Cherie Cone. Clients included *Time, Newsweek, Wired* and *The New York Times*. There he began his work for Microsoft by creating a series of screen fonts such as Verdana and Georgia, recognized as two of the most successful designs created for monitor use thanks to their remarkable legibility even at small sizes. Carter has won numerous accolades: the British Royal Society of Arts made him a Royal Designer for Industry in 1981, the Type Directors Club gave him the TDC Medal in 1997 and in 2011 he received the Lifetime Achievement Award at the Cooper-Hewitt National Design Awards. Carter is one of the craftspeople who has experienced the transitions from physical type to photosetting to digital type creation, and his career has transcended the technological advances of type development and printing.

Date: 1937–
Nationality: British
Notable typefaces:
ITC Galliard (see p.127)
Verdana (see p. 303)
Bell Centennial (see p. 217)
Snell Roundhand (see p. 614)

Below. Carter's Verdana typeface was adopted in 2009 by Swedish furniture giant IKEA for all print and media use, creating a wave of controversy over the decision to change from Futura.

Opposite top. Carter's Georgia typeface showing the bitmapping (hinting) process at work (left); Bell Centennial for the Bell Telephone Company used in directories across the USA (right).

Opposite middle and far right. MoMa Gothic, house font to the Museum of Modern Art, New York.

Opposite bottom left. Matthew Carter's contribution to the field of type design is inestimable.

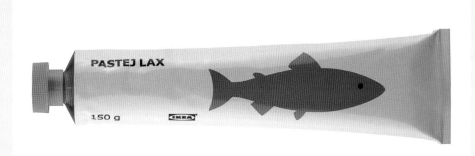

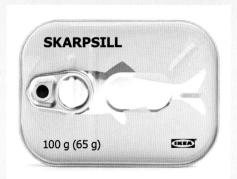

Bell Centennial
Name & Number

ABCDEFGHIJK
LMNOPQRSTU
VWXYZ&1234
567890abncdef
ghijklmnopqrst
uvwxyz.-,:;$?!

Commissioned by AT&T and released in 1978.

MoMA

NEW
PHOTOGRAPHY
2012

MICHELE ABELES, BIRDHEAD,
ANNE COLLIER, ZOE CROSHER,
SHIRANA SHAHBAZI

Bazar

ABCDEFGHIJKLMNOPQRSTUVWXYZ
abcdefghijklmnopqrstuvwxyz
1234567890 !@#?:;"*&

Foundry: Stempel
Designer: Imre Reiner
Designer Nationality: Hungarian
Date: 1956

Hungarian emigré Imre Reiner designed this 1950s painterly and very expressive script typeface. Bazar was digitized later by German designer Klaus Sutter. It was then revived in 2005 by Patrick Griffin for Toronto-based Canada Type, and released under the name 'Boondock'.

Bradley Texting

ABCDEFGHIJKLMNOPQRSTUVWXYZ
abcdefghijklmnopqrstuvwxyz
1234567890 !@#?:;"*&

Foundry: Monotype
Designer: Richard Bradley
Designer Nationality: British
Date: 2016

Richard Bradley designed Bradley Texting in the same vein as his previous fonts Bradley Hand (1995) and Bradley Type (2010). Its open counters and a large x-height make this friendly, marker-pen font very legible, particularly when used at small sizes, and on screens and devices.

Bradley Type

ABCDEFGHIJKLMNOPQRSTUVWXYZ
abcdefghijklmnopqrstuvwxyz
1234567890 !@#?:;"*&

Foundry: Monotype
Designer: Richard Bradley
Designer Nationality: British
Date: 2010

Bradley Type is designed to be used as a complement or counterpart to Richard Bradley's casual handwriting font Bradley Hand (1995). Bradley Type is more refined and slightly more condensed, making it better suited to text usage. It is available in three weights.

Bruno JB

ABCDEFGHIJKLMNOPQRSTUVWXYZ
abcdefghijklmnopqrstuvwxyz
1234567890 !@#?:;"*&

Foundry: Adobe
Designer: Jill Bell
Designer Nationality: American
Date: 1999

Los Angeles-based lettering artist Jill Bell named Bruno after the biggest of her three cats. She was inspired by a note that she had written to remind herself to buy cat food. It is an informal handwriting script with an unusual lowercase 'a', which is available in Regular and Bold weights.

Cariola Script

ABCDEFGHIJKLMNOPQRSTUVWXYZ
abcdefghijklmnopqrstuvwxyz
1234567890 !@#?:;"*&

Foundry: Image Club Graphics
Designer: James West
Designer Nationality: American
Date: 1882 / 1993

This is one of a number of revivals of Carpenter Script, designed by Scottish-American punch-cutter and type designer James West and originally published by Cleveland Type Foundry in 1882. Cariola Script has the same elegant swashes and fine detailing as the original.

Cavolini

ABCDEFGHIJKLMNOPQRSTUVWXYZ
abcdefghijklmnopqrstuvwxyz
1234567890 !@#?:;"*&

Foundry: Monotype
Designer: Carl Crossgrove
Designer Nationality: American
Date: 2017

This casual handwriting font (not dissimilar to Comic Sans) has been developed for use on small screens. Cavolini is available in roman, bold and italic in regular and condensed, its large x-height, clearly defined apertures and open character spacing make it very legible at small sizes.

Chauncy

ABCDEFGHIJKLMNOPQRSTUVWXYZ
abcdefghijklmnopqrstuvwxyz
1234567890 !@#?:;"*&

Foundry: Chank Co.
Designer: Chank Diesel
Designer Nationality: American
Date: 1996

Chank Diesel's Chauncy is available in two weights: Deluxxe is the medium and Fatty is the bold. It is a playful font based on the left-handed penmanship of an artist to resemble children's handwriting. Chauncy Pro was released in 2012, in two weights plus matching italics.

Comic Sans

ABCDEFGHIJKLMNOPQRSTUVWXYZ
abcdefghijklmnopqrstuvwxyz
1234567890 !@#?:;"*&

Foundry: Microsoft
Designer: Vincent Connare
Designer Nationality: American
Date: 1994

An informal comic-book script, Comic Sans has been supplied with Microsoft Windows since the introduction of Windows 95. It is perhaps the most-talked-about typeface ever, its widespread use – often in situations for which it was not intended – having made it the subject of discussion.

Dom

ABCDEFGHIJKLMNOPQRSTUVWXYZ
abcdefghijklmnopqrstuvwxyz
1234567890 !@#?:;"*&

Foundry: American Type Founders
Designer: Peter Dombrezian
Designer Nationality: American
Date: 1951

Peter Dombrezian's approachable type family is comprised of three styles: the upright Dom Casual and slanted Dom Diagonal, plus Dom Bold.

The fonts were a popular choice for TV-show titles during the mid 20th century, appearing everywhere from *Looney Tunes* to *Sesame Street*.

Enviro

ABCDEFGHIJKLMNOPQRSTUVVXYZ
abcdefghijklmnopqrstuvwxyz
1234567890 !@#?.:"*&

Foundry: Letraset
Designer: F. Scott Garland
Designer Nationality: American
Date: 1982

Enviro is a sans serif display font similar to the Tekton family released in 1989, with fine strokes, rounded terminals and an architectural feel, but it is slightly more geometric in structure. Certain letterforms are unusual in their construction; the uppercase 'S' and 'W' are particularly distinctive.

Escript

ABCDEFGHIƷKLMNOPQRSTUVWXYZ
abcdefghijklmnopqrstuvwxyz
1234567890 !@#?:;"*&

Foundry: Linotype
Designer: Hans-Jürgen Ellenberger
Designer Nationality: German
Date: 1994

This handwriting-inspired font was designed by Hans-Jürgen Ellenberger and was a winner in Linotype's International Digital Type Design Contest 2003; it was included in the TakeType 4 Collection of typefaces the following year as a result. Escript is best suited to informal display use.

FF Erikrighthand

ABCDEFGHIJKLMNOPQRSTUVWXYZ
abcdefghijklmnopqrstuvwxyz
1234567890 !@)#?.;"*&

Foundry: FontFont
Designer: Erik van Blokland
Designer Nationality: Dutch
Date: 1990

FF Erikrighthand was developed by Dutch type designer Erik van Blokland in 1990. Working with Just van Rossum, he created the typeface from examples of his own handwriting, pioneering a new, naturalistic style of font made possible by developments in type-design technology.

FF Providence

ABCDEFGHIJKLMNOPQRSTUVWXYZ
abcdefghijklmnopqrstuvwxyz
1234567890 !@#?:;"*&

FF Providence was first designed in 1987 for use within a comic, with its serif and sans serif styles being used for narrative and dialogue respectively.

The typeface was expanded by designer Guy Jeffrey Nelson for release by FontFont in 1994, creating a family of four styles.

Foundry: FontFont
Designer: Panos (Panagiotis) Haratzopoulos / Guy Jeffrey Nelson
Designer Nationality: Greek / American
Date: 1987 / 1994

Fine Hand

ABCDEFGHIJKLMNOPQRSTUVWXYZ
abcdefghijklmnopqrstuvwxyz
1234567890 !@#?:;"*&

British calligrapher and lettering artist Richard Bradley designed Fine Hand based on his own handwriting. It includes a range of alternate characters, which provide scope for a varied approach to typesetting. First published by Letraset, the font has since been digitized.

Foundry: Letraset
Designer: Richard Bradley
Designer Nationality: British
Date: 1987

Fineprint

ABCDEFGHIJKLMNOPQRSTUVWXYZ
abcdefghijklmnopqrstuvwxyz
1234567890 !@#?:;"*&

Fineprint includes a number of swash characters and alternates, reflecting the irregularity of designer Steve Matteson's handwriting, on which it is based.

The axis on which its letterforms are set varies slightly throughout. It is included in the Monotype Library OpenType Edition.

Foundry: Monotype
Designer: Steve Matteson
Designer Nationality: American
Date: 1999

Flight

ABCDEFGHIJKLMNOPQRSTUVWXYZ
abcdefghijklmnopqrstuvwxyz
1234567890 !@#?:;"*&

Tim Donaldson designed Flight for Letraset and it was published in the mid 1990s, when new type design technology enabled the design of fonts that mimicked the irregularity of informal handwriting. Its stroke junctions are thickened throughout, giving the appearance of pooling ink.

Foundry: Letraset
Designer: Timothy Donaldson
Designer Nationality: British
Date: 1995

Ford's Folly

ABCDEFGHIJKLMNOPQRSTUVWXYZ
abcdefghijklmnopqrstuvwxyz
1234567890 !@#?:;"'*&

Foundry: Ascender
Designer: Jim Ford
Designer Nationality: American
Date: 2009

Based on forms written in Sharpie marker by designer Jim Ford, Ford's Folly is an amiable handwriting font available in two weights with corresponding italics. Ford developed an extensive character set for the typeface, which includes Latin, Greek and Cyrillic alphabets.

FS Sammy

ABCDEFGHIJKLMNOPQRSTUVWXYZ
abcdefghijklmnopqrstuvwxyz
1234567890 !@#?:;"'*&

Foundry: Fontsmith
Designer: Phil Garnham / Satwinder Sehmi
Designer Nationality: British / Kenyan
Date: 2009

A hand-drawn script with a chalky texture, FS Sammy was originally drawn for a drinks manufacturer. It was made by creating handwritten impressions on textured watercolour paper with a soft pencil, with the aim of having the breezy, spontaneous air of real handwriting.

Full Moon BT

ABCDEFGHIJKLMNOPQRSTUVWXYZ
abcdefghijklmnopqrstuvwxyz
1234567890 !@#?:;"'*&

Foundry: Bitstream
Designer: Mary Trafton / Charles Gibbons
Designer Nationality: American
Date: 2001

This casual script is a collaboration based on lettering by illustrator Mary Trafton and designer Charles Gibbons. Its weights are named after folk names for the Moon. The family members include Falling Leaves and Black Cherry. It won the Type Directors Club Type Design Competition in 2003.

GFY Kersti

ABCDEFGHIJKLMNOPQRSTUVWXYZ
abcdεfghijklmnopqrstuvwxyz
1234567890 !@#?:;"'*3

Foundry: Chank Co.
Designer: Chank Diesel
Designer Nationality: American
Date: 2002

GFY Kersti is part of Chank Co. foundry's GFY (Go Font Yourself) Handwriting Fontpak, which is a collection of twenty-one handwritten alphabets digitized by Chank Diesel. It falls into the 'unusual and quirky' category along with GFY Aunt Susan, GFY Kimberly and GFY Michael.

GFY Loopy

ABCDEFGHIJKLMNOPQRSTUVWXYZ
abcdefghijklmnopqrstuvwxyz
1234567890 !@#?;"*&

Foundry: Chank Co.
Designer: Chank Diesel
Designer Nationality: American
Date: 2002

Forming part of Chank Co. foundry's GFY (Go Font Yourself) Handwriting Fontpak, a collection of twenty-one handwritten alphabets drawn by real people and digitized by Chank Diesel, GFY Loopy falls into the 'girly bubble letters' category.

GFY Marcie

ABCDEFGHIJKLMNOPQRSTUVWXYZ
abcdefghijklmnopqrstuvwxyz
1234567890 !@#?;"*&

Foundry: Chank Co.
Designer: Chank Diesel
Designer Nationality: American
Date: 2002

Falling in to the 'mature woman's penmanship' category in Chank Co. foundry's irreverent collection of handwritten typefaces, GFY Marcie has a more connected appearance in its lowercase with a looser irregular structure to the capital letterforms, and little consistency in the bowls and counters.

GFY Palmer

ABCDEFGHIJKLMNOPQRSTUVWXYZ
abcdefghijklmnopqrstuvwxyz
1234567890 !@#?;"*&

Foundry: Chank Co.
Designer: Chank Diesel
Designer Nationality: American
Date: 2002

The GFY Palmer font is one of twenty-one handwritten alphabets that make up the GFY (Go Font Yourself) Handwriting Fontpak from the Chank Co. foundry digitized by Chank Diesel. It is part of the 'loose casual' category alongside GFY Brutus, GFY Hey Steve and GFY Josie.

Gillies Gothic

ABCDEFGHIJKLMNOPQRSTUVWXYZ
abcdefghijklmnopqrstuvwxyz
1234567890 !@#?;"*&

Foundry: Bauer
Designer: William S. Gillies
Designer Nationality: American
Date: 1935

William S. Gillies created Gillies Gothic in 1935 for Bauer. It is known as Flott in Germany, Bolide in France and Vigor in Spain. It comes in four weights: Light, Bold, Extra Bold and Extra Bold Shaded. Freda Sack designed the Extra Bold for Letraset in 1980, and Phillip Kelly the Extra Bold Shaded in 1982.

Indy Italic

ABCDEFGHIJKLMNOPQRSTUVWXYZ
abcdefghijklmnopqrstuvwxyz
1234567890 !@#?:;"*&

Foundry: Letraset
Designer: Charles E. Hughes
Designer Nationality: American
Date: 1990

Indy Italic is a stylized lightweight script, whose lowercase letters are linked to imitate handwriting. Lettering designer Charles E. Hughes also designed Century Nova for American Type Founders in 1966, a variation on Century Expanded (1900), one of the last metal typefaces.

ITC Arnova

ABCDEFGHIJKLMNOPQRSTUVWXYZ
abcdefghijklmnopqrstuvwxyz
1234567890 !@#?:;"*&

Foundry: ITC
Designer: Genevieve Cerasoli
Designer Nationality: American
Date: 1997

ITC Arnova is a calligraphic script with pronounced stroke contrast and rough contours. The script is inspired by the distinctive brush style of Japanese sign-painting. Its characters have pointed strokes and lean both towards and away from one another, giving the typeface a dynamic and energetic feel.

ITC Ballerino

ABCDEFGHIJKLMNOPQRSTUVWXYZ
abcdefghijklmnopqrstuvwxyz
1234567890 !@#?:;"*&

Foundry: ITC
Designer: Viktor Solt-Bittner
Designer Nationality: Austrian
Date: 1990

Although inspired by various 18th-century calligraphic styles, Ballerino is not based on any specific typeface. The rough texture of its edges combines with its lowercase swash ascenders and descenders to give it a distinct handwritten feel. The swash caps should be used with the lowercase characters only.

ITC Berranger Hand

ABCDEFGHIJKLMNOPQRSTUVWXYZ
abcdefghijklmnopqrstuvwxyz
1234567890 !@#?:;"*&

Foundry: ITC
Designer: Éric de Berranger
Designer Nationality: French
Date: 1999

Although it has roots in chancery calligraphy, Berranger Hand resembles contemporary handwriting, written quickly with a felt-tip pen on absorbent paper. Some of the lowercase counters are narrow or filled in completely, and the uppercase letters are made without swashes, so they can be combined.

ITC Blackadder

ABCDEFGHIJKLMNOPQRSTUVWX
abcdefghijklmnopqrstuvwxyz
1234567890 !@#?:;"*&

Foundry: ITC
Designer: Bob Anderton
Designer Nationality: British
Date: 1996

Popular in the late 1990s, this so-called 'vampire' script is based on the signature of the orchestrator of the Gunpowder Plot of 1605, Guy Fawkes, after he had been tortured. Bob Anderton captures the scrolls and curlicues of his 16th-century handwriting, and added the sinister tremble.

ITC Coconino

ABCDEFGHIJKLMNOPQRSTUVWXYZ
abcdefghijklmnopqrstuvwxyz
1234567890 !@#?:;"*&

Foundry: ITC
Designer: Slobodan Miladinov
Designer Nationality: Serbian
Date: 1998

Serbian font designer Slobodan Miladinov created ITC Coconino using a freemouse technique, inspired by the 'surprising and confusing' music of Serbian hip-hop artist Voodoo Popeye. It is an unconventional script with strokes that have a deliberate irregularity and rather chaotic feel.

ITC Coolman

ABCDEFGHIJKLMNOPQRSTUVWXYZ
abcdefghijklmnopqrstuvwxyz
1234567890 !@#?:;"*&

Foundry: ITC
Designer: Per Ellstrøm
Designer Nationality: Swedish
Date: 1999

This quirky, informal font is the work of the Swedish font designer Per Ellstrøm, an accomplished musician as well as a typographer, who goes by the stage name of Pelle Piano. It is inspired by lettering styles of the 1950s found on B-movie posters, pocketbooks and cartoons.

ITC Cyberkugel

ABCDEFGHIJKLMNOPQRSTUVWXYZ
abcdefghijklmnopqrstuvwxyz
1234567890 !@#?:;"*&

Foundry: ITC
Designer: Timothy Donaldson
Designer Nationality: British
Date: 1997

Although it looks very organic and takes inspiration from his love of writing with an extra-fine ballpoint pen, ITC Cyberkugel was created by Timothy Donaldson entirely digitally, using a Wacom tablet. The name originates from a combination of cyberspace and *Kugelschreiber*, the German word for 'ballpoint pen'.

ITC Dartangnon

ABCDEFGHIJKLMNOPQRSTUVWXYZ
abcdefghijklmnopqrstuvwxyz
1234567890 !@#?.;"*&

Foundry: ITC
Designer: Nick Cooke
Designer Nationality: British
Date: 1998

Nick Cooke started his design for ITC Dartangnon by doodling using a chunky pencil. The resulting typeface is a spontaneous and swashbuckling script that retains many of the quirks and idiosyncrasies present in handwriting. The energetic script is surprisingly legible even at small point sizes.

ITC Django

ABCDEFGHIJKLMNOPQRSTUVWXYZ
abcdefghijklmnopqrstuvwxyz
1234567890 !@#?.;"*&

Foundry: ITC
Designer: Wayne Thompson
Designer Nationality: Australian
Date: 2000

Wayne Thompson based ITC Django on the handwriting of an acquaintance who called himself Django, after jazz guitarist Django Reinhardt. Thompson said the lively script has a split personality, with the looseness of the lowercase contrasting with the edginess of the uppercase characters.

ITC Humana Script

ABCDEFGHIJKLMNOPQRSTUVWXYZ
abcdefghijklmnopqrstuvwxyz
1234567890 !@#?.;"*&

Foundry: ITC
Designer: Timothy Donaldson
Designer Nationality: British
Date: 1995

British typographer Timothy Donaldson designed Humana Script for ITC in 1995. It was digitized from lettering first drawn on paper with a broad-tipped pen. It comes in Light, Medium and Bold weights, and is part of the ITC Humana family that also contains sans serif and serif typefaces.

ITC Kloegirl

ABCDEFGHIJKLMNOPQRSTUVWXYZ
abcdefghijklmnopqrstuvwxyz
1234567890 !@#?.;"*&

Foundry: ITC
Designer: Scott Carslake
Designer Nationality: Australian
Date: 2006

Australian fashion designer Chloé Papazahariakis commissioned Scott Carslake, co-founder of Australian agency Voice Design, to create an identity for her brand. He created ITC Kloegirl inspired by her handwriting. It comes in two versions: Lotus and New York.

ITC Kulukundis

ABCDEFGHIJKLMNOPQRSTUVWX
abcdefghijklmnopqrstuvwxyz
1234567890 !@#?:;"*&

Foundry: ITC
Designer: Daniel Pelavin
Designer Nationality: American
Date: 1997

US designer Daniel Pelavin's ITC Kulukundis is a single-weight connecting script whose lowercase letters all connect in the same way via a diagonal join creating a continuous line. It was inspired by French upright scripts and the chrome lettering found on old cars.

ITC Mattia

ABCDEFGHIJKLMNOPQRSTUVWXYZ
abcdefghijklmnopqrstuvwxyz
1234567890 !@#?:;"*&

Foundry: ITC
Designer: Giuseppe Errico
Designer Nationality: Italian
Date: 2007

Giuseppe Errico's Mattia, released by ITC in 2007, is a distinctive, informal handwriting font that is somewhat scrawled but highly legible. Its lack of a consistent baseline gives the feel of real handwriting. Errico, who was born in Italy, has designed three typefaces for ITC.

ITC Musclehead

ABCDEFGHIJKLMNOPQRSTUVWXYZ
abcdefghijklmnopqrstuvwxyz
1234567890 !@#?:;"*&

Foundry: ITC
Designer: Timothy Donaldson
Designer Nationality: British
Date: 1997

British type designer, calligrapher and author Timothy Donaldson designed the single-weight, heavy handwriting font ITC Musclehead in 1997. It was drawn using a ruling pen because Donaldson wanted to show that this tool could be used on something robust rather than skinny.

ITC Out Of The Fridge

ABCDEFGHIJKLMNOPQRSTUVWXYZ
abcdefghijklmnopqrstuvwxyz
1234567890 !@#?:;"*&

Foundry: ITC
Designer: Jochen Schuss
Designer Nationality: German
Date: 1996

Jochen Schuss drew ITC Out Of The Fridge in 1996. It is a single-weight, imperfect sans serif script with a scratchy feel and slight drips visible in places, most notably inside the capital 'O'. Schuss, who was born in Marburg, Germany, has released with ITC, Linotype and Typic.

ITC Samuel

ABCDEFGHIJKLMNOPQRSTUVWXYZ
abcdefghijklmnopqrstuvwxyz
1234567890 !@#?:;"*&

Foundry: ITC
Designer: Phill Grimshaw
Designer Nationality: British
Date: 1998

Phill Grimshaw entered type design thanks to Tony Forster, his teacher at Bolton College of Art. When Grimshaw died in 1998, he had released forty-four typefaces through Letraset and ITC, including ITC Samuel, which was one of his last. It is a light, delicate brush script in one weight.

ITC Santangeli

ABCDEFGHIJKLMNOPQRSTUVWXYZ
abcdefghijklmnopqrstuvwxyz
1234567890 !@#?:;"*&

Foundry: ITC
Designer: Guiseppe Errico
Designer Nationality: Italian
Date: 2007

Guiseppe Errico based this face on 18th-century manuscripts written by the Italian calligraphy master Benedetto Santangeli. ITC Santangeli is a baroque, decorative script font in a single weight. It features long, curvaceous ascenders and descenders and many alternate characters.

ITC Studio Script

ABCDEFGHIJKLMNOPQRSTUVWXYZ
abcdefghijklmnopqrstuvwxyz
1234567890 !@#?:;"*&

Foundry: ITC
Designer: Robert Evans
Designer Nationality: British
Date: 1991

A retro, friendly monoline script face, ITC Studio Script was developed by British type designer Robert Evans in 1991. It was initially released by ITC, and there is also a version by the foundry Elsner+Flake. It comes in one weight and features a wide range of extra alternate characters.

ITC Viner Hand

ABCDEFGHIJKLMNOPQRSTUVWXYZ
abcdefghijklmnopqrstuvwxyz
1234567890 !@#?:;"*&

Foundry: ITC
Designer: John Viner
Designer Nationality: British
Date: 1995

This eponymous typeface by British designer John Viner is, as the name suggests, based on his own handwriting. Viner worked as a font designer for Letraset but also released fonts with ITC, such as Viner Hand, which is a single-weight, informal script that adds a personal touch to any application.

ITC Zemke Hand

ABCDEFGHIJKLMNOPQRSTUVWXYZ
abcdefghijklmnopqrstuvwxyz
1234567890 !@#?:;"*&

Foundry: ITC
Designer: Deborah Zemke
Designer Nationality: American
Date: 1997

US illustrator Deborah Zemke designed Zemke Hand in 1997. The monoline handwriting font is friendly and highly legible. Zemke is primarily an author and illustrator of children's books. However, she has developed two other fonts for ITC, both of which are cartoon dingbats.

John Handy

ABCDEFGHIJKLMNOPQRSTUVWXYZ
abcdefghijklmnopqrstuvwxyz
1234567890 !?:;"*&

Foundry: Letraset
Designer: Timothy Donaldson
Designer Nationality: British
Date: 1995

British designer Timothy Donaldson created John Handy for Letraset in 1995. It is an informal, slightly rough but elegant script based on the designer's own handwriting. It is an apt choice for letters, greeting cards and menus. Donaldson started a foundry called Shapes for Cash in 2018.

JP2

ABCDEFGHIJKLMNOPQRSTUVWXYZ
abcdefghijklmnopqrstuvwxyz
1234567890 !@#?:;"*&

Foundry: ITC
Designer: Franciszek Otto
Designer Nationality: Polish
Date: 2008

JP2 by Polish designer Franciszek Otto takes its name from a fellow Pole, Pope John Paul II, and Otto based it on the pontiff's handwriting. Available in one weight, JP2 is a lively, realistic script that features an inconsistent baseline, long ascenders and a low x-height.

Jump

ABCDEFGHIJKLMNOPQRSTUVWXYZ
abcdefghijklmnopqrstuvwxyz
1234567890 !@#?:;"*&

Foundry: Linotype
Designer: Sine Bergmann / Lenore Poth
Designer Nationality: German
Date: 2008

Jump by German designers Sine Bergmann and Lenore Poth is a single-weight, light-hearted handwriting typeface initially released by Linotype. It is based on the kind of informal notes written quickly by hand. Jump takes its name from the effect of letters having different baselines.

Katfish

ABCDEFGHIJKLMNOPQRSTUVWXYZ
abcdefghijklmnopqrstuvwxyz
1234567890 !?:;"*&

Foundry: Letraset
Designer: Michael Gills
Designer Nationality: British
Date: 1994

Michael Gills's Katfish is a quirky script that features sharp letters – some of which incorporate a pair of dots – a variety of ligatures, many alternate characters, and three illustrated dingbats of a cat face, a fish and a dolphin. Gills worked at Letraset from 1988 to 1995.

Kloi BT

ABCDEFGHIJKLMNOPQRSTUVWXYZ
abcdefghijklmnopqrstuvwxyz
1234567890 !@#?:;"*&

Foundry: Bitstream
Designer: Boris Mahovac
Designer Nationality: Croatian
Date: 2004

Kloi BT, released by Bitstream in 2004, is the work of Boris Mahovac, the founder of Alphabet Design based in Ontario. It is a chunky, friendly and somewhat naive monoline handwriting font. Kloi BT has varied capital sizes and the appearance of writing drawn with a felt-tip pen.

Leon Kinder

ABCDEFGHIJKLMNOPQRSTUVWXYZ
abcdefghijklmnopqrstuvwxyz
1234567890 !@#?:;"*&

Foundry: Dmitry Rastvortsev
Designer: Dmitry Rastvortsev / Lev Rastvortsev
Designer Nationality: Ukrainian
Date: 2014

Leon Kinder is a friendly, childlike handwriting font. It was designed by Ukrainian typographer and designer Dmitry Rastvortsev (with assistance from his relative Lev) and released by his eponymous foundry in 2014. It is available in a single weight and features many ligatures.

Linotype Cadavre Exquis

ABCDEFGHIJKLMNOPQRSTUVWXYZ
abcdefghijklmnopqrstuvwxyz
1234567890 !?:;"&

Foundry: Linotype
Designer: Wiebke Hoeljes
Designer Nationality: German
Date: 1997

Wiebke Hoeljes's Cadavre Exquis font is included in Linotype's Halloween Value Pack of thirty-three spooky fonts. The font was picked up by Linotype in 1997 when it was an entry in the company's International Digital Type Design Contest. It features spindly letters of different weights and styles.

Linotype Colibri

ABCDEFGHIJKLMNOPQRSTUVWXYZ
abcdefghijklmnopqrstuvwxyz
1234567890 !@#?.;"*&

Foundry: Linotype
Designer: Hans-Jürgen Ellenberger
Designer Nationality: German
Date: 1999

Available in light and regular, Hans-Jürgen Ellenberger's Linotype Colibri is a light-hearted, informal script with an inconsistent baseline and a chunky monoline, which gives the effect of writing done with a thick, felt-tip pen. It has a childlike feel due to its quirks and imperfections.

Linotype Ego

ABCDEFGHIJKLMNOPQRSTUVWXYZ
abcdefghijklmnopqrstuvwxyz
1234567890 !@#?:;"*&

Foundry: Linotype
Designer: Jörn Rings
Designer Nationality: German
Date: 1999

German creative Jörn Rings, who also goes by Jörn Lehnhoff, designed Linotype Ego in 1999. It is a sharp, imperfect handwriting font with contrast, available in a single weight. Rings, who is based in Düsseldorf, founded an agency called Zellteilung and an art gallery.

Linotype Elisa

ABCDEFGHIJKLMNOPQRSTUV
abcdefghijklmnopqrstuv wxyz
1234567890 !@#?."*&

Foundry: Linotype
Designer: Christopher Young
Designer Nationality: New Zealander
Date: 1999

Elisa, designed by the New Zealand-born Christopher Young in 1999, is a delicate, refined handwriting typeface with wide capitals and long ascenders and descenders. It comes in two weights; Regular and Bold. Young moved to Germany in 1996 and then relocated to Perth, Australia in 2002.

Linotype Notec

ABCDEFGHIJKLMNOPQRSTUVWXYZ
abcdefghijklmnopqrstuvwxyz
1234567890 !@#?.;"*&

Foundry: Linotype
Designer: Franciszek Otto
Designer Nationality: Polish
Date: 1999

An attractive, connecting handwriting script, Notec mimics the spontaneity and inconsistent nature of scribbled writing and has a non-uniform stroke width. By Franciszek Otto, Notec came second in the display category of Linotype's 3rd International Digital Type Design Contest in 2000.

Linotype Sallwey Script

ABCDEFGHIJKLMNOPQRSTUVWXYZ
abcdefghijklmnopqrstuvwxyz
1234567890 !@#?:;"*&

Foundry: Linotype
Designer: Friedrich Karl Sallwey
Designer Nationality: German
Date: 1980

Linotype released German designer Friedrich Karl Sallwey's eponymous script in 1980; it is a distinctive, slightly inclined non-connecting script in a single weight with diamond-shaped tittles. Sallwey began his career as an assistant to Heinrich Jost, art director of the Bauer type foundry.

Linotype Tapeside

ABCDEFGHIJKLMNOPQRSTUVWXYZ
abcdefghijklmnopqrstuvwxyz
1234567890 !@#?:;"*&

Foundry: Linotype
Designer: Stephan B. Murphy
Designer Nationality: British
Date: 1997

Tapeside, which was selected by Linotype at its International Digital Type Design Contest in 1997, is a childlike sans serif with inconsistent stroke widths. Available in Light, Regular and Bold weights, all of which have obliques, it is the only typeface Stephan B. Murphy has released.

Liorah BT

ABCDEFGHIJKLMNOPQRST
abcdefghijklmnopqrstuvwxyz
1234567890 !@#?:;"*&

Foundry: Bitstream
Designer: Holly Goldsmith
Designer Nationality: American
Date: 2000

A wide and curly connecting script, Liorah was released by Bitstream in 2000. This elegant typeface by Holly Goldsmith is slightly oblique and comes in a single regular weight. Goldsmith worked for Mergenthaler Linotype and Xerox before starting her studio called Small Cap Graphics.

Malibu

ABCDEFGHIJKLMNOPQRSTUVWXYZ
abcdefghijklmnopqrstuvwxyz
1234567890 !?:;"*&

Foundry: ITC
Designer: Alan Meeks
Designer Nationality: British
Date: 1992

Alan Meeks's Malibu, named after the famous beach city just outside Los Angeles, California, is a chunky, inclined non-connecting script. The typeface has an energetic, angular feel and manages to evoke the atmosphere of the beach with which it shares its name.

Manu

ABCDEFGHIJKLMNOPQRSTUVWXYZ
abcdefghijklmnopqrstuvwxyz
1234567890 !@#?:; "*&

Foundry: Typotheque
Designer: Peter Biľak
Designer Nationality: Slovakian
Date: 2016

Manu is based on Peter Biľak's handwriting. It is available in four styles: a hand-drawn sans, Formal; a connecting script, Informal; a bold, handwritten uppercase, Emphasis; and a dingbat font, Symbol. Formal and Informal were drawn with a 0.7 mm pen and Emphasis with a chunky marker.

Markerfield

ABCDEFGHIJKLMNOPQRSTUVWXYZ
abcdefghijklmnopqrstuvwxyz
1234567890 !@#?:; "*&

Foundry: Typodermic
Designer: Ray Larabie
Designer Nationality: Canadian
Date: 2010

Ray Larabie's Markerfield, released by Typodermic in 2010, is a single-weight handwritten script that achieves the texture and thickness of lettering drawn with a heavy, black marker pen. Larabie included many ligature options, which help produce a more realistic handwriting feel.

Matthia

ABCDEFGHIJKLMNOPQRSTUVWXYZ
abcdefghijklmnopqrstuvwxyz
1234567890 !@#?:; "*&

Foundry: Linotype
Designer: Dieter Kurz
Designer Nationality: German
Date: 1994

German designer Dieter Kurz's Matthia is a reasonably compact brush script inspired by lettering used in advertising in the 1950s. Linotype inducted it into its TakeType Library when it was a category winner in the company's first International Digital Type Design Contest in 1994.

Missy BT

ABCDEFGHIJKLMNOPQRSTUVWXYZ
abcdefghijklmnopqrstuvwxyz
1234567890 !@#?:; "*&

Foundry: Bitstream
Designer: Holly Goldsmith
Designer Nationality: American
Date: 2000

Holly Goldsmith designed Missy for Bitstream in 2000. It is a single-style, informal handwritten sans serif, which has a naive, childlike energy. Its vertical strokes all begin below the baseline. Missy is one of six fonts Goldsmith released with Bitstream between 2000 and 2001.

Mistral

ABCDEFGHIJKLMNOPQRSTUVWXYZ
abcdefghijklmnopqrstuvwxyz
1234567890 !@#?:;"*&

Foundry: Fonderie Olive
Designer: Roger Excoffon
Designer Nationality: French
Date: 1957

Mistral, one of the world's most popular script typefaces, was designed for the French Fonderie Olive in 1957. A loose joined-up script, Mistral is based on Roger Excoffon's handwriting and has the texture of brush or felt-tip pen lettering. It comes in Light and Regular weights.

Nevison Casual

ABCDEFGHIJKLMNOPQRSTUVWXYZ
abcdefghijklmnopqrstuvwxyz
1234567890 !@#?:;"*&

Foundry: VGC
Designer: Thomas J. Nevison
Designer Nationality: American
Date: 1965

Nevison Casual, designed for the Visual Graphics Corporation (VGC), is a script in the style of informal handwriting. The uppercase characters are typically open and bountiful, while the lowercases are narrower and more reserved, giving the font a dynamic contrast when set in text.

One Stroke Script

ABCDEFGHIJKLMNOPQRSTUVWXYZ
abcdefghijklmnopqrstuvwxyz
1234567890 !@#?:;"*&

Foundry: ITC
Designer: Paul Clarke
Designer Nationality: British
Date: 1991

One Stroke Script is a casual script in which the letterforms imitate the broad strokes of a brush. The font family, which includes Regular, Bold and Shaded styles, resists a formal structure and instead favours the loose curves often associated with hand-lettering.

Papyrus

ABCDEFGHIJKLMNOPQRSTUVWXYZ
abcdefghijklmnopqrstuvwxyz
1234567890 !@#?:;"*&

Foundry: Letraset
Designer: Chris Costello
Designer Nationality: American
Date: 1983

Papyrus was drawn over six months, using a calligraphy pen on textured paper. It is a script designed to imitate the appearance of ancient handwriting. The distinctive characters feature rough outlines, tall ascenders, and a combination of roman and calligraphic styles.

PL Trophy

ABCDEFGHIJKLMNOPQRSTUVWXYZ
abcdefghijklmnopqrstuvwxyz
1234567890 !© #?:; "*&

Foundry: Monotype
Designer: Frank Bartuska
Designer Nationality: American
Date: 1950

PL Trophy is Monotype's digital revival of Frank Bartuska's Trophy Oblique, a script designed in 1950 for the Photo-Lettering foundry. Unlike most scripts, which reference calligraphic forms, these handwritten characters are informal in shape and low in stroke contrast.

Rage Italic

ABCDEFGHIJKLMNOPQRSTUVWXYZ
abcdefghijklmnopqrstuvwxyz
1234567890 !@# ?:; "*&

Foundry: ITC
Designer: Ron M. W. Zwingelberg
Designer Nationality: American
Date: 1984

Rage Italic is a handwritten script font, and one of the first designs to purposely feature a rugged outline that imitates the texture of ink on parchment. The cursive letterforms also utilize a low x-height and looping ascenders and descenders for clarity at small sizes.

Ru'ach

ABCDEFGHIJKLMNOPQRSTUVWXYZ
abcdefghijklmnopqrstuvwxyz
1234567890 !?:;"*&

Foundry: ITC
Designer: Timothy Donaldson
Designer Nationality: British
Date: 1990

Ru'ach is a script font designed in the style of handwriting. The letterforms, which are distinctive in their dry brush texture, are the result of Timothy Donaldson's numerous investigations into the effects of using different writing instruments on a variety of surfaces.

Scooter

ABCDEFGHIJKLMNOPQRSTUVW
abcdefghijklmnopqrstuvwxyz
1234567890 !@#?:;"*&

Foundry: Ascender
Designer: Steve Matteson
Designer Nationality: American
Date: 2009

Scooter is a script designed in the style of colloquial handwriting. The font shares its name with a 'bashful but lovable' Labrador Retriever and intends to convey friendliness in objects, such as badges, T-shirts or even a personalized dog's bed, or in communications via cards and memos.

Skippy Sharp

ABCDEFGHIJKLMNOPQRSTUVWXYZ
abcdefghijklmnopqrstuvwxyz
1234567890 !@#?:;"*&

Foundry: Chank Co.
Designer: Skippy McFadden / Chank Diesel
Designer Nationality: American
Date: 1995

Skippy Sharp is a script designed to imitate the appearance of writing by hand with a marker. The characters were initially drawn by Skippy McFadden, who later sent them by fax to designer Chank Diesel, who then adjusted the kerning and filled the gaps in the font's character set.

Staehle Graphia

ABCDEFGHIJKLMNOPQRSTUVWXYZ
abcdefghijklmnopqrstuvwxyz
1234567890 !@#?:;"*&

Foundry: Linotype
Designer: Walter Stähle
Designer Nationality: German
Date: c. 1960

Staehle Graphia is a script face modelled on correspondences produced on private printing presses in the 19th century. The letterforms combine calligraphic flourishes, which are seen primarily in the capitals, with the direct vertical strokes found in the lowercase forms.

Teebrush Paint

ABCDEFGHIJKLMNOPQRSTUVWXYZ
abcdefghijklmnopqrstuvwxyz
1234567890 !@№?:;"*&

Foundry: Linotype
Designer: Tomi Haaparanta
Designer Nationality: Finnish
Date: 2002

Designed to imitate the quirks of hand-painted lettering, Teebrush Paint is a script designed in two versions, Teebrush Paint and Teebrush Paint Alternate. When combined, the two styles, which feature only slight differences in design, mitigate inauthentic character repetition.

Terry Junior

ABCDEFGHIJKLMNOPQRSTUVWXYZ
abcdefghijklmnopqrstuvwxyz
1234567890 !@#?:;''*&

Foundry: Monotype
Designer: Terrance Weinzierl
Designer Nationality: American
Date: 2018

Terry Junior is a handwritten script designed to convey a childish playfulness. Initially, Terrance Weinzierl drew the letterforms as part of a Monotype Font Marathon before expanding them digitally to comprise a family of five fonts, including Deluxe, Inline and Rotalic versions.

Trackpad

ABCDEFGHIJKLMNOPQRSTUVWXYZ
abcdefghijklmnopqrstuvwxyz
1234567890 !?:;"*&

Foundry: ITC
Designer: Timothy Donaldson
Designer Nationality: British
Date: 1995

Trackpad is a handwritten script that combines an informal character with a functional shape. The colloquial letterforms, which feature large x-heights, upright strokes and varying slants, were designed to maintain both readability and personality in the smallest of text sizes.

Wiesbaden Swing

ABCDEFGHIJKLMNOPQRSTUVWXY
abcdefghijklmnopqrstuvwxyz
1234567890 !@#?:;"*&

Foundry: Linotype
Designer: Rosemarie Kloos-Rau
Designer Nationality: German
Date: 1992

Based on the style of the designer's own handwriting, Wiesbaden Swing is an informal script designed in Regular and Bold weights. The letterforms, which remain resolute and legible in either display or text sizes, are complemented by a full set of convivial dingbats.

Wola

ABCDEFGHIJKLMNOPQRSTUVWXYZ
abcdefghijklmnopqrstuvwxyz
1234567890 !@#?:;"*&

Foundry: Monotype
Designer: Franciszek Otto
Designer Nationality: Polish
Date: 2017

Wola is a handwritten script designed for digital and printed headlines. The letterforms integrate the high-contrast stroke style of Bodoni with the vigour of hand-painted figures, which engenders a structured yet informal appearance in both the upper and lowercases.

Yellabelly

ABCDEFGHIJKLMNOPQRSTUVWXYZ
abcdefghijklmnopqrstuvwxyz
1234567890 !@#?:;"*&

Foundry: Chank Co.
Designer: Chank Diesel
Designer Nationality: American
Date: 1998

Chank Diesel's Yellabelly is a handwritten script that simulates the effects of writing cursive left-handed. For right-handed writing, the pen trails across the page; by contrast, a left-handed writer is forced to push the pen, which can result in irregular, stuttering, letterforms.

Index of Typefaces

Index of Designers

Index of Foundries

Picture Credits

3 tl: Bibliothèque. 3 br: Creative Direction and Design: Astrid Stavro, Pablo Martín. 5 tl: Barnbrook / V&A Publishing. 8 tl: Creative Direction and Design: Astrid Stavro, Pablo Martín. 8 bl: Otl Aicher / From the private collection of Alessandro Rinaudo via www.munich72collected.com objects being the exclusive property of the IOC. 15 tl: Walter Nurnberg / SSPL / Getty Images. 15 tr, b: Hank Walker / The LIFE Picture Collection / Getty Images. 16 tl: Apic / Getty Images. 38: Noa Bembibre / Noa Bembibre Oy / www.noabembibre.com. 39: Johnny Brito / Vertentes Coletivo. 44 bl: Ward / Fox Photos / Getty Images. 44 bc: Neil Spence / Alamy. 44 br: Jock Kinneir Library and Stanley Gibbons Archive. 45 t: Kieran McGlone. 45 bl: Copyright © the Design Museum. 45 br: Micha Klootwijk / Dreamstime.com. 51: Cartlidge Levene / Marcus Ginns Photography. 52 l: Magus Tamm / www.tammtamm.net. 52 r: Mikhail Rul. 54 b: Big Fish Design / Dorset Cereals. 55: Penrodas Collection / Arista Records. 58: Design: Paula Scher / Pentagram; Photo: Peter Mauss / Esto. 61: Barnbrook / V&A Publishing. 62 bl: Private Collection / John Aster. 62 br: Courtesy of the Herb Lubalin Study Center. 63: Courtesy of the Herb Lubalin Study Center. 77: Schmidt / Thurner / von Keisenberg for Weingut Zähringer. 94: Blok Design. 96 cl: TRÜF / trufcreative.com. 96 bl: TRÜF / trufcreative.com. 96 br: The Martin Agency. 110: AF Fotografie / Bridgeman Images. 135: Timothy Dundas. 136 b: BFA / Warner Bros / Alamy. 164-165: Courtesy of the Herb Lubalin Study Center. 170: David Correll / Sacred Bones Design. 175: Penrodas Collection / Penguin Books. 178 br: Zürcher Hochschule der Künste / Museum für Gestaltung Zürich / Grafiksammlung. 180: The Times / News Licensing. 181: Photo by Nick Sherman. 184: BFA / Swiss Dots / Alamy. 189 br: Wim Wiskerke / Alamy. 189 crb: Hemis / Alamy. 189 br: Kim Kaminski / Alamy. 194 bl: AF Fotografie / Bridgeman Images. 194 br: Mike Ashworth Collection.

181 tr, cl, br: Cartlidge Levene and Studio Myerscough / Photography: Richard Learoyd. 185 br: Uber Bilder / Shepard Fairey / Alamy. 202 bl: Photo Roland Smithies / luped.com. 202 br: Courtesy of the Herb Lubalin Study Center. 203 tl: Penrodas Collection / Doyle Dane Bernbach / Audi AG. 198: Design: Shepard Fairey / Uber Bilder / Alamy218 br: BFA / Fox Searchlight Pictures / Alamy. 220 tr: BFA / Alamode Film / Alamy. 230 bl: Experimental Jetset. 230 br: Estudio Husmee. 238: NeoCon: Client: TheMart; Creative director: Giona Maiarelli; Designer: Fionn Breen; Copywriter: Rob Bywater. 239 tl, tr: Stereo Associates. 239 cl, cr, bl, br: Morphoria. 241 l: Jon Buelow / Westminster. 241 c: Reid Miles / Blue Note. 241 r: Ola Lager and Rune Söderqvist / Polar Music AB. 246 br: Amnesty international. 249: From the private collection of Alessandro Rinaudo via www.munich72collected.com, objects being the exclusive property of the IOC. 255 cl: Royal National Lifeboat Institution (RNLI). 264 br: Erik Spiekermann / PUBLIC bikes. 268: Zürcher Hochschule der Künste / Museum für Gestaltung Zürich / Grafiksammlung. 276 bl: Mike Ashworth Collection. 276 crb: Brian Lawrence / Alamy. 276 br: Typoretum. 284: Bunch / Fogg mobile AB. 290-291: Zürcher Hochschule der Künste / Museum für Gestaltung Zürich / Grafiksammlung. 293: R&G Strategic Communications. 304: Erik Spiekermann / Berliner Verkehrsbetriebe. 305 tl, br: Erik Spiekermann. 305 tr: Johannes Erler. 305 bl: Erik Spiekermann / Nokia. 315 cl: The Fly (1986) dir. David Cronenberg / Twentieth Century Fox. 315 cr: Starship Troopers (1997) dir. Paul Verhoeven / TriStar Pictures. 315 bl: Johnny Mnemonic (1995) dir. Robert Longoi / TriStar Pictures. 315 br: WALL·E (2008) dir. Andrew Stanton / Walt Disney Studios. 415: Dídac Ballester. 416: Lesli Ink Ltd. 435: Baden Powell / MPS Records. 437 c: Bibliothèque. 514 bl: Hearst Magazines. 514 bc: 20th Century Fox. 514 br: Netflix. 515 tl, tr, bl: Courtesy of

the Herb Lubalin Study Center. 515 bc: Greig Cranna. 515 br: Photo-Lettering, Inc. / Courtesy of the Herb Lubalin Study Center. 533: Justin Kase zsixz / Alamy. 540: Zürcher Hochschule der Künste / Museum für Gestaltung Zürich / Grafiksammlung. 541 tl: Paul Huf / MAI. 541 tr: Collection Dutch Graphic Designers Archives Foundation / National Library of the Netherlands. 541 bc, bl: Digital image, The Museum of Modern Art, New York / Scala, Florence. 541 br: Zürcher Hochschule der Künste / Museum für Gestaltung Zürich / Grafiksammlung. 554: Michael Bierut / Pentagram. 574 bl: Rochester Institute of Technology, New York, USA. 575 tl, tr: Rochester Institute of Technology, New York, USA. 575 cl: Boris15 / CanStock Photo. 575 bl: The Art Archive / Shutterstock. 575 br: Photo by Nick Sherman. 616: Inter IKEA Systems B.V.. 617 tl: Microsoft Corporation. 617 tr: Roland Smithies / Matthew Carter / Mergenthaler Linotype. 617 cl: The Museum of Modern Art. 617 bl: Ralph Gibson. 617 br: The Museum of Modern Art, New York / Scala, Florence.

All other images:

2 t: © Commercial Type. 2 bl: © Solo Design, Madrid. 3 br: © Yevgeniy Anfalov. 4: © MuirMcNeil. 5 tr: © Emigre. 5 bl: © Fontsmith. 5 br: © BB-Bureau. 6 t: © Dalton Maag. 6 bl: © Jeremy Tankard. 6 br: © Frere-Jones Type. 7 tl: © Fontsmith. 7 tr: © Typotheque. 7b bl: © Tim Mein Architects. 7 br: © Milieu Grotesque. 8 br: © Atelier Pedro Falcão. 13: © Frere-Jones Type. 16 bl: © Fontsmith. 16 br: © Typotheque. 24: © Emigre. 30–31: © Grilli Type. 38: © Cats Let Nothing Darken their Roar. 39: Vertentes Coletivo © 2018. 67: © Fontsmith. 74: © Typotheque. 81–82: © Frere-Jones Type. 91–92: © Typotheque. 93: © Emigre. 99–100: © Emigre. 107–108: © Emigre. 125–126: © Commercial Type. 143: © Commercial Type. 153–154: © Jeremy Tankard. 163–164: © Jeremy Tankard. 172: © Emigre. 178 © Grade Design. 186–187: © Colophon; 188: © Neutura.

190: © Émigré. 196 tr: © Barbican Centre/North. 196 all other images: © Cartlidge Levene. 198 br: Mika Vainio + Ryoji Ikeda + Alva Noto. 199 tl: © Atavist Magazine. 199 bl: © Como Design/ Joan Sodupe. 199 r: © 2019 J. Walter Thompson, New York. 210–211: © Colophon. 214: © Atelier Pedro Falcão. 215: © Dalton Maag. 218 br: © 2019 Swissted. 217: © Tako Chabukiani/Pragmatika Design. 226: © Fontsmith. 229 bl: © Bisgràfic. 229 br: © Leslie Chan Design Co., Ltd. 231: © Konstantin Eremenko. 232–233: © Monotype. 248: © Konstantin Eremenko. 250: © Thomas Berger, Thomas Hirter, Andrea Stebler. 255 tr: © Jeremy Tankard. 255 bl: © Jeremy Tankard. 255 br: © Jeremy Tankard. 261 l: © Courtesy of Intégral Ruedi Baur Paris and Andreas Körner. 255 r: © Typotheque. 266: © Nick Kapica/SV Associates. 269: © Metapur AG. 272–273: © Fontsmith. 285 t: Grade Design. 285 b: © Patrick Myles. 298–299: © Millieu Grotesque. 307: © Typotheque. 311–312: © Playtype. 322: © MuirMcNeil. 330: © MuirMcNeil. 335–336: © MuirMcNeil. 369: © Fontsmith. 387–388: © BB-Bureau. 407: © Patrick Myles. 408: © MuirMcNeil. 411: © MuirMcNeil. 412–413: © MuirMcNeil. 414: © Dalton Maag. 417: © Neutura. 421: © Neutura. 426: © Patrick Myles. 429: © Typotheque. 435: © MuirMcNeil. 437: © BB-Bureau. 439: © Neutura. 440 l: © Miguel Mesquita. 440 r: © BB-Bureau. 441: © Neutura. 442–443: © MuirMcNeil. 444–445: © MuirMcNeil. 458–459: © Frere-Jones Type. 463 ct, cb, tr, br: © Solo Design, Madrid. 472–473: © Neutura. 480: © Jim Ford / Monotype. 483: © Jeremy Tankard. 486: © Neutura. 498–499: © Or Type. 506: © Or Type / Photography © Max Creasy. 521: © Forgotten Shapes GbR. 526–527: © Forgotten Shapes GbR. 532: © Neutura. 545: © Typodermic. 547: © BB-Bureau. 549: © MuirMcNeil. 560: © Dalton Maag. 587: © Dalton Maag. 594–595: © Dalton Maag.

About the Author

Peter Dawson worked as a designer and then creative director at a number of design studios after studying graphic design at Kingston University. He went on to found Grade Design in 2000, a London-based graphic design studio specializing in typography, editorial and book design, corporate identity and art direction for the art, commercial, charitable and publishing sectors.

He has designed for a diverse and extensive range of clients over the years, including the British Museum, Historic Royal Palaces, The National Museum of Qatar, Rolex, Royal Mail, Thames & Hudson, the V&A and Yale University Press.

Peter has designed a number of best-selling and recognized illustrated book titles, and his awards include British D&AD annual inclusion, several ISTD Certificates of Excellence and a Premiere Award, and, in recent years, 'Best Jacket', 'Best Book Series' and 'Best Trade Illustrated' in the British Book Design and Production Awards.

A Fellow of the ISTD, and a former Chair and board member, he has been a visiting typography and design lecturer at a number of universities in the UK and overseas.

Peter is co-author of the book *Graphic Design Rules* (Frances Lincoln) and author of *The Field Guide to Typography* (Thames & Hudson) and has written articles on design and typography for several industry journals.

www.gradedesign.com

Acknowledgments

Writing and creating a book of this extent and complexity has been without doubt, a team effort and I could not have done it without the contributions, hard work and generosity of many dedicated and skilled individuals and organizations. My deepest gratitude goes to my publisher Philip Cooper of White Lion Press, who commissioned me for such an undertaking. He, together with my managing editor Jennifer Barr, provided valuable guidance and support throughout the challenge of creating the *Type Directory*. Thank you also for the efforts of my editor Carol King, whose dedication and diligence in checking facts when historical references were unclear or contradictory went beyond the norm in helping us make sense of it all.

My thanks also go to my team of contributing writers for the quarter-page typeface profiles: the ever-patient Caroline Roberts, writer, editor and founder of *Grafik* magazine, who headed up the team; freelance graphic designer and writer Theo Inglis; design writer, editor and lecturer Anna Lisa Reynolds and design historian Alex J. Todd. They collaborated in a seamless manner while under pressure to meet deadlines, despite having a proverbial typographic mountain to climb. Thanks also to Mike Daines at eLexicons for his assistance with historical research.

My special thanks go to my colleagues at Grade Design, who worked so hard to help research, compile, design and build the book. My everlasting thanks go to both Katie Holmes and to Alice Kennedy-Owen. Their unwavering enthusiasm, patience, insight and dedication – with never a complaint – over the year it took to create the *Type Directory* has been immeasurable.

Thank you to Luped Limited for their assistance and aid in the never-ending quest for images and permissions.

Very special thanks go to Tobias Frere-Jones for very kindly providing time, insight and advice in writing the Foreword to the *Type Directory* and advising on other areas of the book's content. Thanks also go to Christine Bateup in organizing the Frere-Jones Type contributions to feature within the *Type Directory*.

Of course, a book on typefaces could not come to fruition without the generous contribution, time and expertise given by the type designers and foundries who have very kindly provided content for the book. My heartfelt thanks go to (in no preference of order): Benoît Bodhuin of BB-Bureau; Anthony Sheret and Edd Harrington of Colophon Foundry; Paul Barnes, Christian Schwartz and Emil Martirosian of Commercial Type; Bruno Maag, Kathrin Heimel, Katy Smith and Beatrix Fletcher at Dalton Maag; Rudy VanderLans and Zuzana Licko of Emigre; Jason Smith, Tamasin Handley and Stuart de Rozario of Fontsmith; Stephan Müller of Forgotten Shapes / Lineto; David Quay and Freda Sack of The Foundry; Noël Leu and Thierry Blancpain of Grilli Type; Charles Nix, Andy Rodgers and Jim Ford of Monotype; Jeremy Tankard of Jeremy Tankard Typography; Timo Gaessner and Maiko Gubler of Milieu Grotesque; Paul McNeil and Hamish Muir of MuirMcNeil; Alexander McCracken of Neutura; Guðmundur Úlfarsson and Mads Freund Brunse of Or Type; Mathias Jespersen and Annemarie Friislund of Playtype Foundry; and Peter Bil'ak of Typotheque.

A big thank you for the generosity and expertise of Alexander Tochilovsky at The Herb Lubalin Study Center of Design and Typography, who went out of his way checking and suggesting images and to his colleague Laura Mircik-Sellers.

I also want to pay a debt of gratitude to those graphic designers, studios and organizations who have allowed us to showcase their work within the book as examples of particular typefaces: Pedro Falcão of Atelier Pedro Falcão; Professor John McMillan, Emeritus Professor of Graphic Design at Ulster University; Clare Playne at the International Society of Typographic Designers (www.istd.org.uk); Patrick Myles; Konstantin Eremenko of Eremenko Visual Communication, Russia; Margus Tamm; Tako Chabukiani of Pragmatika Design, Georgia; Chantal Manella of Metapur AG, Germany; Solo, Spain; Mikhail Rul; Blok Design, Canada; Trüf Creative, United States; Sacred Bones Records; The Martin Agency, United States; Bisgràfic, Spain; Leslie Chan Wing Kei, Taiwan; Maiarelli Studio, United States; Stereo Associates, Denmark; Morphoria Design Collective, Germany; Intégral Ruedi Baur Paris, France; Erik Spiekermann; Nick Kapica, SV Associates; Typoretum, United Kingdom; Bunch Design, United Kingdom.

Finally, I would like to pay tribute to Freda Sack, my close friend, colleague and mentor, who passed away during the writing of this book. I had the great pleasure and privilege of working with Freda for many years while we were members of the board for the International Society of Typographic Designers (ISTD). However, we first met many years before, just after I left college, and I was always impressed and inspired by her enthusiasm, generous spirit and immense talent. Freda was not only a highly skilled and accomplished type designer and typographer but also contributed inestimably to typographic and design education through her long-standing commitment to the ISTD. She will be greatly missed by all who knew her and this book is in small part a humble tribute to her.

Peter Dawson
London, 2019

For Frederick

First published in the United Kingdom in 2019 by
Thames & Hudson Ltd, 181A High Holborn,
London WC1V 7QX

© White Lion Publishing 2019

Book art direction: Peter Dawson
Book design and layout: Peter Dawson, Katie Holmes, Alice Kennedy-Owen,
gradedesign.com

All Rights Reserved. No part of this publication may be reproduced or transmitted in
any form or by any means, electronic or mechanical, including photocopy, recording
or any other information storage and retrieval system, without prior permission in
writing from the publisher.

British Library Cataloguing-in-Publication Data
A catalogue record for this book is available from the British Library

ISBN 978-0-500-24154-7

Printed and bound in China

To find out about all our publications, please visit
www.thamesandhudson.com
There you can subscribe to our e-newsletter, browse or download our current
catalogue, and buy any titles that are in print.

T = top; B = bottom; M = middle, L = left; R = right; BL = bottom left; BR = bottom right; TL = top left, TR = top right.

Page 2. T: Bespoke typeface for Umbro by Commercial Type for the England football team kit; BL: Promotional print for Skate Agora, using Druk by Commercial Type, design by Solo Design Studio, Madrid; BR: Editorial design by Yevgeniy Anfalov using Mineral by BB-Bureau.

Page 3. T: Identity and branding for the London-based Redchurch Brewery, employing Separat by Or-Type, design by Bibliothèque; B: Poster series by Design by Atlas for Museu del Disseny using Graphik by Commercial Type.

Page 4. Optical/geometric type system Nine by MuirMcNeil.

Page 5. TL: Albertus as used by Barnbrook studio in the book *David Bowie Is*; TR: Program promotional design by Emigre; BL: Lost & Foundry typeface collection by Fontsmith; BR: BB-Bureau's ZigZag in use for Antigel Festival 2014, design by Pablo Lavalley.

Page 6. T: Preparatory workings for Dalton Maag's Blenny font; BL: Pembroke serif by Jeremy Tankard Typography; BR: Empirica by Frere-Jones Type.

Page 7. TL: FS Benjamin by Fontsmith; TR: The innovative History type system by Typotheque employed in shop window display, design by Pentagram NYC; BL: Berthold Akzidenz Grotesk employed on architect's Tim Mein's website, design by Sons & Co. / Timothy Kelleher; BR: Chapeau type specimen by Milieu Grotesque.

Page 8. T: Wayfinding and information graphics by Design by Atlas for Museu del Disseny using Graphik by Commercial Type; BL: Detail showing *DieseWoche* poster employing Univers, designed by Otl Aicher for the 1972 Munich Olympics; BR: *Habitar* poster by Atelier Pedro Falcão using Akkurat Pro.